The American Civil War is often said to have predicted the way in which later wars such as the Boer War and the First World War would be fought. As a result, the British Army has been criticised for not heeding its lessons, a view that can be traced back to the 1930s.

This book challenges that long-held view, and demonstrates that the responses to the lessons of the war in the British Army were more complex, better informed, and of higher quality, than normally depicted.

Key to this new interpretation is that it takes a 19th Century perspective rather than pre-supposing what the British should have seen based upon hindsight from the South African veldt or the Western Front trenches. It demonstrates that strategists and policy-makers reacted to the changes in the nature of warfare suggested by American experience, looks at how officers in the cavalry, infantry, artillery, and engineers applied their observations in America to the technical and tactical issues of the day, and even examines the war's influence on the development of aeronautics.

In studying how the Civil War changed the Late-Victorian British Army, the book provides insight into its learning process, and concludes that although sometimes flawed, its study of the American Civil War meant that it was better prepared for the wars of the 20th Century than previously acknowledged.

Michael Somerville graduated with a First-Class degree in History from Fitzwilliam College, Cambridge. Alongside a professional career as an Information Technology Consultant, much of his spare time has been spent reading and researching military history. His particular areas of interest are the American Civil War and 19th Century European wars; the First World War; the Balkans; and naval history. In August 2017 he was awarded a doctorate by the University of Buckingham for his thesis on the influence of the Civil War on the Victorian British Army.

Michael is a trustee of the American Civil War Round Table UK, for which he has produced a number of presentations and articles. He lives in Wimbledon, London, with his wife Gillian who fortunately shares his love of American history and war cemeteries.

Bull Run to Boer War

How the American Civil War Changed the Victorian British Army

Wolverhampton Military Studies No. 32

Michael Somerville

Helion & Company

Helion & Company Limited
Unit 8 Amherst Business Centre
Budbrooke Road
Warwick
CV34 5WE
England
Tel. 01926 499619
Email: info@helion.co.uk
Website: www.helion.co.uk
Twitter: @helionbooks
Visit our blog at http://blog.helion.co.uk/

Published by Helion & Company 2019
Designed and typeset by Mach 3 Solutions Ltd (www.mach3solutions.co.uk)
Cover designed by Paul Hewitt, Battlefield Design (www.battlefield-design.co.uk)

ISBN 978-1-912866-25-0

British Library Cataloguing-in-Publication Data.
A catalogue record for this book is available from the British Library.

For details of other military history titles published by Helion & Company Limited, contact
the above address, or visit our website: http://www.helion.co.uk

We always welcome receiving book proposals from prospective authors.

Contents

List of Plates

The Wolverhampton Military Studies Series

Series Editor's Preface

As series editor, it is my great pleasure to introduce the *Wolverhampton Military Studies Series* to you. Our intention is that in this series of books you will find military history that is new and innovative, and academically rigorous with a strong basis in fact and in analytical research, but also is the kind of military history that is for all readers, whatever their particular interests, or their level of interest in the subject. To paraphrase an old aphorism: a military history book is not less important just because it is popular, and it is not more scholarly just because it is dull. With every one of our publications we want to bring you the kind of military history that you will want to read simply because it is a good and well-written book, as well as bringing new light, new perspectives, and new factual evidence to its subject.

In devising the *Wolverhampton Military Studies Series*, we gave much thought to the series title: this is a *military* series. We take the view that history is everything except the things that have not happened yet, and even then a good book about the military aspects of the future would find its way into this series. We are not bound to any particular time period or cut-off date. Writing military history often divides quite sharply into eras, from the modern through the early modern to the mediaeval and ancient; and into regions or continents, with a division between western military history and the military history of other countries and cultures being particularly marked. Inevitably, we have had to start somewhere, and the first books of the series deal with British military topics and events of the twentieth century and later nineteenth century. But this series is open to any book that challenges received and accepted ideas about any aspect of military history, and does so in a way that encourages its readers to enjoy the discovery.

In the same way, this series is not limited to being about wars, or about grand strategy, or wider defence matters, or the sociology of armed forces as institutions, or civilian society and culture at war. None of these are specifically excluded, and in some cases they play an important part in the books that comprise our series. But there are already many books in existence, some of them of the highest scholarly standards, which cater to these particular approaches. The main theme of the *Wolverhampton Military Studies Series* is the military aspects of wars, the preparation for wars or their prevention, and their aftermath. This includes some books whose main theme is the technical details of how armed forces have worked, some books on wars and battles, and some books that re-examine the evidence about the existing stories, to show in a different light what everyone thought they already knew and understood.

As series editor, together with my fellow editorial board members, and our publisher Duncan Rogers of Helion, I have found that we have known immediately and almost by instinct the kind of books that fit within this series. They are very much the kind of well-written and challenging books that my students at the University of Wolverhampton would want to read. They are books which enhance knowledge, and offer new perspectives. Also, they are books for anyone with an interest in military history and events, from expert scholars to occasional readers. One of the great benefits of the study of military history is that it includes a large and often committed section of the wider population, who want to read the best military history that they can find; our aim for this series is to provide it.

Stephen Badsey
University of Wolverhampton

Acknowledgements

This book started life as a thesis for a Doctorate in Military History at the University of Buckingham, so the first people I need to thank are my tutor, Dr Spencer Jones of the University of Wolverhampton, and Professor Saul David of the University of Buckingham for their support, encouragement, and guidance in the preparation of that thesis. Also my two examiners, Professor Gary Sheffield of the University of Wolverhampton and Professor Edward Spiers of the University of Leeds, were not only good enough to pass my efforts, but also provided input on areas to improve them, some of which have been further developed in writing this book.

I would further like to thank Andrew Bamford, my editor at Helion, and Stephen Badsey from the editorial team of the Wolverhampton Military Studies Series, for their assistance and valuable input when turning a dry academic thesis into something more suitable for general readership.

Any researcher into the military legacy of the Civil War owes a debt to Professor Jay Luvaas for his initial work on this subject, and I would like to thank Linda Sowers Luvaas for permission to quote from her late husband's work, particularly his unpublished theses and letters. Amy McDonald at Duke University, North Carolina arranged for the digitisation of Professor Luvaas' original PhD thesis, which is now available to future scholars online as a result. Katrina DiMuro at King's College, London helped with access to his MA thesis and to unpublished correspondence with Sir Basil Liddell Hart; my thanks to her and the other staff at Kings, and to the Trustees of the Liddell Hart Archive for permission to quote from the material there.

A number of other libraries and archives have been consulted. My thanks to Jacqui Grainger and her predecessor Tony Pilmer at the RUSI library, London; to Mark Bunt at the Hove Public library for his help with material from the Wolseley archive; to Ruth Cox at the New Brunswick Museum for providing the correspondence between Generals Sir William Fenwick and Sir Hastings Doyle (happily discovered even though not in the museum's catalogue); to James Capobianco at the Houghton Library, Harvard, for identifying and sending me the correspondence between Lord Dunmore and President Jefferson Davis; to Cathy Wright at the American Civil War Museum, Richmond for pinning down Dunmore in the 1862 Richmond newspaper records; and to Paul Evans at the Firepower museum, Woolwich, for locating the parliamentary reports on artillery from the 1860s. A large amount of my research was done in the British Library, London, and The National Archives, Kew, where the staff were always helpful and efficient. The University of Wales at Aberystwyth and Dr Patrick Craddock kindly granted access to his unpublished doctoral thesis. The University of South Dakota, Brookings, and the University of Missouri, Springfield, were kind enough to give me use of their library facilities while in the United States.

The illustrations for the work are primarily taken from the Anne S.K. Brown Collection at Brown University, Providence, and from the Library of Congress collections of Civil War Photographs. Additional thanks are due to Linda Sowers Luvaas, and to Lianne Smith and the Trustees of the Liddell Hart Archive at Kings College, London; Kate Swann at the National Army Museum, London; Barry Smith at the RAF Museum, Hendon; Peter Donnelly at the Kings Own Royal Regiment, Lancaster; Paul Johnson at The National Archive, Kew; and Chris Rawlings and Andrew Gough at The British Library, London; for their assistance and for permission to use additional images from their collections.

I have been interested in the Civil War since my undergraduate days at university, but my academic interest was renewed on joining the American Civil War Round Table of the UK in 2011. Thanks are due to all of the excellent speakers at conferences and meetings since that date for providing inspiration, to Derek Young, Greg Bayne, and Charles Rees, the current and former presidents, and to all the other officials and members of the society for providing such a fertile environment for discussion and the sharing of research. Particular mentions go to Tony Margrave for pointing me to the Canadian leave returns in the National Archives as a source of information, and for providing me with a copy of his then unpublished articles on British observers, and to David Kirkpatrick for providing me with his article on Civil War forts.

My greatest thanks must go to my wife Gillian. She first pointed me to the Military History Faculty at the University of Buckingham and encouraged me to enrol there, and subsequently has supported the conversion of the thesis into this book. She has had to suffer losing me at weekends, evenings, and during holidays to lectures, libraries, archives, or simply to the computer in the study. Finally, she has also been kind enough to proof read my output, in all of its various incarnations over that time, a true labour of love, and to make suggestions for improving its readability and content. Fortunately we have a mutual interest in American history, if not the detailed military aspects of my subject. It can truthfully be said that without her this book would not exist.

Michael Somerville, July 2019

Note on Terminology and Sources

Nineteenth Century British accounts usually referred to the American Civil War as 'The American War', only relatively rarely referring to it as a war of secession or a civil war. I have generally used the term 'American Civil War' or simply 'Civil War' throughout, but have occasionally used the term 'War of Secession' or 'American War' when the original source or context seemed to make these alternative descriptions appropriate.

The terms 'English' and 'British' were used virtually synonymously in the 19th Century, even the Scottish nobleman the Earl of Dunmore being referred to as an 'Englishman'. I have mostly used the term 'British' throughout, but retained the original usage in some indirect references where it seemed appropriate, and in all direct quotations, without recourse to the frequent use of '[sic]', even when the term 'English' is clearly referring to individuals of Scottish or Welsh heritage. Those of Irish descent were usually identified as such.

I have used the modern term 'Canada' rather than the contemporary 'British North America', except where the latter is included in formal titles. Technically the term 'Canada' at the time referred only to modern Ontario (ON) and Quebec (QC). I have used the modern names and abbreviations for these provinces rather than Canada West (C.W.) and Canada East (C.E.) as being more accessible and less confusing to modern readers. Newfoundland, New Brunswick, and Nova Scotia were under separate administration in this period, so their usage generally meets both contemporary and modern expectations.

Officers in British Guards regiments held two ranks, a regimental rank reflecting their seniority within the regiment, and a second, higher rank, which represented their seniority within the Army hierarchy. Thus, a mere Ensign in the Guards held an effective rank of Lieutenant within the Army, a Lieutenant that of Captain, and a Captain that of Lieutenant-Colonel. I have used the higher Army rank when referring to Guards officers as being more reflective of their overall seniority and influence, but it should be noted that these were more junior officers in terms of years of service than their Army rank indicated.

Contributions to *Blackwood's Edinburgh Magazine* and several other periodicals quoted herein were published anonymously or under pseudonym. All attributions for the authorship of such articles are taken from the *Wellesley Index to Victorian Periodicals* (Toronto: University of Toronto Press; London: Routledge, 1966-89) unless otherwise indicated.

Several journals changed their names during the period, or now exist under different, and usually shorter, titles. I have gone for a mixture of brevity, consistency and contemporaneous context, thus for example *R.E. Professional Papers* rather than *Papers on Subjects Connected with the Duties of the Corps of Royal Engineers*; *United Service Magazine* rather than *Colbourn's United Service Magazine*; but *Journal of the [Royal] United Service Institution* rather than *RUSI Journal*, except where referring to modern articles.

Introduction

There is a scene in the film *Gettysburg* (1993) in which probably the most famous British observer of the American Civil War, Lieutenant Colonel Arthur Lyon Fremantle of Her Majesty's Coldstream Guards, strolls through the Confederate camp at daybreak. Behind him a group of Southern soldiers are lined up to drill, their grey uniforms blending slightly into the morning mist. These amateur soldiers are nonetheless thoroughly modern and know their business; to paraphrase the words of Garnet Wolseley, another British visitor to the Army of Northern Virginia, they look like work. Fremantle himself, standing out in his bright scarlet dress uniform, comes from another era. Aristocratic, formal, he is not portrayed as the professional soldier he would consider himself to be, but almost as a figure of fun. In his hand he even holds a cup of tea!

This image typifies much of the popular, and even academic writing, about the American Civil War and the Victorian British Army. What comes across are the contrasts. On the one hand is the American military experience from the Civil War, a war fought by 'amateurs' that at the same time is modern and innovative: the mobilisation of the whole nation for war, massed armies, trenches, skirmish lines, tactics modified to respond to the firepower of new weapons. On the other is a view of war as waged by the European 'professionals', who are nevertheless obstinately conservative, believe in open warfare waged by parade ground formations of brightly coloured infantry and cavalry, and in the traditional power of 'cold steel' as the battle-winning weapon. One is a vision of a terrible 20th Century future; the other a vision clinging to the past that will make that future all the more tragic.

It is a comparison in which the British Army almost invariably comes in for severe criticism. A browse across the internet will find many websites that say that the British Army tried to fight the Boer War using the tactics of Waterloo. If only the British had studied the American Civil War, goes the argument, then they would have been better prepared for that war, and would have realised that the war between the great powers of Europe in 1914-18 would reproduce the trench warfare seen towards the end of the Civil War, only on an even greater scale.

When in 2011 my wife persuaded me that I should utilise my interest in military history to study for a post-graduate degree, I considered this view and questioned its validity. Many historians of the First World War now suggest that the generals in that conflict actually performed better than they have been given credit for, under unprecedented conditions. At the same time, some historians of the Civil War have pointed to ways in which that war retained many traditional features of Napoleonic warfare alongside its apparent modernity. Yet no-one, it seemed, had combined these two arguments to revisit the influence of the Civil War on the military thought of those who would fight the European wars of the 20th Century. Were the professional soldiers of Europe – specifically Britain – really so incompetent as to dismiss completely the lessons from across the Atlantic? This was the idea that I pitched and had accepted for my thesis, and which in turn constitutes the basis for this book.

It was possible that the traditional view was justified. Military organisations are a product of the society in which they operate, and European societies in the late 19th Century had many differences from those of the United States. The image of Fremantle from *Gettysburg* has some truth in it: the British officer corps was drawn almost exclusively from the landed classes (and its rank and file from the labouring ones); was politically and socially conservative; could progress through social rank, wealth, and seniority, rather than ability; and had a strong sense of tradition. American armies, both North and South, were more 'democratic', certainly in the ranks, although officers were still mostly either West Point trained or from the wealthier classes of society, and many of them rose in rank as a result of their political and personal connections as much as through their military record. The rapid expansion of the American armies required the enlistment of new men and officers, outside of the old regular US Army traditions, at a rate unknown in the British Army until Kitchener's New Army of 1914-16.

During the second half of the 19th Century it has been reckoned that the British Army was fighting, somewhere in the world, almost every year.[1] As a result there is a rich seam of military disasters and mistakes that can be used to anecdotally demonstrate the poor quality of British generalship, inappropriate tactics, inadequate equipment, and, by inference, to condemn the whole system. Success on the other hand is usually attributed to mere technical superiority. This is arguably a lesson from the Civil War – that technical and economic superiority overcomes mere bravery and 'natural' fighting skill. It also both belittles Britain's opponents, who were often tactically adept, and some of whom were also quite well-armed, and underestimates the ability of the British generals to adapt their own tactics to local conditions. Britain lost many battles, but won most of her wars. This implies that the British Army actually learnt lessons quite well, at least in the short term, and that some individuals amongst her professional soldiers were therefore good at their jobs. As in the Civil War, the right men were not necessarily in command at the start, but talent could rise to the top.

---

1   Edward M. Spiers, *The Late Victorian Army 1868–1902* (Manchester: Manchester University Press, 1999), pp.335-336 lists a campaign for every year except 1883; W. Baring Pemberton, *Battles of the Boer War* (London: Batsford, 1964), p.32 says that there had been fighting every year of Victoria's reign except 1862; Byron Farwell, *Queen Victoria's Little Wars* (Ware: Wordsworth, 1999, originally published 1973), pp.364-71 lists a war in every year.

Moreover, the British Army differentiated between so called 'civilised' and 'savage' warfare – terms that are uncomfortable to modern sensibilities, but in practical military terms meant that it was fully appreciated that tactics which would work against 'native' troops, where the Army had a technical superiority, would be suicidal against European armies armed with modern weapons. Demonstrating old-fashioned tactics being used against the former gives no indication of how the Army intended to fight a modern war.

Initially I had intended to cover the period up to the First World War, but I decided early on in my research to finish at the start of the Boer War. Aside from practical limitations of length for a thesis, there were also historical reasons for the decision. Firstly, although the British had some experience of fighting opponents with magazine rifles prior to South Africa, that war exposed the British Army for the first time to an army of European extraction and equipped with the full range of European weapons, though not, it needs to be remembered, fighting using European tactics or on European terrain. The Boer War, and the wars in Manchuria and the Balkans that followed it, offered a new set of lessons that seemed to replace, but which were sometimes just as difficult to interpret as, those of the Civil War. Most importantly, the Boer War was soon followed in the new century by changes in the strategic objectives of the British Army as a result of the changing European political situation and the *Entente Cordiale* with France. Since it was an essential part of my approach to evaluate the study of the Civil War by the British Army in terms of how it related to contemporary tactical, operational, and strategic problems, the fact that all of these changed substantially after the Boer War made the start of that conflict a logical endpoint. I include some examples from the conventional opening campaigns of the Boer War in 1899-1900, before the Boers adopted a strategy of purely partisan or guerrilla warfare, to illustrate British military thinking at the end of the period under study.

Even finishing in 1900, this book is not a comprehensive review of every aspect of change in the British Army over the period in question. That would require a much larger work, and one different in concept and focus. It does not re-assess the military significance of the Civil War itself within the development of military practice and thought, nor does it re-examine or judge the arguments of each side in debates such as the *arme blanche* controversy in the cavalry, which have been covered by other scholars. Nor, I hope, does it try to excuse military failure where it occurred, though it will try and point out some examples of military success, and demonstrations of where lessons had been learnt, which are usually either ignored or put down to mere technical or numerical superiority.

Instead, it tries to reassess the learning process of the Victorian British Army through its reaction to one particular external source of lessons, the American Civil War. Thus some very significant changes, such as the Cardwell reforms, are not covered because there is no discernible connection between them and what happened during the Civil War. However, many technical, tactical, and strategic developments can be seen to have been influenced by the changes that were seen or believed to have taken place in America between 1861 and 1865.

The book raises a number of questions and challenges several widely held views. Did the British Army fail to recognise significant trends in military technology and tactics demonstrated by the Civil War, or did it not only see them but successfully incorporate them to achieve its own global military obligations? Was it selective in its interpretation due to social prejudices, lack of understanding or defective leadership? Or did it in fact assimilate key lessons that enabled it to transform and meet ever more complex and threatening technical and geo-political challenges? Through using a range of contemporary sources, and by relating them to contemporary challenges rather than 20th Century conflicts, the British reaction to the war can be seen in its true context, and the Civil War can be seen to have had a greater influence in shaping British responses to military problems than has been acknowledged previously. The resulting new interpretation better reflects the importance of the lessons of the Civil War in the Victorian British Army.

1

The *Military Legacy* of Jay Luvaas

The American Civil War is generally held to be one of the pivotal events in the development of the art of war, 'the first of the modern total wars',[1] and the direct antecedent of the First World War.[2] As a result of this widely held view, historians when reviewing the Civil War's influence on the European military thought have largely followed a common theme: that there were substantial lessons to be learnt, which often contradicted those taken from other conflicts of the time; that the European military establishments failed abjectly to recognise them; and that their negligence in this respect was a major contribution to the tragedy of the First World War.[3]

The problem with this approach is that it fails to put the learning process in its true historical context, judging the decisions of the day with perfect hindsight. It is also guilty of viewing history mostly from a single perspective: that of the Western Front in 1914-18. However, just as there was a unique set of circumstances that formulated the conduct of the American Civil War, a second set of unique circumstances dictated how the First World War was fought. These circumstances were not all obvious before the event. Moreover, the British Army in particular was never designed or expected to wage total war on a continental scale during the period between these two wars. It had many different objectives, mostly incompatible with the political context of a war of secession. The British military establishment did examine the Civil War, but in the context of its own military problems and scenarios. As one modern authority on

---

1   T. Harry Williams, *Lincoln and his Generals* (London: Hamish Hamilton, 1952), p.3.

2   J.F.C. Fuller, *War and Western Civilization, 1832–1932: A Study of War as a Political Instrument and the Expression of Mass Democracy* (London: Duckworth, 1932), p.84; Edward Hagerman, *The American Civil War and the Origins of Modern Warfare: Ideas, Organization, and Field Command* (Bloomington: Indiana University Press, 1992), pp.xi–xii.

3   Brian Holden Reid 'British Military Intellectuals and the American Civil War: Maurice, Fuller and Liddell Hart' in *Studies in British Military Thought: Debates with Fuller and Liddell Hart* (Lincoln: University of Nebraska Press, 1998), pp.133-49 identifies British military writing in the inter-war period as the initial source of this view.

the war has recently suggested, it is necessary to re-evaluate the influence of the Civil War on the British Army looking at it not from the viewpoint of the 20th Century, but from that of the 19th.[4]

The view of the American Civil War as a predictor of the nature of 20th Century warfare can mostly be traced back to the writings of British historians after the First World War, and especially to those of J.F.C. Fuller and Basil Liddell Hart. In the aftermath of what was then the largest and costliest war in British history there appeared to be some clear similarities between the two conflicts.[5] The prolonged battles and the extensive use of field works in 1861-65 could both be seen as a precursor to the trench systems and months long battles of 1914-18. Both had been four-year conflicts where the grand strategy of the war was equivalent to a siege, and both were ultimately decided through remorseless attrition rather than through a single overwhelming tactical defeat. All this was portrayed in contrast to the relatively short European wars of the mid-19th Century that were concluded by decisive military victories. This idea that the experience of the American Civil War was somehow different from and more 'advanced' than European war has been given wide acceptance in subsequent works. One author for example has written that 'the practice of the art of war was given a much greater influence from events in the Civil War in America than from the dozen or so wars that took place in other continents, for the American war gave a preview of developments some fifty years ahead'.[6]

Fuller portrayed the war as one of technical modernity, identifying a number of weapons used in the Civil War that predicted those of the Great War.[7] He also highlighted the emergence of Ulysses S. Grant as the supreme commander of the war. Grant's appointment to command all of the Union armies in March of 1864, answerable only to President Abraham Lincoln, had a parallel in the appointment of Ferdinand Foch as overall Commander-in-Chief of the Allied armies in 1918, both would successfully apply their superiority in numbers and resources in contrast to the failed attempts at coordinated strategy earlier in the two wars. Grant has also been

4   Brian Holden Reid, "'A Signpost That Was Missed'? Reconsidering British Lessons from the American Civil War', *The Journal of Military History*, 70 (April 2006), pp.385–414 (p.414).
5   Basil Liddell Hart, *The British Way in Warfare* (London: Faber and Faber, 1932), Chapter 4, 'The Signpost That Was Missed', pp.74–92; Fuller, *War and Western Civilization*, Chapter 4, 'First of the Modern Wars', pp.84–100. The chapter on the Civil War in Fuller's *The Conduct of War, 1789–1961* (London: Eyre and Spottiswoode, 1961), pp.95-112 is largely an update to his 1932 text.
6   David Woodward, *Armies of the World 1854-1914* (London: Sidgewick and Jackson, 1978), p.13; see also H.W. Koch, *Modern Warfare* (London: Bison, 1983), p.140.
7   J.F.C. Fuller, *The Generalship of Ulysses S. Grant* (London: John Murray, 1929), p.66 describes the technology of the Civil War as a prediction of the First World War. Fuller's *War and Western Civilisation*, p.85 and *The Conduct of War 1789-1961*, p.106 give more extensive lists.

seen as the first proponent of the strategy of attrition, the wearing down of an enemy through sheer numbers and economic superiority.[8]

Liddell Hart was motivated by a desire to understand and avoid a re-occurrence of the trench warfare of the Western Front, and drew somewhat different conclusions from Fuller. For him, William Tecumseh Sherman, not Grant, was the most 'modern' general to emerge from the war. In Liddell Hart's analysis Sherman had not engaged in the war of attrition, but by use of an 'indirect approach' had focussed on the enemy's economic and productive capability rather than its armies. Such a view was appealing to a British audience seeking to avoid a repeat of 1914-18. Liddell Hart's *Sherman,* published in 1929, specifically criticised the pre-war European establishment for neglecting the 'War in the West' in preference to analysing the battles in Virginia between Grant and Robert E. Lee which were 'imitated with even greater lavishness and ineffectiveness on the battlefields of France'.[9]

The most important book on the subject however is Jay Luvaas' *The Military Legacy of the Civil War: The European Inheritance,* which was published in 1959. Using not only English sources but also works published in French and German, this remains the only comprehensive study of the foreign observers in the war and the subsequent European interpretation of its significance. Luvaas took a largely chronological approach to the study, beginning with the experiences of the observers and then tracing the subsequent influence of the American conflict on military thought in the years up to and after the First World War. In the case of Britain, the narrative trajectory of Luvaas' work is that initial interest in the war was followed by a transfer of focus in the 1870s to the study of the German wars of unification which took place between 1864 and 1871. This was then reversed by a reaction against German influence in British military thought in the 1880s. According to Luvaas, a rediscovery of the Civil War occurred in this period principally due to the writings of G.F.R. Henderson, possibly the most prominent military historian and theorist in the British Army during the last decades of the century. Largely as a result of Henderson, the war continued to form a substantial part of the military history syllabus at the Staff College and at the Royal Military College, Sandhurst, through to the First World War. However, in Luvaas' view the assimilation of lessons was undermined by a focus on a limited number of campaigns,

---

8   Reid, 'British Military Intellectuals and the American Civil War', p.141; Koch, *Modern Warfare,* p.151; Henry Coppée, *Grant and his Campaigns: A Military Biography* (New York: Charles B. Richardson 1866), p.268; Fuller, *The Generalship of U.S. Grant,* p.224; A.L. Conyer, *The Rise of U.S. Grant* (New York: Century, 1931), pp.327-28, 332; James Marshall-Cornwall, *Grant as Military Commander* (London: Batsford, 1970), p.135; Russell F. Weigley, *History of the United States Army* (London: Batsford, 1968), p.251; Russell F. Weigley, *A Great Civil War* (Bloomington: Indiana University Press, 2000), p.329.

9   Jay Luvaas, introduction to Sir Basil Liddell Hart, *Sherman* (New York: Da Capo, 1993), p.vii; Albert Castel, 'Liddell Hart's *Sherman*: Propaganda as History', *The Journal of Military History,* 67 (2003), pp.405–426 (pp.408-09); Sir Basil Liddell Hart, preface to *Sherman,* pp.xiii-xiv.

especially those of Henderson's hero Lieutenant General Thomas 'Stonewall' Jackson, and an education system that encouraged 'cramming' rather than serious analysis. Luvaas' ultimate conclusion was that European observers and writers on the war saw in it evidence to re-enforce existing doctrines and prejudices, and failed to grasp its true meaning and significance.[10]

Because Luvaas' work seemed so thorough in its examination of the published sources, it has remained largely unchallenged by subsequent literature. Viscount Montgomery of Alamein wrote of the lessons of the war that 'the professional soldiers of Europe refused to take them seriously because they said that the war was fought by amateurs'.[11] H.W. Koch's *Modern Warfare* (1983) is a further example of a popular history that followed the line that the Europeans largely ignored any lessons from North America, assigning the war to a chapter headed 'The Forgotten Wars'.[12]

Amongst more academic works, William McElwee's *The Art of War: Waterloo to Mons* (1973) drew its interpretation of the war almost entirely from Luvaas. Howard Bailes, in his 1984 lecture and article *Technology and Tactics in the British Army 1866-1900*, considered that 'the work of Jay Luvaas makes it unnecessary to do more than mention the American Civil War in passing'. If Luvaas' views were not used as the basis for the relevant section of a book, then the subject was usually omitted altogether. Michael Howard's *War in European History* (1976) and John Gooch's *Armies in Europe* (1980) stuck to analysing only European conflicts of the age, although Hew Strachan's *European Armies and the Conduct of War* (1983) did touch briefly upon British interpretation of the strategy of the Civil War. In particular Strachan pointed out the common European and American heritage in military thought, which at this time were both largely based upon the teachings of the Swiss theoretician Antoine-Henri Jomini, and the new strategic elements introduced by cavalry raids and the railway. Luvaas warranted a brief footnote entry in Edward Hagerman's *The American Civil War and the Origins of Modern Warfare* (1992), but *Military Legacy* did not even make the bibliography of Azar Gat's *A History of Military Thought: From the Enlightenment to the Cold War* (2001), while Addington (1994), Gates (2001), and Black (2006) discussed the new developments seen in the Civil War but did not analyse any European assimilation of these.[13]

---

10 Jay Luvaas, *The Military Legacy of the Civil War: The European Inheritance* (Chicago: University of Chicago Press, 1959), particularly pp.115-17, 186-90, 233. Hereafter Luvaas, *Military Legacy*.
11 Viscount Montgomery of Alamein, *A History of Warfare* (London: Collins, 1968), p.440.
12 Koch, *Modern Warfare*, pp.140-51.
13 William McEllwee, *The Art of War Waterloo to Mons* (London: Weidenfeld and Nicholson, 1974), pp.147-83; Howard Bailes, 'Technology and Tactics in the late Victorian Army' in *Men Machines and War*, ed. by R. Haycock and K. Neilson (Waterloo: Wilfred Laurier University Press, 1988), pp.21-47 (p.29); Michael Howard, *War in European History* (Oxford: OPUS, 1976), pp.94-113; John Gooch, *Armies in Europe* (London: Routledge and Kegan Paul, 1980), pp.81-108; Hew Strachan *European Armies and the Conduct of War* (London: Allen & Unwin, 1983), pp.73-75, 120-22; Hagerman, *The American Civil War*

Given that Luvaas' work is now over 60 years old it is pertinent to consider it in its historiographic context and the limitations this may have imposed on his interpretations. Luvaas was a close friend and protégé of Sir Basil Liddell Hart, a relationship that had its origins in the genesis of *The Military Legacy of the Civil War*. Although the book was not published until 1959, Luvaas had begun began his research in 1950 as a 22-year-old MA student studying at Duke University, North Carolina. In its initial form it was a dissertation on British military historians of the Civil War. In 1950 Luvaas had limited experience both as a general historian and as a student of war. Indeed, military history as a modern academic study was still in its infancy at the time, Luvaas' supervisor Theodore Ropp being one of a small number of exceptions.

On the advice of another great contemporary American military historian, Douglas Southall Freeman, Luvaas turned for help and guidance to Liddell Hart, one of the foremost British military thinkers of the day, and the author of the critically acclaimed study of Sherman.[14]

From their initial correspondence onwards, Liddell Hart thus had a significant role in structuring the way that Luvaas approached his subject, particularly on the overall quality of British thought prior to the First World War. By 1950 Liddell Hart's view of this was decidedly negative. He acknowledged that G.F.R. Henderson had first sparked his interest in the Civil War, was an 'exceptionally deep' thinker, and was still widely read. However, he raised the criticism that Henderson had mostly focussed his attention on the eastern theatre. More

Jay Luvaas as an MA student at Duke University, 1951. (Liddell Hart Archive, Kings College, London)

and the Origins of Modern Warfare, p.336; Azar Gat, *A History of Military Thought: From the Enlightenment to the Cold War* (Clarendon: Oxford University Press, 2001); Larry H. Addington, *The Patterns of War since the Eighteenth Century*, 2nd edn (Bloomington and Indianapolis: Indiana University Press, 1994), pp.68-94; David Gates, *Warfare in the 19th Century* (Basingstoke: Palgrave, 2001), pp.140-45; Jeremy Black, *The Age of Total War* (Westport and London: Praeger Security International, 2006), pp.29-42.

14   Kings College London Archive (KCL), Morten Jay Luvaas, 'Through English Eyes: The Impact of the American Civil War on British Military Thought' (Thesis for the degree of Master of Arts, Duke University, 1951)

importantly, the idea of the Civil War as the precedent for the First World War was presented to Luvaas at this early stage of his investigation.

> It was the negative lesson of World War 1, and the experience of the trench deadlock there, that quickened my interest in the ways in which a somewhat similar deadlock had been overcome in the American Civil War, particularly in the West, and by Sherman.[15]

Liddell Hart went on to recommend to Luvaas several of his own works which would support this view of Sherman as the true innovator of the war who 'appeared to bear out and illuminate the trend of my thought about future mobile warfare'.[16] One of these, the chapter on the Civil War in *The British Way in Warfare* (1932) entitled 'A Signpost That Was Missed?', provided the title for Luvaas' chapter in his MA dissertation on British writers between Henderson and the First World War. Others works by Liddell Hart that were referred to in their correspondence included *The Strategy of Indirect Approach* (1941), and *Thoughts on War* (1944) which Luvaas thought particularly enlightening. Later Liddell Hart recommended *The Ghost of Napoleon* (1933) for a summary of European military thought. Luvaas' correspondence shows that he avidly sought out and read his mentor's works, and he told Liddell Hart that he frequently found himself in agreement even when he had tried to formulate his own ideas in advance. The conclusion can be drawn that Liddell Hart's theories provided the underlying understanding of the history of military thought on which Luvaas based his work. Furthermore, Liddell Hart's writings became the benchmark against which those who had preceded him would be judged and failed. '[Y]ou alone have incorporated what you learn from Sherman into your philosophy of war'.[17]

The focus of Luvaas' original thesis was firmly in the 20th Century, reflecting the paramount place that the First World War had in forming Liddell Hart's philosophy. The first chapter was primarily on observers, plus some early writers in the immediate aftermath of the war, and the second on Henderson. The third was on 1900-14; the next on post-war writers including Fuller, and the final one on Liddell Hart, who was thus presented as the last word on British military thought about the Civil War. In terms of the deficiencies of the British study of the war, Luvaas highlighted three, all with associations to his mentor: the lack of attention to the western theatre (remedied

---

15   KCL, Liddell Hart Papers, LH 1/465 fols 3-6, Liddell Hart to Luvaas, 7 September 1950.
16   KCL, Liddell Hart Papers, LH 1/465 fols 3-6, Liddell Hart to Luvaas, 7 September 1950.
17   KCL, LH 1/465 fols 10-11, Luvaas to Liddell Hart, 28 January 1951. In a later letter Luvaas told Liddell Hart that he was 'my intellectual Godfather', LH 1/465 fols 101-03, Luvaas to Liddell Hart 31 December 1952. References to Luvaas' collecting of Liddell Hart's writings include LH 1/465 fols 40-41, Luvaas to Liddell Hart, 4 November 1951, fols 63-64, Luvaas to Liddell Hart, 23 March 1952 and fols 101-105, Luvaas to Liddell Hart, 31 December 1952. Liddell Hart frequently provided Luvaas with copies of his books and articles.

by Liddell Hart's *Sherman*); not appreciating the strength of the defensive, particularly in the form of entrenchments (a major tenet of his theories in the 1930s); and not understanding the revolutionary use of cavalry (which was associated to his ideas on 'deep penetration'). Luvaas included as an appendix to his original thesis a memorandum which Liddell Hart had written in 1935 about cavalry in the western theatre, an appendix which also appears in *The Military Legacy of the Civil War*.[18] Luvaas also whole-heartedly accepted Liddell Hart's concept of the 'indirect approach', which he referred to frequently in their correspondence.[19]

In 1990 Luvaas defended his former mentor against the criticisms of John Mearsheimer, which included the suggestion that Luvaas and other young historians were deliberately used by Liddell Hart to restore his reputation after the Second World War. It is not necessary however to accuse Liddell Hart of such cynical manipulation of his protégé to explain his influence. It is clear from their long correspondence, which continued through to Liddell Hart's death in 1970, that the two men had a deep and genuine friendship, but it was a relationship that was also built upon mutual advantage. Liddell Hart gave the young Luvaas intellectual support and validity, and a way into his own network of contacts in the military, academic, and publishing spheres. Luvaas, through his positive analysis of Liddell Hart's work and thought, provided publicity and apparent academic approval for his theories. Luvaas included a chapter on Liddell Hart in another of his classic works, *The Education of an Army: British Military Thought, 1815–1940* (1964), a chapter which Liddell Hart reviewed and edited prior to publication. While Luvaas did include some criticism of his mentor, *The Times Literary Supplement* commented that 'his final estimate on Captain Liddell Hart's thinking and influence is highly favourable'. The last words of the chapter are 'surely the time has come to recognise the greatness of Liddell Hart?'[20]

The overall effect of this relationship on *Military Legacy* was that Luvaas' and Liddell Hart's ideas became mutually re-enforcing, with any alternative interpretations of the lessons that might have been drawn from the Civil War being either ignored or dismissed.

Aside from any bias introduced by his relationship with Liddell Hart, the number of Victorian writers and sources covered by Luvaas in his original MA thesis was quite

---

18   Luvaas, 'Through English Eyes', pp.138-46; *Military Legacy*, pp.237-244; originals in KCL, LH 11/1935/80 and 11/1935/84, both dated May 1935.
19   An early example is LH 1/465 fols 57-60, Luvaas to Liddell Hart, 18 February 1952. Luvaas also wrote of a paper he produced on the Battle of Bentonville at this time that '[m]y treatment of Sherman's generalship smacks suspiciously of Liddell Hart' (LH 1/465 fol. 53, Luvaas to Liddell Hart, 23 December 1952).
20   John J. Mearsheimer, *Liddell Hart and the Weight of History*, (London: Brassey's Defence, 1988), pp.11, 15, 209; Jay Luvaas, 'Liddell Hart and the Mearsheimer Critique: A "Pupil's" Retrospective', *Parameters* 20 (March 1990), pp.9-19 (pp.18-19); 'Brain Battles': review of Jay Luvaas' *The Education of an Army* in *The Times Literary Supplement*, 15 April 1963; Jay Luvaas, *The Education of an Army: British Military Thought, 1815–1940* (Chicago: University of Chicago Press, 1964), p.424.

limited. Having passed his examinations, Luvaas went on to expand the subject area for his PhD. The main aspect of this was the addition and comparison of French and German sources, but he also extended the breadth of his research on British writers. During this period, Liddell Hart's influence is less marked, but Luvaas retained the overall narrative and conclusions of his initial thesis. The work of Prussian observer Julius Scheibert particularly impressed him, and he thought that initial German analysis of the war was superior to that of the British prior to Henderson. He also favourably compared French cavalry thought to that of the British. From the fact that the official observers sent to America were officers in the Royal Engineers and Royal Artillery, he concluded that the British, and other Europeans, had approached the war from a narrow technical perspective, and missed the more profound changes in tactics and strategy later seen by Liddell Hart. 'You and Henderson will sort of be the heroes of the study', he wrote to his mentor.[21]

The biggest problem with Luvaas selection of sources however was that it focussed on writings directly referring to the Civil War. Although he assumed that his sources would reveal doctrinal changes due to the war, only occasionally did he look at material on general military matters that might have indirectly referred to the war, or to the general trends in military technology and thinking. So rather than a study of whether the British Army had changed *as a result of* the war, both of his theses are in effect bibliographic studies of what the British wrote *about* the war. In particular, he assumed that the lack of writing on the Civil War between 1870 and 1886 meant the suppression of lessons from the war in favour of wholesale adoption of Prussian practices. Luvaas also only used published material (allowing in this categorisation government reports produced for limited circulation). Since it is mainly published views that influence others this approach was largely justified, and few unpublished reports or letters from observers seem to have survived. The few that have however do give some insight into British officers' private views, such as their attitudes to the South, which were not always reflected in published articles, particularly those for popular consumption.[22]

In 1953 Luvaas became concerned that he might have a rival in the field when Canadian historian R.A. Preston, following on from the discovery of a previously unpublished letter by a British observer, produced an article that directly examined the question of the military lessons that the British took from the war. Preston accepted

21   Morten Jay Luvaas, 'Through Foreign Eyes: The American Civil War in European Military Thought' (Thesis for the degree of Doctor of Philosophy, Duke University, 1956); KCL, Liddell Hart Archive, LH/1/465 fols 40-43, Luvaas to Liddell Hart, 4 November 1951, fols 63-64, Luvaas to Liddell Hart, 23 March 1952, fols 65-66, Luvaas to Liddell Hart 6 April 1952, fols 134-135, Luvaas to Liddell Hart, 23 February 1954, fols 136-37, Luvaas to Liddell Hart, 18 May 1954, fols 156-57, Luvaas to Liddell Hart, 17 December 1954.

22   Luvaas himself recognised the bibliographic nature of his work, see 'Through Foreign Eyes', p.402; for Luvaas' comments on sources, *Military Legacy* p.13.

the view that the Civil War was the prototype for modern warfare, but said that it had been largely forgotten in continental thought because it was so quickly followed by the great upheavals of the German wars of unification between 1864 and 1871. In Britain, however, Preston noted that the legacy of the war continued to be studied, and had had an important influence. He thought that a focus upon the Southern cause and mode of fighting, and on *élan* rather than firepower, mean that late 19th Century writers drew false conclusions. This repeated and reinforced the views of Fuller and Liddell Hart.[23] Luvaas considered Preston's article 'superficial in spots', but wrote that it approximated his own conclusions. He consulted Preston on his work and was relieved to find that the Canadian did not intend to pursue it further, leaving Luvaas a clear opportunity to publish, and to become the prime authority in the field.[24]

Luvaas intended his work to be part of a trilogy, the second part to cover the legacy of the war in American military thought, and the third to be on naval affairs.[25] Sadly he did not produce these two studies, but *The Military Legacy* can be seen as part of a more informally linked series of works dealing in whole or in part with the writings of G.F.R. Henderson. On the back of his MA and PhD research Luvaas published an article 'G.F.R. Henderson and the American Civil War' in 1956, and this was followed up by the publication, with interpretative notes from Luvaas, of a number of Henderson's works in *The American Civil War: A Soldier's View* in 1958. Finally, Henderson was one of the British military thinkers that Luvaas covered in *The Education of an Army*. Luvaas' view on Henderson and his influence did not change substantially throughout this period.[26]

* * *

Luvaas' work was part of the great flood of books appearing at the time of the Civil War Centennial, primarily of course from American writers. As such it pre-supposed the importance of the Civil War, that it was in some way unique and special, and that

23   Captain Edward Osborne Hewett RE., letter to his mother, 3 December 1862, published in R.A. Preston, 'A Letter from a British Military Observer of the American Civil War', *Military Affairs*, 16 (1952), pp.49-60. Hereafter referred to as Preston, 'Letter'; R.A. Preston, 'Military Lessons of the American Civil War', *Army Quarterly*, 65 (January 1953), pp.229-237.
24   KCL, LH 1/465 fols 104-05, Luvaas to Liddell Hart, 30 January 1953, fols 111-13, Luvaas to Liddell Hart, 20 March 1953.
25   Luvaas, *Military Legacy*, p.viii; KCL, LH 1/465 fols 260-62, Luvaas to Liddell Hart, 1 February 1960, fols 278-80, Luvaas to Liddell Hart, 22 December 1960. He appears to have considered this again in 1988, Jay Luvaas, *The Military Legacy of the Civil War: The European Inheritance*, 2nd edn (Lawrence: University of Kansas Press, 1988), p.xxviii
26   Jay Luvaas, 'G.F.R. Henderson and the American Civil War', *Military Affairs*, 20 (Fall 1956), pp.139-53; Jay Luvaas, *The Civil War: A Soldier's View. A Collection of Civil War Writings by Col. G.F.R. Henderson* (Chicago: University of Chicago Press, 1958); Luvaas, *Education of an Army*, pp.216-247.

this was missed by the European establishment. In a 1964 review the British historian Marcus Cunliffe, while recognising the quality of Luvaas' book, suggested that he was guilty of special pleading – 'anxious to insist upon the value of his war – as against others for example the Franco-Prussian War – for soldiers in search of object lessons'. Cunliffe questioned whether the Europeans were not already aware of the technologies deployed in America such as railways and the telegraph. He also queried Luvaas' interpretation of the importance of American cavalry tactics, and doubted whether a greater knowledge of American practice would have made any difference in 1914-18.[27] Some of these ideas have recently been restated by A.D. Harvey, in a modern critique of the depiction of the American Civil War as the first modern war, who concluded that '[i]t is very natural that the American Civil War should loom large in the consciousness of the American people and of American historians, but from a European perspective it was simply one more episode in the evolution of warfare'.[28] Harvey's article is a useful reminder that many of the features of the Civil War were also recognisable features of contemporary European conflicts, and that contemporary writers were not necessarily wrong if they saw continuity rather than revolution.

In 1959 the Unionist interpretation of the war as exemplified by T. Harry Williams and Bruce Catton was at its height. This accentuated the message taken from Liddell Hart and Fuller that Grant and Sherman were the geniuses of the war and that their campaigns were the true source of any lessons to be learnt.[29] Luvaas' work also predated the revisionist views of later writers on the place of the Civil War in military history. The work of Paddy Griffith, which challenged orthodox views on the weaponry and tactics of the armies engaged, is significant when considering both what the observers and theorists of the day should have noted, and what conclusions later writers should have drawn.[30] More recently Bruce Nosworthy has questioned the uniqueness of much that was seen in America, arguing that the weapons and doctrines used evolved from contemporary European models, and that the tactics developed by the Prussians in the 1860s were at least as innovative as anything in the Civil War.[31] Another revisionist is Earl J. Hess, who has challenged the view that it was increased infantry firepower that led to the adoption of entrenchments in America. Hess notes that armies in America had a tradition of field fortification that pre-dated the Civil War, that

27   Marcus Cunliffe, 'Recent Writing on the American Civil War', *History*, 50 (1965), pp.26-35 (pp.33–34).

28   A.D. Harvey, 'Was the American Civil War the First Modern War?', *History*, 97 (2012), pp.272-280 (p.280).

29   See Thomas J. Rowland, *George B. McClellan and Civil War History* (Kent: Kent University Press, 1998), pp.5-8 for a critique of how the Unionist view has come to dominate popular Civil War historiography.

30   Paddy Griffith, *Rally Once Again: Battle Tactics of the American Civil War* (Ramsbury: Crowood Press, 1987); Paddy Griffith, *Battle in the Civil War* (Camberley: Field Books, 1986).

31   Brent Nosworthy, *The Bloody Crucible of Courage* (New York: Carroll and Graf, 2003) particularly pp.629-40.

armies dug in even when mainly armed with smooth-bore muskets, and that it was the continued proximity of the armies in 1864-65 rather than the nature of their weapons that led to the extended use of temporary works. Again, there is evidence of continuity rather than revolution.[32] This is particularly relevant when re-assessing the technical observers, of whom Luvaas was so dismissive, and the subsequent adoption or otherwise of American technology and weapons. The British were much less inclined to see American exceptionalism, still less superiority, than is perhaps customary for modern popular works to do. Yet, conversely, they were not adverse to evaluating, adopting, and over time developing, technology from the other side of the Atlantic if they saw it as useful, and did so to a greater extent than Luvaas saw, due to his focus on Civil War historiography.

Not until 40 years after the publication of *Military Legacy* was there any real attempt to revise any of Luvaas' conclusions, and then indirectly. In 1998, M.D. Welch wrote a short book on the early history of the Royal United Service Institution (RUSI), an early military 'think tank' founded by the first Duke of Wellington in 1831. The final chapter of this work dealt with the response of the Institution to the American Civil War. Welch's main target was not Luvaas, but Fuller's idea that there was a Victorian intellectual 'dark age' during which the British Army ignored military history and science, and remained wedded to obsolete tactics and technology. In particular he stressed the importance of Sir Henry Whatley Tyler, an engineer officer who gave a series of lectures at the Institution between 1858 and 1864. Luvaas had briefly mentioned one of these, but in Welch's opinion had understated Tyler's importance in introducing scientific method to military analysis. Welch also saw the military debates of the period in the context of an overall Victorian concept of scientific progress. '[T]echnological change would lead to the perfected ideal form of warfare as imagined by the advanced Victorian mind'. Judged by the events of 1914-18 this view might have been mistaken, but it was not blind to the evidence of conflicts such as the Civil War.[33]

In a 2006 lecture, Brian Holden Reid looked at the effect of the Luvaas – Liddell Hart relationship, and questioned the accepted interpretation that the rest of the

32 Earl J. Hess, *The Rifle Musket in Civil War Combat: Reality and Myth* (Lawrence: University of Kansas, 2008) particularly pp.197-224. The alternative view that it was the rifle that changed the Civil War battlefield is put by Major Richard E. Kerr Jr (USA), 'Wall of Fire – The Rifle and Civil War Infantry Tactics' (Thesis for the Degree of Master Of Military Art And Science, U.S. Army Command and General Staff College, Fort Leavenworth, Kansas, 1990). Also Earl J. Hess, *Trench Warfare Under Grant and Lee* (Chapel Hill: University of North Carolina Press, 2007) pp.xiv-xv; and Earl J. Hess, *Field Armies and Fortifications in the Civil War: The Eastern Campaigns 1861-64* (Chapel Hill: University of North Carolina Press, 2005), pp.42-43, and pp.309-310 where he analyses the proportion of engagements involving fortifications before and during the Civil War. Hess' views had precedents in the work of Charles Cornwallis Chesney in the 1860s.

33 M.D. Welch, *Science and the British Officer: The Early Days of the Royal United Service Institute for Defence Studies*, (London: Royal United Institution for Defence Studies, 1998), particularly pp.8-9, 58-73; Luvaas, *Military Legacy*, pp.105-06.

world had either 'ignored or misinterpreted' the lessons of the American Civil War. He chose not to challenge Luvaas' detailed analysis of the tactical and operational lessons that the British took from the conflict, but argued that the war did in fact form a major part of the strategic framework of British military thought in the late 19th Century, particularly in relation to how a modern democratic state could prepare for the kind of war that might arise in the future. 'American problems and their solutions fertilized British thinking and stimulated new responses largely because the questions asked of the American experience helped frame the way military thinkers arrived at the answers to European problems.'[34]

Aside from Reid's re-appraisal, only one other historian has published anything directly associated with the British view of the war since Luvaas, Hugh Dubrulle with his article 'A Military Legacy of the Civil War: The British Inheritance' in 2003. Dubrulle challenged Luvaas' assertion, in the latter's foreword to the reprint of his work in 1988, that 'nothing has appeared since 1959 that casts new light upon the impact of the American experience upon European armies or the lessons that individual soldiers thought they had learned'. Dubrulle proposed that there were two distinct theories that were derived by the British, a 'semi-official' interpretation that the North had beaten a more skilful Southern military establishment solely by brute force, and a version held by the more radical press extolling the military values of Northern democracy. This followed on from his work on pro-Southern sentiment within the British media which highlighted the affinity British observers felt for the apparently more aristocratic South. Dubrulle saw this in part as a reaction to the challenge that the failures in the Crimea had posed to the aristocratic leadership of the Army. Dubrulle's articles mostly examine the politics of the day rather than military doctrine as such, and are based upon newspapers and popular journals rather than military writings, but he significantly tries to look at the subject from a 19th Century perspective without judging the success or failure of the lessons learnt. While on the whole Dubrulle probably overstates his case – for example, the observers had made note of the hospitality and civility of Northern officers and civilians as well as that of the Southerners – the role of political and class prejudice in drawing military lessons from the Civil War is an aspect that must be considered.[35]

There is also an unpublished doctorate thesis by an American student studying in the United Kingdom, Patrick C. Craddock's 'The American Civil War and its Influence on the British Army, 1865-1902' (2001). Craddock identified four main themes for his thesis: the retention of an officer corps drawn from a social elite; the

---

34   Luvaas, *Military Legacy*, p.227; Reid, "A Signpost That Was Missed", p.388.
35   Hugh Dubrulle, 'A Military Legacy of the Civil War: The British Inheritance', *Civil War History*, 49 (June 2003), pp.153-80; Hugh Dubrulle, '"We are Threatened with Anarchy … and Ruin": Fear of Americanization and the Emergence of an Anglo-Saxon Confederacy in England during the American Civil War', *Albion*, 33.4 (Winter 2001), pp.583–613, particularly p.604, hereafter Dubrulle, 'Anarchy … and Ruin'; Luvaas, *Military Legacy*, 2nd edn, p.xv.

primacy of the bayonet as the principal infantry weapon; that only mounted, offensive minded, cavalry was effective; and that there were no valuable lessons to be gained from an unprofessional army. These chosen topics were limited, and like his choice of campaigns and battles in Africa to analyse British tactics in the latter part of the century, highly selective. He arrived at the conclusion that the British only learnt the lessons of the Civil War through the debacle of the Second Boer War. Though he did not look at military thought after 1902, Craddock, like Luvaas, saw the Civil War through 20th Century eyes. Where he adopted a different approach from Luvaas was in looking at whether the tactics and culture of the British Army changed in practice, rather than what British military authors wrote about the Civil War. While this book rejects Craddock's conclusions, it does use and build upon his methodology, in particular the use of drill manuals to try and identify whether tactical lessons of the war were implemented by the British Army. Aside from the official Field Exercises and Drill Manuals, there are also several unofficial works which can be used to obtain an idea of how the Civil War affected the thinking of British writers.[36]

Historians covering the history of the British Army, or of specific services within it, have not written in any depth on British understanding of the Civil War. Edward Spiers' *The Late Victorian Army 1868-1902* (1999) did note the influence of the Civil War on the writings of Sir Patrick MacDougall, Sir Garnet Wolseley, Sir John Frederick Maurice, and G.F.R. Henderson, and in the debate on the role of cavalry. The Marquess of Anglesey's comprehensive study of the mounted arm covered American influence only briefly, though Stephen Badsey, in his influential work on British cavalry doctrine, considers the influence of the Civil War and the historical debates it inspired over the role of the cavalry to have been significant. There are similarly few references to any influence of the war in standard reference works on the Royal Artillery, the Army Ordnance Corps, and the Royal Engineers. Ian Beckett's studies of the 19th Century Volunteer movement did not discuss at any length the conclusions drawn from the Civil War by British supporters or detractors of the movement, while his 1989 lecture 'The Pen and the Sword: Reflections on Military Thought in the British Army, 1854-1914' did not mention the Civil War as an influence.[37]

---

36   Patrick C. Craddock, 'The American Civil War and its Influence on the British Army, 1865-1902' (Unpublished PhD Thesis, University of Aberystwyth, 2001).
37   Spiers, *The Late Victorian Army*, pp.244, 247, 249-251, 255-258; Marquess of Anglesey, *A History of the British Cavalry: 1816-1919*, 8 vols (London: Leo Cooper, 1973-1997), *Vol. 2 1851-1871* (Barnsley: Pen and Sword, 1998, originally published London: Leo Cooper, 1975), pp.447-52; Stephen Badsey, *Doctrine and Reform in the British Cavalry 1880-1918* (Aldershot: Ashgate, 2008), pp.42-47, 65-67; Major General A.A. Forbes, *History of the Army Ordnance Services*, 3 vols (London: Medici Society 1929); Major General. Sir C.E. Callwell and Major General Sir J. Headlam, *History of the Royal Artillery*, 3 vols (London: Royal Artillery Institution, 1931-40); Major General Whitworth Porter, *History of the Corps of Royal Engineers*, 3 vols (London: Longmans, Green, and Co, 1889-1915); Ian F.W. Beckett, *Riflemen Form* (Barnsley: Pen and Sword, 2007, originally published in 1982), pp.177-78, 182. Ian F.W. Beckett, *The Amateur Military Tradition 1558-1945*

Hew Strachan, in *Wellington's Legacy: The Reform of the British Army 1830-54* (1984) and *From Waterloo to Balaclava: Tactics, Technology and The British Army* 1815-54 (1985), examined the process of change in the early Victorian Army but stopped short of the period reviewed in this book. However, some of the developments and issues that Strachan noted, particularly the role of the bayonet; the impact of new infantry weapons of precision on training and tactics; the role of cavalry and how it should be armed; and the strategic challenge of providing an army reserve to match those of potential enemies; are shown to have pre-dated the Civil War, and these continued to be relevant into the second half of the century.[38]

A number of contemporary British sources have either been reprinted in modern editions by American academic publishers or quoted in general works and anthologies. The writings of several first hand observers, particularly Lieutenant Colonel Arthur James Lyon Fremantle, Lieutenant Colonel Garnet Wolseley, and Captain Fitzgerald Ross, are well known and frequently referenced.[39] However, for the most part they have been used to provide description or narrative rather than analysis. These popular accounts are of visits to the Confederacy and this has tended to support the idea that British observers favoured the South, and were subsequently more influenced by Confederate methods and tactics.[40]

* * *

Although Luvaas' original work concluded that the European armies had failed to respond to the lessons of the Civil War, he did not elaborate on what a successful

(Manchester: Manchester University Press, 1991), p.180; Ian F.W. Beckett, 'The Pen and the Sword: reflections on Military Thought in the British Army, 1854-1914', paper delivered at the British Commission for Military History Conference, Camberley, October 1989, printed in *Soldiers of the Queen*, 68 (March 1992), pp.3-7.

38   Hew Strachan, *Wellington's Legacy: The Reform of the British Army 1830-54* (Manchester: Manchester University Press, 1984); Hew Strachan, *From Waterloo to Balaclava: Tactics, Technology and the British Army 1830-54* (Cambridge: Cambridge University Press, 1985).

39   Lieutenant Colonel A J.L. Fremantle, *Three Months in the Southern States, April-June 1863* (Electronic edn) (Chapel Hill: University of North Carolina 2000; first published Mobile, SH Goetzel, 1864); 'An English Officer' [Lieutenant Colonel Garnet Joseph Wolseley], 'A Month's Visit to the Confederate Headquarters', *Blackwood's Edinburgh Magazine*, 93 (1863), pp.1-29; Fitzgerald Ross, *A Visit to the Cities and Camps of the Confederate States* (Edinburgh and London: Blackwoods, 1865). The British-born Ross was a serving officer in the Austrian army.

40   See for example Stanley Horn, *The Robert E. Lee Reader* (New York: Smithmark 1995, originally published 1949), pp.259-261, 316-21, 323-26, 329-32; Richard B. Harwell, *The Civil War Reader: The Confederate Reader* (New York: Konecky and Konecky, n.d.; originally published 1957), pp.177-87, 25-229, 236-241; Richard Wheeler, *Witness to Gettysburg* (New York: Harper and Row, 1987), pp.167-68, 183, 245-46. Amanda Foreman, *World on Fire* (London: Allen Lane, 2010) is more recent example of the integration of these popular sources, and others, into a narrative history.

response to those lessons would have been, other than the implication from his work that the interpretations of the 1920s and 1930s were in some way correct whereas earlier analysis was flawed. By the time the second edition of his work appeared in 1988, Luvaas admitted in a new introduction that perhaps the ways in which an army would demonstrate learning were more complex than his original study allowed. He also posed the questions whether a lesson implied a solution; and whether lessons from one conflict were universally applicable elsewhere, although without modifying his original text.[41] He was perhaps influenced in these observations by the emergence at around the same time of a new genre of military studies that began to apply theoretical models from the social sciences to investigate how military organisations change over time.[42] There are now several contending theories of thought in this area. One common theme, however, is that military organisations are difficult to change. While this is true of most large bureaucracies, it is emphasised in the military because of their hierarchical and disciplined structures, which mean dissent occurs with risk to the reputation of the individual or their unit. Failure in wartime can also lead to truly fatal consequences, resulting in a tendency to stick to trusted methods.[43]

Some modern research has suggested that the British Army has a unique culture and military heritage which has influenced the way in which it has learnt. Comparison of the German and British armies in the First World War suggests that the former had a centralised organisation and a formal 'lessons learnt' process which allowed it to quickly disseminate lessons from combat, but which did not foster radical change; whereas the British had a more devolved and informal, but not necessarily less successful, learning structure.[44] Another study, looking at the British Army's experi-

---

41   Luvaas, *Military Legacy*, 2nd edn, p.xv.
42   The three main models used have been balance of power theory, organisational theory, and learning theory. Richard D. Downie, *Learning from Conflict: The U.S. Military in Vietnam, El Salvador and the Drug War* (Westport: Praeger, 1998), pp.29-34 is a good summary.
43   For a summary, see Adam Grissom, 'The Future of Military Innovation Studies', *The Journal of Strategic Studies*, 29 (2006), pp.905-34 (pp.908-19). For resistance to change in the military, see Stephen Peter Rosen, *Winning the Next War: Innovations and the Modern Military* (Ithaca: Cornell University Press, 1991), p.2; Williamson Murray, 'Innovation Past and Future' in *Military Innovation in the Interwar Period*, ed. by Williamson Murray and Allan R. Millett (Cambridge: Cambridge University Press, 1998, originally published 1996), pp.300-28 (p.301); Theo Farrell and Terry Terriff, 'The Sources of Military Change' in Theo Farrell and Terry Terriff (Eds.), *The Sources of Military Change: Culture, Politics, Technology* (Boulder: Lynne Riener, 2002), pp.3-17 (p.4); J.A. Nagl, *Learning to Eat Soup with a Knife: Counterinsurgency Lessons from Malaya and Vietnam* (Chicago: University of Chicago Press, 2005), p.8-9; Theo Farrell, 'Improving in War: Military Adaptation and the British In Helmand Province', *The Journal of Strategic Studies*, 33/4 (2010), pp.567-94 (p.571).
44   Rosen, *Winning the Next War*, p.4; Robert T. Foley, 'Dumb donkeys or cunning foxes? Learning in the British and German armies during the Great War', *International Affairs* 90 (2014), pp.279-98. Stuart Bruce Taylor Mitchell, 'An Inter-disciplinary Study of Learning in the 32nd Division on the Western Front, 1916-1918' (PhD Thesis, University

ence in Malaya in the 1950s, concluded that because its culture had been honed in small colonial wars, with roots at least as far back as the Edwardian army, it was a more successful learning organisation than the US military in Vietnam, which remained wedded to conventional doctrines. In contrast, recent studies of the British Army's performance in Afghanistan have suggested that its reputation for excellence in counter-insurgency and low intensity conflict had concealed significant flaws in its learning process, in particular a poor institutional memory which means that it has had to continually re-learn lessons.[45]

There are considerable problems trying to apply these concepts and views to the 19th Century. For example, in modern theory significant change is defined as being reflected through doctrine. Elsewhere however studies have suggested that in the 19th Century the British Army lacked a formal doctrine in the modern sense of the word. This has then been met with the counter-argument that modern standards cannot be applied to the Victorian or Edwardian period.[46] In the absence of a formally stated doctrine, evidence of learning has to be identified through other sources; such as the curricula of military schools, new structures, new organisations, and other institutional responses to change.[47] Some of these will be seen in the British Army's responses to the Civil War, particularly in relation to technology. The term 'doctrine' is therefore used throughout this book in a more informal sense of the stated standard British military practice, in particular as identified through instructional manuals. This is a concept that would be more comprehensible to the Victorian military mind than modern definitions.[48]

It has also been suggested that the British Army's practices and learning processes were driven not by doctrine, but by an *ethos*, a universal philosophy based upon shared values of loyalty, self-confidence, courage, obedience, moral virtue, and sacrifice, representing the cultural spirit of the nation. In particular there was a notion that officers also had to be 'gentlemen', and the British class structure was reflected in the

of Birmingham, 2015), pp.272-76, concluded that the command structure, battle experience, and leadership, rather than top down instruction drove learning in the British Army in 1916-18.

45   Nagl, *Learning to Eat Soup with a Knife,* pp.ix, xii, xxii, 9-11; Foley, et al. 'Transformation in Contact', pp.259-62; Farrell, 'Improving in War', p.591, Sergio Catignani, 'Coping with Knowledge: Organizational Learning in the British Army?', *The Journal of Strategic Studies,* 37 (2014), pp.30–64 (p.32).

46   Shelford Bidwell and Dominick Graham, *Fire-Power: The British Army Weapons and Theories of War 1904-1945* (Barnsley: Pen and Sword, 2004, first published London: Allen & Unwin, 1982), pp.2-3. For a summary of the arguments see Mitchell, 'Learning in the 32nd Division', pp.30-31.

47   Nagl, *Learning to Eat Soup with a Knife,* p.7.

48   Luvaas, *Military Legacy,* p.233 seems to use the word 'doctrine' in this more informal sense. However, in his 1988 introduction Luvaas stated that drill manuals did *not* constitute doctrine, but then seems to suggest a concept of 'informal doctrine' which he applied to Civil War practice as well as the French and German ideas of 1914 (*Military Legacy,* 2nd ed., p.xviii).

military hierarchy. An *ethos*, by its nature, is a more difficult thing to change than doctrine. There was perhaps no need for the British to change theirs, since by relying on philosophical principles of *ethos* rather than on a rigid, scientifically deduced doctrine, the British Army's culture deliberately rejected standardised solutions in favour of independent thinking, allowing its officers to adapt to local conditions when fighting anywhere in the world. The most recent work on the subject, again focussed on the First World War, suggests that a combination of *ethos* and personal networks, largely based upon a common social upbringing amongst the officer class, gave the British Army an effective learning system.[49] It may however have resulted in resistance to foreign practices that were seen to be at odds with these underlying principles, and therefore characteristically 'un-British'. Much of the rejection of German practice from the 1890s onwards seems to have stemmed from such a feeling, and not from the renewed study of the Civil War.[50] It may also have led to a particular, and negative, interpretation of the more 'democratic' nature of American society, and its impact on military effectiveness.

Doctrine and *ethos* are not mutually exclusive, nor are they in themselves necessarily either enablers or obstacles to change. Learning and learning processes exist in some form in all organisations, and the questions that need to be asked are how the late Victorian British Army learned and why; what it learnt; and how that aligned to its mission and strategy.[51]

In 1861 the British army had just emerged from two conflicts which had severely undermined its self-confidence and prestige. The Crimean War of 1854-1856, the first fought against a European adversary in nearly 40 years, had exposed serious shortcomings in its organisation and leadership. The Indian Mutiny of 1857-1859 had raised similar concerns on its fitness for purpose to fulfil its imperial duties.[52] The conservative establishment could resist but not ignore the rise of a new breed of military professionals needed to fight a modern, technological war. During the 1850s a number of new institutions appeared which reflected the need for a more professional, scientific

---

49   Albert Palazzo, *Seeking Victory on the Western Front* (Lincoln and London: University of Nebraska Press, 2000), pp.9-13; Aimée Fox, *Learning to Fight: Military Innovation and Change in the British Army, 1914-1918* (Cambridge: Cambridge University Press, 2018), particularly pp.20-28, 37-45, 49-72.

50   T. Miller Maguire, 'Our Art of War as "Made In Germany"', *United Service Magazine*, n.s., 13 (1896), pp.124-133, 280-291, argued for the teaching of *British* military history rather than the war of 1870-71. The objections that Prussian practices were 'un-English' can be dated at least as far back as 1873, Colonel Lumley Graham, introduction to Wilhelm Carl Friedrich Gustav Johann von Scherff, *The New Tactics of Infantry*, translated by Colonel Lumley Graham (London: Henry S. King & Co., 1873), pp.v-vii.

51   This approach is suggested by Anthony J. DiBella, Can the Army Become a Learning Organization? A Question Reexamined', *Joint Force Quarterly*, 56 (2010), pp.117-22 (p.119).

52   Michael Barthorp, *The Armies of Britain 1485-1980* (London: National Army Museum, 1980), pp.155-56, 175-77, 183-84.

approach to warfare. The adoption of the Minié bullet and the Enfield Rifle Musket led to the creation of the Hythe Musketry School in 1853, while the development of rifled artillery led to the opening of a School of Gunnery at Shoeburyness in 1859. The Army's educational establishment was re-organised with the formation of the Staff College in 1858. The United Service Institution, originally founded in 1839, transformed itself during the 1850s into an organisation which actively supported scientific and technical thought within the military. The Institution first published its Journal in 1857, recording lectures held in the Institution on contemporary military concerns, and was given Royal patronage in 1860.[53]

The Civil War also occurred towards the beginning of a period of rapid innovation in military technology that transformed warfare, and which would have occurred with or without a war in America. From the widespread adoption by armies of the rifled musket in the 1850s, through the introduction of breech-loading firearms in the 1860s and 1870s, to the magazine rifles of the 1890s, infantry firepower increased five or six-fold.[54] Advances in metallurgy, projectile design and explosives similarly transformed the destructive power of artillery. Defensive technologies were emerging such as wire entanglements, land and sea mines – 'torpedoes' in the contemporary parlance – and the use of iron in fortifications.

As the war in America finished, a third dynamic was introduced. The wars of German unification between 1864 and 1871 dramatically altered the balance of power in Europe, and ended the previous dominance of French military thought in favour of Prussian. The rapid victories of the Prussian armies naturally led to a search for the reasons for their success. 1864 and 1866 were relatively easy to attribute to the superiority of the Prussian breech-loading rifle to its opponents' muzzle-loaders. Yet in 1870 the French, heirs to the Napoleonic tradition, were beaten as much by the Prussian military system as by technology. The Franco-Prussian War (1870-71) in particular was a significant shock as the defeated French army, though raised through a form of conscription rather than voluntary enlistment, was nevertheless more similar to the British Army model of a professional army than that of Prussia which included large numbers of short service conscripts.[55]

53   Barthorp, *Armies of Britain*, p.176; Strachan, *From Waterloo to Balaclava*, pp.27-31; Strachan, *Wellington's Legacy*, pp.131-132; John Atkins, 'Early History of the Army School of Musketry in Hythe, Kent', *Black Powder* (Winter 2007), pp.35-37 (p.35); Brian Bond, *The Victorian Army and the Staff College, 1854–1914* (London: Eyre Methuen, 1972), p.82; < http://www.rusi.org/history > [accessed 19 September 2015]; Welch, pp.39-42.

54   Trained infantry armed with a smoothbore musket or Enfield rifle had a normal rate of fire of around two rounds per minute (Paddy Griffith says up to five in well trained hands but this would be exceptional). Infantry armed with breech-loading rifles could fire twelve rounds per minute. The BEF in 1914 was trained to fire 15 aimed rounds per minute with the magazine Lee-Enfield rifle. Griffith, *Rally Once Again*, pp.74-75; Hess, *The Rifled Musket in the Civil War*, pp.100-03; Kerr, 'Wall of Fire', p.22.

55   Michael Howard, *The Franco-Prussian War* (London: Methuen, 1981), pp.29, 455. Most of the significant engagements of the war took place in 1870.

These three drivers of social change, technological change, and the replacement of French military dominance in Europe with that of Prussia, come together in consideration of how the British Army's structure and tactical doctrine changed between 1861 and 1900. The response included both major immediate changes such as the Cardwell reforms, and an ongoing political debate as to the ability of the army to fight a modern war.[56] As well as the potential invasion threat to Britain from a continental power, whether it be the traditional enemy France or the new power of Imperial Germany, in the 1870s the geopolitical balance was further altered by the expansion of Russia in Asia which raised the additional prospect of a direct military threat to India. As well as this, the American Civil War itself raised the spectre of a first-class military power with a land border adjacent to British territory. British military theorists tried to interpret all of these external threats in a national and imperial context.[57]

* * *

The second half of the 19th Century was a time of rapid changes in both military technology and thinking. The lessons of the American Civil War were not always obvious, nor was their applicability relevant in all circumstances, and their adoption would be constrained as a result. Previous views taken by historians of how the British Army learnt or failed to learn from it have presented an incomplete picture, and all of them have been influenced by historiographic bias. In particular the works of Fuller and Liddell Hart were overly influenced by their experience of the First World War and their use of the Civil War to exemplify their military philosophies. Luvaas' seminal work was then in turn also heavily influenced by his mentor Liddell Hart, and is overdue a critical review.

Luvaas wrote in 1959 that 'the trail of ideas at times is faint and difficult to follow'.[58] His treatment of the subject appeared so comprehensive that few have queried the trail he blazed. Most have accepted his conclusions and not followed up the subject. Others have ignored the Civil War, in favour of analysing the development of the art of war from a primarily continental European viewpoint. The few that have explored further have mostly focussed on the tactical, and evaluated the British assimilation of the Civil War from the viewpoint of the Transvaal or the Western Front.

This ignores the prominent place that Civil War study held in the British Army at the end of the 19th Century, a substantially different situation to the continental

---

56 Enacted by Edward Cardwell, Secretary of State for War 1868-74, these included the abolition of purchased commissions and flogging, short term enlistments, and the reorganisation of the regimental system into local recruitment areas. See Spiers, *The Late Victorian Army*, pp.2-24 for a full discussion.
57 Christopher Clark, *The Sleepwalkers: How Europe Went to War in 1914* (London: Allen Lane, 2012), pp.136-39.
58 Luvaas, *Military Legacy*, p.13.

European military establishments.[59] The aim of this book is to re-examine the British Army's evaluation of the Civil War without the hindsight of these later conflicts. It looks at the process by which the British Army took on the lessons of the Civil War and how this prepared it for the challenges of war in the 20th Century.

---

59   Luvaas, *Military Legacy*, pp.133-37, 164-65, for the study of the Civil War in France and Germany. For a modern study of the latter see Lieutenant Colonel Kay Brinkmann (German Army), 'German Observations and Evaluations of the U.S. Civil War: A Study in Lessons Not Learned' (Thesis for the Degree of Master of Military Art and Science, U.S. Army Command and General Staff College, Fort Leavenworth, Kansas, 2000).

2

Lessons Ignored or Misunderstood? – The Observers

It is impossible to know precisely how many officers and men of the British Army observed the American Civil War first hand. Some men left British service to enlist in the armies of the warring states, others used periods of personal leave to review the conflict, while a few were sent under instruction (though never as official representatives of the government) with a view to examine particular aspects of military development. This chapter looks at the first hand experiences of British observers. It first looks at the context for the observers to the conflict. Why were they there, who were they, how did they travel and how did this influence what they saw? What bias did these viewpoints introduce? Many of the most frequently cited accounts are written by observers in the South, and the reasons behind this and its implications for the conclusions that have been drawn are examined. Finally, what did they see and how perceptive were they in their observations, and what impact did they have, if any, on the major debates of the day?

All of the major European nations sent observers of some form or other to the American Civil War. Britain, however, had more reasons than most to be interested in the events across the Atlantic. *The Times* declared that 'civil war in the US affects our people even more generally than the Indian Mutiny'.[1] Despite the growing diversity of the American population, the two countries were still closely linked culturally, politically, socially, and economically. The textile mills of Lancashire were especially dependent upon Southern cotton, which had supplied over three-quarters of their raw material in 1860. The Confederacy's initial policy of blocking its export in the hope of forcing overseas recognition, followed by the impact of the Union blockade of Southern ports, were among the main causes of a severe economic depression in the area, dubbed the 'cotton famine'. This caused the closure of over 300 factories, put over 400,000 workers out of work or on short time, and cost the cotton trade around £65 million. Perhaps surprisingly, many cotton mill workers nevertheless supported

---

1   *The Times*, 21 August 1862, quoted in R.J.M. Blackett, *Divided Hearts: Britain and the American Civil War* (Baton Rouge: Louisiana State University Press, 2001), p.4.

the Unionist cause. The industrial north of England had a Radical political tradition which supported the extension of democracy, and an evangelical Christian tradition of abolitionism, that made its population more inclined to support the Union rather than the aristocratic and slave-holding Confederacy. This did not prevent the port and shipyards of Liverpool, which had originally grown rich on the slave trade and subsequently on the cotton trade, from having a decidedly pro-Southern bias.[2] These links had a significant influence on the views that the British participants formed of the conflict. A large proportion of the American population had been born in Britain or Ireland, and many more were of British or Irish descent.[3] More than one British writer saw the warring sides as reflective of their own Civil War of the 17th Century, a fight between 'the descendants of cavaliers and the descendants of roundheads'.[4]

Historic associations are also reflected in the racial subtexts which run through the writings of the period. While no writer could overtly come out in favour of slavery, which had finally been abolished throughout the British Empire by 1843,[5] they could refer to the British experience of emancipation in the West Indies as a reason not to interfere in the workings of the 'Peculiar Institution', which one writer even went so far as describing as 'a way of getting an inferior and superior race to live together somehow in nearly equal numbers'.[6] Alongside the assumption of the inferiority of the African races there also ran the idea of the superiority of the Anglo-Saxon race. This would be evidenced by the poor regard generally shown for troops of Irish or German extraction and an inflation of the martial prowess of the 'Anglo-Saxon' South.[7]

2   Blackett, *Divided Hearts* p.7-9; W.O. Henderson, 'The Cotton Famine in Lancashire', *Transactions Of The Historic Society Of Lancashire And Cheshire*, 84 (1932), pp.37-62; Debrulle, 'Military Legacy', pp.155-56.

3   In the 1860 census 2,197,277 people in the United States were British or Irish born. Of these, 2,087,345 were in states that remained in the Union. Ella Lonn, *Foreigners in the Union Army and Navy* (Baton Rouge: Louisiana State University Press, 1951), p.663.

4   [Marquess of Lothian], *The Confederate Secession* (Edinburgh: W. Blackwood & Sons, 1864), p.12; Wolseley, 'A Month's Visit', p.25; Blackett, *Divided Hearts*, p.15; Tom Vallely, 'Why Liverpool and Manchester supported different sides in the American Civil War', *Crossfire*, 118 (Winter 2018), pp.20-24.

5   Although the Slavery Abolition Act was passed in 1833 and came into effect the following year, this did not cover territory governed by the East India Company, where the practice was only abolished in 1843.

6   Sir James Fitzjames Stephen, 'England and America', *Fraser's Magazine*, 68 (1863), pp.419-37 (p.437). The *Illustrated London News* described slavery as repugnant to the English mind, W. Stanley Hoole, *Vizetelly Covers the Confederacy (Confederate Centennial Studies Number 4)* (Tuscaloosa: Confederate Publishing Company, 1957), p.74. On West Indian abolition, Wolseley, 'A Month's Visit', p.3; William Watson, *Life in the Confederate Army: Being the Observations and Experiences of an Alien in the South During the American Civil War* (London: Chapman and Hall, 1887), pp.28-30; Blackett, *Divided Hearts*, pp.37-38.

7   Dubrulle, 'Anarchy ... and Ruin', pp.598-601.

Economic ties between the countries were strong, and could dictate positions on the war. The cotton trade was the most substantial of these, affecting up to five million people in Britain according to the *Army and Navy Gazette*. In the view of many Southerners this was a reason in itself to expect Britain to side with their cause and an influence upon their behaviour towards the observers, although Americans on both sides attached great importance to British support. This affected the views of the observers as their hosts on both sides, but particularly in the South, aimed to influence and impress them.[8]

Alongside these political and social aspects, however, it can be forgotten that there were pressing military reasons to take an interest in the war. At a time of rapid techno-logical change, it was highly desirable to see new weapons in action. This particularly applied to the technical branches of the service who were interested in, for example, the practical effects of new artillery pieces on fortifications.

War between the United States and Britain was also considered a serious possibility by the military and political writers of the time. The War of 1812 was within living memory, and there had been a history of minor squabbles between the two countries ever since – the Canadian rebellion of 1837 when American sympathisers occupied Navy Island in the Niagara River and erected batteries there; the Maine dispute of 1843; the Oregon dispute which came to a crisis in 1845; the Mosquito protectorate in 1856; and the so-called 'Pig War' over San Juan Island in modern Washington state as recently as 1859.[9] In the heightened tension brought about by the Civil War, many scenarios were envisaged by British writers. Some predicted a war instigated by the North to reunify the states on the back of patriotic fervour, or the acquisition of British territory to compensate for the lost territory of the South – a not entirely unreasonable fear when the New York press was calling for the annexation of Canada as early as 1861.[10]

8   *Army and Navy Gazette*, 28 June 1862, p.405; [Robert Bourke], 'A Month with the Rebels', *Blackwood's Edinburgh Magazine*, 90 (1861), pp.755-67 (p.762); Wolseley, 'A Month's Visit', p.25; [Lieutenant Colonel Henry Charles Fletcher], 'A Run Through the Southern States', *Cornhill Magazine*, 7 (1863), pp.495–515 (p.499); Edward Dicey, *Six Months in the Federal States*, 2 vols (London and Cambridge: Macmillan, 1863), Vol.II, p.39; William Howard Russell, 'Recollections of the Civil War', *North American Review*, 166 (1898), pp.234-49, 362-73, 491-502, 618-30, 740-50 (p.365); Stephen, 'England and America', p.419.

9   William Forsyth, 'The American Crisis', *Quarterly Review*, 111 (January 1862), pp.239-280 (pp.259-262). The San Juan Island dispute was not resolved until 1872, see San Juan Island National Historical Park webpage 'The Pig War', <http://www.nps.gov/sajh/historyculture/the-pig-war.htm> [accessed 26 March 2015].

10 Forsyth, 'The American Crisis', pp.272, 275-76; Stephen, 'England and America', p.420; Wolseley 'A Month's Visit', p.23; Major General Sir George Bell, *Soldier's Glory: Being Rough Notes of an old Soldier*, ed. Brian Stuart (London: Spellmount, 1991, originally published London: Day, 1867), p.298.

More likely perhaps was a precipitation of war through incidents resulting from the blockade which the North had placed upon Southern ports. In November 1861 just such an incident occurred when a US Navy vessel, the USS *San Jacinto* stopped the British mail packet *Trent* and removed two Confederate agents from on board. The British government protested the act as a violation of the rights of neutral shipping under international law. For anti-American writers the *Trent* affair was 'an act of outrage which leaves us no alternative but reparation or war'.[11] In February 1863 a further incident involving the seizure of the *Peterhoff*, a British merchantman deemed by the United States to be a blockade runner, renewed the tensions between the two countries.[12] In 1864 Lord Lyons, the British Ambassador in Washington, wrote requesting permanent military staff to be added to the legation there in order to monitor the military and naval forces of the United States, so that appropriate measures could be taken at a moment's notice in the event of a declaration of war.[13]

Whatever the possible cause of a new Anglo-American conflict, the war made the US military a serious threat to the security of British North America and many observers viewed war as inevitable.[14] The duration of the fighting saw two missions to review Canadian defences, one in 1862 and the second in 1863-64. The *Trent* affair resulted in a significant deployment of troops to Canada, many of whom were not withdrawn until 1867.[15] The pre-war American army and navy were small in comparison to the military resources of the British Empire and may have been perceived to be of little consequence, but the wartime forces of the Union consisted of half a million

11   William Forsyth, 'The American Crisis', p.259. See also ibid, pp.259-62, 272, 275-76;
     Robert Cecil, 'The United States as an Example', *Quarterly Review*, 117 (January 1865),
     pp.249-86, (p.250).
12   Hove Public Library (HPL), Wolseley Archive, 163/3/26, Wolseley to his brother
     Richard, Montreal, 7 August 1863; J.G. Randall, *Lincoln the President: Midstream* (New
     York: Dodd, Mead & Co., 1952), pp.334-38.
13   Kew, The National Archives (TNA), CO 880/6/1, *Canada: Defences of Canada*, Lord
     Lyons to Lord Russell, Washington, 4 July 1864. This enclosed a letter from Lieutenant
     Colonel Gallwey RE to Lyons dated 27 May 1864 on the probable operations in the event
     of war.
14   [Robert Bourke], 'Canada – Our Frozen Frontier', *Blackwood's Edinburgh Magazine*, 91
     (1862), pp.102-17 (p.102); [George Robert Gleig], 'Defence of Canada', *Blackwood's
     Edinburgh Magazine*, 91 (1862), pp.228-58 (p.228); Anon, 'Canada – Its Several Invasions'
     in *Journal of the Household Brigade for the year 1862* (London: W. Clowes and Sons, 1863),
     pp.150-51; HPL, Wolseley Archive, 163/3, Wolseley to his brother Richard, Montreal, 29
     November 1861; Montreal, 6 August 1862; Baltimore, 21 September 1862; and Montreal,
     7 August 1863.
15   TNA,WO 33/11/0185, *Report of the Commissioners Appointed to Consider the Defences of
     Canada* (1862); TNA, WO 33/15/0265, Lieutenant Colonel Jervois RE, *Report on the
     Defence of Canada, made to the Provincial Government on the 10th November 1864, and of
     the British Naval Stations in the North Atlantic: Together with Observations on the Defence
     of New Brunswick, etc.* (London: HMSO, 1865), hereafter referred to as Jervois, *Defence
     of Canada*; TNA, WO 33/11/0155, *List of Troops and Stores Embarked for British North
     America*; Callwell and Headlam, *History of the Royal Artillery*, I (1931), p.47.

men and nearly six hundred vessels, which was clearly a different matter.[16] The British therefore had both the motive and opportunity to observe a powerful potential enemy.

In the early days of the war most observers were non-military men – particularly reporters such as William Howard Russell of *The Times*, Edward Dicey of the *Spectator*, and Samuel Philips Day of the *Morning Herald*. Some reporters, including Russell and Day, did manage to travel through the Southern states in 1861, but the majority of their observations were constrained to information from the North.[17] The experiences and views of the journalists are of interest to the general history of the war, for background as to how British people saw the conflict, and for insight into the media representation of the conflict, but are of little value for assessing how the British Army reacted and learnt from the conflict, so the focus of this chapter is on the military observers.

The history of British observation can be broadly classified into three phases, roughly coinciding with the overall course of the war, although each individual observer's experience was unique. The first phase can generally be taken to run from the start of hostilities at Fort Sumter, South Carolina, in April 1861 through to the Seven Days battles in front of the Confederate capital at Richmond, Virginia in June 1862. During this period both sides had to build up their military organisations almost from scratch, a process in which the North had a distinct advantage in resources. The South won the morally significant battle of First Bull Run (known as Manassas in the South) outside the Union capital, Washington DC, in July 1861, as well as a number of lesser actions which prevented the immediate collapse of the new Confederacy. The balance of success for the first year of the war nevertheless lay with the Union. The border states of Missouri and Kentucky were secured; Western Virginia (later acceding to the Union as a new state in 1863) occupied; and several strategically important locations on the coast were seized, the most significant of which was the largest city in the South, New Orleans, which secured the mouth of the vital Mississippi river for the North. Major General Thomas 'Stonewall' Jackson caused consternation in Washington from March to June 1862 with a campaign in the Shenandoah Valley

16   TNA, WO 33/14/0229, Lieutenant Colonel T.L. Gallwey RE and Captain H.J. Alderson
     RA, *Report upon the Military Affairs of the United States of America*, p.32. 'It is impossible
     to ascertain the strength of the Federal Army, it is popularly believed to amount to nearly
     a million men but in reality the numbers cannot reach to half that figure.' The report goes
     on to calculate the Federal strength at 450,000 men. Hereafter referred to as the Gallwey
     Report. TNA, FO 881/1254, *Report by Captain Goodenough, R.N. on the Naval Resources of
     the United States*, Cabinet Paper dated 20 May 1864, estimated the strength of the navy of
     the United States built and building at 588 vessels, including the Mississippi squadron.
17   William Howard Russell, 'Recollections of the Civil War', *North American Review*, 166
     (1898), pp.234-49, 362-73, 491-502, 618-30, 740-50; Dicey, *Six Months in the Federal
     State*; Samuel Philips Day, *Down South: or, An Englishman's Experience at the Seat of the
     American War* (London: Hurst and Blackett, 1862); Major F. Miller, 'Military Sketch
     of the Present War in America', *Journal of the Royal United Service Institution*, 6 (1863),
     pp.241-62 (p.253).

in northern Virginia that seemed to threaten the city, but elsewhere the fortunes of war favoured the Union. A Confederate counter-offensive in the West was fought off at the battle of Shiloh (April 1862). The following month the North's senior general, George B. McClellan, began a campaign on the Virginian Peninsula which most foreign experts expected to take Richmond and end the war with a Northern victory.

That victory was prevented through Robert E. Lee's victory over McClellan in the Seven Days battles. This initiated the second phase of the war, which was characterised by a series of Confederate successes against a succession of Union commanders in the eastern theatre of the war in Virginia, in particular the battles of Second Bull Run (August 1862), Fredericksburg (December 1862), and Chancellorsville (May 1863). However, tactical victories did not lead to strategic success in the form of either Northern submission or foreign recognition of the Confederacy. Twice in this phase of the war Lee took his Army of Northern Virginia northwards into Union territory, but on both occasions his encounters with the Army of the Potomac, the principle army of the North, failed to result in decisive victory. The drawn battle of Antietam (October 1862) led directly to President Lincoln issuing the Emancipation Proclamation, which declared slaves in seceded territory to be freed, while defeat in the three-day encounter at Gettysburg in July 1863 forced Lee back onto the strategic defensive. In the western theatre Southern armies had also initially met with some success, carrying the war back into Kentucky with the Perryville campaign of October 1862, and successfully defending a number of attempts by Major General Ulysses S. Grant to seize Vicksburg, now the most important strategic point on the Mississippi. The eventual fall of that city on the 4 July 1863, coming the same day as Lee began his retreat from Gettysburg, marked the end of this phase of Confederate ascendancy.

Although the South was still capable of winning tactical victories after July 1863 (most importantly the Battle of Chickamauga in September 1863, which resulted in the main Union army in the West becoming besieged in the strategic communication hub of Chattanooga, Tennessee), the third phase of the war is primarily the story of gradual Confederate decline. It is also the story of the rise to ascendency of Ulysses S. Grant. In November Grant successfully broke the siege of Chattanooga, reversing the strategic results of Chickamauga. Appointed by Lincoln to overall command of all the Union forces in February 1864, Grant finally made effective use of the North's superior resources by organising a series of more or less co-ordinated campaigns which wore down the military and economic strength of the South. These campaigns were conducted at huge cost to both sides. A new offensive in Virginia, nominally led by the victor of Gettysburg, Major General George Meade, but in practice managed by Grant in person, pinned Robert E. Lee's Army of Northern Virginia through a series of bloody actions such as the Wilderness and Spotsylvania (May 1864) and Cold Harbour (June 1864). Meanwhile in the eastern theatre Major General William Tecumseh Sherman advanced from Chattanooga against the communications and industrial centre of Atlanta, Georgia. Both of these campaigns were characterised by the extensive use of temporary earthworks as the Northern armies tried to manoeuvre those of the South out of defensive positions. Grant's campaign then stagnated into siege warfare at Petersburg, Virginia, from July 1864 onwards, raising Southern hopes that the North might become war-weary and vote Lincoln out of office in the elections due in November, bringing about a negotiated peace and independence. At Atlanta, however, Sherman was able to manoeuvre the Southern army under General John Bell Hood out of its defences. While Hood then attempted another raid into Northern territory which ended in bloody failure at the battles of Franklin (November 1864) and Nashville (December 1864), Sherman took the war to the economic heartland of the Confederacy by marching through Georgia to the port of Savannah. Other significant Union victories were won by Rear Admiral David Farragut at Mobile, Alabama, (August 1864) and by Major General Philip Sheridan in the Shenandoah Valley (August-October 1864). The cumulative effect of these successes both won the election for Lincoln in November 1864, and crippled the Southern economy and logistics, bringing about its total collapse the following spring.

* * *

Probably the first British officer to visit the United States during the war was Major General Sir George Bell, a veteran of both the Peninsular War and the Crimean War as well as the Canadian expedition of 1837, who arrived from Canada in the summer of 1861. Bell believed from what he saw that the conflict would soon be settled in favour of the North and chose not to travel further south than Washington, where he had met Lieutenant General Winfield Scott, Major General George B. McClellan, and, briefly, President Lincoln, as well as William Russell. Notwithstanding Russell's much publicised report of the Bull Run debâcle in July 1861, which was greeted by detractors of Northern democracy in Britain as proof of its decadence and shortcomings in its means of making war, throughout this period there was still a perception that the North would recover and overwhelm the South through its economic strength.[18] Bell was certainly of this opinion, showing none of the Southern bias of which later British observers were accused. Though critical of the Americans as braggarts, and at times of the soldiers ('ragged fellows with arms'), he was impressed by the health of the troops, and by McClellan. Bell believed McClellan was 'just the man to lead them – young, vigilant, quiet in manner and address – popular and with a kind word for everyone'. He thought that the fortifications around Washington made it secure and that the Confederacy had missed an opportunity to take the city offered them by their victory at Bull Run.[19]

18   William Howard Russell in *The Times*, 16 August 1861, published in *The American Civil War: Extracts from The Times 1860-1865*, ed. by Hugh Brogan, (London: Times Books, 1975), p.15, hereafter Brogan, *Extracts from the Times*.
19   Bell, *Soldier's Glory*, pp.308-312.

From all I can see and learn, the Federal army are now in the ascendant, and will win the day. There is money at command, the capital secure, an increasing army, and good commissariat, learning their new trade, and united heart and voice.[20]

After Bull Run in July there was indeed a steady progression of Northern successes during the remainder of 1861 which secured the contested border states of Missouri and Kentucky for the North. Edward Dicey, another perceptive Northern sympathiser, also felt that criticism of the Federal government for not sweeping all before it had underestimated what it had managed to achieve in mobilising the people of the Northern states for war.[21]

As a retired officer, Bell's assessment of the capability of the Union army at this time perhaps carries more weight than those of the journalists, and he probably shared it both with the British Ambassador in Washington, Lord Lyons, and with the British commander in Canada, Lieutenant General William Fenwick Williams. In the spring of 1862, a number of serving army officers, particularly those based in Canada as a result of the *Trent* affair and the heightened military tension, began to travel to the seat of the war. As the expectation was still that the North would soon be victorious these observers largely confined themselves to the operations of McClellan's Army of the Potomac. In April the special correspondent of *The Times* reported reviewing troops camped at Alexandria, Virginia, in company with Colonel Wetherall, Chief of Staff in Canada, 'who has been attracted here by the desire of seeing the vast army which his neighbours have put in the field'.[22] Later that month officers serving in the Scots Fusilier Guards in Montreal visited Washington hoping to see the army but found that it had left for Yorktown.[23]

Lieutenant Colonel Henry Charles Fletcher and Lieutenant Colonel Edward Neville, also from the Scots Fusilier Guards, and who obtained a two month leave of absence from their regiment in Canada in March 1862, were more fortunate. On McClellan's invitation these two officers were granted exceptional permission to accompany the army as he started his campaign against Richmond in the spring of 1862. They left Washington in the company of Brigadier General Van Vliet, Chief Quartermaster to the Army of the Potomac, on 2 April, and disembarked at Fortress

20   Bell, *Soldier's Glory*, p.310.
21   Dicey, *Six Months in the Federal States*, Vol.II, pp.6-7, 22-23.
22   'A Glance at the Federals', *Army and Navy Gazette*, 5 April 1862, p.220. Up until June 1862 the *Army and Navy Gazette* was still predicting imminent Northern victory at Richmond, *Army and Navy Gazette*, 17 May 1862, pp.308-09, and 14 June 1862, p.373. The latter, published after the Seven Days battles, illustrates the time delay for news to reach Britain from America.
23   'R.D.' [probably Captain Robert Augustus Dalzell] 'Boston, New York and Washington' in *Journal of the Household Brigade for the year 1862*, 192-96. Dalzell along with Lieutenant Sir Richard Cunliffe took leave from their regiment from 8 April to 1 May, which fits with the dates in the *Journal*, see TNA, WO 17/1566, *Monthly Returns to the Adjutant General, Canada, 1862*.

British guards officers with the Army of the Potomac, Camp Winfield Scott, Yorktown, Virginia, 1862. Henry Fletcher is seated on the right. (Library of Congress)

Monroe at the end of the Virginia Peninsula on 4 April. Both overstayed their leave and remained present at McClellan's headquarters through to his defeat by General Robert E. Lee in the Seven Days campaign, not leaving the Union army until 1 July.[24] Several engineering and artillery officers also visited McClellan's army at this time to investigate the technology being used by the army at this stage of the war. Their experiences and observations, being largely confined to technical matters, will be covered in the next chapter.[25]

24   Lieutenant Colonel Henry Charles Fletcher, 'Visit to the Army of the Potomac' in *Journal of the Household Brigade for the year 1862* (London: W. Clowes and Sons, 1863), pp.197-99; Lieutenant Colonel Henry Charles Fletcher, *History of the American War*, 3 vols (London: R. Bentley, 1865–66), Vol.I, p.v.; William Howard Russell *My Diary North and South* (Boston: T.O.H.P. Burnham, 1863), pp.597-99; London, British Library (BL), Layard Papers, Add. 38988, fols 190-95, General William Fenwick Williams to Sir Austen Henry Layard, Montreal, 11 July 1862; WO 17/1566.

25   TNA, WO 33/11/0174, *Report of Officers of the British Army on American Arms August 1862*; Captain F. Beaumont RE, 'On Balloon Reconnaissance as Practised by the American Army', *R.E. Professional Papers*, 12 (1863), pp.94-103.

The only record of a serving officer travelling into the Confederate states prior to June 1862 is Lieutenant the Earl of Dunmore, serving with the Scots Fusilier Guards. Dunmore went absent without leave from his regiment on 21 April, and according to the *Richmond Examiner*, arrived in the South on Tuesday 29 April 1862, having ran the blockade on board the *Nashville*. This story was reported in *The Times* on 3 June with the caption 'ENGLISH ENTERPRISE', and received widespread circulation in the British press at the start of June. If Dunmore's actions seem foolhardy, it should be noted that he had only just turned 21, his coming of age celebrations were held *in absentia* on his Scottish estates in March 1862. In July several British newspapers reported that the Confederate authorities had allowed him access to watch their operations, and that he had met with several generals. According to this subsequent report, Dunmore had recorded his experiences in a journal, which had been reviewed by the authorities in Canada and would shortly be published.[26] Its existence was further confirmed by the Guards' Brigade house journal for 1862, which stated that '[t]he promised Journal of his Lordship not having arrived in time for insertion in this volume, we shall hope to present to our subscribers in the next'.[27] But the promised article did not appear the following year, and the journal is presumably lost. Further evidence for the visit exists in the form of a letter from Dunmore to President Jefferson Davis thanking him for his assistance in helping him leave the South. Dunmore had left via Norfolk for Fortress Monroe, but had been put under guard by the Union commander of that post while it was decided what to do with him. He managed to escape and make his way back to his regiment in Canada.[28]

There is a marked contrast in the character and content of the observation in the second period. Lee's victory in the Seven Days changed the nature of the war in British eyes. From this point through to the Battle of Gettysburg in July 1863, the South seemed to be not only holding its own in the struggle but even to be superior to the North in many military aspects. The Confederacy now appeared to be 'winning' – at least tactically and in the eastern theatre. There was an increased number of people not only writing about these Southern victories but actually crossing the front lines or running the blockade and visiting the South. Throughout this second period a number of British officers made their way through the Northern lines and observed the Confederate forces first hand.

26 *Dundee Courier*, Wednesday 26 March 1862; *Richmond Examiner*, 1 May 1862; *The Times*, 3 June 1852, *Falkirk Herald*, Thursday 5 June 1862 and Thursday 24 July 1862; copies of the same articles appeared in several other local newspapers, available through www.britishnewspaperarchive.co.uk.

27 *Journal of the Household Brigade for the year 1862* (London: W. Clowes and Sons, 1863), p.237.

28 Harvard University, Houghton Library, Dearborn Collection, bMS Am 1649.24 (232), Dunmore to Jefferson Davis, probably written sometime after 1 June 1862. According to the Canada leave records Dunmore was back with his regiment by that date, and the *Journal of the Household Brigade 1862* p.133 recorded him playing cricket for his regiment against the Grenadier Guards on 5 June.

Again it was civilians who had first blazed this trail. Lord Edward St Maur, son of the Duke of Somerset, had succeeded in making his way through the Union lines to Richmond at the end of June when the Seven Days battles were still raging.[29] The Marquis of Hartington, accompanied by his brother Lord Edward Cavendish who was serving as a Lieutenant with the 1st Battalion of the Rifle Brigade in Canada, did so at the end of the year.[30] All three were aided by the services of William Wilton Glenn, a Baltimore newspaper owner and Southern sympathiser, who subsequently assisted many of the observers in their journey south. Glenn had distinctly ulterior motives, having 'determined to devote myself to giving intelligent Englishmen every facility for acquainting themselves thoroughly with the true condition of Southern affairs and the spirit of the Southern people', in the belief that only foreign intervention would bring a speedy end to the war.[31]

Hartington was certainly the sort of Englishman that Glenn was looking for. He was the eldest son of the 7th Duke of Devonshire, and the MP for North Lancashire, an area suffering economically from the cotton famine. Although one biographer thought that his 'judgements often seem shallow and immature' at this time, including one ill-judged incident involving a female Southern sympathiser, and some insensitive letters, Hartington made some interesting observations on the war.[32] At first he wrote to his father that he was more unionist than previously, since the North seemed to be moderate towards the South and would accept them back, whereas the South 'appears from what one hears to hate the North more than the devil.'[33] In New York Hartington observed that the people there hated the abolitionists more than Southerners, while the people he met in Baltimore (his circle of acquaintances influenced presumably by Glenn) he thought more earnest than those in the North. He also thought that the Union could not survive without the Southern ports and the Mississippi river, and would splinter into half a dozen republics if they lost. Hartington thus recognised the

29   [Lord Edward Percy St Maur], 'Ten Days in Richmond', *Blackwood's Edinburgh Magazine*, 92 (1862), pp.391-402 (the *Wellesley Index* wrongly attributes this to E[dward] A[Dolphus] St Maur); Ella Lonn, *Foreigners in the Confederacy* (Chapel Hill and London: University of North Carolina Press, 2002, originally published 1940), pp.353-54.

30   Luvaas, *Military Legacy*, pp.18-20; Bernard Holland, *The Life of Spencer Crompton Eighth Duke of Devonshire 1833-1908, 2 vols*, (London, Longmans, Greene and Co, 1911), Vol.I, pp.39-54; Patrick Jackson, *The Last of the Whigs: A Political Biography of Lord Hartington, Late Eighth Duke of Devonshire (1833-1908)* (London and Toronto: [Fairleigh Dickinson University Press] Associated University Presses, 1994), p.20. Lord Edward Cavendish took leave from 31 August to 31 December 1862, TNA, WO 17/1566, extended to 31 January 1863, TNA, WO 17/1567, *Monthly Returns to the Adjutant General, Canada, 1863*.

31   William Wilton Glenn, *Between North and South*, ed. by Bayly Ellen Marks and Mark Norton Schaz, (London: Associated University Press, 1976), pp.64-65, 78-79.

32   Jackson, *The Last of the Whigs*, p.20. William Willis Blackford, serving with J.E.B. Stuart, was also not impressed by Hartington, see Lieutenant Colonel W.W. Blackford (CSA) *War Years With Jeb Stuart* (New York: Charles Scribner, 1946), p.199.

33   Holland, *Life of Spencer Crompton*, p.41 citing letter Hartington to his father, 2 September 1862.

interdependency of the slavery and union questions. At this stage, before visiting the Confederacy, he still expected the North to win through the exhaustion of the South, and he liked McClellan very much.[34]

Having first visited the Antietam and Fredericksburg battlefields while in the North, it was not until mid-December that Hartington and Cavendish crossed the lines to go South, spending Christmas in Richmond. By then fighting had ceased for the winter, so they did not see any actual battles. After trying to leave from Charleston, they were assisted back across the Potomac by Glenn, and Hartington then wrote to his father that he was 'decidedly very Southern', even though this 'would not at all suit my constituents'.[35] When he returned to England he was offered and accepted the post of Under-Secretary at the War Office. In this capacity he was responsible for putting forward the Volunteer Bill in May 1863, and in speeches in Parliament he compared these British volunteers to the Confederate army. In committee he spoke on the technical merits of different rifles, the effects of which he had seen or heard about on American battlefields, and he became Secretary of State for War in February 1866.[36]

St Maur, who at 20 was even younger than Dunmore, published a short account of his visit to the Confederacy in *Blackwood's Edinburgh Magazine*, considered by historian Hugh Dubrulle to have changed the British perception on the war. However, his only military rank was as a captain in the 6th Wiltshire Rifle Volunteers, so both his military insight and his influence were at best minimal. More importantly though he returned home via Canada and there met with regular army officers, most notably the future British Commander-in Chief, Field Marshal Lord Garnet Wolseley.[37] Lieutenant Colonel Wolseley, as he was then, had been posted to Canada as Assistant Quartermaster General in November 1861, and took a keen interest in the progress of the war. Influenced by St Maur's conversation Wolseley made up his mind, as he related much later, 'by hook or by crook, to reach the army of Virginia then commanded by that greatest of all modern leaders, General Lee'.[38] He eventually obtained leave and made the trip in September 1862, initially accompanied by Sir William Muir, Principal Medical Officer in Canada. Leaving Muir in the North to observe the medical facilities there, Wolseley crossed into the South in the company of *The Times'* new correspondent to Richmond, Frank Lawley, and arrived in the camp of the Army of Northern Virginia shortly after the Battle of Antietam (17 September 1862). Wolseley wrote of his trip both in a contemporary article (again published in

34 Holland, *Life of Spencer Crompton*, pp.44–46.
35 Holland, *Life of Spencer Crompton*, pp.52–54
36 Jackson, *Last of the Whigs*, pp.33–34.
37 Tony Margrave 'British Officers Observe the Civil War in America', Part 2, *Crossfire*, 105 (Summer 2014), pp.13-19 (pp.13-15); Dubrulle, 'Anarchy ...and Ruin', p.590. St Maur did not turn 21 until August 1862.
38 Field Marshal Viscount Garnet Joseph Wolseley, *Story of a Soldier's Life*, 2 vols (Westminster: Archibald Constable, 1903), Vol.II, p.120; Halik Kochanski, *Sir Garnet Wolseley: Victorian Hero* (London: Hambledon Press, 1999), pp.34-36.

Blackwood's) and in his memoirs written at the end of the century, but although he visited the Richmond battlefields he did not in either account record that he witnessed actual combat.[39]

Another British officer visited the Antietam battlefield itself in October 1862, Captain Edward Osborne Hewett of the Royal Engineers. Like Fletcher and Neville he took leave of absence on 'private affairs', from 1 October to 15 November, and there is no evidence whether he was acting under instruction or on his own expense, but like Fletcher he wrote a report for his superiors on his return which cannot now be found. Unlike Fletcher he did not publish an account of his exploits, but a personal letter to his mother, discovered in the 1950s, provided details of his travels though the timeline is somewhat imprecise.[40] Hewett travelled first to Washington where he obtained a pass to view the fortifications, and reported that he then stayed with McClellan's army. He also wrote of visiting Pennsylvania and then Kentucky where he met with the Union Major General Don Carlos Buell around the time of the Battle of Perryville (October 1862), and he tried unsuccessfully to make contact with John Hunt Morgan's Confederate guerrillas. Hewett also claimed to have visited Fredericksburg, 'the scene of the last great Yankee thrashing'.[41]

Henry Fletcher was also granted leave again from October to December and travelled through the South at this time, publishing an account of his trip in the *Cornhill Magazine* in 1863. Whereas in his earlier visit he had visited the eastern theatre, on this occasion he travelled down the Mississippi from St Louis to Memphis, where he met with Major General William Tecumseh Sherman. Ten miles from Memphis he encountered the Confederate army at Hernando, Mississippi, and went on to visit Major General Earl Van Dorn's headquarters at Abbeville. From here he went on to several key Southern cities including Vicksburg, Jackson, Mobile, Montgomery, Charleston, Wilmington, and Weldon, before finally arriving at Richmond. He was thus able to observe the earthworks before Richmond from both the Union and Confederate side.[42]

Returning through the lines to Washington, Fletcher met with another Guards officer, Captain Henry Charles Eden Malet of the Grenadier Guards. Malet had taken leave from 18 November 1862 to 1 January 1863, ostensibly to visit his brother Edward who worked at the British legation in Washington, but on his arrival he had immediately obtained a pass to visit the Army of the Potomac in the lines around Fredericksburg. He never published his observations but they can be found in personal

---

39   Wolseley, 'A Month's Visit', passim; *Story of a Soldier's Life*, Vol.II, pp.124-44.

40   Hewett, in Preston, 'Letter', passim.

41   Hewett, in Preston, 'Letter', p.55. Since the letter is dated 3 December and the 'thrashing' occurred on 11-13 December this must have been a later alteration to the manuscript. Strangely Preston did not pick up on this anomaly in his otherwise detailed notes in which he tried to date Hewett's progress.

42   Fletcher, 'A Run Through the Southern States', passim.

letters sent to Sir Austen Henry Layard, a senior diplomat back in London, and to his parents. Malet was regarded as a keen observer by Lord Lyons and by others.[43]

Malet may have intended to try and cross into the Confederacy as well, but does not appear to have done so, perhaps because of ill health or perhaps because of his brother's position in Washington.[44] However, two of his fellow Grenadier Guards officers were present on the Confederate side of the lines at Fredericksburg. Captains Lewis Guy Phillips and Edward William Lloyd Wynne had both taken leave from their regiment in October, and made their way across into Virginia using the same network as Hartington, St Maur, and Wolseley. On 9 December 1862 Phillips was with the Army of Northern Virginia near Fredericksburg and remained so during the battle of 11-13 December, in which he took an active role and where his hosts recorded he was 'perfectly cool' although it was his first time under fire. Wynne missed the fighting due to sickness but joined Phillips shortly afterwards on 17 December. Yet another Grenadier Guards officer, Captain Thomas Harvey Bramston, was also on leave at this time and visited the Confederate army in January, but is not recorded as being present during the December fighting.[45]

Meanwhile, Phillips and Wynne had begun their journey back to Canada, arriving at Leesburg on 27 December where they separated in order to cross the Potomac back into Maryland. Yet this did not represent safety, as Phillips had become sufficiently committed to the Southern cause that he had unwisely agreed to carry sensitive documents through the lines. Phillips brazened his way past the Union guards at Baltimore station, but Wynne, travelling some six hours later, missed the train. Detained by suspicious guards, he was arrested and imprisoned in the Old Capitol Prison, New York. After three days, he contrived to escape and make his way back to William Glenn's house in Baltimore. From here he managed to make his way back

---

43   WO 17/1566 for Malet's leave. BL, Layard Papers, Add. 39104, fols 225-28, Henry Malet to Sir Austen Henry Layard, 27 December 1862; BL, Malet Papers, RP.886 Reel 1, folder H12, fols 239-42, J.R. Crauford to Lady Malet, 26 January 1863; Malet Papers, RP.886 Reel 5, (no further sub-references), Edward Malet to his father, Washington, 20 November 1862, Edward Malet to his father, 2 December 1863 enclosing letter from Henry, and Henry Malet to his father, 16 December 1863. This last letter is unsigned and on Edward's notepaper, but appears to be from Henry. The originals of the Malet Papers are held by Duke University, Raleigh, NC.
44   In his letter to Layard, Malet states that he was recovering from scarlet fever. The following year he indicated a desire to go to the Confederacy, see BL, Malet Papers, RP.886 Reel 1, folder H12, fol. 105, Henry Malet to his mother, 24 August 1863.
45   Glenn, *Between North and South*, pp.73-78; Heros Von Borcke, *Memoirs of the Confederate War of Independence*, 2 vols (London: William Blackwood and Sons, 1866), Vol.II, pp.87, 113, 150, 174; Blackford, *War Years With Jeb Stuart*, pp.187, 192; WO 17/1566; WO 17/1567; Barrie Almond, 'Captain Lewis Guy Phillips', *Crossfire*, 84 (August 2007), <http://www.acwrt.org.uk/uk-heritage_Captain-Lewis-Guy-Phillips.asp> [accessed 19 November]; Tony Margrave 'British Officers Observe the Civil War in America', Part 3, *Crossfire*, 106 (Winter 2014), pp.12-16 (pp.12-15).

via Pennsylvania and Ohio, where the story of his adventures was made public in February 1863.[46]

Probably the most famous of the British observers in this second period was another Guards officer, Lieutenant Colonel Arthur Fremantle of the Coldstream Guards. Unlike most of his predecessors Fremantle did not travel from Canada but sailed from England in March 1863 and arrived in the Confederacy in April by way of Havana and the port of Matamoros on the Mexican bank of the Rio Grande. Fremantle's three month journey took him across Texas, Louisiana, and Mississippi to Mobile in Alabama, on to Braxton Bragg's headquarters at Chattanooga, then via Charleston and Wilmington to Richmond, and up the Shenandoah Valley finally joining Lee's army on 22 June 1863 just before the Battle of Gettysburg.[47] Fremantle's experience of the South was therefore more extensive than many officers who were constrained by a shorter leave of absence from their regiments in Canada, though he did not see much actual combat other than at Gettysburg. Already pre-disposed towards the Southern cause, this predisposition was reinforced by the prolonged period in which Fremantle experienced Southern hospitality. Robert Lawley, a British MP and the elder brother of *The Times*' Richmond correspondent Francis Lawley who had accompanied Wolseley across the Potomac in 1862, identified three genres of writing on the war – the stately procession, the anonymous visit, and remote observation. Lawley believed that the first of these, typified by Fremantle, resulted in the greatest bias.[48]

In Virginia, Fremantle had met with another compatriot, Fitzgerald Ross, of British birth but Austrian upbringing, and a cavalry officer in the Austrian Army. Ross had entered 'Secessia' in May 1863, one of the last to do so using Glenn's network, and was also present with Lee's army at Gettysburg. He then travelled much the same route as Fremantle but in the opposite direction, visiting Wilmington, Charleston, the Army of Tennessee outside Chattanooga, then Savannah and Mobile before leaving the South via Savannah and spending some time in the North. Ross published his memoirs through *Blackwood's* magazine, and then in book form through the same publisher. *Blackwood's* did the same with the memoirs of Colonel Heros von Borcke, a German soldier of fortune who served on J.E.B. Stuart's staff and who played host to a number of the British visitors to the South. While technically neither Ross nor von Borcke were British army observers, this gave them a wide audience in the British

46   BL, Malet Papers, RP.886, Reel 3, EBM Private Papers, Wynne to Edward Malet, Montreal, 19 February 1863; Glenn, *Between North and South*, pp.74-78; Almond, 'Captain Lewis Guy Phillips'; Margrave 'British Officers', Part 3, pp.13-14.

47   Lieutenant Colonel A.J.L. Fremantle, *Three Months in the Southern States, April-June 1863*, Electronic edn (Chapel Hill: University of North Carolina 2000; first published Mobile, SH Goetzel, 1864). All references hereafter to Fremantle are to this edition unless otherwise noted. Part of this work was previously published as 'The Battle of Gettysburg and the Campaign in Pennsylvania: Extract from the Diary of an English Officer present with the Confederate Army' in *Blackwood's Edinburgh Magazine*, 94 (1863), pp.365-94.

48   Robert Neville Lawley, 'The Prospects of the Confederates', *Quarterly Review*, 115 (April 1864), pp.289-311 (pp.289-92).

establishment. Their works provide additional perspectives on some military aspects of the war, and form part of the opus of the British learning experience from the conflict.[49]

By the start of 1864 interest in the war had started to wane in Britain. In Europe the Polish uprising in January 1863, and subsequently the Schleswig-Holstein crisis between Prussia and Denmark, where war broke out in February 1864, were much closer conflicts to which military theorists could turn their minds. There was a 'perceptible relaxation of the interest with which our countrymen first watched the vicissitudes of the American war'.[50] The South had suffered significant reverses in all theatres during the second half of 1863, and although adherents continued to back their cause and commentators still wrote of potential strategies for victory, the attraction of visiting what had been the winning side had waned. Running the blockade had also become more difficult as the war progressed. As previously related, Captain Edward Wynne was caught and imprisoned by the Northern authorities returning North in December 1862, and George Alfred Lawrence, a reporter for the *Morning Post*, was captured and imprisoned for eight months after trying to cross from Maryland to Virginia at around the same time. William Wilton Glenn, the Confederate sympathiser who had assisted many of the observers in their journey south, was forced to flee Maryland, and the 'underground railway' through the border was effectively closed. Fremantle made a point of handing himself over to Union troops, saying that he had done so deliberately in order not to break the blockade, when he crossed back into Federal lines.[51]

During the third period of observation, through to the end of the war, access to the Confederacy became more difficult and the final group of observers primarily turned their attentions to the Federal side of the lines again. There was also a tendency for them to come from the more technical branches of the service, reflecting the change in the tactical nature of the war, where sieges and fortifications were becoming as important as field battles. An example of this was the significant interest taken by the British in the operations at Charleston, South Carolina, and later at Petersburg, Virginia. Further missions were also sent as a response to the ongoing possibility of a war with the United States. The use of Canada by Confederate sympathisers to mount raids on Northern states, and the Federal response to these, posed a plausible cause of conflict between Britain and America at this time. There was a second

49   Fitzgerald Ross, *A Visit to the Cities and Camps of the Confederate States* (Edinburgh and London: Blackwood, 1865). All references hereafter to Ross are to this edition, cited as Ross, *Visit*. Previously published under the name 'A Cavalry Officer' in *Blackwood's Edinburgh Magazine*, 96 (1864), pp.645-70 and 97 (1865), pp.26-48, 151-76. Von Borcke's *Memoirs* had originally been serialised in *Blackwood's* from September 1865 – June 1866. Von Borcke in particular was occasionally cited during discussions in Military Societies in the 1880s, some of which are discussed later.

50   Cecil, 'The United States as an Example', pp.249-50.

51   George Alfred Lawrence, *Border and Bastille* (New York: W.I. Pooley, 1863), passim; Glenn, *Between North and South*, pp.86-97; Fremantle, *Three Months in the Southern States*, p.148.

review of Canadian defences in 1863-64, and while this was in part occasioned by the forthcoming confederation of the Canadian provinces, the only conceivable military threat was what many in Britain perceived as an expansionist and now militarised United States. In early 1864 a mission was sent to look at American fortifications and ordnance. Since these formal missions focussed primarily on technical matters, they are again covered in more depth in the next chapter.[52]

These generalisations however overlay an enormous variety of observers in this period. Around December 1863 Fitzgerald Ross met with 'a young English officer of engineers here, who, with but a very short leave of absence, crossed the lines on foot with a small kit, saw the army in Northern Virginia, visited Charleston, Wilmington, &c., and is now going to walk across the lines again on his return', adding that '[w]ith the exception of Colonel F[remantle], no other 'tourist' as far as I am aware, has visited the country since I have been here'.[53] This young engineer is most likely to have been 22-year-old Lieutenant William Innes RE, who was posted to the garrison in Nova Scotia and who published an account of the siege of Charleston in the *Royal Engineers' Professional Papers* the following year. The Nova Scotia leave records suggest that Innes visited the United States twice during the war, the first time in November 1862 and the second from 11 November 1863 to 21 January 1864, which would coincide with Ross' report.[54]

A contemporary of Innes was either less fortunate or more foolhardy. Lieutenant Henry Rooke, serving in the Royal Artillery in Nova Scotia, obtained leave to visit the United States at roughly the same time as Innes, from 4 November to 20 December 1863. The return of January 1864, however, records him as being Absent Without Leave and imprisoned in Fort Lafayette in New York, having been arrested 'under suspicious circumstances', and his case was in the hands of Lord Lyons, the British Ambassador. The British Consul in New York provided Lord Lyons with a report produced by the Americans, detailing the conditions in which Rooke and the other prisoners were held. It seems that Rooke was found with papers on his person from Confederate sympathisers in Baltimore, with the possible implication that he had been caught trying to cross into the South.[55]

52   *The Times*, 10 February 1865, published in Brogan p.163; Cecil, 'The United States as an Example', pp.252, 263; WO 33/14/0229, Gallwey Report.; WO 33/15/0265, Jervois, *Defence of Canada*.
53   Ross, *Visit*, p.220; Lonn, *Foreigners in the Confederacy* p.353. 'Colonel F' is clearly Fremantle as Ross had first recorded meeting with him at Gettysburg, Ross, *Visit*, p.46.
54   Lieutenant Innes RE, 'Notes on the Defences of Charleston, South Carolina', *R.E. Professional Papers*, 13 (1864), pp.16-24; TNA, WO 25/3913, Military service record of William Innes; TNA, WO 17/2409 *Monthly Returns to the Adjutant General, Nova Scotia, 1862*; TNA, WO 17/2410 *Monthly Returns to the Adjutant General, Nova Scotia, 1863*.
55   WO 17/2410; TNA, FO 5/1150 *Report of a Board of Officers convened at Fort Lafayette, New York Harbour, February 17 1864*. The story of the incriminating papers comes from the evidence of another inmate of Fort Lafayette, James McHugh. McHugh claimed that he was falsely accused of having these papers which had been carried by Lieutenant

Fort Lafayette, New York, where Lt. Rooke was imprisoned. (Library of Congress)

A year later another young officer from the Royal Engineers also managed to make his way into the South, this time to Petersburg. Lieutenant Albany Featherstonhaugh may have found it rather easier than most of the observers to travel through Virginia as he had family connections in the state. His father was George William Featherstonhaugh, an Englishman who had migrated to America in 1806 and had become the first Geologist to the US Government, and his mother was Charlotte Williams Carter, who was a niece of Robert E. Lee. Their son joined the Royal Engineers as a cadet, studied at the Royal Military Academy in Woolwich, and became a lieutenant on 22 June 1859. He took leave from his post in Chatham on 15 August 1864, and presumably arrived in Petersburg sometime in September. Featherstonhaugh is silent on precisely how he managed to enter and leave the Confederate lines, but like Innes he was unable to take any papers with him on departing and wrote up his observations from memory. He most probably entered through Northern Virginia where he would have had contacts through his mother's family, he may have returned the same way or may have travelled south and ran the blockade.[56]

Rooke, though he incorrectly identifies Rooke as a Royal Navy officer. See in *British Parliamentary Papers*, 1864, 62 (cmd 299), pp.461-79, a letter from Mr. McHugh to Lord Lyons dated Fort Lafayette, 13 February 1864, cited on the Irish Emigration Database, <http://www.dippam.ac.uk/ied/records/34395> [accessed 15 June 2015]. Samuel Negus, "A Notorious Nest of Offence": Neutrals, Belligerents and Union Jails in the Civil War Blockade-running Trade', *Civil War History*, 56 (2010), pp.350-85 (p.372) erroneously identifies Rooke as a 'reserve Royal Artillery second lieutenant'.

56   Lieutenant Featherstonhaugh RE, 'Notes on the Defence of Petersburg', *R.E. Professional Papers*, 14 (1865), pp.190-94 (p.190); WO 25/3913, Military service record of Albany Featherstonhaugh; TNA, WO 17/2412 *Monthly Returns to the Adjutant General, Nova Scotia, 1865;* Edmund Berkeley and Dorothy Smith Berkeley *George William*

The threat of war with the United States led to other technical officers arriving in North America under instruction. Captain (later General) Richard Harrison accompanied Lieutenant Colonel William Jervois, Deputy Inspector General of Fortifications, to Canada in September 1863 in order to survey the defences of Canada and Nova Scotia, and both took the opportunity to also visit the defences of the north-eastern United States. Their travels were initially limited to the cities of Portland, Boston, New York, and Washington, in all of which they examined the fortifications, but Harrison took then leave in the first week of November to visit the Army of the Potomac (now under Major General George Meade, the victor of Gettysburg) in its winter quarters on the Rappahannock. He also briefly crossed the front line in Virginia to converse with a Confederate cavalry picket. The two men left for England on 7 November 1863, but the following year Jervois returned to Canada and Harrison again accompanied him. They left Liverpool on 5 September 1864 and arrived in Halifax nine days later. On 1 October they were in Ottawa, from where Jervois went back to Quebec while Harrison travelled further west, through Kingston, Toronto, Hamilton, and thence to London, Ontario. Here Harrison again took a week's leave to visit the war in Missouri. He appears to have entered America on 14 October from Windsor, Ontario, and managed to get as far as Washington, Missouri, where he was almost lynched as a spy by a Northern picket in the surrounding countryside. He left there on 18 October, returning to meet Jervois in Toronto by the same route he came. Although he failed to see any actual fighting, he is one of relatively few British observers to have visited the western theatre.[57]

Another group of Guards officers visited the Army of the Potomac at roughly the same time as Harrison. These were Lieutenant Colonel Earle and Lieutenant Lord Castle Cuff of the Grenadier Guards, and Captain Cecil Lennox Peel and Captain Stephenson of the Scots Fusilier Guards. They left Washington on 14 November 1863 with letters of introduction to Major General Meade, who they met at Alexandria. They travelled by railway to Bealton, over the Bull Run and Bristoe Station battlefields, and from there rode via Brandy Station to Meade's headquarters on the Rappahannock, where their presence was recorded by Lieutenant Colonel Theodore Lyman, an officer serving on Meade's staff. Peel, who was the nephew of the former Prime Minister, Robert Peel, also published a record of the visit in the house journal of the Guards Brigade. As well as a description of Meade's field operations during the minor action at Mine Run on 28-29 November, Peel's account covered a wide variety of military topics, including armament, medical matters and signals, even remarking on administrative details such as the procedure for regimental returns, and the use of

Featherstonhaugh: The First US Government Geologist (Tuscaloosa and London: University of Alabama Press, 1988), pp.88, 246 for Featherstonhaugh's relationship to the Lee family.

57   'An Officer of the Royal Engineers' [Lieutenant Richard Harrison], 'A Trip to Meade's Army on the Rappahannock', *United Service Magazine*, 428 (July 1864), pp.329-39; General Richard Harrison, *Recollections of a Life in the British Army* (London: Smith Elder, 1908), pp.106-15.

'repeating pads' to duplicate orders for distribution. It is an interesting counterpoint to Fremantle's 'stately procession' that demonstrates both the breadth of interest of the informal observers, and that not all of them were outright Confederate sympathisers.[58]

While Peel and his colleagues were cordially treated by Meade, a formal mission comprising Lieutenant Colonel Gallwey of the Royal Engineers and Captain Alderson of the Royal Artillery, sent from England at the start of 1864 to look at the technological advances being made in the US Army, experienced great difficulty gaining access to the front line because in the spring of 1864 the government in Washington suspended the issuing of nearly all passes. In April, Colonel Francis Lambton and Lieutenant Colonel George Hay Moncrieff of the Scots Fusilier Guards, who had taken leave from their regiment from 28 March to 20 May presumably with the specific intent of visiting the Army of the Potomac, were refused permission to do so. Although Gallwey and Alderson had previously received passes, and although Lord Lyons argued that they were representatives of the British Government rather than independent observers visiting out of curiosity, Lyons was informed by Secretary of State William H. Seward that the same restrictions would apply and their passes would not be renewed.[59]

This ban, which coincided with the start of Grant's Overland Campaign against Richmond, applied even to those visitors whose interests lay outside of the front line. William Muir, the Medical Officer who had accompanied Wolseley to the United States in 1862, was also turned down for a pass in 1864. However, a Welsh veterinary officer with the Royal Artillery, Lieutenant Henry Evans, who had been granted leave of absence from 20 June to 2 August 1864 on the intention of going south, did manage to obtain one. Evans' success in this matter seems to have been the result of the influential personal network he managed to create. One letter of introduction he carried was to Dr Austin Flint in New York, a friend of Generals Grant, Meade, and George Henry Thomas. Flint wrote him further introductions to all three generals, while Professor Joseph Henry of the Smithsonian Institute, who knew Evans from the Medical School in Montreal, introduced him to President Lincoln. The President thought that Evans 'seemed like an honest man' and the following day (25 June) he was given a pass to go wherever he pleased on the condition that he rendered medical assistance should it be needed. Evans visited both the Army of the James as a guest of Major General Benjamin Butler, and the Army of the Potomac under Major General

58 'CLP' [Captain Cecil Lennox Peel], 'A Short Campaign With the Federal Army of the Potomac', *Journal of the Household Brigade for the year 1863* (London: W. Clowes and Sons, 1864), pp.190-99; George R Agassiz (ed.) *Meade's Headquarters 1863-1865. Letters of Theodore Lyman From The Wilderness to Appomattox,* (Freeport NY: Books for Libraries Press, 1970), pp.48-50. WO 17/1567 *Monthly Returns to the Adjutant General, Canada, 1863* shows these officers on leave in November, and Peel as AWOL in December.

59 TNA, FO 5/948; Lyons to Seward, Washington, April 20 1864; Seward to Lyons, Washington, April 20 1864; R.S. Canby to Seward, Washington, April 20 1864; Lyons to Seward, Washington, April 20 1864; WO 33/14/0229, Gallwey Report, pp.ix-x.

Meade, as well as meeting Lieutenant General Grant.[60] According to his biographers Evans also had an elaborate story of meeting Major General Thomas, but since Thomas was in Georgia and not Virginia in July 1864 this claim must surely be fictitious, perhaps added because Thomas was of Welsh descent.[61]

Other visits on 'personal affairs' were also still being made. Artillery officer Henry Knollys recorded that he had met with Brigadier General William Barry, the Union Inspector General of Artillery, during the war. If the Canadian leave records are correct this can possibly be dated to a period of leave that Lieutenant Knollys took from 23 December 1863 to 10 January 1864.[62] It would be possible to travel from Canada to Washington and back in such a short time, and opens up the possibility that many of the short periods of leave taken by other officers in Canada did involve otherwise unrecorded visits to the United States. Major Henry Smyth, also of the Royal Artillery, obtained two rather longer leaves of absence, the first being from 5 November to 10 December 1864. During this time he visited the Army of the James south of Petersburg. Captain H.H. Pierce of the 1st Connecticut Artillery, which constituted the siege artillery for the army, reported test firings of a new incendiary shell and concussion fuse attended by 'a Major of the 'Royal Artillery' and an English gentleman, guests of General Butler' and this is confirmed by Lyman.[63] Smyth's second period of leave was granted from 5 January to 5 July 1865, and he was possibly the last British observer of the war, being present at the fall of Petersburg on 2 April 1865, at which time he reported that he was the only European still with the Army of the Potomac.[64]

60   Jean Ware and Hugh Hunt, *The Several Lives of a Victorian Vet* (London: Bachman & Turner, 1979), pp.68, 74-87; Bangor, University of Wales, (UWB), Extracts from Evans' diary 29 June 1864 – 8 July 1864 (typescript copy).

61   Ware and Hunt, *Victorian Vet*, pp.85–87. This also throws into some doubt the meeting with Grant, since neither event is in the Diary.

62   Captain Henry Knollys RA, *The Elements of Field Artillery* (Edinburgh and London: William Blackwood and Sons, 1877), p.106; TNA, WO 17/1568, *Monthly Returns to the Adjutant General, Canada, 1864*.

63   WO 17/1568; TNA, WO 17/1569, *Monthly Returns to the Adjutant General, Canada, 1865*; Captain Pierce to Colonel H. L Abbott, 24 November 1864, recorded in Major Samuel P. Hatfield, *History of the First Connecticut Artillery and of the Siege trains of the Armies Operating against Richmond, 1862-65* (Hartford: Case, Lockwood and Brainard, 1893), p.123; David W. Lowe (ed.), *Meade's Army: The private notebooks of Lt. Col. Theodore Lyman* (Kent: Kent State University Press, 2007), p.297. The 'English gentleman' is revealed by Lyman to be a Mr Lunn from Montreal, though Lyman says that they were guests of General Humphreys. Lyman records two other English civilian visitors to the Army in November 1864, (*Meade's Army*, p.296), and a Royal Engineer, Lieutenant Satterthwaite in December, (ibid, p.305). Satterthwaite is also identified in WO 17/1569, and WO 25/3913.

64   Major H.A. Smyth, 'Account of the Final Attack and Capture of Richmond, by the Federal Army, Commanded by General Grant', *Minutes of the Proceedings of the Royal Artillery Institution*, 4 (1865), pp.363-70. WO 17/1569 is confusing on the dates of Smyth's second leave. Each return starts with a list of officers granted leave the previous

One other visitor to the Union lines before Petersburg is worthy of note. This was the most senior British officer to visit the American army during the war, the British commanding officer in Nova Scotia, Sir Hastings Doyle. Doyle visited Meade's command in October 1864 and was cordially received within the Union lines, even by Major General Butler, which the British press attributed to the fact he wore his full dress uniform throughout. The Americans in contrast thought Doyle's appearance somewhat comical. Lyman wrote in his diary that he 'wore a uniform, like the undress of the Guards, and, in his little gold-laced cap, looked like a military punchivello'. Doyle made a second visit in the following year, taking a particular interest in the winter quarters of Grant's army.[65]

*   *   *

Relatively few of the observers wrote about their experiences. For many of them it would seem that the motivation was as much a search for excitement as a quest for knowledge. Most were young, in their twenties or early thirties, and for a young officer based in Canada, visiting the South was the equivalent of their counterparts in India taking 'shooting leave' in Central Asia – it fulfilled their desire for adventure, danger and visiting exotic locations. While many were veterans of the Crimea, for more junior ranks it would have been their first opportunity to see a war first hand. Although some accounts say that Wolseley went south as a result of a 'toss up' with his travelling companion, Sir Edward Muir, as to who would stay in the North and who would travel to the South, it is probable that the choice had been decided beforehand. Wolseley clearly relished the excitement of travelling to the South while Muir, who was the principal medical officer in Canada, equally clearly had an interest in medical affairs that was best served in the North.[66] On his return Wolseley wrote to

month; but Smyth does not appear on this list either in January or February. The January return for the regiment shows him as present, as would be expected since his leave started during the month, and the February regimental return shows him absent with his leave dates recorded as 5 January until 5 July. However, the March and April returns both show him as present for duty. While it is not impossible he could have returned to Canada briefly in early March it seems unlikely, while the April return is incompatible with Smyth's own report of being present at the fall of Petersburg. Lyman records that he left the Army of the Potomac on 15 April (Lowe, *Meade's Army*, p.374) and he was back in Montreal by 30 April, the date he submitted his report.

65   *Army and Navy Gazette*, 12 November 1862, p.729, reprinted in *Army and Navy Journal*, 3 December 1864, p.231; Luvaas, *Military Legacy*, p.31; Lowe, *Meade's Army*, p.279; see also Aggasiz, *Meade's Headquarters*, p.244 for a second description of Doyle; New Brunswick Museum (NBM), Letter from Sir Hastings Doyle to Sir Willian Fenwick, Halifax, Nova Scotia, 29 March 1865.

66   Charles Rathbone Low, *General Lord Wolseley of Cairo: A Memoir*, 2nd edn (London: Richard Bentley, 1883), p.160, and John Lehman *All Sir Garnet: A Life of Field Marshal Lord Wolseley* (London: Jonathan Cape, 1964), pp.117-18, both give the coin toss version. Compare Wolseley, *Story of a Soldier's Life*, Vol.II, p.124. For the medical advances in the

his brother that 'I ran the blockade and have enjoyed myself beyond description', while Fremantle admitted to visiting the South 'for my own amusement'.[67] In 1861 at least one Sandhurst cadet had written to the Duke of Cambridge, Commander in Chief of the British Army, requesting deployment to Canada, presumably for the opportunity to see conflict, while Edward Hewett had resigned his position as an assistant instructor at the Royal Military Academy, Woolwich, in December 1861 in order to come to Canada with the reinforcements sent as a result of the *Trent* incident.[68]

One striking feature of the recorded instances of British observers, particularly in the second period, is the large number of Guards officers among them. Engineer and Artillery officers also appear prominently, but some of these were sent under instruction and there were clear professional reasons why officers in these regiments should take an interest in the technical innovations displayed in the war. The reasons why the war held such an attraction for the socially elite Guardsmen are not so obvious.

The various Guards' officers all moved in the same social circle. Henry Malet knew Henry Fletcher and other officers in the Scots Fusilier Guards, including Lord Abinger and the Earl of Dunmore. They also associated with the émigré Confederate community in Montreal, particularly the family of former US Navy Commodore, George Allan Magruder. Wolseley also knew the Magruders and other 'nice Southern families' in Montreal, and it was his liaison with them that first set him thinking about visiting the South. Lord Abinger would eventually marry one of Commodore Magruder's daughters in December 1863, while Dunmore had a mildly scandalous affair with another, the widow of a Confederate officer who had died in November 1862. These associations may have motivated them to see first-hand the fighting and to investigate the issues being discussed over the dinner table. Lord Abinger is known from photographic evidence to have visited the Army of the Potomac between April and May 1863, though there is no evidence that he crossed into the Confederacy, and he seems to have left no other record of his visit. The self-confidence of the upper ranks of the British aristocracy may also have made them more likely to run the risk of capture by entering the South on the expectation that the British diplomatic corps would come to their assistance. Captain Wynne was assisted when captured and held by the US authorities by the British Ambassador Lord Lyons and by Malet's brother

North at this time see *The Times*, 25 January 1862, published in Brogan, *Extracts from the Times*, pp.50-53. Muir was to make further visits to the United States later in the war (see HPL, Wolseley Archive, 163/3, Wolseley to his brother Richard, Montreal, 19 November 1862; Montreal, 31 January 1863 and Montreal, 14 February 1863) but was refused a pass in 1864, see Ware and Hunt, *Victorian Vet*, p.68.

67   HPL, Wolseley Archive, 163/3/11, Wolseley to his brother Richard, Montreal, 24 October 1862; Fremantle, *Three Months in the Southern States*, p.56.

68   TNA, WO45/289, *Letter Book of the Commander in Chief*, Engineers papers [*sic*]; request from Lieutenant Nolan RA at Sandhurst dated 24 December 1861 for employment in Canada (but there is no record of a Lieutenant Nolan in the Canada returns); Dictionary of Canadian Biography Online <http://www.biographi.ca/en/bio/hewett_edward_osborne_12E.html> [accessed 5 April 2015].

Lord Abinger and group of officers at headquarters, Army of the Potomac, Falmouth, Virginia, April 1863. (Library of Congress)

Edward, though Wynne contrived to avoid their embarrassment by escaping from captivity and making his way back to Canada.[69]

Guards officers seem to have taken a rather higher level of leave than officers in the line regiments stationed in Canada. On a number of occasions significant numbers of Guards officers were absent from their units, these coincide with the known periods of observation in May and December of 1862. The average number of Guards officers requesting leave was around twice that of those in line regiments, though the same seasonal variation is seen. Leave during winter was relatively rare, and the most popular time was the late summer. This could have been related to the campaigning season or simply the social calendar and the climate. Of the large number of Guards who took leave in November 1862 for example, some are known to have gone to the battles in Virginia, but others appear to have returned to England for the fox-hunting

69   HPL, Wolseley Archive, 163/3/4, Wolseley to his brother Richard, Montreal, 21 May 1862; BL, Malet papers RP.886, Reel 1, folder H12 fol.112, Henry Malet to his mother, Montreal, 6 November 6 1863.; *Crossfire*, 103 (December 2013), p.33 and 106 (Winter 2014), p.16; *The Peerage* genealogical website <http://www.thepeerage.com/p4805.htmi48050> [accessed 4 April 2015]; WO 17/1567; BL, Malet Papers, RP.886, Reel 3, Wynne to Edward Malet, Montreal, 19 February 1863; Almond, 'Lewis Guy Phillips'; Margrave, 'British Officers', Part 3, p.16.

season, or maybe just to avoid the Canadian winter.[70] It is probable that officers in the Guards possessed greater financial means than officers in less fashionable regiments which would have enabled them to make extended trips to the United States, and the cost of travel would also have influenced the locations which observers could visit. Fremantle's three month leave and journey from England must have entailed considerable expense, although some of it would have been recouped from the proceeds of the publishing fees for his memoir.[71]

The historical record may be biased in favour of the recording of visitors from more prestigious regiments. While a few are known from their own writings, many have been identified only from references in other works such as Russell, Ross, and von Borcke. Stories of associating with senior members of the British aristocracy added to the appeal of popular memoirs, while their implied support was good propaganda for the Confederate cause, and therefore more likely to be commented upon in Confederate records. In the case of the Earl of Dunmore the accounts of his having visited the South have been elaborated. Various unsubstantiated sources claim that Dunmore not only visited the Confederacy in 1862 and was captured by the US authorities, which facts are borne out by other evidence, but also that he served on Lee's staff and even captained the blockade runner *Nashville*, which are patently untrue. Some may even be a case of mistaken identity; it was certainly not unknown for British soldiers of fortune to fabricate or exaggerate their social background.[72] There is also evidence from Glenn that he was very conscious of what benefit the South might secure from the considerable risk that he was taking in assisting British visitors to run the blockade. When Wynne and Phillips came to him, he wrote that he 'did not think that either of them were men to influence public opinion or take even the trouble to write out their experiences for publication'.[73] In this judgement Glenn was to be proved correct, and it is possible that only their social position persuaded him to take the risk of assisting them.

---

70   This is from analysis of the leave records of units in Canada held in the *Monthly Returns to the Adjutant General*, TNA, WO 17/1566 through to WO 17/1569. The average leave requests for each line regiment was 1.3 per month; that for the Grenadier Guards 2.3 and for the Fusilier Guards 3.1. James Morris Morgan, *Recollections of a Rebel Reefer* (Boston and New York: Houghton Mifflin, 1917), p.104, met officers returning for the fox-hunting.

71   Francis Dawson, who travelled from England to the South in 1861 to fight for the Confederate cause was unable to afford the fare to Nassau and worked his passage on the CSS *Nashville*; Francis W. Dawson, *Reminiscences of Confederate Service* (Charleston SC: The News and Courier Book Presses, 1882), pp.3-24. Fremantle did travel part of the way on a British warship which may have saved some money.

72   Morgan, *Recollections of a Rebel Reefer*, pp.104-05 the details Morgan gives are however incorrect; Kate Mason Rowland 'English Friends of the Confederacy', *Confederate Veteran*, 25 (June 1917), pp.198-202 (p.201); Lonn, *Foreigners in the Confederacy*, pp.185, 353; Margrave, 'British Officers', Part 2, pp.18-19. Dawson described a British cavalry sergeant who passed himself off as an aristocrat, Dawson, *Reminiscences*, pp.134-35.

73   Glenn, *Between North and South*, p.73.

A final consideration is that officers in the Guards were sometimes more conscientious about their trade than they are given credit for. The very fact that some members of the aristocracy only served with these regiments for short periods of time, almost as a rite of passage, before advancing their careers in other areas of public life meant that there was a relatively high turnover of commissions in the Guard regiments. This meant that for those who were serious about the military profession, provided that they could afford the expense of joining and serving in these prestigious regiments in the first place, there were opportunities to get more rapid promotion than might be possible in less fashionable units.[74] Some of the Guards officers who visited the United States not only showed themselves to be keenly interested in the technical details of what they saw in the American armies, but when they returned to Britain continued to apply their experiences to the military questions of the day, as will be seen later.

There are a few references to officers from infantry regiments other than the Guards visiting the United States. Several served as soldiers of fortune in the Southern ranks, amongst them Captain Bradford Smith Hoskins, who was a veteran of the Crimea where he had served in the 44th Foot, and who died fighting with the renowned guerrilla leader John Singleton Mosby in Virginia in June 1863.[75] Captain Stephen Winthrop of the 22nd Foot resigned his commission to serve in the Confederate Army and fought at the battle of Knoxville in November 1863, and Ensign Henry Wemyss Fielden of the 42nd Foot (Black Watch), became assistant adjutant general in the Army of Tennessee.[76] However, these young men were in America for adventure, not as observers.[77] More significantly, Lyman recorded in his diary for 29 March 1865 that 'a couple of English Greenies were along' during the last days at Petersburg. According to Lyman, these were Lieutenants Reginald Talbot and Abercromby. Lieutenant Ralph Abercromby was indeed granted personal leave from his regiment, the 4th Battalion, 60th Foot (Kings Royal Rifle Regiment), from 14 March to 15 April 1865, but Lyman seems to have been mistaken in describing Talbot as a 'Greenie' (rifleman). There is no mention of a Talbot in the records of the 60th Foot, and it would seem that the visitor was probably the Honourable Reginald Talbot. He was serving as a Lieutenant in the Life Guards at this time so would have visited the United States from England.[78]

---

74   Stephen Badsey 'The Boer War (1899-1902) and British Cavalry Doctrine', *Journal of Military History*, 71 (2007), pp.75-98 (p.80).

75   Foreman, *World on Fire*, pp.387, 470; TNA, FO 115/394 fol.10.

76   Dawson, *Reminiscences*, pp.109-10, though Dawson mistakenly reports his regiment as the 44th, see *Hart's Army List No. 87, July 1860* (London: John Murray, 1860), p.171; 'Stephen Winthrop – Rebel Without A Cause', <http://www.acwrt.org.uk/uk-heritage_Stephen-Winthrop---Rebel-Without-A-Cause.asp> [accessed 16 July 2018], originally published *Crossfire*, 45 (April 1993); Foreman, *World on Fire*, pp.387-391.

77   From genealogical research on Ancestry.com, Hoskins was about 29 in 1862 and Fielden about 24. Winthrop was 23.

78   Lowe, *Meade's Army*, p.351. If this is correct, Talbot went on to command the Heavy Camel Brigade in the 1884 Sudan campaign.

These were still people from highly privileged backgrounds, Talbot was the third son of the Earl of Shrewsbury, and Abercromby the son of a Scottish baronet. Lyman's diary entry does however open up the possibility that more officers outside of the Guards, Artillery, and Engineers did take advantage of their posting and their leave to visit the war, but that evidence of their visits remains undiscovered or unrecorded. There is one further previously unexamined source that supports this view. The leave returns for the Canadian station record the majority of leave as being on 'private affairs', with only rare indication of the underlying reason or destination. The garrison in Nova Scotia however was much smaller, and the reporting officers were much more conscientious, recording in accordance with the official instructions more complete reasons for why leave had been requested.[79] Between the arrival of troops following the *Trent* affair in December 1862 and the end of the war in April 1865 there were a total of 286 requests by officer for leave from the station. 20 of these (seven percent) gave no other reason than private affairs, but the remainder gave an indication of where they were travelling. Nearly half those requesting leave (111, or 39 percent of requests) returned to England, while in a further 121 requests (42 percent) the officers declared that they intended to travel in Canada, the various Nova Scotia dependencies or the West Indies. However, 34 of the officers requesting leave (12 percent), specifically stated that they intended to travel to the United States.[80]

This does not of course mean that all of these officers who declared an intention to visit the United States did so in order to observe the fighting, nor that they managed to do so. However, the names include Major General Hastings Doyle; Captain Osborne Hewett; Lieutenant Innes, and Lieutenant Rooke; all of whom are known from other records, and it seems very probable that several of those for which no other evidence exists also travelled to America out of professional interest in the conflict taking place there. Circumstantial evidence for this can be seen in the pattern of when officers made these visits, which occur at critical times in the Civil War and match the timings of visits of officers who did leave published accounts of their travels. The first instance of a visit to the United States by officers from Nova Scotia occurred in June 1862, and a second group went in November 1862. There was a third series of visits around June 1863, and another in October-November of that year. Then there was a long break, which corresponded to the period when passes were difficult to obtain, before visits resumed in September. Exactly half of the total happened in the last nine months of

79   In 1862-65 the government and military station in Nova Scotia was distinct from that of Canada. The returns for Nova Scotia and its dependencies included the modern Canadian provinces of Newfoundland and New Brunswick, and from 1863 also included Bermuda.

80   Leave statistics have been derived from WO 17/2409, *Monthly Returns to the Adjutant General, Nova Scotia, 1862*; WO 17/2410, *Monthly Returns to the Adjutant General, Nova Scotia, 1863*; WO 17/2411, *Monthly Returns to the Adjutant General, Nova Scotia, 1864*; and WO 17/2412, *Monthly Returns to the Adjutant General, Nova Scotia, 1865*. Included in the 34 are those requesting leave to travel in the United States, the United States and Canada, and the United States and West Indies.

Interior of Fort Sumter, Charleston, September 1863, the scene that Lt. Innes would have observed. (Library of Congress)

the Civil War. This is suggestive that officers were taking a last opportunity to see the war as it was coming to a close. In March 1865 out of nine officers requesting leave no less than five intended to travel to the United States whereas the following month, out of the same number of leave requests, none did so.[81]

An analysis of the individual officers making these visits is also interesting. The officers visiting the United States from Nova Scotia were mostly junior. Aside from Major General Doyle, only Lieutenant Colonel Spencer Westmacott of the Royal Engineers had a rank higher than captain. Almost half of them were from the Royal Artillery or Royal Engineers, while most of the others came from the four British line regiments based on the station. None of the officers in locally-raised units sought leave to visit the United States. The small group of engineers based on station made a disproportionate number of the visits, eight in all, including two by Lieutenant Innes and two by Lieutenant Keith. Looking at it another way, one-third of the engineers serving in Nova Scotia who took leave during the Civil War did so to visit the United States. In the artillery the proportion was one in six, and in the foot regiments one in ten. This reinforces the view that technical officers took a particularly keen interest in

81   WO 17/2409, WO 17/2410, WO 17/2411, WO 17/2412. 18 out of the 34 visits took place after August 1864.

the conflict, but it also suggests that young officers even in the less fashionable regiments were also interested in observing what was happening in the war.[82]

Thirty-four leave records is a small sample from which to draw conclusions. Yet the fact that the leave patterns and the importance of the technical arms amongst the observers are supported by the other known evidence suggests that the patterns seen in Nova Scotia may be applicable to Canada as a whole. This would suggest that around 50 anonymous officers from the Line and Rifle regiments stationed in Canada may have taken the time to visit the United States in this period; and maybe 16 Royal Artillery officers and five Royal Engineers.[83]

* * *

At the start of the war many British observers had claimed indifference to the politics of the war, or even a pro-Northern stance.[84] Fremantle in the preface to his book professed such sympathy, and the reasons why it changed.

> At the outbreak of the American war, in common with many of my countrymen, I felt very indifferent as to which side might win; but if I had any bias, my sympathies were rather in favour of the North, on account of the dislike which an Englishman naturally feels at the idea of slavery. But soon a sentiment of great admiration for the gallantry and determination of the Southerners, together with the unhappy contrast afforded by the foolish bullying conduct of

82   Of 135 regimental officers recorded as being on station in January 1862, 36 were in the artillery, 5 in the engineers and 69 in the three line regiments then present; the other 7 being in units raised locally. Seven requests to visit the United States were made by Royal Artillery officers and eight by Royal Engineers. The line regiments on station were the 2/2nd Foot (one request), 1/15th Foot (eight requests), 2/16th Foot (three requests), 2/17th Foot (five requests), and the 39th Foot in Bermuda (no requests), 17 requests in all. One request was from a Staff Assistant Surgeon (equivalent to captain in rank) in the Royal Army Medical Corps and the other was Major General Doyle. The latter was in February-March 1865, Doyle's earlier visit to the Army of the Potomac is not shown as leave.

83   Based upon leave requests identified in the Canadian leave registers, WO 17/1566 through to WO 17/1569; and the ratios visiting the United States from the Nova Scotia registers WO 17/2409 through WO 17/2412. At various times and excluding the Guards, the following British regiments served in Canada during this period: 1/16th Foot, 1/17th Foot, 1/25th Foot, 30th Foot, 47th Foot, 4/60th Rifles, 62nd Foot, 63rd Foot and 1/ Rifle Brigade. Collectively there are 504 leave requests on 'personal affairs' in the period for these regiments, 10 percent of these would give 50 officers visiting the United States. There were 100 leave requests by Artillery officers, the one in six ratio seen in Nova Scotia would imply 15 visits. The thirteen requests by Engineers implies four to five visits; two visits (Hewett and Satterthwaite) are verified from other sources.

84   Robert Cecil, 'The Confederate Struggle and Recognition', *Quarterly Review*, 112 (July 1862), pp.535-70 (pp.536-37); [E.W. Head], 'The American Revolution', *Edinburgh Review*, 116 (October 1862), pp.549-94 (p.561).

the Northerners, caused a complete revulsion in my feelings, and I was unable to repress a strong wish to go to America and see something of this wonderful struggle.[85]

Other convertees to the Confederate cause were influenced in their opinions by the reception given them by their Southern hosts. Glenn noted that Lord Hartington's sympathies were initially Northern, and that Edward St Maur was 'quite Northern too and not really very anxious to undertake the enterprise' of going south. On his return Hartington was 'better informed', and 'thoroughly Southern'. Edward Malet in the British legation in Washington described Hartington on his return from the South as 'enthusiastically secesh' and noted the annoyance of the Northern authorities who were 'very much put out at our soldiers going South and then returning rampant Secessionists'.[86]

Coming from the cultural elite of the British Army, Guards officers, as well as the sons of peers like Hartington and St Maur, were naturally drawn to and sympathised with what was universally portrayed by the British media as the aristocratic South. This affiliation was perhaps boosted for those of lesser means by the commercial opportunity provided for pro-Southern pieces in journals back home.[87] A majority of the British press was favourable to the South, so observers were obliged to come down on the side of the South in order to be published.[88] In contrast, Dicey's pro-Northern views meant that his book received a 'lukewarm reception' and poor reviews.[89] Members of the social elite published in periodicals such as *Blackwood's*, *Frasier's*, and the *Edinburgh Review*, all of which had a pro-Southern stance. John Blackwood was even said to have passed pieces to James Mason, the Confederate envoy to Britain, for approval.[90] Engineers and artillery officers were more likely to submit their reports

85   Fremantle, *Three Months in the Southern States*, p.3.
86   Glenn, *Between North and South*, pp.64, 78; BL, Malet Papers, RP.886, Reel 5, (no further sub-references), Edward Malet letters to his mother, Washington, 26 January 1863, and 10 February 1863.
87   Garnet Wolseley's article in Blackwood's Edinburgh Magazine based upon his travels earned him £40. Henry Fletcher was paid an advance of £50 per volume and 50 percent of the profits for his history of the war, while journalist George Alfred Lawrence was advanced £200 by the Morning Star to visit the South. Wolseley, *Story of a Soldier's Life*, Vol.II, p.126; BL, Bentley Papers, Add. 46618, f.4, Record of agreement dated 6 February 1862; Glenn, *Between North and South*, p.83. £40 was roughly equivalent to £4,300 in 2017 prices. <http://www.bankofengland.co.uk/education/Pages/resources/inflationtools/calculator/index1.aspx >.
88   Anon [Sir Bruce Hamley?], 'Our Rancorous Cousins', *Blackwood's Edinburgh Magazine*, 94 (November 1863), pp.636-52 (p.637); Stephen, 'England and America', p.424; Russell, 'Recollections', p.366; DuBrulle, 'A Military Legacy of the Civil War: The British Inheritance', p.160.
89   Charles L. Graves, *Life and Letters of Alexander MacMillan* (London: Macmillan, 1910), p.205.
90   Dubrulle, 'Anarchy ... and Ruin', p.594.

to professional journals than the general press. Innes and Featherstonhaugh both published in the *Royal Engineers' Professional Papers*, while Smyth published in the *Minutes of the Proceedings of the Royal Artillery Institution*.

Since the official news arriving from America was most likely to come from the North, reports from the South made better press regardless of a journal's political bias. One reason that Dunmore's arrival in Richmond was so widely reported in British newspapers was the anticipation that it would lead to first hand news from the South.[91] Not only were the stories more exotic but partaking in the Southern attempt to 'forge a new nation', to use Gladstone's words,[92] was a far more romantic narrative than a description of the logistical superiority of the Northern forces. This tendency to romanticise and favour narratives from the South would continue after the war. In 1890 the popular children's author G.A. Henty published a 'Boys' Own' adventure story entitled *With Lee in Virginia*. Writing such a narrative about campaigning with Grant's army simply would not have resonated with the British public, or British publishers. While Henty could give Grant credit for his magnanimity in victory, it was the heroic struggle against overwhelming odds that made the war of 'peculiar interest' to his young readers.[93]

Ella Lonn wrote in her study of foreigners who served in the Union forces that a natural English sympathy for the weaker side meant that it did not provide its quota of 'soldiers of fortune' to the North.[94] There is contemporary evidence for this as a source of Southern bias. A commentator back in Britain wrote that 'English feeling naturally takes the weaker side, and when the weaker side is adorned by characters of the grandeur of 'Stonewall' Jackson and Lee, the sympathy which follows its course warms into enthusiasm'.[95] This was also the view of the *Richmond Examiner* which spoke of 'the natural inborn British love of the just cause and the weak side'.[96] Because most of the fighting was in the seceding states Southern sympathisers could also portray the North as the aggressor, further appealing to the English sense of fair play. Evans openly admitted to President Lincoln that his sympathies were with the South because 'they were putting up a good fight for their freedom'.[97]

Another factor influencing the military observers was the Southern culture of military values to which they could readily relate. 'The qualities of the modern soldier – bravery, military knowledge, honourable feeling towards friends and foes alike,

---

91   *Falkirk Herald*, Thursday 24 July 1862, 'It to be hoped that, through its help, [i.e. that of Dunmore's Journal] the sealed book of Southern experiences will soon be opened to us'.
92   W.E. Gladstone speech given at Newcastle-on-Tyne on 7 October, cited in Francis M. Carroll, 'The American Civil War and British Intervention: The Threat of Anglo-American Conflict', *Canadian Journal of History*, 47 (2012), pp.87-115 (p.107).
93   G.A. Henty, *With Lee in Virginia: a story of the American Civil War* (London: Blackie and Son, 1890), pp.v-vi.
94   Lonn, *Foreigners in the Union Army and Navy*, p.300.
95   Cecil, 'The United States as an Example', p.249.
96   *Richmond Examiner* quoted in Dawson, *Reminiscences*, p.131.
97   Ware and Hunt, *Victorian Vet*, p.72.

chivalry, humanity – have been as remarkable on the side of the South as the absence of them has been on that of the North' wrote one commentator back in Britain.[98] Southerners went to military academies, were more likely to take up the military profession, and in the proving ground that was the war appeared to produce more men of military genius. Even successful Northern commanders could be depicted as reinforcing this view of Southern military prowess. Ulysses S. Grant was a Kentuckian, George Thomas a Virginian, and David Farragut a Louisianan. Prior to the war the South had also provided a majority of West Point educated regular army officers, who were regarded by the British as superior to volunteer officers in bearing and in attitude.[99] Hewett wrote that

> [t]he regular officer on both sides can be detected in a moment, as the education has made [them] gentlemen to a very great extent, or most, (whether born so or not) and their soldier-like manner and bearing towards officers of other armies who they meet, and the less prejudiced and more enlarged views about every subject and people is very striking in comparison with that of the volunteer-officers [sic].[100]

Some of the supposed Southern bias however appears to be the result of serious geopolitical concerns as much as an emotional preference for the Southern way of life. Wolseley, later accused by an American historian of writing about the war through 'Confederate spectacles' claimed in private to have 'no great love for the South', but supported recognition of the Confederacy because it would weaken England's potential enemy, the United States. In later life he would attribute the secession crisis to the self-interest of the Southern slaveholders.[101] The British commander in Canada, Lieutenant General William Fenwick Williams, was no friend of the North, and after the 1862 Peninsular campaign predicted their defeat and bankruptcy, but the following year showed that he had no love for the South either when he wrote to a friend in London supporting the British government's policy of formal neutrality. 'Be assured of one thing – the 'South' hate us as cordially as the 'North' – all the dirt we have eaten (as we Turks say) for half a century has been Southern

98   Marquess of Lothian, *The Confederate Secession* (Edinburgh: W. Blackwood & Sons, 1864), pp.115-16.
99   Russell, 'Recollections', p.370. The veneration of military life in the South is noted in Hagerman, *The American Civil War and the Origins of Modern Warfare*, p.101.
100 Hewett, in Preston, 'Letter', pp.51-52.
101 Arthur Lockwood Wagner *The Campaign of Königgrätz: A study of the Austro-Prussian Conflict in the Light of the American Civil War* (Fort Leavenworth: [n.pub.], 1889), p.4; HPL, Wolseley Archive, 163/3, Wolseley to his brother Richard, Montreal, 8 May 1863 and Baltimore, 21 September 1862; HPL, Wolseley Archive, SSL, hand annotations to copy of *Story of a Soldier's Life*, Vol.II, p.116.

Statesmen's insolence.'[102] Fenwick's equivalent in Nova Scotia, Sir Hastings Doyle, used similar words, writing that 'I sympathise with neither, for I think they both hate us cordially'.[103]

Numerically, far more British observers visited the Northern rather than the Southern armies, and the supposed Southern bias of the British establishment does not seem to have influenced the way in which they were received by their Northern hosts, which seems to have been mostly cordial throughout the war. Sir George Bell recorded the civility and kindness shown by the Americans, even though writing in late 1861 when Anglo-US tension was high. Edward Dicey, admittedly a Northern sympathiser, remarked upon the courtesy of the US officials even though denied permission as a journalist to accompany the Army of the Potomac, while Fletcher and his colleagues travelled with the army under the direct invitation of Major General McClellan, and formed personal friendships with the Northern officers. In his preface to his history of the Civil War, Fletcher considered this to be a possible source of bias *towards* the North, which he then wrote was offset by his admiration for the gallantry of the Confederates in the field. Henry Malet, visiting the Army of the Potomac in late 1862 wrote that 'the mere fact of being an English Officer is sufficient to ensure courtesy and kindness from nearly everyone in this country with whom one is likely to be thrown in contact'.[104]

Even Wolseley, who wrote in his published article that all Englishmen in the border states were viewed as smugglers or rebel sympathisers, in his private letters remarked that the few Northerners he had met were 'courteous and obliging'.[105] A year later Cecil Peel and his fellow officers were also treated with great courtesy.

> On our arrival at head-quarters, we were received by all with the most marked kindness and hospitality, the officers of the general and personal staffs vying with each other in the heartiness of their welcome, and in many cases, I fear, stripping their own tents of their camp furniture to make ours comfortable.[106]

The officers who visited Meade's army in late 1864 and early 1865 were similarly warmly received and shown every courtesy. According to Smyth he was an intimate acquaintance of Meade, even privy to the army dispatches, while Sir Hastings Doyle

102 BL, Layard Papers, Add. 38989, fols 18-21, General William Fenwick Williams to Sir Austen Henry Layard, Montreal, 12 January 1863. The reference to 'we turks' presumably refers to Williams' service with the Turkish army at the defence of Kars in 1855.
103 NBM, Letter from Sir Hastings Doyle to Sir William Fenwick, Halifax, Nova Scotia, 29 March 1865.
104 Bell, Soldier's Glory, p.324; Dicey, *Six Months in the Federal States*, Vol.II, p.34; Fletcher, *History*, Vol.I, p.v-vi; BL, Layard Papers, Add. 39104, fols 225-28, Letter from Henry Malet to Sir Austen Henry Layard, 27 December 1862.
105 Wolseley 'A Month's Visit', p.2; HPL, Wolseley Archive, 163/3/9, Wolseley to his brother Richard, Baltimore, 21 September 1862.
106 Peel, 'A Short Campaign', p.191.

visited Meade and his wife socially on at least one occasion after the war. Theodore Lyman thought that Doyle's Irish roots made him favourably disposed to the North.[107]

*   *   *

Those observers serving in Canada had a number of options available to them to visit the United States. Most observers went via Washington, not only because of its obvious political and military significance but also because of the practical necessity of acquiring passes from the US Government. The most direct route between Montreal and Washington was to travel by train down to New York City by the Hudson River Railroad from where a train could be caught to Washington or Baltimore. An alternative railway route ran from Toronto through Niagara, and then to Williamsport (PA) which had rail links to Baltimore, Washington, Philadelphia, and New York. It was possible to do this in three days by rail, though probably more usual to make overnight stops on the way. Wolseley took a different route, by steamer across Lake Champlain and Lake George to Saratoga and Philadelphia, and down the Hudson by steam boat, from Albany to New York. This journey took Wolseley five days, with two rests at New York and Philadelphia. So travel from Canada to the eastern theatre was simple and achievable during short periods of leave.[108]

Travellers to the West such as Dicey and Hewett also usually started in Washington, and this meant a long train journey.[109] Travel away from the railway was difficult. Hewett, searching for the warring armies in Kentucky, wandered about the country for 10 days, including one day on which he claimed to walk an incredible 48 miles 'which is the longest walk I have ever done or certainly ever will do if I can help it'![110] Harrison took a less well travelled route to the Mid-West from London (Ontario) crossing the border at Windsor and travelling on to Chicago before going south to St Louis. Remarkably he was able to do this while taking only a week's leave.[111]

Those observers arriving from England usually sailed to New York, a voyage taking around 12 days, and picked up the overland routes from there, even if their ultimate destination was the South. Some civilians did run the risk of the naval blockade and travel to Southern ports. For example Frank Vizetelly, a journalist with the *London Illustrated News* who was based in the South from September 1862, travelled home

107 Smyth, 'Account of the Final Attack and Capture of Richmond', p.363; Lowe, *Meade's Army*, pp.239, 392.
108 Tony Margrave 'British Officers Observe the Civil War in America', Part 1, *Crossfire*, 104 (Spring 2014), pp.13-20 (p.15); WO 33/11/0174, *Report of Officers of the British Army on American Arms, August 1862*, p.2; 'R.D.' 'Boston, New York and Washington', pp.192-94; HPL, Wolseley Archive, 163/3/9, Wolseley to his brother Richard, Baltimore, 14 September 1862.
109 Dicey, *Six Months in the Federal States*, Vol.II, pp.34-119; Hewett, in Preston, 'Letter', pp.51, 54.
110 Hewett, in Preston, 'Letter', p.58.
111 Dicey, *Six Months in the Federal States*, Vol.II, pp.34-119; Harrison, *Recollections*, p.113.

from Wilmington to England via Bermuda in 1864 and returned later the same year via Nassau in the Bahamas. It is possible that Albany Featherstonhaugh ran the naval blockade in similar fashion, particularly in leaving the Confederacy as his first posting after his leave was to Bermuda, but there is no firm evidence of this, and the returns for the Bermuda station have him as arriving on 6 January 1865 from Canada. Running the blockade was highly risky by that time and could have caused an international incident if a serving officer had been captured doing so. As already noted, Fremantle chose to use the longer but physically and politically safer route through Mexico, and when leaving the South formally surrendered himself to the US authorities in Virginia.[112]

Crossing to the South in Maryland also involved significant risk, whether achieved by boat across the Potomac or on foot. Wolseley had several 'disagreeable interviews' with the United States cavalry before being smuggled across the river past the gunboat patrols. The front line in the West was longer and more difficult for the Northern authorities to guard but could be equally dangerous to cross. Hewett was continually followed by Northern patrols looking for the guerrilla leader John Hunt Morgan, and though he was able to evade them, Kentucky was a dangerous place for a stranger out of uniform. Harrison related how he was nearly lynched as a Confederate spy in Missouri during Sterling Price's 1864 invasion. In 1862 Fletcher had found it rather easier to cross the lines in the West, having received a pass from Major General Sherman in Memphis at the start of his journey through the Confederacy. Railways were less well developed in the West whereas river transport was more common, and Fletcher travelled down the Mississippi on board a steamer which also carried both Union and Confederate officers. By late 1863 any visit to the major eastern theatre of war around Chattanooga or Atlanta meant a long and difficult journey either by rail through the Confederacy, as Ross had done, or along the Union military supply route, which no British observer seems to have attempted.[113]

Luvaas was critical of subsequent British writers for their focus on the eastern theatre of the war, which may be attributable to the influence of Liddell Hart, whose study of Sherman in the 1930s emphasised the supposedly superior tactics and strategy of the western theatre.[114] This criticism cannot reasonably be levelled at the observers of the time. It is true that a high proportion of observers did visit the armies in northern Virginia, but this was largely down to these practical reasons of transport. Commentators back in Britain fully understood the strategic importance of the western theatre, but observers on the ground were more limited in what they could view. The north-eastern United States was the most accessible to visitors from both

112   WO 33/14/0229, Gallwey Report, p.ix; Hoole, *Vizetelly Covers the Confederacy*, pp.112-18; WO 25/3913 Featherstonhaugh military service record; TNA, WO 17/2412, *Monthly Returns to the Adjutant General, Nova Scotia, 1865*, Fremantle, *Three Months in the Southern States*, p.148.
113   Wolseley, *Story of a Soldier's Life*, Vol.II, pp.128-31; Hewett, in Preston, 'Letter', pp.59-60; Fletcher, 'A Run through the Southern States', pp.495-96.
114   Luvaas, *Military Legacy*, p.202.

Canada and Britain, and those on a short stay of leave would have had little time to venture much further afield, although Harrison demonstrated that it was possible. The armies in Virginia were perceived to represent the best equipped, largest, and most efficient of the forces engaged, while in the case of the North the political authorities often made it difficult to visit areas that they considered sensitive. The vast geographical scale of the conflict, and the associated transportation problems, limited what the observers could see. Travel to the West was simply extremely difficult. In spite of these difficulties, observers did manage to visit locations as far apart as Galveston, Shreveport, Memphis, Jackson, Mobile, Chicago, St Louis, Chattanooga, and Charleston, as well as the north-east and Virginia.

* * *

Such then were the motives and opportunities for British direct observation of the war. What was the quality of that observation? A number of common themes can be observed. The first thing recognised was the sheer difficulty of conducting war in America. The poor quality of infrastructure made even simple manoeuvring difficult. Wolseley considered his journey to Fredericksburg to be along 'the very worst road I ever travelled on' while Edward Dicey thought them 'hardly roads in our sense of the word', though he also wrote that McClellan had over-exaggerated the difficulty of movement by the roads in Virginia.[115] Transport was worsened by the devastation of several years of war. Fitzgerald Ross took five days to travel 70 miles when he crossed into northern Virginia in June 1863, 'owing to the devastation of the country we had passed through' but the roads were also bad when Ross accompanied Lee's army north into Pennsylvania.[116] In October that year he found that the roads in the western theatre around Chickamauga were impassable to wagons due to the rains, and he attributed the poor roads in the South to lack of sufficient stone.[117] Ross noted how well the American troops coped with these difficult conditions.

> I was surprised to see how well the men were shod. The weather was fine now, but it had been horribly bad. The mud on the roads had been ankle-deep, and several rivers and streams had been waded and forded. Many a European army would have been half without shoes, but here there were very few barefooted men, and during our halt these few were supplied by stores sent up from the rear.[118]

115 Wolseley, 'A Month's Visit', pp.7, 15; Dicey, *Six Months in the Federal States*, Vol.II, pp.18-19. For further comments see Fletcher, 'A Run through the Southern States', p.513; Harrison, 'A Trip to Meade's Army', p.337; von Borcke, *Memoirs*, Vol.I, p.29.
116 Ross, *Visit*, p.15.
117 Ross, *Visit*, pp.15, 36, 42, 73, 166.
118 Ross, *Visit*, pp.95-96. In contrast Major General Sheridan, who accompanied the Prussian army in France in 1870, commented that 'campaigning in France – that is the marching, camping and subsisting of an army – is an easy matter, very unlike anything we had in

The tactical implications of the thickly wooded terrain were observed. Major General Bell remarked to William Russell that a general 'could no more handle his troops among these woods than he could direct the movements of rabbits in a cover'.[119] Wolseley visited the battlefields around Richmond and elaborated further on the difficulties faced by an American commander.

> Most of the country fought over was very thickly wooded, so that, without accurate knowledge of the ground, to direct any operation well would be impossible. No general could see what was going on to his right or left; nor without closing upon his enemy could he form that just estimate of the numbers of those opposed to him, or the position of reserves &c, which is so essential to success.[120]

A further geographical constraint was the strategic limitations imposed by the enormous distances. 'In so vast a space of country armies can retreat in any direction they please and fight wherever they happen to be'.[121]

A second set of general observations concerned the quality of troops. European commentators are sometimes dismissed as regarding Civil War armies as amateurs or even mere 'armed mobs' but the reality of the observers' remarks is more complex.[122] There seems to have been a universally high regard for the physical and mental qualities of the rank and file soldiers on both sides, who were considered much better than Europeans – 'none of the miserable undersized half starved creatures that we are glad in times of pressure to take to recruit our armies with'.[123] The high level of literacy also contrasted markedly to European experience. Observers in the early part of the war recorded that every man was able to read or write, that most were married, and most had some form of education. The men's attitude and deference to women was also noted.[124] Others such as Guards officer Henry Malet qualified their opinions.

> Physically the American troops are much the finest that ever I saw and I see no reason to doubt that they are as brave as any soldiers that ever stepped – but there

the War of the Rebellion'. Quoted in T. Miller Maguire 'Guerrilla or Partisan Warfare', *United Service Magazine*, n.s., 23 (1901), pp.127-34, 264-271, 353-364, 473-485, 583-592 (p.355).

119 Russell, 'Recollections', p.748.
120 Wolseley, 'A Month's Visit', p.11.
121 Dicey, *Six Months in the Federal States*, Vol.II, p.39; Stephen, 'England and America', p.432.
122 Montgomery, *History of Warfare*, p.440; Luvaas, *Military Legacy*, p.2.
123 BL: Layard Papers, Add. 39104, fols 225-28, Henry Malet to Sir Austen Henry Layard, 27 December, 1862. See also Bourke, 'A Month with the Rebels', p.769; Dicey, *Six Months in the Federal States*, Vol.II, p.7.
124 Bell, *Soldier's Glory*, p.313; St Maur, 'Ten Days in Richmond', p.392. The high numbers of letters posted by Federal troops was reported in *The Times*, 25 January 1862, published in Brogan, *Extracts from the Times*, p.51; Dicey, *Six Months in the Federal States*, Vol.II, pp.10, 243-44; Wolseley, *Story of a Soldier's Life*, Vol.II, p.125.

ends all I can say, they are dirty, careless of their arms, (which are generally in a filthy state) and most slovenly, and ignorant on outpost duty.[125]

Racial and social prejudices clearly affected the views put forward on American troops, particularly those on the Union side. Wolseley made references to Irish and German 'mercenaries' in the North, comparing them unfavourably with the patriotic (and, not explicitly but by inference, Anglo-Saxon) Southerners. There is an interesting paradox here that Wolseley also regarded regulars as superior to irregulars, but the majority of the US Regular Army in 1861 was composed of Irish or Germans. Other writers painted a more favourable view of foreigners in the armies. Fremantle commented upon a group of Confederate Regulars at Fort Sumter as 'more soldier-like' than the normal volunteers before noting that 'a great proportion of them are foreigners'.[126] The pro-Northern Dicey thought that the proportion of foreigners in the Northern armies was at most 10 percent – though allowing that the Germans might form a majority in some western states. He also believed that the July 1862 levies came primarily from the wealthier classes rather than poor immigrants, since there was no general distress forcing the poor into the army. This was also the view of an 1863 article in *The Times*, a newspaper which was normally Southern leaning. Dicey did however consider the variety of nationalities in the Northern armies contributed to the difficulties of discipline.[127]

The picture painted of the Southern soldier was more consistent and more positive, he was usually portrayed as the gallant volunteer fighting for his country, and observers visiting the South remarked on the presence of gentlemen in the ranks.[128] The following passage from Wolseley is typical of the comments as to their quality, and illustrates that the observers were on occasion prepared to look beyond 'spit and polish' when judging what they saw.

125 Dicey, *Six Months in the Federal States*, Vol.II, pp.7, 243-44; Wolseley, *Story of a Soldier's Life*, Vol.II, p.125; BL, Layard Papers, Add. 39104, Malet to Layard, 27 December, 1862.
126 Wolseley, 'A Month's Visit', p.23; Lonn, *Foreigners in the Union Army and Navy*, p.85; Fremantle, *Three Months in the Southern States*, p.92. Richard P. Weinart Jr, *The Confederate Regular Army* (Shippensburg: White Mane, 1991), pp.86-89 records that Company C 15th South Carolina Heavy Artillery Battalion, a regular unit, was in the Charleston region in the first half of 1863 and these may have been the troops Fremantle saw. The unit was a mixture of men from Maryland and South Carolina. Weinart supports Fremantle's observation that the Confederate regular units included a high percentage of foreign-born men, ibid p.112.
127 Dicey, *Six Months in the Federal States*, Vol.II, pp.9, 19-20, 290; Antonio Carlo Napoleone Gallenga in *The Times*, 8 August 1863, published in Brogan, *Extracts from the Times*, p.122. Lonn, *Foreigners in the Union Army and Navy*, pp.656-57, concluded that only 20-25 percent of Union soldiers were foreign born. Russell, 'Recollections', p.618, referred to foreigners taking a leading part. Fletcher in 'A Run through the Southern States', p.502, remarked that there were less foreigners in the South than the North.
128 Wolseley, 'A Month's Visit', p.23; Watson, *Life in the Confederate Army*, p.174; Ross, *Visit*, p.54; St Maur, 'Ten Days in Richmond', p.392; Bourke, 'A Month with the Rebels', p.764.

[E]ach man had that unmistakeable look of conscious strength and manly self-reliance, which those who are accustomed to review troops like to see.

I have seen many armies file past in all the pomp of bright clothing and well-polished accoutrements; but I never saw one composed of finer men, or that looked more like *work*, than that portion of General Lee's army which I was fortunate enough to see inspected.[129]

The supposedly pro-Southern Wolseley however, while praising the Confederate army, also wrote of what he termed the 'Southern race' as being 'indolent', that they 'despised all manual labour', and were of a 'listless disposition'.[130] The Southern soldier was portrayed as drilled to manoeuvre fast and used to handling guns by virtue of his upbringing, but he was criticised for wastefulness and straggling on the march.[131]

Observers universally considered the discipline of the Americans on both sides poor, though their analysis of the cause and remedy varied. Russell made several comments on poor discipline in the early stages of the war, and stated that McDowell admitted to him that his army in 1861 was not fit to fight. Short service was largely attributed as being the source of the problem, particularly in the North. Wolseley later wrote of this as a 'serious evil' and said that General Lee had argued for enlistments being for the duration of the war. St Maur thought that the high level of individual intelligence amongst Southern soldiers offset the lack of discipline, but given their background from elite regiments of the British army, it is perhaps unsurprising that for the professional military men, inexperienced officers and lack of *esprit de corps* were considered the weak point.[132]

Fletcher, also writing about the Southern troops, records that the officers of the old army serving the Confederacy complained that their men had little military spirit, and that pride in the regiment was substituted by 'neighbourly feeling of each man for his comrade'. Fletcher concluded that '[t]here is no time to make them good regular troops; therefore latitude in discipline must be allowed in order to make them good volunteers'.[133] Completely the opposite view was taken by his friend Henry Malet in his observation of the Army of the Potomac.

The first of my observations at that time and subsequently is this, that great results cannot be achieved by volunteer armies unless the day that war breaks out the military authorities shall utterly ignore the difference between them and regular troops and deal 'equally without fear favour or affection' if anything

---

129 Wolseley, 'A Month's Visit', p.24.
130 Wolseley, 'A Month's Visit', pp.13, 16-17.
131 Bourke, 'A Month with the Rebels', pp.765, 773; Fletcher, 'A Run Through the Southern States', p.507; Fremantle, *Three Months in the Southern States*, pp.59, 63.
132 Russell, 'Recollections', pp.500, 618, 620, 741; General Viscount Wolseley, 'General Lee', *MacMillan's Magazine*, 55 (1887), pp.321-31 (p.326)
133 Fletcher, 'A Run through the Southern States', p.507.

rather harder with the volunteers than the regulars, as wanting it more licking into shape.[134]

Malet and Fletcher met after Fletcher's journey through the South, from which Malet understood that discipline was stronger in the Confederate Army than in the Union Army. This he attributed to the Southern officer class being drawn from the higher social classes. Given that Wolseley in his near contemporary account of the Southern army was still criticising the election system and men of property serving under their social inferiors, Malet's social prejudices probably led to him overstating the case for an army he had not directly observed. He also bemoaned the lack of corporal punishment, which does seem to have been rare. Ross however reported in 1863 that gamblers were flogged in the Army of Northern Virginia.[135]

George Robert Gleig, a veteran of the war of 1812, wrote in *Blackwood's* at this time in respect of the problems of defending Canada that '[a]n American army, when it first takes the field, may be little better than a rabble, but give it the experience of a year or two, and it becomes able to hold its own against the best troops in the world'.[136] This was perhaps the fairest and best conclusion that could have been drawn from the reports emanating from America, and a good example of not underestimating a potential enemy. Later observers acknowledged that the Federal army had improved during the war. They did however still retain the notion that poor discipline limited the value of the US forces. This was thought to be particularly demonstrated on the march, where straggling was rife, and through the high rates of desertion, which were attributed to the bounty system. Cecil Peel concluded that European standards of discipline were impossible due to the institutions and manners of the country.

> Their discipline appeared to me to be rather that of men who had learned by experience the necessity, for their own sakes, of obeying their leaders under certain circumstances, than to spring from that unquestioning obedience to authority that should exist through all ranks of an army.[137]

This belief in the inferiority of a volunteer army to European regulars was maintained right through to the end of the war, as the following comment from the mission of 1864 illustrates.

> The soldiers are well behaved and their bravery indisputable. Properly disciplined and well commanded the Federal Army would be second to no army in the world, but as presently constituted, with so many great defects, it must as a whole be

---

134 BL, Layard Papers, Add. 39104, Malet to Layard, 27 December 1862.
135 BL, Layard Papers, Add. 39104, Malet to Layard, 27 December 1862; Wolseley, 'A Month's Visit', pp.22-23; Ross, *Visit*, p.193.
136 Gleig, 'Defence of Canada', p.254.
137 Gleig, 'Defence of Canada', pp.198-99.

considered greatly inferior to European armies, and not at all approaching that value which is represented by numbers alone.[138]

* * *

American cavalry was particularly poorly regarded. The traditional interpretation of this view has been that the British were fixated on the mounted charge and failed to recognise that modern firearms had rendered traditional shock tactics obsolete.[139] This is simplistic, and ignores the significant level of expertise of the observers, and their recognition of the problems faced by the Americans in raising large bodies of cavalry. Even if it is accepted that British aristocrats did not recognise the revolution in fire-arms, they did know something about horseflesh and horsemanship. Particularly in the North the level of both of these was seen as low. In contrast to the cavalier traditions of the South, the use of horses in the Northern states was primarily as draft animals, so they had significant problems getting good cavalry mounts and in getting horses to stand fire. Even in the South the horses were not trained for military work and one British volunteer serving with the Confederacy in 1862 wrote that they reacted badly to the noise of military music. Federal troopers are frequently described as barely able to sit their mounts, and as not being used to looking after them. Peel thought the Union cavalry horses in poor condition, less well looked after than those in the artillery, and 'evidently overweighted'. Hewett recorded that he escaped from a 'Yankee Cavalry' patrol because he knew them incapable of jumping a 3-feet fence. Thomas Morley, a veteran of the Light Brigade serving in the Union Army, considered himself the only person in his volunteer regiment who knew cavalry tactics, and while he was certainly a self-publicist this may well have been true.[140]

The Southern cavalry was more highly regarded, although even Fremantle, an advocate of the Southern cause and an admirer of its leaders, thought that 'Stuart's cavalry can hardly be called cavalry in the European sense of the word', going on to qualify this by saying that 'the country in which they are accustomed to operate is not adapted for cavalry'.[141] Wolseley thought that all the men 'rode well', Harrison described the Confederate picket he met as looking like 'a thorough light horseman', and Fletcher recorded seeing a 'soldierlike body of cavalry' but even the Southern cavaliers were not

138 WO 33/14/0229, Gallwey Report, pp.32-33.
139 For the 'traditional' view, Luvaas, *Military Legacy*, particularly pp.4-5, 17-18, 177-78, 193-97; Craddock, 'The American Civil War and its Influence on the British Army', particularly pp.1, 69-72, 118-24, 219-23.
140 Russell, 'Recollections', p.621; Wolseley 'A Month's Visit', p.27; Watson, *Life in the Confederate Army*, p.170; Fremantle, *Three Months in the Southern States*, p.151; Peel, 'A Short Campaign', p.199; BL, Layard Papers, Add. 39104, Malet to Layard, 27 December 1862; Hewett, in Preston, 'Letter', p.60; Tony Margrave, '"brits in blue or gray" [*sic*]: Thomas Morley, 12th Pennsylvania Cavalry', *Crossfire*, 96 (August 2011), pp.6-12.
141 Fremantle, *Three Months in the Southern States*, p.143.

seen as comparable to European troopers. Heros von Borcke thought himself a better horseman than Stuart, relating how he had jumped a difficult fence that Stuart would not attempt.[142]

When it came to fighting, the cavalry of both sides was considered timorous with some justification during the early period of the war. There were a high number of skirmishes but few attacks were truly pressed home. Fremantle described their actions as 'miserable affairs' and remarked that there was no use of bayonets or sabres, and that the cavalry was incapable of following up broken infantry – one of cavalry's most important roles in European military thinking. He was however complimentary about the skirmishing tactics he saw in the West.[143]

None of the serving British officers who published their observations of the war were from the cavalry, but one British cavalryman did write about his experiences in the war. Fitzgerald Ross was a serving officer in a hussar regiment of the Austrian Army, and he also reported that the American cavalry were not dashing, and never charged mounted even when the opportunity arose. Ross also believed that the fact the Confederates supplied their own horses influenced their decision to fight mainly on foot. That this was not entirely simple European prejudice is shown by Ross's reporting of Lieutenant General James Longstreet's views on the cavalry. Longstreet apparently believed that the cavalry relied too much on artillery and this encouraged them to play 'long bowls' and demoralised them when it came to offensive action.[144]

Von Borcke wrote of the demoralisation of levies under artillery fire and how the action of artillery could be decisive in cavalry skirmishes, giving an example of Pelham's battery at Poolesville on 10 October 1862. He also described cavalry defending a turnpike using entrenchments and artillery, while 'a genuine cavalry fight with sabres crossing and single combat' was clearly exceptional, and even under the gallant von Borcke's leadership units of the supposedly superior Confederate cavalry refused to charge home during the Battle of Brandy Station in June 1863.[145]

The observers did not, however, deduce from this that the Americans were wrong in their use of their mounted arm. Von Borcke believed along with Fremantle that the terrain did not favour cavalry, and Ross considered that their use as mounted infantry was entirely appropriate.

> There has been no time to put them through a regular cavalry drill, and teach the efficient use of the sabre – the true arm of real cavalry – whilst with the use of

---

142 Wolseley, 'A Month's Visit', p.27; Harrison, 'A Trip to Meade's Army', pp.337-38; Fletcher, 'A Run through the Southern States', p.502; Von Borcke, *Memoirs*, Vol.I, p.322.

143 Fremantle, *Three Months in the Southern States*, pp.126, 87.

144 Ross, *Visit*, pp.30, 88, 99.

145 Von Borcke, *Memoirs*, Vol.I, pp.24, 113-14, 305-07, see also Vol.I, pp.173, 211; Heros von Borcke and Justus Scheibert *Die Grosse Reiterschlacht bei Brandy Station*, translated by Stuart T. Wright and F.D. Bridgewater (Winston-Salem: Palaemon, 1976, originally published Berlin, 1893), pp.64-65, 89-90.

the rifle they have been familiar from their earliest youth. To handle a rifle efficiently, of course, a man must dismount. On the whole, I think they have acted judiciously in taking their men as they found them, and not trying to establish the European system.[146]

Wolseley compared the Confederate horsemen to irregular regiments raised by the British in India, the practice of each man providing his own horse being an obvious comparison, and also felt them 'admirable adapted for the service required of them' – as scouts, and not used as masses of horsemen. Equally importantly the Federals, through their lack of horsemanship, were reported as being poor scouts and as a result ignorant of the enemy location.[147]

Peel was also reminded of Indian irregulars when he visited the Army of the Potomac at the end of 1863, and Harrison 'did not [...] think much of the Federal cavalry as seen at this time, and, in my humble opinion, they would disgrace some of our wildest Irregulars raised in the north of India at the time of the mutinies in that country'.[148] Harrison described both traditional and new models of the mounted arm. His description of the Confederate picket dwelt on his dress and gentlemanly aspect, but the more slovenly Federal cavalry, ragged, poorly mounted and ill-disciplined, were well-armed; in particular with that remarkable 'Yankee device' the Spencer carbine, which could fire seven shots without reloading and be operated by one hand.[149] Harrison was a more even handed observer than many, as he was even more disparaging of the Confederate cavalry serving under Major General Price in Missouri in October 1864 than he had been of the Federals the previous year, writing that 'by all accounts [they] were little better than banditti and had no discipline or cohesion'.[150]

* * *

The infantry was somewhat better thought of, and some of the Southern regiments were quite highly regarded. Both Fletcher in 1862 and Fremantle in 1863 commented favourably on the drill of regiments on garrison duties in the West.[151] Wolseley praised the troops of Longstreet's Corps in the autumn of 1862, which although poorly equipped and ragged marched smartly 'with an elastic tread, the pace being somewhat slower than that of our troops' and he 'had never seen troops that looked

---

146 Ross, *Visit*, p.30.
147 Wolseley, 'A Month's Visit', p.27.
148 Peel, 'A Short Campaign p.199; Harrison, 'A Trip to Meade's Army', pp.337.
149 Harrison, 'A Trip to Meade's Army', pp.337-38.
150 Harrison, *Recollections*, p.115.
151 Fremantle, *Three Months in the Southern States* p.12; Fletcher, 'A Run through the Southern States', pp.496, 560.

so much like *work*.[152] Both Fletcher and Ross commented on the wide range of arms used in the Confederate western armies, and Edward St Maur attributed the aggressive Confederate tactics to their inferior arms, the shorter range of which meant that they had to close with their enemies.[153]

Russell was highly critical of the untrained Federal infantry at First Bull Run, in particular their fear of cavalry and 'masked batteries', but raw Canadian volunteers when first engaged in battle six years later during the Fenian raids were to show an equally disproportionate fear of cavalry. Wolseley believed the Americans also unduly fearful of artillery fire since they lacked a tradition of charging batteries. Hewett thought the American armies unable to manoeuvre under fire and, like the cavalry, reluctant to close, resulting in large numbers of skirmishes and few casualties other than in the big battles.[154] Fremantle may have adopted his Southern hosts' contempt of the enemy, to which hubris he attributed their defeat at Gettysburg, when he wrote of captured Union troops with poor fitting uniforms as being dirty, slovenly and 'bad imitations of soldiers'.[155]

The pro-Northern Dicey was more positive. While recognising there was a 'slouching gait about the men, not soldier like to British eyes', he thought them 'more business-like' and believed a Pennsylvania regiment of six weeks service to be trained to 'to the average of our best trained volunteer troops, as far as marching and drill exercise went'.[156] By contrast, Harrison in 1863 still considered the infantry of the Army of the Potomac 'not better, if as good, as one of our moderate County Volunteer Regiments in England' and 'chiefly composed of undrilled, undisciplined conscripts'.[157] The following year he saw two regiments of '100 day men' in Chicago which he described as 'the dirtiest, most undisciplined and worst body I ever saw that called themselves soldiers', and remarked on sentries being placed around camps to prevent desertion. Travelling by train between Chicago and St Louis, he observed a group of conscripts 'being marched along between rows of bayonets, and guarded with as much care as convicts'. On the other hand, Harrison saw some regiments 'said to be as good as any in the American army and chiefly composed of veterans', and concluded that 'their movements were smart, something like French troops'.[158] These were probably Major

---

152 Wolseley, 'A Month's Visit', p.27.
153 Ross, *Visit*, pp.151-54; St Maur, 'Ten Days in Richmond', pp.392, 395-96; St Maur to his Father (11th Duke of Somerset), Washington, 25 July 1862, in *Letters of Lord St. Maur and Lord Edward St. Maur, 1846 to 1869*, ed. Guendolen Ramsden, (London: n. pub. 1888), p.257.
154 William Howard Russell, *The Times*, 6 August 1861, dateline Washington 22 July 1861, published in Brogan, *Extracts from the Times*, pp.15-35; Mary Beacon Fryer, *Battlefields of Canada* (Toronto and Reading: Dundurn Press, 1986), pp.217-18; Wolseley 'A Month's Visit', pp.11-12; Hewett, in Preston, 'Letter', pp.56-57.
155 Fremantle, *Three Months in the Southern States*, pp.138,147.
156 Dicey, *Six Months in the Federal States*, Vol.II, pp.6-8.
157 Harrison, 'A Trip to Meade's Army', pp.333, 335.
158 Harrison, *Recollections*, p.114.

General A.J. Smith's Division, veteran's from Sherman's army who had been posted to St Louis to defend against Major General Sterling Price's invasion, and the similarity of their drill to that of the French attributable to the fact that the standard American drill manual, Hardee's *Rifle and Light Infantry Tactics* of 1855, was essentially a translation of the pre-war French manual.[159] Another more generous view of the quality of the American infantryman was provided by Peel.

> They take an evident pride in their drill, and do their best to show themselves to advantage in this respect; and though the movements I saw were slow, and always confined to marching past and deploying from a double column of companies into line and vice versa, they were more steadily executed than I expected, – quite equal, I should say, to those of our own Volunteers at home.[160]

The observers rarely got to see major battles, and were limited by geography and opportunity as to what they could observe when they did. Ross commented that at Gettysburg the Confederates operated using more extended lines than the Federals, who he regarded as being held in too compact masses and therefore suffering from the execution of artillery and superior musketry by Confederates. Von Borcke describes the Texans as advancing in a 'wild indian fashion'. In general, though, it seems that there was nothing exceptionally unusual observed in American infantry tactics.[161]

* * *

The artillery on both sides was regarded as the best arm. '[The cavalry] is utterly worthless the infantry are <u>rather</u> better and the artillery better again – I saw <u>some</u> batteries which were really in tolerable order', wrote Henry Malet of the Federals at Fredericksburg, while Wolseley also thought the Confederate artillery was better drilled than their infantry, and that 'for all practical purposes, its manoeuvres were executed in the most satisfactory manner'.[162] Peel witnessed an artillery bombardment at Mine Run, Virginia, on 30 November 1863 when 'every shot fired seemed to tell' and the heavy 20-pounders and siege guns 'also made wonderful practice … at 2000 yards' range'.[163] Professional prejudice would appear to have biased Henry Smyth's view of the competence of the Federal batteries at Petersburg however. His American host believed that he 'came on purpose to criticise American gunnery' and

159 Albert Castel, *General Sterling Price and the Civil War in the West*, Paperback edn (Baton Rouge: Louisiana State University Press, 1993), p.208; Nosworthy, *The Bloody Crucible of Courage*, pp.79-81.
160 Peel, 'A Short Campaign', p.198.
161 Ross, *Visit*, pp.65-66; Von Borcke, *Memoirs*, Vol.II, p.106.
162 BL, Layard Papers, Add. 39104, Malet to Layard, 27 December 1862, original emphasis; Wolseley, 'A Month's Visit', p.23.
163 Peel, 'A Short Campaign', p.199.

was pleased to report to his superior that 'he [Smyth] looked through the sight, and seeing it directed at the very center of the building, remarked, "We allow for drift in our service." Informed him that the sights were already adjusted for drift, and surprised him somewhat'.[164]

Wolseley also discussed the composition of the batteries, considering the Confederate four-piece establishment to be a limitation, and seeing nothing remarkable in the equipment with the possible exception of the few Blakely rifles which were highly regarded. Ross provided an extensive analysis for his readers of the artillery of the Army of Tennessee where he noted the preference for the smooth-bored Napoleon cannon over rifled guns, while *The Times'* Richmond correspondent, Frank Lawley, noted the preference for case over solid shot in the Battle at Fredericksburg. However, the only thing thought uniquely American seems to have been the arrangement of the artillery into battalions rather than allocating it by battery to divisions.[165]

* * *

When it came to officers, the election of officers was universally condemned, as was the preferential advancement of volunteers over regulars which led the latter to resign their US Army commissions to take up appointments from their states. The observers tended to have a high opinion of anyone with formal military qualification, regular officers in the Federal army being described as more gentlemanly, soldier-like, and less prejudiced than volunteer officers. Major General McClellan is an excellent case in point. British observers who met him formed a high regard for McClellan. He fitted perfectly into the British view of an acceptable American – a West Point educated professional soldier and engineer, who had experience of European warfare in the Crimea, was imposing drill and discipline on the hastily formed army, and favoured accommodation rather than annihilation of the South. Hewett considered that McClellan was the only person the North had who was capable of handling 300,000 men. Wolseley was rather more balanced in his judgement, being critical of McClellan's excessive caution, but recognising his organisational skills, and believing him the only Federal general who could have fought the Battle of Antietam. Wolseley thought that the need for 'idols' such as McClellan was indispensable for American armies.[166]

164 Major Birnie to Colonel H.L. Abbott, Fort Brady VA, 24 November 1864, published in Hatfield, *History of the First Connecticut Artillery*, p.123.
165 Wolseley, 'A Month's Visit', p.23; Ross, *Visit*, pp.151-54; Frank Lawley in *The Times*, 23 January 1863, and 18 August 1863, published in Brogan, *Extracts from the Times*, pp.100, 126.
166 Fremantle, *Three Months in the Southern States*, p.31; Wolseley, 'A Month's Visit', pp.22, 19, 28; Wolseley, 'General Lee', p.326; Harrison, 'A Trip to Meade's Army', p.335; Hewett, in Preston, 'Letter', pp.51, 56; Bell, *Soldier's Glory*, p.310.

More especially the British praised the Southern commanders. The greatest praise was of course reserved for Lee, described by Wolseley as 'a splendid specimen of an English Gentleman', the 'handsomest man of his age I ever saw', and 'cast in a grander mold'; and by Fremantle as 'a perfect gentleman in every respect'.[167] Nevertheless, Wolseley could be critical even of Lee, regarding his calculations before Antietam to be faulty and, in private, the Confederate invasion of the North strategically unsound. He was also critical of Lee's junior officers and staff, writing that overall the army lacked cohesion and the efficiency of a regular army, and that bad staff work had allowed McClellan to escape during the Seven Days.[168] By comparison Fremantle described Lee's staff as 'composed of gentlemen of position and education, who have now been trained into excellent and zealous staff officers'. When it came to field officers though, Fremantle noted their tendency to expose themselves to fire to the point of recklessness.[169] While personal bravery made the Southern leaders popular heroes, the limitations of this to personal command were recognised when injury or death led to the breaking of the chain of command at critical times.[170]

* * *

Since the use of entrenchments is often cited as evidence that the Civil War represented a significant change in the conduct of war at a tactical level, and one that was ignored in European warfare, it is worth considering what the observers had to say on the matter. Russell remarked on the 'rapidity and skill' with which the Americans raised earthworks, but other early commentators were much less favourable. Dicey, whose military experience was admittedly limited to some observation of the wars in Italy, considered Manassas the 'rudest and poorest description of earthworks', and a great Confederate fort (possibly Fort Donelson on the Cumberland River in Tennessee) as being 'of no great military strength'.[171] Hewett, who as an instructor of engineering can be assumed to have a better knowledge of what constituted good fortifications, thought that the defences at Cincinnati were capable 'not only of being taken by infantry but also by cavalry' and rode his horse over them to prove it. This exploit was interpreted by Canadian historian R.A. Preston as evidence of the British belief in shock tactics, and a failure to understand the effect of increased firepower, but as an engineer Hewett would not have expected cavalry to charge properly built

167 Wolseley, 'A Month's Visit', p.18; Fremantle, *Three Months in the Southern States*, p.375.
168 Wolseley, 'A Month's Visit', pp.12, 18, 22; Wolseley 'General Lee' p.328; HPL, Wolseley Archive, 163/3, Wolseley to his brother Richard, Montreal, 4 July 1862 and Baltimore, 21 September 1862.
169 Fremantle, *Three Months in the Southern States*, pp.131-32.
170 Frank Lawley in *The Times*, 18 August 1863, published in Brogan, *Extracts from the Times*, pp.127-28.
171 William Howard Russell in *The Times*, 16 August, 1861, published in Brogan, *Extracts from the Times*, pp.20-21; Dicey, *Six Months in the Federal States*, Vol.II, pp.28, 75.

and defended fortifications. A more obvious explanation is that he was simply demon-strating the poor construction of these works. Hewett was also critical of the defences at Washington at this time, which were 'not particularly well placed nor is the design much good'.[172]

Other writers were likewise critical of the fortifications at Richmond. Fletcher described a 'very small trench and earthworks' on the Virginia Peninsula, while other works were 'insignificant compared with the works round important European towns but are as strong or stronger than the lines of Yorktown', which in turn *The Times* described as 'most slovenly'.[173] However, Fletcher considered those constructed at Memphis by Sherman using black labour to be well made.[174] Wolseley and Ross both visited Winchester where they found the defences poorly sited and commanded by hills. Wolseley thought that this 'speaks very poorly for the engineering talent of the North', which is surprising given the prominence of engineering in the West Point syllabus.[175]

Later defence works were acknowledged to have been better constructed. Ross considered the Federal lines at Chattanooga in the autumn of 1863 too strong to assault, and at about the same time Harrison wrote of Meade's defences in northern Virginia that he 'would rather have to defend than attack them'.[176] When Meade took the offensive, the group of Guards officers with him reported that in a single night the enemy had erected 'a formidable earthwork; regular parapets, riveted with pine logs and embrasured, had been thrown up for his guns; and his front was dotted with a succession of rifle-pits, while the river had been dammed up so as to make it about five feet deep'.[177] Gallwey's mission in 1864 found, in contrast to Hewett, that the defences of Washington by that time were formidable.[178] However, Lieutenant Featherstonhaugh whose opinion as an engineer, even though much more junior, must also be given some weight, wrote that the impregnability of the Petersburg fortifica-tions was exaggerated – 'the works on the north side of the James were certainly strong if defended by adequate forces; but the lines in front of Petersburg and to the south west of it [...] were by no means formidable either in trace or in profile'.[179] Good

---

172 Hewett, in Preston, 'Letter', p.51.
173 [George Alfred Townsend], 'Richmond and Washington during the War', *Cornhill Magazine*, 7 (1863), pp.93-102 (p.101); Fletcher 'A Run through the Southern States', pp.510, 496, 512; *The Times*, 30 August 1861, published in Brogan, *Extracts from the Times*, p.83.
174 Fletcher, 'A Run through the Southern States', pp.510, 496.
175 Wolseley, 'A Month's Visit', p.22; Ross, *Visit*, p.25.
176 Ross, *Visit*, p.150; Harrison, 'A Trip to Meade's Army', p.333.
177 Peel, 'A Short Campaign', p.196.
178 WO 33/14/0229, Gallwey Report, pp.1-4.
179 Featherstonhaugh, 'Notes on the Defence of Petersburg', p.190. Much later, Featherstonhaugh, by then a Major, repeated these views. 'I saw the defences of Petersburg, and they were very slight. In the place where most of the fighting was the troops were about 300 yards apart, and the rifle firing went on day and night to prevent surprise. In

British siege works and mortar battery at Sebastopol, 1854. (Library of Congress)

Union mortar position at Petersburg, 1864. (Library of Congress)

or bad, there is no evidence that any of the observers thought earthworks particularly innovative or notable other than in the speed with which they were erected. One exception comes from Fremantle, who clearly found it unusual that 'the artillery-men in charge of the horses dig themselves little holes like graves, throwing up the earth at the upper end. They ensconce themselves in these holes when under fire.'[180]

* * *

What influence did the war have on those who witnessed it, and what did they take back to their regiments and to the Army as a whole? On the basis of the published evidence, the short-term impact must be considered very limited. Only a minority of those who are known to have made the journey published any accounts. Some of those who did lived out their lives in relative obscurity. Lieutenant Innes died fighting insurgents in Perak, in modern day Malaysia, in November 1875, while Featherstonhaugh returned to North America as part of the Commission delineating the Canada – United States border in the 1870s and eventually made Lieutenant Colonel in the regiment, but was not influential.[181]

The Guards officers by virtue of their higher social standing were most likely to rise to prominent positions in the army and in government. Abinger, Dunmore, and others were already in such positions by birth, but Dunmore left the Army in 1864, and Abinger's American wife seems to have been the only significant outcome of his Canadian posting. Both Phillips and Wynne rose to general rank, but nothing in their careers was anything out of the ordinary. Fremantle saw combat in Egypt in 1882, and later became Governor General of Malta, but there is nothing to indicate that his experiences in the Confederacy were of any influence on his career.[182]

Major Henry Smyth was a more serious career soldier, who was to play a substantial role in important decisions taken on military equipment. Not only did he rise to general rank, commanding troops in Zululand in 1887-88, but he also went as an observer to the Franco-Prussian War, and again published his observations in the *Minutes of the Proceedings of the Royal Artillery Institution*. He served on army committees responsible for the selection of guns in India, another for the review of siege operations, and in the 1880s on the Ordnance Committee in Woolwich that recommended the adoption of

the other parts where certainly better no serious attempt was made to attack them. That siege lasted seven months and Petersburg was never taken in the real sense.' Comments in response to lecture at the Royal United Service Institution, Friday May 7 1886, by Major H. Elsdale. 'The Defence of London and of England', *Journal of the Royal United Service Institution*, 30 (1886), pp.601-670 (p.665).

180 Fremantle, *Three Months in the Southern States*, p.129.
181 Captain Featherstonhaugh, 'Narrative of the Operations of the British North American Boundary Commission, 1872–76', *R.E. Professional Papers*, 23 (1876), pp.24–69; WO 25/3913, Military service record of Albany Featherstonhaugh.
182 Margrave, 'British Officers', Part 1, p.16; Gary W. Gallagher, introduction to Fremantle, *Three Months in the Southern States* (Lincoln: University of Nebraska Press, 1991), p.xi.

steel rifled guns. There is no specific evidence of whether his observations in America had an influence on his opinions, although in 1870 he did challenge some of the German theories arising from the Franco-Prussian War, especially the idea that cavalry would be able to charge home 'against fire like that of the English infantry' and the wisdom of the battalion column as an infantry formation in the face of modern fire-arms.[183]

Captain Richard Harrison also went on to a distinguished career, reaching the rank of General. This included service on the staff under Wolseley in both South Africa and Egypt, and under Sir Evelyn Wood in the Sudan campaign, followed by staff appointments in Aldershot and as Governor of the Royal Military Academy, Woolwich.[184]

The experiences of Lieutenant Colonel Henry Fletcher were perhaps more relevant to his subsequent achievements. After returning to England Fletcher published a three-volume history of the war, and like Smyth was a prominent member of a number of technical committees. In 1869 he had provided written evidence regarding the instruction of new officers to the Commission on Military Education, presided over by Lord Dufferin, and when the latter was appointed Governor of Canada he took Fletcher with him as his military secretary. Fletcher was then influential in organising the Canadian militia, and in particular establishing the Royal Military College of Canada in 1875 along the lines of West Point, before he died at only 46 years of age in 1879.[185] The first commandant of the new college was Edward Hewett, by then promoted to major, who held the post until 1885. Returning to England, Hewett held further important educational posts, including command of the School of Military Engineering at Chatham and governor of the Royal Military Academy at Woolwich.[186]

Most significantly, Garnet Wolseley became Commander-in-Chief of the British Army, and his continued interest in the American Civil War was evident throughout the period. American historian James A. Rawley, who edited a modern collection of Wolseley's writings on the war, considered that Wolseley had 'force (if not brilliance) of intellect, clearness of foresight, ingenious adaptability and high executive capability'

---

183 R.H. Vetch and Rev. James Lunt, 'Smyth, Sir Henry Augustus (1825–1906)', *Oxford Dictionary of National Biography*, first published 2004, online edn, Jan 2008, <http://www. oxforddnb.com/view/article/36174 > [accessed 1 February 2014]; Major H.A. Smyth, 'Some Observations Amongst German Armies During 1870', *Minutes of the Proceedings of the Royal Artillery Institution*, 7 (1870), pp.184-202 (pp.199-200).

184 Harrison, *Recollections*, pp.190-315.

185 Dictionary of Canadian Biography Online <http://www.biographi.ca/en/bio/fletcher_ henry_charles_10F.html> [accessed 5 April 2015]; House of Commons, *First Report of the Royal Commission Appointed to Inquire into the Present State of Military Education and into the Training of Candidates for Commissions in the Army*, 1868-69 (cmd 4221), p.57. See footnote above for Fletcher's *History*. Fletcher's involvement in technical committees will be covered in the next chapter.

186 Dictionary of Canadian Biography Online <http://www.biographi.ca/en/bio/hewett_ edward_osborne_12E.html> [accessed 5 April 2015].

and that his interest in the war exerted substantial influence. Luvaas on the other hand was dismissive of Wolseley's analysis, concluding that he 'ought not to be regarded as a profound student of the war', but this again seems to have been influenced by 20th Century thinking. Wolseley was not a theorist like Luvaas' mentor Liddell Hart, nor someone who tried to codify the operations of war like his contemporary Sir Edward Bruce Hamley, whose writings on the war will be discussed in later chapters, nor someone who tried to create didactic works based upon history like G.F.R. Henderson. He was a practical soldier who used his own experiences and observations to come up with practical solutions to specific problems. One example of this is his *Soldier's Pocket-Book*, a field manual for officers covering a range of practical subjects that often used the Civil War as a source of examples. As will be shown in subsequent chapters, between 1887 and 1892 Wolseley published a number of articles in various magazines on subjects related to the Civil War and took lessons from the Civil War in a number of technical, tactical, and strategic matters. Wolseley also gathered around him a range of promising intellectual officers and his patronage of Henderson, perhaps the most important British historian of the American Civil War in this period, sprang from his own interest and from the belief that the conflict could be used to illuminate military issues of the day.[187]

Luvaas started out with the objective of trying to see why people had not learnt apparently obvious lessons from the American Civil War. However, in taking an approach informed by hindsight, he did not place the British observers in their historical context. By not considering what the British intentions were, he underestimated how much they did in fact assimilate. The observers certainly saw, in Fletcher's words, 'many things consequent on the state of society in America, and the rough organisation of the volunteer force, which strikes a European officer as rather odd', but there is no reason to conclude from this that they failed to understand what they saw.[188] Rather, as R.A. Preston admitted, British observers 'thoroughly understood what they were talking about', and they were used to observing alien cultures, of which America was just one more. For example, Wolseley had served in the Crimea, India, Burma, and China and had visited both the Taiping court and Japan, and seems to have learned from all of these experiences. They recognised the value of both volunteers and irregulars, and deemed the Americans more successful when they tried not to adopt strict regular practice. While critical of ill-discipline as detrimental to military efficiency, they were not always obsessed by drill and ceremony, and recognised the importance of speed of movement both tactically and strategically.[189]

---

187 James A. Rawley (ed.), *The American Civil War: An English View* (Charlottesville: University Press of Virginia, 1964), pp.ix-xvii, xix; Luvaas, *Military Legacy*, p.51; Colonel Garnet Joseph Wolseley, *Soldier's Pocket Book*, 2nd edn (London and New York: MacMillan, 1871, originally published 1869).
188 Fletcher, 'A Run Through the Southern States', p.497.
189 For criticism of the observers, Luvaas, *Military Legacy*, p.12; Craddock, 'The American Civil War and its Influence on the British Army', pp.2-3; Preston, 'Military Lessons of the American Civil War', p.234. For Wolseley, *Story of a Soldier's Life*, Vol.II, pp.88-100;

The British did not go to America because they thought the conflict would teach them radical new lessons in the art of war. Their reasons for being there were firmly rooted in the issues of the day. America was important because its expanded army and navy were a potential threat to British interests, and it was necessary to assess the potency of that threat. At a time of rapid technological change, the war gave the technical branches of the Army an opportunity to observe new weaponry in action. It offered the opportunity for personal advancement, and fulfilled a desire for adventure and action that was appealing to young military personnel. That appeal was reinforced by a common language and cultural history, and even, in some cases, by personal ties.

If they did not see a different type of war, this was because much of what they saw was familiar. Graduates of the academies at Woolwich and Chatham did not need to be educated in the importance of field fortifications, nor veterans of the Crimea in the efficacy of rifled muskets. Much American practice, particularly in the early years of the war, was an imitation of European manuals and the observers exhibited the experienced profession-al's disdain for the enthusiastic amateur. Their greatest prejudices were those of national and racial arrogance. These could be waived when they were impressed by anything, and excellence attributed as being down to the common Anglo-Saxon heritage.[190]

Nor were they dismissive of the war's lessons. This was, after all, the largest war fought between English-speaking peoples. There was much of interest to be seen, and the American soldiers' intelligence, courage, and pragmatism were recognised just as strongly as their indiscipline and lack of training were criticised. When considered against the reasons for their presence in America at the time, and the limitations of what they were allowed to or able to see, the observers on the spot were quite successful in achieving their objectives and perceptive in what they found.

Within six years, however, interest in the American war was overwhelmed by the upheavals that took place in the military balance of power in Europe. The following chapters will examine to what extent it is true that the developments in warfare seen in America were discarded or forgotten as a result, and to what extent they continued to have an influence. The first of these will examine how effectively the British evaluated and adopted the new technologies observed during the war, and how they applied these through to the end of the century.

Charles Rathbone Low, *General Lord Wolseley of Cairo: A Memoir*, 2nd edn (London: Richard Bentley, 1883), pp.148-50.

190 Wolseley recorded 'a sincere feeling of thankfulness and pride that I belong to the race from which sprang the soldiers and sailors who fought upon both sides in this memorable struggle'. General Viscount Wolseley, 'An English View of the Civil War', *North American Review*, 148 (1889), pp.538-63 and 149 (1889), pp.30-43, 164-81, 278-92, 446-59, 594-606, 713-27 (p.727).

3

Ordnance versus Earthworks – The Artillery and the Engineers

The commonly held view of the American Civil War as the 'first modern war' also represents it as being innovative in technology.[1] This chapter examines whether the British succeeded or failed to take up new technologies pioneered in America, and how the technical arms of the British Army – the Royal Artillery and Royal Engineers – responded to what they saw in America. It covers the evaluation of artillery and its growing effectiveness against temporary and permanent fortifications; the changing nature of those fortifications; and new methods of supplementary defence in the form of mines and wire entanglements. It looks at British attitudes to the machine guns, and the debate over whether these should be artillery or infantry weapons. Since it was also primarily a technical concern, it also covers small arms developments and the introduction of breech-loading and repeating weapons. Finally it looks at the adoption of the telegraph for military use.

It is reasonable to assume that in these matters of technology, any racial, social, and political bias was largely excluded from consideration. Observers during the war who came from the technical branches of the British Army were mostly concerned with the Northern armies; and seem to have had good relations with their counterparts in the Union service. Furthermore the explicit technical nature of the observations and reports meant that there was little motivation for such bias in the adjudication of purely scientific and engineering matters. Had the observers considered that American technology represented an imminent threat to Britain they would surely have represented this in no uncertain terms. This also gives some credence to ongoing criticism of the lack of discipline in the Union army, as the threat to Canada was regarded as being lower than the sheer numbers of troops available would have indicated, although the

---

1   See for example the website <http://www.civilwarhome.com/civilwarfirsts.htm,> [accessed 1 July 2013], which cites as its source Burke Davis, *The Civil War, Strange and Fascinating Facts* ([n.p.]: Random House, 1988) which is in turn a reprint of *Our Incredible Civil War* ([n.p.]: Holt, Riehart and Winston, 1960), see <http://www.encyclopediavirginia.org/Davis_Burke_1913-2006> [accessed 1 July 2013].

possibility of an inherent professional prejudice against 'amateur' soldiers does need to be considered.

Many of the British observers during the war came from the technical arms of the service. Aside from those officers who took leave to visit the United States, Royal Engineer and Royal Artillery officers were twice sent on formal missions to America with instructions to observe and report back upon technical developments in the war. The first of these was sent at the request of the Duke of Cambridge, the Commander in Chief of the Army, and was made up from officers serving in Canada. Lieutenant General William Fenwick Williams, commanding in British North America, selected Captain Thomas Mahon, the Inspector of Warlike Stores in Canada, to head the mission. He was accompanied by Captain R. Grant of the Royal Engineers, and Lieutenant T.C. Price of the Royal Artillery. The three officers left Montreal on 9 May 1862, arriving at Washington on 12 May where, with the assistance of Lord Lyons, they obtained permission to proceed to the headquarters of the Army of the Potomac, then advancing up the Yorktown Peninsula towards Richmond. While waiting for transport to take them to Fort Monroe, they visited the Washington Arsenal and Navy Yard, as well as the defensive works around the city. On 21 May they departed the capital, and having acquired transport up the York River from Major General Wool at Fortress Monroe, they arrived at McClellan's headquarters on 24 May. McClellan granted them 'every facility for seeing the disposition and organisation of the army; we were thus enabled to procure much information on the Artillery Branch of the service, as well as other subjects of general interest'.[2] By 5 June, having witnessed a number of engagements, the mission decided that there was nothing further to be gained from staying with the army, and returned north to Washington, inspecting the defences of Yorktown and Fortress Monroe on route. Here they received permission to visit a number of arsenals, including those at Pittsburgh, Philadelphia, New York, Troy, and Springfield, finally returning to Canada on 7 July.[3]

Two years later in 1864 a second mission was sent directly from Britain to report on the further progress made in the United States on a wide range of technical advances. On this occasion the members, Lieutenant Colonel Thomas Lionel Gallwey RE and Captain Henry James Alderson RA, were selected directly by the Secretary of State for War, the Earl de Grey and Ripon. Lieutenant Colonel Gallwey and Captain Alderson were also issued with very precise instructions by their respective heads of service as to the information which they were required to gather. While sponsored at the highest level, however, the mission did not have any official status and the two officers were told not to press matters if information was withheld. In response to

2   WO 33/11/0174, *Report of Officers of the British Army on American Arms, August 1862*, p.2.
3   WO 33/11/0174, *Report of Officers of the British Army on American Arms, August 1862*,
     pp.2-6. This is the untitled report referred to by Luvaas as being in the PRO; Luvaas,
     Military Legacy, p.23. Hereafter referred to as the Mahon Report. The report is referred to
     in TNA, WO 33/12/0186 *Abstracts of Proceedings of the Ordnance Select Committee from 1st
     October to 31st December 1862*, p.538.

a question in the House of Lords, Earl de Grey and Ripon made it clear that these were technical representatives sent to obtain information about *matériel*, not military operations, and that they were not official Commissioners. He also said that this was the reason for their presence in the North, since aside from the difficulties of access to the South, the greater technical resources were in the North.[4]

Arriving in New York on 11 February, the two officers travelled to Washington and presented themselves to Lord Lyons. While they obtained passes to visit the Army of the Potomac, since at that time it was in winter quarters, they decided to defer this and instead visited the Department of the South, under Major General Quincy Adams Gilmore, who had his headquarters at Hilton Head, South Carolina, from where they were able to visit the siege works at Charleston. Returning north in early April they were informed that their passes to visit the Army of the Potomac had been withdrawn. Like the 1862 mission they therefore made a number of visits to foundries and arsenals in the North, as well as the permanent fortifications at Portland, Boston, New York, and Baltimore which were mapped and drawn in detail.[5]

In addition to these missions to the United States, and reflecting the tension between Britain and America and the possibility of war, Lieutenant Colonel William Jervois RE was sent in 1863 to produce a review of the Canadian defences, with a further visit in 1864. Jervois was accompanied by Captain Richard Harrison RE, and according to Harrison's account they used the opportunity to reconnoitre American defences as well.[6]

To modern eyes, it seems remarkable that the United States allowed a potential enemy to make such detailed observations of their military affairs. Indeed the 1864 report specifically thanked the various Heads of Departments and Staff Officers for the readiness with which they had furnished information. Gallwey's instructions had, it is true, allowed him to be equally free with the provision of information pertaining to British practices. At the time the sharing of information and the sending of observers to foreign wars and manoeuvres was common practice. Prior to the war, a Royal Engineer officer had openly recommended the detailed observations of fortifications during peacetime as a means of compensating for the difficulty of doing so in war due to the increased range of rifled artillery and small arms, and the activities of the 1864 mission perfectly fits his description.

4   *Hansard*, 173, pp.856-858.
5   WO 33/14/0229, Gallwey Report, pp.ix-x. Letters from Captain Alderson to the Ordnance Select Committee covering many of the key findings are also referenced in TNA, WO 33/14/0230 *Abstracts of Proceedings of the Ordnance Select Committee for the Quarter Ending 30 June 1864*, pp.262-63. Manuscript copies of the instructions for the British Officers are held in TNA, FO 115/402 fols 96-118.
6   General Richard Harrison, *Recollections of a Life in the British Army* (London: Smith Elder, 1908), pp.106-09; WO 33/15/0265, Jervois, *Defence of Canada*, p.5.

By collecting in time of peace correct plans of all the fortresses in the world, [...] in fact, all the information in regard to them that it is necessary to be possessed of in time of war [...] and having it ready for use when wanted [...] it would certainly be worth a vast deal more to obtain such information than the pay and expense of the two or three officers who might be employed in procuring it.[7]

The main recipient of these observations back in the War Office was an organisation called the Ordnance Select Committee. As the name suggests, the members of this committee were appointed primarily from the Royal Artillery but included representatives from the Royal Engineers and the Royal Navy.[8] The Committee had a wide-ranging oversight of all technical matters including the evaluation of artillery, fortifications, and small arms, as well as more exotic innovations such as aeronautics and more mundane equipment such as ammunition boxes. The activities of the Committee were mostly initiated by external correspondence, which was then followed up through minutes drawn up in the War Office. This correspondence could come from a number of sources, including officers within the army putting forward proposals for improvements to equipment, civilian inventors submitting their ideas for new weapons, reports on tests carried out at government proving grounds, and intelligence from the War Office and Foreign Office based upon observation of overseas developments. Gallwey was himself on the Committee, which indicates the importance given to the 1864 mission.[9]

The military mind has a reputation for conservatism, and a cynical view of the Committee's work was that it existed to pour cold water on new ideas and stifle innovation.[10] Nevertheless, the Ordnance Select Committee provided a permanent and formal process for the review of, and learning from, new technology, in contrast to the complete absence of any formal bodies for reviewing strategic or tactical developments. Therefore, its records can be used to get a good indication of the relative importance given to affairs in America.

7   Captain Tyler RE, 'The Effect of the Modern Rifle Upon Siege Operations, and the Means Required for Counteracting it', *Journal of the United Service Institution*, 2 (1858), pp.225-53 (p.238). Lecture delivered on Friday, 16 April, 1858

8   In 1862 the Committee comprised Brigadier General J. St George RA; Captain Sir W. Wiseman RN; Lieutenant Colonel C. Hogge, late Bengal Artillery; Lieutenant Colonel F.A. Campbell RA, Lieutenant Colonel R.S. Baynes, 8th Foot; and Lieutenant Colonel T.L. Gallwey RE. The secretary was Lieutenant Colonel Lefroy RA.

9   Gallwey later became Commandant of the School of Military Engineering (17 August 1869 to 31 October 1875) and Inspector General of Fortification and Director of Works (1 August 1880 to 9 June 1882). Major General Whitworth Porter, *History of the Corps of Royal Engineers*, 3 vols (London: Longmans, Green, and Co, 1889-1915), Vol.II, pp.95, 195. Alderson later became president of the Ordnance Committee, with the acting rank of major general, *London Gazette*, 27 October, 1891 p.5586.

10   Porter, *History of the Corps of Royal Engineers*, Vol.II, p.189

An interesting point to note is that there is not a single reference to the military operations in America in the proceedings of the Committee until the last quarter of 1862. For example, one standing agenda item was a review of intelligence about foreign artillery. During 1861 and early 1862 the committee considered intelligence about French, Italian, Prussian, Spanish, Russian, Dutch, Belgian, and even Würtemburger artillery, but not American.[11] Given the nature of the war in this early period, and the improvised armaments of the hastily raised armies, the British saw nothing of importance to learn from the early conflict in America. From 1862 onwards this was to change as the increasing military strength of the North became a concern, and as more modern and innovative technology started to appear. The result was the 1862 mission. Its report was completed by 1 August 1862 and received by the Ordnance Select Committee on 10 October 1862.

*   *   *

Within the field artillery the focus of attention was on the use of rifled guns. The American Civil War was not the first time these had been used. The British themselves had made limited use of guns rifled on the Lancaster system in the Crimea, and had also used the more advanced Armstrong breech-loading guns in China in 1860, but with limited success. On a larger scale, France had extensively re-equipped her forces with muzzle-loading rifled artillery which had proved superior to the Austrians' smoothbore cannon in the Franco-Austrian War fought in northern Italy in 1859. However, the American war represented the most extensive use of rifled artillery to date.[12] Because of the urgent need to procure large numbers of guns, the devolution of procurement across Federal and State governments, and the 'private energy and enterprise of the American people' several different systems of ordnance had been pressed into service.[13] In 1862 there were still a number of different ideas being proposed for the manufacture of rifled guns as well as debate over their tactical use. These included several different systems for rifling and for the form of the projectiles, systems for the re-boring and conversion of old smoothbore weapons, and new patterns for fuses.[14] The Army of the Potomac in 1862 therefore promised to provide a kind of laboratory in which their various merits could be observed in the field.

11   TNA, WO 33/11/0159, *Abstracts of Proceedings of the Ordnance Select Committee from 1st October to 31st December 1861*; TNA, WO 33/11/0163, *Reports and Papers on Foreign Artillery* (1861); TNA, WO 33/11/0164, *General Index to the Abstracts of Proceedings and Reports of the Ordnance Select Committee for the Year 1861*. Württemberg had procured the latest Krupp steel breech-loading guns. The American *Army and Navy Journal* for 23 January 1864, p.338, noted that when the war began there was not a single rifled cannon in American service.
12   WO 33/14/0229, Gallwey Report, p.77.
13   WO 33/11/0174, Mahon Report, p.9; WO 33/14/0229, Gallwey Report, p.34.
14   Nosworthy, *The Bloody Crucible of Courage*, pp.73-76, 103-08, 161; Colonel H.C.B. Rogers, *A History of Artillery* (Secaucus NJ: Citadel Press, 1975), pp.93-95.

The British mission of 1862 recorded a great deal of information about the numbers and organisation of the artillery in the Union army. Five principal types of rifled ordnance were identified in Federal Service: the 3-inch Ordnance Rifle, the 10-pounder and 20-pounder Parrott guns, the Wiard gun, the James gun and Government 6-pounder rifles. A detailed breakdown of the different types in use in the armies in Virginia was provided, but only a high-level assessment of the numbers in the West. The bronze 6-pounder rifles were no longer in service in the Army of the Potomac, but James guns were reported as being attached to some of the coastal expeditions. The British were also unable to observe the Wiard gun in action, although they received good reports on its accuracy from American officers who had seen it in the West. Opinions were found to be divided on the merits of the other weapons. The 10-pounder Parrot had less recoil (attributed to it being a heavier piece) but being of cast iron was considered by most American ordnance officers to be less reliable than the regulation 3-inch Ordnance Rifle. The British report concluded that there was little to choose between them. The 20-pounder Parrott appeared to be less effective, with a number of shells failing to take the rifling. The British report concluded that 'a more varied description of artillery than was prudent' had been introduced into the field, and that this was contrary to the advice given by the professional officers in the US Army. One outcome of this was that large orders for ammunition had to be placed with many different contractors, which led to considerable problems of ammunition supply, quality and transportation.[15]

In the end the observation of the use of artillery in the field proved unsatisfactory for the mission's intended purpose of determining the effectiveness of the new weapons. Although the British observed 'every action or skirmish along the entire line of the Federal army that occurred during our stay, and of which we could obtain sufficient information to reach the place in time', and took the opinions of several Union officers, including McClellan's chief of artillery Brigadier General W.F. Barry, they concluded that it was 'very difficult to pronounce with confidence on the relative merits of these rifle guns'.[16] It was hard to observe the effects of the guns in the wooded terrain, either the guns or the target were hidden from view. The fuses and powder were of inconsistent quality. One particular problem identified was that the use of fuses designed for round shells in the rifled guns, which had less windage, meant that they did not ignite on firing, and the conclusion was drawn that 'a concussion fuze [sic] is indispensable for shell, to secure any certainty of a proper bursting of the projectile'. Concussion fuses were later experimented with in America, and Major Henry Smyth RA was present at test firings in 1864.[17]

---

15   WO 33/11/0174, Mahon Report, pp.9-11, 15.
16   WO 33/11/0174, Mahon Report, p.15. Margrave, 'British Officers', Part 1, p.18, notes that the Official Records lists fourteen battles during the period of their stay.
17   WO 33/11/0174, Mahon Report, pp.10, 15, 39, 44; Hatfield, *History of the First Connecticut Artillery*, p.123. Windage is the gap between the barrel and the shell, the flame from the charge passing the shell to ignite the fuse. The 3-inch Ordnance Rifle, having less

'Want of skill in the management of their artillery' was considered 'the chief cause of failure in the Federal army, the guns being manned principally by men who were but little versed in the principles of gunnery'. The regular batteries were thought to conduct 'firing that was well sustained and seemed effective', but while volunteer batteries were well-horsed and performed simple manoeuvres well enough their general efficiency was considered 'not good, and the firing made by them was generally inferior'.[18]

The mission eventually decided that more valuable information about the new rifled guns could be obtained from visiting manufacturing sites than staying with the army.[19] Due to the large consumption of powder, and its sourcing from many different manufacturers, the quality and strength of powder in the United States service was also observed to be very uncertain at this stage in the war which hindered observation in the field. 'To arrive at a true knowledge of their qualities, they should be fired under similar circumstances, and in positions where the ranges could be accurately determined, the same description of powder used and of the kind best adapted for rifle guns.'[20]

Symptomatic of all of these factors was the American preference for the simple light 12-pounder 'Napoleon' smoothbore gun as the weapon of choice. The 1862 report noted that since the principal work of the artillery was shelling woods, and the Napoleon was particularly effective as a shell gun, as a result it was more widely used than any of the rifled guns. Brigadier General Barry had originally proposed that one-third of the guns should be smoothbore but now believed a greater proportion of smoothbores would be advantageous. The following year, Fitzgerald Ross would report similar opinions as part of a detailed discussion on the artillery in use in the Confederate Army of Tennessee. Mahon also wrote a further private letter on 27 November 1863 which stated that in relation to artillery the Americans 'reject anything complicated and aim at being eminently practical'.[21]

By the time of the second mission to America in 1864, the Federal army had standardised its rifled artillery on the 10-pounder Parrot and 3-inch Ordnance guns but the smoothbore Napoleon still remained highly popular. The mission reported that the ratio of these to rifled guns had increased since 1862 as it was 'the best gun of the two for canister, and therefore better adapted to the nature of the country in which the fighting is carried out'.[22] Breech-loading guns such as the British Whitworth, while recognised as being best for accuracy and range, were disliked by the Americans

---

windage than the Parrott design, was more prone to shells failing to explode, the solution resorted to was to cut grooves in the lead base of the shell.

18   WO 33/11/0174, Mahon Report, pp.3, 14.
19   WO 33/11/0174, Mahon Report, p.3
20   WO 33/11/0174, Mahon Report, p.15.
21   WO 33/11/0174, Mahon Report, p.10; Ross, *Visit*, p.152; TNA, WO 33/13/0214, *Abstracts of Proceedings of the Ordnance Select Committee from 1st October to 31st December 1863*, p.569.
22   WO 33/14/0229, Gallwey Report, pp.34-35

because of the tendency for the breech mechanisms to clog. Some had been abandoned at Yorktown when McClellan's army was re-embarked. 80-pounder Whitworths were observed at Charleston, but the Americans preferred the simpler Parrott guns here as well, again due to the problems of jamming. Ross had reported similar conclusions from the Confederate side: the Whitworth was acknowledged to be highly accurate but required great care on campaign, with many reported to have their breeches blown off or disabled. The Whitworth rifling system (a hexagonal bore rather than grooving imparted spin to the projectile) required special and precisely manufactured ammunition which further diminished its utility in the field.[23]

The peculiar geographical conditions of the war, as well as the need to rapidly expand the number of guns available to the armies, were thus seen as exceptional and dictating the Americans' choice of weapon.

> In the late American campaigns considerable numbers of S.B. [*sic*] guns were employed by both sides, but this may be easily accounted for; the country is so densely wooded that case-shot ranges are frequently the only ones practicable, and, no doubt, both sides were obliged to use any guns that they could procure.[24]

Cavalryman Fitzgerald Ross considered the Confederate practice of massing their field artillery and organising them into battalions worthy of note, but in general artillerists took very limited direct lessons from American tactical or organisational practice, even when aware of them. At Petersburg, artilleryman Henry Smyth made no comment on the use of artillery bombardments, though he did note the preference of the field artillery to engage at close range. After the war, Lieutenant Henry William Lovett Hime wrote an essay on modern artillery tactics in the early 1870s which used only the Napoleonic and recent European wars as historic examples, though he was clearly aware of American artillery manuals, as one is cited when recommending the use of railway cuttings when siting guns. Captain Henry Knollys RA had visited the United States during the war, and had met with Brigadier General Barry, but his work on modern artillery published in 1877 again refers only to European examples, except with regards to rockets, of which he noted that the Americans had made only limited use before discarding. The developments in field artillery during the 40 years

23 WO 33/14/0229, Gallwey Report, pp.69-70. WO 33/13/0214, p.569; TNA, WO 33/14/0234, *Abstracts of Proceedings of the Ordnance Select Committee for the Quarter Ending 31st September 1864*, p.451; Von Borcke, *Memoirs*, Vol.II, pp.32-33; Ross, *Visit*, p.152; Nosworthy, *The Bloody Crucible of Courage*, pp.162-63. See also Captain H. Schaw, 'The Amount of Advantage which the New Arms of Precision Give to the Defence over the Attack', *Journal of the Royal United Service Institution*, 14 (1870), pp.377-94 (p.380) for the comparative merits of rifled and smooth bore artillery in America.

24 Major C.H. Owen RA, 'The Present State of the Artillery Question', *Minutes of Proceedings of the Royal Artillery Institution*, 5 (1867), pp.212-249 (p.223); reprinted from *Journal of the Royal United Service Institution*, 9 (1865), pp.342-370.

following the war were substantial, and further appeared to limit the relevance of lessons around the use of artillery in the American Civil War. The European wars of the time, particularly the major actions at Sadowa (Königgrätz) in 1866 and Sedan in 1870, seemed to offer more useful lessons than the conservative American practice. Even American authors seem to have accepted that there was nothing especially forward looking in American artillery tactics. Military historian Arthur Lockwood Wagner wrote that offensive artillery tactics in 1866 were 'not yet understood in any army'. A modern authority has concurred that America was a follower rather than a leader in artillery tactics in the 1860s.[25]

* * *

Although the American experience may have favoured the smoothbore, the superior range and lighter weight of the rifled gun resulted in its universal adoption by the British Army in 1865. This was not without some resistance, the Select Committee of the House of Commons had recommended the use of smoothbore guns by the Royal Horse Artillery in 1862 because of its short range effect.[26] The universal adoption of rifled guns in preference to smoothbores and the increased range of infantry rifles presented a problem for the artillerist because it limited the use of his most potent short range weapon: grape shot or canister. This form of ammunition consisted of a tin canister packed with small cast iron balls; on firing the canister split open and a cone of shot resulted which could be devastating at close range. Considerable interest was taken in the potential of 'multi-barrelled breech-loading guns', the precursor of what we now know as the machine gun, to replace its effect. These were frequently at this time called by their French name, *mitrailleuse*, (anglicised to 'mitrailleurs'), which derived from the word *mitraille* – grape shot.[27]

The first of these weapons to come to the British attention was the 'Union Repeating Gun' which was used in the Virginia Peninsula, and a detailed description of which was provided in the 1862 report. This was the .58 calibre Agar gun, and it was

25   Ross, *Visit*, p.153; Smyth, 'Account of the Final Attack and Capture of Richmond', p.365; Lieutenant Henry William Lovett Hime, *The Minor Tactics of Field Artillery* (London and Woolwich: [n.pub.], 1872), p.5, reprinted in booklet form from the *Proceedings of the Royal Artillery Institution*, 7 (1872); Knollys, *The Elements of Field Artillery*, pp.141-63, and for the Americans' use of rockets p.106; Wagner, *The Campaign of Königgrätz*, p.97; Nosworthy, *The Bloody Crucible of Courage*, p.159.

26   Callwell and Headlam, *History of the Royal Artillery*, Vol.I, p.148; House of Commons, *Report from the Select Committee on Ordnance, together with the Proceedings of the Committee, Minutes of Evidence, Appendix, and Index* (ordered to be printed 23 July 1863), p.vi.

27   Captain H. Schaw, 'The Present State of the Question of Fortification', *Journal of the Royal United Service Institution*, 10 (1866), pp.442-62 (p.449); Hime, *The Minor Tactics of Field Artillery*, p.9; Nosworthy, *The Bloody Crucible of Courage*, p.64; Lieutenant Colonel G.S. Hutchison, *Machine Guns: Their History and Tactical Employment* (London, MacMillan, 1938), p.9.

The Union Repeating (Agar) Gun, drawing from the Mahon Report, 1862.
(The National Archives)

considered unreliable by the observers. 'It might be useful in the defence of a narrow passage or bridge, but it is questionable whether it would be of any great practical utility in the open field of battle.'[28] In comparison, the Ordnance Select Committee were 'favourably impressed with the results obtained' in a trial of a similar weapon at Woolwich in September 1862 and showed some interest in obtaining further examples, but acquisition was held up by a dispute over the ownership of the patent.[29] The 1864 report recorded that the gun was no longer in use in America, McClellan's men 'did not think them worth taking trouble about, and abandoned them sooner than fight for them', and further investigation appears to have been dropped.[30] Some years later Lieutenant Colonel Henry Fletcher, who had been an observer at McClellan's headquarters in 1862, stated that the machine guns had not been bought to the front as the Army of the Potomac already contained an undue proportion of artillery. In Fletcher's opinion the machine gun was not suitable to be attached to infantry units primarily because it was only effective against troops in the open, whereas modern tactics involved more use of cover and defences. The machine guns of the time, being

---

28   WO 33/11/0174, Mahon Report, pp.43-44. For technical details of the Agar gun, see Ian
      V. Hogg, *Weapons of the Civil War* (New York: Military Press, 1986), p.52; Ian Drury and
      Tony Gibbons, *The US Civil War Military Machine* (Limpsfield: Dragon's World, 1993),
      pp.64-65.
29   TNA, WO 33/12/0192, *Abstracts of Proceedings of the Ordnance Select Committee From 1st
      January to 31st March 1863*, p.132.
30   WO 33/14/0229, Gallwey Report, p.72.

relatively large and immobile weapons, were therefore ill-suited to the needs of the infantry attack as opposed to static defence.[31]

Meanwhile, Colonel Henry Sebastian Rowan of the Royal Artillery reported in November 1862 from New York that 'the Americans are producing multiple guns in great varieties', in particular one of 25 barrels. This was the Billinghurst or Requa gun, on which Rowan provided more detailed information the following August.[32] The use of these weapons at Charleston was noted in several reports and accounts, including their mounting on picket boats in place of howitzers. Again they were thought effective for limited purposes, particularly the defence of bridges, breaches and flanks, or 'the defence of earthworks in a level country' but not for general purposes.[33] The Ordnance Select Committee concluded that the guns were not an effective substitute for field guns and of limited use for 'multiplying and accelerating infantry fire in the field', but they were seen as being of value in defensive positions. Further trials were not progressed with since 'such instruments could be readily devised by our own mechanisms, without applying to the United States for them'.[34]

This was not the end of the Committee's involvement with multiple barrelled guns from America however. In 1864 Brigadier General Vanderburgh from New York submitted a proposal for his design of volley gun and offered to demonstrate it at his own expense.[35] Vanderburgh had earlier given a lecture at the Royal United Service Institution on his theories for his invention's use, from which it is clear that it was intended as an artillery weapon to supersede the use of canister fire.

[T]wo modes of projection are theoretically and practically required to meet the two conditions of an enemy: one, the means to assail him when protected by defensive works, either on land or water, which the largest single shot and shell gun furnishes; the other, to meet him when uncovered, in the condition of attack. The system which I now make public, is intended to meet the last-named requirement.[36]

31   Lieutenant Colonel H.C. Fletcher, 'The Employment of Mitrailleurs during the Recent War and their Use in Future Wars', *Journal of the Royal United Service Institution*, 16 (1872), pp.28-52 (p.34).

32   WO 33/12/0186, pp.568-69; WO 33/12/0192, p. 146; TNA, WO 33/12/0203, *Abstracts of Proceedings of the Ordnance Select Committee from 1st July to 30th September 1863*, p.458.

33   Anon, 'Siege of Charleston', *United Service Magazine*, 439 (June 1865), pp.177-83 (p.177); WO 33/14/0229, Gallwey Report, pp.72, 24.

34   WO 33/12/0203, p.458.

35   TNA, WO 33/13/0226, *Abstracts of Proceedings of the Ordnance Select Committee for the Quarter Ending 31st March 1864*, p.156; TNA, WO 33/15/0255, *Abstracts of Proceedings of the Ordnance Select Committee for the Quarter Ending 31st March 1865*, p.174.

36   General O. Vandenburgh (NYSM), 'A New System of Artillery for Projecting a Group or Cluster of Shot', *Journal of the Royal United Service Institution*, 6 (1862), pp.378-90 (p.379). The gun was manufactured by Robinson and Cottam in London.

The use of these primitive machine guns in the American Civil War itself was not that widespread, but the fact that they received significant attention from the British at this early stage is evidence of a willingness to consider and accept technical change which contrasts to the traditional view of resistance to the adoption of the machine gun.[37] Following the introduction of a *mitrailleuse* by the French army, in August 1869 the War Office appointed a Committee under Colonel Wray of the Royal Artillery to report upon comparative utility of the French Montigny system and the Gatling gun. The latter had seen only very limited use in the American Civil War, in 1864 when Major General Benjamin Butler had acquired some privately for use in the Army of the James, but it had been brought to the attention of the War Office in January 1867, and a gun had immediately been acquired for trial. The Ordnance Select Committee had retained at that time the same view as they had of the earlier guns, that it was a valuable weapon in fixed defences but not appropriate for field service.[38]

Wray's Committee (to which Lieutenant Colonel Henry Fletcher was appointed in January 1870) took a much more positive view of the Gatling gun, and recommended its immediate adoption for use in the field as well as in field works. Further notable recommendations were the provisions of 'musket-proof shields' for the gun carriages and the adoption of a calibre such that the ammunition would be interchangeable with the new Martini-Henry rifle being adopted.[39] A report a year later, having considered the further evidence provided by the Franco-Prussian War (where French *mitrailleuse* deployed in the manner of traditional field batteries had been outranged and outgunned by Prussian field artillery), still advocated a role for the Gatling gun in the field but principally for 'the defence of entrenched positions and villages, or for covering roads, defiles, bridges, or other narrow places, along which an enemy may be expected to pass'. Although considered superior to shell fire at short range, in response to the objections from the Director of Artillery, it was expressly recommended that 'the Field Artillery should not be reduced by a single gun or horse for the sake of substituting mitrailleurs'. Furthermore 'mitrailleurs should invariably be so entrenched as to bid defiance to the fire of field guns, and be kept masked until the attack is fully developed and the enemy well within effective range'. They were looked

---

37   For example, Tim Travers, 'The Offensive and the Problem of Innovation in British Military Thought 1870-1915', *Journal of Contemporary History*, 13 (1978), pp.531-53 (pp.532-33).

38   TNA, WO 33/22/454, *Report of the Special Committee on Mitrailleurs*, November 1870, pp.1-5; TNA, WO 33/22/445, *Minute by the Director of Artillery, upon the Report on the Special Committee on Mitrailleurs*, dated 28 October 1870, p.2. For the use of the Gatling gun in the Civil War see Drury and Gibbons, *The US Civil War Military Machine*, p.65 and Hogg, *Weapons of the Civil War*, p.52.

39   WO 33/22/454, p.4. Fletcher was also president of the Committee charged with examining the adoption of the Martini-Henry Rifle. TNA, WO 33/22/450, *Martini Henry Rifles* (War Office, 1871), p.1.

upon as a supplement to infantry fire in defence, and the report was strongly opposed to its use for attacking in any form.[40]

Given the state of development of the technology at this stage, the British analysis of their usefulness and method of deployment seems sensible rather than shortsighted. The mobility of the mitrailleurs on the battlefield was limited and there was at the time no effective mechanism to traverse the gun effectively, so they put a high volume of fire down but in a narrow field of fire. They also had limited effectiveness against troops taking cover behind obstacles or folds in the ground. To view them as a long range replacement for the old canister round, and to recommend them for use as defensive artillery was therefore entirely appropriate.[41] They were not underestimated in this role. They had the advantages over artillery that they could be fired through loopholes, and within buildings or locations where the recoil of a normal artillery piece made deployment impossible. Captain H. Schaw, Professor of Fortifications and Artillery at the Staff College, wrote in 1870 that one mitrailleur was superior to two or three field guns in providing enfilading fire on a flank, a view supported by experimentation.[42] Schaw also predicted how in future a combination of artillery, machine guns, infantry and field defences would make frontal assaults impossible.

> [T]he works, if well designed, should give such security to their defenders that even after a heavy cannonade the assailants, if attacking by day, ought to find themselves under fire of securely-posted artillery for the maximum distance which the features of the ground will allow, and this fire ought to increase in intensity as they approach, and be supplemented by the terrible aid of mitrailleurs, and, finally, of the infantry manning the works, under whose close and rapid fire, and probably also an enfilading fire of artillery and mitrailleurs, they

40   TNA, WO 33/24/0539, *Second Report of the Special Committee on Mitrailleurs*, November 1871, pp.3-5; WO 33/22/445, *Minute by the Director of Artillery*.

41   Knollys, *The Elements of Field Artillery*, pp.108-10, citing as authority Boguslawski, *Tactical Deductions*. As late as 1886 Lieutenant G.E. Benson RA, who had experience of Gardner guns at Suakin in the Sudan, wrote that 'machine gun fire partakes more of the nature of artillery shrapnel fire than of infantry fire'. He explained the technical reason for this view; they created a zone of fire; this zone extended out to 1700 yards whereas infantry fire ceased to be effective at 900-100; the fire could be concentrated onto one spot; and that the guns 'have no nerves' so every bullet could tell. Benson did not consider them limited to static defence however, he thought that they could have the mobility and effect of horse artillery if properly equipped. Lieutenant G.E. Benson 'A Machine-Gun Battery and its Equipment', *Journal of the Royal United Service Institution*, 30 (1886), pp.69-76, (pp.69-71).

42   Colonel H. Schaw, *Defence and Attack of Positions and Localities, being the substance of some lectures delivered by him at the [Staff] College in 1875*, 5th edn (London: Kegan Paul, Trench, Trübner, 1893, originally published 1875), p.49; Schaw, 'New Arms of Precision', p.385; Captain T. Fraser RE, *The Defence of a Position Selected as a Field of Battle: Royal Engineer Prize Essay for 1875* (Woolwich: [n.pub.], 1875), p.23 (footnote). The service Gatling fired 400 rpm, the equivalent of 22 Martini-Henry rifles, and at 300-1,000 yards scored as many hits on a target as two 9-pdr field-guns.

would have to overcome the obstacles placed outside the line of works. Such an attack could have but one result, and no-one would probably have the temerity to attempt it after the numerous failures which occurred during the late American war.[43]

While the artillery and infantry saw relatively limited opportunities for the use of early machine guns, and did not advise them to be allocated at battalion level, in the cavalry the potential was seen for the machine gun to be an effective weapon at a regimental level. Here it was thought that they could be useful on outposts, piquet duty, and patrols. In retreat, they could augment the firepower of a cavalry force to make it independent of other arms, especially in towns. In attack they could provide 'most effective support', fulfilling the role of traditional horse artillery in weakening formed bodies of troops in preparation for the cavalry charge. Moreover, the machine gun offered a further advantage over traditional artillery because guns could be assimilated without any increase into the existing regimental establishment. Since the cost of maintaining cavalry regiments was high, and they were often under-strength, this was a major consideration and shows the capacity of some officers to think of innovative technological solutions to financial and administrative constraints, as well as to tactical issues. The original adoption of the machine gun was merely adapting new technology to fulfil existing artillery functions to traditional roles. In the cavalry, although having some precedent in the horse artillery, it supported potential new and extended forms of combat for mounted troops.[44]

> '[T]wo machine-guns per squadron would be a wonderful increase of power, and would prove invaluable for outposts, detached posts, advance and rear guards, for holding defiles and bridges, also in attacking the latter, clearing and holding streets.[45]

There were also at an early stage a few visionaries who could see the possible future of hand weapons that would 'pour out such a stream of shot as would sweep a hostile regiment from the field in a space of a hundred seconds', but these were purely speculative

---

43   Schaw, 'New Arms of Precision', p.383.
44   Memorandum by Major General Cameron Shute, late commander 4th Dragoon Guards, included in Fletcher, 'Employment of Mitrailleurs', pp.53-55; Fraser, *Defence of a Position*, p.23; Benson, 'A Machine-Gun Battery and its Equipment', p.76; Colonel Liddell, 10th Hussars, comments on lecture by Captain R.H. Armit, 'Machine-Guns, Their Use and Abuse', *Journal of the Royal United Service Institution*, 30 (1886), pp.37-68 (pp.62-63). For 'adaption' and 'innovation' in modern parlance see Farrell, 'Improving in War', pp.567-69.
45   Major M.R. West, RHA, 'Suggestions for the Adoption and Adaption of the Single-Barrel Machine-Gun for the various branches of Land Service', *Journal of the Royal United Service Institution*, 30 (1886), pp.21-36 (p.23, also pp.27-28, 30).

at this time and in no way derived from actual war experience or existing technical capabilities.[46]

Volunteer units also became supporters of the machine gun. By 1893 there were 19 guns in the hands of volunteer regiments, all privately purchased – reminiscent of Major General Benjamin Butler's private experimentation with the Gatling gun in 1864.[47] One such example was the purchase of two rifle-calibre Nordenfelt guns by a London volunteer unit in June 1882.

> Lieutenant Colonel Alt, commanding the Central London Rangers, came to the conclusion that this arm was particularly adapted to that very species of work that our volunteers may be called upon to perform, such as repelling landing parties on a coast, defending fixed positions, mountain passes, roads, and bridges.[48]

Alt purchased the guns without first seeking sanction; if this was in anticipation of resistance from central authority it was well founded. The War Office told Alt that these were not infantry weapons, and the Rangers were not allowed to use them on parade. Liddell Hart and others have taken this as further evidence that the conservative Army establishment was short-sighted and opposed to the new weapon. If considered in the context of the time however, the War Office position becomes more understandable. The Nordenfelt guns were multi-barrelled, hand cranked weapons, bulky, and mounted on wheeled carriages with a separate ammunition limber, not at all like the infantry machine guns of the two World Wars. They had been adopted by the Royal Navy but not by the Army. Put in that light, the idea that they were not infantry weapons made some sense, they were not part of the infantry drill, and it seems that the aim of the Volunteers, like the cavalry, was indeed to have an element of attached artillery to increase their firepower. Also to the War Office's credit, in 1884 Alt's men were allowed to take them on manoeuvres at Aldershot, though not on parade. Perhaps someone had spotted that this enabled the Army to experiment with the tactical use of the new weapons without incurring their expense on the Army Estimates. The Volunteers were certainly prepared to experiment, Alt invented a special carriage to overcome the problems of a separate ammunition limber, protected by steel plate as suggested by Wray's Committee in 1870, and drawn by a team of men rather than horses to reduce their vulnerability to fire. Later the 26th Middlesex Regiment would mount machine guns on bicycle trailers.[49]

46   Lieutenant A. Steinmetz, 'The Past and Future of Cavalry', *United Service Magazine*, 439 (June 1865), pp.159-79 (p.164 (footnote)).

47   Beckett, *Riflemen Form*, p.200; see also 'HCW', 'Future Infantry Tactics', *Illustrated Naval and Military Magazine* 4 (1889), pp.418-432 (p.423).

48   Armit, 'Machine-Guns, Their Use and Abuse', p.44.

49   Sir Basil Liddell Hart, *Thoughts on War* (London: Faber and Faber, 1944), p.111; Beckett, *Riflemen Form*, p.200; Hutchison, *Machine Guns*, pp.47-53; 'HCW', 'Future Infantry

Machine gun section of the Central London Rangers, 1896. (*Army and Navy Magazine*)

Allowing the Volunteers to take their guns on manoeuvres did pay dividends. Two years later in 1886, Captain Armit of the Rangers gave a paper at the Royal United Service Institution which presented the lessons that the regiment had learnt from the experiment. Some of this was critical of existing thought, for example the imposition of escorts on the machine guns which limited their freedom of action, an essential part of machine gun tactics. 'Guns in my opinion should, when in action, creep or sneak, or move at the double to seize positions.'[50] Others show the continued limitations of the technology of the day, in particular that it was not an individual weapon – to generate sustained fire for any length of time the Nordenfelt guns required a crew of at least 10 men to continually refill the ammunition hoppers. Armit suggested the creation of a dedicated Machine Gun Corps, mainly because the training of the crews was so different from normal infantry training. Also, six rifleman were attached to each gun in order to provide protection against cavalry. 'The mitrailleuse', Armit said, 'is neither a pure infantry arm nor a pure artillery arm. It is not an offensive weapon; this is an especially important point [...] It must be used against massed troops.'[51] He

Tactics', p.424; Armit, 'Machine-Guns', p.45. Armit had served in the Royal Navy before joining the Volunteers.

50   Armit, 'Machine-Guns', pp.48, 56.
51   Armit, 'Machine-Guns', p.53.

observed that the magazine rifle, which was preferred in continental armies to the machine gun, was by comparison a true small-arm and the infantry equivalent of the machine gun.[52]

Mechanical guns like the Nordenfelt or the Gatling were prone to jam and hence unreliable, cumbersome to bring into and out of action, difficult to supply with ammunition, and difficult to operate. Most importantly they were considered inaccurate. Their operation shook the gun violently, and Major (later Lieutenant General) Edward Hutton, who had used Nordenfeldt guns mounted on railway wagons with the cavalry brigade in Egypt in 1882, reported how very minor variances in the plane of the weapon on the wagon significantly affected the fall of the bullets, resulting in the danger of friendly fire. As well as the issues of concealment and mobility, this largely explains why they were considered ill-suited to being used in support of infantry attacks.[53] This view was not universally held however. Frederick Thesinger, Lord Chelmsford, commander of the British forces in the Zulu War of 1879, is not generally regarded as one of the most able Victorian generals, but based upon his experience of the use of machine guns in that war he was of the opinion that it was an infantry weapon, able to provide covering fire in the final attack.[54]

Within a few years the technology available had changed and the Army's views on the weapon changed with it. The appearance of the recoil-operated Maxim gun in 1884 resolved many of the practical problems. First demonstrated to the Army on 3 February 1885, its adoption was relatively rapid. Significantly, the Committee entrusted with its development, though still under the Department of the Artillery, was entrusted to Colonel Arbuthnot, who was the Superintendent of the Royal Small Arms Factory, and after July 1885 the weapon is no longer mentioned in the minutes of the *Proceedings of the Department of the Director of the Artillery* (the successor to the Ordnance Select Committee). Following a debate at the Royal United Service Institution on 13 November 1885, Wolseley announced from the chair that the Army had concluded that it must have machine guns, and that they should to be treated as a small arm, an infantry weapon. By 1888, instruction in the Maxim gun was taking place at Hythe, and the first use of the Maxim in the field took place in November the same year during an expedition in Sierra Leone, the guns being carried by porters through the West African jungle. It was not until the Boer War, however, that the

---

52   Armit, 'Machine-Guns', p.53. It is worth noting that Lieutenant Colonel Alt, speaking from the audience, did not agree with all Armit's conclusions. He thought all infantry could be trained in the use of machine guns and that they could be used offensively, ibid, pp.60-61.

53   Captain F.G. Stone, *The Maxim Machine Gun, Lecture to Aldershot Military Society, Friday July 6 1888* (Aldershot: Gale and Polden, 1888), pp.10-11. Stone was the Instructor in Fortification at the Royal Military College, Sandhurst.

54   Hutchison, *Machine Guns*, p.39.

tripod completely replaced wheeled carriages, allowing the machine gun to approach the mobility, and more important the concealability, of the rifleman.[55]

* * *

In comparison to the limited lessons that the Royal Artillery thought could be learnt from the American field artillery, and their even more limited view regarding the utility of the machine gun, great interest was taken in the technical development of US heavy artillery. The very first item that Captain Alderson was instructed to look at in 1864 was 'the system which is adopted by the United States of employing guns of very large calibre of cast iron'. Britain, along with most other European countries, regarded cast iron as insufficiently durable for use in large guns, but it did offer the prospect of substantially cheaper ordnance for siege, coastal, and naval artillery than did other materials.[56] The 1862 mission had also looked at the construction of cast iron ordnance, while several items of intelligence relating to such artillery had been acquired since then. The 1864 report in particular is highly technical and very detailed; eight specimens of iron ore were sent with the report, as well as four specimens of iron obtained from ordnance factories. Both reports included detailed descriptions of manufacture, including temperatures and timings of components in the casting process and details of the rifling process. From all of the information provided it was expected that the experimental establishments in Britain would be able to ascertain the effect of Federal artillery in service. However, British interest did not stop with the procurement of intelligence and metallurgy samples. In November 1863 the Royal Navy tried to secretly purchase two large Parrott guns from America through a Liverpool businessman, which would have been delivered to Woolwich, and in Washington Colonel Henry Rowan also endeavoured to procure specimens of the large guns. With the war at its height and the US government keeping every gun possible for its own use, this proved impossible. The order from the Navy was finally cancelled in May 1865.[57]

---

55 Ian V. Hogg, *Machine Guns: A Detailed History of the Rapid-Fire Gun 14th Century to Present* (Iola WI: Krause, c. 2002), pp.30-37; Hutchison, *Machine Guns*, pp.39-51; Wolseley speaking at the Royal United Service Institution, Friday 13 November 1885, at lecture by Major M.R. West, 'Single-Barrel Machine-Gun', pp.34-35; Stone, *The Maxim Machine Gun*, p.9. Paradoxically machine guns were a relative failure in South Africa, where there were few massed targets, which may have limited its further adoption in the early 20th Century, Spencer Jones, *From Boer War to World War: Tactical Reform of the British Army 1902 – 1914* (Norman: University of Oklahoma Press, 2012), pp.101-04.

56 The prime motive behind the American use of iron as their material of choice seems to have been strategic rather than financial, since they possessed high quality iron but limited resources of copper and tin. Hogg, *Weapons of the Civil War*, p.73.

57 WO 33/11/0174, Mahon Report, pp.16-19, 26-29; WO 33/12/0186, p.539; WO 33/13/0214, pp.568-69; WO 33/13/0226, pp.103, 152; WO 33/14/0229, Gallwey Report, pp.58, 75; TNA, WO 33/14/0230, *Abstracts of Proceedings of the Ordnance Select Committee*

A 15-inch Rodman smoothbore and a 200-pounder Parrot rifle in the Washington defences, c. 1863. (Library of Congress)

Certain details of American designs were seen as superior to current British prac-tices. In particular due to a combination of iron carriages, the balance of the gun, and a simple but highly efficient elevating mechanism they required only one-quarter the crew of a British gun of the same weight. In technical terms the American guns had little or no 'preponderance': rather than being heavier at the breach to give stability, they were balanced at the trunnions and relied upon friction to keep them in place. Iron carriages and casting guns without preponderance were two of the three items the 1864 report recommended for further investigation and experiment; the third recommendation being trial of firing at iron embrasures as constructed in Federal fortifications. The main concern over cast iron as a material for gun manufacture was that the endurance of American guns was believed suspect, resulting in the use of low charges in actual combat which limited their effectiveness. The US Navy, in order to try and achieve penetration of iron plated vessels with the Dahlgren 11-inch gun, had found it necessary to increase the size of charges such that 'it becomes extremely unsafe to fire it', while large numbers of heavy cast-iron Parrott guns were observed to have burst at Charleston, even when re-enforced with wrought iron banding around the breech.[58]

for the Quarter Ending 30th June 1864, pp.259-64; TNA, WO 33/14/0249, *Abstracts of Proceedings of the Ordnance Select Committee for the Quarter Ending 31st December 1864,* pp.717-19; TNA, WO 33/15/0259, *Abstracts of Proceedings of the Ordnance Select Committee For the Quarter Ending 30th June 1865,* p.364.
58   WO 33/11/0174, Mahon Report, p.37; WO 33/14/0229, Gallwey Report, pp.39-40, 55.

In 1865 the Committee finally concluded that while the Americans possessed a formidable number of heavy guns, that they bore 'no comparison' to the best British models and that cast iron was unsuited for the manufacture of large-calibre rifled ordnance, although the 1864 report had recommended continued monitoring of American progress in heavy gun manufacture from time to time. A contemporary report from Captain Goodenough RN came to a similar conclusion. British naval practice was to deliver a small shot with high velocity, whereas the Americans used larger guns, smaller charges and lower velocities. The latter was not seen as superior to British practice, but its simplicity, cheapness and quickness of manufacture was recognised as being appropriate for the large volunteer force that the United States had called into being.[59]

Within a few years steel guns had made cast iron as obsolete as bronze, and large calibre, low velocity, guns proved to be a technological dead end.[60] The importance of the British interest in these guns and methods is not whether they were adopted or not, but the readiness of the British establishment to look at American technology and to evaluate it on its merits.

Previously-rejected ideas were also reviewed as a result of intelligence received from America. One example was the mounting of ordnance on railway stock. In November 1862 the Committee directed

> a reconsideration [...] on the locomotive revolving battery proposed by Messrs Baker and Casbourne, as it appears that in the battles near Richmond a heavy rifled gun on railway track with iron screens of similar thickness to plates on "Merrimac" was run up by the Confederates to the Federal position, and played an important part during the action.'[61]

It was concluded that locomotive batteries might be of use if Britain were invaded, but that as they could be constructed at short notice there was no need for a permanent peacetime establishment or trial. It did recommend drawing up designs and possibly constructing models, 'one class exhibiting a light locomotive shield to carry one gun and resist field artillery, one to carry one gun, and resist naval artillery at moderate distances'.[62] The mounting of heavy artillery using armoured cupolas was

---

59   WO 33/14/0229, Gallwey Report, pp.xi, 34; WO 33/15/0259, p.364; FO 881/1254, p.5. The Americans, not unsurprisingly perhaps, took the view at the time that their own ordnance was better than that of the British, *Army and Navy Journal* 23 January 1864, p.338.

60   Rogers, *History of Artillery*, pp.103-04.

61   WO 33/12/0186, p.539. The action in question was presumably that at Savage's Station on 29 June 1862. Robert Underwood Johnson and Clarence Clough Buel (eds), *Battles and Leaders of the Civil War*, 4 vols (Secaucus NJ: Castle, 1983, originally published 1887), Vol. II, pp.373-74.

62   WO 33/12/0186, p.539.

A railroad gun at Petersburg, 1864. (Library of Congress)

also considered, but since it would be limited by weight only 'very sparing use' could be made of such heavy batteries. The Committee observed that a cupola of the form designed by Captain Cowper Coles RN, which was similar to the turret used on the USS *Monitor*, weighed 40 tons and therefore considerable study would be needed to develop such a railway battery.[63]

In 1865 Gallwey described the Federal use of railway-mounted artillery at Petersburg in 1864, including a 13-inch mortar observed by a Colonel Simmons, while the Committee received another letter from a civilian, via Horse Guards, pointing out the value of railway batteries for defence. They did not change their position from that of 1862, minuting that 'whenever railways run within gunshot distance of the coast they will naturally be employed in defence, but their special construction is out of the question'.[64]

*   *   *

Gallwey's instructions in 1864, issued by the Inspector General of Fortification, Field Marshal Sir John Burgoyne, not surprisingly directed him to look at the attack and defence of fortifications as his prime object. Specific questions included the effects of

63   WO 33/12/0186, p.539.
64   TNA, WO 33/15/0266, *Abstracts of Proceedings of the Ordnance Select Committee for the Quarter Ending 30th September 1865*, p.696. Lieutenant Colonel Gallwey, 'The Influence of Rifled Guns on the Attack and Defence of Fortresses', *R.E. Professional Papers*, 14 (1865), pp.25-55 (p.55).

rifled canon, the application of iron, and the construction of new permanent works. Burgoyne's instructions specifically refer to ascertaining the 'general *principles* of construction [...] from which we might perhaps imbibe useful lessons for ourselves in fortification'.[65] The importance of this to the British was both defensive (the protection of the country's major fleet bases and magazines was an important issue at the time) and offensive (how would the Royal Navy and the Army fare against the enemy's fortifications in time of war). Burgoyne explicitly told Gallwey to 'avoid prying into any details in which the authorities desire to maintain any degree of mystery or reserve', and there is nothing in the formal instructions to imply that the United States might be a potential enemy, but Gallwey also submitted an informal report to Lord Lyons with his opinions on the operations of United States forces in the event on war with England [*sic*], and several sections of the report to the War Office also seem to anticipate war with the United States.[66] Because of the small charges used in American guns, British experiments indicated that the armour of Royal Navy ironclads was proof against the American 8-inch smoothbore and 100pdr rifles which were in use at some of the forts in New York. Gallwey concluded that the New York defences, though strong were not insurmountable and that ironclads could run past them into the harbour.[67] At Portland it was noted that the defences had been strengthened since 1862, when its possession 'would have been a matter of easy accomplishment', and it now represented a danger to neighbouring British harbours which would be within range of a fleet of monitors based there. However, the Portland defences were thought even more open to attack than those at New York.[68]

This observation of the possible defects of the defensive measures at specific harbours, which seems to have exceeded Gallwey's official remit, were not seen as a general principle or lesson to be learnt from the conflict overall. Operations in the Baltic and Black Sea during the Crimean War had already demonstrated to the British that warships could not contend with forts if conditions were anything like equal, but some pre-war opinion had thought that the introduction of ironclads would tilt the balance back in favour of ships.[69] Gallwey's report disagreed with this. 'In order to reduce a well constructed fort, it is now generally conceded that a force must be landed, and siege batteries (armed with heavy guns) erected.'[70] Events at Charleston, where due to the weak armament of the forts the conditions favoured the attacking ironclad fleet but it was still unsuccessful, were held to support this view. Weak or poorly sited

65   WO 33/14/0229, Gallwey Report, p.77. Original italics.
66   TNA, CO 880/6/1, *Defences of Canada*, Gallwey to Lord Lyons, New York, 27 May 1864.
67   WO 33/14/0229, Gallwey Report, pp.9, 13. Schaw, 'New Arms of Precision', p.389 also observed that the war demonstrated steam ships could run past shore batteries at speed unless prevented by obstacles in the channel.
68   WO 33/14/0229, Gallwey Report, pp.13-14.
69   WO 33/14/0229, Gallwey Report, p.12; Anon, 'Ironclad Ships of War and our Defences', *Blackwood's Edinburgh Magazine*, 89 (1861), pp.304-17 (pp.304, 306).
70   WO 33/14/0229, Gallwey Report, p.13.

fortifications, however, even one as powerful as Fort Fisher at Wilmington NC, could be successfully attacked.[71]

When looking at sieges by land, the first lesson was that exposed brickwork was easily breached, this was evidenced at Fort Pulaski near Savannah, a case study referenced by both the 1862 and the 1864 reports, and also the subject of books and articles by Major General Gillmore, who had commanded the siege operations there, that were widely read in Britain.[72] However the British were already carrying out experiments on Martello towers at Eastbourne in this respect, and it was considered that 'the practice of the English artillery will bear favourable comparison with that of the Americans'.[73] Furthermore the vulnerability of exposed brickwork was a general principle of siege engineering: the only difference at Fort Pulaski was the range at which the breach was achieved due to the new rifled ordnance. Prior to the war, Captain Henry Whatley Tyler had anticipated the increased vulnerability of traditional fortifications to the new rifled artillery, as well as predicting the use of heavier ordnance by besieging forces (previously the defence had usually had the advantage of possessing the larger calibre guns).

> It is evident that, by the employment of rifled guns of the heavier calibres, the besieger will be able to destroy all the ordinary defences of a fortress that are exposed to his fire, with greater facility, and from greater distances, than before. We have still much information to acquire in regard to the relative penetration into earth and masonry, at different distances, of round and elongated projectiles; but we know the accuracy with which the latter may be thrown; and we can foresee, without difficulty, that the aggregate effect of a given number of shot will be materially increased, for this reason, at anything but short ranges.[74]

71   The events at Charleston were closely observed by Britain, see WO 33/14/0229, Gallwey Report, pp.20-25; WO 33/13/230, pp.261-62; also 'W.C.', 'On the Defence of our Dockyards against Iron-Plated Vessels', *United Service Magazine*, 428 (July 1864), pp.339-44 (p.340). Schaw, 'New Arms of Precision', p.389 for observations on Fort Fisher.
72   WO 33/11/0174, Mahon Report, p.49; WO 33/14/0229, Gallwey Report, pp.19-20. The latter report shows that a book by Gillmore, referred to as *Siege of Fort Pulaski* was delivered as an attachment (Gallwey Report, p.viii), this probably refers to Brigadier General Q.A. Gillmore, *Official Report of the United States Engineer Department of the Siege and Reduction of Fort Pulaski, Georgia* (New York: Van Nostrand, 1862), extracts from which were subsequently published in *R.E. Professional Papers*, 13 (1864), pp.147-52. See also Luvaas, *Military Legacy*, p.44.
73   Callwell and Headlam, *History of the Royal Artillery*, Vol.I, p.148; WO 33/14/0229, Gallwey Report, p.19.
74   Captain H.W. Tyler, 'The Rifle and the Rampart; or, the Future of Defence,' *Journal of the Royal United Service Institution*, 4 (1861), pp.331-63, (p.347). Lecture delivered on Friday, 2 March 1860.

Tyler went on to state that 'it will not be desirable to construct any walls in future permanent fortifications, when we can avoid it, that are not well protected from distant fire'.[75] He would certainly not have been surprised by the fall of Fort Pulaski, other than perhaps by the speed with which it took place. The British were scathing of the 'wretched inefficiency' of the Confederate defence, the 'ineffective fire' of the fort, and a surrender which was 'hardly necessary'. In marked contrast, Fort Sumter was held to show 'what an amount of battering a casemented fort will endure even if made of brick'.[76]

The US engineers were found to have adopted iron embrasures in response to rifled artillery. The observers in 1864 received good access to Brigadier General Barnard, Chief Engineer of the Department of Washington, who did not foresee a general substitution of masonry by iron in the construction of permanent fortifications. The importance of traditional masonry casemate forts had also been demonstrated by the war. However the British thought that the detailed construction of American casemated works had weaknesses, and the use of multi-tier casemates was considered inappropriate for some sites where successive tiers of fortification would have been more appropriate.[77] In 1866 Jervois authored a memorandum on the construction of casemated structures with iron shields which considered the progress the Americans had made in this field, along with other major powers (aside from three small works at Portsmouth built in the 1860s, Britain had not built a casemated fort since the time of Henry VIII). Forts Pulaski and Sumner, Jervois noted, were built entirely of brick due to the unavailability of local stone, and were not designed to resist modern artillery. The stone defences at Boston, New York, and Newport were superior, but even the new works at Portland and New York that had been observed by Gallwey, and possibly by Jervois himself, were still believed to be inadequately protected against modern rifled artillery. The British ran a series of experiments between May and December 1865 at Shoeburyness, and Jervois then applied statistics from the US Navy's bombardment of Fort Sumter to estimate how resilient the proposed new structures would be under battle conditions as opposed to the artificial environment of the firing range. From this he concluded that the resilience of the proposed British design for granite structures with iron embrasures was sufficient for most purposes. In line with Barnard's view, Jervois thought that works wholly plated with iron would be superior, but generally not worth the additional expense unless the work was isolated and unsupported. He did however include drawings of a turreted iron structure in the report that in design is very similar to that used in US Navy monitors, as a solution to mounting very heavy guns and to maximise their angles of fire.[78]

75   Tyler, 'The Rifle and the Rampart', p.350.
76   WO 33/14/0229, Gallwey Report, pp.19-20, 23; WO 33/11/0174, Mahon Report, p.49.
77   WO 33/14/0229, Gallwey Report, pp.4-5.
78   TNA, WO 33/17A/0299, W.D.F. J[ervois], *Experiments upon a Casemated Structure for Granite, with Iron Shields at the Embrasures, carried on at Shoeburyness in May and November 1865*, Memo dated October 1866. See also Colonel [William F. Drummond] Jervois,

Gallwey's instructions also explicitly referred to how far had 'any alterations been made in the construction of field or siege works, arriving from the effect of rifled cannon upon them'.[79] While some mention of this has been made in the previous chapter, the conclusions of this official report are worth noting here. Fieldworks were the very first item written about. Their extensive use, both in entrenching towns and camps and as tactical earthworks on taking up of new positions, was commented upon, and when well-constructed they were reported to 'have generally enabled the defensive force to withstand the most determined attacks'. On more extensive works, the use of traverses and well framed bomb-proofs and magazines was complimented, it was also remarked that the abundance of timber mean that these were both economic and quick to build. Abattis and similar timber obstructions were also quickly and efficiently constructed.[80] However 'there seemed to be no modification of profile consequent on the introduction of rifled artillery'. The more permanent defences such as those at Washington were constructed on the same principles as Torres Vedras, field forts within range of each other so that fire swept intervening spaces; connected by light parapets. The analogy with Wellington's Torres Vedras lines, constructed to defend Lisbon in Portugal during the Peninsular War, was made by Brigadier General Barnard, and not by Gallwey or Alderson, though Barnard may have been making the comparison in deference to his British guests. Gallwey's very complete description seems to go beyond discussion of 'principles' and can be interpreted as a detailed analysis of the strength of the Washington defences ('very powerful') should an attack be necessary.[81]

Half-way between the field works and the permanent casemated forts, the 1864 report noted the creation of extensive earthen batteries. These mounted the heaviest guns available, but came in for criticism for having the guns *en barbette* – elevated to fire over, rather than through an embrasure in, a parapet, and therefore very exposed to shell fire. The US engineers had not yet resolved this problem, though there was some expectation that some arrangement of turrets would be the solution. The vulnerability of earthen forts with batteries mounted *en barbette* were demonstrated during the US Navy's bombardment at Fort Fisher in January 1865, where most of the Confederate heavy guns were disabled before the assault. While not dismissing the significance of earthworks for the future, the limitations of inadequately laid out defences such as those at Fort Fisher were pointed out by authorities such as Schaw.[82]

The willingness of the British to adopt earthen fortifications is further demonstrated by the recommendations made by Jervois as a result of his review of the defences of

---

'Coast Defences, and the Application of Iron to Fortification', *Journal of the Royal United Service Institution*, 12 (1868), pp.549-69.

79   WO 33/14/0229, Gallwey Report, p.77.
80   Abattis was an obstacle formed of the branches of trees laid in a row with the sharpened tops directed outwards, frequently used during the Civil War.
81   WO 33/14/0229, Gallwey Report, pp.1-4.
82   WO 33/14/0229, Gallwey Report, p.7; Schaw, 'New Arms of Precision', pp.389-90.

British 150-pounder Armstrong rifle, Fort Fisher, 1865. (Library of Congress)

Canada. In part this was down to simple budgetary constraints. This was the second report on the defence and fortification of Canada to be produced during the war, and in his instructions to the earlier Royal Commission of 1862 Sir John Burgoyne had explicitly instructed that permanent works be kept to a minimum so as to keep down the expense. A further indication of Burgoyne's thinking was the suggestion that defensive battlefields could be identified that if 'previously well studied could no doubt be rapidly entrenched and made very formidable'.[83] Written in February 1862 this view predates any observation of widespread entrenchment during the Civil War.

Jervois' report, presented in January 1865, is of particular interest as it is perhaps the only document that explicitly considered how the British would need to go about conducting a war with the United States at the height of its military power during the Civil War. A defensive war in Canada was clearly envisaged in which the initial forces that would be available there to the British would be significantly outnumbered. As an engineer, Jervois perhaps naturally concluded that 'it is only by availing ourselves of the advantages of works of fortification that we can provide against the Canadian

83   TNA, WO 33/12/0185, J.F. Burgoyne, *Memorandum of General Information to the Commission to report on the Defence of Canada*, 24 February 1862, in *Report of Commission on Defences of Canada* (Montreal, 1 September 1862), pp.39-40 (p.40); J.F. Burgoyne, *Memorandum by Sir J.F. Burgoyne, on the Defence of Canada – February 1862*, 15 February 1862; ibid pp.41-46 (p.46) and also archived in WO 33/11/0165.

forces being overpowered'. Troops were still expected to make use of field entrenchments, but he anticipated that these would be liable to having their flanks turned
and forced to retreat. Minor defensive works, some of which had been proposed in
1862, were advised against as they would be overwhelmed, while forts with batteries
en barbette were also identified as vulnerable. [84] The basis of Jervois strategy was the
concentration of forces in defence of one or two major strategic points.

> It is proposed that the vital points of the country should be protected by works of
> fortification, chiefly earthworks, constructed in the form of extensive entrenched
> camps, each of which would form a focus of refuge and action for troops employed
> in the defence of that section of the country in which it is situated.[85]

An example of the extent that Jervois considered these camps could cover was Toronto,
where the earthworks were expected to be over nine miles long and require some
50,000 men to defend. While these were large numbers in the context of the forces
available in Canada, Jervois noted that the defences of Washington were some thirty-
five miles in length. Toronto, along with Montreal and Hamilton, were the only locations where he envisaged the construction of major new permanent fortifications,
while at Quebec some existing defences were recommended to be strengthened and
Kingston would have casemented works with iron embrasures for sea defence [*sic*].[86]
Jervois described the envisaged new defences at Montreal in more detail than most.

> Considering the necessity of them being executed with rapidity, the shortness of
> the working season in Canada, and the advisability of rendering them as inex-
> pensive as possible, they should be of a less permanent character than it would be
> desirable to adopt under other circumstances. With this view it is proposed that
> at Montreal the main part of the works should be of earth, with detached walls
> in the ditches, which should be flanked by caponiers of masonry. Bomb-proofs of
> wood and earth may be added behind the ramparts at a time of expected attack.
> The forts might further be strengthened by masonry keeps, from which a fire
> could be brought to bear over the whole of the interior of the work; these keeps
> would be well covered by the earthen ramparts of the main work and they should
> be of economical construction.[87]

This description reflects a mix of American practice in the form of earthen
ramparts and bomb-proofs, and conventional European practice in the form of stone
strongpoints. Jervois referenced the Washington defences in his report, but also the

---

84   WO 33/15/0265, Jervois, *Defence of Canada*, pp.14, 17, 19-20.
85   Jervois, *Defence of Canada*, p.15.
86   Jervois, *Defence of Canada*, pp.17, 25.
87   Jervois, *Defence of Canada*, p.25.

operations at Sebastopol in 1854, and at Düppel during the Prusso-Danish War of 1864. This is a good example of how the lessons of the Civil War were not considered in a vacuum, but compared and merged with experience from other recent conflicts and applied to specific strategic and tactical problems.[88]

A key assumption in Jervois' strategy was that the entrenched camps would need to be sufficiently strong only to survive the relatively short campaigning season in Canada, since it was expected that it would be impossible to maintain a siege during the Canadian winter.[89] Some permanent fortifications were required because Jervois did not underestimate the capacity of the US Army for waging war, nor overestimate the value of the Canadian militia. He anticipated that any Canadian force would be inferior in both numbers and efficiency, and hence there would be a need for permanent fortifications supplemented by temporary defences thrown up in the event of war.

> It should be observed that there is a great deal of difference in the power of resistance of temporary earthworks and of permanent fortifications with earthen ramparts. The former require many more men and a much better disciplined force to defend them than the latter.[90]

A final example of the significance that the British placed on the extended use of earthworks is the Ordnance Select Committee review in 1864 of the composition of the siege train, particularly the provision of rifled guns. Although the Commander in Chief himself believed that smoothbore guns were more effective than rifles against masonry or iron, the decision was made in favour of the rifled guns because of their greater effect against earthworks. Since Gallwey was a member of the committee it is hard to believe that his American experience did not influence the decision. In an article in a professional journal published shortly after his return from the United States, he referred to shells being as good as solid shot against brickwork, and only inferior against granite and iron. The American war he considered 'a good stock of information respecting the effect of guns on brickwork' but of little value with regards to the effect on earthworks due to the poor fuses.[91]

* * *

Of equal or greater importance to any evidence from America therefore were the extensive experiments carried out by the British at Newhaven around this time, with various fuses, guns and types of shell, in order to determine the best way to destroy

88   Jervois, *Defence of Canada*, pp.21, 17.
89   Jervois, *Defence of Canada*, p.14.
90   Jervois, *Defence of Canada*, p.17.
91   TNA, SUPP 6/12, *Extracts from the Reports and Proceedings of the Ordnance Select Committee Vol. 2. January–December 1864* (London: HMSO, 1865), p.327; Gallwey, 'Influence of Rifled Guns', p.39.

earthworks. Also worthy of note is that the British had gained direct experience of the effectiveness of rifled guns (in this case Armstrong breech-loaders) in tearing away earthworks at Kagemushi in Japan in August 1863. The Newhaven experiments had concluded that smoothbores were of little use, and that the most effective method was the fire of the largest possible guns with full charges, detonating on the parapet of the earthwork to destroy it. Heavier shells detonating lower down only displaced the earth without causing a breach. Lighter shells created only local damage which could easily be repaired. Schaw concluded that field guns would be ineffective against earthworks, which meant that these would need to be taken either by siege or by surprise.[92]

Over 20 years later Major Sir George Sydenham Clarke pointed to the experiences of the American Civil War, which he thought were 'full of interest and have perhaps received insufficient study', and thought that British works constructed since the war had not followed American experience.[93] Luvaas quoted this in *Military Legacy* as evidence that the war did not materially alter British practice, but this needs to be qualified.[94] The invasion scares of the 1850s and 1860s had led to many fortifications built to defend the south coast of England during the 1860s, largely supervised by Jervois, and due to their cost these were hugely controversial even at the time of their construction. The evidence shows that Jervois paid a great deal of attention to American practice, and that his designs specifically referred to applying that experience.[95] The main thrust of Clarke's book was a criticism of expensive works designed around theoretical models. American experience was significant in that it showed instances of where temporary works had resisted assault or siege as well as permanent works, but Clarke also drew the same conclusion from European wars of the period, and even from Wellington's defences at Torres Vedras.[96]

In the case of British works constructed since 1859, while they had the advantage of being constructed after the appearance of rifles, Clarke criticised them as 'large, elaborate and costly', and as a waste of money because in Britain land defences were subordinate to sea power in national defence.[97] The defences designed by Jervois around the Solent on the south coast, protecting the naval base at Portsmouth, incorporated several instances of earthwork batteries. These included those at Southsea, Eastney, and Lumps in the inner defences; almost all the defences on the Isle of White except the casemated fort at Sandown; the Cliff End, Hatherwood, and Warden Point

---

92   TNA, WO 33/12/0204, *Report of Ordnance Select Committee No.3065 6th November 1863: The Relative Penetration into Earth of Projectiles From Rifled and Smooth Bore Guns, and on Several Varieties of Percussion Fuze;* WO 33/13/0226, pp.68-71; SUPP/6/12, pp.17-18, 45-50, 93; Gallwey, 'Influence of Rifled Guns' p.42; Schaw, 'New Arms of Precision', p.385.

93   Major Sir George Sydenham Clarke, *Fortification: its Past Achievements, Recent Development, and Future Progress* (London: John Murray, 1890), p.43.

94   Luvaas, *Military Legacy*, p.45.

95   See footnote 78 above.

96   Clarke, *Fortification*, pp.40-51 for operations in the Civil War, pp.52-73 on European Wars, p.17 on Torres Vedras.

97   Clarke, *Fortification*, p.79.

batteries covering the Needles; Purbrook, Widely, Southwick, and Nelson among the outer works; and Forts Grange, Rowner, Brockhurst, and the Hillsea lines around Portsmouth. Some of these earthworks included bomb-proof casemates or caponiers similar to Jervois' suggestions for the Canadian defences, while some of the guns at Southsea were behind iron shields. At other key strategic points it is true that the majority of defences were casemates; but at Cork, in southern Ireland, they were entirely earthworks with iron shields for guns.[98] Clarke however restricted his criticism to features of the permanent fortifications. This does not mean that his criticism was wrong – there was a continuing technology race between artillery and fortifications and many features of the forts were obsolete by the time Clarke wrote. Nevertheless he wrote with hindsight, and it was by no means an accepted fact in 1867 either that Britain could not be invaded, or that her ports would be secure without some form of permanent works.

* * *

The peripheral defences around the fortifications in America also drew British attention. Schaw wrote about the American habit of constantly raising fortifications in woods, and that, when covered with abattis 'the experience of the American civil war [sic] proves that such a line, if properly defended, is impregnable'.[99] Also commented upon was the use of two innovations often cited as predicting the First World War, wire entanglements and land mines. Wolseley gave precise instructions on the setting up of wire entanglements in the Soldier's Pocket-Book, based upon his observation of their use in America and concluding that 'a work or battery surrounded by such an obstacle is difficult to storm'.[100] Schaw was teaching their use at the Staff College during the following decade, and an 1878 article on the defences at Plevna in Bulgaria, the siege of which from July to December 1877 was the main action of the Russo-Turkish War of 1877-78, commented upon the absence of wire there, implying its use was considered normal by that time. Instructions for their erection continue to appear later in the century, including the 1889 infantry drill manual.[101] By 1891 the use of the newly invented barbed wire to further strengthen the obstacle was also being proposed.[102]

---

98   WO 33/17A/0297 Lieutenant Colonel William F. Drummond Jervois, Report with Reference to the Progress Made in the Construction of the Fortification for the Defence of the Dockyards and Naval Arsenals of the United Kingdom (London: HMSO, 1867), pp.12-16, 25.
99   Schaw, Defence and Attack, pp.119, 123.
100 Wolseley, Soldier's Pocket Book, p.330.
101 Schaw, Defence and Attack, pp.77, 130; Fraser, 'Defence of a Position', pp.39-40; Lieutenant Francis Welch, 'Military Notes Around Plevna and on the Danube, During December, 1877, and January, 1878', Journal of the Royal United Service Institution, 22 (1878), pp.328-49, (p.341); Anon, Infantry Drill, 1889 (London: HMSO, 1889), p.432.
102 Captain J.W. Malet, Handbook for Field Training in the Infantry (London: Gale and Polden, 1891), pp.87-88. Barbed wire was first automatically manufactured in 1874, Edward L Katzenbach Jr, 'The Horse Cavalry in the 20th Century: A Study in Policy

Wire was frequently recommended for the protection of defensive lines, but mention of the use of mines on land is less common. Although observed at Fort Wagner in 1863, they were not thought to have done much damage by the 1864 observers, and one commentator thought that they rendered the defence too passive as they prevented sorties, but Schaw later considered them of great value, including the moral effect of the small red flags used to mark their position.[103] Their presence was also noted at Fort Fisher where they were intended to be detonated electronically, but as the wires to do so were only three feet deep they had been cut by artillery.[104]

The use of artificial obstructions was not only the subject of theoretical lectures in the Staff College, there is some evidence that practical soldiers in the field observed and learnt from the American experience. One officer writing about the Umbeyla campaign of 1863 on the North-West Frontier of India – about as far as it was physically possible to get from the battlefields of Georgia or Virginia – reflected on the use in America of abattis and telegraph wire entanglements and remarked that 'this was exactly what was required here'. He also referred to the Americans using artificial light in both attack and defence of entrenched positions and thought that 'some simple contrivance for producing and directing light in such a country as this [India] would be of the greatest advantage'.[105] No other British military journals of the period seem to have recorded the use of searchlights in America, but a calcium light was reported as being mounted at the Federal Battery Gregg overlooking Fort Sumter, Charleston, by an unnamed British officer whose observations had been printed in *The Times* in January 1864.[106]

In 1875 the title for the Royal Engineer Prize Essay competition was 'The Defence of a Position Selected as a Field of Battle'. The winning entrant, Captain T. Fraser RE,

Response' in *American Defense Policy*, 4th Edn ed. by John E. Endicott and Roy W. Stafford Jr (Baltimore and London; John Hopkins University Press, 1977), pp.360-73 (p.361), originally published in *Public Policy*, 7 (1958).

103 WO 33/14/0229, Gallwey Report, p.22; Anon, 'Siege of Charleston', p.182; Schaw, 'The Present State of the Question of Fortification', pp.443, 449. Schaw's comments were based upon the observations of Lieutenant Featherstonhaugh at Petersburg.

104 Capt Harding Steward RE, 'Notes on the Employment of Submarine Mines in America During the Late Civil War', *R.E. Professional Papers*, 15 (1866), pp.1-28 (pp.26-27).

105 Captain D.C. Fosbery, 'The Umbeyla Campaign', *Journal of the Royal United Service Institution*, 11 (1868), pp.548-68 (p.566).

106 'The Southern Confederation', in *The Times*, Friday, 1 January 1864, p.7. The correspondent's dateline was Richmond November 19, the original visit by the officer to Fort Sumter was on 15 November 1863. The item appeared in several British local papers as well as the American *Army and Navy Journal*, 23 January 1864, p.346, this last version being cited by Luvaas, *Military Legacy*, p.34 (without noting the use of searchlights). Luvaas identified the officer as different from Lieutenant Innes and his visit being earlier, but since Innes' leave was from 11 November 1863 to 21 January 1864, and in view of Ross' comments quoted earlier that he knew of no other 'tourists' at the time, it is possible that the unnamed officer was also Innes. See also <www.history.com/news/history-lists/8-unusual-civil-war-weapons> [accessed 31 December 2014].

described comprehensively how artificial obstructions should be used. He recommended abattis as the first choice of obstacle, since it was not destroyed by artillery fire, and was often readily available (apart from its extensive use in America, Fraser noted it had been used in the Franco-Prussian war at both Metz and Paris). Next best were wire entanglements, though the materials to construct these were not at that time carried by the Royal Engineers in the field; and finally pointed stakes, which had been seen in China. He advised that wire entanglements should have bells attached to warn of an enemy attacking at night. *Fougasses* or mines, usually fired mechanically or chemically when trodden on, were useful to defend passes or against night attacks. They could also be fired by electricity, either controlled manually or on contact, and each company of engineers had an electric dynamo for this purpose. To illuminate the enemy 'lime lights may occasionally be posted in salient positions.'[107] Overall, Fraser described a comprehensive defensive network in which the enemy's potential lines of advance would be covered with obstacles and mines, and be swept with field guns and mitrailleurs. This was a vision both reflecting the lessons of the Civil War, and anticipating the elaborate defensive positions of the First World War.

Schaw also remarked that the American war had shown the use of floating mines, more commonly referred to as 'torpedoes' in this period, to be 'very effective in the defences of rivers and harbours'.[108] The British Army's involvement and interest in this aspect of warfare has been largely ignored, probably because it is now mostly a subject covered by naval historians. Luvaas touched upon it briefly, but another eminent modern American historian, James A. Rawley, noted with a little surprise that Wolseley considered the operations around Charleston as being the most important source of lessons for both Europeans and Americans from the Civil War.[109] If this is considered from a 19th Century perspective however, rather than from any pre-conceived view of the Civil War's importance in history, the significance of these developments to the British becomes easy to understand. The single most important role for the Army was the defence of the home country. Since Britain could only be threatened by seaborne invasion, the protection of the coast, and in particular of harbours and naval arsenals, was of paramount importance to British strategy, to a much greater extent than any other European power. The construction, maintenance, equipping and manning of Britain's coast defences were an Army not a Navy responsibility, and the invasion scares of the period and the construction of a number of defences around the coast; had sparked contentious debate at the time about the best form of coastal defence. Senior engineer officers would have keenly observed foreign practice as part of this debate. Jervois himself expected torpedoes to be deployed in conjunction with the Solent defences, since the war in America 'has shown the great

---

107 Fraser, *Defence of a Position*, pp.39-40.
108 Schaw, 'The Present State of the Question of Fortification', pp.457, 459. The term torpedo will be used here for submarine devices, to distinguish them from land mines.
109 Luvaas, *Military Legacy*, pp.30, 44; James A. Rawley, introduction to *The American Civil War: An English View*, p.xx; Wolseley, 'An English View of the Civil War', p.595.

value of submarine mines [*sic*] employed in connection with forts'.[110] The projection of British power overseas also depended upon the ability of the Navy to transport her forces across the globe, which in turn depended upon holding dozens of strategic bases overseas.

The various designs of floating torpedoes used in America by the Confederates were recorded by the 1864 mission, but even before this the War Office had established a Committee (which included Gallwey among its members until February 1864 when he was appointed to lead the mission to the United States) 'to consider and report on the use which may be made of Floating Obstructions and Submarine Explosive Machines in the Defence of Channels'. The first Chairman of the Committee was Rear Admiral Wellesley of the Royal Navy, but he was succeeded in 1865 by Colonel William H. Askwith of the Royal Artillery.[111] The first report produced under Askwith's direction was for the production of 'extemporised torpedoes' with simple mechanical fuses much as seen in the Confederacy, the use of which was proposed for the defence of colonial harbours including those in Bermuda and Australia. This was followed up by two much more substantial documents, one into the use of 'passive' obstructions such as booms, and the other into 'active' obstructions which covered both moored torpedoes and those designed to be attached to vessels. Later, in 1870, a second committee was established to determine the most effective technology for the defence of harbours, and in particular the use of electrical firing.[112]

The use of floating obstructions was not an American innovation. The reports described how the British had encountered Russian 'infernal machines' at Cronstadt [*sic*], Sveaborg, and Sebastopol in 1854. Since then the Russians, Austrians, Prussians, and others had also experimented with their own devices, for example Gallwey's report includes a description of a Russian electrically fired torpedo which was obtained from a Norwegian officer visiting America. By the end of the decade the European powers had made significant improvements on the primitive contact mines developed by the Confederacy. However, while British interest cannot be said to have been driven entirely by their use in America, the observations in 1864 clearly contributed. None of the contemporary European wars since 1854 had involved any extensive combined

---

110 WO 33/17A/0297, p.10.
111 WO 33/14/0229, Gallwey Report pp.29-31; TNA, WO 33/19/0305, *Report on Passive Obstructions For The Defence Of Harbours And Channels, by the Committee on Floating Obstructions and Submarine Explosive Machines* (1866), Memorandum from Edward Lugard to Rear Admiral Wellesley, War Office, 8 September 1863).
112 TNA, WO 33/19/0300, *Memorandum by Floating Obstructions Committee on Extemporizing Torpedoes*, 25 September, 1865; WO 33/19/0305, *Report on Passive Obstructions;* TNA, WO 33/19/0357, *Report on Active Obstructions For The Defence Of Harbours And Channels, Etc., and on the Employment Of Torpedoes For Purposes Of Attack, by the Committee on Floating Obstructions and Submarine Explosive Machines* (London: HMSO, 1868); TNA, WO 279/860, *Report of the Torpedo Committee appointed 29 July 1870 by HRH the Field Marshal Commanding in Chief for the Purpose of Deciding on the Form, Composition and Machinery of Torpedoes.*

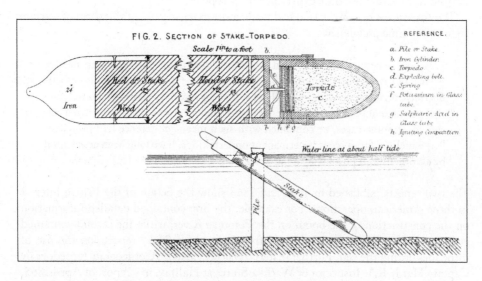

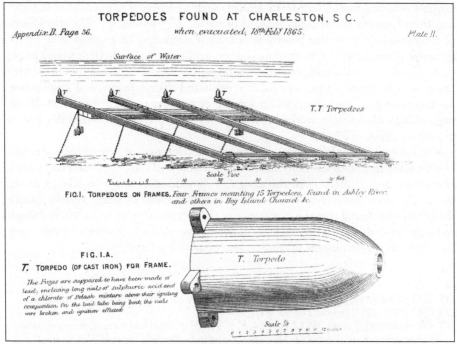

Underwater defences observed at Charleston, from the 1868 report on the defence of harbours. (The National Archives)

operations, so there were fewer lessons, either supportive or contradictive, to be derived from actual wartime experience in Europe.[113]

The Americans by comparison had made more extensive use of this form of warfare than at any time previously.

> It is now generally admitted that we cannot rely upon our sea-going fleet to protect our naval ports, and that these works must be defended by works of fortifications, or, where fixed works will not suffice, by auxiliary floating batteries, and that permanent obstacles and extemporized submarine and floating obstructions should, in some cases, be combined with such means of defence [...] principles [...] which, so far as regards permanent undertakings, have long been acted upon by all other naval powers; by none to a greater extent than the United States.[114]

The two reports published in 1866 and 1868 show the extent of the British interest in those American operations. For example, the first contained detailed information on the construction of the boom on the Potomac River, while the second contained even more extensive material derived from official US Navy reports on the use of torpedoes during the war. Further material was provided on Confederate torpedoes by Captain Hardy RA, Inspector of Warlike Stores at Halifax, in a report of April 1865, possibly obtained from Confederate émigrés seeking refuge in Canada after the war; and from Captain E. Harding Steward of the Royal Engineers.[115] The conclusions of the committee were that passive obstructions needed to be guarded from attack by active defences in the form of torpedoes, artillery, floating batteries, and patrol boats. On the tactical use of active obstructions, the committee found that these were 'most invaluable auxiliaries to permanent coast and river-defences, and as affording the means of defending positions on a coast, or small channels or rivers, which are unprovided with defensive works' but were most effective 'if bought to bear as adjuncts to artillery defences'.[116]

When it came to making decisions about the development of new weapons though, as with other technologies, experimentation at home still comprised the main source of evidence and opinion. Even the design of something as simple as a boom could be rapidly made obsolete by the increased size and speed of steam vessels. Hence the committee 'found that the experience of the recent civil war in America, though certainly favourable to the employment of booms as a defensive expedient, throws very little light on the best means of constructing or applying them'.[117]

---

113 WO 33/19/0357, pp.viii, x, xxvii, 8, 15, 17; WO 33/14/0229, Gallwey Report, pp.29-31.
114 WO 33/15/0257, Jervois, *Defence of Canada*, p.36.
115 WO 33/19/0357 citing WO Letter 84, H 678 (4 May 1865) and Committee on Floating Obstructions Report dated 26 May 1865, Captain E. Harding Steward 'Notes on Submarine Mines', all cited in WO 33/19/0357, pp.44, 21.
116 WO 33/19/0305, pp.ix, xii; WO 33/19/0357, pp.xi-xii.
117 WO 33/19/0305, pp.v-vi.

An important recommendation to come out of the Committee's work was the establishment of regular torpedo training classes, open to both the Army and the Navy, at the School of Military Engineering in Chatham. The first such course had been run in the summer of 1867, in particular drawing from previous experience of field telegraphy and the electronic detonation of mines. The Army also arranged for the training of Royal Navy personnel in torpedo service at the Chemical Department in Woolwich during 1867. The advent of torpedoes did not introduce a new mission or a new organisational structure into the Army, but there was an institutional response indicating willingness to adopt new technology when demonstrated to be necessary.[118]

*   *   *

In the case of small arms, which at this time also came under the direction of the Ordnance Select Committee, there is also nothing to suggest that the readiness to adopt new technology was substantially more advanced in America than in Britain during this period. The American War Department had advocated adopting breech-loaders in December 1860, but by the same year the British already had breech-loading carbines in service. The American Sharps carbines had been tested at Hythe as early as February 1855, and following trials with the East Kent Mounted Rifles, a yeomanry regiment, 6,000 had been ordered. These were issued to five regular cavalry regiments, and some saw service during the Indian Mutiny in 1857-58. Later the British Terry carbine was issued to the 18th Hussars, and a further three regiments received the British Westley-Richards carbine in 1861. The infantry was slower to adopt breechloading, but converting the Enfield rifle to a breech loader was considered as early as April 1861, and the British were actively experimenting to determine for infantry weapons the relative merits of different rifling systems, a smaller bore size, and breech-loading against muzzle-loading. These experiments were much more significant in British decision making than observation of the American conflict, which was largely fought with weapons no better than those in service with the British Army.[119]

The success of the Prussian breech-loading Dreyse rifle against muzzle-loader armed troops in the Prusso-Danish War of 1864, as well as the introduction of breech-loaders by several smaller European countries, was further reason for action. In June 1864 a special committee was set up to consider the general adoption of breech-loaders. One

118 WO 33/19/0357, pp.xli-xlii.
119 C.H. Roads, *The British Soldier's Firearm 1850-1864* (London: Herbert Jenkins 1864), pp.276-298; Clayton R. Newell and Charles R. Schrader, *Of Duty Well and Faithfully Done: A History of the Regular Army in the Civil War* (Lincoln: University of Nebraska, 2011), p20; D.W. Bailey, *British Military Longarms 1715-1865* (New York, London: Sydney: Arms and Armour Press, 1986), pp.107-08, 136; Forbes, *History of the Army Ordnance Services*, Vol.II, p.111; WO 33/12/0186, pp.548-52. WO 33/14/0234, p.424 records that cavalry officers considered the Westley-Richards carbine an excellent weapon.

of the appendices to the committee's report was the observations of Gallwey's mission
to the United States. The committee was informed that there were 63 different kinds
of muzzle-loading muskets (a term which encompassed rifled as well as smoothbore
arms) in service in the Union army, compared to seven breech-loaders (although for
carbines the ratio was six to 17). While the exact numbers had not been ascertained,
'by far the larger portion of the infantry are armed with muzzle-loaders', but breech-
loaders were favourably regarded for use by selected troops. In particular the observers
had spoken to a number of American officers who had experience of breech-loading
firearms, including the use of the Spencer repeating rifle at the Battle of Olustee in
Florida in February 1864. This rather obscure action in February 1864 was given as an
example because it formed part of the operations of Major General Gillmore's Army
of the South based at Charleston, which had been visited by the British observers in
March that year.[120]

While the effectiveness of the Spencer was acknowledged, Brigadier General
Seymour, commanding at Olustee, was reported by Gallwey as believing that breech-
loading weapons should be allocated only to specialist or flank companies, and in
favour of the rest of the infantry being armed with smoothbore muskets.[121] Arming
specialist companies of more highly skilled and trained men with the best available
weapons was common practice in both Confederate and Union armies, was remarked
upon in the latter by Ross, and has been confirmed by modern research – although
Sherman wrote that in practice there was no real distinction between the flank companies and the rest of the regiment. When 4,000 breech-loading rifles were purchased
in America by the Canadian authorities in 1866 to defend against the Fenian incur-
sions, they appear to have been allocated to specialist companies in this way.[122] Some
modern opinion has also defended the retention of smoothbore small-arms during the
Civil War. Like the short range firepower of the Napoleon cannon, 'buck and ball'
(a combination of smoothbore musket ball and several smaller .30 calibre buckshot
pellets) was a lethal combination at close range, while the smoothbore musket did not
require as accurate aiming as the new rifles. Furthermore the heavily wooded terrain

120 The first-hand account by Major General Rawley (USV) in *Battles and Leaders*, Vol.IV,
     pp.79-80 confirms the use of Spencer carbines, but in spite of this the result was a Federal
     defeat – attributed to the Confederates 'having the great advantage, with modern weapons,
     of being on the defensive and ready'.
121 TNA, WO 33/17B, *Report on Arming of infantry with Breach Loading Rifles* (1864),
     pp.6-7; WO 33/14/0229, Gallwey Report, pp.58-59. Luvaas mentioned the favourable
     observations on the Spencer rifle, but not the more conservative aspects of the evidence,
     including General Seymour's view that the remainder of the infantry should be armed
     with smooth bore muskets, Luvaas, *Military Legacy*, p.45.
122 Ross, *Visit*, p.155; Nosworthy, *The Bloody Crucible of Courage*, pp.185-86; General William
     Tecumseh Sherman (USA), *Memoirs*, 2 vols (New York: Appleton, 1875), Vol.II, p.384; Sir
     John William Fortescue, *A History of the British Army*, 13 vols (London: Macmillan, 1899-
     1930), Vol.XIII (1930), p.548; Fryer, *Battlefields of Canada*, p.215.

encountered on many American battlefields meant that the greater range of the rifled musket could not always be made to tell.[123]

The decision of the committee after only four sessions to recommend unequivocally the adoption of breech-loading arms universally and immediately throughout the service demonstrates that the British were not averse to taking bold technology decisions when the evidence showed it necessary. The details of the recommendation and the way in which it was implemented are worth considering, as they shed light on the overall status of breech-loading technology at the time and on the British military system. The recommendation for universal use was not accompanied by any preference for any specific technical solution, of which there were many at the time, but it did recommend that the transition to a breech-loading arm should be accomplished as soon as possible, while investigating the adoption of the 'most perfect arm for the infantry' following a more exhaustive experimentation and selection process.[124]

The first stage was achieved through conversion of large numbers of the standard muzzle-loading Enfield rifle to breech-loaders through application of the Snider breech-loading mechanism. While this short term expedient was applied, the British experimented with, and debated the characteristics of, a purpose-designed breech-loader (the Martini-Henry, itself a combination of technologies from different suppliers, being the chosen weapon). The idea that the British after 1866 or 1870 were enthralled by all things Prussian is not born out by the rejection of the Prussian needle-gun mechanism, an obvious 'off the shelf' solution, as being an inferior system not suitable for British service. Equally the British did not look to America for such a solution. This was due in part to poor experience with the Sharps carbine used by the British cavalry, which demonstrated a significant escape of gas from the breech (the rim-fired metallic cartridge being part of the cause for this), and American weapons were in general seen as being applied 'experimentally' for military use.[125]

Also worth noting is that although the British adopted a single-shot weapon in the Martini-Henry, the invitation to tender proposals for the new breech-loading weapon did not preclude the adoption of a repeating arm.[126] The Ordnance Select Committee

123 Nosworthy, *The Bloody Crucible of Courage*, pp.373-77; Earl J. Hess, *The Rifle Musket in Civil War Combat: Reality and Myth* (Lawrence: University of Kansas, 2008), pp.58-59; Griffith, *Rally Once Again*, pp.145-50.

124 TNA, WO 33/15/0242, *Report of Ordnance Select Committee on various plans of Breech-Loading Small Arms Submitted between 1859 and 1864*, Memorandum by Earl de Grey, 1st August 1864; Captain V.D. Majendie RA, 'Military Breech-Loading Small Arms', *Journal of the Royal United Service Institution*, 11 (1867), pp.190-217 (p.195).

125 Majendie, 'Military Breech-Loading Small Arms', pp.192-96; Captain J.H. Selwyn RN, 'Breech-Loaders, with Reference to Calibre, Supply and Cost of Ammunition', *Journal of the Royal United Service Institution*, 11 (1867), pp.16-26 (p.19).

126 War Office Notice, 22 October 1866: 'To Gunmakers and others. The Secretary of State for War is desirous of receiving proposals from gunmakers and others for breech-loading rifles, either repeating or not repeating, which may replace the present service rifles in future manufacture.' Selwyn, 'Breech-Loaders', p.16.

had obtained a specimen of the Spencer repeating rifle in June 1864 and had conducted a trial. It was considered to be ingenious and to work well, but the recommendation was made not to proceed further. This was partly because of its weight, partly because it was thought liable to rust, and partly because it was inferior in precision to the Westley-Richards, but primarily because the ammunition contained its own means of ignition. At the time it was a fundamental axiom in British military practice that cartridges containing their own ignition were not admissible for military use. The belief was that such cartridges were more liable to accidental explosion in storage, and that the explosion of a single cartridge would cause a chain reaction throughout the stored barrels of ammunition. This was not evidence of a uniquely British conservatism, as the balance of American and other foreign opinion also favoured keeping the fulminate priming charge separate from the cartridge (the exception was Prussia, where the paper cartridge used in the needle-gun contained its own fulminate). It was not any act of war but investigation into the cause of a gunpowder magazine explosion that occurred at Erith near Woolwich on 1 October 1864 which gave rise to experiments on the liability of cartridges (in this case the ordinary muzzle-loading Enfield rifle cartridge) to explode in bulk. When it was established by experimentation that the explosion of a single cartridge would not result in a general explosion, the British were subsequently quick to adopt the metallic cartridge which had already become the standard in American use.[127]

Safety concerns continued to be a contributing factor to the debate over the adoption of magazine rifles. After self-igniting ammunition was accepted, the British would still not countenance systems where the cartridges were held end to end, rather than side by side in a clip. These systems were also believed to required lighter, and therefore weaker, cartridges This view was apparently endorsed when trials with a Winchester rifle resulted in a magazine explosion in 1880. 'Health and Safety' could of course have been an excuse to justify inherent conservative tendencies, but these opinions demonstrate that the debate over the new rifle technology was more complex than has sometimes been suggested, and the technical factors cannot be dismissed. Weapons such as the Spencer are generally held to have had a significant effect on the conduct of the Civil War, but contemporary opinions of their technical superiority were varied.[128]

---

127   WO 33/14/0230, pp.345-46; WO 33/14/0234, p.523; Majendie, 'Military Breech-Loading Small Arms', p.193-94; General William H. Morris (USA) 'On the Best Method of Arming, Equipping and Manoeuvring Infantry', lecture delivered at the Royal United Service Institution 20 April 1866, *Journal of the Royal United Service Institution*, 10 (1866), pp.209-24 (p.215); Captain J. O'Hea, 'Cartridges for Breech-Loading Small Arms, and the Best Form of Projectile', lecture delivered at the Royal United Service Institution 16 March 1868, *Journal of the Royal United Service Institution*, 12 (1868), pp.105-26 (p.107).

128   TNA, SUPP 5/908, 'Trials of Magazine Rifles in England from 1879', Memorandum by Colonel C.G. Slade, dated 13 January 1887, published by War Office 7 February 1887; Colonel Sir Henry St John Halford, *New Service Magazine Rifle, Lecture to Aldershot Military Society, Thursday 2 February 1888* (Aldershot: Aldershot Military Society, 1888).

The following two passages illustrate that even supporters of the breech-loading revolution had mixed views on the suitability of repeating firearms at this time for general service.

[Magazine rifles] though very attractive to the uninitiated, are not capable of giving more rapid fire in the long run than an ordinary breech-loader which, like many of these, will fire 16 or 17 shots per minute. It is only where combined with a power of loading and firing single shots, that the magazine becomes of practical utility, and even here as the weight is constantly varying – and would be excessive in a full-sized infantry arm – the conditions are not favourable to accurate shooting. Add to this, that the dust storm would here be especially dangerous, and I think it will be evident that however applicable it may be for cavalry and artillery the magazine gun does not yet take rank as a serviceable weapon for infantry.[129]

The direction in which repeaters generally err, is in complexity of construction; but if this defect can be overcome, a magazine-rifle would present immense advantages over the simple breech-loader, not merely for those services, such as the navy, the cavalry and artillery, in which an intensely rapid fire is generally required for a few decisive moments, but for the universal equipment of troops. It is in arms of this class, that breech-loading tends towards its highest development; and to this principle of action I believe we must look for the ultimate solution of the breech-loading question.[130]

The author of the first passage may have shown bias as he had his own design of single-shot rifle to promote, but the second comes from Captain V.D. Majendie, the Assistant Superintendent of the Royal Laboratory at Woolwich, and shows that the British military establishment was not fundamentally opposed to the magazine rifle.

129 Selwyn, 'Breech-Loaders', p.21. The view on comparative rates of fire was to some extent upheld by trials, though Selwyn overstated the rates of fire achievable with single shot weapons unless handled by very well trained troops. The British trial of the Spencer rifle in 1865 concluded that the total time to fire seven shots was one minute 15 seconds – 55 seconds to load the magazine and 20 seconds to fire it (WO 33/13/0230, p.346). The average rate of fire achieved using single shot breech-loaders by six men of the Scots Fusilier Guards during comparative trials with the Gatling gun in August 1870 were approximately eight rounds per minute with the converted Snider and 12 per minute with the new Martini-Henry rifle (average per rifleman per minute from three firings of two minutes each). The maximum achieved in two minutes with the Snider was 19 shots, and with the Martini-Henry 30 shots. WO 33/22/0454, pp.7-8. The problem of balance was also noted by Colonel Halford, *New Service Magazine Rifle*, p.6.
130 Majendie, 'Military Breech-Loading Small Arms', p.204.

Concern over the firing away of ammunition is sometimes cited as the major reason for the delay in adopting breech-loading or repeating small-arms.[131] Amongst those like Majendie who were actually involved in evaluating the technology, such arguments clearly did not prevail. Fire discipline had always been essential to prevent wasted ammunition, and would continue to be necessary. Once a solution was available that overcame the balance problem and also allowed single-shot firing, officers were conscious that it would 'be very demoralising to troops to feel they only have a single shooter when their enemy has a rifle that will fire some eight or nine shots' – feelings which Confederate troops must have had when facing the seven-shot Spencer when armed only with muzzle-loaders.[132] Although emphasizing that when using aimed fire it was not possible to get off more than two or three rounds per minute more than with a single shot breech-loader, and that magazine fire should only be allowed at close quarters, at critical moments the tactical advantage of an eight shot magazine that could be fired in less than half the time of a single-loader was clear.[133]

The British approach in the years after the adoption of the breech-loader was therefore to monitor and experiment with advances in magazine technology, but not to rush into the premature re-arming of the majority of its troops with what were considered to be insufficiently proven weapons. In a time of crisis, Britain's superiority in manufacturing capacity was relied upon to remove any technology deficit in an acceptable period of time. In the strategic situation of the late 19th Century, with no immediate military threat from a technically superior rival, and financial constraints on army expenditure, this was an understandable policy. It mirrors the American policy of favouring proven, simpler to operate, weapons in preference to advanced technologies that were difficult to maintain in the field, and it is worth noting that the universal adoption of breech-loaders was not formally recommended by the US War Department until almost the end of the Civil War, on 1 March 1865 – after the equivalent decision had been made in Britain. The Americans also adopted the approach of converting their existing stocks of muzzle-loaders to breech-loaders, and retained single shot arms for general use until 1892.[134]

* * *

Artillery, fortifications, and small arms were all traditional military technologies, and even torpedoes had clear military antecedents. A further feature of the period was the growing importance and application of civilian devices in warfare. Of particular significance, given the increasing size of armies and distances on the battlefield, were

---

131 Nosworthy, *The Bloody Crucible of Courage*, pp.60, 610-11; Luvaas, *Military Legacy*, p.73; Craddock, 'The American Civil War and its Influence on the British Army', pp.156, 172.
132 Halford, *New Service Magazine Rifle*, p.6.
133 Halford, *New Service Magazine Rifle*, pp.6-7.
134 Nosworthy, *The Bloody Crucible of Courage*, p.628; Gregory J.W. Urwin, *The United States Infantry: An Illustrated History* (London: Blandford, 1988), pp.121, 134.

those associated with signals and communications. Although the American Civil War is sometimes credited with the first military telegraph, the British were actually the first to make use of this technology in the trenches in the Crimea. During the Indian Mutiny telegraph wires were laid as the army advanced and even onto the battlefield (Wolseley claimed to have seen workmen 'laying it actually under a fire of canister'), and in 1862 it had been formally adopted by the British as part of the Engineer Field Equipment.[135] Its use in America reinforced its importance, and in 1864 a committee was set up in to review 'the whole question of ARMY SIGNALS AND TELEGRAPHY' [sic]. Included in its deliberations was the examination of Lieutenant Sir Arthur Mackworth RE, who had visited the United States in 1864, and who gave detailed information on the signals organisation and equipment of the American armies. The evidence from Mackworth that was published in the report was not about the new electronic telegraph however, but around more traditional methods in use in America, and about the organisation of their Signal Corps.[136] The Committee's recommendations, published in December 1865, included the establishment of a separate electric telegraph branch, as well as the adoption of portable signalling apparatus comprising a system of flags and torches 'as used by the American armies during the late war' for when obstacles or time prevented the laying down of a telegraph wire. In order to operate the telegraph, a body of trained operators to maintain the lines and signal stations would be needed, who would need to be mounted and supplied with suitable transport when in the field.[137] It was however the Franco-Prussian War that finally spurred the creation of a separate telegraph troop.[138]

'A careful study of the late wars in America and Bohemia will give the student an idea of its immense value in military operations' wrote Wolseley regarding the telegraph in the *Soldier's Pocket Book* a few years later.[139] He also recommended a number of tricks that had been used in America related to the telegraph, including the tapping of wires to read enemy communication, which was capable of obtaining more news than could be done from traditional spies, and misleading the enemy by sending false information, a tactic particularly recommended by Wolseley for the cavalry advance

---

135 Captain Schaw RE, 'Military Telegraphs', *R.E. Professional Papers*, 11 (1862), pp.111-24 (pp.114-16); Wolseley, *Soldier's Pocket Book*, pp.316-17; Captain R.H. Stothard, 'The Electric Telegraph and Visual Signalling in Connection with Future Military Operations', *R.E. Professional Papers*, 18 (1870), pp.100-106 (p.100).

136 TNA, WO 33/15/0268, *Report of Committee on Signals and Telegraphy* (1865), pp.14-15. Capitalisation in the original. Mackworth inherited his baronetcy in 1857. His service record shows him as making lieutenant on 1 July 1861 and serving at Chatham throughout the Civil War. His time in America therefore seems to have been during a month's leave from 13 January to 14 February 1864. He was only 21 years old at the time. WO 25/3913, military service record of Sir Arthur Mackworth.

137 WO 33/15/0268, pp.3-5.

138 Porter, *History of the Corps of Royal Engineers*, Vol.II, p.120. Wolseley, *Soldier's Pocket Book*, p.317.

139 Wolseley, *Soldier's Pocket Book*, p.317

guard in emulation of the Confederates. Wolseley advised officers to be discrete in revealing their plans and to use ciphers to counter these tactics.[140]

Wolseley also proffered some more general views on the adoption of technology which are worthy of note, as they relate directly to his belief that the Civil War was a source of valuable information. The following appeared in a series of articles that he wrote about the war in the *North American Review*.

> It is never very safe, however, to assume that anything will take place in war precisely as the result of peace trials would lead one to believe. It would be no good reason, however, for refusing to adopt new plans or novel inventions in our next war because they have not been tried and found to answer well in some former one. To act upon such a principle would be to handicap very heavily the nation that adopts it. It would be to hand over many great advantages to a more courageous, a more intelligent, and a more enterprising enemy. But it is only possible safely and usefully to apply the results of peace experiments to war preparations by studying as closely as we can the experience with which past wars supply us.[141]

* * *

There was during this period a constant re-evaluation of technology and the strengths of the offense and defence, particularly regarding the balance between ships and forts, which was critical to British security at home. The American Civil War was only one of a large number of inputs into the decision making progress, the others being technical trials, commercial propositions, other foreign intelligence, and the actions of British forces overseas. The fact that Luvaas found no 'concrete evidence that the several reports on the arms and the equipment of the Union army induced the British to make changes in their own matériel' is for the very good reason that the overall conclusion the British drew from the American war was that there was nothing in the technology used that was particularly new or superior.[142] Many technologies often claimed as 'firsts' for the American Civil War such as torpedoes, the telegraph, and railway guns, had actual or theoretical precedents, and the British reaction to their use in America was to conduct reasoned evaluations and then utilise the technologies as appropriate.

To an extent, the British imitated the American establishment's drive for simplicity, which was appropriate for an army whose equipment needed to function in a wide range of climates and physical conditions. An example is the apparently retrograde

---

140 Wolseley, *Soldier's Pocket Book*, pp.81-82, 140. By contrast the American military writer Arthur Wagner criticised the use of the telegraph in the Austro-Prussian War, citing Hamley, Grant and Sherman to this effect. Wagner, *The Campaign of Königgrätz*, p.98.
141 Wolseley, 'English View', pp.594-96.
142 Luvaas, *Military Legacy*, p.45.

decision to revert to muzzle-loading artillery while the Prussians and others were adopting breech-loading technology, which has a parallel in the American preference for the Napoleon smoothbore. The British and American experience with the more advanced weapons in the 1860s had been that whatever their advantages on the proving ground, they did not stand up to the trials of campaign, and this caution, rather than any innate technical conservatism, informed many decisions over technologies as diverse as artillery, magazine rifles, and electrically detonated torpedoes. At the same time the British were on occasion prepared to make bold decisions such as the rapid adoption of the breech-loading rifle, and the adoption of the machine gun even when its actual effectiveness in battle had been questionable.

The majority of the arms used by the American armies were technically obsolescent or even obsolete in a European context by 1865, and a large proportion of the high technology weapons such as breech-loading artillery were imported weapons. When the Americans adopted low technology expedients on the grounds of cost, appropriateness, and simplicity it was explicitly recognised, and not criticised, by the British. What they also recognised was American ingenuity where it mattered, whether in 'high-tech' innovation such as the Spencer rifle, 'mid-tech' developments such as iron gun carriages, or 'low-tech' expedients such as wire entanglements and explosive torpedoes. The American war did not constitute a revolutionary technical watershed that the British failed to see, but its innovation did contribute to the ongoing process of reviewing and adopting new technologies.

4

Tradition versus Technology – The Cavalry

The most significant departure of American military practice in the Civil War from that of contemporary Europe was in the use of cavalry. The key tactical question of the day was the adoption of fire tactics by the mounted arm, and Luvaas considered those adopted by the Americans as both revolutionary and largely ignored by the British establishment. In his view the American armies, recognising the superiority of the new firepower and the impossibility of mounted shock action, developed a new kind of cavalry force that dismounted to make itself effective tactically, and adopted a new strategy of independent action to threaten the enemy's line of communication. In contrast he portrayed European cavalry as remaining fixated with outmoded shock tactics using sword and lance – the *arme blanche* – and to a battlefield role that limited its strategic mobility.[1] In Luvaas' account a few early British visionaries were recognised as having understood the American methods, notably Henry Havelock and George Denison, but they were portrayed as 'maverick' outsiders, and were said to have been ignored by the establishment.[2]

Luvaas' views on the cavalry were strongly influenced by Liddell Hart, who had portrayed British cavalry officers not only as reactionaries devoted to the charge but also in great part responsible for the futile offensive tactics of the First World War, and in the words of Gervase Phillips made them a scapegoat for the British war dead.[3] This is a view that while challenged by some academics remains the popular perception to this day. Even the British cavalry's best known modern historian, the Marquess of Anglesey, otherwise inclined to support the reputation of the mounted

---

1 The French term *arme blanche* (literally 'white weapon') refers to any weapon whose application is only through human force, and not through an explosion. <(http://fr.wikipedia.org/wiki/Arme_blanche>; <http://en.wikipedia.org/wiki/Cold_weapon>.
2 Luvaas, *Military Legacy*, pp.108-15, 232, on which Luvaas identifies Liddell Hart as another such outsider. Preston, 'Military Lessons of the American Civil War', p.234, suggested Denison was ignored in part because he was a provincial soldier.
3 Gervase Phillips, 'Scapegoat Arm: 20th Century Cavalry in Anglophone Historiography', *Journal of Military History*, 71 (2007), pp.37-74, (pp.57, 62-63).

arm, has followed this argument, and some have been even more critical than Luvaas of the British cavalry establishment.[4] As a result the British are generally portrayed as entering the war in South Africa in 1899 with an archaic concept of cavalry action. The case is exemplified by the charge of the 21st Lancers at Omdurman in the Sudan in 1898, and by the failure of the British cavalry to defeat a fraction of their numbers of Boers in South Africa.[5] However, as with other aspects of the British learning experience from the American war, the story is more complex.

Other studies have reviewed the contemporary *arme blanche* controversy in some depth and challenged Luvaas conclusions, particularly with respect to the role of cavalry in the First World War, so this will not be reconsidered in detail here.[6] Nevertheless, in any full assessment of how the British learnt from the Civil War the cavalry lessons must be considered. This chapter looks at how the British saw the nature of the mounted forces raised in America; and what they learnt or failed to appreciate from the tactical use of cavalry in the Civil War, both dismounted and mounted; and from their strategic role. It will look at how European, American, and British experience drove the debate, and will demonstrate that American lessons were adopted in British practice to an extent not previously acknowledged.

* * *

Much of the heat of the 19th Century debate seems to have revolved around military name-calling. Traditionally, cavalry had always been regarded as an offensive arm relying upon shock tactics, speed, and *morale* to defeat the enemy. This offensive tradition could be traced back through the armies of Napoleon, Frederick the Great, and Gustavus Adolphus to the medieval knight and even further.[7] Implicit in this tradition was a reliance on mounted action using the sword or the lance as a

---

4   Marquis of Anglesey, *A History of the British Cavalry: Vol. 2 1851-1871* (Barnsley: Pen and Sword, 1998, originally published London: Leo Cooper, 1975), p.452, *Vol. 3 1872-1898* (Barnsley: Pen and Sword, 2004, originally published London: Leo Cooper, 1982), pp.406-07; Brian Bond, 'Doctrine and Training in the British Cavalry, 1870–1914' in *The Theory and Practice of War: Essays Presented to Captain B H Liddell Hart*, ed. Michael Howard (London: Cassell, 1965), pp.97-125 (p.98) (Bond's reference is Luvaas' *Military Legacy)*; Gerard J. De Groot, *Douglas Haig 1861-1928* (London: Unwin Hyman, 1988), pp.30-31. Anglesey was influenced by Bond, to whom his third volume is dedicated.

5   Preston, 'Military Lessons of the American Civil War', pp.234-35; Craddock, 'The American Civil War and its Influence on the British Army', pp.69-83, 219-25, 255-56, 291-92, 294.

6   Stephen Badsey, 'Fire and the Sword: the British Army and Arme Blanche Controversy 1871-1921', (PhD Thesis, University of Cambridge, 1982), together with his more recent book *Doctrine and Reform in the British Cavalry 1880-1918* (Aldershot: Ashgate, 2008) remains the keystone for historical discussion on the subject. See also Badsey 'The Boer War and British Cavalry Doctrine'.

7   Denison's *History of Cavalry*, originally written as an entry in a competition sponsored by the Tsar of Russia, traced the history of cavalry back to the days of the chariot. Lieutenant

primary weapon. Alongside this purely offensive arm, many armies in history had given mounts to troops who normally fought on foot in order to make them more mobile, as mounted infantry. Complicating the terminology further was a third tradition of light horsemen, who fought mounted and performed some of the functions of cavalry but who used firepower rather than edged weapons as their main arm. In the 19th Century such troops were termed 'mounted rifles', a term applied both in the US and British service.[8] Unfortunately this term was so close to that of 'mounted infantry' that the two often became synonymous in the debate.[9] As a result, the discussion on how mounted troops should be trained, armed, and used became not just a technical or tactical matter, but an emotive one which at times appeared to threaten the traditions and even the very existence of an entire arm of the service.

Were the Americans 'merely mounted infantry', as Edward Hewett had described them in 1862, or a new breed of cavalry? For Wolseley, they were most definitely mounted infantry, even if the Americans did have a high regard for their 'cavalry'. Wolseley wrote of Bedford Forrest, the most well-known Confederate cavalry leader in the western theatre, that he was a leader of 'dragoons'. This term was not meant by Wolseley as derogatory; but was used in its original technical sense based upon the sound military precedent of the dragoons of the 17th and 18th Centuries, whose primary weapon was the dragoon musket, but who were mounted to give them mobility in battle.[10] Nor did he consider the Americans inferior in the circumstances to regular cavalry. In Canada Wolseley had served with Major (later Lieutenant Colonel) George Denison who had led a troop of Canadian militia during the Fenian raids of 1866, and who later became a strong supporter of dismounted cavalry tactics. Wolseley's extolled the benefits of these irregular mounted troops in his autobiography. Denison, 'a born cavalry leader', with three

Colonel George T. Denison, *A History of Cavalry: From the Earliest Times, With Lessons for the Future* (London: MacMillan, 1877).

8   The 3rd US Cavalry originally went by the name of Mounted Riflemen, as did many volunteer units raised during the Mexican War, Gregory J.W. Urwin, *The United States Cavalry: an Illustrated History* (Poole: Blandford, 1983), p.89. Irregular cavalry units raised in the British colonies were also named 'mounted rifles'. The most famous, often raised in discussions on the cavalry arm, was probably the Cape Mounted Rifles – which had been formed in 1827 from an Infantry Regiment. <http://www.forces-war-records.co.uk/units/5147/cape-mounted-rifles> [accessed 6 November 2014].

9   See Jean Bou, 'The Evolution and Development of the Australian Light Horse, 1860-1945' (Thesis submitted for the degree of Doctor of Philosophy in the School of Humanities and Social Sciences, University of NSW, 2005), pp.19-20; Jean Bou, *Light Horse: A History of Australia's Mounted Arm* (Cambridge: Cambridge University Press, 2010), pp.ix-xi, 7-8; and Andrew Philip Winrow, 'The British Regular Mounted Infantry 1880 – 1913: Cavalry of Poverty or Victorian Paradigm?' (DPhil Thesis, University of Buckingham, 2014) pp.5-8.

10   This historic description did not apply to the contemporary British dragoon regiments, which were regarded as heavy cavalry in British terminology. Strachan, *From Waterloo to Balaclava*, p.77.

officers and 55 men armed with Spencer carbines, had patrolled 32 miles of frontier, and in Wolseley's opinion 'no similar number of regular cavalry could have done that duty'. In the same way Wolseley thought that no regular cavalry could have done as well as Forrest's scouts.[11]

During the later stages of the Indian Mutiny, Wolseley had seen the British struggle due to a lack of mobility, and he regretted 'that it never occurred to anyone at the time [...] to make use of mounted infantry. That lesson we were to learn four years later from the War of Secession in the United States'.[12] This understates the extent to which the British were already experimenting with mounted infantry during the Mutiny and elsewhere in the Empire, albeit on very ad hoc basis, but it shows the profound influence that his American experiences had on Wolseley's views, as does the following more extensive passage from 1886.[13]

> The first time I saw a large force of mounted infantry in the field it was not counted by companies or by hundreds, but by thousands; that was in America. I there saw the largest force of mounted infantry ever put into the field. They were nominally called cavalry by those who did not know what cavalry were, but they were purely and simply infantry in every way, and armed and drilled as infantry. They had the locomotive power, or a certain amount of the locomotive power of cavalry; the most distinguished of all their leaders was an infantry Officer, General Sheridan. That force of mounted infantry, made such good use of in the American War, was improvised in a very short time, and I am quite sure what was done in America from 1862 [sic] to 1865 could be as well done in this country[.][14]

Wolseley had probably never seen Sheridan's cavalry himself, and was wrong both with regards to their armament (usually a short-barrelled carbine, not a long infantry rifle and bayonet) and in saying that they were drilled as infantry, but this passage typifies the British view of the time. Wolseley himself considered that it took two years to

11   Hewett, in Preston, 'Letter', p.52; Field Marshal Viscount Garnet Joseph Wolseley, 'General Forrest', *United Service Magazine*, n.s., 5 (1892), pp.1-14, 113-24 (pp.1-3); Wolseley, *Story of a Soldier's Life*, Vol.II, pp.148, 163; Lieutenant Colonel George T. Denison, *Soldiering in Canada: Recollections and Experiences*, 2nd Edn (Toronto: George N Morang, 1901), pp.119-20. According to Denison, Wolseley had retained his irregulars in preference to replacing them with a regular regiment, the 13th Hussars, ibid, p.133-34.
12   Wolseley, *Story of a Soldier's Life*, Vol.I, p.361.
13   For early use of mounted infantry see Winrow, 'The British Regular Mounted Infantry', pp.11-12. A more contemporary summary of early experiments is Lieutenant General Sir Frederick Middleton, 'Mounted Infantry', *United Service Magazine*, n.s., 5 (1892), pp.178-84 (p.179-80).
14   Wolseley, speaking at the Royal United Service Institution 2 June 1886 in discussion on a lecture given by Major E.T.H. Hutton, 'Mounted Infantry', *Journal of the Royal United Service Institution*, 30 (1886), pp.695-738, p.736.

convert a civilian into a cavalryman, others allowed for slightly shorter periods, but in all cases it was recognised that cavalry training took time.[15] This was one of the prime reasons given by British authors for the way in which Civil War troopers fought, the other being the limited opportunity for traditional cavalry action in the heavily wooded terrain in which most of the war took place.

> As we all know, in the American Civil War, the so-called cavalry were as a rule little more than infantry on horseback, partly because the nature of the country was wholly unsuited for cavalry proper, and partly because there was neither the time nor the opportunity to give men the training which true cavalry soldiers require.[16]

So it was simply pragmatic, as Captain Ross had recognised in 1863, for the Americans to organise their 'cavalry' as irregular mounted rifles armed with carbines and revolvers. If mobile, mounted forces were to be rapidly raised and trained in wartime these could only be mounted rifles or mounted infantry within the definition of the terms being used. In comparison to the two years required to train a cavalryman there was an example from the Indian Mutiny of 1857 of a mounted infantry regiment, the 300-strong Peshawar Light Horse, being formed and trained in as little as four months.[17]

The first post-war assessment of the American cavalry emerged from this Indian mounted infantry tradition, and was written by Major Henry Havelock in his book *Three Main Military Questions of the Day*, published in 1867.[18] He was the son of Major General Henry Havelock, whose campaigns to raise the sieges of Cawnpore and Lucknow during the Indian Mutiny in 1857 had made him a national hero, and the younger Havelock had himself won the Victoria Cross (VC) as a lieutenant for his gallantry at Cawnpore. During later campaigns in India, in 1858, Havelock had led a force of mounted infantry, as well as briefly commanding Hodson's Horse, a famous

15   Colonel Valentine Baker, formerly 10th Hussars, 'Organisation and Employment of Cavalry', *Journal of the Royal United Service Institution*, 17 (1873), pp.375-410 (p.377); Wolseley, 'General Forrest', p.3; Steinmetz, 'Past and Future of Cavalry', pp.160-61; Lieutenant Colonel Evelyn Wood, *Mounted Riflemen: A Lecture Delivered at the Royal United Service Institution, March 4 1873* (London: W. Mitchell & Co, 1873), p.17.

16   Major Frank S. Russell, 14th Hussars, 'Cavalry', *Journal of the Royal United Service Institution*, 20 (1876), pp.179-95 (p.189).

17   Major S. Boulderson, 17th Lancers, 'The Armament and Organisation of Cavalry and their Influence on its Tactics', lecture delivered at the Royal United Service Institution 5 April 1878, *Journal of the Royal United Service Institution*, 22 (1878), pp.378-96 (p.38). The Peshawar Light Horse were raised by Colonel Francis Augustus Fane (1824–1893) an infantry officer in the 25th Foot. <http://en.wikipedia.org/wiki/Francis_Fane_(soldier)> [accessed 20 October 2014].

18   Major Henry M. Havelock, *Three Main Military Questions of the Day* (London: Spottiswoode, 1867).

Indian cavalry regiment.[19] The three military questions of the title were firstly how to provide an army reserve; secondly how to secure India more economically; and thirdly the impact of breechloading arms on cavalry. Luvaas gave prominence to the third of these, declaring Havelock 'the first English soldier to indorse whole-heartedly the tactics of Civil War cavalry'.[20]

Havelock was certainly damning in his criticism of the British cavalry of 1867. Whereas 'our Artillery leaves little to be desired', and 'our Infantry is almost perfect',

> when we come to the cavalry, we find not only a theory of action, and conse-
> quently of instruction, apparently behind and at variance with the spirit of the
> times, but symptoms, only too evident, of an intention to shut the eyes to the
> manifest direction in which all progress in military practice and art is tending;
> and a determination, which recent events appear to pronounce to be mistaken,
> to adhere to a tactical system that originated in a state of things which has long
> passed away, once and for ever.[21]

This error Havelock attributed to a focus on the purely cavalry actions in Bohemia in 1866 during the Austro-Prussian War, and to reforms that had aligned British practice to that of Austria. Against the obsolete 'charging school' of cavalry, he set the American experience, but also that of recent European conflicts where cavalry had failed in attacks against infantry. It was the general introduction of the rifled musket in the early 1850s, not the Civil War, that had been the 'first great blow given to the supremacy of what we may call a purely 'sabre cavalry'. Havelock described both the stand of the 93rd Highlanders at Balaclava in October 1854 and the failures of the French cavalry in Italy in 1859 to demonstrate this, before going on to analyse the American cavalry, and then the Austro-Prussian war.[22]

At the start of the Civil War, Havelock agreed with the observers that cavalry had been organised upon European lines and of little use. However, 'the apparent inefficiency of Cavalry against rifled arms, which early struck the practical American mind', led the Americans to adopt rifle-fire as their main weapon. In particular Havelock singled out the Union cavalry of 1864-65 for praise. The main feature of their doctrine, and the one which differentiated them from European cavalry, was that they were primarily organised for, and drilled, in the practice of fighting on foot, always where possible from behind cover. At the same time, according to Havelock,

---

19   R.H. Vetch 'Allan, Sir Henry Marshman Havelock-, first baronet (1830-1897)' *Oxford Dictionary of National Biography*, 60 vols (Oxford: Oxford University Press, 2004), Vol.I, pp.753-754 (hereafter DNB); Fortescue, Vol.XIII, p.397-98.
20   Luvaas, *Military Legacy* p.111.
21   Havelock, *Three Main Military Questions*, pp.33-34.
22   Havelock, *Three Main Military Questions*, pp.44-53. Luvaas in *Military Legacy* p.109 represents the quotation (Havelock, p.44) as referring to the Civil War, which is misleading.

they kept mounted supports always ready to hand to attack an exposed flank, either with an opportunistic charge or by creating a destructive cross-fire.

> Troops thus armed, trained, and instructed, were equal to any contingency, and could act upon any sort of ground. Though called Cavalry, they were, in fact, Mounted Riflemen, and the breech-loading or repeating rifle [sic] their principal arm.[23]

Havelock then went on to include an entire chapter describing and analysing Major General Sheridan's pursuit of Lee's army after the fall of Richmond, which he considered to be the finest achievement of the American cavalry and quite beyond anything that European horse would have been capable of.[24]

> [N]o British Cavalry that he [Havelock] has ever been associated with have either the arms, training, equipment, or instruction, to have enabled them, under similar circumstances, to play this part of independent and unsupported self-sufficing action at a distance from the other two arms.[25]

Havelock's treatise had not set out to be an analysis of American cavalry practice. It was an attempt to provide a holistic solution to all three of the military questions he posed, and as such was rooted in specifically British problems. The adoption of the Mounted Riflemen as effectively a new arm in the army – since Havelock intended to retain the traditional cavalry, though they too would be armed with breech-loading rifles – was a key part of this solution. It would improve the efficiency of the Regular cavalry and of the Yeomanry (a part-time reserve force of cavalry raised on a county basis and equivalent to the Militia in the infantry), but more importantly it meant that the army in India could become much more mobile, and this would mean that it would be possible to maintain a smaller garrison there. 'Five thousand picked British "Mounted Riflemen" might literally-ride from one end of India to the other at twenty-five miles a day, carrying all before them.' Havelock proposed that this would allow the release of between 8,000 and 10,000 men from the India garrison, and these men would be added to the home reserves as part of his solution to the first of his three questions. The tactical introduction of Mounted Riflemen would thus have much more widespread impact, 'removing it far from the comparatively low level of mere tactics into the higher fields of politics and statecraft'.[26]

Although Havelock had led cavalry in India for a short period, he was an infantry officer, and it was infantry battalions in India that he proposed to replace with his new

---

23 Havelock, *Three Main Military Questions*, pp.47–48.
24 Havelock, *Three Main Military Questions*, pp.66-114.
25 Havelock, *Three Main Military Questions*, p.79.
26 Luvaas, *Military Legacy*, pp.109-111; Havelock, *Three Main Military Questions*, pp.26-27, 112, 206.

formations. His use of the term 'mounted riflemen' or 'mounted rifles', and its connotations of 'mounted infantry' was therefore problematic in a treatise that dealt in part with cavalry reform. His description of the American practice, with their ability for mounted action, went beyond the concept of mounted infantry, but in addition to the new troops he also referred to the retention of Regular Cavalry, although he proposed that these should also be armed with breech-loading rifles.[27]

The formal manual for the mounted infantry, when it appeared in the 1880s, also included some ambiguity on this matter. On the one hand it made it clear that there was a difference between mounted infantry and cavalry proper: 'It must be distinctly recognised that a Mounted Infantryman fights on foot, and that his horse is intended as a means of placing him with rapidity in some desired or chosen position where he can use his rifle to advantage.'[28] On the other, the limited numbers of true cavalry available to the British meant that the mounted infantryman needed to have 'a good practical knowledge of what is required of mounted men when acting as a covering force to front' and to be trained in reconnoitring, vedette, and outpost duties.[29] A great fear in the British establishment was that permanent bodies of such troops would aspire to become cavalry, and in doing so would become both inferior cavalry and inferior infantry.[30]

Such statements introduced into the debate the politics of regimental and intra-service rivalry. The professional cavalry officer was not necessarily dismissive of mounted infantry when used for certain roles – one noted that many thought highly of them 'judging chiefly from the experiences of the American War'. Yet the same officer also argued that they needed to be thought of as infantry, and could not to be considered as the equal of true cavalry with respect to duties such as reconnaissance, as this was an activity that needed trained horsemen.[31]

Mounted infantry was believed by others to be a valid, essential and potentially battle-winning arm. Sir Edward Bruce Hamley agreed with Havelock on the inability of cavalry to face up to infantry even in small detachments, and on the inability of infantry to move quickly enough in many circumstances.

> Some force which should combine the celerity of cavalry with the formidable fire of infantry would exactly suit the case; and such is to be found in a corps of *mounted riflemen*. [...] For seizing a post or a defile before infantry could arrive there, and which cavalry would be incompetent to hold – for rapidly turning a flank – for executing distant enterprises against communications, – mounted

27   Havelock, *Three Main Military Questions*, p.202.
28   Anon, *Regulations for Mounted Infantry, 1889* (London: HMSO, 1889), p.21.
29   Anon, *Regulations for Mounted Infantry* (1889), p.3.
30   Lieutenant General Sir Edward Bruce Hamley speaking at the Royal United Service Institution, 2 June 1886, in Hutton, 'Mounted Infantry', p.720.
31   Boulderson, 'The Armament and Organisation of Cavalry', p.381.

riflemen seem the inevitable solution of a problem the conditions of which are, speed of movement, with ability to contend with any kind of force.[32]

Hamley believed that the Prussian alternative of arming their cavalry with improved firearms would only produce a less effective and more expensive mounted rifleman. 'Size and weight of man and horse are worse than superfluous where celerity, accuracy of aim, and readiness in obtaining cover, are the requisites.'[33] In contrast, a corps of true mounted riflemen would be 'a force of infinite value, such a force as, if it were in preponderating numbers on the battle-field might well turn the scale of victory'.[34]

Sir Redvers Buller was another infantryman who, like Havelock, had commanded mounted infantry and irregular horse, in his case in South Africa during the Zulu War (1879) where he had also been awarded the VC. Drawing on his experience here and later in the Sudan (1884-85), Buller was positive about the ability of the cavalry but still believed that 'as in the last great war, the value of cavalry was very much more fully recognized, so in the next great war will the value of mounted infantry be the most noticeable feature'.[35] Somewhat ironically, Buller would initially lead that 'next great war', in South Africa, in which his performance would generate immense controversy and ultimately lead to the loss of his reputation.

Probably the most significant proponent of mounted infantry in the British Army was Lieutenant General Edward Hutton, who as a lieutenant colonel became the Commandant of the Mounted Infantry School at Aldershot in 1889.[36] The Civil War featured prominently among his influences: in January 1891 as a member of the audience at a lecture on cavalry Hutton expressed astonishment that the speaker had not mentioned the use of cavalry in that war.[37] In an article in 1895 he made it clear that he viewed the American Civil War as a significant break from previous cavalry traditions.

> The reason for the success of such leaders as Stuart, Grierson, Forrest, Sheridan and others is yet not far to seek. It was that, unfettered by traditions of the past, the Americans armed their Cavalry with a repeating rifle [sic], and developed

---

32   Major General Edward Bruce Hamley, *The Operations of War Explained and Illustrated*, 4th edn (Edinburgh and London: W. Blackwood, 1878, originally published 1866), p.439, original italics. The text was introduced in the 1873 edition. Hereafter all references are to 4th edition unless otherwise noted.
33   Hamley, *Operations of War*, p.439.
34   Lieutenant General Edward Bruce Hamley, speaking at the Royal United Service Institute, 2 June 1886 in discussion on Hutton, 'Mounted Infantry', p.720.
35   Major General Sir Redvers Buller, Hutton, 'Mounted Infantry', p.723.
36   Winrow, 'The British Regular Mounted Infantry', pp.3, 12 (footnote), 426.
37   Major W.C. James, *The Development of Modern Cavalry Action in the Field, Lecture to Aldershot Military Society, Thursday January 8 1891* (Aldershot: Gale and Polden, [1891]), pp.27-28.

their power of independent action in a manner which has not hitherto been equalled in modern times.[38]

Hutton believed that the European powers had overlooked the Civil War. 'What nation has such a record to show as these great strategic feats, successfully achieved by masses of mounted troops'[39] In his view Americans were superior to the Prussians in understanding the importance of rifle fire for mounted troops. His ideas on mounted infantry were also clearly influenced by Havelock's *Three Main Military Questions of the Day*, which 'read by the light of our present development of military expediency in this respect, reads almost like a prophecy'.[40]

Hutton, an infantryman from the King's Royal Rifle Corps, was usually careful to differentiate between mounted infantry and mounted rifles and to insist upon distinct roles. The former, he declared, were infantry pure and simple, but using rapid means of transportation (such as horses, camels, carts, or bicycles) for mobility. Their tactics should be those of infantry on an extended scale, and they should not be equipped with swords, or with other cavalry accoutrements such as boots and spurs. Mounted rifles he described as horsemen trained to fight on foot, and to perform all the duties of cavalry except 'the shock'. Mounted infantry could be indifferent horsemen, whereas mounted rifles had to be good riders.[41]

> [W]e shall find, if we only put it to the test, that this country can furnish as numerous and as efficient a body of improvised mounted troops, organized and drilled as mounted infantry, with equal if not greater facility than did the Americans in 1862-64 [*sic*].[42]

Contemporary defenders of the American horse soldiers who claimed that they were true cavalry did so by arguing that they had in fact carried out mounted action. The Prussian veteran Heros von Borcke claimed that Stuart's cavalry had been obliged

38   Major General Hutton, 'The Tactical and Strategic Power of Mounted Troops in War', *United Service Magazine*, n.s., 10 (1895), pp.431-49 (p.438). Paper read before New South Wales United Service Institution, Sydney, 28 August 1894. Like Wolseley, Hutton was wrong to say that the American cavalry were armed with a repeating rifle, they normally carried the Spencer repeating *carbine*, a cavalry rather than an infantry firearm.
39   Hutton, 'Mounted Troops in War', p.439.
40   Major E.T.H. Hutton, *Mounted Infantry its Present and Future: Lecture to Aldershot Military Society, Thursday March 21 1889* (Aldershot: Gale and Polden, 1889), p.6.
41   Hutton, *Mounted Infantry its Present and Future*, pp.3, 7, 17; Hutton, 'Mounted Infantry', pp.701-703; Lieutenant Colonel E.T.H. Hutton, 'The Mounted Infantry Question in its Relation to the Volunteer Force of Great Britain', *Journal of the Royal United Service Institution*, 35 (1891), pp.785-814 (p.787). In practice, Hutton did extend the role of mounted infantry into traditional cavalry roles. See Winrow, 'The British Regular Mounted Infantry', particularly pp.6, 77-78, 116.
42   Hutton, *Mounted Infantry its Present and Future*, p.8.

during the ride around McClellan's army in 1862 to 'fight all our way through, charging continually and dispersing again and again, sabres in hand, the hostile cavalry', although the earlier description of the same action in his memoir had referred to pistol and carbine shooting but had not mentioned the use of sabres.[43] Later in the same memoir he wrote of 'a genuine cavalry fight with sabres crossing and single combat – *incidents that very rarely occur in modern warfare*'.[44]

The 19th Century American military writer Arthur Wagner, who considered American cavalry in 1865 far superior to its European counterparts in 1866 or 1870, also took offence at the mounted infantry description, and pointed to the sabre charges of Wesley Merritt, George Armstrong Custer, and Thomas Devin, as evidence that it was much more than that.[45] In America the new tactics were adopted after the Civil War, but old tactics persisted, and there existed a 'cavalry school' which still believed in the traditional mounted charge with the sabre in preference to dismounted conduct, and which held to the belief that the horse was an essential part of the cavalryman's 'weapon system', rather than a mere mode of transport as it was for the mounted infantryman.[46] Merritt, who remained in the US Army until after the Spanish-American War of 1898, was amongst those American officers who continued to support mounted action, he suggested that 'the effect of breech-loading firearms is greatly exaggerated', and was a firm believer 'in the value of the sabre'.[47]

British writers sometimes expressed similar views about the American cavalry. In 1889, during one of Hutton's lectures on mounted infantry, General James Keith Fraser, Inspector General of Cavalry, noted that the Americans were hostile to the term, and that 'our [British] cavalry are both Mounted Infantry and Mounted Rifles. They ought to fulfil both functions. If they cannot, the sooner they are done away with the better'.[48] Fraser recommended study of American war and insisted that the Union cavalry of the Army of the Potomac were true cavalry, because they had not been armed with rifles, and were able to charge mounted. Among the Confederate leaders he dismissed Morgan and Forrest as guerrillas, saying that they could not be grouped together with Stuart, who he accepted as a pure cavalry general; as were Custer, Merritt, John Gregg, Judson Kilpatrick, and Alfred Pleasonton, on

43   Von Borcke to Lieutenant General Fraser, quoted in Captain W.H. James, *The Role of Cavalry as Affected by Modern Arms of Precision* (Aldershot: Gale and Polden, 1894), pp.7-8 (hereafter James, *Role of Cavalry*); referenced in Luvaas, *Military Legacy*, p.58; but see Von Borcke, *Memoirs*, Vol.I, p.39.
44   Von Borcke, *Memoirs*, Vol.I, p.104, emphasis added.
45   Wagner, *The Campaign of Königgrätz*, p.92.
46   Katzenbach 'The Horse Cavalry in the 20th Century', pp.361-63; Perry D. Jamieson, *Crossing the Deadly Ground: United States Army Tactics, 1865-1899* (Tuscaloosa and London: University of Alabama Press, 1994), pp.85-90. Jamieson's account of the different opinions and arguments in the US Army parallels those in Britain.
47   Quoted in Jamieson, *A Treatise on the Tactical Use of The Three Arms*, pp.85, 87.
48   Hutton, 'Mounted Infantry Question', p.800.

the Union side.[49] Hutton was prepared to concede in response that the Americans by the time of the Third Battle of Winchester (September 1864) had the ability to charge, but pointed out that this was after nearly four years of war. Relatively untrained troops such as the British Yeomanry, he thought, still needed to adopt a mounted rifle role.[50]

* * *

The British description of American cavalry as 'mounted infantry', both during the war and afterwards, might at times have been meant as derogatory but is best understood as simply a means of describing how these troops were understood to have been armed and used to a European audience. Even Henry Havelock wrote that 'Sheridan's 10,000 men were in fact – call them Cavalry, Mounted Rifles, or what you will – really *Mounted Infantry*'.[51] Historically, there were very specific tactical functions expected of cavalry. In encampments, it provided the army's outposts, escorts and performed reconnaissance. On the march it formed the advance guard and scouted the flanks. On the battlefield it felt for the enemy, overran shaken troops and broke through the enemies last reserves. In victory, it pursued and collected prisoners; in defeat it sacrificed itself to prevent such a pursuit.[52]

American troopers were thought to be very good at outpost duties and scouting, and even for feeling for the enemy. Occasionally, in defeat, regiments were committed in desperate charges to slow down an enemy advance, notable examples being the 5th US Cavalry at Gaines Mill (June 1862) and the 8th Pennsylvania at Chancellorsville (May 1863).[53] Its failure to otherwise conduct mounted battlefield charges could be put down to a lack of training, unsuitable arms, and unfavourable terrain. However, the main reason the American mounted arm was not considered cavalry was due to its failure to follow up in victory. This became a circular argument in British writings, as

---

49   Hutton, 'Mounted Infantry Question', pp.800-801. See also James, *Modern Cavalry Action In The Field*, p.31, where Fraser, in the chair, commented that while the Americans dismounted in close terrain, in open country 'they rode at the enemy and charged him with great success revolver or sword in hand'.
50   Hutton, 'Mounted Infantry Question', pp.813-14.
51   Havelock, *Three Main Military Questions*, p.74. Original italics.
52   Steinmetz, 'Past and Future of Cavalry', p.160; Wolseley, *Soldier's Pocket Book*, p.245; Colonel F. Chevenix Trench, *Cavalry in Modern War* (London: Kegan Paul, 1884), p.121. William Willis Blackford's description of the duties of cavalry in his memoir of his service with Stuart also conforms to this European ideal – covering flanks, vigorous pursuit, performing delaying charges in the event of defeat, and executing the decisive battle winning charge. Blackford, *War Years with Jeb Stuart*, p.28.
53   Stephen Z. Starr, *The Union Cavalry in The Civil War*, 3 vols (Baton Rouge: Louisiana University Press, 1979-1985), Vol.I: *From Fort Sumter to Gettysburg* (1979), pp.275-76, 359-60. Henry Fletcher blamed the failure of the cavalry at Gaines Mill on their stopping to fire pistols and carbines 'following the traditions of Indian warfare' rather than riding in with the sabre, *History of the American War*, Vol.II (1865), pp.88-89.

The 1st Maine cavalry deployed as dismounted skirmishers, 1863. (Library of Congress)

shown by the following passages. Without cavalry there could be no effective pursuit; since there had been no effective pursuits, there could not have been any real cavalry.

> Many writers who have advocated the systemic conversion of cavalry into mounted infantry have relied much on the experience of the American Civil War. The truth, however, is that the Americans substituted mounted infantry for cavalry proper, partly on account of the exceptional nature of the country, partly because they had no time to form a body of cavalry proper. It was owing chiefly to the want of the latter that success was rarely followed up, and that the most important tactical successes had not proportionately large strategical [sic] results. [54]

> Now, we can all look back to the American campaign, and, in looking back, what do we remember? We remember a series of battles, that were decided by the infantry on one side or the other, but which had no results, for they were never followed up. I ask, is it reasonable to suppose that, if cavalry existed which was superior to any cavalry that has ever been organized by any army, this, time after time, could have been the case? I think it is a manifest absurdity. [55]

---

54   Lieutenant Colonel W.W. Knollys, 'The Fighting of Cavalry on Foot', *United Service Magazine*, 589 (Dec 1877), pp.403-10 (p.407). Review of a book by Colonel T. Bonie, 11th French Hussars.
55   Baker, 'Organisation and Employment of Cavalry', p.388.

Few if any of these British theorists had directly observed the cavalry actions of the war, and their views were influenced by classic military theory, but they also looked to American authors to support their views. One such was Colonel F.G. Lippitt, whose views of the American cavalry, written in 1865, are so close to those expressed by British writers that it seems certain that his work must have been known and discussed. Lippitt gave three reasons for the Americans not forming a force of traditional cavalry. Foremost amongst these was the nature of the American terrain, second the nature of modern weapons, and third the time and the cost that it would have taken to train them. The resulting nature of the American mounted troops had a significant influence on the nature of battle.[56]

> The battles of the late War of Rebellion, the earlier ones, at least, were mostly indecisive. One chief cause of this was, that neither side had a sufficient force of true cavalry to enable it to turn a defeat into a rout, and drive the enemy effectually from the field. The cavalry charges were generally such as mounted infantry could just as well have made; charges in which the pistol and carbine played the principal part, instead of the spur and sabre.[57]

Lippitt accepted that a traditional cavalry charge against modern weapons would result in few of the cavalry charging home, but he still believed that 'the success of cavalry in battle depends upon the *impetuosity of its charge*, and its *use of the sabre*'.[58]

Lippitt had spent his service during the war in California, so had little more experience of modern cavalry than the British writers who quoted his views.[59] But George Denison had met and corresponded with a number of Civil War veterans who put forward similar ideas about why a distinctive mode of fighting had appeared in America. General Fitzhugh Lee, nephew of Robert E. Lee and one of the leading cavalry commanders in the Army of Northern Virginia, remarked that the expense had not justified creating a force of heavy cavalry because 'in this country, from its topographical features, opportunities seldom appear for charging with large masses

---

56   Francis J. Lippitt, *A Treatise on the Tactical Use of The Three Arms, Infantry, Artillery, and Cavalry* (New York: Van Nostrand, 1865), pp.129-30. Lippitt's work is directly quoted in Captain H.W.L. Hime, 'Duties of Partisan Cavalry', *United Service Magazine*, 578 (January 1877), pp.1-12. A copy was present in the War Office Library, see Anon, *Catalogue of the War Office Library Vol. 1.2* (London: [n.pub.], 1906), p.728. According to G.F.R. Henderson, Havelock had observed the Civil War, but as Luvaas noted this is unlikely, *Military Legacy*, p.109.

57   Lippitt, *A Treatise on the Tactical Use of The Three Arms*, p.128.

58   Lippitt, *A Treatise on the Tactical Use of The Three Arms*, pp.97, 109. Original italics.

59   Lippitt had also served in the California volunteers in the Mexican War, but also without seeing action. He was given the brevet rank of Brigadier General in 1865, but saw no action outside of Indian fighting. Francis J. Lippitt, *Reminiscences of Francis J. Lippitt, written for his family, his near relatives and intimate friends* (Providence, R.I.: Preston & Rounds Co, 1902), pp.61-76, 108-11.

of cavalry' and also commented on the lack of horsemanship in the North.[60] Another veteran of the Army of North Virginia, Major General Thomas L. Rosser, was also quoted as saying that his forces were 'not cavalry'. Rosser followed the contemporary definition of cavalry (armed with sabre, pistols, and nothing else) and mounted rifles (armed with carbine and revolver).[61] From Mississippi, Lieutenant General Stephen D. Lee, whose cavalry service had been with the Army of Tennessee in the western theatre, wrote to Denison that 'nearly all the cavalry used by the Confederate States, and in fact by both sides, was nothing more than mounted riflemen'.[62] Denison had been a strong Confederate sympathiser both during and after the war, and had also become a close friend of Havelock, whose ideas and work he acknowledged.[63] Yet while Victorian scholarship may have lacked the resources and rigour of modern day analysis, it cannot be entirely dismissed as the result of mere prejudice when Civil War veterans themselves wrote in the same terms.

Americans did talk in terms of cavalry and mounted infantry during the war, and the tactical usage and effectiveness of specific units was dependant to a great extent upon their weapons. However, the distinction between the two had blurred in American practice to an extent not seen in European armies. By 1864 the Federal horsemen were almost universally armed with an effective breech-loading carbine (either the Sharps or the repeating Spencer) that made them particularly suited to fighting on foot, but Stephen Starr's modern study of the Union cavalry has concluded that most mounted regiments still definitely perceived of themselves as cavalry, and that their training and tactics did anticipate the use of the mounted charge even if opportunities for this were rare.[64] Sheridan's campaign in the Shenandoah valley that year was the occasion for several such charges, prompting the British *Army and Navy Gazette* to observe that the United States were now making use of their horsemen as real cavalry, and that this 'marks a period in their military education'.[65] Under the terminology of the day, since they carried a carbine and sabre rather than a long rifle, the Union troopers did conform to the definition of cavalry, or at the very least mounted rifles, rather than mounted infantry. The Confederacy by contrast found more advanced firearms such as the Spencer difficult to procure, and particularly in the west many mounted units,

---

60   Denison, *Modern Cavalry*, p.353.
61   Denison, *Modern Cavalry*, p.362.
62   Wood, 'Mounted Riflemen', p.20; Boulderson, 'The Armament and Organisation of Cavalry', p.387. Boulderson was not a supporter of Denison's views, he may have read his work or may have derived the reference from Wood or others. The original, exact quote from Rosser's letter to Denison, dated 27 January 1868, is 'Neither the Yankees nor the Confederates employed cavalry in the late war, it was all *mounted rifles*' (*Modern Cavalry*, p.368, original italics).
63   Denison, *Soldiering in Canada*, pp.58-82, 140-152; Denison, *History of Cavalry*, p.477.
64   Starr, *The Union Cavalry in the Civil War*, Vol. II: *The War in the East From Gettysburg to Appomattox 1863-1865* (1981), pp.472. See also Jamieson, *Crossing the Deadly Ground*, pp.13-14.
65   *Army and Navy Gazette*, 8 October 1864, p.641.

while they were titled cavalry, were armed with long rifles. This meant that they had to dismount to be effective, and a description of mounted infantry was more appropriate to them. The views of Havelock and Denison on American cavalry were thus overly influenced by their Confederate sympathies and associates in this respect.

Post war, both dismounted and mounted action were considered equally valid as a use of cavalry in America, whereas many European commanders would have regarded mounted infantry as necessary for the former. One example is given in the writings of American Civil War veteran and military theorist Brevet Major General Emory Upton (USA), who observed a field exercise in India where the British mounted their infantry on artillery caissons to move them quickly forward to seize a bridge. Upton's view of this incident succinctly illustrates the difference in British and American views at this time.

> In the same situation we would have sent a company of cavalry, which, in the event of opposition, would have dismounted and fought on foot, and would have thought no more of it. In India, however, few officers appreciate the true use of cavalry, so infantry had to be mounted on artillery-carriages for an exploit which legitimately belonged to cavalry.[66]

Indian cavalry officers may have been particularly conservative, according to Upton the value of the carbine was little appreciated in India. 'Apparently indifferent to the brilliant achievements of the American horse, a majority of the officers still hold to the sabre as the only weapon worthy of the cavalryman.'[67]

* * *

This indifference to firepower was not universal. Well before 1861, the improved range and precision of small arms and artillery had been noticed by the more intelligent amongst British cavalry officers, and it was understood to have changed the balance between the different arms. Captain Lewis Nolan, who died at the battle of Balaclava in the charge of the Light Brigade, was a passionate believer in the ongoing importance of cavalry in war, but in his *History of Cavalry*, written in 1853, he wrote of the threat to traditional cavalry of the new rifled weapons.

66   Brevet Major General Emory Upton (USA), *The Armies of Asia and Europe. Embracing Official Reports On the Armies of Japan, China, India, Persia, Italy, Russia, Austria, Germany, France, and England. Accompanied by Letters Descriptive of A Journey from Japan to the Caucasus* (New York: Appleton, 1878), p.411, quoted in Anon, 'Armies of Asia', *United Service Magazine*, 598 (September 1878), pp.87-95 (p.92) a review of Upton's book which considered the mounted infantry incident an example 'of British pluck and heedless rashness'.

67   Upton, *Armies*, p.77.

The great improvement made in firearms and the increased range of the infantry musket, leave but little chance for cavalry, unless the speed with which they can pounce upon the infantry lessens the number and the effect of the discharges to be received during their advance.[68]

In a footnote later in the work Nolan also foresaw the possible impact of the new breech-loading arms in this context.

The long range gun is not to be despised, and the needle gun of the Prussians, which can be loaded quicker and fired with greater accuracy, and with these advantages combines the long range, is a formidable projectile in the hands of a steady soldier![69]

While Nolan died several years before the Civil War, his book was the first serious work in English on cavalry and it continued to have significant influence on cavalry theory on both sides of the Atlantic after his death. It was reprinted by Evans and Cogswell of Columbia, South Carolina, in 1864; recommended for study by Major General McClellan; and J.E. Roemer's *Cavalry: Its History, Management and Uses in War*, published in New York in 1863, drew heavily on Nolan. Fitzhugh Lee quoted Nolan that cavalry were the 'eyes, ears, feeler and feeder of an army' in his letters to Denison, and much of the historical content in Denison's writings is derived from Nolan's earlier work.[70]

In May 1862, prior to any significant lessons from America, Major Alfred Stowell Jones (another recipient of the VC during the Indian Mutiny, where he had served with the 9th Lancers), wrote in the *Journal of the Royal United Service Institution* about the condition of the British Cavalry and how it needed to modernise. His opening challenge echoed that of Nolan.

While the Artillery and Infantry of all armies have passed, during late years, through the most extensive changes in organization and equipment, and engineers have modified the arrangements of defence to meet these changes in offensive warfare, the Cavalry service has alone stood still, or nearly so, when its progress in the march of improvement is compared with that of the other arms.[71]

68   Captain L.E. Nolan (15th Hussars), *Cavalry: Its History and Tactics*, 3rd edn (London: Bosworth & Harrison, 1860), p.78. Originally published 1853.
69   Nolan, *Cavalry*, p.310, (footnote).
70   See Jon Coulston's introduction to a 2007 reprint of Nolan (Yardley PA: Westholme, 2007), pp.xxi-xxii; Denison, *Modern Cavalry* p.360; Nolan p.61. Instances of Denison using Nolan's examples are shown later in this chapter.
71   Major Alfred Stowell [Stovell] Jones VC, 'Present Condition of Our Cavalry; With Some Suggestions as the Practicality of Increasing its Efficiency in the Field', *Journal of the Royal*

While believing that nothing had changed to influence cavalry charges against other cavalry, Jones saw these as rare. The superior range and precision of modern rifles and shells had however made massed charges on infantry or artillery impossible –'no extensive formation or deployment of Cavalry can take place under a heavy fire of segment shells and conical bullets'.[72] Jones recommended a clear distinction between heavy and light cavalry. The former would be reserved for the charge, but could no longer stand in the front line while waiting for this opportunity, and needed to be bought rapidly to the front when it occurred, so needed to be given more mobility. He suggested several simplifications to the drill manual to achieve this, including operating in single rank ('rank entire'), moving in fours rather than threes (adopted in the 1865 manual), and non-pivot drill (adopted in the 1870s). However, he was still looking for ways to achieve victory in the charge over infantry, even in square, for which he proposed to lighten the heavy cavalry's equipment so as to increase its speed and momentum – each squadron becoming 'a living projectile'.[73]

Jones was disparaging of the British light cavalry, in part because it was also trained for the charge in line, since from motives of economy it was often used as a makeshift heavy cavalry, but also because of its poor marksmanship and inefficient carbines. In order to be able to compete with opposing light troops armed with rifles he proposed a radical change in the nature of light cavalry.[74]

> In the first place then, the Light Cavalry, *par excellence*, should be brought to regard their horses chiefly as means of rapid locomotion, not as fighting animals. The men should be light, energetic, quick-sighted, and, above all, good marksmen. They should be armed with the best breechloading rifle, with sling, and sword bayonet, and they should ride active, wiry ponies, trained to stand rooted to the spot when the riders dismount.[75]

In 1862 Jones was the Deputy Assistant Quarter-Master General at the Cape of Good Hope, and his model for the ideal light cavalry was a colonial one. The major difference between Jones' proposals and later supporters of mounted infantry was that his light cavalry was expected to be used in scouting and outpost drill only; he was not proposing it for battlefield use, and therefore thought that it would not need to be strong in numbers. Jones was not anticipating the cavalry tactics of the Civil War, nevertheless this was a description of the mounted infantry type armed with long rifle

United Service Institution, 6 (1862), pp.423–35 (pp.423). The copy was communicated to the magazine on 29 May 1862.
72 Jones, 'Present Condition of our Cavalry', pp.424.
73 Jones, 'Present Condition of our Cavalry', pp.423-425, 427-432.
74 Jones, 'Present Condition of our Cavalry', pp.424-26.
75 Jones, 'Present Condition of our Cavalry', p.234.

and bayonet several years before the writings of Havelock or Denison, and based upon the experiences of a British cavalry officer.[76]

Havelock, while critical of the British cavalry as 'behind and at variance with the spirit of the times', also thought that mounted rifles were 'not an original arm with our trans-Atlantic brethren'. He pointed to the rifle volunteers formed in Hampshire and Devonshire in 1859, and to the Cape Mounted Rifles in South Africa, as evidence that they were an essentially English arm, combining the love of the horse with the love of shooting.[77]

Comments from Wolseley in the *Soldier's Pocket Book* also demonstrate the uncertainty over cavalry tactics at the end of the 1860s as a result of the new firearms. While he listed one function of cavalry as 'to check a serious attack of infantry by forcing it to form square', he was critical of a case in China where Royal Marines armed with rifles formed square against Tartars armed only with bows and arrows, and attributed this both to the moral effect of massed horse on foot soldiers and to overly rigid drill. In the *Soldier's Pocket Book* Wolseley also included in the cavalry's roles the '[g]rand charge in force against infantry' but warned that 'these grand charges are but a waste of men and horses, if made against infantry armed as at present' unless the infantry were either shaken by artillery or of inferior quality.[78]

The Duke of Cambridge, usually regarded as a conservative whose position as Commander in Chief held back progress within the Army, reacted to a lecture on the American campaigns of 1864 by Captain Charles Cornwallis Chesney, the Professor of Military Art and History at the Royal Staff College, Sandhurst, by saying that 'whereas it was considered in former years that cavalry should be of a very heavy calibre, they ought now to be made as light as possible' although he would not go so far as to say that heavy cavalry should be given up entirely as 'heavy cavalry at the critical moment may be very useful and necessary'.[79] At another lecture, in 1876, he recognised the futility of frontal charges.

> I do not think that any large body of cavalry would ever be sent to the front against the firepower of the present day, because they [*sic*] are so destructive that really at the end of any distance it is impossible to assume that many men or horses would be in a condition fairly and strongly to carry out a direct charge.[80]

---

76   Jones, 'Present Condition of our Cavalry', pp.434–35.
77   Havelock, *Three Main Military Questions*, p.33, 65. For the tactics of the Cape Mounted Rifles see Strachan, *From Waterloo to Balaclava*, pp.89–90.
78   Wolseley, *Soldier's Pocket Book*, pp.244-46.
79   Captain C.C. Chesney, 'Sherman's Campaign in Georgia', *Journal of the Royal United Service Institution*, 9 (1865), pp.204-20. For the Duke of Cambridge's conservatism, see Kochanski, *Sir Garnet Wolseley: Victorian Hero*, p.53; Spiers, *The Late Victorian Army*, pp.31-32, 69-70, 156; Koch, *Modern Warfare*, p.82. However, Strachan, *Wellington's Legacy*, p.27, notes that before the Crimean War the Duke had been seen in the press as a reforming young officer.
80   Comment from the chair at Russell's lecture at the Royal United Service Institution, 3 March 1876, Russell, 'Cavalry', p.192.

In comparison Lieutenant John Frederick Maurice, Instructor of Tactics and Organisation at the Royal Military College, Sandhurst, and generally regarded as a progressive thinker, saw a need to retain traditional cavalry in the context of winning the cavalry fight against a European opponent. In 1871 Maurice was the winner of a prize offered by the 2nd Duke of Wellington for the best military essay on the subject of 'The System of Field Manoeuvres Best Adapted for Enabling our Troops to meet a Continental Army'. In his submission he was of the same opinion as the traditional cavalrymen that 'it seems exceedingly unlikely that now more than before mounted riflemen [*sic*] can be made into good cavalry'. He also wrote that 'while light cavalry on outpost duty are supported by mounted riflemen, the light cavalry on the field of battle should be supported by a powerful force of cuirassier regiments'.[81] This reflected the lessons of the Austro-Prussian and Franco-Prussian wars where victory in cavalry *mêlées* had been seen to go to the heaviest horsemen.[82]

The retention of traditional charging cavalry was also proposed by Denison, who in many ways remained a traditional thinker, and not the overlooked prophet that Luvaas, drawing largely from Denison's own autobiography, portrayed him to be. Denison's early writing before the Civil War stressed the historic role of cavalry as a decisive and attacking force, quoting Napoleon that cavalry would break infantry if resolutely led, as well as the English military writer Sir Patrick Leonard MacDougall in his *Theory of War* (1856) that '[n]o formation of infantry can resist the shock of horses ridden as English Dragoons do ride in earnest'. Denison's belief at this time in the ability of cavalry to decide the fate of battles even extended to examples of successful cavalry attacks in the past on entrenchments and squares.[83]

While some of his views changed after observing the tactics of the Civil War, Denison did not completely abandon these beliefs. In *Modern Cavalry*, written in the immediate aftermath of the American Civil War, he wrote that

the great changes in the firearms of the infantry, and in the field artillery, have considerably affected the power of cavalry proper to overcome the other arms of

81   Lieutenant F. Maurice, *Wellington Prize Essay on The System of Field Manoeuvres Best Adapted for Enabling our Troops to meet a Continental Army* (Edinburgh and London: William Blackwood, 1872), p.157. Hereafter Maurice, *Wellington Essay*. Amongst a number of authorities on continental wars, on p.xiv Maurice also listed Chesney and Denison.

82   Captain J.C. Russell (10th Royal Hussars), 'Essay 3', in *Essays Written for the Wellington Prize* (Edinburgh: Wm. Blackwood & Sons, 1872), pp.99-188 (p.170); Denison, *Modern Cavalry* pp.17, 36-37, 46-47; Denison, *History of Cavalry*, pp.487-89.

83   Luvaas, *Military Legacy*, pp.111-14; Craddock, 'The American Civil War and its Influence on the British Army', pp.151-52; Adrian Preston, 'British Military Thought 1856-1890', *Army Quarterly*, 88 (1964), pp.57-74 (p.66); Preston, 'Military Lessons of the American Civil War', pp.234-35; George T. Denison, *The National Defences: or, Observations on the Best Defensive Force for Canada* (Toronto: [n.pub.], 1861), pp.14-17, 24-25. Also Denison, *Modern Cavalry*, pp.165-66.

the service, still there can be no doubt that it is carrying the principle too far to say that these improvements are to do away with cavalry proper for ever.[84]

Denison still thought that cavalry could not only overthrow unsupported artillery, but also suggested that by adopting the revolver it would also have a means of attacking and defeating formed infantry. The rifles that in the hands of the mounted arm would make it capable of repeating the feats of Sheridan's men, were nevertheless portrayed as overrated in the hands of infantry faced with a fast moving and resolute cavalry. Denison was of the opinion that infantry accustomed to fight at long range would not stand to receive a determined mounted charge, and would lose heart if their fire did not have the anticipated effect. He quoted von Borcke on the unreliability of volley fire, and gave examples of successful charges by Confederate cavalry. In particular he observed that 'with the breach-loading weapons the waste or consumption of ammunition is frightful'.[85] The following passage is quoted at length because it illustrates how much Denison shared the views of the 'traditional' cavalry school.

> Still, however, when the ground is open and clear, when there are no obstacles to prevent the rush of the advancing squadrons, no shelter behind which the infantry can protect themselves, but a fair field between the two arms, then cavalry carefully trained, properly armed, and with a strong esprit-de-corps, riding at infantry with a will, with their minds made up to go in, will always succeed. All they want is the spur and the spear and the sabre, and the native courage of the blood horse to depend on, and when they fight, it should be with the rush of the whirlwind. Their horses pushed to their utmost speed, the men leaning forwards in their saddles, and their eyes bent upon the enemy. The shock should be as the crash of the thunderbolt, and although many may fall, all will not, and the survivors will win a glorious victory, and amply avenge their comrades.[86]

Denison proposed the division of cavalry into 'Line', who should be as heavy as possible and trained only to fight at close quarters and in the mounted charge, and 'Dragoons' armed for dismounted service. The former force would be expensive to maintain, but Denison thought that 'the result of success [of a charge] will be so great as to amply compensate for the trouble and expense in preparing to profit by them' and advocated that between one-third and one-quarter of the mounted force with an army should be 'cavalry proper'.[87] In support of this view, Denison quoted Major General Rosser, who in their correspondence had written that 'The cavalry soldier should never be

84   Denison, *Modern Cavalry*, p.72.
85   Denison, *Modern Cavalry*, pp.153-55, 174-85, 51 (quote). Also Denison, *History of Cavalry*, pp.522-23.
86   Denison, *Modern Cavalry*, pp.162-63.
87   Denison, *Modern Cavalry*, p.72. Also Denison, *History of Cavalry*, pp.514-15.

dismounted to fight, if you expect him to ride over masses of infantry, but be educated to the belief that *nothing can withstand a well-executed charge of cavalry*, and should feel perfectly "at home" on horseback'.[88] Rosser had also differentiated between mounted rifles, which should be responsible for all picketing, and escort duty and cavalry of the line meant for charging, which should be *'always kept in mass, and used in the charge alone'*.[89] The latter 'should be carefully educated in the idea that the fighting does not commence until they begin to ply their swords or use their lances or revolvers'.[90]

Rather than the American Civil War, it was the Franco-Prussian War that made Denison change his original view that cavalry could defeat unbroken infantry. Examples of mounted charges against infantry in America were too few in number, and their failure too easy to attribute to the unsuitability of the terrain or the lack of training of the troops, to strongly influence European thinking. In 1870 however the failures of the cavalry, on both sides, were frequent and clear to see.

> The question of cavalry charging infantry with breech-loaders is, I think, settled conclusively by this campaign. Wherever it has been tried by the 8th and 9th French Cuirassiers at Woerth [6 August], by the 7th Prussian Cuirassiers at Vionville on the 16th August, or by the two French light cavalry brigades on their extreme left at Sedan [1 September], the result has been the same – a fearful loss of life with no result whatever.[91]

It is true that British drill manuals did continue to stress the use of cavalry as an offensive, mounted arm – 'the ultimate and main object of the cavalry being to ride down the enemy, the practice of the charge is the culminating point in the instruction of the squadron'.[92] However, this does not mean that they endorsed the use of sword and lance against unbroken infantry armed with rifles and machine guns. The 1876 regulations stated very clear circumstances in which it was appropriate for cavalry to charge infantry. These were: when it was demoralised or inferior; if it was possible to surprise them and to charge from a short distance thus limiting their fire; when they were broken, or out of ammunition; and in order to force skirmishers to close ranks and create a more vulnerable target for other arms.[93] By 1891 the last of these situations had been removed, presumably in recognition of the further increase in

---

88   Denison, *Modern Cavalry*, p.20. Original italics. This quote was also used by Hutton, 'Mounted Infantry', p.701.
89   Denison, *Modern Cavalry*, p.20. Original italics.
90   Denison, *Modern Cavalry*, p.49.
91   Denison, *History of Cavalry*, p.503.
92   Anon, *Cavalry Drill, 1891* (London: HMSO, 1891), p.276.
93   Anon, *Regulations for the Instructions and Movement of the Cavalry, 1876* (London: HMSO, 1876), pp.185-86, (hereafter, *Cavalry Drill* (1876));Luvaas, *Military Legacy*, p.199; Craddock, 'The American Civil War and its Influence on the British Army', pp.222-23.

infantry firepower resulting from the introduction of magazine rifles. However, while acknowledging that 'the attack of [sic] intact infantry, well supplied with ammunition, will almost invariably be accompanied with heavy losses' it also stated that under some circumstances results might justify the loss.[94]

The manuals also stated that when it came to charging artillery, 'a plan of attack should be adopted which will offer the smallest advantage to the fire of modern field guns' and that 'when circumstances are favourable, the mounted attack upon artillery in position may also sometimes be supported by the fire of dismounted men'.[95] Finally, by the 1890s the manual included the instruction that 'machine guns will, as a rule, be attached to every force of cavalry acting in the field', primarily for offensive use as a substitute for carbine or infantry fire to support the attack. This was expected to be particularly important in broken or enclosed country where the mobility and long-range fire of horse artillery would be limited.[96] The machine gun was put forward as a technological solution to the tactical problem of whether to engage in mounted or dismounted action.

> The accuracy and volume of machine gun fire will largely save the employment of dismounted cavalry for both attack and defence and the cavalry commander can thus keep all his men mounted ready, when the favourable moment comes, either to attack or deliver a counterblow on a threatening enemy.[97]

The tactical quandary for the cavalry was that to be effective the charge needed to be well timed, rapid and sudden. 'The opportunities for making an attack with cavalry quickly pass away. Whenever they occur they must be instantly seized'.[98] However, the increased range of modern weapons meant that the cavalry initially needed to keep great distance. The cavalryman's solution to this, which was essentially an extension of Jones' observations about the need for mobility in 1862, was that they needed to be trained to move at a uniform rate over considerable distances and over a variety of ground, which in turn needed highly trained and practised horses inured to exertion. It was these characteristics that were admired in the Prussian cavalry.[99]

They were not however the characteristics of mounted infantry, which was seen as a defensive or supporting arm. The 1884 drill book for the Mounted Infantry explicitly

---

94 Anon, *Cavalry Drill* (1891), pp.284-85; Anon, *Cavalry Drill, 1896*, 2 vols (London: HMSO, 1896), Vol.II, p.207.
95 Anon, *Cavalry Drill* (1876), p.184.
96 Anon, *Cavalry Drill* (1891), pp.477-88, especially pp.477-78; Anon, *Cavalry Drill* (1896), Vol.II, pp.202-03.
97 Anon, *Cavalry Drill* (1896), Vol.II, pp.202-03.
98 Anon, *Cavalry Drill* (1876), p.189.
99 Anon, *Cavalry Drill* (1891), pp.276-77; Captain Frederic Natusch Maude, 'Rise, Decay and Revival of the Prussian Cavalry' in *Attack or Defence: Seven Military Essays* (London: J.J. Keliher, 1896), pp.19-21.

stated that they were not cavalry, and would operate together with cavalry who would engage any significant numbers of enemy horse. Not equipped to fight on horseback, mounted infantry were instructed to seek broken ground if threatened whilst mounted. Once dismounted however, 'cavalry will not attack the fighting line of Mounted Infantry except in extended order, and if coolness and steadiness is displayed such an attack will be readily repelled'. If seriously threatened, the infantry were instructed to fix swords (i.e. bayonets) and form round the horses, in the manner of the traditional rallying square used by skirmishers, while if escape were blocked they were to advance firing by volleys leading their horses.[100] This perception of mounted infantry as lacking both the offensive power of 'real' cavalry and, perhaps more importantly, their offensive tradition, was a crucial part of the cavalry's argument for their own retention.

The traditional role of cavalry was as an offensive arm, and traditionalists were concerned that by dismounting, troopers would lose their offensive spirit. One of the criticisms levelled at Denison was that 'his sympathies are so much on the side of the infantry system of tactics that whenever possible he gives the virtue to that arm'.[101] The concern was that to be effective in shock action, cavalry had to be trained above all to believe in power of their own arm to overcome the opposition. One fear was that if dismounted they were more likely than infantry to be impressed by a cavalry charge and therefore offer weaker resistance on foot. There is some evidence of this from the action of the cavalry battalions that formed part of the Camel Corps in the Sudan campaign of 1884, which were reported to have stepped back during the assault on the British squares at Abu Klea.[102]

How was the square broken? you will say. Well, there are various opinions; one is, that it was a mistake to turn cavalry into infantry, and make them fight in square with an arm with which they were not accustomed to. Add to this, the cavalry were detachments from different regiments, only bought together a few days before we left Korti. A cavalry man is taught never to stand still, and that a square can be broken. How can you expect him in a moment to forget all his training, stand like a rock, and believe no one can get inside a square? Then the cavalryman has a short handy carbine; he is given a long rifle and a bayonet, and uses them for the first time in his life when a determined enemy is charging him.[103]

---

100 Anon, *Regulations for Mounted Infantry, 1884* (London: HMSO, 1884), pp.17, 23.
101 Russell, 'Cavalry', p.189; Anon, [Review of Denison's] 'A History of Cavalry', *United Service Magazine*, 586 (September 1877), pp.15-22 (pp.19-20). It would appear that the reviewer was unfamiliar with Denison's earlier works.
102 Knollys, 'The Fighting of Cavalry on Foot', p.410; John H. Waller, *Gordon of Khartoum: The Saga of a Victorian Hero* (New York: Atheneum, 1988) p.426.
103 Sir Charles Wilson, *From Kurti to Khartoum*, 4th edn (London: Blackwood, 1886), p.33.

'Sudan Campaign 1884: Officers and men of the Household Cavalry forming part of the Light Camel Regiment during the Khartoum Expedition', by Orlando Norie. (Anne S.K. Brown Military Collection)

Those who were near the Heavies told me that as the men fired they moved back involuntarily – not being taught, as infantry men are, to stand in a rigid line; they thus got clubbed together, and Burnaby tried to open them out so as to get a greater development of fire and let the Gardner [machine gun] play.[104]

Another concern was that hit and run tactics based around the long range rifle as seen in America would lead cavalryman to thinking of his horse only as a means of escape, resulting in a further reduction in moral and offensive spirit. 'Genuine cavalry should guard against the practice of always having recourse to the rifle instead of the sabre'.[105] A tactical weakness of dismounted troops was their led horses, physically they could not always be protected and were vulnerable to attack, and morally they made their

104 Wilson, *From Kurti to Khartoum,* p.34. However, Wilson also quoted an article by the commander of the Heavy Cavalry Brigade, Lieutenant Colonel The Honourable R. Talbot, 1st Life Guards, in the *19th Century Review*. 'Afterward thirty dead horses were counted on the spot where the advance was made, which tends to show that the shooting of the Heavy Camel Regiment was not so indifferent as has been implied.' (ibid, p.317). This was probably the same R. Talbot who had visited Petersburg in 1865.
105 Lieutenant Colonel W.W. Knollys, 'What we have Learnt From the War', *United Service Magazine*, 591 (February 1878), pp.135-43 (p.142). Knollys was writing of the Russo-Turkish War, although he also recognised that conflict had justified the use of troops armed as dragoons.

owners less stubborn in defence through concern for their means to escape. In support of this view, the Civil War veteran Heros von Borcke was quoted as having said that he would have had the horses of mounted infantry shot to prevent the men running away.[106]

More practically, mounted infantry, were generally perceived to be poor horsemen when compared to true cavalry, viewing their horse as a mere means of conveyance and not an essential part of their equipment. Within a few days of campaigning, it was argued, the majority of mounted infantry would be dismounted and no better than normal infantry. This sounds very similar to the criticism by the early observers in America of the inferior horse management of the poorly mounted and trained Union cavalry. However, poor management of horses on campaign was also not unknown within the regular British cavalry regiments in South Africa.[107]

Dismounted action was still seen as a secondary role for true cavalry, but the 1876 drill manual for the cavalry included six pages on the subject, which compares favourably with the 10 pages devoted to the mounted charge, given that the instructions for the latter are much more prescriptive. Indeed, precisely because it was difficult to lay down exact rules for dismounted service the regulations advised that cavalry 'should consequently be practised on every description of ground and squadron and troop leaders should be allowed considerable scope for the exercise of their intelligence and discretion'.[108] General guidance was given on how to carry out dismounted action successfully – it should not render the troops vulnerable to mounted attack, should not expose the led horses to fire and these should be readily available in case of the necessity to retreat, a steady fire needed to be maintained (which meant that trained troops were needed), and rapidity of movement was essential. The precise regulations for mounting and dismounting on the drill ground were expressly stated as unnecessary for such action in order to achieve this.[109]

These guidelines are very similar to those given by Colonel F. Chevenix Trench eight years later for when to use dismounted action. They contradict Luvaas' claim that Chevenix Trench's work was an exception, and that the official manuals were 'reluctant to adopt the theories advanced by Havelock and Denison'.[110] On one thing the 1876 regulations are very clear however, that dismounted cavalry were not to consider themselves 'skirmishers' in the infantry sense of leading an assault upon

106 Lieutenant Colonel G.F.R. Henderson, 'The Tactical Employment of Cavalry' in *The Science of War* (London: Longman Green, 1905), pp.51-69 (pp. 59-60). Letter reported as received from Heros von Borcke by Lieutenant General Keith Fraser, in discussion on Captain W.H. James' lecture *The Role of Cavalry as Affected by Modern Arms of Precision*, p.7.

107 General Shute, at Major Russell's lecture at the Royal United Service Institution, 3 March 1876, Russell, 'Cavalry', p.193; BL Layard Papers Add. 39104, fols 225-28, Henry Malet to Sir Austen Henry Layard, 27 December 1862; Marquess of Anglesey, *A History of the British Cavalry, Vol. 4: 1899-1913* (London: Leo Cooper, 1986), pp.356-60.

108 Anon, *Cavalry Drill* (1876), p.143.

109 Anon, *Cavalry Drill* (1876), p.142.

110 Trench, *Cavalry in Modern War*, p.191; Luvaas, *Military Legacy*, p.114.

enemy infantry – dismounted action was primarily to check enemy cavalry through holding important defensible positions.[111] This still reflected the role assigned to the cavalry by Nolan in 1853.

> Dismounted cavalry have done good service in covering a retreat, in defending defiles and passes against cavalry, and in pushing forward to seize bridges and dismounting to maintain them; but they would be quite out of place if used in storming positions, or if expected to take their post in line of battle with the infantry.[112]

The dismounted regulations remained essentially unchanged in subsequent manuals, and it was generally accepted by the end of the century that a great deal of the cavalry's operations would entail dismounted action. That role though still did not envisage *extensive* dismounted action, which would be the role of cheaper and more expendable mounted infantry.[113] Cavalry officers still feared moves to convert any part of the small British cavalry force to this mounted infantry role.

* * *

Uncertainty over the future tactical use of cavalry inevitably led to a great deal of discussion of how troopers should be armed. This was an issue that had been identified once again by Nolan, well before the outbreak of the American Civil War.

> The devices of armament have made progress in the infantry, and enormous strides in the artillery, but in the cavalry, where the subject is of vital importance, nothing has yet been suggested likely to make it more formidable in action.[114]

Part of the problem facing reformers throughout the period was that to undertake any discussion on armament was to challenge 'long standing customs, traditions, regimental prejudices, and very possibly the bulk of popular opinion in the cavalry arm'.[115] One of Denison's most controversial views, and one which he predicted would result in criticism from his brother officers, was his advocacy of the revolver rather than the sword as the best close-quarter weapon for mounted forces.[116]

This was not in itself a new debate. Nolan had commented in 1853 on the tendency for Indian Regular Cavalry to rely upon their (single shot) pistols rather than their

111 Anon, *Cavalry Drill* (1876), p.146.
112 Nolan, *Cavalry: Its History and Tactics*, p.66.
113 James, *Role of Cavalry*, p.3.
114 Nolan, *Cavalry: Its History and Tactics*, p.100.
115 Colonel F.J. [F.T.] Graves (20th Hussars), 'Cavalry Equipment, Organisation and Distribution', *Journal of the Royal United Service Institution*, 34 (1891), pp.695-712 (p.707).
116 Denison, *Modern Cavalry*, p.62.

sabres, and believed that the Irregulars were more effective as a result. Twenty years later Colonel Valentine Baker, formerly of the 12th Lancers and the 10th Hussars, could still write that 'notwithstanding assertions made by American Officers [...] a pistol is a demoralizing and dangerous weapon for a cavalry soldier'.[117] This idea that firearms had a demoralising effect on the offensive 'cavalry spirit' and that cavalry prepared to charge home would always defeat those relying upon their firearms could be justified with historical examples dating back at least to the Thirty Years War in the 17th Century.[118] Denison had also initially believed in the superiority of the sabre, although he had proposed that cavalry should also be armed with Colt revolvers. The following quote comes from a pamphlet he wrote in 1861.

> Unless cavalry are dismounted the officer in command should never let them use their pistols, and if when opposing cavalry, the enemy attack with firearms, he should at once fall on them, sword in hand, for the mere fact of a dragoon regiment trusting to firearms when they have good swords is a sign that they are altogether deficient in the requisite qualities of a cavalry corps.[119]

Denison's views were changed by his observations on the 'confederate war for independence' [sic]. Although he still maintained that 'the cavalry of the line should undoubtedly be armed with a sabre' he questioned whether the revolver might not be better, and gave a number of comparisons of battles during the Civil War with sabre and revolver to show the superiority of the latter. In particular he quoted from Colonel Harry Gilmor's *Four Years in the Saddle* (1866), John Scott's *Partisan Life with Mosby* (1867), Heros von Borcke's memoirs, and from correspondence with Stephen D. Lee who stated that since his cavalry had been nothing more than mounted riflemen, the sabre had been a dispensable weapon.[120] Yet it is worth noting that several of Denison's examples of how few casualties were caused by the sabre come not from the Civil War, but directly from Nolan, who had used them not to demonstrate the superiority of the revolver, but of Indian cavalry and swords over their inferior European counterparts.[121]

---

117 Nolan, *Cavalry: Its History and Tactics*, p.100; Baker, 'Organisation and Employment of Cavalry', p.384. See Strachan, *From Waterloo to Balaclava*, pp.62-63 for further contemporary views to Nolan's on the revolver.
118 Denison refers to Gustavus Adolphus training his men 'to depend upon the keen edge of the sword, and the shock of the charging men and horses, and he was therefore the first to revive the ideas of Alexander and Hannibal, and to introduce into modern Europe the true principles of cavalry tactics': Denison, *History of Cavalry*, p.259.
119 Denison, *The National Defences*, pp.31-32.
120 Denison, *Modern Cavalry*, pp.29, 362-64; *History of Cavalry*, pp.518-19.
121 Nolan, *Cavalry: Its History and Tactics*, pp.105-15. Nolan describes the effectiveness of Indian cavalry swords and those of the Sikh horsemen and compares the action of Bergen and Egmont-op-Zee, on 2 October 1799, between British and French cavalry, and which resulted in few casualties, with that of the 3rd Dragoons at Chillianwalla in the Sikh War who lost 46 casualties. Nolan also refers to a near bloodless cavalry *mêlée* at Heilsberg, on

One anonymous reviewer of *A History of Cavalry* summed up the traditionalist case for rejecting the evidence of the American Civil War in favour of firearms.

> We have not space to discuss this question properly; but we may simply point out that the revolver has always been a favourite American weapon, and the sword never. It need not therefore be a matter for surprise that men who not only never knew how to use a sword, but had a dislike of it, would be easily defeated by others armed with weapons the former dreaded to see in the hands of opponents! Pistols and revolvers are keep-me-off weapons, and weapons of that description have seldom proved effective arms in the hands of cavalry well led.[122]

Denison himself had acknowledged the American familiarity with and preference for firearms, and had suggested that the *morale* effect of the sabre charge did not exist in America because of contempt for that weapon, particularly in the Confederate army. As to Denison's view that a cavalry force armed with revolvers was more likely to break infantry than one with sabres, the same reviewer disputed the effectiveness of mounted fire, and claimed that the evidence of history was that cavalry trained to depend upon pistols lost their sense of superiority and did not charge home. Another, while accepting that the use of firearms dismounted was accepted doctrine and beyond debate, also criticised Denison's 'evident American sympathies' in his support of the use of firearms mounted. Like his anonymous contemporary, he put this down to American familiarity with firearms; but also once again to their lack of cavalry training and to the terrain.[123]

Possibly even more controversial in Britain than whether the use of the revolver lessened the cavalry's *élan* in the charge was debate over the use of the lance. Although outside the main context of the discussion about American influence on the British Army, the lance became the iconic weapon for supporters of the *arme blanche*. In 1892 it was universally adopted for the front rank of all regiments except hussars, then dropped throughout the army in 1903, before being re-introduced in 1909 within lancer regiments.[124] Lessons from America regarding the lance were severely limited, if the revolver was an American weapon, the lance was definitely not. Only one unit of significance, the 6th Pennsylvania Cavalry (popularly known after their commander

---

18 June 1806, between the French and Prussians. The two Napoleonic examples, but not that from the Sikh War, were selectively used by Denison, *Modern Cavalry*, pp.32-34, and *History of Cavalry* pp.517-18.

122 Anon, [Review of Denison's] 'A History of Cavalry', p.21.

123 Anon, [Review of Denison's] 'A History of Cavalry', p.20; 'JWH', [Review of Denison's] 'History of Cavalry', *Journal of the Royal United Service Institution*, (1878), pp.1225-32 (p.1230). The probable author is Major John Wallace Hozier (1834-1905), Royal Scots Greys; ibid, p.iv; Edward Almack, *The History of the Second Dragoons 'Royal Scots Greys'* (London: Alexander Moring, 1908), p.207.

124 Anglesey, *History of the British Cavalry*, Vol.III, p.401; Vol.IV, pp.409-410.

as Rush's Lancers) used the lance during the Civil War, briefly and without success in Virginia in 1862. This would not have been a surprise to British observers, as the lance was a difficult weapon to master and not particularly well suited to the close terrain found in Virginia. Nolan in 1853 had dismissed it as unfit for military use for this very reason. Denison favoured the lance as an impact weapon, but also recognised that it was only effective in the hands of well-trained troops, using the example of Rush's Lancers to demonstrate its ineffectiveness in untrained hands.[125]

British lancer regiments until 1873 were equipped with obsolete single-shot pistols, and as late as 1877 only around six carbines were issued per squadron.[126] Yet even though lancer officers retained faith in their weapon as the pre-eminent weapon for cavalry action, this did not mean that they did not recognise that tactics needed to change as a result of modern technology. Valentine Baker disapproved of the pistol, but recognised the lance was unsuitable for outpost duties and the need therefore to arm lancers with carbines for 'temporary' dismounted service, leaving their lances slung on their horses.[127] Major Samuel Boulderson of the 17th Lancers considered a hypothetical encounter between lancers and hussars in which the hussars held the lancers with fire to front while attacking mounted on their flanks, saying that 'plenty of ground can be found where such tactics could be employed with advantage'.[128] These were tactics reminiscent of those used by American commanders, such as Bedford Forrest at Okolona (February 1864) and Brice's Cross Roads (June 1864).[129] In order to be successful, Boulderson postulated that the lancers needed to pin the dismounted force, then defeat the mounted troopers and threaten the horses of the dismounted men so as to drive them off. Hence he proposed to arm half of all lancers with firearms to meet the dismounted fire on equal terms, the remainder armed with lances could then beat the mounted hussars.[130]

Boulderson's solution was of course based around his personal belief in the superiority of the lance over the sword as a *mêlée* weapon (or indeed over the revolver, which he thought discouraged shock action and risked hitting your own men in close combat), and in the primacy of mounted conflict in action. Most participants in the discussion which followed his lecture questioned the practicality of mixed-arm regiments, particularly where a specialist arm such as the lance was concerned. Some

125 Nolan, pp.121-33; Denison, *Modern Cavalry*, pp.39-48. Denison's source regarding Rush's Lancers was Von Borcke, and has been challenged by Starr, *The Union Cavalry in The Civil War*, Vol. I, p.270. See Strachan, *From Waterloo to Balaclava*, pp.57-59 for the adoption of the lance into British service.

126 Field Marshal Sir William Robertson, *From Private to Field Marshal* (London: Constable, 1921), p.15.

127 Baker, 'Organization and Employment of Cavalry', p.384.

128 Boulderson, 'The Armament and Organisation of Cavalry', p.384.

129 Forrest's action at Okolona had been covered in Denison, *History of Cavalry*, p.459-60. Although not referenced directly by Boulderson, there is no European example of similar tactics in the literature.

130 Boulderson, 'The Armament and Organisation of Cavalry', p.384.

maintained that lancers should never dismount and should only be equipped with swords or revolvers, others that lancers were too expensive and should be done away with altogether. What is of interest is that Boulderson's lecture sparked a lively debate between officers in his audience, from all sections of the army, about such tactical issues. It was not a simple matter of a few visionaries fighting a conservative establishment. Lancer regiments do however seem to have been particularly reluctant to break with tradition, in 1877 they began to be equipped with Martini-Henry carbines, but the 9th Lancers still needed to undergo further musketry training when deployed to Afghanistan two years later.[131]

Age appears to have been a factor in officers' assessment of the relative merits of different weapons. The officers who had recommended the breech-loading carbine to the Ordnance Select Committee in 1864 were colonels or lieutenant colonels, and included Valentine Baker, then aged 37.[132] Commenting on Boulderson's presentation at the Royal United Service Institution in 1878, 29-year old Lieutenant Graves of the 20th Hussars extolled the virtues of the revolver quoting examples from the American Civil War of the successes that revolver-armed Confederates, particularly under leaders such as Mosby, had over Federal cavalry relying upon sabres. In his arguments Graves cited a number of examples used by Denison in his *History of Cavalry* published the same year, to which he was surely referring. Graves was clearly well-read and interested in his profession, and well acquainted with the American Civil War. He went on to reference comments made by Wolseley about Sheridan's troopers the previous year – 'bad cavalry and only middling infantry', but able to take and hold strategic points, and in their operations against Lee's rear-guard during the Appomattox campaign 'thoroughly instructed in the use of their arms'. Twelve years later, Graves was still using the same examples from the American Civil War to argue for the arming of cavalry with revolvers.[133]

Graves' interest in modern arms may also have reflected his regimental background. The 20th Hussars had been formed after the Indian Mutiny from the 2nd Bengal European Light Cavalry, an East India Company regiment. Amongst its officers was Frederick Chevenix Trench, the third British writer in this period singled out by Luvaas as recognizing the importance of the American cavalry, and as an advocate of mounted infantry and firearms. Trench, a veteran of the Mutiny, remarked at a lecture in 1877 upon the deadly efficiency of the revolver, and on the inability of the sabre to

131 Boulderson, 'The Armament and Organisation of Cavalry', pp.381-82; Captain F. Chevenix Trench (20th Hussars) 'On the Progress that has Been Made During Recent Years in Developing the Capabilities of Cavalry', *Journal of the Royal United Service Institution*, 21 (1877), pp.990-1011 (pp.1004-07); Anglesey, *History of the British Cavalry*, Vol. III, p.227.
132 TNA, WO 33/14/234, *Abstracts of Proceedings of the Ordnance Select Committee for the Quarter Ending 30th September 1864*, p.424.
133 Lieutenant Graves comments in discussion following Boulderson's lecture delivered at the Royal United Service Institution, 5 April 1878, p.392; Graves, 'Cavalry Equipment', p.709.

hold its own against it, a fact 'known long ago to those who have seen any actual hand to hand fighting'.[134]

More senior officers tended to favour the sabre for close combat, but were not blind to the changes that technology was forcing upon cavalry armament and tactics. One senior general, Sir Charles Beauchamp Walker – veteran of the Crimea, the Indian Mutiny, and China, an observer with the Prussian army in both 1866 and 1870, and recently appointed Inspector General of Military Education – expressed the opinion that 'using carbines on the field of battle is nothing short of insanity' based upon the historic experience of the Peninsular War, and as evidence that cavalry armed with carbines would rather fire than 'cut in' with the sword he referenced an 1860 inspection of Indian cavalry. However, he then went on to state that 'the times have changed' and to agree that all cavalry must be armed with firearms due to the wider range of roles which they had to fulfil; the increased importance of cavalry in shielding and scouting meaning that they needed firearms to hold points of advantage.[135] Another Crimean veteran, Sir Montagu Steele, also put the view that cavalry without firearms were useless, and advocated common armament across all regiments for flexibility. Both argued against the use of the lance, regarding it as an expensive and limited weapon.[136] Furthermore, in 1869 General M.W. Smith wrote a book on modern tactics that barely mentioned the American campaigns, but accepted the need for cavalry to carry firearms, and therefore that the most effective means of using them needed to be found.[137]

Smith accepted that there was a role for cavalry trained to use rifled firearms in the correct tactical circumstances, and discussed at length how the cavalry carbine should be carried so as to be readily available for dismounted use. He saw little value in mounted fire either by skirmishers or *en masse*, but on the basis of American operations predicted the need for a body of men that could move rapidly to a strong position in order to check the progress of the enemy. Recognising that there were strong prejudices against mounted infantry, he suggested the equipment of a portion of the cavalry to render this service.[138] Smith had been an officer in the 3rd Dragoon Guards and in the 15th Hussars, and had served in the Crimean War, but attached to the Turkish

---

134 Trench, 'Capabilities of Cavalry', pp.990-1011. Trench was present at the capture of Lucknow in 1858.
135 Sir Charles Beauchamp Walker in discussion on Major Boulderson's lecture delivered at the Royal United Service Institution, 5 April 1878, Boulderson, 'The Armament and Organisation of Cavalry', p.394; E.M. Lloyd and Rev. James Lunt, 'Walker, Sir Charles Beauchamp Pyndar (1817-1894)', DNB, Vol.LVI, pp.818-19.
136 Sir Montagu Steele in discussion on Major Boulderson's lecture, Boulderson, 'The Armament and Organisation of Cavalry', p.394.
137 General M.W. Smith, *Modern Tactics of the Three Arms* (London: W. Mitchell, 1869).
138 Smith, *Modern Tactics*, pp.x-xii, 161, 295-302. See also Major General Michael W. Smith, 'Cavalry: How Far its Employment is Affected by Recent Improvements in Arms of Precision', *Journal of the Royal United Service Institution*, 12 (1868), pp.147-68, hereafter Smith, 'Cavalry Employment'.

forces. He had also served in Central India during the Mutiny. Although a member of the cavalry establishment, his campaign experience perhaps allowed him to recognise the value of less regular tactics.[139]

Smith's suggestions for improving the cavalry mostly comprised highly technical developments in drill, but he also looked to how cavalry could benefit from the new arms of precision. Apart from dismounted action, he saw the main benefit to cavalry in the improved power of artillery, and cited an American work, Roemer's *Cavalry: Its History, Management, and Uses in War*, to support him in this.

> Thus if the improved tactics of infantry have given them an advantage over the cavalry, the latter are even greater gainers by the improvements of the artillery, which, by accompanying them, affords them those favourable occasions, when to dare is to conquer.[140]

Smith also cited in his support the recently published first edition of Colonel Edward Bruce Hamley's *Operations of War*, which suggested that by combining their distinct capabilities, a combination of cavalry and horse artillery together had the power of both attack and defence.[141] The use of horse artillery was of course not a new concept, and ongoing developments in artillery and infantry firepower quickly made many of Smith's arguments and solutions for the continued effectiveness of mounted cavalry action open to question. What is notable is that even traditionally minded cavalry officers like Smith were recognising that improved firearms and artillery were a challenge to that action, and that improving the firepower of the cavalry force had to be part of the solution.

When it came to long cavalry firearms, well before 1861 the British had been experimenting with breech-loading carbines, with a shorter barrel than the infantry rifle and therefore especially suitable for mounted use. Many of these were of American manufacture, in 1856 a contract had been placed for 6,000 Sharps carbines, around half of which had been issued to five regiments of cavalry serving in India. British manufactured arms included the Calisher and Terry carbine issued to the 18th Hussars, and those using the Westley-Richards system, also trialled by the 18th Hussars as well as the 10th Hussars and the 6th Dragoon Guards.[142] The British military were also fully aware of the French experience in North Africa which encouraged the development of dismounted fire tactics and the introduction

139 E.M. Lloyd and Rev. Roger T. Stearn, 'Smith, Michael William (1809-1891)', DNB, Vol. LI, p.259, concluded that 'Smith was not only a practical soldier, but thought and wrote with some originality on military, especially cavalry, matters'.
140 Smith, 'Cavalry Employment', p.148.
141 Smith, 'Cavalry Employment', pp.148-50. Hamley was an artillery officer.
142 Bailey, *British Military Longarms*, pp.126-130, Strachan, *From Waterloo to Balaclava*, pp.85.

of musketry training into cavalry regiments before the outbreak of war in America.[143] By the 1870s the Commander in Chief, the Duke of Cambridge, speaking at the National Rifle Association said it was essential that a cavalry soldier should shoot as well as an infantry soldier could, and at the same distances, and the musketry regulations were modified to allow for more dismounted training for the cavalry. By 1889 a few cavalry regiments were even reported to be beating some infantry regiments in shooting contests.[144]

The nature of that firearm would be hotly debated for many years. There was no question that mounted infantry should have a long rifle and a bayonet; this was the very essence of their function, but ideas on how a cavalry trooper should be armed were many and varied. Nolan, who had dedicated several pages to the carbine, its means of carriage and its use, had considered that accuracy of fire was more important than rapidity, and favoured a short, handy, rifled weapon sighted to only 300 yards, since one of the greatest difficulties in combat was to get men to hold their fire.[145] Denison concurred that long range fire had a 'very demoralising tendency', and thought that sighting to 400 yards was sufficient. In his opinion the Spencer was the best weapon of its time, followed by the Sharps and then the British Snider. But he also quoted at length Brigadier General Basil W. Duke's history of Morgan's cavalry since 'as they are the opinions of an officer of great experience [...] and as they are contrary to the popular ideas on the subject, they will probably be of interest to the reader'. Duke had been Morgan's second in command and, like Robert E. Lee, argued against breech-loading weapons in favour of muzzle-loaders, as the fire was more controlled. While conceding that the Spencer was a good weapon on horseback or defending works, he thought it encouraged wild firing. As for Denison, although his views on the mounted use of the revolver had changed, he still believed that carbines should not be used mounted, and even that '[c]avalry of the line should not have carbines'.[146]

Colonel Valentine Baker, in spite of his support of the *arme blanche* for mounted action, held the completely opposite view from Denison regarding long range fire.

143 Lieutenant A. Steinmetz, 'Musketry Instruction For The Cavalry Carbine And Pistol, Recently Issued To The French Cavalry With Suggestions For The Training Of Cavalry, And Its Important Functions In Future Battles', *Journal of the Royal United Service Institution*, 5 (1861), pp.454-96 (p.455).

144 Lord Elcho during discussion at Major Boulderson's lecture delivered at the Royal United Service Institution, 5 April 1878, p.390; Trench 'Capabilities of Cavalry', pp.1004-07; Major J.R. Mecham, comment during discussion on Hutton lecture to Aldershot Military Society, Thursday March 21 1889, Hutton, *Mounted Infantry its Present and Future*, p.23. An alternative view was held by Field Marshal Sir William Robertson, who had risen from the ranks of a lancer regiment, and was dismissive of the musketry training given to the cavalry due to the limited amount of practice ammunition made available. Robertson, *From Private to Field Marshal*, p.15.

145 Nolan, *Cavalry: Its History and Tactics*, pp.121-23.

146 Denison, *Modern Cavalry*, pp.49-56; also Denison, *History of Cavalry*, p.531.

In the Henry-Martini [*sic*] carbine we shall have a beautiful arm, having the advantage of easy loading and long range. The latter, I consider a most important point for cavalry, as the instances must be very few where they could, or should, use their carbines at short ranges.[147]

It was no coincidence that Baker's regiment, the 10th Hussars, was one of the most innovative and enterprising when it came to dismounted action. Their development of dismounted tactics during the 1870s included the adoption of the American practice of one man in four, rather than one in three, acting as horse-holders.[148] Another officer in the regiment recognised that the new demands placed upon the cavalry required more than the traditional cavalry values of heroism and dash, it required a higher level of individual intelligence from officer and men alike.

Every trooper who is armed with a carbine should be trained and accustomed to act dismounted as effectively as when mounted; the special intelligence of each man must be developed, and a thorough confidence in his own resources impressed as well on the individual as on the mass.[149]

Earlier historical precedents than the Civil War could also be used. In one example, a writer used the fact that Frederick the Great's famous cavalry general, Seydlitz, had trained his cavalry to act on foot as well as mounted to support the view that cavalry should be armed with rifles like the infantry. This was on the grounds that a cavalryman armed with a carbine that could shoot indifferently at 500 yards could not engage an infantryman armed with a rifle that was effective to 1,500.[150] British cavalry officers sometimes drew on the Civil War, sometimes other historical justification, sometimes on their own experience. Yet they were not blind to the need for change. One review of a French discourse on dismounted cavalry, with which the author was far from agreeing, put the traditional cavalryman's point of view succinctly.

We are prepared to admit that many eminent generals have used their cavalry dismounted. Equally are we ready to admit that dismounted cavalry are far more formidable now than formerly, and that in many cases can be employed with excellent results. The real question at issue is, should dismounted service be considered normal or exceptional.[151]

From these examples it is clear that a simple narrative, in which there were a handful of visionaries such as Denison who were ignored by a conservative or even reactionary

147 Baker, 'Organization and Employment of Cavalry', p.383.
148 Badsey, *Doctrine and Reform in the British Cavalry*, p.9.
149 Captain J.G. Russell, 'Essay 3' in *Essays Written for the Wellington Prize*, p.133.
150 Russell, 'Cavalry', p.189.
151 Knollys, 'The Fighting of Cavalry on Foot', p.410.

majority, greatly oversimplifies the variety of individual views held. An officer who disagreed with the value of mounted infantry on the grounds that they did not have an affinity with the horse and that 'the result would be that after a few weeks of a campaign they would be dismounted', could nevertheless believe that the rifle was a more valuable weapon for the cavalry soldier than the lance.[152] Another suggested that some of the Rifle Volunteers should be the exemplar for a model cavalry corps, and proposed the long rifle for cavalry based upon his colonial experience in the Cape.[153]

* * *

The Yeomanry had for several years prior to the American Civil War recognised the importance of dismounted training. Originally raised in 1794 as a volunteer force against French invasion, it drew its officers from the landed nobility and its ranks largely from their tenants and servants. In times of war it would function as a reserve to the regular cavalry, but in peacetime its duties were to act in support of the civil powers.[154] This meant that they would often be required to act dismounted in order to force their way into enclosures or buildings, or to clear blocked roads, acting in small detachments to do so. While the regular cavalry could hanker after the decisive battle-winning charge, the Yeomanry's practical experience was more likely to be similar to the policing duties of the pre-war American regular cavalry when serving on the western plains. Their equipment, training and tactics reflected this. The carbine exercise was identified 'as necessary for the Cavalry as for the Infantry soldier', and they were instructed to use cover without regard for regular dressing of the ranks. For deployment against domestic disturbances, single rather than double rank was recommended in order to achieve greater freedom of movement and to maximise the number of carbines (not sabres) that could be used.[155]

One or two Yeomanry regiments had been converted to mounted rifles experimentally in 1853, and this role was considered by some officers to be the correct one for the Yeomanry, since 'good cavalry they will certainly never become'.[156] It was also practical on account of the type of operations which they might be expected to perform, since 'England is a country which affords even fewer opportunities for purely cavalry

152 General [Sir Charles Cameron] Shute in discussion on Major Russell's lecture at the Royal United Service Institution, 3 March 1876, Russell, 'Cavalry', p.193. Shute was a veteran of the Heavy Brigade, and MP for Brighton.
153 Colonel Bower in discussion on Major Boulderson's lecture delivered at the Royal United Service Institution, 5 April 1878, p.391.
154 Marquis of Anglesey, *A History of the British Cavalry: Vol. 1 1816-1850* (London: Leo Cooper, 1973), pp.76-78.
155 Anon, *Yeomanry Regulations, 1853* (London: HMSO, 1853), pp.24, 97-98, 197.
156 Lieutenant General Sir Percy Douglass, speaking at the Royal United Service Institution 14 March 1873 in response to Valentine Baker 'Organisation and Employment of Cavalry', p.397, see also Hutton, 'Mounted Infantry', pp.708-09; Strachan, *From Waterloo to Balaclava*, p.90.

combat than even Virginia'.[157] Havelock was of this view. If under modern conditions only really well trained and well mounted cavalry could have the speed, discipline and horsemanship to be effective in the charge, Yeomanry regiments training for a few days a year could never become this proficient. If on the other hand they were to train as mounted rifles, they would become 'the most formidable body of guerrilla combatants in the world'.[158]

One Yeomanry officer, Colonel Charles Edwards, 2nd West Yorkshire Yeomanry Cavalry, agreed with Havelock on the latter, but took exception to the idea that the Yeomanry could never become good cavalry. His comments below, responding to remarks in a lecture by Hutton, further demonstrate the sensitivity of the terms 'mounted infantry' and 'mounted rifles'.

> The Officers of the Yeomanry are not averse to their men acting as mounted riflemen, but they do not want them to be converted into mounted infantry for this reason, that in the first place the Yeomanry wish to serve primarily as mounted troops, and in the second, mounted infantry must be the very perfection of infantry merely temporarily mounted for tactical purposes, and to this standard of efficiency neither the Yeomanry nor the mounted men attached to Volunteer Corps can hope to attain. On the other hand, this force presents the very best material for mounted riflemen, and I hold that from the Yeomanry could be made as reliable and efficient a body of mounted riflemen as you will find in any country out[side] of South Africa.[159]

The sentiments reflect the social and military prejudices of the cavalry establishment, but is also similar to some of the accounts given by Starr of the reaction by America units when their cavalry status was threatened.[160]

The chief problem with the Yeomanry that led regular cavalryman to look down on them as 'poor cavalry' was that much depended upon the individual Yeomanry colonel as to how the unit was drilled. Those who sought to emulate the regular cavalry manoeuvres and focus on the mounted charge were arguably those who created the least efficient formations. Since there were limited opportunities for drill there were varying levels of horsemanship, and since there was also no consistent means of providing mounts, these 'charges' on training days were the subject of some ridicule.

---

157 Lieutenant Colonel G.F.R. Henderson 'The American Civil War, 1861-1865' in *Science of War*, pp.230-79 (p.278). Originally two lectures to the Aldershot Military Society, 9 and 16 February 1892. Reprinted in Jay Luvaas, *The American Civil War: An English View* (Chicago: University of Chicago Press, 1958), pp.174-224.

158 Havelock, *Three Main Military Questions*, pp.63-65.

159 Comments made by Colonel Charles Edwards at Hutton's lecture to the Royal United Service Institution 2 June 1886, Hutton 'Mounted Infantry' (1886), pp.731-732, including footnote.

160 Starr, *The Union Cavalry in The Civil War*, Vol.I, pp.111-12; Vol.II, pp.132-33.

More progressive members of the Yeomanry force, while resisting suggestions that they should be converted into mounted infantry, did recognise the opportunity of the force to transform its role.[161]

Major Edwards was one of those progressive thinkers amongst the Yeomanry commanders. Three years before the observations quoted above, he had given a lecture at the Royal United Service Institution proposing how the Yeomanry should be employed and trained. While their quality naturally varied due to their territorial nature, in general he characterised them as young (19-30 years old), fair shots, good horsemen, well-educated, and with very good self-discipline. He was critical of the authorities for making them too much like regular cavalry, setting 'a standard which, save under exceptional circumstances, cannot be obtained, and which is not really desirable'.[162] He believed that they would never become effective shock troops, but were ideally suited to performing detached duties as scouts, where their knowledge of the local countryside and their intelligence gave them the ability of 'noticing and forming deductions from natural and physical signs'.[163] He gave examples of drills, which were more dismounted than mounted, and proposed that 'instead of being trained, dressed, and equipped purely as regular cavalry, they should be trained and armed, &c., as Mounted Rifles'.[164] However, he did not propose conversion to mounted infantry, believing that the time available for training, which was too limited to make them good cavalry, would also prevent them from being made into good infantry.

What is most interesting is that Edwards' model for this new role was directly taken from the American Civil War. Unable to perform either traditional cavalry or infantry roles, their main activity would be partisan warfare, since they were 'in "constitution," &c., not unlike the horsemen who under Jackson, Morgan, Stuart, Pleasanton, Mosby, and others, performed such signal service in the American War of Secession'.[165] If they formed line, it should not be to charge, but to 'pour hot fire into the enemy', in order to do which he recommended a reduction in the regulation number of horse-holders. He thought swords of little use, citing Mosby and Gilmor as his authorities (possibly an indication that he had read Denison), and he would have armed the Yeomanry with revolvers and magazine rifles. The latter had been 'proved to be of startling efficacy in the American War', and when used by the Turkish cavalry

161 Major W.A. Baillie Hamilton (Lothian and Berwickshire Yeomanry), 'The Truth about the Yeomanry Cavalry', *United Service Magazine*, n.s., 3 (1891), pp.433-40.
162 Major C.J. Edwards, 2nd West York Yeomanry Cavalry, 'The Yeomanry Cavalry as an Auxiliary and Reserve Force', lecture given Wednesday 14 March 1883, *Journal of the Royal United Service Institution*, 27 (1883), pp.329-356. Lieutenant General Sir Charles Beauchamp Walker was in the chair.
163 Edwards, 'Yeomanry Cavalry', p.331.
164 Edwards, 'Yeomanry Cavalry', p.333.
165 Edwards, 'Yeomanry Cavalry', p.334.

in the Russo-Turkish War.[166] The 'value of such equipment for such troops was proved in a thousand instances during the War of Secession'.[167]

While demonstrating once again that Havelock and Denison were not the only ones to see in American practices the solution to specific British problems, this did not of course mean that Edwards' ideas were immediately and enthusiastically adopted. Again, the terminology and rigidity of definitions was part of the problem. Edwards himself was very clear that the Yeomanry thought of themselves as horse soldiers, and that 'if the term [Mounted Rifles] is repugnant to the traditions of the force' they should be styled 'as Dragoons, in the original sense of the word'.[168] However, in his audience was Colonel Mussenden, the Inspecting Officer for Auxiliary Cavalry at Aldershot, who held more traditional views. Mussenden disputed that the Yeomanry were unable to charge, thought that their shooting was poor, and insisted that if given a long rifle then this meant that they needed to be mounted infantry – there was no compromise in between. Furthermore '[n]o body of Mounted Infantry should ever be detached without having a strong cavalry support at hand'.[169] Mussenden did however note that a troop of the Middlesex Yeomanry were to be armed with a long rifle and equipped as mounted infantry as an experiment. On another occasion a Yeomanry officer argued that the Yeomanry should be armed with swords in order to fight cavalry, saying that they were happy to take on the same role as American cavalry, but in that case they should have the same weapons.[170]

Major Baillie Hamilton of the Lothian and Berwickshire Yeomanry also went into print against Hutton's proposals for converting the Yeomanry to mounted infantry, accusing the infantryman of 'having a hit' at the Yeomanry. He argued that the criticism of them was outdated; that it was now impressed upon them that outpost and reconnaissance work, and not the charge, was their most important role; and that they must shoot as well as ride well. Combat with Regulars in the open 'must obviously be beyond them', but this was 'only one of the manifold functions of cavalry'.[171] Although he did not reference the Civil War explicitly in his article, his description of how the Yeomanry would operate in the countryside of south-east England in the event of invasion nevertheless has similarities to cavalry operations in America.

> There are numberless points on any line of march from the coast where there is ample scope for the action of small bodies of cavalry [...] it is not invariably necessary for a regiment, or even a brigade of cavalry, to have an open plateau of several square miles to manoeuvre upon [...] a squadron or troops of cavalry

166 Edwards, 'Yeomanry Cavalry', p.339.
167 Edwards, 'Yeomanry Cavalry', pp.340.
168 Edwards, 'Yeomanry Cavalry', pp.333, 341.
169 Edwards, 'Yeomanry Cavalry', pp.344-45.
170 Colonel Crichton, at Hutton's lecture at the Royal United Service Institution, 1891, Hutton, 'Mounted Infantry Question', pp.799, 800 (footnote).
171 Baillie Hamilton, 'The Truth about the Yeomanry Cavalry', p.436.

properly handled, whether Regulars or Yeomanry, could work with the greatest effect in a close country, especially if the object in view were to harass a body of troops upon the line of march, when the more "serried" the enemy's squadron, the better chance would a few dismounted Yeoman have of making good practice at it.'[172]

*   *   *

British cavalry theory could not and did not develop in splendid isolation driven only by the observation of the American Civil War. It also had to take note of developments on the continent, with a view to both offensive and defensive actions against potential continental opponents. To assess whether it is true that the lessons from America were forgotten or ignored in favour of misplaced confidence in traditional tactics, based upon misunderstood interpretations of continental wars – more specifically the Franco-Prussian War of 1870 – it is therefore necessary to look briefly at contemporary changes in European cavalry at this time and how the British viewed them.

Initially it is true that European armies did not respond to the new tactics observed in America. Descriptions in contemporary British works of cavalry fights in the Austro-Prussian War of 1866 could easily be from half a century earlier.[173] British writers such as Denison and Chevenix Trench observed that only after 1870 did some of the lessons of the American Civil War take fruit. Prussian uhlans had been forced to arm themselves with French Chassepot rifles and to become mounted riflemen in order to combat the *francs-tireurs* in 1870, although they lacked the training to operate effectively in this role. The Russians took similar lessons from their operations against the Turkish *bashi-bazouks*.[174] During the 1870s European armies gradually responded to the evidence that cavalry needed to adopt fire tactics, such that one of the reviewers of Denison's *History of Cavalry* in 1877 challenged Denison's statement that European cavalry held the view that cavalry relying upon firearms were worthless.[175]

Foremost among the countries re-organising their cavalry were the Russians. Their lancer and hussar regiments adopted the mixed armament solution of lance, sword, and revolver for front ranks and carbine for the second rank, but the Russians went further in following American practice in arming their dragoon regiments as mounted rifles; specially trained to fight on foot.[176] This was recognised by contemporary observers to

172 Baillie Hamilton, 'The Truth about the Yeomanry Cavalry', p.437.
173 Smith, *Modern Tactics of the Three Arms*, pp.107-18; Denison, *Modern Cavalry*, pp.44-48 (but compare pp.56-59 on the Prussian use of breech-loading carbines mounted).
174 Denison, *History of Cavalry*, pp.485-91, particularly p.490 'the experience of that [the American Civil] war seems to have had no effect on the system of warfare in Europe', and p.494; Trench, *Cavalry in Modern War*, p.166; Russell, 'Cavalry', p.189; Boulderson, 'The Armament and Organisation of Cavalry', p.379-80.
175 Hozier, 'History of Cavalry', p.1230.
176 Trench, 'Capabilities of Cavalry', pp.990-1011.

have been effective. Trench wrote in 1884 that the necessity for cavalry to be prepared to fight on foot had been proven by the experiences of recent European campaigns, and even one sceptic on the dismounted use of cavalry admitted that the Russian dragoons had proved their value on occasion during the Russo-Turkish War.[177]

The French dropped the lance as a weapon after 1871 and produced some strong advocates for dismounted action such as Colonel T. Bonie. The ideas of French reformers were not met favourably by those who saw dismounted action as demoralising to cavalry proper.[178] The German cavalry was more conservative, possibly because they thought it took too long to train short-service troops to fight both mounted and on foot, but nevertheless by 1877 they were observed to have adopted a new carbine and to be practising infantry drill, and they had also attached mounted pioneers to their cavalry formations, increasing their ability to operate independently.[179] The Austrians largely copied the Germans, but had allocated carbines, as well as revolvers, to some lancers, and also adopted mounted pioneers. They also provided for mounted infantry in their cavalry divisions.[180]

The completeness of the Prussian victory over France in 1870-71 did result in some focus on the success of the German cavalry. However the idea that the one successful traditional charge against infantry, that of von Bredow's brigade at the battle of Mars La Tour (July 1870), bought in a doctrine that cavalry could still defeat unbroken troops is largely a modern interpretation.[181] While Denison's critics did use von Bredow and other supposed Prussian successes in 1870 to argue against his views, that charge was normally used as an example of what could *potentially* still be achieved, even in the face of modern weaponry, by well led cavalry using cover and speed to achieve surprise.[182] It was recognised that poorly led cavalry committed to futile charges had been and would be slaughtered. Denison himself thought that the opportunities for a charge were rare, and they would be accompanied by heavy

177 Trench, *Cavalry in Modern War,* p.164; Knollys, 'What we have Learnt From the War', p.142. This is the same article in which Knollys advises that cavalry should avoid recourse to always fighting on foot. The two views were not considered inconsistent.

178 Boulderson, 'The Armament and Organisation of Cavalry', p.381; Richard Knotel, Herbert Knotel and Herbert Sieg, *Uniforms of the World* (New York: Charles Scribner and Sons, 1980), p.107. The French re-adopted the lance in the 1890s in response to Prussian practice, which also enhanced its popularity in Britain, Graves, 'Cavalry Equipment', pp.707, 712. For rejection of Bonie see Lieutenant Colonel W.W. Knollys, 'The Fighting of Cavalry on Foot', passim.

179 Smyth, 'Some Observations Amongst German Armies During 1870', p.200; Trench 'Capabilities of Cavalry', pp.990-1011.

180 Trench, 'Capabilities of Cavalry', pp.990-1011; General Sir Evelyn Wood, *Achievements of Cavalry* (London: George Bell & Sons, 1897), p.247.

181 Michael Howard, *The Franco-Prussian War* (New York: Dorset Press. 1990, originally published 1961), p.157; William McEllwee, *The Art of War Waterloo to Mons* (London: Weidenfeld and Nicholson, 1974), pp.94, 224, Michael Glover, *Warfare from Waterloo to Mons* (London: Cassell, 1980), pp.138, 214.

182 Anon, [Review of Denison's] 'A History of Cavalry', p.20.

casualties such as those suffered by von Bredow's brigade, but he also accepted the 'cavalry spirit' had always included an element of gallant self-sacrifice, justifiable by results.

> The lesson the war of 1870-71 teaches, therefore, is, that at the cost of immense loss of life, and probable destruction of the cavalry force, time may be gained, an attack checked at the critical moment, and the fortune of the day turned while trembling in the balance; and of course, if a victory is won by the sacrifice, it is worth the cost. But the conditions of modern warfare are such that the occasions when these sacrifices may be demanded are likely to be rare, and the opportunity of using them to advantage seldom met with. The action of cavalry on the battle-field, especially on the old system, has consequently been very much narrowed.[183]

Colonel W.W. Knollys, writing in 1887, was one of those who disagreed with the view that sabre charges were a thing of the past. Knollys had served in the Scots Fusilier Guards and the 93rd Highlanders. He was a regular contributor of military articles to newspapers and magazines including *The Times*, the *United Service Magazine*, and the *Edinburgh Review*, and perhaps unusual for being an infantry officer who thought that mounted cavalry could still be effective. Although he admitted the great loss of life that had occurred in the cavalry charges of 1870, like Denison he believed that some had nevertheless met with tactical success. He was nevertheless critical of the tactics used by the German cavalry in 1870, and thought that rather than massed attacks in close order, 'swarm' or '*en fourrageur*' formations would have been equally effective.[184]

> Our own idea is that cavalry should rarely attack infantry in large bodies, but rather as a rule content themselves with making sudden short swoops from under cover, to which they should quickly return, only squadrons or troops being employed.[185]

Knollys went on to specify in detail the circumstances when it might still be possible for large bodies of cavalry to attack, and the tactics to be used when doing so. The infantry should have been shaken by fire, or be in disorder due to obstacles. The cavalry should have a short distance to go; over favourable ground that nevertheless contained undulations so as not to give the infantry a clear field of fire; and they should obtain surprise by emerging from such depressions, or from mist, woods or enclosures. They should charge in rank entire with considerable intervals between the men, closing up only at the moment of contact. The charge should be made from a flank or obliquely,

183 Denison, *History of Cavalry*, p.514.
184 Colonel W.W. Knollys, 'Lessons Taught by the Franco-German War', *United Service Magazine*, 705 (August 1887), pp.93-119 (p.105).
185 Knollys, 'Lessons Taught by the Franco-German War', p.115.

and the cavalry should keep close to their opponents, presumably to deter supporting fire. It was also 'eminently desirable that when cavalry make a charge infantry should invariably co-operate', since the threat of attack from cavalry would drive the enemy into groups and provide a denser target for infantry fire.[186] Knollys maintained the traditional belief in the offensive power of mounted cavalry, but this was not blind faith in the *arme blanche* and the speed of the horse, it was an attempt at reasoned analysis of how cavalry might still operate with success on a modern battlefield.

> It is quite clear that in the present day cavalry have little chance of success against even infantry in extended order unless under certain favourable conditions, such as those we have mentioned.[187]

Sources show that other cavalry officers understood that the battlefield charge, if not a thing of the past, had become much more difficult. Major Frank Russell of the 14th Hussars said in 1876 that 'there is no quality in a Cavalry Officer so fatal as bravery, unless it is tempered with discretion'. He went on to say that huge bodies of cuirassiers could not break though unbroken infantry, but that scattered bodies of infantry late in the day and short of ammunition could be charged if surprised.[188]

In 1888, Colonel R.S. Liddell, former commanding officer of the 10th Hussars, suggested that by exploiting ground, cavalry could advance unseen and make use of surprise to attack the enemy's flanks. This sounds very much like the tactics of von Bredow, but rather than opening up opportunities for a charge, Liddell seems to have envisaged the result more in terms of the traditional cavalry role of forcing infantry to form squares, which would then be vulnerable to firepower. 'The very appearance of cavalry frequently frightens infantry into masses', wrote Liddell, at which point the cavalry could dismount with carbines, any attached mounted infantry could do the same, while the 'machine guns of the cavalry would also pour in their volleys'.[189] He still believed at heart that cavalry could break a square, but that it was 'most undesirable' that they should attempt to do so, and that the losses would be disastrous. Having forced the infantry into a solid formation, artillery, infantry and machine guns should do the rest.[190]

This was a proposal for a doctrine of combined mounted and dismounted action, where firepower and not the charge was the decisive element. Liddell also mentioned the performance of his own regiment at the Battle of Tamai, in the Sudan, on 13 March 1884. Rocks and ravines meant that the ground here had not been suitable for a charge, but when a British square was broken, one of the hussar squadrons had

186 Knollys, 'Lessons Taught by the Franco-German War', p.115.
187 Knollys, 'Lessons Taught by the Franco-German War', p.112.
188 Russell, 'Cavalry', p.188.
189 Colonel R.S. Liddell, *Modern Cavalry on the Field of Battle, Lecture to Aldershot Military Society, Monday August 6 1888* (Aldershot: Gale and Polden 1888) p.8.
190 Liddell, *Modern Cavalry*, p.13.

dismounted and created a diversion by firing on the enemy flank. Liddell listed both Denison and Chevenix Trench amongst his authorities, showing again that these writers were not as isolated in their views as Luvaas implied.[191]

The 1896 cavalry manual stated that 'the attack of intact infantry, well supplied with ammunition, will almost invariably be accompanied with heavy losses'. The following year Sir Evelyn Wood, in his *Achievements of Cavalry*, noted that at the time there were two contrary deductions being drawn from von Bredow's charge, one that the Prussian cavalry could have wrecked the entire French corps if it had been properly handled, the other that the heavy losses showed the folly of the attack.[192] Though a supporter of mounted infantry, Wood was very much of the traditional school when it came to cavalry proper, and he disagreed with those who believed that cavalry could be trained to fight effectively on foot. Citing Rosser in support of this view, he produced the usual arguments of familiarity with firearms, unsuitable terrain, and lack of training to dismiss the tactics of the Americans.[193] He wrote his book in support of cavalry because he believed that the umpiring at field days was overestimating the effects of rifle and artillery fire (which seems to indicate that whatever the sentiments of the cavalry, the overall consensus in the army was not in favour of the *arme blanche*). Yet he was not a believer in futile charges, recording the failed attacks of the French on the same battlefield as von Bredow's success, and regarded it as essential that 'cavalry officers should know when and how to charge, and when to refrain from attack'.[194]

Focus on the interpretation of von Bredow's attack obscures the equally important assessments that were being made of the cavalry's value during the Franco-Prussian War regarding the relative performance of the French and German practices in relation to scouting and protecting the armies. The conclusion drawn was that cavalry would become *more* important in future – not on the battlefield itself, but because there would be larger scope for cavalry activity preceding the battle. Rapidity of concentration was the all-important lesson from 1870, and the expectation was that significant advantage would be conferred on the winner of early cavalry actions, not least through prestige and *morale*.[195] One of Liddell's reasons for lecturing on the role of modern cavalry on the battlefield was to redress the fact that after 1870 the attention of most writers had been directed at this extended use of the cavalry arm, rather than its battlefield role. Training in shooting, teaching of advanced duties, outposts,

---

191 Liddell, *Modern Cavalry*, pp.12, 15.
192 General Sir Evelyn Wood, *Achievements of Cavalry* (London: George Bell & Sons, 1897), p.238. Wood discussed the details of the charge at length, pp.224-38.
193 Wood, *Achievements of Cavalry*, pp.245-247. Wood used G.F.R. Henderson's observation at his Aldershot lecture of 9 February 1892, that American cavalry charged in column at Brandy Station, as evidence of their poor training.
194 Wood, *Achievements of Cavalry*, pp.v, 243-245, 218-220.
195 Anon, [Review of Denison's] 'A History of Cavalry', p.23; Trench, 'Capabilities of Cavalry', p.991; Trench, *Cavalry in Modern War*, pp.69, 78-79.

reconnaissance, and dismounted work had all been extended. Liddell also spoke of the American Civil War as being the catalyst for this revival of the cavalry arm, after the Crimean War had initially raised doubts upon its future.[196] Prussian and American lessons did not need to be mutually exclusive.

The real backlash in favour of traditional mounted action, and against the proponents of mounted infantry school, came not in the immediate aftermath of the Franco-Prussian War but in the late 1880s. This did arise in emulation of a new school of thought in Germany, one that emphasised the importance of *morale* as being the decisive factor in battle, and suggested that the greater mental stress which the new weapons placed upon infantry would make them more vulnerable to the *morale* effect of the sudden massed cavalry charge.[197] Foremost amongst the British advocates of offensive tactics for the cavalry was Frederic Natusch Maude, a prominent if controversial military writer towards the end of the century whose work was also published in America. Rather than simply ignoring the events of the American Civil War, Maude again explained away the behaviour of the American cavalry through the special circumstances prevalent in America, and argued that their experience and tactics therefore had little relevance to European cavalry. He also described these as points that it was 'customary to overlook', which once again implies that other writers of the time were more influenced by, and supportive of, American practices and precedents than has otherwise been portrayed.[198] Recognising that the Americans had raised enormous forces he questioned their quality along the same lines as had the contemporary observers, considering Southern and Western troopers relatively good, and those from the Eastern states 'very bad'. The contemporary criticism of lack of discipline and routine was repeated, and was said to have meant that care of the horses was very poor (though given that the Southern cavalry provided their own horses, this criticism was presumably intended to be limited to Northern horsemen). While Maude believed that the intention upon raising the forces was to make them cavalry – that is, trusting to shock tactics – and that the prairie states reached 'a very fair degree of cavalry efficiency' in this respect, he also concluded that it was impossible in the timescale, and with the *matériel* available, for the Americans to develop squadrons well enough trained to do so. The 'uniformity and precision of movement necessary to seize opportunities was not in existence on the spot at the right time'. Otherwise, argued Maude, men of the calibre of Sheridan, Sherman, Fitzhugh Lee, and Stuart would have taken advantage of them. As a result different methods had been employed, principally the

196 Liddell, *Modern Cavalry*, pp.4-5.
197 Captain G.F. Leverson RE, 'The Cavalry Division as a Body in the Fight', *Journal of the Royal United Service Institution*, 34 (1890), pp.46-100 (especially p.51); F.N. Maude, 'Cavalry on the Battlefield', *United Service Magazine*, n.s., 3 (1891), pp.310-23 (pp.319-20).
198 Lieutenant Colonel Frederic Natusch Maude, *Cavalry: Its Past and Future* (London: William Clowes, 1903), p.184.

cavalry raid, which was particularly suitable in light of the sparsely settled (and therefore sparsely garrisoned), well-watered terrain, with poor communications in the way of roads, railways, and telegraphs. Similar conditions, according to Maude, and excepting the abundance of water, prevailed in South Africa.[199]

When it came to European operations, Maude was a passionate believer in knee to knee shock tactics, and wrote in their support and against the mounted infantry school which was then in the ascendency. 'In England, the current of opinion has set very strongly against the cavalry'.[200] In other articles he argued for the historic ability of cavalry to overcome even formed infantry; that the enormous advances made by the German cavalry in the quality of horses and precision of manoeuvre enabled large masses of horsemen to be rapidly manoeuvred to achieve decision on the battle-field; that because cavalry could cross ground exposed to the enemy's fire faster than infantry that they would therefore take fewer casualties, and would therefore succeed in an assault where infantry would fail; that dispersed formations resulted in less fire-power per frontage; and that the reduced stopping power of modern bullets against horses meant that mounted charges remained viable. He claimed that the German cavalry had 'practically invariably' ridden down French infantry in 1870.[201]

Maude did accept that the square was 'an almost inconceivable formation', and the prime reason for his belief in the continuing shock value of cavalry was that the extended lines of 'more or less shaken skirmishers' would be vulnerable to such tactics. In order to take advantage of this, he argued that cavalry had to be trained to believe in their ability to ride down even unshaken infantry.[202] Maude may have taken this to the extreme, but other writers recognised the issue. Wolseley had written similarly in the Soldier's Pocket Book that 'it should be instilled into the mind of every cavalry soldier that his arm of the service is invincible', while G.F.R. Henderson, who in general thought there would be limited opportunities for the application of shock tactics in the face of the breech loader and the rifled cannon, nevertheless thought that in order to be effective when called upon to use them the cavalryman had to consider himself 'first and foremost the soldier of the charge and of the mêlée' and to retain the 'cavalry spirit' and dash that differentiated him from other arms.[203]

199 Maude, Cavalry: Its Past and Future, pp.184-86.
200 Captain Frederic Natusch Maude, Cavalry versus Infantry (and other Essays) (Kansas City: Hudson–Kimberley, 1896), p.94.
201 Maude, Cavalry versus Infantry, pp.9-10; Maude, 'Rise, Decay and Revival of the Prussian Cavalry' in Attack Or Defence, pp.19-21; Maude, 'Field Fortifications and Intrenched Camps' in Attack Or Defence, p.37, reprinted from Operations of the Military Engineering of the International Congress of Engineers, 1894; Maude, 'Cavalry on the Battlefield', pp.322-23; Maude, Cavalry: Its Past and Future, pp.182, 260; Lieutenant Colonel F.N. Maude, 'Notes on the Evolution of Cavalry', United Service Magazine, n.s., 23 (1901), pp.5-23, 111-126, 229-247 (p.241).
202 Maude, Cavalry versus Infantry, p.20.
203 Wolseley, Soldier's Pocket Book, p.247; Lieutenant Colonel G.F.R. Henderson, 'The Tactical Employment of Cavalry', in The Science of War, pp.51-69 (pp.55, 60-61). Originally published in Encyclopaedia Britannica ([n.d.]).

Henderson took a different view both to Maude and to the advocates of mounted infantry. He did not believe that as cavalry the Americans 'would have been able to cope with good European troops in open terrain', but equally 'no European cavalry would have been able to touch them on their own ground'. Nor, when dismounted, did he think them to be as efficient as the ordinary infantry. Yet he did not dismiss them as mounted infantry, allowing that they preferred to fight on horseback whenever possible. The key for Henderson was adapting the tactics to suit the terrain. It was the combination of mobility and firepower that made the 'mounted riflemen of America [...] practically a new feature in modern war'.[204] Henderson also recognised that these tactics had taken time to evolve. 'It was as much the length of the War of Secession as native ingenuity which enabled the Americans to work out so many military problems to their logical conclusion'.[205] While at the start of the war their cavalry may have been indifferent, by the end Henderson believed that it was capable of everything that could be asked of it, fulfilling all the classic cavalry roles of pursuit (Appomattox, 1865); screening the army (Wilderness, 1864), pitched battle (Brandy Station, 1863); defensive delaying action (Spotsylvania, 1864); and decisive offense (Shenandoah Valley, 1864). Key to all this he believed was its ability to combine both dismounted and mounted action.[206]

Much of Henderson's writing by the end of the century emphasised the priority of fire tactics for cavalry. In particular he advised that the traditional roles of pursuit and delay were better carried out through firepower and position than through the *arme blanche*. In this he echoed Havelock's writings three decades earlier. It was a 'pious expectation' that horsemen could advance on mass on a shaken enemy and rout them, only bad troops would so break, and it would only take 'a few cool and intelligent riflemen' to 'easily hold at bay far larger number of mounted troops', while artillery and machine guns would occupy positions to stem the attack. In pursuit, it was therefore necessary to adopt the tactical defensive, to occupy positions blocking the line of retreat and holding the enemy to be encircled and forced to surrender, exactly as Sheridan had done at Appomattox in 1865. In retreat, 'fire is a far better means of gaining time and keeping the foe at a distance than shock, and a retreat from position to position, making full use of the rifle and the machine gun may be less glorious but much more effective than the supreme self sacrifice'.[207] This doctrine of firepower for the cavalry was to be adopted, albeit after the further experience of the Boer War, in the 1902 *Combined Training* manual:

---

204 Henderson, 'The American Civil War, 1861-1865', in *Science of War,* pp.247, 266, 275.
205 Henderson, 'The Tactical Employment of Cavalry', in *Science of War,* p.55.
206 Henderson, 'The Tactical Employment of Cavalry', in *Science of War,* p.56.
207 Henderson, 'The Tactical Employment of Cavalry', in *Science of War,* pp.65, 67. See Havelock, *Three Main Military Questions,* pp.69-111 for an earlier and more extended British appreciation of Sheridan's tactics in 1865; Denison, *History of Cavalry,* pp.474-83 acknowledges his later study is based upon Havelock's work.

Artillery altogether, infantry almost wholly, and cavalry to a very great extent make use of fire to bring about the enemy's overthrow. All movements on the battlefield have but one end in view, the development of fire in greater volume and more effectively than that of the opposing force.[208]

However, even Henderson was not prepared to break entirely with the cavalry tradition. Rapid, decisive, mounted action was still considered an essential option for cavalry. While the rifle had proved superior to the carbine (unless a repeater), he still wrote that Sheridan's cavalry in 1864 had beaten their rifle-armed opponents because they were also willing to charge with the sabre. Against infantry 'unless surprised, shock tactics have very little chance of success', but 'in dealing with a dismounted [cavalry] force [...] shock tactics may play a most important part'.[209] As with much of Henderson's thought, this particular piece of reasoning turned around the moral side of combat.

Given that there was such a range of discussion and thought about how the cavalry arm should face the challenges of modern warfare, how is it that its most prominent historian, the Marquis of Anglesey, concluded that 'the average cavalry colonel's views [sic] as to how to use his regiment was no different in 1898 from what it had been a century before'?[210] The action which prompted this statement was the charge of the 21st Lancers at the Battle of Omdurman, fought in the Sudan against the Mahdists on 2 September 1898, which has become an icon for the conservatism of the British cavalry. This is largely due to the disproportionate casualties suffered by the regiment in what was a very one-sided battle. It is also due to the later comments of its most famous participant, Lieutenant Winston Spencer Churchill, who in the 1930s wrote that '[o]f course there would be a charge. In those days, before the Boer War, British Cavalry had been taught little else', and also quipped that after the charge the commanding officer of the Lancers 'remembered for the first time that we had carbines'.[211]

The action was certainly flawed, though it is hard to believe that given the same situation, facing an apparently disordered and defeated enemy, most Civil War cavalry generals such as Stuart, Merritt, or Custer, would not have given the order to charge. A more generous interpretation than Churchill's is nevertheless possible. Far from demonstrating that the British cavalry was only trained in the charge, when the initial impact failed to break the Mahdist infantry the Lancers rapidly transitioned from shock tactics to dismounted fire tactics (the entire action was over in around 30 minutes). This indicates the flexibility of British doctrine by this time. Having

208 Anon, *Combined Training* (London: HMSO, 1902), pp.14-15.
209 Henderson, 'The Tactical Employment of Cavalry', in *Science of War*, p.60.
210 Anglesey, *History of the British Cavalry*, Vol.III, p.407.
211 Churchill, *My Early Life* (1930), pp.208, 203, cited in Anglesey, *History of the British Cavalry*, Vol.III, p.384-385. The Lancers lost 21 killed and 50 wounded, out of a total of 482 casualties in the entire army.

attempted the first form of action and discovering that the enemy was too strong for those tactics to succeed, the Lancers were immediately able to adopt the second to complete the defeat of the enemy. Further evidence of the tactical flexibility in British cavalry thinking had already been seen that morning at Omdurman when the Egyptian Cavalry and Mounted Infantry (on camels), British-trained and led, had conducted a fighting withdrawal using fire and movement tactics supported by artillery and machine guns, as well as at least one mounted charge against enemy horse.[212]

*   *   *

While tactical issues have become the focus of much modern debate about the cavalry, the strategic role of cavalry, and the appropriate organisation that should ensue, was equally if not more important in contemporary articles. Once again the American Civil War informed a great deal of that discussion. There was a strong argument that cavalry would play a larger role than ever, especially prior to battle being joined. Increased ranges of engagement had extended the size of the battlefield. The near impossibility of direct frontal assault meant that flanking manoeuvres would become essential. The general who could keep his intentions hidden from the enemy while securing knowledge of his opponent's location therefore had a huge advantage, and cavalry superiority was vital to conceal flanking movements and enable envelopment, as evidenced by actions such as Chancellorsville. The strategic use of cavalry in Europe, in 1866 and 1870, was acknowledged as being substantially inferior to that of the Americans, whose lessons 'would seem to have been overlooked alike by the Austrians, the French and the Germans'.[213]

Moreover, the military thinkers of the day recognised that the increased size of armies and their long lines of battle rendered them more sensitive to attacks on communication. The new technologies of the railway and the telegraph actually increased this vulnerability, and the cavalry raid launched against the enemy's line of communications was recognised as something new to warfare introduced by the Americans – 'a turning point, or the beginning of a new chapter in the history of what cavalry may be trained to achieve'.[214] Wolseley's *Soldiers Pocket Book* described

---

212 Anglesey, *History of the British Cavalry*, Vol.III, pp.375-77. Douglas Haig was amongst the British officers with the Egyptian cavalry.

213 General William H. Morris (USA), 'On The Best Method Of Arming, Equipping, and Manoeuvring Infantry', *Journal of the Royal United Service Institution*, 10 (1866), pp.209-24 (p.217); James, *Role of Cavalry*, p.3; Major General Hutton, 'Mounted Troops in War', *United Service Magazine*, n.s., 10 (1895), pp.431-49 (pp.432, 438); Lieutenant Colonel G.F.R. Henderson, 'Tactics of the Three Arms Considered', in *Science of War*, pp.70-86 (p.77). Originally published in *Encyclopaedia Britannica* ([n.d.]); Lieutenant Colonel G.F.R. Henderson, *Stonewall Jackson and the American Civil War*, 2 vols (Secaucus NJ: Blue and Grey Press, n.d, originally published London: Longmans, 1900), Vol.II, pp.418, 425, 435-37.

214 Trench, *Cavalry in Modern War*, p.53.

Sherman's men destroying railway tracks, 1864. (Library of Congress)

the extensive use in America of cavalry operations to destroy railways and disruption of enemy communication. Whenever the future role of cavalry was discussed, it was common for the formal training of troops in the destruction of railways and telegraphs to be proposed.[215]

More attention was shown in Europe towards these operations in America than has been acknowledged. It is true that in 1866 and again in 1870 relatively little use was made of detached cavalry and the armies were criticised for keeping their cavalry to the rear rather than in front of the armies, but the Prussians had sent cavalry on a limited scale to attack railways in 1870, and subsequently laid plans to initiate cavalry raids at the start of any future war to disrupt enemy mobilisation; to prevent the provisioning of fortresses; to break railway lines and telegraphs; and to spread false intelligence. Once again, Prussian and American lessons did not need to be mutually exclusive.[216]

215 Wolseley, *Soldier's Pocket-Book*, pp.301-07, 317; General Shute at Major Russell's lecture at the Royal United Service Institution, Russell, 'Cavalry', pp.192-94; Major J.C. Ker Fox (South Staffordshire Regiment), 'The Training of the German Cavalry as Compared with that of the English', *Journal of the Royal United Service Institution*, 34 (1891), pp.805-828 (pp.819, 824, 827).
216 Trench, 'Capabilities of Cavalry', p.991; Trench, *Cavalry in Modern War*, pp.69, 78-79, 216.

Western Europe was expected to offer little opportunity for extensive detached action, but the circumstances to the east, where there were large areas of sparsely settled land with limited communications, meant that the Russians adopted mounted infantry tactics and independent strategic operations in the 1870s. The Russian cavalry executed long range raids on manoeuvres in 1876 to the south-west of Warsaw. The exercise was recognised as being carried out 'after the American fashion' with practice at hindering the enemy mobilisation, seizing railways, protecting friendly mobilisation and railway communications, and conducting reconnaissance. The invading cavalry suppressed or bypassed infantry garrisons with ease, some units covering 200 miles in 48 hours. Another exercise was carried out in 1883. Similar real operations met with mixed success in the Russo-Turkish War of 1877-78, but Lieutenant General Joseph Vladimirovich Gourko's operation of July 1877 in Bulgaria was regarded as a classic operation on a par with those undertaken in America.[217]

The strategic importance of cavalry was being expounded by other British military writers. Another of the submissions for the Wellington Essay Prize of 1871 was from Captain J.C. Russell of the 10th Hussars. While covering the general question, Russell focussed in particular on how the cavalry arm should be used. Although his direct references to the American conflict are limited to a comment on the value of light troops acting independently of an army, and the efficacy of 'partisan' troops such as cossacks, Spanish guerrillas, the Prussian uhlans, and the 'raiders of the great American struggle', his observations are very much in line with the use of cavalry in America. Amongst the detailed comments are statements that in enclosed country cavalry should be massed and march independently; employed so as to be the first portion of the army to meet the enemy; that the actions of small numbers of cavalry are never of much value; the detachment of cavalry to perform partisan works and manoeuvre; and its use for reconnaissance in force and to screen the movements of the main army.[218]

Russell's conclusion was that rather than being a declining force, in future cavalry should have a more extended role than it was usually assigned. Its use should not be solely confined to the climax of the battle, or on outposts, or even in combination with other arms. 'It must be considered as a force able to move and manoeuvre independently, and at a distance from other support, finding in itself every resource necessary to meet different contingencies.'[219] This would require substantial training of the troops and especially a high level of competence amongst officers. 'The true way "to cover an army on the march and to gain intelligence of the enemy" is to employ for the purpose a mass of cavalry, as an independent force, acting under the command of

217 Trench, 'Capabilities of Cavalry', pp.1001-04; Trench, *Cavalry in Modern War*, pp.73 (footnote), 217-24, 227; Hutton 'Mounted Troops in War', p.439.
218 Captain J.C. Russell, 'Essay 3' in *Essays Written for the Wellington Prize* (Edinburgh: Wm. Blackwood & Sons, 1872), pp.99-188, (pp.119-120, 130-31).
219 Russell, 'Essay 3', p.133.

a trusted leader.'[220] While not explicit, it would be hard to find a better description of the way in which American cavalry had operated at its best under Stuart or Sheridan, or more at odds with the limited deployments of British mounted forces in the course of the century.

Russell was not alone in proposing new and often much more independent roles for mounted troops. In 1876 his namesake in the 14th Hussars proposed that an independent cavalry division should be included in any expeditionary force, on expectation of large cavalry actions at outset of any European war, and that the cavalry should be trained in the use of the telegraph and in the destruction of railways, in emulation of American practice. Boulderson suggested that mounted infantry could be used as divisional cavalry, either to be massed or dispatched on raids, since they were 'better able than cavalry proper to take care of the flanks of their own divisions and to assist in turning the flanks of the enemy'. Such mounted infantry would provide support to advanced artillery and cavalry.[221]

The practical opportunity for any large strategic manoeuvres against enemy lines of communication by British cavalry was limited. In the event of an invasion of home soil, the enemy's communications would primarily be by sea. Large scale operations on the continent by Britain's army were rare, and would likely be opposed by superior numbers of enemy cavalry. Against colonial enemies there simply were no highly vulnerable communications in the form of railways or telegraphs to attack, rather the British faced the more difficult task of trying to defend such extended lines. In addition, budgetary and geographic constraints meant that British cavalry were unable to train realistically for war, as there was insufficient space for cavalry to play a strategic role during field manoeuvres. Even the opportunities to practice outpost and reconnaissance duties were very limited in Britain.[222]

Even so, British writers did recommend, and more importantly generals in the field did make some use of, strategic operations by mounted troops. In the 1882 campaign in Egypt the cavalry division under Major General Drury-Lowe was used after the Battle of Tel-el-Kebir to seize Cairo in 'a bold exploit, which may vie in its results with anything which cavalry has achieved by prompt and rapid action in any modern campaign', capturing 10,000 of the enemy without a shot being fired purely by moral effect.[223] Less successfully, Wolseley formed a flying column of all arms, including mounted infantry in the form of the Camel Corps, in the Sudan in 1884 in an attempt to cross the desert, seize the village of Metemmeh, and advance on Khartoum ahead

220 Russell, 'Essay 3', p.135. The phrase in double quotes is from the original text and is one of the specific subject areas asked in the Wellington Essay question.
221 Russell, 'Cavalry', pp.183,190, 194; Boulderson, 'The Armament and Organisation of Cavalry', p.385.
222 Trench, *Cavalry in Modern War*, p.47; Trench, 'Capabilities of Cavalry', pp.999, 1006-07; Baker, 'Organisation and Employment of Cavalry', p.386.
223 Hutton, 'Mounted Troops in War', p.440; Trench, *Cavalry in Modern War*, p.225; Anglesey, *History of the British Cavalry*, Vol.III, pp.303-04, 320-21.

of the river column advancing down the Nile.[224] On a smaller scale, in the operations in Matabeleland in 1893-94 a small mounted column of less than eight hundred men was able to defeat the Matabele nation, using light artillery and machine guns to substitute for traditional infantry firepower.[225] None of these were raids in direct imitation of the American Civil War, although Hutton considered Drury-Lowe's action as 'the latest and best illustration of the system which the American leaders had initiated twenty years before', but they all demonstrate a readiness of the British military to adapt to new strategic and tactical realities.[226]

* * *

Past discussion of the *arme blanche* debate has usually focussed on the regular cavalry establishment. But this only reflects one component of the British mounted arm, and ignores not only the Yeomanry but also the imperial dimension. Denison, Havelock, and Chevenix Trench all came from an imperial background. Havelock's *Three Main Military Questions of the Day* devoted the majority of its pages to India, and his ideas on mounted infantry were primarily aimed at reducing the cost of the army's Indian establishment. Throughout the 19th Century, and into the 20th, Britain relied upon large numbers of auxiliary and irregular mounted troops, and their tactics and training were more similar to those found in the American war than to anything in Europe.[227]

[N]o uniform, most of them wearing their own leather-patched patrol jackets [...] open-necked flannel shirts, brown cord breeches and a slouch hat around which was wrapped a strip of coloured cloth to distinguish the regiment [...] no overcoats or raincoats, only one blanket, strapped to the saddle. They carried no swords, and were armed for the most part with revolvers and [...] carbines.[228]

224 Anglesey, *History of the British Cavalry*, Vol.III, pp.320-21.
225 Hutton, 'Mounted Troops in War', p.440.
226 Hutton, 'Mounted Troops in War', p.440. Although cavalry raids did have precedents in the Napoleonic Wars, in the context this would appear to be a case of identifying new ways in which the cavalry would operate or use its forces on campaign, and therefore to constitute innovative change under one modern definition, that of Rosen, *Winning the Next War*, p.6. Paradoxically Rosen used the US cavalry as an example of how large organisations resist change, ibid, p.2.
227 Havelock, *Three Main Military Questions*, pp.31-32, 114, 115-26. For earlier experiments with mounted infantry, and for earlier dismounted cavalry action in a colonial context, see Strachan, *From Waterloo to Balaclava*, pp.87-90.
228 Anglesey, *History of the British Cavalry*, Vol.III, p.188. This is a composite description by Anglesey from several sources, but reflects the appearance and equipment of the Frontier Light Horse in 1879.

The Frontier Light Horse on vidette duty in Zululand, drawing by Captain Laurence of the King's Own Regiment, 1879. (King's Own Royal Regiment Museum, Lancaster)

This could easily have been written by Fremantle or Ross, describing a Confederate trooper in 1863. In fact it describes the Frontier Light Horse in South Africa during the Zulu War of 1879. Temporary mounted infantry units were also formed from men taken from the regular infantry units available in South Africa, mounted upon locally purchased horses, and armed with a rifle and bayonet. One volunteer officer thought that 'this sort of cavalry will be the force of the future for Africa, as they are as good as any others and far cheaper'.[229]

Many Indian Army officers were traditionalists who favoured the *arme blanche* and mounted action. Indian cavalry regiments continued to carry the sword or lance, both traditional local weapons, and the number of regiments armed with the lance actually increased over the period. However, Indian regiments were raised through the *sillidar* system where each man provided his own horse and equipment, and as a result the latter was much lighter and more practical than that of British regulars. The greater mobility of the Indian horse meant they were preferred to European regiments for use in local law enforcement and in the frequent minor frontier expeditions of the period which were not dissimilar to those carried out by post-war US Cavalry on the Great Plains. This led to Indian cavalry becoming skilled in reconnaissance and outpost work, and in operating on foot as well as mounted. Carbines were sometimes carried

229 Anglesey, *History of the British Cavalry*, Vol.III, p.184, quoting W H.Tommason.

slung across the back, and in 1896 one Bombay regiment even privately purchased its own Maxim gun.[230]

British regiments posted to India also learned the need to adopt fire tactics in combination with mounted charges in the difficult terrain. At Fatehabad, in April 1879, the 10th Hussars expended over one thousand rounds of ammunition in a small action against Afghan tribesmen. When it came to a mounted action the same day, the native Guides regiment, operating in a looser formation, were found more effective against the skirmishing tribesmen than the hussars charging *en masse*. Indian cavalry also showed itself highly mobile on campaign, the 6th Bengal Cavalry force-marched for three days without a single straggler during the Tel-el-Kebir campaign in Egypt in 1882. An American observer wrote that '[c]avalry capable of such performance is not cavalry to be thought lightly of'.[231]

By the end of the century, Dominion troops were also becoming prominent in British thinking. Wolseley's views on Denison represent an early example of this. Henry Charles Fletcher, the observer of 1862, became Military Secretary in Canada in the 1870s and recognised that though there was little use in Canada for cavalry based upon European lines, there might be considerable scope for mounted infantry. He emphasised the need for the study of recent campaigns especially the 'great American civil war [*sic*]' and quoted Sheridan as having the view that mounted infantry should be augmented at the expense of artillery.[232] In Australia too, little use was seen for traditional cavalry but mounted infantry was seen as a natural arm for the colony. This mounted infantry, it was made clear, 'must by no means be looked upon as cavalry – no charging or fighting on horseback' but could nevertheless operate effectively as scouts and vedettes.[233]

When Hutton chose, in 1895, his ideal example of a well-balanced mounted force it was neither a formation from the British nor from the Indian army, but the New South Wales Brigade. This contained not only a traditional shock element (lancers) and mounted infantry, but also mounted engineers and its own attached medical and

230 Upton, *Armies*, p.77; Anglesey, *History of the British Cavalry*, Vol.III, pp.147,150, 159-160, 164-65, 218, 226-27; Boris Mollo, *The Indian Army* (Poole: New Orchard, 1986, originally published Blandford, 1981), pp.114-22; Major E.A. De Cosson, *Fighting the Fuzzy-Wuzzy: Days and Nights of Service with Sir Gerald Graham's Field Force in Suakin* (London: Greenhill Books, 1990, originally published London: John Murray, 1886), pp.61, 98; General Sir James Hope Grant, speaking at the Royal United Service Institution, 26 March 1873 in discussion on Colonel Valentine Baker's lecture 'Organisation and Employment of Cavalry', p.405.

231 Anglesey, *History of the British Cavalry*, Vol.III, pp.215-17,166. Anglesey does not name the American source.

232 Colonel Henry Charles Fletcher, *A Lecture delivered at the Literary and Scientific Institute, Ottawa, February 1875* (Canadian Institute for Historical Microproductions, 1981, microfiche in British Library), p.10.

233 Lieutenant Colonel R. Elias, 'The Land Forces of Australia', *Journal of the Royal United Service Institution*, 34 (1890), pp.205-28 (pp.212-13).

supply detachment. Thus it represented a self-contained force ideally suited to independent strategic operations. Moreover, Hutton directly compared the challenges of the size of the country in the defence of Australia to those faced by America in 1862, and the Australian forces to the Confederacy's 'magnificent force of improvised mounted troops'.[234]

*　*　*

The British cavalry in the late 19th Century had its faults. With the further hindsight of the Boer War, Henderson himself would become one of its strongest critics, comparing it unfavourably to the American horsemen of the Civil War.[235] Yet the picture of a uniformly conservative body clinging to outmoded tactics is unfair, and the evidence used to support this view is selective. A cavalry in which its most prestigious regiments, mostly officered by peers or the sons of peers, detached volunteers to create a composite battalion of camel-mounted infantry cannot be condemned as unreceptive to change.[236] Nor can it be said that the British establishment assumed that 'only European wars counted'.[237]

The impact that modern firepower would have on future cavalry tactics was already being recognised prior to the American Civil War, and its implications were gradually reflected in doctrine and tactics throughout the period. All the writers on the cavalry from Nolan onwards recognised this impact; the challenge was how to meet it. A focus on the *arme blanche* controversy has given overdue prominence to the immediate battlefield role of cavalry, and in particular the retention in cavalry tactics of the mounted charge at the climax of battle. However, the most significant change in cavalry thinking arising from the Civil War, and from the European wars of the following decade, was the recognition that in future the main role of mounted troops would be in the action leading up to and at the fringes of the battlefield, rather than on the battlefield itself. No longer capable of delivering by itself a massed, battle-winning charge, cavalry nevertheless now had a greater role to play in screening the movements of the new massed armies, and in penetrating those screens to find out the enemy's intent. Once battles lines were formed, flanking movements, encirclements, and attacks on the line of communications were the key to breaking those lines, and the mobility of the mounted arm was expected to be essential in bringing this about.

234 Hutton, 'Mounted Troops in War', p.441. Hutton was however talking to an Australian audience. For Hutton's development of the Australian Mounted Arm see Bou, *Light Horse*, pp.27-31.
235 Henderson, 'Foreign Criticism', in *Science of War*, pp.376-77; Lieutenant Colonel G.F.R. Henderson, 'The British Army', in *Science of War*, pp.382-434 (pp.414, 417, 420).
236 Anglesey, *History of the British Cavalry*, Vol.III, pp.321-22; Winrow, 'The British Regular Mounted Infantry', p.421 for detailed analysis of officers in the Camel Corps.
237 Bond, 'Doctrine and Training in the British Cavalry', p.98.

The lessons from America were not and could not be the only factor in this change because the British cavalry had to plan to operate in many different theatres and against many different foes, but they were a major component in that debate throughout the period. The Civil War was still being used as a source for examples into the 1890s when the further development of technology could have been taken to render those lessons obsolete. The very factors that the cavalryman used to dismiss the Americans as mounted infantry were relevant to the British because their establishment of trained 'proper' cavalry was so limited compared to continental armies. The Americans were not true cavalry because of limited time for training – the same would be true of any large body of mounted troops raised in time of war, and of those improvised on colonial service. The close terrain of America did not favour mounted action – the same would be true of south-east England in the event of invasion, so the Yeomanry and cavalry needed to be able to fight dismounted. The Americans were more familiar with firearms than with traditional cavalry weapons such as sabre and lance – the same was true of many colonial mounted troops such as the Australians.

Men like Havelock, Denison, and Chevenix Trench were not isolated voices ignored by a conservative establishment; they represented part of a spectrum of views around how to equip and train mounted troops in this new era. Denison in particular was far more conservative than modern writers, or indeed his contemporary critics, have acknowledged. Even the supporters of traditional cavalry accepted that mounted infantry – troops trained in contemporary infantry tactics for defence and attack, armed with long rifles and the bayonet, but using the mobility conferred upon them by the horse to place them in a favourable tactical position – had a place in modern war. What they doubted was that such troops had the horsemanship and the quickness of movement to replace the cavalry in its traditional mounted roles, or to defeat well-trained and well-armed cavalry in the all-important opening battle in a European theatre. The competent cavalry officer also recognised that the key to victory could no longer be just the *élan* and discipline of the charge, though these were still important, but was a combination of mobility, surprise, firepower, and flexible tactics. By the end of the century British cavalry doctrine, while still believing in mounted action to defeat the enemy's cavalry in the opening engagements of the campaign, progressively emphasised the use of mobile firepower to bring about overall tactical success in support of the other arms.

5

The Bullet and the Bayonet – The Infantry

Just as cavalry theorists sought to find a way to preserve their traditions and their role on the battlefield in the face of the new firepower, so too did those concerned with the infantry. The traditional image of British infantry tactics during this period is one of the continued use of unsuitable, obsolete, close order formations that had no place in modern war.[1] However, the increasing number of professional and educated officers present in the British Army following the mid-century reforms could see that the improved range and rate of fire of modern weaponry would significantly change warfare. This chapter explores to what extent the lessons of the American Civil War influenced this change. It looks at the attitude to entrenchments and the influence of the American war on the debate over offensive and defensive tactics. By examining the changes in the British tactical manuals it evaluates whether there really was a rejection of the lessons learnt in America in response to the European campaigns of the 1860s and 1870s, and concludes with an examination of the state of British tactical theory at the end of the century, and how much it was based upon the tactics of the Civil War.

In 1867 a new infantry drill manual was published. The immediate reason for its appearance was the replacement of the old Enfield muzzle-loading rifle with the new Snider-Enfield breech-loader. Based solely on the evidence of this document, it would appear that as far as the British military were concerned, the war in America might never have happened. Changes were limited almost solely to the technical impact

---

1   Craddock, 'The American Civil War and its Influence on the British Army', p.204, citing David Clammer, *The Victorian Army in Photographs* (London: David and Charles, 1975), p.6; Pemberton, *Battles of the Boer War*, p.30. The view is perpetuated by modern web-sites, for example https://www.britishbattles.com/great-boer-war/battle-of-colenso/ [accessed 24/05/2018], 'At the outbreak of the [Boer] war British tactics were appropriate for the use of single shot firearms, fired in volleys controlled by company and battalion officers; the troops fighting in close order'; 'The idea of fire and movement on the battlefield was largely unknown, many regiments still going into action in close order'; and 'Britain engaged volunteer forces from Britain, Canada, Australia and New Zealand who brought new ideas and more imaginative formations to the battlefield.'

of the new rifle, such as reducing the complexity of the firing drill down from nine pages to only three. The 1867 manual presented no new formations for manoeuvre or fighting, which were replicated in their entirety from the 1861 instructions. The basic formation both in defence and in attack remained the traditional British close order line in two ranks.[2]

The following year the American War Department issued their new drill manual, largely the creation of Brevet Major General Emory Upton (USA), who had emerged from the war as the most important American tactical theorist. Upton and his new manual have been seen as the start of a distinctive American school of tactics. The manual particularly stressed its application to all arms and its simplicity, abbreviating training time being 'of great importance in its relation to the volunteer force'. It also specifically aimed to deal with the difficulties of performing complicated manoeuvres in the wooded and obstructed country that could be expected in America, and to provide for the single rank tactics that were appropriate to the new breech-loaders, as well as a new system of skirmishing.[3]

In contrast to the British drill book, the American manual was directly based upon, and therefore reflected, wartime experience. It was clearly a more progressive document than its contemporary, but Upton's manual remained in parts as traditional as the British. It was, above all, a drill manual with a large proportion of its pages concerned with the basic training by rote of raw troops at an individual level.[4] It contains instructions not only for the new breech-loaders, but also for the obsolete muzzle-loading Springfield rifle. It still assumed that many manoeuvres by unengaged troops would be in traditional double line formation and even column. Perhaps more surprisingly, given the view that the war had supposedly introduced a radical new doctrine for cavalry into American military thought, it still dedicated several pages to the forming of squares and other defensive formations against cavalry.[5] Squares had rarely been formed during the Civil War, but while the Americans could have faced conventional charging cavalry in wars against Mexico or Britain, this retention of shoulder to shoulder formations to repel such attacks indicates that the ability of firepower alone to hold off cavalry was not a clear conclusion taken from the war.[6]

2   Anon, *Field Exercises and Evolutions of Infantry* (London: HMSO, 1861), hereafter *Field Exercises* (1861); Anon, *Field Exercises and Evolutions of Infantry* (London: HMSO, 1867), hereafter *Field Exercises* (1867).
3   Brevet Major General Emory Upton (USA), *A New System of Infantry Tactics Double and Single Rank, Adapted to American Topography and Improved Fire Arms* (New York: D. Appleton, 1868), p.iii-iv. For Upton's importance in American tactical thought, see Perry D. Jamieson, *Crossing the Deadly Ground: United States Army Tactics 1865–1899* (Tuscaloosa: University of Alabama Press, 1994), pp.3-11.
4   Upton, *Infantry Tactics*, pp.8-66. Compare Anon, *Field Exercises* (1861), pp.4-58.
5   Upton, *Infantry Tactics*, pp.27-34, 203-09, 289-94, 297.
6   There are very few firm instances of squares being formed during the Civil War. *The War of the Rebellion: a Compilation of the Official Records of the Union and Confederate Armies* electronic edn (Cornell University, 2015) <http://ebooks.library.cornell.edu/m/moawar/

The Civil War had given the Americans enormous practical evidence of the power of the new rifled muskets to influence their new tactics, though it needs to be remembered that the majority of troops had been armed with the muzzle-loading Springfield, or its imported equivalents, rather than breech-loaders. The British by comparison had relatively limited experience of what could be considered modern warfare. Rifled muskets had been used during their campaigns in the Crimea, India, and China. However, in each case the enemy had not been armed with the new weapons, so British troops had not been on the receiving end of the improved firepower. Without the impetus of a major war against an equally well-armed enemy, which was not to occur until the Boer War of 1899-1902, it was perhaps to be expected that the 1867 manual did not introduce widespread innovation.[7]

There were also strong conservative elements in the army that were resistant to change. Foremost amongst their objections was that a loss of courage and aggressive spirit would result from the longer ranges at which fire would be initiated. This is not dissimilar to the views expressed by the more aggressive American generals, who believed that *élan* and the bayonet could still carry a defended position, and that holding defensive positions weakened their men's resolve. The counter-argument to this was that winning the fire-fight through effective long range fire was necessary before the infantry could close.[8] A more technical objection was the lower stopping power of the smaller bullets used in the new rifles. Noted as early as 1857, this would be a recurring motif throughout the remainder of the century as the increased rate of fire of the new rifles required an increase in the number of rounds to be carried, and a corresponding reduction in calibre. In particular the stopping power of the smaller bullets against cavalry would be a matter for debate.[9] A further claim was that the

waro.html> (hereafter 'OR') identifies three: the 69th New York at First Bull Run (OR Series 1, Vol. 2, p.370); the 25th Iowa in a skirmish in Alabama in October 1863 (OR Series 1, Vol. 31, p.24) and the 37th US Colored Troops in operations before Richmond in October 1864 (OR Series 1 Vol. 42, p.815). On none of these occasions was the square attacked. Henry Kyd Douglas remembered that during the Third Battle of Winchester, on 19 September 1864, while most of the Union cavalry assaults were met in line, '[f]or the first time I saw a division of Infantry, or what was left of one, form a hollow square to resist cavalry', Henry Kyd Douglas, *I Rode with Stonewall* (London: Putnam, 1940, originally written 1899) p.309-10, referenced in Starr, *The Union Cavalry in The Civil War*, Vol.II, p.276. Douglas wrote that the charge was repulsed, a modern website suggests the charge was successful, <http://www.fortcollier.com/history.htm>, [accessed 5 July 2018].

7   The Anglo-Transvaal War of 1880-81 had earlier demonstrated the effectiveness of Boer rifle fire, but the size of actions does not merit classification as a major war. In the Anglo-Egyptian War of 1882 the British faced an enemy well-equipped with modern weapons but poorly trained, and its short duration means that the conflict cannot be classified as major.

8   Lieutenant Colonel R.A. Dixon, 'The Rifle – Its Probable Influence on Modern Warfare', *Journal of the United Service Institution*, 1 (1857), pp.95-120 (p.112).

9   Lieutenant Colonel Wilford, 'On The Rifle; Showing the Necessity for its Introduction as a Universal Infantry Weapon', *Journal of the United Service Institution*, 1 (1858), pp.238-53

new weapons would be too difficult to master by the average soldier, in particular that they would be unable to judge ranges. In 1857 this element of the debate in Britain centred on whether all soldiers should be issued with the new rifled weapons or, as was the practice adopted in many American regiments at the start of the Civil War, only a small number of elite marksmen. Once this was settled in favour of a single universal arm, the argument moved on to how to control the fire of the troops, particularly those relatively lacking in training. The lack of control, it was feared, would nullify the advantages of the improved accuracy of weapons and improved marksmanship.[10]

These concerns raised by the conservatives in the Army did not mean that the British ignored the impact of the new weapons. The most significant practical evidence of this is the establishment of the School of Musketry at Hythe in 1853, which recognised the need for improved training in order for troops to use the new weapons effectively.[11] Theorists in the late 1850s and early 1860s were already predicting the changes that were to manifest themselves in America. This started from a general recognition that the new weapons had increased the power of the defensive, and resulted in a number of subsidiary questions. The first of these was over the use and value of earthworks. Second, since it was assumed that at some point troops would have to leave their fortifications to attack, came a debate over how to increase the speed and mobility of troops in order to decrease the time during which they came under fire. This led to a third discussion of how to adapt formations that would enable troops to survive the greater volumes of fire. Finally, there was the changing balance of the role of infantry compared to those of cavalry and artillery, neither of which, it was predicted, could stand against infantry armed with the new rifles. All of these issues were under consideration well before both the American Civil War and the European wars of the 1860s.[12]

*   *   *

(p.251); Lieutenant Colonel F.N. Maude, *Cavalry: Its Past and Future* (London: William Clowes & Co, 1903), p.182.

10   Wilford, 'On The Rifle', passim; Dixon, 'The Rifle', pp.103-06; and comments by Dixon in Lieutenant Colonel Lane Fox, 'On the Improvement of the Rifle as a Weapon for General Use', *Journal of the United Service Institution*, 2 (1859), pp.453-493, 485-486; For arming of elite companies with rifles see Griffith, *Rally Once Again*, pp.78-79, and James R. Arnold, *The Armies of U.S. Grant* (London: Arms and Armour Press, 1995), p.20. The Confederate Army organised its sharpshooters at brigade level, see Philip Katcher, *The Army of Robert E. Lee* (London: Arms and Armour Press, 1994), p.123.

11   John Atkins, 'Early History of the Army School of Musketry in Hythe, Kent', *Black Powder*, (Winter 2007), pp.35-37 (p.35), <http://www.mlagb.com/blackpowder/200704_hythe.pdf> [accessed 31 May 2014]; Wilford, 'On The Rifle', pp.246-47.

12   Colonel Bainbridge, 'Notes on the Changes in Field Operations Likely to be Caused by the Adoption of Rifled Arms, and their Effect on the Engineer Equipment', *R.E. Professional Papers*, 11 (1862), pp.240-42.

The first of these concerns to be recognised through formal incorporation into the British drill manuals was the importance and use of field works. Prior to the outbreak of the war in America, at least one British writer had already recognised that the new rifle would result in greater use of entrenchment as a defence. Captain Henry Whatley Tyler of the Royal Engineers had given a series of lectures at the United Service Institution in the late 1850s, one of which predicted the increased use of temporary fortifications. Paradoxically Tyler suggested that this would lead to more close fighting, in spite of the increased range of weapons, as fortified posts would be more fanatically defended. Every post, captured position, and exposed position would need to be entrenched. The extensive use of earthworks and temporary fortifications in America was therefore not something entirely new or unforeseen, but validated earlier theoretical predictions which anticipated the intensity of trench combat seen in the First World War.[13]

The writings of officers from the technical branches of the Army during and after the Civil War emphasised both the speed at which the American troops created defences and the virtual invulnerability of such fortifications to frontal assault. What was also noted as novel by observers such as Major Henry Smyth at Petersburg was that the American soldiers created their entrenchments with little need for supervision and used the entire unit to do so. As a result, the progressive element within the British Army anticipated a need for all troops to be trained in the preparation of field works, rather than just engineers and pioneers as had previously been the practice. Tyler had recommended this in 1858, and in 1870 Sir John Burgoyne advised that all troops should be required to set to work on fortifications immediately after a march, just as had been observed in America.[14] Wolseley also recommended, based upon his observations in America, that staff officers should know as much about field fortification as engineers in order to guide their construction. 'The most skilled workmen will be often little better than useless unless their own officers can direct them.'[15] As contemporary observers had noticed, while swiftly raised, defences in the Civil War had often been poorly sited due to lack of trained officers.[16]

13   Captain Tyler RE, 'The Rifle and the Spade, or the Future of Field Operations', *Journal of the Royal United Service Institution*, 3 (1859), pp.170-94, (particularly pp.178, 184), lecture delivered on Friday, 1 April 1859; the other lectures were 'The Effect of the Modern Rifle upon Siege Operations', op.cit., and 'The Rifle and the Rampart', op cit.

14   Smyth, 'Account of the Final Attack and Capture of Richmond', p.365; Captain H. Schaw, 'The Present State of the Question of Fortification', *Journal of the Royal United Service Institution*, 10 (1866), pp.442-62 (p.448); Schaw, 'New Arms of Precision', pp.379-80; Tyler, 'The Rifle and the Spade', p.185; Sir John Burgoyne, 'On Hasty Entrenchments in the Field', *R.E. Professional Papers*, 18 (1870), pp.93-96 (p.94).

15   Wolseley, *Soldier's Pocket Book*, p.327.

16   Colonel Gerald Graham, 'Shelter Trenches or Temporary Cover for Troops in Position', *Journal of the Royal United Service Institution*, 14 (1870), pp.448-78 (p.471). Graham quoted a report from the Army of the Potomac on the difficulty of taking up proper lines of defence due to lack of experienced officers, but gave no exact reference.

In order to achieve the training required by officers and men, and recognising the growing importance of protecting troops from fire, a shelter trench drill was included in the 1870 drill manual.[17]

> Taking into consideration the long range, extreme accuracy, and great rapidity of fire of the rifled guns and small arms now in use, it may be desirable to shelter the troops as much as possible from unnecessary exposure, provided this can be done without harassing the men [...] It is self evident that troops behind cover must have a considerable advantage over an enemy advancing, unprotected, against them.[18]

Although fortifications had been used in the past, these had primarily been to obstruct the final infantry assault, not to diminish the effect of the opponent's firepower. The fortifications now being recommended were by contrast explicitly intended to stop the enemy at a distance, and to protect their occupants against the enemy's long range rifle fire and the increased shellfire from modern artillery. Experiments carried out on Dartmoor demonstrated that shelter trenches reduced casualties by 75 per cent.[19]

Inevitably, there were objections to the new use of field entrenchments in battle. The principal concern was that troops in trenches would become demoralised and reluctant to attack, fearing exposure to fire. This latter argument had been raised in the British Army following the experience of trench warfare at Sebastopol in 1854, but was also prevalent amongst the more aggressive American generals a decade later, most notably John Bell Hood, commander of the Confederate Army of Tennessee during bloody and unsuccessful assaults around Atlanta in July 1864 and at Franklin in November 1864.[20] Even Sherman remarked that 'the habit of intrenching [sic] certainly does have the effect of making new troops timid' and justified the failed assault in June 1864 on the strongly fortified Confederate position at Kennesaw Mountain north-west of

17   Anon, *Field Exercises and Evolutions of the Infantry, 1870* (London: HMSO, 1870), pp.280-305; hereafter *Field Exercises* (1870).
18   Anon, *Field Exercises* (1870), p.280.
19   Captain C.F. Clery, *Minor Tactics* (London: Henry S. King, 1875), p.107; Major J.W. Savage, *The Application of Fortification to the Requirements of the Battlefield; Lecture to Aldershot Military Society, Thursday 21 February 1889* (Aldershot: Gale and Polden, 1889), pp.3, 9.
20   Tyler, 'The Rifle and the Spade', p.171; [General A. Cunningham Robinson], *Field Intrenching* (Edinburgh: Thomas and Archibald Constable, 1878), p.12; Lieutenant General John Bell Hood (CSA), *Advance and Retreat* (Edison NJ: Blue and Grey Press, 1985, originally published 1880), p.342. For a modern view, see McWhiney and Jamieson, *Attack and Die*, pp.109-10. Robinson's anonymous essay was entered for the Royal United Service Institution prize competition of 1878. Its authorship is confirmed by the minutes of the 1880 Annual Meeting of the Institute in *Journal of the Royal United Service Institution*, 22 (1880), p.ix, and a copy signed by Robinson is held in Hove Public Library, Wolseley Archive under the reference RWY 3/2).

Shelter trench drill, from *Field Exercises and Evolutions of the Infantry, 1870.* (British Library)

Atlanta on the grounds that his men had 'settled down into a conviction that he would not assault fortified lines'.[21] Wolseley firmly believed that it was a lesson from the war that defensive tactics had a tendency to make soldiers unfit for offensive action, claiming Jackson, Grant, and Lee as supporters of this view.[22]

The British drill manual sought to diminish this risk by instructing that 'it must be distinctly impressed upon the men that the object of these shelter-trenches is merely to afford cover from the fire of the enemy, until the moment arrives for advancing against him', and that 'the shelter trench exercise is invariably to conclude with a charge'.[23] The British proponents of field fortifications saw shelter trenches as having 'rather the character of offensive than of defensive fortifications' and used Sherman's Atlanta campaign as their main reference for this mode of use.[24] Burgoyne wrote that as a result of increased firepower a 'very essential requirement will be the best practicable means for obtaining cover, to prevent a possibility of being mowed down before coming into contact with the enemy'.[25] At a practical level, Burgoyne wrote that shallow trenches were preferable to built-up works if intending to attack, as they provided less of an obstruction. This reiterated advice from Tyler in 1859 that

21   Captain Emilius Clayton RA, 'Field Intrenching', *Journal of the Royal United Service Institution*, 23 (1879), pp.281-338 (pp.289, 285), quoting W.T. Sherman, *Memoirs*, Vol.II, pp.61, 396.
22   General Viscount Wolseley, 'An English View of the Civil War', p.283.
23   Anon, *Field Exercises* (1870), pp.285, 299.
24   Colonel Gerald Graham, 'Shelter Trenches, or Temporary Cover for Troops in Position', *Journal of the Royal United Service Institution*, 14 (1870), pp.448-78 (pp.448, 452).
25   Burgoyne, 'On Hasty Entrenchments in the Field', p.95.

temporary entrenchments needed to allow for the opportunity to attack.[26] The *Field Exercises* stated that '[i]n the present day it will doubtless also be advisable to provide hasty and temporary shelter for troops, even when in line of battle and prepared to act on the offensive'. It went on to say that it was impossible to lay down exact circumstances when such methods would be necessary, but the key condition was that the trenches should not offer an obstacle to any subsequent advance.[27]

Colonel Henry Schaw, Professor of Fortifications and Artillery at the Staff College, was more precise in describing the occasions when 'hasty entrenchments' (defined as those taking less than six hours to construct) were necessary in an offensive battle. These were: to cover the enemy's front with trenches while moving the bulk of the army to attack the flank ('such tactics were frequently adopted during the late American war, and were specially favoured by the wooded nature of the country'); to prepare an attacking position during the night previous to the actual assault; to secure positions won against counterattack; and to cover a possible retreat. Schaw observed that the last three of these were used by both sides in 1870-71, while elsewhere he had noted that the tactics of using successive lines of trenches during a retreat 'were frequently used during the late American war'.[28]

Instruction manuals of the period gave fairly precise indications of the size of force required to hold a given frontage. The 1877 manual, for example, recommended three men per yard for a battalion in defence – split into a firing line, supports and a reserve. The 1889 version retained the need for three infantry per yard, but in addition recommended an overall all-arms strength of five men per yard. By the use of trenches to defend part of the position this number could be reduced. Schaw suggested that they could lower the number of troops needed to hold a defensive line by more than half. Thus field fortifications were seen as a defensive measure, but also as a means of enabling offensive action, by freeing up troops to achieve numerical superiority at the decisive point.[29]

> A general may wish to combine the conditions of an advantageous defence with those favourable for obtaining opportunities of employing his reserves in making such a vigorous counter-attack as, if successful, would inflict on his adversary a decisive defeat. In such cases his intrenchments should be so arranged as to offer temptations for the undue lateral extension of the enemy's line.[30]

26   Tyler, 'The Rifle and the Spade', pp.180-81.
27   Anon, *Field Exercises* (1870), p.280.
28   Schaw, *Defence and Attack*, pp.59, 65, 68-82; Captain H. Schaw, 'New Arms of Precision', pp.380-81.
29   Schaw, *Defence and Attack*, p.65.
30   Robinson, *Field Intrenching*, pp.13-21.

These are very similar to the tactics attributed by one modern writer to Stonewall Jackson.[31] The 'undue lateral extension of the enemy's line' was a feature of Grant's use of entrenchments at Petersburg, though British commentators do not seem to have drawn upon this particular example. Sherman's use of entrenchments during the Atlanta campaign, to hold a position with part of his army while turning Johnston's flank with other troops, was however used by a British writer to show how field fortifications could enable offensive operations.[32] Major Robert Home's *A Precis of Modern Tactics* (1873) also made reference to the American use of trenches to hold to the front and then move around the flank, considering this a 'legitimate' use of fortifications to enable a small body of men to resist a larger one, or to secure a portion of the army from attack, while attacking a flank with the remainder. His example for this was Lee's victory at Chancellorsville.[33]

The concept of a defensive-offensive tactical stance based upon the use of field defences was therefore an explicit component of British military thought by the 1870s. Indeed, it could be seen as the natural British mode of fighting given the Wellingtonian tradition and the belief in the historic defensive capability of British soldier. Tyler had noted this in his lectures, pointing out that while Wellington and his generals had largely relied upon natural terrain to provide cover they had on occasion, such as at Fuentes de Oñoro in the Peninsular War (May 1811), constructed temporary entrenchments, while Wellington had also constructed the extensive strategic defence works at Torres Vedras in 1810 to defend Lisbon. Lieutenant John Frederick Maurice also pointed out this British defensive tradition in his influential Wellington Prize Essay of 1871.[34]

In spite of the supposed success of Prussian offensive tactics in 1870, the evidence of European wars at this time did not result in British writers ignoring the importance of defensive works. The presence or the absence of field defences was recognised as being a significant factor in the outcome of battles in both the Austro-Prussian and the Franco-Prussian wars, for example by Maurice who noted that the French had not appreciated 'the advantage of a war of American shelter trenches'.[35] Captain Fraser, in his prize-winning essay of 1875, used the Franco-Prussian War almost exclusively for his examples, but this was not out of ignorance of the American Civil War. Fraser also shared the 1877 Royal United Service Institution Essay Prize, the subject of which was 'Field Intrenching'. This choice of subject probably reflected the nature of

---

31   Bevan Alexander, *Robert E. Lee's Civil War* (Holbrook, MA: Adams Media, 1998), pp.38-39.
32   Clayton, 'Field Intrenching', p.287.
33   Major Robert Home RE, *A Precis of Modern Tactics* (London: HMSO, 1873), pp.137-78. Home cited Charles Cornwallis Chesney's writings on the war, such as *Campaigns in Virginia and Maryland* and his articles in the *Edinburgh Review*.
34   Tyler, 'The Rifle and the Spade', p.182; Maurice, *Wellington Essay*, p.84.
35   Maurice, *Wellington Essay*, p.20.

the fighting seen in the Russo-Turkish War of 1877-78, but entries in this competition showed significant awareness and appreciation of the American experience.[36]

There was one slightly dissenting view on the subject of American field fortification. Charles Cornwallis Chesney explained the use of entrenchment during the Civil War as primarily being due to the terrain and national temperament, rather than to new weapons. Because of the heavily wooded country the movement of the enemy army could only be guessed at, and the opposing front lines could be very close. Hence troops entrenched overnight for security, and this developed into entrenching during battle itself to avoid surprise, particularly from flank attacks, with troops creating breastworks every few hundred yards. '[T]he fighting, in fact, had grown to resemble rather the last part of a siege on a grand scale.'[37] Chesney pointed to an American tradition of entrenchment which went back to the War of Independence, which he exemplified by the Battles of Bunker Hill (1775) and New Orleans (1815); and to a fear of being outflanked, which Chesney dated back to Brandywine and Germantown (1777). This view, which anticipated that of modern historian Earl J. Hess, provided an alternative rationale which does not seem to have been shared or repeated by other authorities at the time. Chesney did not in any case say that entrenchment was in itself wrong or to be discouraged, although he thought that Americans were temperamentally disinclined to assault.[38]

Since entrenching was a recognised tactic in the British Army during this period, why was it so infrequently used?[39] This was more due to the nature of the campaigns,

36 Schaw, *Defence and Attack*, pp.2, 65; Graham 'Shelter Trenches', pp.451-52; Lieutenant T. Fraser, 'Notes on the Combined use of Intrenchments, Defended Posts, and Redoubts for Strengthening Positions, War of 1870-71', *R. E. Professional Papers*, 21 (1873), pp.17-25; Fraser, *Defence of a Position*, p.3, but see pp.18-19, 43 for awareness of the American Civil War; Brevet Major T. Fraser, 'Field Intreching: its Application on the Battlefield and its Bearing on Tactics', *Journal of the Royal United Service Institution*, 23 (1880), pp.339-401; Clayton, 'Field Intrenching', op.cit.; Robinson, *Field Intrenching*, op.cit.; *Journal of the Royal United Service Institution*, 22 (1880), p.ix.

37 Charles Cornwallis Chesney, 'Recent Changes in the Art of War', in C.C. Chesney and Henry Reeve, *The Military Resources of Prussia and France and Recent Changes in the Art of War* (London Longmans Green and Co. 1870), pp.1-57 (p.49), reprinted from *Edinburgh Review*, 123 (1866).

38 Charles Cornwallis Chesney, 'The Military Life of General Grant', in *Essays in Modern Military Biography* (London: Longman, Green and Co., 1874), pp. 214-95 (p. 268), originally published in *Edinburgh Review*, 129 (1869); Lieutenant Colonel Charles Cornwallis Chesney, 'The Compte de Paris' Campaigns on the Potomac', *Edinburgh Review*, 164 (1876), pp.79-103 (p.82). The 1876 article, the last Chesney ever wrote, also suggested that entrenchment was one of a series of American traits going back to the revolution. For modern analysis, Hess, *Field Armies and Fortifications 1861-64*, op. cit.; Hess, *The Rifle Musket in Civil War Combat*, op. cit.

39 For criticism of the British failure to entrench during colonial conflicts in Africa see Craddock, 'The American Civil War and its Influence on the British Army', pp.254, 263-64, 272, 284; though he does acknowledge the general use of the tactical defensive on p.260.

the strategic circumstances in which the British found themselves, and the characteristics of their opponents, than to doctrinal considerations. In the Zulu War of 1879 the British normally adopted a tactical defensive, and where successful this often involved some form of fortification. The British did not entrench at the final and decisive Battle of Ulundi in July 1879, but this was hardly 'unnecessary exposure', given the limitations of Zulu firepower and the expectation of an advance after the Zulu assault. Lord Chelmsford's decision not to entrench can further be argued to be in line with the instructions of the drill manual, as it could have led his army to exposure to surprise attack and would have been unnecessary 'harassing' of the men.

Against the Mahdist tribes of the Sudan, the British also on occasion adopted the tactical defensive, but in the form of squares and zaribas rather than entrenchments.[40] Tofrek (March 1885) and the opening engagement at Omdurman (September 1898) were in defence of zaribas, while the battles of El Teb (February 1884), Tamai (March 1884), and Abu Klea and Abu Kru (both January 1885) notably featured the use of squares. In these engagements the essentially defensive squares were used during attacking manoeuvres, protecting the troops' flanks and rear while bringing overwhelming British firepower to bear on Sudanese counterattacks or ambushes. Again, the threat of enemy firepower, though much more substantial than that of the Zulus (the Mahdist weapons included American Remington rifles captured from the Egyptians), was less of a concern than the need for tactical mobility. Battles fought over strategically vital water sources, such as Abu Klea, required an offensive use of firepower, and not an entrenched static defence that would have sacrificed the initiative to the enemy. Other battles were in defence of slow moving and vulnerable transport columns, which it would have been impractical to entrench.[41]

In the Anglo-Transvaal War of 1880-81, the British notably failed to fortify their position on top of Majuba Hill which contributed to the Boer victory there. This is again usually attributed to Major General George Pomeroy Colley's wish not to further fatigue the men after a night march. It was also due to the expectation that when obviously outflanked their Boer opponents would evacuate their position rather than counterattack. This was the behaviour the British had observed of volunteer troops in America. Colley had previously entrenched his camp at Mount Prospect and also the temporary camp at the foot of Majuba, though the latter entrenchments were extremely weak. Although there is no evidence that Colley extensively studied the American Civil War, as will be shown later he was not dismissive or unaware of its lessons. One of these was the strength of the defensive, and he possibly considered the natural strength of the position on Majuba to be a sufficient deterrent to Boer attack.

---

40   A zariba was a fence using thorn bushes used to fortify a camp or village in the Sudan. Its use was similar to that of abattis, an obstacle formed of the branches of trees laid in a row with the sharpened tops directed outwards, during the Civil War.
41   Michael Barthorp, War on the Nile (Poole: Blandford, 1984), pp.85-88, 103-108, 121-122, 159-161.

Underestimation of the enemy and restrictions of the terrain, rather than a lack of doctrine, determined the fateful decision.[42]

Trenches were adopted by the British in the Boer War of 1899-1902 when troops were besieged, besieging, or otherwise required to hold positions, but as an offensive tactic they were of relatively limited value against a highly mobile enemy. What was needed were mounted troops to force the abandonment of positions by threatening the lines of retreat, and not the progressive development of siege entrenchments as seen at Atlanta or Petersburg in 1864. Buller's suggestion that the Boer lines on the Tugela could only be taken by siege was viewed as a loss of nerve.[43] More avoidable factors were also to blame however, which could perhaps have been anticipated from studying commentaries on the Civil War. Limited opportunities for training, the fact that the infantry did not carry their entrenching tools on their person, and a reliance upon the Royal Engineers to plan and execute serious entrenchments, all contributed to both a lack of expertise and a lack of appreciation of the benefits of artificial cover amongst officers and men alike. At Spion Kop in February 1900, in a situation not dissimilar to that of Majuba, the British did try to entrench the position they had taken, but the troops lacked the proper equipment, the terrain prevented more than an extremely shallow trench and a stone breastwork, and the position marked up by the Royal Engineers and taken up by the infantry was tactically flawed, being overlooked and outflanked. As in the Civil War, the quality of entrenchments increased as men experienced the effects of modern artillery and rifle fire first hand, and in some units entrenching became second nature as it had in America.[44]

In India, punitive expeditions formed the greater part of British operations on the Indian frontier, and mobility was again considered more useful than the protection offered by entrenchment. Defensive tactics were still sometimes the order of the day when pitched battles did occur, such as the defeat at Maiwand (July 1880). In that action only the Bombay Sappers entrenched out of the British force engaged, though the 66th Foot did make use of a dried-up riverbed for cover. The un-entrenched sepoy regiments suffered significantly heavier casualties. The commander once again put tactical flexibility and the option for reverting to offensive action above the defensive advantages of fortifications, particularly when operating against less well armed foes. The failure to create or improve temporary cover by some units nevertheless seems

42   Louis Creswicke, *South Africa and the Transvaal War*, 6 vols (Edinburgh, T.C. and E.C. Jack, 1900-01), Vol.I (1900), p.87; Joseph Lehman, *The First Boer War* (London: Military Book Society, 1972), p.239; Oliver Ransford, *The Battle of Majuba Hill* (London: John Murray, 1967), pp.44, 80, 82-83.

43   Rayne Kruger, *Good-bye Dolly Gray: The Story of the Boer War* (London: Pan, 1974, first published 1959), p.143; Thomas Pakenham, *The Boer War* (London: Weidenfeld and Nicholson, 1979), p.239; Geoffrey Powell, *Buller: A Scapegoat?* (London: Leo Cooper, 1994), pp.152-153.

44   Jones, *From Boer War to World War*, pp.106-08. For the trenches on Spion Kop see Kruger, *Good-bye Dolly Gray*, p.187-89; Pemberton, *Battles of the Boer War*, p.173-74.

British troops entrenched at the Orange River during the Boer War, c.1900.
(National Army Museum)

an inexplicable error, but given the situation at Maiwand, where the British were surrounded by Afghan forces superior in numbers and artillery, the likely outcome of adopting a purely defensive entrenched stance would still have been eventual defeat. On other occasions during this campaign, shelter trenches were constructed to protect encampments.[45]

Faulty tactics aside, there was a further practical reason for the failure to entrench, which was that the Army's logistical organisation in this regard was not aligned to its tactical requirements. Speaking at Aldershot in January 1889, Major General Richard Harrison, who had observed the Civil War as a captain in 1863-64, noted that while there was an entrenching tool designed to be carried by the individual soldier, it was not clear under what circumstances this was to be done, although the matter had been under consideration for some time. According to Harrison, the tool was neither published in the official list of War Kit (probably because its weight would have raised the soldier's load beyond what he could efficiently carry), nor provided for in the regimental transports. The following month Major J.W. Savage, the Instructor in Field

45   Leigh Maxwell, *My God – Maiwand!* (London: Leo Cooper, 1979), pp.127-28, 263.

Fortification at the School of Military Engineering, Chatham, reported that a large number of different tools had been tried at Chatham, and that tools were carried in the battalion transports (which is where Wolseley's *Soldiers Pocket Book* advised they should be placed) but only enough for three companies. He also observed that although soldiers of overseas powers carried entrenching tools 'and so do we, at least on paper', they were not universally carried on manoeuvres.[46]

* * *

Defensive tactics were all very well if an enemy could be forced into a position where he had to attack or else suffer strategic defeat, but the prevailing view was that this was a strategic situation that the Army was unlikely to meet on foreign service. Outnumbered by most of its actual or prospective opponents, the British sought a means of obtaining quick decisive victories. It was therefore still essential to determine a means of successfully dislodging an enemy who would not obligingly attack himself, but held a tactically or strategically vital position. The problem when faced by an enemy armed with modern weapons was how to bring the firing line into decisive range without taking excessive casualties. The extended range of the new rifled muskets meant that troops were exposed to effective fire for a longer period of time. The solution would mean increasing the speed of movement over the ground, and enabling troops to manoeuvre more quickly. It would require troops to take greater advantage of cover, and use of concealed routes of approach.[47]

The traditional formation of manoeuvre when speed was required was the column, and this had initially been adopted by European nations as a solution to the problem. It formed the basis of French offensive tactics in 1859 against the Austrians in Italy, and was not unknown as an assault formation in the American Civil War when speed of advance and concentration of force was considered to be of the essence, for example at Spotsylvania (May 1864) and Kennesaw Mountain (June 1864), and at the final assault on Petersburg in April 1865. However, the increased accuracy of the new rifles meant that in the hands of skilled troops more shots would hit such dense targets, while the penetrative power of new weapons meant that a single bullet could go through more than one man. Long range artillery fire was also increasingly a threat to

---

46   Wolseley, *Soldier's Pocket Book*, p.54; Major General Richard Harrison, *The Organization of an Army for War, Lecture to Aldershot Military Society, Thursday 3 Jan 1889* (Aldershot: Gale and Polden, 1889), p.9; Savage, *Application of Fortification*, p.4. Major General Harrison was in the chair for Savage's lecture. The soldiers load, comprising food, arms, clothing and equipment was 56 lbs, reduced to 48 in the tropics, a shovel weighed around 5 lbs (Harrison, *Organization of an Army*, p.9; Savage, *Application of Fortification*, p.16). However, one officer recommended that 'our infantry should never be far from their entrenching tools, and when there is a likelihood of these being required they must be carried on the men's backs', 'HCW', 'Future Infantry Tactics', p.431.

47   Dixon, 'The Rifle', pp.111-12.

large masses of infantry. So it was soon realised that these dense column formations would become highly vulnerable.[48]

With fire action the main element in deciding battle, the challenge was now to find a formation for the attack that could develop the maximum fire, with the highest possible mobility, while presenting the most difficult target. Traditional British lines were famous for their firepower, and were less vulnerable than compact columns, but did not constitute a formation that could be rapidly manoeuvred. The slowness of British movement had been observed by the Russian Lieutenant Colonel (later Major General) Todleben at the Battle of the Alma (September 1854) during the Crimean War, and was compounded by the rigidity of the British drill book and its parade ground insistence upon the correct ordering of files and ranks. Nevertheless, the 1867 infantry drill manual, introduced in the wake of adopting the Snider breech-loading rifle, did not change the tactical formations or manoeuvres in which the British Army was trained other than observing that cavalry could now be met in line, or at worst a two deep square, in view of the new breech-loader's firepower and the increased vulnerability of squares to artillery.[49]

In 1866 William H. Morris (USA), who had served as a Brigadier General with the Army of the Potomac and had published a book on infantry tactics after the war, lectured at the Royal United Service Institution and observed that 'some of the evolutions so admirably executed at Aldershot appeared to me susceptible of simplification, and I thought time might have been saved by avoiding intermediate movements'.[50] Morris recommended to his audience the practice of manoeuvring by column of fours, which was already allowed for and authorised in the British manual primarily for manoeuvring around obstacles. 'Fours' had been the basis of skirmisher formations in Hardee's *Rifle and Light Infantry Tactics* (1855), the standard American tactical manual before the Civil War, and manoeuvre by fours was the basis of tactical movements in Upton's new drill manual of 1868.[51] Proposals to operate in fours also appeared in British works in the 1870s including one by a volunteer officer, J.H. MacDonald,

48 Sir Patrick MacDougall, *Modern Warfare as Influenced by Modern Artillery* (London: J. Murray, 1864), p.188.
49 'R.R.', *British Infantry Drill as it Might Be* (London: Simpkin Marshall and Co, 1868) p.iii; MacDougall, *Modern Warfare*, pp.4-5. See also Captain A.F. Becke, *An Introduction to the History of Tactics 1740-1905* (London: Hugh Rees, 1909), p.40; Anon, *Field Exercises* (1867), p.229. Demands for simplification of the drill-book had a long history, see Strachan, *From Waterloo to Balaclava*, pp.16-19.
50 Brigadier General William H. Morris (USA), 'On the Best Method of Arming, Equipping, and Manoeuvring Infantry', *Journal of the Royal United Service Institution*, 10 (1866), pp.209-24 (p.218).
51 Morris, 'On the Best Method of Arming, Equipping, and Manoeuvring Infantry', pp.215, 220; Anon, *Field Exercises* (1861), pp.241-45; Kerr, 'Wall of Fire', p.39, referencing William J. Hardee, *The Rifle and Light Infantry Tactics: For the Exercise and Manoeuvres of Troops*, 2 vols (Philadelphia, Lippincott, Grambio & Co., 1855), Vol.II, pp.168-78; Jamieson, *Crossing the Deadly Ground*, pp.9-10.

looking to simplify drill. Another critic of the British system wrote at some length indirectly supporting Morris' observations and comparing the simplicity and speed imparted by this American system with that of the British, which still relied largely upon wheeling the line, a manoeuvre difficult for volunteers. Certain sections of the drill book, he wrote, would lead to heavy loss of life, as irregulars would panic when changing formation under fire, while even steady regulars would suffer more casualties than necessary due to the slowness of the drill.[52]

By 1877 the British drill book included several references to the use of column of fours when rapid movement was needed, particularly when marching to the flank and even when forming square. These cannot be definitively ascribed to adoption of American practice, but Upton's manual was certainly known to the British, copies being held in the War Office library.[53] At another lecture held at the Royal United Service Institution, in 1878, MacDonald presented his new system for the infantry based upon four-man files, which Wolseley, the chairman for the evening, observed was very similar to the American system of skirmishing.

> With reference to the Americans, most of their formations are in fours. For many years past they have adopted a great simplicity of drill, which I am glad to see the authorities of England are becoming alive to the necessity of adopting also; indeed that great rigidity of movement, which we had borrowed from Prussia is, I think, gradually disappearing from our drill book.[54]

Not unnaturally though, the greatest influence in British infantry tactics at this time did come from Prussia, in the wake of the European wars waged by her army between 1864 and 1871. There were several reasons for favouring European over American experience. Firstly, the Prussian victories over Austria in 1866 and France in 1870-71 had substantially changed the European balance of power through a series of remarkably swift campaigns and apparently overwhelmingly decisive victories against leading military powers. '[The] tactical facts of the late campaign in France [...] were calculated to startle every soldier interested in his profession',[55] and therefore far more likely to dominate the thinking of British and European military theorists than a distant conflict fought between volunteer armies. Secondly, these were wars fought

---

52   Sir Patrick MacDougall, *Modern Infantry Tactics* (London: Edward Stanford, 1873), p.46; Lieutenant Colonel J.H. MacDonald, *Memorandum of Instruction for a New System of Infantry Attack* (Edinburgh and London: Wm. Blackwood and Son, [1884]), p.16; 'R.R.', *British Infantry Drill*, pp.iv, 6, 11.

53   Anon, *Field Exercises and Evolutions of Infantry, 1877* (London: HMSO, 1877), pp.146, 148, 175, 183, 194; Anon, *Catalogue of the War Office Library, Vol. 1.2* (London: [n.pub.], 1906), p.1202.

54   Lieutenant Colonel J.H.A. Macdonald, 'On the Best Detail Formation for Infantry in Line', *Journal of the Royal United Service Institution*, 22 (1878), pp.556-82 (pp.563, 581).

55   Maurice, *Wellington Essay*, p.3.

over European terrain and with European standards of supply and communication networks. The tactical and strategic circumstances of the battles were therefore seen as more relevant than those fought across the American wilderness.

Finally, these European conflicts were fought with more up to date technology. The close nature of the American terrain had encouraged the retention of weapons that were becoming seen as outmoded in European armies, such as the smooth-bore Napoleon cannon which sacrificed the long range and accuracy offered by the new rifled artillery pieces for close range volume of fire.[56] More important for the infantry was the debate over the impact on tactics of breech-loading small arms. Although the British were aware of the breech-loading weapons used in America and their possible impact for the future, and had taken the decision to re-equip the infantry with breech-loaders in 1864, it was still true that for most people the breech-loading rifle 'first came prominently into notice in the campaign of 1866' as a major factor in the Prussian victory over the Austrians armed with muzzle-loaders.[57] Most significantly the victories of 1870 had been achieved over a French army armed with one of the most up to date rifles in the world. In comparison the majority of troops in the American war, even in the later campaigns, had still been armed with muzzle-loading weapons.[58]

The breech-loader introduced additional tactical factors into the equation between attack and defence. It was the breech-loader that introduced the increase in the *volume* of fire that was so significant on those occasions when it was used in the Civil War, and subsequently on a far greater scale during the wars of 1866 and 1870-71. With the universal adoption of the new breech-loader, precision and rapidity of fire now went together, whereas previously precision had only been bought at the expense of rapidity.[59] Troops armed with muzzle-loading rifles were peculiarly vulnerable to sustained long range fire because they were unable to respond without halting their advance, which was a significant factor in enhancing the superiority of the defensive in America. Since the breech-loader could be fired in confined spaces and while lying down, the attacker could in theory take more advantage of cover during the advance. This led some theorists to conclude that following their introduction 'the defence has gained greatly, but the offensive has, relatively speaking, gained still more'.[60] This was not a call for an out-and-out offensive regardless of casualties, culminating with

56   Smyth, 'Account of the Final Attack and Capture of Richmond', p.365.
57   Clery, *Minor Tactics*, p.99.
58   Paddy Griffith, *Battle in the Civil War* (Camberley: Field Books, 1986), p.33; Griffith, *Rally Once Again*, pp.76-81.
59   Lieutenant Colonel Henry William Lovett Hime, *Stray Military Papers* (London, New York and Bombay: Longmans, Green, and Co, 1897), p.58.
60   Major Robert Home RE, *A Precis of Modern Tactics* (London: HMSO, 1873), p.71, referenced in 'an adjutant of Militia', *British Infantry Tactics, or the Attack Formation Explained with Some Introductory Remarks on Infantry Tactics in General* (London: Mitchell & Co, [1877]), p.6.

the bayonet charge, but recognition that the breech-loader made possible a change in offensive tactics.

From early on, Wolseley had been an advocate of the need for widespread reform as a result of these changes in technology. In 1869 he wrote in the *Soldier's Pocket Book* that it would be impossible in the future to attack in lines, such as those used by the British at the Alma, against an enemy armed with breech-loading rifles. 'In future, attacks will be made more by the line of skirmishers than by the line supporting them.'[61] According to Wolseley the necessity was to form up within striking distance of the enemy a force equal to the regular line, but without its rigidity. To do this the assailants would need to use cover and folds in ground, which was made easier with the adoption of the breech-loader, and to be assisted by every available field gun. Wolseley stated, however, that it was now impossible to take a battery within 800 yards of formed infantry. This meant that the close support artillery tactics favoured in the Civil War, and made possible largely due to the heavily wooded terrain, were obsolete. The attacking force needed to have the flexibility of command to find and exploit weaknesses in the enemy's defence and, when he retired, to attack the flanks of stronger positions that held out. To bring about this vision Wolseley believed that an 'entire change in our system of skirmishers, and in our offensive tactics is absolutely necessary'.[62]

The need for rejection of the traditional British line was recognised by other reformers. Maurice agreed that the line was not viable over long distances without an unachievable perfection in drill. Since modern weapons meant that attacks must be over long distances, if the army was to attack at all then it must be in skirmishing order. Maurice noted that although the Prussians had won in 1870 by taking the offensive, the Franco-Prussian war nevertheless demonstrated 'strangely successful defensive tactics'. Conventional attacks had taken heavy losses, and inflicted few up until the point of victory. Yet in order to gain the advantage of the defensive, it was necessary to undertake tactical offensives to seize critical positions that the enemy must in turn attack. 'The superiority of armies on the defensive favours bold offensive strategy, and therefore invasion.' In spite of acknowledging the advantage of the defensive, Maurice wrote that 'troops cannot take the field which are not able to attack an enemy's position'.[63]

Appreciation of the new firepower can also be seen in another influential book, *Minor Tactics*, published in 1875 by Captain (later Major General) Cornelius Francis Clery, the Professor of Tactics at the Royal Military College, Sandhurst. This book was based upon his lectures to sub-lieutenants at the college, so represents the basic military training given to junior officers in this period. Clery was criticised by Luvaas for not incorporating examples from the Civil War, but it is difficult to see how

61   Wolseley, *Soldier's Pocket-Book*, p.250.
62   Wolseley, *Soldier's Pocket-Book*, pp.241–43.
63   Maurice, *Wellington Essay*, pp.78, 72.

his conclusions would have differed had he done so. They included the observation that shelter trenches were 'now an almost indispensable provision for troops on the defensive';[64] the impossibility of moving in masses under fire; and that local superiority was to be won by force of fire, rather than force of numbers. 'The fire action of infantry could [*sic*] no longer be confined to preparing the attack with the bayonet, but must become the main element in deciding the battle.'[65] Defensive fire was to be used at the longest effective range in order to prevent an enemy closing with the defenders position, and not, as under traditional tactics, to be reserved for close range. Only in the belief that the breech-loader gave increased firepower to the attack as well as the defence was there any real departure from Civil War experience.[66]

The increased volume of fire generated by all troops in the war of 1870-71, rather than by the minority which had been armed with breech-loading weapons in the Civil War, simply accentuated the lessons of the earlier conflict. Under the intense fire generated by the breech-loader the supporting troops behind the initial skirmish line had also dissolved into further lines of skirmishers. The British view was that this had not been the *doctrine* of the Prussian army in 1870, which was still that of close order company columns feeding the skirmish line to bring about decisive fire superiority, instead the behaviour had been instinctive by the troops. In the same way, Sherman had identified his troops' natural tendency to adopt looser formations – 'although our lines were deployed according to tactics, the men generally fought in a strong skirmish line'.[67]

The need for the adoption of a looser formation was universally acknowledged by the 1870s as part of a general need to change tactics. 'Single rank in open order had now become the legitimate fire formation of Infantry armed with breech-loaders, not only because it gave sufficient development to their fire, but because it is the least vulnerable formation.'[68] Single rank close order – the formation recommended by Upton from his experience of the Civil War – was largely bypassed in European military thought. It was natural that the most influential model would be an army that had recently pressed home successful attacks in the face of modern breech-loading firepower, which meant copying the German army of 1870 rather than the armies of the Civil War. In the British drill book of 1877, extended order is officially defined as the appropriate formation for all but the final assault. The drill instructions for a company forming extended order are prefaced with the following.

Extended order is applicable both to the formation for the attack and for skirmishing, but with the general difference that *in the attack,* the object is to

---

64 Clery, *Minor Tactics*, p.107.
65 Clery, *Minor Tactics*, p.100.
66 Clery, *Minor Tactics*, pp.106-07, 154. For criticism of Clery, Luvaas, *Military Legacy*, p.193.
67 Clayton, 'Field Intrenching', p.290, quoting W.T. Sherman, *Memoirs*, Vol.II, p.294; Clery, *Minor Tactics*, p.100.
68 Hime, *Stray Military Papers*, p.55.

gradually bring up the battalion, with as little loss as possible, to a point suffi-ciently near the position of the enemy, whence the hottest fire can be poured in, and the final assault by the battalion, *as a compact body*, can be made; whereas *in skirmishing* the object is either to cover a body of troops not formed for attack, or to *feel* for an enemy when advancing through an enclosed or wooded country.[69]

There were, however, three problems arising as a result of adopting extended order tactics, all revolving round the loss of cohesion compared to close formations. The first was the problem of controlling men in a battalion that was spread over a greater frontage than ever before. The second was how to arrange the fighting line, its supports and reserves, in order to retain unit integrity and *morale*. The third was how to keep up the momentum of the attack when men were dispersed.

* * *

The problem of control was an issue readily recognised by the officers of the day as a result of their own battle experience. Some of these are recorded in the discussions that took place after lectures upon tactics at the military societies. Wolseley remarked that he had lost control of his company of only 100 men in India when extended to four-pace intervals, while another veteran doubted the possibility of commanding a battalion spread out over 875 yards. The solution to this was recognised as being the devolution of control to smaller unit organisations and to more junior officers. By 1892 the infantry regulations explicitly stated the need for officers at company level to use their initiative, for example 'leaders of supports and reserves will choose such formations as are best suited to the ground and the exigencies of the moment' while 'the leader of the second line will, throughout, adopt those formations that are most suitable to the requirements of the moment'.[70]

This practice was greatly influenced by Prussian practice. However, Wolseley had anticipated it while serving in Canada: in the *Soldier's Pocket Book* he had written that the rigidity of movement imposed by the current infantry drill book was impossible for battalions of 1,000 men, and that control needed to be devolved, as in the cavalry drill manual of the time. Wolseley also seems to have been aware of and interested

69   Anon, *Field Exercises* (1877), p.91 (original italics).
70   Anon, *Infantry Drill (Provisional)* (London: HMSO, 1892), p.85; Wolseley in discussion on Lieutenant Colonel J.H.A. Macdonald's lecture, 'On the Best Detail Formation for Infantry in Line', *Journal of the Royal United Service Institution*, 22 (1878), pp.556-82 (p.580); Lieutenant General Sir [John] Lintorn [Arabin] Simmons, in discussion on Captain H. Brackenbury RA, 'The Tactics of the Three Arms as Modified to Meet the Requirements of the Present Day', *Journal of the Royal United Service Institution*, 22 (1878), pp.618-47 (p.643). Although not explicit in earlier manuals, there is some evidence that the light infantry tradition in the British Army had fostered individual initiative at company level much earlier, see Strachan, *Wellington's Legacy*, pp.34-35.

in practical British experience along the same lines. Among Wolseley's professional papers in The National Archives at Kew is a report on an operation on the North-West Frontier of India that shows British officers in the field were recognising the need to devolve responsibility in the 1860s. The standing orders explicitly stated that each body of men were to support the one in front of it without orders from the Brigade Headquarters, and also that the supporting companies were to assist the skirmish line without waiting for orders. They also instructed the skirmishers to get as near to the enemy as possible while keeping cover, and that the enemy needed to be shaken by artillery fire before the assault. The lessons of the Civil War, European wars, and colonial operations were all pointing to the need to devolve authority and encourage initiative on the modern battlefield, particularly for junior officers.[71]

Sound precedents and support for this could also be found in the Army's historical traditions, in particular those of the Light Brigade during the Peninsular War.

> Sir John Moore and the colonels of the Light Brigade intended, when they instituted their system of discipline, of instruction, and of command, *to form in the persons of their company officers a body of intelligent and zealous assistants, capable of carrying out their plans and anticipating their wishes*; and not merely a body of docile subordinates capable of obeying orders to the letter, but untrained to resolute initiative.[72]

One senior officer went further, suggesting that in order to cross the zone of fire on the modern battlefield, all those involved needed to be clear on how the attack was to be made.

> When we have got our instructions we shall have to think out how our part of the attack is to be made; then hand those instructions down through all the ranks to the private soldier, who by this excellent system will always have some commander to look to when in the field.[73]

Now not only junior officers but the ordinary soldiers as well needed to act on their own initiative. This had been codified to a limited extent in the 1870 infantry manual,

---

71   Major General Sir Frederick Maurice, 'How Far the Lessons of the Franco–German War are out of Date', *United Service Magazine*, n.s., 10 (1895), pp.555-77 (pp.563-64); Wolseley, *Soldier's Pocket Book*, p.251; TNA, WO 147/49, Brigadier General A. Wilde, 'Report on equipment of the Hazarrah Field Force', September 1868.
72   G.F.R. Henderson, 'The Training of Infantry for Attack', in *Science of War*, pp.338-61 (p.348) originally published in *United Service Magazine*, n.s., 19 (1899), pp.491-512. Original italics.
73   Major General Clive, comment upon lecture by Colonel Lonsdale Hale, *The Spirit of Tactical Operations of To-day, Lecture to Aldershot Military Society, Wednesday 11 April 1888* (Aldershot: Aldershot Military Society, 1888), p.20.

which in the section on company skirmishing stated that individual men, while remaining under the general supervision of their section commanders, should 'act on their individual judgement in choosing cover, advancing, halting, or retiring'.[74] Successive versions of the manual further emphasised that the commanders of supports and reserves should be given great latitude in choosing their formations in order to minimise casualties. This was a feature of the examinations for junior officers.[75]

The 1870 manual also noted in its section on skirmishing that 'the object of moving in extended order is to enable the soldier to take advantage of cover'.[76] However, field-craft was more difficult to teach than simple spacing between files, which could be practiced through drill. One veteran of both the 1881 Transvaal War and the North-West Frontier of India observed the deficiencies of the British infantryman in this respect.

> Attention should be particularly directed to the training of infantry in shooting from behind cover accurately and rapidly without exposing themselves. The Boers and some of the natives of South Africa, and also most Pathans, excel in this art, whereas the average British infantryman usually exposes half his body to the view of his enemy, and frequently puts himself into such position that he can neither aim accurately nor shoot quickly. This is one of the criticisms most frequently heard among the Boers and colonists of South Africa.[77]

In part this lack of fieldcraft was a result of to the occupational and social back-ground of the British soldier. The Civil War observers had commented on the natural soldierly abilities of the Southern and Western soldiers with their culture of hunting and shooting, abilities that would also be later attributed to British colonial troops such as the Australians and Canadians, but which were lacking in the agricultural labouring classes that made up the majority of recruits to the rank and file of the regular army recruited in Britain. It was also a function of deficiencies in doctrine and in the training process. The concern of the conservative element in the army about

---

74   Anon, *Field Exercises* (1870), p.94.
75   Lieutenant W.R. Clifford (Cheshire Regiment), *A Resume of the Tactical Portions Contained in parts VI, VII, VIII and IX of the 'Infantry Drill, 1889'* (London: William Clowes, 1890), p.44. This pamphlet was written for promotion candidates based upon on Clifford's own revision notes, so is a good indication of what junior officers were being taught and examined upon.
76   Anon, *Field Exercises* (1870), p.53. This wording is presented by Craddock ('The American Civil War and its Influence on the British Army', p.207) as being from William J. Hardee's *Rifle and Light Infantry Tactics* (New York: J.O. Kane, 1862) and to have been 'overlooked or discouraged' in the British army. I have not been able to find similar text in Hardee's manual, and Craddock's source is in fact the British manual, as his own footnote indicates.
77   Unnamed source quoted in Henderson, 'The Training of Infantry for Attack', in *Science of War*, pp.350-51.

the use of extended formations in the assault, as well as skirmishing, was that battles would become 'mere rifle duels without manoeuvre' as observed in the later operations in America. Dispersed infantry allowed to seek cover were thought to have a tendency to engage purely in a fire-fight, and to be reluctant to advance.[78]

The primary solution to this was the act of training and drill itself. This harks back to the British observers' concerns over the lack of drill and discipline shown by the hastily formed American levies of 1861 which in their view was one of the reasons for battles being indecisive. It was a concern still prevalent among American commanders after the Civil War as Upton's drill manual showed.

> In battle it should always be the aim of the colonel to preserve command throughout; which can only be done by keeping the men in ranks; the file-closers will, therefore, closely observe the men in their front; allow them to break neither to the front nor the rear; and permit no man to fall out unless wounded.[79]

In the face of modern firepower, with extended formations, in order to carry out any form of organised operation, it was deemed more necessary than ever to train men to carry out actions under fire instinctively. The British manual of 1889 explained the ongoing need for drill.

> Men who are in ordinary times taught and frequently practised to act in a particular manner, will, from acquired habit, under somewhat similar circumstances, do the same in moments of great mental strain, and will, even under heavy fire, act, as it were instinctively, according to well established custom.[80]

Yet this did not mean that the intention was to attack in parade ground formations, as the manual later went on to state 'this method of fighting [in extended order] demands not only greater individual exertion and intelligence, but far higher and more complete instruction and training both of officers and men than mere parade ground movements'.[81] For the progressive element in the Army, training in close order drill needed to be retained not because this was how men were expected to attack an enemy armed with modern weaponry, but as a necessary pre-requisite for developing the intelligence and steadiness to succeed in looser formations. 'Mechanical instruction

---

78   Lieutenant A. Steinmetz, 'On the Formation of Troops for Battle with Reference to the Modern Improvements in Firearms', *United Service Magazine*, 429 (September 1864), pp.11-21 (p.17); Lieutenant Colonel G.F.R. Henderson, 'Battles and Leaders', in *The Civil War: A Soldier's View. A Collection of Civil War Writings by Col. G.F.R. Henderson*, ed. by Jay Luvaas (Chicago: University of Chicago Press, 1958), pp.130-73 (pp.157-58), originally published in the *Edinburgh Review*, April 1891, reprinted in *Science of War*, pp.187-229.
79   Upton, Infantry *Tactics*, p.143.
80   Anon, *Infantry Drill, 1889* (London: HMSO, 1889), p.205.
81   Anon, *Infantry Drill* (1889), p.340.

is indispensible [but] it is only the foundation on which an intelligent infrastructure is to be raised' wrote MacDougall, while Wolseley expressed similar sentiments in the *Soldier's Pocket Book*. 'Drill is but a means to an end, i.e. to enable you to carry out with ease, certainty and precision, the tactical combinations which you consider most suited to the occasion.'[82]

In fact, far from the drill manuals enforcing rigid, out of date tactics, a contemporary criticism was that this devolution of responsibility to regimental level resulted in the creation of a multitude of local practices. This might have been desirable if they reflected local conditions and new technical developments, but one group of officers criticised the formation being taught at Chelsea Barracks as being a 'billiard table' formation, suitable for the open plain but 'unsuitable elsewhere, preposterously so for an enclosed country like England' and suggested that its author had never seen a field exercise with modern weapons. Furthermore, when the commanding officer changed, or when battalions were brigaded in the field, lack of cohesion and confusion resulted. These critics argued not for a single attack formation, which it was recognised would not meet all the circumstances that the army might face, but the teaching of the rationale behind recommendations in the manuals, the standardisation of low level commands, and establishment of common practices to meet common problems such as how to reinforce the firing line in the face of casualties.[83]

A further problem with extended order was the intermingling of units and the difficulty of providing effective supports. On several occasions during the Civil War the intermingling of units and the inability to effectively deploy reserves from the same units were a significant factor in the failure of assaults. At Shiloh in April 1862 the formation of the three assaulting Confederate corps in successive lines had led to confusion at the highest level of command. At Fredericksburg successive brigade-level attacks had been thrown in piecemeal by the Union command, whereas the Confederate reserves had been distributed so that supports were available from the same organisations as formed the fighting line. At Spotsylvania the assaulting troops had adopted greater depth, but the resulting confusion from the intermingling of units after the initial attack had enabled the defenders to regroup.[84] 'Attacks in which each line was formed of a single division appear to have been far more productive of confusion, and were never so thoroughly successful, as those where each division was

82   Major General P.L. MacDougall, *Modern Infantry Tactics* (London: Edward Stanford, 1873), p.vi; MacDougall, *Modern Warfare*, p.418; Wolseley, *Soldier's Pocket Book*, p.iv.
83   'Q', a Company Officer, 'The Critics and the Infantry Attack', *United Service Magazine*, n.s., 13 (1896), pp.238-253 (pp.238-40, 243); 'Three Field Officers', 'The Critics and the Infantry Attack', *United Service Magazine*, n.s., 13 (1896), pp.368-374 (pp.369-70, 373).
84   Henderson, 'The Campaign of Fredericksburg', *Soldier's View*, pp.91, 105, 208. Shiloh was not explicitly used as an example by any British writers, Fletcher, *History of the American War*, Vol.I, pp.377-379, put the confusion there down to the general inexperience of both officers and men.

drawn up in three lines, as at Chattanooga.'[85] Although the British had assimilated the Prussian 'skirmisher swarm' tactics of 1870, these were seen by some contemporaries as particularly subject to the problem of units becoming intermixed. As individual unit commanders, down to company level, used local initiative to continue the assault on a position, and as further lines of skirmishers re-enforced from the rear, it was feared that command of the fighting line by higher command would become impossible. MacDougall observed that Prussian writers accepted the intermingling of battalions and even brigades, but he favoured the allocation of a defined front for a unit to reduce disorder. Several volunteer officers wrote in the 1880s criticising the tactics of the current drill manual because it resulted in confusion between companies and made it impractical to reform units after attack.[86]

The traditional British three-deep succession of lines, which had also been a common formation in America, also meant that the lead battalion would bear the brunt of the fighting from the start and suffer heavy loss. This was observed in the Civil War where some battalions suffered over 80 percent casualties.[87] Deeper formations for the battalion were suggested in Britain in the 1870s so as the battalion could support its own skirmishers. The 1889 drill manual changed in response to these concerns. Companies were to be self-supporting, with two sections in the firing line and two in support. As this formation approached the enemy, initially in extended order, it would advance by alternate sections, until at a point where concentrated fire could be poured into enemy. The reserve would be from the same half-battalion.[88] The traditional British line where battalions formed up side by side in close order, as seen at the Alma, and as described in the manuals of 1861 and 1867, was now recognised in the new training manual as a thing of the past for fighting a European enemy armed with modern weapons, although it would continue to be used in colonial actions until the end of the century.[89]

* * *

85   Henderson, 'The American Civil War, 1861-1865', in *Science of War*, p.265.
86   MacDougall, *Modern Infantry Tactics*, p.28; Lieutenant Colonel J.H.A. MacDonald (Queens Edinburgh Rifle Volunteer Brigade), *Memorandum of Instruction for a New System of Infantry Attack* (Edinburgh and London: Wm. Blackwood & Sons, [1884]); Captain Edgar J. Mayer (2nd Volunteer Battalion, The Hampshire Regiment), *The Attack Formation by Sections: as it can be Carried out in Accordance with 'Field Exercises, 1884' Without Mixing Companies* (London: T.G. Johnson, 1885); Colonel Bethune Patton (2nd Volunteer Battalion, Prince Albert's Somerset Light Infantry), *Attack Formations* (London: Wm. Clowes, 1885).
87   The 1st Texas lost 82.3 percent at Antietam and the 1st Minnesota 82 percent at Gettysburg. There were 115 instances of individual regiments sustaining over 50 percent casualties in a single battle in the Civil War. Terraine, *The Smoke and the Fire*, p.47.
88   Lieutenant Colonel W.J. Williams RA, 'On Infantry Tactics', *Journal of the Royal United Service Institution*, 16 (1872), pp.768-73; Captain H.R. Gall, 'Infantry', *Illustrated Naval and Military Magazine* 2 (1889) pp.1223-26; Anon, *Infantry Drill* (1889), pp.343-359.
89   At the Atbara in 1898, for example, the lead battalion, the 1st Cameron Highlanders, formed all eight companies in line, with the supporting battalions in column of companies behind. Barthorp, *War on the Nile*, p.146.

The manuals frequently stated that one of the objectives of the new formations and tactics was the avoidance of casualties in the approach and the need to maximise firepower. There were, however, aspects of the manuals that contained instructions which were deliberately intended to maintain the momentum of the offensive, even though they would have the effect of incurring greater losses. In the 1877 instructions, men were told not to take cover in the attack if it would mean losing their intervals; failing to move to the front; or when only under artillery fire. This is similar in intent to Upton's advice to colonels in 1868, quoted above, about retaining control of their men. The 1889 manual also advised that within 500 yards of the enemy, which was the decisive range for the firefight, troops would not as a general rule be allowed to fire while lying down. One further aspect of this might have been that the Martini-Henry rifle was difficult to fire in a prone position.[90]

The need to keep troops in hand also contributed to the apparently regressive adoption of volley firing during the period. The 1861 manual, while giving the commanding officer of a unit the discretion to use whatever mode of firing was appropriate, had warned that volley fire should be used with caution, as it could waste ammunition and lower morale if it failed. File firing was 'the usual and for general purposes the most effective mode of firing', a fact proven by contemporary trials.[91] The Prussian observer to the Civil War, Heros von Borcke, had written that 'little effect is often produced by volley firing'.[92] However by the end of the decade, Wolseley in the *Soldier's Pocket Book* was discouraging the use of independent fire in favour of volley fire because of the impossibility of stopping the former when required to charge. By 1889 volley firing was now advised to be 'more immediately effective than a group of shots fired by an individual' at ranges over 500 yards due to the 'cone of fire' laid down by the bullets.[93]

The benefits of volley fire were deemed to be fourfold: it was the only method of firing allowing complete control; it admitted correction of elevation/direction by observation of where the bullets stuck; it regulated ammunition expenditure; and it kept the men steady.[94] Once again these considerations echo the advice given in Upton's manual based upon the lessons of the Civil War.

> As the strength of troops armed with breechloaders lies in the volume and effect of their fire when well delivered, so their weakness will lie in the very superiority of their weapon when allowed to deliver their fire injudiciously at long range; the officers therefore should keep the men always under their control, see that

---

90 Anon, *Infantry Drill* (1889), pp.346-47. For the problem of firing the Martini-Henry lying down see Maxwell, *My God – Maiwand!*, p.130.
91 Anon, *Field Exercises* (1861), p.196. For contemporary experiments see Kerr, 'Wall of Fire', p.26. The experiments cited by Kerr are those by the United States War Department in February 1860.
92 Von Borcke, *Memoirs*, Vol.II, p.243-44.
93 Wolseley, *Soldier's Pocket Book*, p.249; Anon, *Infantry Drill* (1889), p.214.
94 Clifford, *Resume of the Tactical Portions*, p.9.

they husband their ammunition, and by teaching them confidence in their arm and deliberation in aiming, enable them always to hold their fire until the enemy shall be within deadly range.[95]

One further consideration in the selection of mode of fire was the continued presence of smoke from gunfire on the battlefield at this time. In the attack the instructions advised one volley to be fired at each halt, followed by an immediate advance to utilise the cover of the resulting smoke. Once the advance could not take place 'without unnecessary exposure' independent firing would be ordered. This provided the cover for the second line to make the final assault. 'The advantages of independent fire at the final stage, from the cover which its smoke affords to the Second Line to push forward to the attack, are self evident'.[96]

When the introduction of smokeless powder removed this concealing effect of the infantry's own gunfire, the British experimented with artificial means of providing it. An exercise was carried out on 7 August 1890 at Fort Cumberland, Portsmouth, using the regulation attack in the 1889 Infantry Drill, but with each man in the front-line battalions equipped with three smoke cannisters in place of half of their ammunition allowance. The plan was for the left-hand company of each battalion to throw their cases at 500 yards, then fire a volley. The right-hand company would make a rush forward under cover of the smoke and repeat the process. In this way, advancing by turns and picking up and re-throwing the cases as they advanced, the front line would advance to 150 yards. At this point they would commence independent fire, throw their final cannisters, and finally the battalions in the reserve line would assault through the smoke. In practice, this orderly process fell into utter confusion. The act of throwing the cannisters detracted from that of firing and slowed the advance. The cannisters overloaded the men and were unpopular and the smoke did not effectively conceal the firing line but had the opposite effect of obscuring the defenders. An observer of the exercise concluded that it was doubtful such a frontal attack would succeed.[97] The exercise does however indicate that the British fully understood the difficulty of a frontal attack on magazine rifles, and were looking at technical solutions as one means of overcoming this.

Decisions regarding fire tactics were not merely based upon subjective opinions, they were also arrived at through experimentation. The introduction of the Martini-Henry rifle was accompanied by trials with the new weapon at Gravesend, which produced some interesting statistics. On average, volley fire at 800 yards scored 50 percent hits on target, while on one occasion four men firing by volleys at 600 yards achieved 85 percent hits. According to Lieutenant Stephens RE, the Assistant Musketry

95   Upton, *Infantry Tactics*, p.297.
96   Anon, *Infantry Drill* (1889), pp.341, 346-47.
97   Mark Hamilton, 'The Smoke Attack: As Shown to the German Emperor by Colonel Crease on the 7th August', *United Service Magazine*, n.s., 1 (1890), pp.551-55.

Instructor, independent fire at long distances 'although good, was not so effective as volley firing, and on service would cause great waste of ammunition'. At closer range though, five men firing independently at 300 yards placed 112 out of 121 shots into the target, or 92 per cent. Captain Drake RE, the senior Musketry Instructor, calculated that if 400 men tried to advance on 100 defenders in a shelter trench from 600 yards away, that within two minutes there ought not to be an assailant left standing.[98]

In 1888 Colonel Lonsdale Hale predicted a similar outcome from an attack on a shelter trench. Hale's lectures at the Staff College on the Franco-Prussian War were used by Luvaas as an example of the Civil War being overlooked,[99] so it is worth quoting Hale at length to show that study of European wars did not lead to a lack of appreciation of the strength of defensive firepower and entrenchments that had been demonstrated at Atlanta, Cold Harbor, Franklin, and many other Civil War battles.

> Assume that your battalion is in a shelter trench at the top of a hill with gently sloping open ground in front of you, and that 800 men on a front of 300 yards advance to the attack. Will your fire be so ineffective that they will ever reach your shelter trench? Surely not; surely you not only believe, but you know, that those 800 men will be destroyed, decimated, driven back, or bought to a stand still. But what is sauce for the goose is sauce for the gander, and if this is the fate of 800 Germans attacking you, it will be your fate if you and your 800 English attack 800 Germans, and if they are backed up by machine and maxim guns and magazine rifles the result will be even more marked.[100]

*   *   *

Given this recognition of the defensive impact of modern rifle fire, it is a misconception that the British remained fixated during this period on the value of the bayonet as a lethal weapon in its own right, ignoring the evidence of the Civil War, where bayonet casualties were minimal.[101] There were some conservatives who did retain such views. Chesney quoted continental writings about the Civil War by Jomini and his followers, which argued that the American conflict had demonstrated that the bayonet had been 'usually more effective than grape, canister or bullets', and he believed MacDougall's views that firepower had superseded the bayonet were 'contrary to the belief of those who have seen the latest use of both weapons in America'.[102] While presenting the

98   Graham, 'Shelter Trenches', Appendix III on the Martini Henry Rifle, pp.474-75.
99   Luvaas, *Military Legacy*, p.116.
100 Hale, *The Spirit of Tactical Operations of To-day*, p.8.
101 Craddock, 'The American Civil War and its Influence on the British Army', pp.7, 43, 164, 212-13, 291; for bayonet casualties see Griffith, *Rally Once Again*, p.27.
102 Charles Cornwallis Chesney, 'Recent Changes in the Art of War', in Chesney and Reeve, *Military Resources*, pp.35, 39). Chesney's American authority was Lippitt, who was also

new Lee-Metford magazine rifle to an audience at Aldershot in 1892, Colonel Henry St John Halford referred to an officer in his audience who did not believe in rifle fire. Halford wryly observed that the new rifle still had a bayonet, which was 'useful for other purposes [...] A man can skin a sheep with it, eat his dinner with it, or cut up his tobacco'.[103]

The arguments for the bayonet were more commonly sentimental. The British soldier's historic success in close order combat was both a source of national pride and seen as a physical and moral advantage over the enemy. According to Sir William Napier, the historian of Wellington's campaign in the Peninsular War, 'our only real superiority [lay] in our resolute courage to close with the bayonet', and the fear was that this advantage would now be irreparably lost due to the new firearms.[104] Even for Wolseley, the bayonet was part of the British military tradition to be maintained under the new conditions, and the army needed to 'go a step further, and teach our men to charge with the bayonet in skirmishing order'.[105] It was also argued, quoting Major General McClellan as an authority, that the bayonet drill was the best means of developing a soldier, and increasing steadiness in recruits.[106]

Other writers were of the opinion that actual bayonet fights were rare, even historically. One young British officer wrote in 1864 that 'scarcely more than two incidents of regular and downright bayonet charges are on record'. For these writers it was not the physical shock of the bayonet that was important, but the *morale* effect of troops being willing to engage in something which was 'not a mode of contest that man naturally selects' that enabled troops prepared to close with the bayonet to win the day.[107] In

in favour of the bayonet on the basis of his observation of the Civil War where Chesney claimed that it had 'succeeded in nine cases put of ten', ibid, p.35. Lippitt, *A Treatise on the Tactical Use of The Three Arms*, pp.4-26.

103 Halford, *New Service Magazine Rifle*, pp.8-9. Halford's comment is similar to those reported of some Civil War soldiers, Nosworthy, *The Bloody Crucible of Courage*, p.595.

104 Napier quoted in Hime, *Stray Military Papers*, p.61.

105 Colonel Garnet Wolseley ['Ubique'], 'Essay 4', in *Essays Written for the Wellington Prize* (Edinburgh: Wm. Blackwood & Sons, 1872), pp.189-252 (p.229).

106 Captain Sir Sibbald David Scott, 'On the History of the Bayonet', *Journal of the Royal United Service Institution*, 7 (1863), pp.346-47. Debate over the value of the bayonet was not new in Britain. John Mitchell and Sir William Napier had taken opposing views over its effectiveness in the 1830s, see Strachan, *From Waterloo to Balaclava*, pp.27-31, and *Wellington's Legacy*, p.27. However, Mitchell had advocated alternative close quarter fighting weapons to the bayonet (*Waterloo to Balaclava*, p.28) whereas its later opponents stressed the power of rifle fire alone.

107 Lieutenant A. Steinmetz, 'The Soldier's Why and Because: Or the Theoretical Principles of Drill; and the Chief Battalion Movements Exemplified In Battle', *United Service Magazine*, 428 (July 1864), pp.339-44 (pp.346-47). In 1899 an anonymous writer in the *United Service Magazine* acknowledged that the use of the bayonet would be rare in European warfare, but his support of bayonet drill was commended by the editor of the magazine because it would encourage troops to close with the enemy. Anon ['Cold Steel'], 'The Bayonet as a Weapon', *United Service Magazine*, n.s., 18 (1898), pp.82-85.

this view, the bayonet charge had, like the cavalry charge on formed infantry, become something to be delivered against an inferior or demoralised enemy. Maurice put this clearly in his 1871 Wellington Prize winning essay. 'Now the bayonet, or rather the charge, in which the bayonet counts almost for nothing, is only the means by which the fruits of the fire-action are reaped when they are fully ripe.'[108] Another entry in the same competition recommended that a Wellingtonian bayonet charge should not be used against a recoiling attacker, as this would expose the defender to fire. Its author suggested that 'the great rapidity of loading it has made the breech-loading rifle an *offensive weapon* of itself' with a greater moral effect than that of the bayonet charge, and regarded the bayonet attack, again like the cavalry charge, to be of use only on occasion when surprise could be obtained.[109] The winning entry in the Staff College essay competition the same year also wrote that to counter-attack with the bayonet would lead to heavy casualties due to the 'murderous fire of the breech-loader'. This goes against the idea that challenging traditional tactics was discouraged, it could in fact be positively rewarded.[110]

Captain Henry Brackenbury, then Professor of Military History at the Royal Military College, Sandhurst, made it clear the following year that 'the chief aim of modern offensive tactics is to obtain the greatest possible development of accurate fire, as being the surest means of breaking down the enemy'.[111] An engineering officer speaking at the Royal United Service Institution in 1881 went further, stating that he was 'essentially opposed to the use of the bayonet'; that there should be no attempt to physically push the enemy out of his position; and that the attack should put the enemy to flight through superiority of fire alone.[112]

Official doctrine did not go this far, and the 1889 Field Exercises have been criti- cised for continuing to include a bayonet charge to follow up the assaulting lines.[113] However, it was the bullet, not the bayonet, that now formed the basis for the tactics which the British intended to use against a European enemy. 'It is infantry fire which really decides the issue', stated the 1889 manual. 'To demoralise the enemy by the fire of the firing line, and of artillery, may be regarded as a necessary preliminary to a successful assault upon the most important points of his position.'[114] The manual elaborated further.

108 Maurice, *Wellington Essay*, pp.85-86.
109 James F. MacPherson ['An Adjutant'], *An Essay in Tactics* (London: W. Mitchell, 1872), p.72. Original italics.
110 Lieutenant E.H.H. Collen, *The Battle of Worth. Staff College Essay Prize, 1872* (London: W. Mitchell, 1872), p.41.
111 Brackenbury, 'Tactics of the Three Arms', p.619.
112 Captain Walter H. James 'Modern Fire: Its influence on Armament, Training and Tactics', *Journal of the Royal United Service Institution*, 17 (1873), pp.378-403 (p.379).
113 Craddock, 'The American Civil War and its Influence on the British Army', pp.212-13; Preston, 'Military Lessons of the American Civil War', p.235.
114 Anon, *Infantry Drill* (1889), pp.210, 338. The 1892 manual went further, stating that '[t]he firing line crushes and overwhelms the enemy with bullets' and that the attack 'must crush

Victory depends upon the final assault; but experience teaches that before the bayonet charge can be successfully delivered against good troops, the defenders of a position must have been shaken and demoralised by a preparatory artillery or infantry fire directed on the main points of attack; otherwise it will be impossible for the firing line to advance over the fire swept zone.[115]

The bayonet is clearly identified here as a psychological weapon and not a physical one. 'The moral [sic] effect of fixing bayonets is great; it intimidates the enemy and encourages those about to engage in the assault.' Similarly, the purpose of the seemingly anachronistic instruction that the second line should make the assault through the first 'with drums beating and bugles sounding' was to further demoralise a shaken enemy and to encourage the assaulting troops.[116] Handbooks based on the manuals were also clear that the prime purpose of fixing bayonets was its *morale* effect, and that bayonet attacks were always to be preceded by a heavy fire to demoralise and break the enemy.[117] This aligns to the conclusions of some modern authorities that 'shock action' is psychological not physical, and that shock tactics and the bayonet charge could still be effective in the Civil War even if the casualties caused by the bayonet itself were few.[118] The willingness of the American troops in the Civil War to try and close with the bayonet was seen by the British as being superior to the Prussian tactics of relying upon firepower alone.[119]

* * *

In colonial warfare the use of close order lines and squares continued, but should not be seen as evidence of irrational conservatism. The retention of the square by the British has come in for particular criticism, but the square as a defensive formation against cavalry was already becoming recognised as an anachronism by the end of the 1860s. The 1867 regulations instructed that, if formed at all, a two-deep square, rather than the traditional four rank formation, was sufficiently strong for troops armed with breech-loaders to resist cavalry. Moreover, at the discretion of the commanding officer, it was permissible to receive cavalry in line, particularly where there was danger

the enemy's fire and secure the greatest prospect of success'. Anon, *Infantry Drill* (1892), pp.87, 179.

115 Anon, *Infantry Drill* (1889), p.222.

116 Anon, *Infantry Drill* (1889), p.224.

117 For example Captain J.W. Malet, *Handbook to Field Training in the Infantry* (London: Gale and Polden, 1893), pp.21-23, 40.

118 Nosworthy, *The Bloody Crucible of Courage*, pp.594-608; Griffith, *Rally Once Again*, pp.140-45.

119 For superiority of American over Prussian tactics, see G.F.R. Henderson, 'Military Criticism and Modern Tactics', in *Science of War*, pp.108-64 (pp.148-150), originally published under the pseudonym 'The Author of *The Campaign of Fredericksburg*', in *United Service Magazine*, n.s., 3 (1891), pp.396-415, 553-67.

from artillery fire. Upton's contemporary American manual also retained instructions to form square against cavalry, and to form from line to column when cavalry attack might be anticipated.[120]

In contrast, Wolseley wrote in the *Soldier's Pocket Book* that good skirmishers if armed with breech-loaders, and in country broken up by hedges, 'ought to laugh at all partial charges of cavalry', and that squares should only be formed when absolutely necessary since they became 'a mark for every description of fire'. By 1870 the preferred formation to meet cavalry in the open plain was the line, although 'where there is any possibility of cavalry approaching unperceived, the troops should be prepared to form square, two or four deep, at any moment'. The 1877 manual goes further stating that 'although necessary for drill purposes to recognise square formations, it must be borne in mind that they should only be resorted to in extreme cases when infantry is attacked by a very large force of cavalry'.[121]

The adoption of squares against tribal opponents was nevertheless common in Africa throughout the 1870s and 1880s. These were rarely the battalion squares such as had been used at Waterloo, and now stated to be largely obsolete in the drill manuals. Rather, they were usually much larger formations consisting of several units acting as a brigade, and were retained in colonial campaigns on much the same grounds as the advice given in the 1870 manual regarding cavalry. Expeditions operating in unfamiliar territory could be subject to attack from multiple directions from a mobile or concealed enemy, meaning that they needed to be ready for all round defence while maintaining some mobility. Lieutenant General Sir Gerald Graham, who had commanded the Suakin Field Force in the eastern Sudan in 1885, made the reasons for their adoption quite clear.

> [S]quares are only to be used when you cannot protect your flanks and rear by any other formation against an enemy who uses shock tactics. [...] Nor must it be supposed that in our fights near Suakin we were slavishly bound to the square as a fighting formation.[122]

Against troops armed with modern rifles or artillery close order tactics would have resulted in heavy casualties, but in the words of the 1892 manual '[a]gainst untrained and indifferently armed races, closer formations are not only practicable but essential. The power of concentration, which renders a close and intense fire possible, should be

120 Craddock, 'The American Civil War and its Influence on the British Army', pp.213-15; Anon, *Field Exercises* (1867), pp.213, 229, 310; Upton, *Infantry Tactics* (1868), pp.203-09, 249, 289-94.
121 Wolseley, *Soldier's Pocket Book*, pp.250, 285; Anon, *Field Exercises* (1870), p.193; Anon, *Field Exercises* (1877), p.233.
122 Lieutenant General Sir Gerald Graham, 'Infantry Fire Tactics: Attack Formations and Squares', *Journal of the Royal United Service Institution*, 30 (1886), pp.233-274, (p.233)

British square at El Teb, 1884. Obsolete in Europe, squares provided both firepower and all round defence in so-called 'savage' wars. (Anne S.K. Brown Military Collection)

utilised to the fullest extent'.[123] Significantly, the reason given here for adopting these close-order formations was to maximise firepower, not to encourage close combat and the use of the bayonet. When dispersed formations, even those armed with breech-loaders, were heavily outnumbered by an enemy willing to press their attacks regardless of losses, such as the Zulus at Isandlwana in January 1879, they could still be overwhelmed.[124]

Throughout the 1870s and 1880s, British troops were rarely called upon to conduct offensive operations against opponents armed with effective firepower, so there is little actual evidence of the attempted use of the new regulation tactics. The frontal assault on the Boer line at Laing's Nek in January 1881 is sometimes cited to demonstrate the retention of close order tactics by the British in spite of the lessons of recent history, but this was in contravention of the drill-book instructions on correct attack formations, not because of them, and the British infantry (the 58th Foot) did not really deploy into a fighting line. The men were new, short-term soldiers, and most of them,

123 Anon, *Infantry Drill* (1892), p.185.
124 Captain J.S. Rothwell, *Narrative of the Field Operations connected with the Zulu War of 1879* (London: Greenhill Books, 1989, originally published 1881), p.33-38; Ian Knight, *Brave Men's Blood* (London: Guild, 1990), pp.61-67.

including Colonel Deane their commander, had never been under fire.[125] Like other defeats in this war, it was the result of poor leadership, and a lack of training and experience amongst the officers and troops involved, rather than faulty doctrine. A few years later at Kirbekan in the Sudan (February 1885), a British force of similar size was faced with a similar tactical situation with the enemy (in this case Mahdist tribesmen) installed on a ridge and in cover. Major General Earle, a veteran of the Alma, was initially minded to make a frontal assault but was dissuaded by his staff and subordinate officers, who included Colonel Henry Brackenbury, by then one of Wolseley's protégés. As a result of an effective reconnaissance by the small attached cavalry force, a means of turning the position was found and while a demonstration held the Mahdists' attention to the front, the main assault went in from the rear in line – 'open attack formation, none of your Abu Klea squares' and achieved complete success for slight loss.[126]

Both Laing's Nek and Kirbekan were however minor engagements. The only battle in this period where a sizeable British Army encountered an army equipped with modern firearms and artillery, and entrenched behind strong and well-constructed field works, was conducted by Wolseley himself at Tel-el-Kebir in September 1882. Although it is easy to dismiss the conscripted Egyptian infantry in this battle as not of the quality of European or American troops, the position was nevertheless formidable. A six-foot-deep, nine-foot-wide ditch ran in front of a rampart five to six feet high and ten feet thick, stretching for four miles, with an advanced redoubt to the front. The Egyptians were between 25,000 and 30,000 strong and well-armed with American Remington rifles and German Krupp artillery. The terrain fronting their lines was completely devoid of cover. Wolseley himself had less than 18,000 troops available. His tactics in the circumstances show that he had absorbed the lessons of other conflicts. Static confrontation of the enemy behind his own breastworks would have achieved nothing. In foreign territory and with inferior numbers he could not afford to engage in a campaign of attrition. A simple frontal assault, even if successful due to the quality of the troops on each side, would have resulted in a large 'butchers bill' unacceptable to the British public. Wolseley needed a decisive victory, but one relatively cheaply won. To counter the lack of cover, he decided upon a daring night approach that would leave his troops at daybreak some 200 yards from the enemy position, the regulation distance for the final assault. The frontal assault was to be accompanied by an attack on the left flank by the cavalry, supported by infantry, artillery, and machine guns. The attack would be made on a limited frontage, each brigade covering 1000 yards, and in several places the timely bringing up of the reserves was needed to carry the Egyptian positions. Wolseley substituted surprise and speed in the

125 Lehman, *The First Boer War*, pp.151-55; Creswicke, *Transvaal War*, Vol.I, p.82; Craddock, 'The American Civil War and its Influence on the British Army', p.265.
126 Colonel Sir W.F. Butler, *The Campaign of the Cataracts* (London: Sampson Low, Marston, Searle and Rivington, 1887), pp.323-34; Barthorp, *War on the Nile*, p.115, quoting Captain Ian Hamilton (later General Sir Ian Hamilton).

'The Cameron Highlanders charging at Tel-el-Kebir' (1882), by F. Claridge Turner, a typical artistic depiction of British Infantry. (Anne S.K. Brown Military Collection)

attack, rather than superiority in the firefight, to gain the moral ascendency over his enemy but the Battle of Tel-el-Kebir was far from a simple frontal bayonet assault.[127]

* * *

From 1870 until the mid-1880s, the traditional view is that British military thinking became obsessed with all things Prussian and that military writers took their main examples from the war of 1870-71, in particular the battles of Mars-La-Tour/Rezonville (16 August 1870), Gravelotte-St Privat (18 August 1870) and Sedan (1-2 September 1870).[128] It is true that there was very little directly written on the American Civil War in Britain during this period. The renewed interest in the war is usually dated from, and largely attributed to, the anonymous publication of Captain G.F.R. Henderson's *The Campaign of Fredericksburg* in 1886. There were some good reasons behind the lack

127 Michael Barthorp, *War on the Nile*, pp.63-71; Kochanski, *Sir Garnet Wolseley: Victorian Hero*, pp.142-44. In the copy of Cunningham-Robinson's *Field Intrenching* held in the Wolseley Archive, there are hand-written annotations in the margin where the text refers to night attacks; this may indicate that Wolseley had considered this as a tactic for avoiding casualties well before his use of it in Egypt, op.cit., pp.19, 27.
128 Luvaas, *Military Legacy*, pp.115-17; Craddock, 'The American Civil War and its Influence on the British Army', p.161.

of interest in the American war at this time. There was the greater immediacy and relevance of European conflicts discussed previously, and the great number of works produced analysing these wars by continental writers. By comparison, to a large extent there was nothing significant being written in the United States itself as the nation tried to rebuild itself after the conflict. On those occasions when important new material did appear, it usually drew a response from a British writer. For example, from the late 1870s American participants in the war began to publish their memoirs. Most notably both Major General Sherman and General Joseph E. Johnson produced their accounts of the Atlanta campaign in 1875, prompting an analysis from Chesney. When a decade later the *Century Magazine* published its famous *Battles and Leaders* series of articles and debates on the critical campaigns and battles, it drew a series of articles from Wolseley in the *North American Review* based upon their content, and a vigorous debate on Wolseley's opinions from the American participants concerned. Two years later, the death of Sherman prompted an analysis of his career by Wolseley. It was also Wolseley who recognised Henderson's talents on the basis of his volume on Fredericksburg, and got him appointed to the staff of the Royal Military College at Sandhurst. Perhaps most significantly, from 1881 the comprehensive and voluminous *Official Records of the Union and Confederate Armies* began to be published. This wealth of new material created a general revival of interest in the American Civil War in Britain, and the personal and official material offered new sources of lessons and debate.[129]

The lack of publications directly related to the Civil War did not however mean that it played no part in British thinking during the 1870s. As shown, it continued to feature in discourses regarding the use of fortifications, and in 1873 Major George Pomeroy Colley, at the time the Professor of Military Administration and Law at the Staff College, and soon to become a prominent member of Wolseley's 'ring', suggested that it warranted further study.

> We are perhaps a little apt to undervalue American experiences and attribute to want of manoeuvring power and energy of attack on their part, the indecisive results which were really due to stubbornness of defence. But certainly the battles of the great civil war [*sic*] bear out the opinions expressed by American Officers, that no advance can succeed against good troops holding a fair defensive position

---

129 'Line Officer' [Captain G. F. R. Henderson], *The Campaign of Fredericksburg* (London: Gale and Polden, 1886). I have used the more accessible modern reprint in Luvaas, *Soldier's View*, pp.9-119. C.C. Chesney, 'Sherman and Johnston, and the Atlanta Campaign', *Fortnightly Review*, n.s., 18 (1875), pp.611-624. The *Century Magazine* articles were originally issued from 1884 to 1887, and Wolseley's series of articles in the *North American Review* throughout 1889. Field Marshal Viscount Garnet Joseph Wolseley, 'General Sherman', *United Service Magazine*, n.s., 3 (1891), pp.97-116, 193-216, 289-309. For Wolseley's role in Henderson's career see Jay Luvaas, 'G.F.R. Henderson and the American Civil War', *Military Affairs*, 20 (1956), pp.139-53 (p.139); also the introduction in Luvaas, *Soldier's View*, pp.4-5, and Luvaas, *Military Legacy*, pp.170-71.

till these have been not merely shaken, but practically broken and destroyed as a fighting body.[130]

Colley went on to say that the source of victory was in preparation – the final advance merely confirming victory in the fire-fight which was all important. These were not unsound views, even though Colley's own performance in the field six years later in South Africa led to ignominious defeat, and his own death at the hands of the Boers on Majuba Hill.

It is perhaps surprising then that the revised interest in the American Civil War in the 1880s did not re-enforce the recognition of the primacy of defensive firepower as might have been expected. To the contrary, some authorities such as F.N. Maude drew upon the war to support their theories of the offence. For Maude, the study of the Franco-Prussian War had led to false conclusions regarding the effectiveness of the spade, the intensity of fire on the battlefield and the inevitability that formed troops would dissolve under fire. 'A careful study of the incidents in the American Civil War might have corrected these impressions.'[131] As in his views on the American cavalry, discussed in the previous chapter, Maude believed that the conditions of that war had been exceptional. He thought the American troops to have been naturally skilled in the use of the rifle, with the result that their fire 'obtained a degree of precision which has probably never before or since been equalled'.[132] The low degree of manoeuvrability of the armies; the difficult terrain; the lack of effective battlefield communication, 'everything favoured the adoption of cover and defensive tactics generally [...]. The balance of advantage in favour of the defence had then attained a superiority which had never been approached before *or can be expected again*'.[133]

Maude went further, claiming that the Civil War provided evidence that the Americans had succeeded in frontal assaults in spite of the casualties, even though the muzzle-loading rifle greatly favoured the defence. According to his argument, discipline and a willingness to endure casualties were the keys to victory. 'There never were armies in which the average level of intelligence was higher than those which

---

130 Major Colley, speaking at the Royal United Service Institution 31 May 1873, in response to Brackenbury, 'Tactics of the Three Arms', p.636.
131 Captain Frederic Natusch Maude, 'Field Fortifications and Intrenched Camps', in *Attack or Defence: Seven Military Essays* (London: J.J. Keliher, 1896), p.9. Reprinted from *Operations of the Military Engineering of the International Congress of Engineers, 1894.* The comparison between the casualty levels of Napoleonic and Civil War battles was echoed by the American writer Arthur L. Wagner, a great admirer of Maude, see Arthur L. Wagner, 'The Army', in *The United States Army and Navy* (New York: Werner, 1899), pp.15-103 (p.36).
132 Maude, 'Field Fortifications and Intrenched Camps', in *Attack or Defence*, p.15 Maude's view on the superior ability of American troops with firearms has received modern support from Nosworthy, *The Bloody Crucible of Courage*, pp.581-93.
133 Maude, 'Field Fortifications and Intrenched Camps', in *Attack or Defence*, p.16 (emphasis added).

fought in the American Civil War', he wrote, and went on to say that this level of *intelligence* did not vary between First Bull Run and Gettysburg. In between these two battles (and echoing the views expressed by the contemporary observers), Maude argued that the American soldier had learnt *discipline*, which enabled him to stand up to casualties higher than any since Waterloo, and considerably higher than those suffered in European wars from 1866-77.[134] In Maude's view the greatly increased firepower of field artillery by the 1890s, and the ability of assaulting troops armed with breech-loaders to fire while advancing and making use of available cover, would restore the superiority of the offensive, and hasty entrenchments would be obsolete in future wars. 'Works adequate to stop the rush of troops handled as were the Russians before Plevna, or the VII Corps at Gravelotte, would be useless in face of troops of the quality of Pickett's Division at Gettysburg handled by a Napoleon'.[135]

Maude used pseudo-scientific analysis to support his views, for example stating that the chances of troops carrying a position 'varies directly to the square of their discipline' to argue that troops willing to take casualties could be successful even in frontal assaults. Maude even dismissed the idea that close formations were impractical, believing them to be the only way to bring the required number of rifles into the firing line to break the enemy. The Americans were again his model. 'Had breech-loaders suddenly been placed in the hands of both North and South during the war [...] no other change would have been required to place either side on a level with the German tactics as they are now'.[136] In a series of articles published in America, he compared the tactics of the Civil War and the losses incurred with those of the Prussians, and concluded that the American troops were superior. Maude argued that attacks needed to be put in using great numbers and depth, and that three lines advancing at 500 yards intervals would have succeeded where the Prussian Guard had failed, in carrying the French position at St Privat during the battle of 18 August 1870. Referring once again to Pickett's men and 'what losses Anglo-Saxon troops can bear' (according to Maude, four times those of the Prussian Guard), this led him to conclude that 'the experience of both our own army and the Americans proves, that troops with British blood in them require less leading in an attack than those of any other race'.[137]

However, Maude did not promote *élan* above all other considerations. In fact he proposed the two-deep line as the ideal formation because it brought the maximum

134 Maude, 'The Infantry Attack 1892', in *Attack or Defence*, pp.1-2. Reprinted from *United Service Magazine*, n.s., 6 (1893), pp.602-609.
135 Maude, 'Field Fortifications and Intrenched Camps', in *Attack or Defence*, p.47.
136 Maude, 'The Evolution of Modern Drill Books', in *Attack or Defence*, p.23. Re-printed from *Journal of the Military Service Institution*, New York ([n.d.]).
137 Captain F.N. Maude RE, *Letters on Tactics and Organization, or, English Military Institutions and the Continental Systems* (Fort Leavenworth: George A Spooner, 1891), pp.150-151, 59-60, 163.

number of rifles to bear on the enemy.[138] 'All infantry must be trained to believe the bayonet invincible, but all tactical principles must be based upon the fact that fire alone decides.'[139] The final, successful bayonet charge would be the consequence of effective fire preparations, just as Maurice and others had expounded 20 years earlier.

To modern eyes Maude's theories may appear outrageous, but they were widely read on both sides of the Atlantic. He published extensively in America and edited the *Journal of the Royal United Service Institution* for 10 years, although his direct influence on the British Army establishment has been assessed by one modern authority as limited.[140] Maurice dismissed the apparent paradox raised by Maude that casualty rates had fallen with the introduction of arms of precision as a 'feeble fallacy', on the simple grounds that since it was a feature of modern firearms that greater casualties were inflicted in a given period of time, this had a devastating effect on morale, and stopped troops exposing themselves to fire.[141] Another writer expanded upon this.

> What we gather from the facts known of the losses in the principal battles of the first stages of the [Franco-Prussian] war is that, though with the increase in range, accuracy, and rapidity of fire of artillery and small arms, the losses seem to have diminish, the diminution only applies to the totals on the battle-field. Destruction is more concentrated, and the troops closely engaged really lose as large if not a larger proportion of their strength than formerly.[142]

Despite Maude's views that determined and disciplined infantry could still succeed in the assault, neither the official manuals nor most other military writers were under any illusions as to the difficulty of the attack and the casualties that might be inflicted by modern weapons. The instructions for the umpires in determining the results of the mock engagements on field manoeuvres make particularly interesting reading. In order for an attack on an entrenched position to succeed, the necessary superiority required by the attacker over the defender, assuming adequate artillery support, was considered to be three-to-one. Even then the expected loss to the attackers was one-quarter if successful, while the overwhelmed defender would similarly be judged to have lost one-quarter of their number. If the attack was unsuccessful, one-third of the assaulting troops were deemed lost. An un-entrenched but 'well held' position was

138   Maude, 'The Evolution of Modern Drill Books', in *Attack or Defence*, pp.13-14. Maude's theories ignored the penetrative power of the latest high velocity rifles, see Major McCartney, 'Modern Rifle Fire', *United Service Magazine*, n.s., 10 (1894), pp.31-41.
139   Maude, 'The Infantry Attack', in *Attack or Defence*, p.2.
140   Arthur L. Wagner, preface to Maude's *Cavalry Versus Infantry*, op.cit.; Howard Bailes, 'Patterns of Thought in the Late Victorian Army', *Journal of Strategic Studies*, 4 (1981), pp.29-45 (p.33, 41); Spiers, *The Late Victorian Army*, p.246.
141   Maurice, 'How Far the Lessons of the Franco-German War are out of Date', p.562.
142   Knollys, 'Lessons Taught by the Franco-German War', *United Service Magazine*, 705 (August 1887), pp.93-119 (p.119).

rated as somewhat easier to assault but, even then, the attacker was assumed to need a two-to-one superiority for success, and would still lose one-sixth of their strength. The overwhelmed defender was still classed as losing one-quarter. If artillery support was not available, the numerical superiority considered necessary for a successful assault was increased to four-to-one and three-to-one respectively.[143]

The exact origin of the three-to-one ratio as the odds needed to conduct an assault successfully is unknown. G.F.R. Henderson attributed it to the Germans but it has been suggested it was in use as a rough rule of thumb during the Civil War.[144] And losses in these ratios were broadly in line with those recorded for the battles of 1861-65. For example, the casualties given in Henderson's *Campaign of Fredericksburg* for the failed assault on Marye's Hill were 7,000 out of 30,000 Union attackers (23.3 percent) and 1,500 out of 7,400 Confederate defenders (20.3 percent).[145] Casualties for some individual regiments had significantly exceeded these percentages, and every battle and every attack was unique, but losses of 25-30 percent were not an unreasonable expectation for larger assaulting formations as a whole. Casualties approaching the initial strength of the defenders, which are implied by the umpiring guidelines, are also supported by the losses suffered by Major General Wright's VI Union Corps at Petersburg in their assault of April 1865, reported by Major Henry Smyth at the time, and used as an example in the 1870s.[146] Prussian authorities considered that the maximum casualties which could be sustained by a unit and for it to remain effective was 30 percent, a figure also adopted by Maude in his calculations.[147] This would support the three-to-one ratio, as well as being the basis for the one-third losses for assaults.

The influence of G.F.R. Henderson was far greater than that of Maude. His admirers have seized upon the notion he considered that the lessons drawn from the Franco-Prussian War to be overrated, saying that he was 'years ahead of his time' in recognising the value of entrenchments and that American tactics were superior to those of the Europeans, in contrast to the views of the majority of British writers who failed to learn from the Civil War. Detractors have pointed to his focus on the eastern theatre and earlier stages of the war, and suggested that his thinking was essentially conservative and that his advocacy of the moral element in war influenced British thinking in favour of offensive tactics in the first decades of the 20th Century.[148]

---

143 Anon, *Infantry Drill* (1889), p.409; Anon, *Infantry Drill (Provisional)* (1892), p.229.
144 Henderson, 'The British Army', in *Science of War*, p.416; Colonel Trevor N. Dupuy, *Understanding War* (New York: Paragon, 1987), p.31.
145 Henderson, 'Campaign of Fredericksburg', in Luvaas, *Soldier's View*, p.90.
146 Clayton, 'Field Intrenching', pp.287-88, his observation is based upon Wright's report from Petersburg, quoting the work of Belgian writer Alexis Henri Brialmont; Smyth, 'Account of the Final Attack and Capture of Richmond', p.368.
147 Brackenbury, 'Tactics of the Three Arms', p.627; Maude, 'The Evolution of Modern Drill Books', in *Attack or Defence*, pp.13-14.
148 Luvaas, *Soldier's View*, pp.120-28; Preston, 'Military Lessons of the American Civil War', pp.235-36; Luvaas, *Military Legacy*, p.189.

Henderson's views on infantry tactics were much more complex than Maude's and sometimes appear contradictory, not least because he modified them over time. Henderson was not primarily interested in what he called 'minor tactics' and did not consider those of the Civil War to be of very great interest. The formations adopted at the start of the war he identified as derivative of the traditional British line, although the American drill was based upon French practice with their use of rapid movement and skirmishers. These formations, according to Henderson, had proved to be un-manoeuvrable under fire, and like the Prussian attacks in 1870 had dissolved into lines of skirmishers. While crediting the Americans with the invention of this mode of attack by successive skirmish lines, as well as advancing by rushes, these were tactics that 'differed little, if at all, from those now in vogue in Europe'. In particular Henderson recognised that the Russian Major General Michael Skobeleff had adopted the attack by successive lines as the primary means of assault in the Russo-Turkish War.[149]

Henderson certainly recognised the importance of entrenchments in the war, but to suggest that this made him ahead of the time is to misrepresent the body of military thought that preceded him. For example, Henderson's statement in *The Campaign of Fredericksburg* that 'good infantry, sufficiently covered, and with free play for the rifle, is, if unshaken by artillery and attacked in front alone, absolutely invincible' is taken almost verbatim from MacDougall's work *Modern Infantry Tactics* of 1873. Henderson altered the earlier passage in response to the increasing significance of artillery preparation in the attack, which in turn was reflected in the instructions in the 1877 infantry manual that the 'advance of infantry should always be preceded by a concentrated fire of Artillery on the point selected for attack, which fire should be maintained until the last moment possible'.[150]

Also significant is the qualification regarding frontal assault *alone*. Henderson stressed that the main idea of modern tactics was flanking fire (for which he used an example from the Russo-Turkish War, even when writing about the Fredericksburg campaign).[151] He did not countenance an out and out defensive, since the existence of earthworks would simply cause the enemy to avoid them; formidable lines that could be turned or whose lines of communication could be threatened were merely false security. 'It may be very dangerous, under all circumstances, to select your position long beforehand, and to make sure that the enemy will knock his head against it.'[152]

149 Henderson, 'The American Civil War, 1861-1865', in *Science of War*, pp.262-64.
150 Henderson, 'The Campaign of Fredericksburg', in Luvaas, *Soldier's View*, p.103; Anon, *Field Exercises* (1877), p.293. MacDougall's original wording is 'Good infantry, defending a part of a position which must be approached over open ground is, so far as relates to a frontal attack, invincible' (MacDougall, *Modern Infantry Tactics*, p.10). Wolseley also used very similar words in his Wellington Essay entry of 1872, indicating that this was accepted doctrine by the time MacDougall wrote, see Wolseley, 'Essay 4', in *Essays Written for the Wellington Prize*, p.239.
151 Henderson, 'The Campaign of Fredericksburg', in Luvaas, *Soldier's View*, pp.103-04.
152 Henderson, 'Battles and Leaders of the Civil War', in Luvaas, *Soldier's View*, pp.130-73 (pp.148-49), originally published in the Edinburgh Review April 1891 reprinted in *Science*

Henderson's writings in the 1890s became much more inclined to countenance offensive tactics based upon his readings of American campaigns. The Union assaults at Spotsylvania for example seemed to indicate that, given adequate preparation, 'great masses of men, in several lines, one behind the other, as has been shown over and over again, if the ground is at all favourable, and the propitious moment seized, will go through anything'.[153] Henderson disapproved of the adoption in the British manual of the Prussian practice where the skirmish line was the firing line in which company sized units operated independently, extended their formations indefinitely, and intermingled. In his opinion this was a poor model, and he thought that the tactics of 'the last great war waged by English speaking soldiers' were more suited to the British Army.[154] Nevertheless, he recognised that confusion was inevitable in modern war, and that rigid adherence to drill trained troops poorly for it.

> In hot contests over large extents of intricate ground, men of different companies, regiments, brigades, and even divisions, mingle with each other. Soldiers should therefore be drilled, not indeed to fall into such irregularities on principle, but to be ready for them in practice. Soldiers who have not been drilled on this principle, or who have not acquired it by experience, are, when extended under fire, transformed into unmanageable mobs. Skirmishers who understand it will always show a formidable front, and, under the worst possible circumstance, act together in the mighty energy of mutual confidence. Unreflecting mechanical precision is at direct variance with such practice.[155]

Although not as extreme in his views as Maude, Henderson also seems to have regarded the American experience where the bayonet was subordinated to the rifle as exceptional. He stressed the importance of moral factors in war, and therefore supported the more traditional tactics of the 1880s where the old distinctions between skirmish line, supports, and reserve were re-emphasised, and the bayonet charge reinstated as the final arbiter. He accepted that confusion was sometimes necessary and also that in order 'to prepare way for the bayonet' battalion needed to be piled upon battalion.[156]

By 1899, on the eve of the Second Boer War, Henderson was still not proposing any changes to contemporary British tactics, even though these were still based upon the lessons of 1870 and 1877-78. Although new weapons had appeared, he thought

of War, pp.187-229. Henderson, 'The Campaign in the Wilderness of Virginia, 1864', in Luvaas, *Soldier's View*, pp.254-83 (p.279), originally a lecture to the Irish Military Society, 24 January 1894 and reprinted in *Science of War*, pp.307-37.

153 Henderson, 'The Campaign in the Wilderness of Virginia, 1864', in Luvaas, *Soldier's View*, p.270.
154 Henderson, 'Military Criticism', in *Science of War*, p.148.
155 Henderson, 'The Training of Infantry for Attack', in *Science of War*, p.351.
156 Henderson, 'Battles and Leaders', *Soldier's View*, pp.157-59; Henderson, 'Military Criticism', *Science of War*, p.131.

that these 'will not make the battle of the future very dissimilar from anything that has gone before' and concluded that 'consequentially the training of our troops is based upon sound and substantial foundations'.[157] A few years later however, with the evidence from South Africa in front of him, he had come to the opinion that the new weapons had indeed wrought a second revolution (the first being that of the introduction of breech-loaders) in the art of fighting battles. The flat trajectory of the new small bore rifles increased the lethal zone (the part of a bullets trajectory in which it may hit the target, rather than either falling short or passing harmlessly overhead) at any given range, and made long range fire more effective, while the invisibility provided by smokeless powder enhanced the element of surprise. Yet Henderson did not consider that the British had been slow on the uptake on this new revolution.[158] British troops had been some of the first to come under fire from the new weapons, during the Tirah expedition of 1897. This experience from the North-West Frontier had led to a 'general instinct in favour of less rigid methods', and to more attention to the practice of skirmishing and how to reduce losses.[159] In South Africa, 'on hardly a single occasion was the usage of the manoeuvre ground adhered to', the regimental officers 'discarding the dense and regular lines of Aldershot and Salisbury, at once deployed their men at wider intervals, [and] encouraged them to make use of all natural cover, to imitate the Boers in invisibility'.[160]

In fact, the attack over open ground as practised in Aldershot and on Salisbury Plain was more reminiscent of the tactical problems encountered during the 1870 Metz campaign, and those that would be met in South Africa, than those encountered in America. Had more frequent and more realistic exercises been carried out, the British might have been better prepared for the Boer War. Army manoeuvres had been started in 1871 under Cardwell's reforms, but financial constraints meant that large scale manoeuvres were suspended after 1875 and did not resume until 1898, meaning that battalions had rarely trained as part of larger formations.[161] As Henderson noted, the attack over open ground was the most difficult of all operations of war, but it was also one that the British were forced to adopt in South Africa. When properly executed, Henderson thought that the British combined tactics could be surprisingly effective, even in the harsh conditions of the veldt, giving as examples of successful British actions the battles of Talana, Elandslaagte, and Reitfontein, all of which took place in October 1899.[162]

157 Henderson, 'The Training of Infantry for Attack', *Science of War*, pp.338, 340.
158 Henderson, 'Foreign Criticism [of the South African War]', in *Science of War*, pp.365-81 (p.371-73), originally published as introduction to Count Sternberg, *My Experiences of the Boer War* (London: Longmans & Co., 1901).
159 Henderson, 'Foreign Criticism', in *Science of War*, p.372.
160 Henderson, 'Foreign Criticism', in *Science of War*, pp.372-73; [G.F.R. Henderson], 'The War in South Africa', *Edinburgh Review*, 191 (Jan 1900), pp.247-78 (p.274).
161 Spiers, *The Late Victorian Army*, pp.22, 143, 260-63.
162 Henderson, 'The War in South Africa', p.270.

'The 60th (The King's Royal Rifle Corps): The 1st Battalion on manoeuvres c. 1890', by Orlando Norie, showing the loose formations expected to be used in European warfare. (Anne S.K. Brown Military Collection)

By the late 1890s the British Army was beginning to come up against modern weapons even in the hands of non-European opponents, and their tactics had clearly been modified as a result. The new approach was still based upon offensive action; this was dictated both by the strategic context of operations and the necessity to maintain a moral ascendency over native opponents; but it also recognised the need to adopt more open formations. Exemplary of this was the assault by the Gordon Highlanders at Dargai during the Tirah campaign of 1897.

> The Gordon's gave fresh proof that the only way to carry a position in these days of quick firing arms of precision, is to push forward at close intervals line after line of men in extended order and under perfect control.
>
> The enemy cannot shoot down more than a small fraction of the attacking force, and the moral effect of the onward rush of so large a number of men is certain to demoralise the defenders.[163]

At Elandslaagte, Colonel (later General) Ian Hamilton, who had been in the Tirah, deployed his infantry at three-pace intervals. While this has been described as 'a

---

163 Lord Methuen, *Report of the Dargai Attack*, 6 Jan 1898, cited in Stephen M. Miller, *Lord Methuen and the British Army: Failure and Redemption in South Africa* (London: Frank Cass, 1999) p.58. 'Close intervals' refers to the spacing of the successive lines, rather than the files.

much greater dispersion than anything practised at Aldershot',[164] it was the regulation spacing for skirmishing infantry as far back as the 1877 regulations, and troops had previously been deployed at similar distances in the field, such as Wolseley's observation of four-pace intervals during the Indian Mutiny noted above.[165] Spacing between files of three paces was in fact the distance prescribed in the 1889 infantry manual when moving more than 800 yards from the enemy, though the bringing up of supports would close this to one or two paces as the firing line approached between 400 and 150 yards, in order to achieve maximum fire effect and weight in the final assault. The 1892 regulations were not prescriptive on a frontage for attack, it was explicitly left to the local commander's discretion, but although it stated that the firing line needed to be thicker in the attack (to absorb its own casualties and inflict more on the enemy), it was also expected to move in extended order.[166] Both the Devonshire Regiment, who made the frontal assault, and the Gordon Highlanders, who attacked the Boer flank, were also veterans of the Tirah campaign and would have been aware of the need for extended formations under modern rifle fire.[167]

The casualty rates at Elandslaagte, while generally regarded as 'heavy', were substantially lighter than those suffered in most assaults in the Civil War, and in line with those to be adjudicated in Field Manoeuvres. The same was true of other early Boer War battles in 1899, where the percentage losses overall in the British forces involved were usually in single figures. Of course, some individual battalions had suffered much heavier, but this had been predicted by Hale, and officers and generals should have been prepared for it. It could also have been the case that if the attacks

164   Michael Barthorp, *The Anglo-Boer Wars: The British and the Afrikaners, 1815-1902* (London: Blandford, 1987), p.57; see also Kruger, *Good-bye Dolly Gray*, pp.83; Pakenham, *The Boer War*, pp.135-37.

165   Anon, *Field Exercises* (1877), p.93.

166   Anon, *Field Exercises* (1889), pp.365, 373; Anon, *The Attack for a Company, Battalion, or Brigade* (Chester: J. Thomas, 1889) p.5; Clifford, *Resume of the Tactical Portions*, p.43; Anon, *Infantry Drill* (1892), pp.85, 99; Captain H.L. Nevill, *North-West Frontier: British Army Campaigns on the North-West Frontier of India 1849-1908* (London: Tom Donovan, 1992, originally published 1912), pp.278, 282, 284.

167   Lord Methuen, another veteran of the Tirah campaign, also deployed his men in extended formations, see Miller, *Lord Methuen*, pp.92, 145. The most notable (and bloody) exceptions, the Naval Brigade at Graspan (November 1899), and Wauchope's Brigade at Magersfontein, were due to subordinates disobeying or giving faulty orders, ibid, p.100 and pp.140-41 respectively. In spite of acknowledging these extended formations, Miller's otherwise sympathetic account nevertheless perpetuates the idea that the British used '19th Century military tactics against an enemy armed with 20th Century weapons', 'did not take on the implications of new weaponry' (p.107), and in regard to the cavalry 'refused to accept the change' seen by Fletcher and Fremantle in America (p.118, footnote). Miller's sources for these views, including Adrian Preston, Tim Travers, and Howard Bailes, were followers of the Luvaas tradition.

had been pushed harder then greater casualties would have resulted; but equally, it can be argued that greater pressure might have forced more Boer retreats.[168]

The British performance in the Boer War was far from perfect, but in tactical terms it is difficult to see how, in the words of one writer, that 'had the lessons of the American Civil War been studied as diligently as those of the Franco-Prussian War, the Army might have been better prepared to face a terrain of wide-open spaces and an enemy whose tactical philosophy was based primarily on the hit and run principle'.[169] While a few cavalry raiders such as Forrest may have mastered hit and run attacks, these did not decide the American war, and the Confederates never embarked upon a national guerrilla struggle as did the Boer 'bitter-enders'. Very few engagements in the Civil War, and none of those that constituted major or decisive battles, was fought over a terrain of wide-open spaces as found on the South African veldt. After they adopted guerrilla tactics, the Boers did engage in hit and run tactics, including mounted charges firing from the saddle.[170] However, Henderson, the British Army's most distinguished student of the Civil War, saw the Boer tactics during the early more conventional phase of the war as very limited because they acted by fire and fire alone. Because the Boers were incapable of counterattack, Henderson regarded their victories such as that at Modder River (December 1899) as indecisive, the same view as had been taken of defensive victories in America. While fire and envelopment could be effective against a force in the open with an exposed line of retreat, they could not force an enemy out of entrenchments; unless supported by superior artillery. In comparison Henderson noted the 'astonishing success in the earlier battles of the British skirmish line'.[171]

168 British casualties at Elandslaagte are given by Creswicke, *Transvaal War,* Vol.II, p.26 as 41 killed, 206 wounded and 10 missing; by Michael Davitt, *The Boer Fight for Freedom* (New York and London: Funk and Wagnalls, 1902) p.141 as 35 killed, 206 wounded and 10 missing; and by the Official History as 50 killed and 213 wounded (Major General Sir Frederick Maurice and Captain Maurice Harold Grant, *History of the War in South Africa,* 4 vols (London, Hurst and Blackett, 1906-10), Vol.I (1906), p.464. The vast majority of these casualties would have been taken by the assaulting infantry. Also according to the Official History, there were 1,630 infantry at the battle (plus 1,314 cavalry and 552 artillery, with 18 guns and 6 machine guns), giving a casualty rate of approximately 16 percent – roughly that expected for taking a strong but *un-entrenched* position with a 2:1 superiority. The loss in the army overall was 8.7 percent. Figures for the Boer losses, from a strength of about 800-1,000, also vary. The Official History estimates 363 (67 killed, 108 wounded, and 188 captured) while Davitt (p.141) gives 340 (45 killed, 110 wounded and 185 prisoners), both are over one-third the Boer strength, and in excess of the field exercise prediction of 25 percent. Many of the Boer losses in this particular battle would have been inflicted by the pursuing cavalry. The British losses at Modder River and at Magersfontein were about 7 percent of the overall force on each occasion (Miller, *Lord Methuen,* p.110, 145). The entrenched Boers' casualties were much lower in these two battles.

169 Barthorp, *The Anglo-Boer Wars,* p.53.

170 Stephen Badsey, 'The Boer War and British Cavalry Doctrine', pp.94-95.

171 Henderson, 'The War in South Africa', p.275.

Those successes were won immediately prior to a series of disastrous defeats for British arms (at Stormberg, Magersfontein, and Colenso) during the 'Black Week' of 10-17 December 1899. But these defeats were bought about more through faulty leadership, poor reconnaissance, and underestimation of the opposition – combined with intelligent Boer generalship – than from any misconceptions in the regulations on how to fight a modern battle. A general lack of suitably mounted cavalry in sufficient numbers severely limited reconnaissance and intelligence of enemy positions, and the lack of mobility meant frontal assaults were favoured over turning movements. A lack of local knowledge, faulty maps, and compasses that were affected by local magnetic conditions, misdirected the approach marches at Modder River and Magersfontein, and led troops into ambushes while still in close order formations prior to deployment. The disaster that befell Major General Hart's Irish Brigade at Colenso was due to similar failures of reconnaissance, but was exacerbated in this case by poor generalship, Hart refusing to let his men extend their formations. Limited artillery preparation, again in large part due to poor reconnaissance and ignorance of the siting of the enemy's trenches, increased the casualties amongst the infantry.[172] The fact that the Boers simply did not have to stay to defend their positions as a European army might have done meant that the fruits of victory were elusive. Historian Howard Bailes concluded that the faulty tactics and reverses in South Africa were mostly down to the failure of individual commanders to adopt and adapt the formal teachings of Aldershot and Sandhurst, not of applying an outmoded doctrine.[173]

* * *

The idea that the British Army failed to learn the lessons of 1861-65, and intended to fight their wars at the end of the 19th Century still wedded to the close order tactics of those at the start, is an attractive and common explanation for its failures in South Africa in popular histories. It is, however, misplaced. From 1859 onwards the formally prescribed tactics recommended in the drill manuals for wars against a 'civilised' (as opposed to 'savage') enemy changed beyond recognition, replacing parade-ground movements with open formations and devolving command to the officers on the ground. Throughout the period there were three very clear themes in British thinking that fully recognised important lessons from the American Civil War.

First was the recognition that the new weapons of precision had substantially increased the power of the tactical defensive compared to Napoleonic warfare, to such an extent that frontal assaults were now impossible. This was modified but not overturned by the universal adoption of the breech-loader, which it was thought could

172 Kruger, *Good-bye Dolly Gray*, pp.115-16, 126-31, 139-40; Pemberton, *Battles of the Boer War*, pp.59-66, 76-78, 87-85, 115-17, 131-134; Miller, *Lord Methuen*, pp.147-50, though on pp.250-251 he cites more traditional criticisms as the source of British failure.
173 Bailes, 'Technology and Tactics in the British Army 1866-1900', p.46.

enable the local assertion of fire superiority by the attacker either through numbers or flanking fire. Second was the understanding that against an enemy armed with modern weapons the use of cover was essential to minimise casualties. Such cover could be natural, artificial or, as Henderson saw, provided through technology such as artillery.[174] The third was the need for increased training and initiative by individual soldiers, who could adapt their tactics to local conditions. This was seen as especially important for junior officers and it is notable that many of the tracts on open and flexible formations were penned by volunteer officers who had little experience of actual war, but direct knowledge of the nature of irregular and volunteer forces such as had been formed in America.

Set against this progressive view of modern warfare was a conservative one that saw discipline, drill, and more rigid control of troops as a necessity to achieve decisive results. Although the conservative view has been seen as taking its belief in the offensive from the Franco-Prussian War, in contrast to the supposedly novel defensive tactics in America, this is over-simplistic. Open formations and the importance of intelligence and initiative in the individual soldier were lessons from 1871 as much as from 1865. Battles of 1870-71 were used as examples of the success of defensive tactics, while the conservatives also found examples in the Civil War in support of their views. These were often supported by racial and historic subtexts, most significantly in the idea that the steadfastness and discipline of 'Anglo-Saxon' troops would enable them to achieve victory. However, there was not a marked focus on the offensive victories of the Confederacy compared to a more 'modern' defensive approach from Union generals. The victories of Sherman and Grant at Atlanta, Chattanooga, and Spotsylvania, featured in British writing as well as those of Lee and Jackson in Virginia. Henderson, whose study of the Civil War was more complete than any of his contemporaries in Britain, held a complex set of views which mixed both conservative and progressive elements. In *Science of War* he summed up the changes which had taken place in British tactical training in the two decades prior to the Boer War.

> The annual allowance of ammunition for target practice had been largely increased. Drill in close order had been relegated to the proper place; the time given to the practice of spectacular movements had been greatly reduced, and the barrack-square whenever men and space were available, was deserted for the open country. All this was to the good. Fighting was really taught.[175]

The deficiency was that it was not realistic fighting against the weapons that the Army now faced – weapons very different from those of the armies in the Civil War. Although writers had identified and continually talked about the need for individual initiative, it was outside of the competence and experience of many officers and men.

174 Henderson, 'Tactics of the Three Arms Combined', in *Science of War*, pp.78-80.
175 Henderson, 'The British Army', in *Science of War*, p.409.

'It was mechanical discipline [...] that was still the ideal of the British Army in 1899'.[176] This is demonstrated further by another passage in which Henderson quoted a regimental officer who had seen service on the North-West Frontier.

> We at once found out, he says, the deficiencies of our peace training. In the first place, the system of attack (or rather, the systems, for we had recently changed stations, and come under a new general) which we had taken so much trouble to learn, was quite out of place in the hills. In the second place, we had not been in action five minutes before we found that volley-firing was useless, for the targets never remained long enough in position for us to go through all the elaborate preliminaries. In the third place, companies, and even sections, had to a great extent to fight their own battles, for it was impossible to supervise them, and sometimes even to see them; and lastly, both officers and men were very much at sea in the skirmishing tactics which the ground made necessary.[177]

The influence of the conservative school persisted largely because the operational practice of the army meant that the experience of most soldiers had not extended to facing an enemy armed with modern weapons, and peacetime training was inadequate to compensate for this lack of experience. Lonsdale Hale warned his audience in 1888 that the British officer who had seen service against so-called 'savage' foes needed to 'sweep from his mind all recollections of that service, for between Afghan, Egyptian, or Zulu warfare and that of Europe, there is no similarity whatsoever'.[178] When, in South Africa, Britain did fight a significant war against an enemy armed with modern weapons, those who had previously faced an enemy so armed were more able to use their experience, for example through the use of extended formations, while those who had not were often forced to learn the hard way from defeat or heavy casualties.[179] This was not dissimilar to the situation in which the warring parties in America found themselves in 1861, but it was not because the British had ignored the tactical lessons of 1865.

---

176 Henderson, 'The British Army', in *Science of War*, p.410. It should be noted that this was written in February 1903, with the hindsight of the Boer War.
177 Unnamed source quoted in Henderson, 'The Training of Infantry for Attack', in *Science of War*, p.345. It is also notable that in the later essays in *Science of War*, many of Henderson's examples shift from the Civil War and 1870 to the North-West Frontier and South Africa, reflecting the change in technology and the new and different lessons that Henderson saw as a result.
178 Hale, *The Spirit of Tactical Operations of To-day*, p.13.
179 Jones, *From Boer War to World War*, pp.76-78. Henderson, 'The British Army', in *Science of War*, p.413, also suggested veterans of the North-West Frontier were more aware of modern tactical circumstances.

6

The Arm of the Future – The Aeronauts

There is one set of records created under the auspices of the Ordnance Select Committee which are no longer held in the War Office collections in the National Archive. In 1919 they were transferred to the Air Ministry, where they form part of the collections of the Air Historical Branch. The records relate to the early history of the Balloon Corps, which subsequently become the Royal Flying Corps and eventually the Royal Air Force.[1] Tracing the story of the RAF back to the American Civil War may at first sight appear far-fetched, but the suggestion is not entirely new. One modern authority has said of the early pioneers of British ballooning that 'the achievements of this small irregular band of aeronauts directly inspired the first serious agitation for an air arm in the British Army'.[2] Some members of that band were initially, and significantly, influenced by their brief acquaintance with, and observation of, the US Balloon Corps.

Balloons were not a new weapon of war in 1861. Their use went back to the French Revolution, when in 1794, only eleven years after the Montgolfier brothers' first ascent on 5 June 1783, the French had created the world's first balloon corps.[3] The British Army had never used them for military purposes, although in 1855 Sir William Reid, the Governor of Malta, had forwarded to the War Office a proposal from a Dr Collings to use 'spy balloons' in the Crimea. Sir William commented that

1   TNA, AIR 1/2404/303, War Office Ordnance Select Committee: employment of balloons in warfare, (1862-1885).
2   Hugh Driver, *The Birth of Military Aviation: Britain, 1903-1914* (Woodbridge (Suffolk) and Rochester NY: Royal Historical Society (Boydell Press), 1997), p.153.
3   Lieutenant [George Edward] Grover RE, 'On the Use of Balloons in Military Operations', *R.E. Professional Papers*, 12 (1863), pp.71-86, (p.76); Lieutenant B[aden] Baden-Powell, Scots Guards, 'Military Ballooning', lecture delivered at the Royal United Service Institution, 1 June 1883, *Journal of the Royal United Service Institution*, 12 (1868), pp.735-57 (pp.736-37).

as balloons were successfully used more than sixty years back by a French army, they may perhaps be made of some use in the Crimea just now. To raise an observer even 200 or 300 feet above a fortified position might enable assailants to form more correct ideas on inner intrenchments than when only viewing such a position from a height of equal altitude.[4]

In 1861 the case for military ballooning in Britain was taken up again, this time by a young officer in the Royal Engineers, Lieutenant George Edward Grover, in the form of a report to the Ordnance Select Committee. In his submission, Grover pointed to the recent employment of balloons by the Americans, as well as during the 1859 Franco-Austrian War in Italy, as reasons why the British should re-examine their use.[5]

In time, military aviation would quite literally introduce a new dimension in warfare, and with the benefit of 150 years of hindsight, the advantages of being able to observe one's enemy from the air may seem obvious, but it is important to view Grover's proposal from the perspective of the middle of the 19th Century. At the time balloons were as much the subject of early science fiction as of the science of war, and in the context of the Civil War they would be of minor importance. It was not clear whether they could provide sufficient advantages to an army to justify the cost and effort involved in their use. Grover himself recognised their technical limitations.

The time occupied by its inflation, its unwieldly form when filled, causing it, if retained to the earth, to vibrate at the slightest breeze, besides numerous other objections, all point out that this machine will not, in its present state, supply satisfactorily the desideratum for aerial reconnoissances [sic].[6]

What Grover proposed was not the immediate adoption of balloons, but investigation and experimentation to assess and develop their potential.[7]

One of the Committee's responses to Grover was that there was nothing new in his paper. They also regretted that he had not provided details of the use of balloons in America; the absence of solid information being interpreted to mean that they had not been found to be of much use there. It did accept, however, that there were 'many critical occasions when a captive balloon at a moderate elevation might render very valuable service', and proposed to arrange some experimental ascents.[8] When this was referred for approval to Sir John Burgoyne, the Inspector General of Engineers, Burgoyne wrote that since 'other very intelligent nations such as the French & United

4   Grover, 'Balloons in Military Operations', p.75.
5   TNA, AIR 1/2404/303, Ordnance Select Committee Minute 6004, (5 February 1862) and Report 2139 (7 February 1862), with regards to letter dated 8 January 1862.
6   Lieutenant [George Edward] Grover RE, 'On Reconnoitring Balloons', R.E. Professional Papers, 12 (1863), pp.87-93 (p.92).
7   Grover, 'Balloons in Military Operations', p.84.
8   AIR 1/2404/303, Memo. response from Lt. Grover dated 22 March 1862.

States have in some form adopted them, it would be discreditable if we should be totally without any understood system'.[9] However, before he would agree to any experiments he asked for information to be obtained about foreign developments from the Ambassadors in Paris and Washington.

While the Committee deliberated, both newspaper correspondents and officers in the British Army were reporting on the use of balloons in America. One incident identified by Grover as of particular interest was the operation at Island No. 10 on the Mississippi, which was reported by *The Times* of 15 April 1862, and to which he referred in a paper given at Chatham eight days later.

A balloon reconnaissance was made on the 27th March by Professor Steiner, accompanied by Colonel Buford and Captain Maynardier, which established the fact that shells had been thrown at too great a range to be sufficiently effective against the Confederate batteries. This defect in mortar practice has since been remedied.[10]

The effectiveness of the balloons at Island No. 10 was perhaps exaggerated, and Grover himself later wrote that 'from a detailed account given by the special correspondent of the New York Times, and copied into our Times of Wednesday, April 16th, 1862, there is reason to doubt whether the reconnoissance [*sic*] was really so useful as was stated'.[11] Steiner had ascended to 1,200 feet, and was able to observe the Confederate positions and assess the results of the bombardment. Shells had been fired long, and on descending Steiner was able to alert the Federal fleet to this effect.[12] Yet there was not on this occasion, as was later claimed by one British supporter of aeronautics, real time correction of the artillery fire 'communicating the effect of each shot'.[13]

On 8 January 1862 Captain Frederick Edward Blackett Beaumont RE, a veteran of the Crimean War and the Indian Mutiny, arrived in Nova Scotia on the mail steamer *Canada*, as part of the build-up of forces in British North America in response to the *Trent* affair. Once in North America, Beaumont had, like many other British officers, taken advantage of this opportunity to satisfy his interest in the war. What interested Beaumont was balloons – to the extent that he went Absent Without Leave to find out what the Americans were doing with them.[14] The main theatre of the war in which balloons were being used was on the east coast in Virginia, which was

9　AIR 1/2404/303, Memo. from Sir John Burgoyne to Sir E Lugard, 11 April 1862.

10　*The Times*, 15 April 1862, p.6; Grover, 'Balloons in Military Operations', p.79. Grover incorrectly gave the date of the report as 14 April.

11　Grover, 'Reconnoitring Balloons', p.87; *The Times*, 16 April 1862, p.9.

12　Charles M. Evans, *The War of the Aeronauts: A History of Ballooning during the Civil War* (Mechanicsburg PA: Stackpole Books, 2002) pp.159-160.

13　Baden-Powell, 'Military Ballooning' pp.739-40. Baden-Powell also incorrectly identified the aeronaut as James Allan.

14　WO 17/2409; TNA, WO25/1192, Disembarkation returns, 1862.

readily accessible from Nova Scotia, and on 23 May 1862 Beaumont left for America. He went via Washington, recording that once free from officialdom there he was given every possible assistance and hospitality, and he joined McClellan's army in its encampments on the Pamunkey River, a day's march below White House Landing.[15] Beaumont rode forward to find the American balloon hidden in a hollow about seven miles from Richmond and under Brigadier General Stoneman's command. This was probably around 25 or 26 May at Gaines Mill. Beaumont was definitely present for the battle of Hanover Court House, and he may still have been with the Union army at the Battle of Seven Pines the following month, which he later referred to as being important for the use of the telegraph from the balloon during battle. He returned to Nova Scotia on 4 June, when he 'accounted satisfactorily for his absence'.[16]

The Chief Aeronaut of the Army of the Potomac, Thaddeus Lowe, had been assigned to Stoneman's command on 20 May, and had arrived at Gaines Mill on 21 May, and at Mechanicsville on 25 May.[17] Unfortunately he made no mention of Beaumont's presence in his journal which would pinpoint exactly when Beaumont visited. Beaumont certainly met Lowe in person, as he later described their conversations. Lowe made a good impression on Beaumont, who described him as 'a man celebrated in America as a very daring aeronaut'. They discussed Lowe's plans to complete an 'aerial ship' to attempt the passage of the Atlantic, and Beaumont thought that he could 'not see how he can help making a wonderful voyage somewhere, whether across the Atlantic, or not, is another thing'.[18] Moving on to the practical military matters at hand, Beaumont described the organisation of Lowes' small Corps.

> The balloon staff with M'Clellan [sic] consisted of one chief aeronaut whose exact rank I could never quite make out, but it was not lower than a captain, or higher than a brigadier, he was a civilian and by profession an aeronaut, he was very highly paid, the same as a brigadier, and as the military rank, I believe, in America, is in some way attached to, and determined by, the pay received, I fancy Professor Low [sic] must have been a brigadier.[19]

15 Captain F. Beaumont RE, 'Balloon Reconnaissance', *Journal of the Royal United Service Institution*, 8 (1864), pp.52-66, (p.57); Beaumont, 'On Balloon Reconnaissance' p.97. McClellan reached the White House on 16th May, but Beaumont cannot reasonably have been there before 25 May.
16 WO 17/2409 *Monthly Returns to the Adjutant General, Nova Scotia*, 1862.
17 Michael Jaeger and Carol Lauritzen (ed.), *Memoirs of Thaddeus S. C. Lowe, Chief of the Aeronautic Corps of the Army of the United States during the Civil War: My Balloons in Peace and War* (Lewiston, NY; Lampeter: Edwin Mellen Press, c. 2004), pp.123-27. Born in Jefferson Mills, NH, on 20 August 1832, Lowe first flew in 1856 and built his first balloon only four years before the war, but by 1861 he was one of most respected balloonists in the United States. See Robert P. Broadwater, *Civil War Special Forces: The Elite and Distinct Fighting Units of the Union and Confederate Armies* (Santa Barbara: Praeger, 2014), p.69.
18 Beaumont, 'On Balloon Reconnaissance', p.101.
19 Beaumont, 'On Balloon Reconnaissance', p.96.

Lowe's pay, at $10 per day, was actually equivalent to that of colonel, but he never had any official rank in the army, and Major A.A. Humphreys, McClellan's chief topographical engineer, who had been placed in command of the 'Balloon Department' on 25 May, referred to Lowe in correspondence with him simply as 'Prof. Lowe, Aeronaut to the Army of the Potomac, or 'Prof. TSC [*sic*] Lowe, Chief Aeronaut, Army of the Potomac.[20] In fact the 29-year-old Lowe (a year older than Beaumont) had no academic or professional qualifications at all, he had given himself the title of 'Professor' while working as a showman before the war, demonstrating his balloons to the public. Lowe's ambiguous position in the army hierarchy would later cause problems for him. At this time, however, he was being well supported, with about 50 men working for him.

> [U]nder him was a captain of infantry who had been instructed previously at West Point (the American Woolwich) in the art of ballooning. The captain commanded the men, some 50 in number, attached to the machine, and superintended generally every arrangement in connection with its inflation and use; he was also responsible for its transport, and that a due supply of materials was kept ready. The captain never went up himself, indeed he informed me that he liked the work below best, and confined himself entirely to it. Under the captain were a proportion of non-commissioned officers who knew more or less of the management of it, and the men, who, besides having a sort of reverential awe of the machine, knew nothing whatever about it.[21]

Beaumont described the terrain in the Mechanicsville area, and, like other observers, noted the similarity of Virginia to agricultural districts in England, although more undulating and not so extensively cultivated. With nearly half of the country wooded, balloon observations were both highly desirable but also very difficult to make.[22] Although a supporter of the balloons, Beaumont was thus careful not to overstate their case.

> [M]ost anxious enquiries were made from the observers in the balloon, as to the difficulties that lay on the road to Richmond. Were there any fortifications round the place? Where were the camps, and for how many men? Were there any troops in movement near the present position? and many other questions of equal importance. Now these questions were difficult to answer; and even from the balloon many of them could only be replied to with more or less uncertainty.

---

20 Beaumont, 'On Balloon Reconnaissance', p.72; Lowe, *Memoirs of Thaddeus S.C. Lowe*, pp.129-140.
21 Beaumont, 'On Balloon Reconnaissance', p.96.
22 Beaumont, 'On Balloon Reconnaissance', p.97.

He went on the describe in detail both the potential benefits of balloon observation in what amounted to a siege operation, and the practical difficulties associated with their use.

> From the balloon to the Chickahominy, as the crow flies, was about 2 miles; thence on to Richmond, 8 more. At the altitude of 1,000 feet in clear weather an effective range of vision of 10 miles could be got; thus the ground on the opposite side of Richmond could be seen; that is to say, houses, and the general occupation of the land became known. Richmond itself was distinctly seen, and the three camps of the Confederates could be distinguished surrounding the place. Looking closer the wooded nature of the country prevented the possibility of saying whether it were occupied by troops or not, but it could be confidently asserted that no large body was in motion. In the same way, on seeing the camps round the place one could form a very rough estimate of the number of men they were for, but it was impossible to say whether there were men in them or not. Earthworks, even at a distance of 8 miles, could be seen, but their character so far off could not be distinctly stated, though one could with certainty say whether they were of the nature of field or permanent works. The pickets of the enemy could be made out quite distinctly with supports in rear, thrown forward to the banks of the stream. The country from its thickly wooded character was peculiarly unfitted for balloon reconnoissances [sic].[23]

Beaumont was also able to describe the use of the balloon during an actual battle. On 27 May 1862 the battle of Hanover Court House took place to the north-west of Mechanicsville. This action came about because Major General McClellan wanted to secure his right flank, and the route down which he was expecting Major General McDowell's reinforcements to come from Washington, against a Confederate force seen in the area. Beaumont put himself at some personal risk to try and observe the battle but was unsuccessful.

> I happened to be close to the balloon when the heavy firing began. The wind was rather high, but I was anxious to see, if possible, what was going on, and I went up with the father of the aeronaut. The balloon was, however, short of gas, and as the wind was high, we were obliged to come down. I then went up by myself, the diminished weight giving increased steadiness, but it was not considered safe to go higher than 500 feet on account of the unsettled state of the weather. The balloon was very unsteady, so much so that it was difficult to fix my sight on any particular object; at that altitude I could see nothing of the fight. It turned out afterwards that the distance was, I think, over 12 miles, which from 1,000 feet, and on a clear day, would in a country of that nature have rendered the action invisible; had the weather, however, been such as to have allowed the balloon

23   Beaumont, 'On Balloon Reconnaissance', pp.98-99.

to remain at its usual altitude, the position of the engagement from the smoke created could have been shown; and it could have been said that no retreat had reached within a certain distance of the point of observation.[24]

Beaumont's description in this passage gives insight into the constraints of the technology of the day, independent of the problems of the terrain. The balloons had limited lifting power, and limited elevation in high winds. While an observer, even at relatively low altitude, could see considerable distances, other than in perfect conditions the instability of the balloon made observation difficult. Beaumont had difficulty fixing his sight on objects with the naked eye, only a very experienced balloonist in very good conditions would have been able to use a telescope aloft. Furthermore, since the balloon's position was static, the ability to manoeuvre it to where it could be of most use was limited, again particularly in poor weather.

Beaumont also recorded being present when the fire battery of artillery was corrected directly from the balloon, but again considered it a qualified success.

> The balloon being up and the signals preconcerted, the battery opened fire, the people from the car telling the artillerists which way their shot were dropping. The result of the operation was that the Confederates were driven from their cover; but I cannot say in that instance that I was impressed with the advantage of artillery fire directed from the air, though there are cases, no doubt, where a balloon might be similarly and profitably employed.[25]

The technical details of the balloon made up a large part of Beaumont's observations. They illustrate the challenges presented by the immature technology of the period. The first consideration was the fabric used in the construction of the skin of the balloon. This affected its permeability, and thus how long the balloon could stay inflated and retain its lifting capability. The American balloons were made of high-quality silk, covered in a varnish of Lowe's own invention. Although always admitting an amount of leakage, this was nevertheless impermeable enough to keep the balloon inflated for a fortnight and allowed them to be held almost continually ready for use.[26]

An invention of even more interest was Lowe's provision of a mobile gas generator. At the time there were two chief forms of balloons, one inflated with hot air, and one with hydrogen. Although hot air balloons were simpler to operate, their lifting capacity for any given volume of the balloon envelope was less, and many aeronauts were dismissive of 'fire balloons'. Hydrogen had a lower specific gravity and therefore better lifting capabilities, making it, in Beaumont's opinion, 'a sine qua non for a

24   Beaumont, 'On Balloon Reconnaissance', p.99.
25   Beaumont, 'On Balloon Reconnaissance', p.59.
26   Beaumont, 'On Balloon Reconnaissance', p.95.

Professor Lowe's military balloon and gas generators near Gaines Mill, Virginia, 1862.
(Library of Congress)

military aeronaut'.[27] It could be generated by a number of chemical methods, but up until 1862 hydrogen balloons had mostly been inflated from city gas works. One of the Confederate balloons operated at Richmond used this method, and it provided a cheap and practically unlimited source of gas, but it meant that the balloon was not always available where needed, and it limited its mobility.[28] Lowe's generators were simply large tanks of wood with acid-proof copper linings, in which the hydrogen was generated by passing dilute sulphuric acid over iron. Since old iron could be readily found in the army ('the tires of wheels, old shot broken up, &c, was used')[29] only the sulphuric acid had to be specially provided and stored. When generated, the gas was passed through a pair of lime purifiers to absorb carbonic acid and other extraneous gases, and then into the balloon. The purifiers also had the benefit of reducing the temperature of the gas. Each generator required a wagon with four horses to draw it, and each balloon, with ropes and tools, another four-horse wagon. In addition, there was a two-horse wagon to carry the acid. This made the apparatus as mobile as any other part of the army.[30]

27 Beaumont, 'On Balloon Reconnaissance', p.95.
28 Broadwater, *Civil War Special Forces*, p.73.
29 Beaumont, 'On Balloon Reconnaissance', p.95.
30 Broadwater, *Civil War Special Forces*, p.73; Beaumont, 'On Balloon Reconnaissance', pp.95-97.

With this apparatus, Lowe, according to Beaumont, could prepare a balloon for ascent in three hours from the time of the machine being halted. Once inflated, it could be kept secure by a series of sandbags in all but very high winds, in which case it had to be hauled down. If necessary to move it, it was marched along by 25 or 30 men holding the guy ropes, being raised when required to clear any obstacles. Beaumont reported that he had 'frequently seen it carried thus without the least difficulty'. He also noted that around 30 men were needed to control the balloon in its ascent, a significantly higher number than the five or six that Grover was suggesting back in England. Three guy ropes were used, one of which was passed through a block and attached to a tree or other fixed object.[31]

This attention to minor details such as the number of ropes used was significant, and demonstrates the limited practical experience available to the British. Not only did the number of ropes affect the calculations required to determine a balloons buoyancy, and therefore how big a balloon would be needed to be to lift a particular payload, it also affected the safety of the operations. A single mooring rope had been used with one of Lowe's balloons on 10 April 1862 when an ascent had been made by Brigadier General Fitz John Porter, commander of V Corps. Through an accident with the sulphuric acid, this single rope was burnt through and Porter found himself drifting towards the Confederate lines. Only a shift in the wind saved him from the embarrassment of capture.[32]

Lowe operated two different sizes of balloon. The 'Washington' and the 'Constitution', based at Mechanicsville and Gaines Mill respectively, were of the smaller size with a capacity of about 13,000 cubic feet – about the same size that Grover was suggesting back in England.[33] It was in one of these two balloons that Beaumont ascended. Both Beaumont and the Americans preferred the larger sized balloon, 'Intrepid'. Size gave additional stability in the air, greater elevation (buoyancy was needed to offset the weight of the guy ropes), and the ability to take up two people, which the smaller balloons could only do when recently inflated.[34] A further consideration in 1862 was the issue of communication with the ground. The aeronaut could of course descend to give his report, but this took time. A primitive form of air to ground communication could be achieved by messages wrapped around a stone. The best method, though, was to establish a telegraph link to the ground, and only the larger of the balloons had the lifting capability to carry the telegraph equipment and operator as well as the aeronaut.[35]

Beaumont recognised the importance of the telegraph, but apparently did not see its use in person. He was also highly critical of the way in which, in America, the army

31   Beaumont, 'On Balloon Reconnaissance', p.97; Grover, 'Balloons in Military Operations', p.81.
32   Evans, *War of the Aeronauts*, p.181.
33   Grover, 'Balloons in Military Operations', p.83.
34   Beaumont, 'On Balloon Reconnaissance', pp.94-5.
35   Evans, *War of the Aeronauts*, p.226.

chain of command was circumvented in favour of the politicians, and suggested that this should not be the case in the British Army.

> During the first two days of the heavy fighting by the left of the army before Richmond, which ended in its retreat from the [Virginia] Peninsula, a telegraph was taken up in the car, and the wire being placed in connection with the line to Washington, telegraphic communications were literally sent, direct from the balloon above the field of battle, to the government. In place of this the wires should have gone to the Commander-in-Chief's tent, or, indeed, anywhere better than to Washington, where the sole report of the state of affairs should have been received from no one but the officer in command of the army. If balloons or telegraphs are to be turned into means for dividing authority, every true soldier will look upon them as evils hardly unmitigated, but this with us need not be the case, for as military machines they would be solely under the control of the Commander-in-Chief.[36]

Beaumont had also asked Brigadier General Barnard, McClellan's chief of engineers, for his views on the utility of balloons. Barnard 'considered a balloon apparatus as decidedly a desirable thing to have with an army; but at the same time it was one of the first incumbrances that, if obliged to part with anything, he should leave behind'.[37] Beaumont came to an equally guarded conclusion on the value of the balloons in warfare. It was not a magic solution to a general's desire for information, but could on occasion be valuable, it was ultimately a judgement of the benefits against the costs.

> [O]f the utility under certain circumstances of overlooking a tract of country, from a height of 1,000 or 2,000 feet, if necessary, there can be little doubt; at the same time the cost of being able to do so is so trifling that it would appear unwise to neglect the necessary steps to secure the advantage.[38]

It was Lieutenant Colonel Charles Fletcher of the Scots Fusilier Guards, present with McClellan's headquarters at the same time, who provided the official response to Sir John Burgoyne's request for details of the American balloons, through Lord Lyons in Washington. The technical details of Fletcher's report were a summary of Beaumont's findings, making it probable that Beaumont was the original source. Although he reported the use of balloons to signal the fall of shells, Fletcher's conclusion was not particularly positive about their utility.

36 Beaumont, 'On Balloon Reconnaissance', p.100.
37 Beaumont, 'On Balloon Reconnaissance', p.100.
38 Beaumont, 'On Balloon Reconnaissance', p.100.

The advantages in obtaining inform[atio]n are reported not to have been so great as was expected. This may be perhaps owing to the wooded nature of the country, wh[ich] conceals the movements of troops. It is difficult to obtain an idea of fortifications from a balloon as the relief of the works cannot be perceived.[39]

Much of Beaumont's information was also repeated, in summary form with some minor variation in details, in the report produced by Captain Thomas Mahon. Mahon's conclusions were also less than enthusiastic about the success of the United States Balloon Corps, warning that '[t]he stories in the newspapers are exaggerated.'

The practical advantages of the balloon seem hardly commensurate with the expense, but they [the Americans] are enabled to get from it a general notion of the positioned of the enemy, especially at night, when camp fires are plainly seen, and by comparing the number of fires on both sides, they are enabled to form an estimate of the comparative numbers. It has also been found useful in noting the effect and range of artillery when firing over intervening obstacles such as woods.[40]

*   *   *

Beaumont himself left Nova Scotia aboard HMS *Steady* on 23 September.[41] Back in England he presented a paper on his experiences in America at a lecture in Chatham on 14 November, 1862. Together with two articles by Grover, this account was published in the *Royal Engineers' Professional Papers* the following year.[42] The publication of these papers in the Royal Engineers' technical journal was accompanied by growing support for the idea that balloons might be of significant military use after all. In October 1862, while still having reservations over their expense compared to the results that might be obtained, Burgoyne had stated that he was inclined to propose experiments. The following January, swayed by further evidence of overseas developments that included the report received from Fletcher in America, as well as intelligence from France, Prussia, Russia, and Austria, the Ordnance Select Committee decided that 'stores more costly and more difficult of transport balloons are carried in the train of armies upon much more remote probabilities of their services being required', and recommended that experiments should proceed.[43] Beaumont and Grover were

39   AIR 1/2404/303, FO paper dated June 23 enclosing undated report by Fletcher on balloons in America; also in TNA, FO 5/831 fols 124-27, Lyons to Russell, No. 400, Washington, 3 June 1862.
40   WO 33/11/0174, Mahon Report, pp.50-51.
41   TNA, WO 25/1192 Disembarkation Returns 1862-3.
42   Grover, 'On the Use of Balloons in Military Operations'; Grover, 'On Reconnoitring Balloons'; Beaumont 'On Balloon Reconnaissance'.
43   AIR 1/2404/303, OSC minute 7998 15/12/62, Report 2629, dated 2/1/63

seconded onto the Committee as associate members, and at a meeting on 16 February 1863 they were tasked with setting up trials.[44]

In Britain, Beaumont and Grover's fortunes were rising, but in America those of Thaddeus Lowe were in decline. Since he had no official military rank or status, his position was extremely vulnerable to politics within the army, and he lost influence with the reorganisations under Burnside and Hooker. Matters came to a head when in the spring of 1863 there was a demand for Lowe to accept a cut in pay from $10 to $6 – implying a demotion from colonel to captain. Lowe was insulted, and, after protest, resigned. Another aeronaut, James Allen, briefly took over the Corps, but in the absence of Lowe to fight for resources, the equipment deteriorated and interest from the US Army in balloons disappeared. By the end of June the Corps was effectively disbanded, and in the autumn of 1863 the War Department declined to reinstate it. In February 1864, Gallwey's mission reported an advertisement in the Washington press selling Lowe's equipment.[45]

Gallwey's report also noted a further tactical limitation that had been demonstrated in the 1862 Peninsular Campaign, that balloons revealed the army's own positions and intentions to the enemy which a clever opponent could use to his advantage. It told the story of a Federal divisional general who was said to have ascended in the balloon and reported the enemy as about to attack, when in fact they were evacuating Yorktown. 'It is probable that the Confederate General, seeing the balloon in the air, made a feint to the front in order to cover his retreat, and so deceived the Federal Generals [sic] in the balloon.'[46] The Americans did not learn their own lessons well, the use of balloons for observation in Cuba in 1898 during the Spanish-American War was described by one American colonel at the time as 'idiotic' for exposing the American line of march.[47]

At almost exactly the same time as the Balloon Corps was being disbanded in Washington, in England the British Army was finally going ahead with its first balloon trials. In spite of the mixed views of their utility and 'an absence of evidence of their direct value' in America, the Ordnance Select Committee decided that 'it can be readily perceived that it would be difficult to find a seat of war more unsuitable for balloons than a hilly, densely wooded region, like the State of Virginia' and that further experimentation was therefore justified.[48] The British were just as concerned as Comstock over the cost of balloons, but unlike him they saw civilian balloonists as part of the solution, engaging Henry Coxwell to conduct the experiments alongside

44   AIR 1/2404/303, OSC minute 8495 23/2/63, Report 2708, dated 26/2/63; Letter from Horse Guards 7/2/63 approving Grover and Beaumont's employment; Porter, *History of the Corps of Royal Engineers*, Vol.II, p.190.
45   Evans, *War of the Aeronauts*, pp.265-76; WO 33/14/0229, Gallwey Report, p.614.
46   WO 33/14/0229, Gallwey Report, p.31.
47   David F. Trask, *The War With Spain* (New York: Bison Books, 1996, originally published Simon and Schuster, 1981), pp.239-50.
48   WO 33/12/0192, p.127.

Beaumont and Grover. A prominent British aeronaut, in 1859 Coxwell had demon-strated the dropping of explosives from the air, and he later went on to serve with the Prussians in the war of 1870-71.[49]

The first trial ascent took place on 14 July 1863 at Aldershot, on the day of the Royal Review. The day was exceptionally still, and the balloon ascended to 1,200 feet. The observers could both see and hear troops (whereas at ground level the music of the bands was muffled), and 'no body of troops of any consequence could have moved on the roads or occupied the villages or woods without being seen'.[50] It was noted however that it was difficult to make out elevation, even of such a prominent feature in the Surrey countryside as the Hog's Back ridge south-west of Aldershot.[51] The local commander reported to the Commander in Chief, the Duke of Cambridge, that balloons could be 'of most valuable assistance'.[52] The second trial, on 6 October 1863 at Woolwich, was conducted by Beaumont and Grover. This was less successful, as they were unable to make out the positions of troops on the move – though they put a positive spin on it by saying that they were able to tell where they were not! A later, untethered, ascent by the two officers accompanied by Coxwell was more successful.[53]

The Committee's final report on balloons was issued in July 1865. Although noting Gallwey's observations that the use of balloons for military purposes had been discontinued in the United States, the Committee considered that the thickly wooded country in America was not suited to their operation and that 'the value of such a means of obtaining information should not be judged by American experience alone'.[54] Nevertheless, financial considerations won the day, and while the Committee said that balloons reconnaissance by experienced officers could on occasion provide useful information, they did not feel their utility warranted the retention of equip-ment in time of peace.[55]

This decision was probably not unreasonable given the state of ballooning at the time. Even Grover and Beaumont had been careful not to overstate their case. They limited their proposals to the use of balloons for reconnaissance only. There were many schemes being proposed at the time to use balloons to mount artillery batteries, or to drop bombs on fortresses. Coxwell's experiment notwithstanding, these were Wellsian fantasies given the limitations in the technology of the period.[56] Some of these, particularly the need for a suitably robust, impermeable,

49   Driver, *Birth of Military Aviation*, pp.154-155.
50   AIR 1/2404/303, Report from Captain P Twynam, Aldershot, 17 July 1863.
51   Beaumont, 'Balloon Reconnaissance', p.60.
52   Beaumont, 'Balloon Reconnaissance', p.60.
53   Beaumont, 'Balloon Reconnaissance', p.60; WO 33/13/0214, p.591; AIR 1/2404/303, OSC minute 16015, 10/7/65 dated 12 July 1865 [*sic*] published in WO 33/15/0266, pp.613-15.
54   WO 33/15/0266, pp.614.
55   WO 33/15/0266, pp.614-15.
56   Beaumont, 'Balloon Reconnaissance', pp.56; TNA, WO 33/11/0169 *Abstract of Proceedings of the Ordnance Select Committee From 1st January to 31st March 1862*, p164, provides one example, dismissed as 'entirely unworthy of any serious discussion'.

but light material to replace silk for the balloon envelope, and more importantly a means of producing hydrogen gas from a mobile device, have been discussed above. However, the quotation from Grover near the start of this chapter points out that the real difficulty, even if these were resolved, lay in the ability to keep the balloon steady in the air. Beaumont suggested that a cylindrical form, though spherical balloons were simpler and lighter, might give the balloon the ability to 'ride somewhat like a ship in a stream-way', and also suggested that the car should be boat-shaped.[57] An airship involving cylindrical airbags, and propelled without use of motors, had been developed by the American inventor Solomon Andrews in 1863. Andrews offered his invention to the British through Lord Lyons in Washington, who in November forwarded the offer back to London, along with newspaper reports claiming speeds of up to one hundred miles an hour for the airship. The Director of Ordnance asked the Ordnance Select Committee to review the proposal, which they did the following month, but they were quick to dismiss to accounts as 'clearly fabulous', and recommended that no notice be taken of them.[58] Grover and Beaumont took the more conventional view that some form of air-screw was potentially the answer, but these were simply not practical until a machine with a greater power-to-weight ratio than the contemporary steam engine was available.[59]

There was one further direct contribution by a Civil War balloonist to British developments. In 1867 a war broke out in south America between Brazil and Paraguay. The Brazilians asked Thaddeus Lowe to provide a balloon for them, and while Lowe himself declined (it appears that his interest in aeronautics had waned), he put the Brazilians in touch with James Allen. These balloons were of the same design and handled in the same way as Lowe and Allen had used them on the Virginia Peninsula.[60] Soon reports were coming back from the British representative in Buenos Aires of the use of these 'American' balloons.

The engineer in the Argentine [sic] service, [...] owing to his former experience in the United States, has made from it [the balloon] several very important observations. He has been able to see the enemy's line of earthworks in all their detail[.][61]

57 Beaumont, 'On Balloon Reconnaissance', pp.101-92.
58 TNA, FO 5/896 fols 97-104 Lyons to Lord Russell, Washington, 13 November 1863, enclosing letter from Solomon Andrews to Lord Lyons, Perth Amboy, 14 September 1863, and newspaper articles on his airship; WO 33/13/0214, p.620.
59 Grover, 'Reconnoitring Balloons', pp.92-93; Beaumont, 'Balloon Reconnaissance', p.64-65; Beaumont comments at Baden-Powell lecture, Baden-Powell, 'Military Ballooning', pp.753-54.
60 Baden-Powell, 'Military Ballooning', p.740.
61 AIR 1/2404/303, Correspondence from Buenos Aires, 13 December 1867.

Grover seized upon this opportunity to submit a further request for experiments with a full-sized gas generating apparatus, since '[t]hese reconnaissances appear to have attained a fair degree of success'. On 21 June 1868 he wrote to the Ordnance Select Committee again requesting further funds for practical trials. This was rejected, with the response that balloons were only of utility in sieges, and the Committee suspended further trials the same year.[62]

*   *   *

Although rejected once again, Grover's persistence was about to pay off. In 1870, following the outbreak of the Franco-Prussian War, the Royal Engineers Committee was created to consider innovation and improvement in the Engineers' equipment, and in June 1871 a balloon sub-committee was set up comprising Grover, Beaumont, and Frederick Abel, the War Office Chemist, who had been experimenting with methods of generating hydrogen since the 1850s. In 1872 funding was provided for the gas generation apparatus, though not for balloons. Grover did not stay on the committee long enough to see this reward for his efforts however, being replaced in 1870. Beaumont also left the Committee, in 1873, to pursue other interests, and he retired from the Army in 1876 to become an MP.[63]

In 1869 the first edition of Sir Garnet Wolseley's *Soldier's Pocket Book* was published. In it Wolseley wrote in support of balloons, with what appears to be a clear reference to Mahon's observations.

> One of the most effective means of learning the whereabouts and doings of an enemy is by means of balloons, for although the undulations of the ground when viewed from the car of a balloon at an elevation of about 1,000 or 1,200 feet do not show, yet the position of troops can be accurately ascertained in close, still weather. Ascents by night, particularly in wooded countries, are most useful for this purpose, as the fires indicate the enemy's position, and his numbers may be roughly estimated, by allowing ten men to each fire.[64]

---

62   AIR 1/2404/303, Letter from Grover, 4 May 1868 requesting further funds for practical trials. Rejection response as balloons only of utility in siege. TNA, WO 33/20/0364, *Abstracts of Proceedings of the Ordnance Select Committee from 1st October to 7th December 1868*, p.884.

63   Brigadier P.W.L. Broke-Smith, 'Aeronautics, the History of Early British Military Aeronautics', *Royal Engineers Journal*, 66 (1952), pp.1-20, 105-21, 208-226, (pp.2-3); Baden-Powell, 'Military Ballooning', p.741; Colonel C. M. Watson 'Military Ballooning in the British Army', *R.E. Professional Papers*, 28, (1902), pp.39-59 (p.40); Driver, *Birth of Military Aviation*, p.158-9.

64   Wolseley, *Soldier's Pocket Book*, p.201.

There were tentative proposals to make use of balloons on Wolseley's 1873 Ashanti expedition. Lieutenant C.M. Watson RE, who had replaced Beaumont, worked out a means for splitting the gas generating apparatus into 80 lb loads for porter carriage, and Coxwell offered two balloons for the army to use. But the cost was too expensive, and the logistics could not be worked out in time (the weight of the iron needed for generating the hydrogen alone was estimated to be 10,000 lbs). This justified the claims of the aeronauts that balloons could not be extemporised in time of war but needed to be developed during peace. On balance it was probably a good thing that they were not used in the jungles of Ashanti, where they would have been of dubious utility, and failure would have set back the balloonists' cause. There was a further proposal to send a balloon on Wolseley's next major campaign, in Egypt in 1882, but before the detachment could sail Wolseley had already defeated the Egyptian Army, and it was not proceeded with. Here the conditions for observations would have been more suitable, although one sceptical veteran of the campaign, Sir Charles Nugent, questioned how the six-ton carts would have been manoeuvred over sand.[65]

Step by step, the balloon was becoming part of the formal establishment. In 1878 the Balloon Equipment Store was formed at Woolwich. The same year funds were made available to the Balloon Committee for construction of a balloon. Balloons featured in Volunteer reviews at Dover (1879), and at Brighton (1880 and 1883). In September 1880, 24th Company Royal Engineers was detailed for instruction in ballooning, and in 1882 a balloon factory was set up at Chatham as part of the School of Military Engineering, this would later become the School of Ballooning.[66]

Most importantly the two main technical problems were resolved. The linen or silk balloon envelopes that had constituted the best technology available in the Civil War were replaced by ones made of something called 'goldbeater's skin' (ox intestines grafted together in a method similar to that used to apply gold leaf). This reduced permeability, and therefore the loss of gas, and increased the time for which the balloon could remain inflated. The problem of mobility for the gas generator was resolved by pre-generating the gas, compressing it, and storing it in steel tubes – an idea first suggested in 1875 but not proceeded with until 1882.[67]

With these two technologies, several years ahead of other armies at the time, the British finally deployed balloons into the field. On 25 November 1884 a balloon detachment left England for Mafeking in Bechuanaland. Although it did not play any part in fighting, the operations, which started on 6 April 1885, were considered successful. The following year a second detachment was sent to Suakin on the coast of East Africa. On 25 March 1885 a balloon was kept aloft for seven hours to cover the advance of a column to Tofrek, three days after a battle with the Mahdist forces

65 Watson, 'Military Ballooning', pp.41-44; Baden-Powell, 'Military Ballooning', pp.755-76.
66 Baden-Powell, 'Military Ballooning', pp.746, 742; Broke-Smith, 'Aeronautics', pp.2-4;
    Watson, 'Military Ballooning', p.45; Driver, *Birth of Military Aviation*, pp.157-60.
67 Watson, 'Military Ballooning', pp.42-3; Broke-Smith, 'Aeronautics', pp.3-5; Driver, *Birth of Military Aviation*, p.161.

there. This saved scouting, and gave security to the troops and convoys operating in the scrub country. On another occasion a balloon was raised to 2,000 feet, and was able to see artillery fire at Suakin 28 miles away. Coincidentally, Grover was serving in Suakin at this time, though whether he became involved in the use of the balloons there is not recorded.[68]

In 1886 a report produced by Major Henry Elsdale, who had visited Paris ('the centre and focus of the ballooning world') in December 1885, concluded that Britain led the other European powers in military ballooning. This had also been achieved with a significantly lower expenditure than in France, in part because officers like Elsdale were funding research and development out of their own money.[69] However, there was still resistance from the military establishment – once again on the grounds of cost. Wolseley himself, as Adjutant General, was having second thoughts on their utility, and once again America was cited in evidence.

It is possible that balloons may yet be made some use of in war, although as yet no practical benefit to troops in the field has ever yet been derived from them. They were tried on a very extensive scale during the Great American war, and finally abandoned. As yet it has never been found possible to use them in a strong wind. The point I would however wish to raise here is the expediency of our squandering money on these experiments. H. R. H. [the Duke of Cambridge] is of the opinion that the money could be spent upon far more useful objects.[70]

In fairness to Wolseley he was at the time trying to implement proposals for the mobilisation of the British Army in time of war, which can reasonably be considered a more important matter on which to spend the annual budget, and was also perhaps merely reflecting the views of the Duke of Cambridge. That said, his suggestion in the same memo that balloons could be quickly obtained in time of war, and civilian aeronauts employed to man them, was a significant threat to their permanent establishment within the army, and would surely have led to situations such as those faced by Thaddeus Lowe in 1863.

68   TNA, WO 32/6930, *Final Report of Committee on Ballooning* (1904), p.4; Broke-Smith, 'Aeronautics', pp.5-7; Watson, 'Military Ballooning', pp.47-49; Porter, *History of the Corps of Royal Engineers*, Vol.II, pp.191-93; Driver, *Birth of Military Aviation*, pp.163-165; Obituary of Sir George Edward Grover (1840-1893), Institution of Civil Engineers, on website *Grace's Guide to British Industrial History*, https://www.gracesguide.co.uk/George_Edward_Grover#cite_note-1 [accessed 02/10/2017].

69   TNA, WO 32/6067, 'Ballooning: Report of Visit to Paris, from Major Elsdale RE, Chatham 18 December 1885'; TNA, WO 32/6068, Memo by Lothian Nicholson, Inspector General Fortifications, dated 11 September 1886. The funding, by Elsdale and the more famous Captain (later Colonel) James Templer, included payments to secure the secret of goldbeaters skin.

70   WO 32/6067, Memo by Wolseley to Inspector General Fortifications, dated 24 March 1886.

A British T class balloon at Frensham, 1893. (The RAF Museum)

In reply the Inspector General of Fortifications, Sir Andrew Clarke, challenged Wolseley's view and insisted that there needed to be a small permanent nucleus of experienced balloonists in the army in order to be capable of expansion in time of war. As to their utility, he quoted back Wolseley's own words from the *Soldier's Pocket Book*, saying that 'it would be a suicidal policy to neglect this branch of military science on the grounds of the trifling expenditure involved'.[71] The internal debate continued after Sir Lothian Nicholson replaced Clarke as Inspector General of Fortifications later that year. Nicholson continued to argue the potential for the balloon to be of value, while Wolseley kept challenging whether the money could be better spent elsewhere, until in February 1887 the Duke of Cambridge seems to have changed his mind and decided that a small balloon detachment was indeed necessary, and that the costs were to be included in the annual estimates.[72]

In 1889 the balloon detachment took part in the Army Manoeuvres at Aldershot. It was so successful that a Balloon Section of the Royal Engineers was established as a permanent unit the following year. Its work and personnel were supported by a

71   WO 32/6067, Memo by Sir Andrew Clarke, Inspector General Fortifications, dated 18 May 1886.
72   WO 32/6068, Wolseley comment on memo from Sir Lothian Nicholson, IGF, dated 26 February 1887.

balloon factory and school. This can be regarded as the point in which balloons finally stopped being at the experimental stage, and were recognised as a necessary component of the Army.[73] Interestingly, the establishment of the new section was authorised as three officers, three sergeants and 28 men; while the train comprised one balloon wagon, three tube wagons, one equipment wagon for spare balloons and stores, and one water cart. This was not dissimilar in size to Lowe's operation with the Army of the Potomac.[74]

* * *

The story of balloons provides a case study into how the British Army approached technical innovation. At first sight it might appear that Grover, Beaumont, and their successors, were 'mavericks', similar to early 20th Century air-power enthusiasts such as Brigadier General William 'Billy' Mitchell in the United States.[75] Yet while Grover certainly had to overcome resistance, both he and Beaumont were able to enlist the support of men like Sir John Burgoyne, and their appointment as supplementary members of the Ordnance Select Committee meant that they were working within the official processes. It is notable that Grover and Beaumont, while frequently promoting their ideas, were cautious not to overstate their case, and always pointed out the limitations of the technology and the subsequent need for experimentation and development. This added to their credibility, in contrast to the often-dismissive response given by the Committee to civilian proposals for aerial machines. There was, moreover, no external or political element to their campaign. Coxwell, the civilian specialist, was engaged under the Committee's direction in preference to committing government resources to experiments that might amount to nothing, and not as a civilian champion for the cause.

Conversely, innovation may result from senior military leaders recognising what the next war will look like, and how their organisation must change if it is to be won.[76] This process was seen to a limited extent in the case of ballooning. Without Burgoyne's support, the trials in 1863 would never have taken place, and it is to his credit, and to that of the Ordnance Select Committee and of the evaluation process overall, that the apparent failings of the technology in America did not kill these experiments at birth. Wolseley, the future Commander in Chief, was early to spot the

73   Broke-Smith, 'Aeronautics', p.9; Watson, 'Military Ballooning', pp.52-53; Driver, *The Birth of Military Aviation*, p.166.
74   Watson, 'Military Ballooning', pp.51-52; Broke-Smith, 'Aeronautics', p.9.,
75   Grissom, 'The Future of Military Innovation Studies', pp.908-910. This 'maverick' theory was first proposed by Barry R. Posen, *The Sources of Military Doctrine: France Britain and Germany Between the World Wars* (Ithaca: Cornell University Press, 1984).
76   Grissom, 'The Future of Military Innovation Studies', pp.913-16; Stephen Peter Rosen, *Winning the Next War: Innovation and the Modern Military* (Ithaca: Cornell University Press, 1991), pp.19-20.

potential of the balloon for observation, and it is an intriguing fact that on two of his campaigns, in Ashanti and in Egypt, there were proposals to send a balloon unit with the expedition. These proposals came to nothing however, and despite his words in the *Soldier's Pocket Book* Wolseley actually obstructed setting up a balloon organisation in the 1880s. The technology during this period remained too limited in its application for any senior figure to commit a significant level of political capital to its support, although without the support of Sir Arthur Clarke and Sir Lothian Nicholson the new establishment could have fallen victim to budgetary constraints in the 1880s. New organisations were created, and a few officers would base their careers on their involvement with the technology, but such opportunities were limited and this was not on a scale to constitute a new 'theory of victory' for the future.

Competition may drive innovation, especially where a rival organisation may threaten either to usurp traditional roles or to compete for resources, but competition does not explain the development of the balloon in the British Army.[77] The Royal Navy, which would in the early years of the 20th Century develop its own air arm, did not input into the experiments of the 19th other than perhaps through providing ropes from Chatham dockyard for the Army's trials.[78] Competition between different arms within the Army was also lacking. Aerial reconnaissance had not reached a stage of maturity at which it could provoke a response from the cavalry, and while the Royal Artillery might have been expected to have had some interest in balloons for artillery spotting, the experiments remained entirely under the auspices of the Royal Engineers.

Rather than innovation, the story of the balloon is one of bottom-up adaptation and adoption, driven by relatively junior champions in the service, and subject to the winning of certain levels of support from more senior figures.[79] Most significantly the technical institutions, such as the Ordnance Select Committee and the Department of the War Office Chemist, provided input and support which kept experimentation at a level just sufficient to maintain the momentum of progress. Also, as the early champions, Grover and Beaumont, left the scene, the organisational structure put in place through the Royal Engineers Committee enabled their role in driving the adoption process to be taken up by others. Rather than the conservative attitude to new weapons sometimes attributed to the Army – in the case of the machine gun for example – the story of the balloon indicates a readiness to keep an open mind, which then paid off when the technology matured to a point when it could provide valuable service in the field.

77   Grissom, 'The Future of Military Innovation Studies', pp.910-13. The idea that competition between services for resources and military roles derives largely from studies of the US military in the 1950s.
78   WO 33/12/0192, p.128.
79   Grissom, 'The Future of Military Innovation Studies', pp.920-26, discusses bottom-up change; see also Farrell, 'Improving in War', pp.567-69 for discussion of adaption and innovation.

Finally, this adoption process was one of slow, incremental progress. In the case of balloons, it was 23 years between Beaumont's observation of Lowe's activities in Virginia and the British deployments of balloons to Africa, but there is nevertheless a clear line of development between the two events. During this period the Army adapted the existing Royal Engineer organisations to the new technological environment, rather than building a new arm from scratch. This possibly helped protect the fledgling technology. Had it been created as an independent Corps soon after the Civil War it would have had to have fought for its existence, and for funds, in much the same way Lowe had to fight for his funding within the Army of the Potomac. One or two mishaps, or even bad publicity from the failures to deploy to Ashanti and Egypt, and the value of the new arm would probably have been successfully challenged, and it would likely have been lost. By keeping the new technology essentially as a minor part of the engineering train, it was protected from controversy until ready to play a more serious role.

By the outbreak of the Boer War, the balloon had become a recognised part of the Army's array of equipment, and the Balloon Corps a valued if small part of the establishment, which saw some success at Ladysmith, Colenso, Modder River, Paardeburg, and Fourteen Streams.[80] In time military aviation would pass all of the modern tests for being considered innovative, producing new organisations and career paths, and new tactics and strategies for winning wars, but this was still in the future. Aeronautical technology in 1899 was not yet in a position to challenge the roles of the existing three arms as it would in the two World Wars, but it had taken the first small steps to doing so, a process that can be directly traced back to Grover, Beaumont, and their observations on the use of balloons in the American Civil War.

80   Driver, *Birth of Military Aviation*, pp.170-77; TNA, WO 32/6062, 'The Role of English Military Balloons in the South African War', Lecture given at Paris on the 27th March, 1902, by Colonel Arthur Lynch of the Boer Army; translation of article in *L'Aeronaut*, April 1902. Lynch was an Irish MP who volunteered to serve with the Boers.

7

Railways, Volunteers, and Imperial Defence – Strategic and Operational Lessons

The American Civil War's place in military history is not defined only by its supposed technological innovation and break with traditional tactics. Some have seen in it the start of a fundamental change in the nature of war itself.[1] If it is taken as an accepted fact that the conflict was the first of the modern, total wars, then those 19th Century commentators who failed to see in it the future direction of conflict are condemned, as a consequence, to be seen as backward thinking and unobservant. Such has been the traditional verdict on many of the major British military writers of the 1860s and 1870s and their treatment of the war. Captain Charles Cornwallis Chesney, the Professor of Military History at the Royal Military College, Sandhurst, and subsequently at the Staff College, is considered by one authority to have laboured under 'basic misconceptions' about the American conflict and as a result 'could not penetrate deeply into, or analyse clearly, the real significance of the operations for the future'.[2] Chesney's predecessor at the Staff College, Lieutenant General Sir Edward Bruce Hamley, whose work on strategy, *The Operations of War*, was published the year after the Civil War ended, in 1866, drew praise from Robert E. Lee and William T. Sherman but has been criticised as conservative and unoriginal, his work described as over-rated.[3] Even Lieutenant Colonel G.F.R. Henderson, who from the mid-1880s onwards influenced future British military historiography on the war perhaps more

1   Fuller, *The Conduct of War*, pp.95, 99, 107–108; James M. McPherson, 'From Limited War to Total War' and Edward Hagerman, 'Union Generalship, Political Leadership, and Total War Strategy' in *On the Road to Total War: The American Civil War and the German Wars of Unification*, ed. Stig Förster and Jörg Nagler (Cambridge: Cambridge University Press, 1997), pp.141–69, 295–309.
2   Preston, 'British Military Thought 1856-1900', pp.63-64.
3   Preston, 'British Military Thought 1856-1900', pp.68-69; Luvaas, *Education of an Army*, pp.143-46.

than any other historian, is accused of an undue focus both on the early period of the war, and on its eastern theatre.[4]

These views on the British failure to draw strategic lessons from the war rely, as do the views upon the tactical and technological legacy, upon a particular view of warfare in the first half of the 20th Century, and how successfully, or rather unsuccessfully since the opinions are usually critical, the British Army had adapted. For those seeking to find the seeds of the Western Front in the Civil War, Grant's strategy of attrition in the 1864 Overland Campaign and the subsequent adoption of trench warfare at Petersburg held the key. For those like Liddell Hart seeking to find ways to avoid such a stalemate, Sherman's campaigns in Georgia the same year showed that mobility could still have a role in modern warfare. But both these campaigns, as well as others from the American war, had previously been examined and used by 19th Century authors to provide evidence of their own theories of war.

Modern military doctrine draws clear distinctions between strategy, which is defined as the process of integrating all aspects of national power to achieve a theatre, national or multinational objective; operations, which describes the conduct of campaigns bringing tactical forces to bear to achieve the strategic objectives; and tactics, the application and arrangement of combat forces to achieve missions through battle.[5] While the last of these would have been familiar to 19th Century writers, the concept of 'strategy' was much less clear, while in spite of the title of Hamley's work the term 'operations' was rarely used in any analytical context. Although famous for his description of war as an extension of policy, Clausewitz's definition of strategy as 'the employment of the battle as the means towards the attainment of the object of the War' is more aligned to the modern concept of operations than to geopolitics and strategy.[6] Henderson adopted an even looser definition of the term, describing it simply as 'war on the map', with the justification that this was both short and comprehensive.[7] It is also a rather accurate description of much of the early strategic observations on the Civil War that were written in Britain at the time, which very much depended upon the interpretation of the movements of armies across the map of America with

4   Luvaas, *Military Legacy*, p.200.
5   US Army, *Field Manual FM 3–0, Operations* (Washington: Department of the Army, 2008), pp.6 – 2, 6 – 3, 6 – 4.
6   Carl von Clausewitz, *On War*, trans. by F.N. Maude, ed. by Anatol Rapoport (London: Pelican, 1968, originally published 1832, translated 1908), p.241.
7   Lieutenant Colonel G.F.R. Henderson, 'Strategy and Its Teaching', *Journal of the Royal United Service Institution*, 42 (1898), pp.761-86 (p.761). Henderson's source for this may have been Jomini's *The Art of War*, which also describes strategy as the art of making war on the map, see Stephen Badsey, 'Forum II: Confederate Military Strategy in the U.S. Civil War Revisited', *Journal of Military History*, 73 (2009), pp.1,273-1,278. Referring to Henderson's *Science of War*, Badsey suggests that the term 'grand tactics' has parallels with modern 'operations'; but also that 'operations' meant campaigning in the widest sense of the word in 19th Century British writings, citing Hamley, who included both strategy and tactics in *Operations of War*.

limited or no direct knowledge of the territory being fought over. Again, in modern parlance most of these writings are more operational than strategic in their focus. The war did however also give rise to some more generic analyses which indicate a more truly strategic view emerging in Britain of how wars might be waged in the future. Nevertheless, to avoid imposing 21st Century concepts onto 19th Century thought, the term 'strategy' will be used in this chapter in both its operational and strategic contexts as used by the original authors.

This chapter will look at four principal themes: the quality of the contemporary British commentary and analysis of the progress of the war; the operational lessons derived from the use of railways and combined operations; the raising of a massed volunteer army in America as a result of the war, and how this resonated with and informed the British response to the emergence of mass conscript armies in Europe; and the understanding of how the nature of the conflict influenced the way in which it was fought. If 20th Century hindsight is stripped away, how well did the British military establishment understand the significance of the war in America? Was the war misunderstood, misinterpreted or ignored in favour of European lessons? Finally, why *should* the British Army have regarded a civil war across the Atlantic, on a continent where its own military presence was strictly limited, as being of significance for its military activities in the future?

The substantial interest which the British had in the war was reflected in the volume of newspaper reports crossing the Atlantic, coming both from the American press and from the special correspondents of leading British journals resident in America. However, military writers in Britain trying to make sense of how the war was being fought noted the difficulty of relying upon these reports. Besides the necessity for reporters to make their stories interesting for their readers, which was often at odds with providing informed and impartial analysis, it was largely the Northern view of war that initially made it into the British press. Offsetting this reliance on Northern sources, a great deal of the British establishment took a pro-Southern stance due to its political leanings and distrust of American democratic tendencies. Reports from America were therefore often viewed with a high level of incredulity.[8] Chesney thought that the numbers fighting at Antietam had 'been much exaggerated' although he accepted that it had been 'a very important battle'.[9] Another commentator wrote regarding the lack of news from the Federal expedition to New Orleans in 1862 that

8   Major F. Miller, 'Military Sketch of the Present War in America', *Journal of the Royal United Service Institution*, 6 (1863), pp.241-62 (pp.241, 253); [Sir Edward Bruce Hamley], 'Books on the American War', *Blackwood's Edinburgh Magazine*, 94 (1863), pp.750-68 (pp.750-51); Anon [Sir Edward Bruce Hamley?], 'Our Rancorous Cousins', *Blackwood's Edinburgh Magazine*, 94 (1863), pp.636-52 (p.637); Dubrulle, 'Anarchy ... and Ruin', p.588.
9   Captain C.C. Chesney, *A Military View of Recent Campaigns in Virginia and Maryland* (London: Smith, Elder, and Co., 1863), p.806

'so entirely is the press in the power of the [United States] Government that silence cannot mean success'.[10]

These anti-American prejudices were accentuated during the opening months of the war by a level of professional contempt for the operations of what were seen as ill-led, undisciplined levies. Hamley's biographer quoted a letter written on 12 December 1861, in response to a request Hamley received from the pro-Southern publisher John Blackwood for an article on the war to go into *Blackwood's Edinburgh Magazine*.

> It appears to me that the calm judicial style is altogether unsuitable to the discussion of American affairs. If their proceedings – civil, military and popular – met the derision they deserve they might come to a more correct estimate of their own position; and when they saw that they were making themselves ridiculous, they might cease this absurd war.[11]

Early commentators therefore saw the war as politically significant but militarily of little instructional value. As the war progressed and the campaigns became more sophisticated and more extended, military writers were obliged to provide for their readership more extensive opinions of how the fighting had and would progress, whether in professional or popular journals. This required a more analytical approach than the initial outpourings, and an application of Hamley's 'calm judicial style'.

The writers who produced the most substantial articles and books on the war in the 1860s were military academics, meaning that they were army officers who held positions as professors or lecturers at the military colleges, or had mostly made their reputations as military commentators rather than as field commanders. They came with their own preconceptions of the principles of war, but they were also actively trying to identify what the conflict could tell them about modern warfare. Major Frederick Miller VC, presenting at the Royal United Service Institution in April 1862, aimed to use the military history of the war to 'point out how far principles were vindicated by the results of observing or neglecting established rules, and how any new weapon or any new features in the equipment of an army influenced its movements or affected its achievements'.[12] The meeting was chaired by Lieutenant General W.T. Knollys, the Vice-President of the Council of Military Education. In a similar vein,

---

10   Miller, 'Military Sketch', p.259.
11   Alexander Innes Shand, *The Life of General Sir Edward Bruce Hamley*, 2 vols (Edinburgh and London: William Blackwood and Sons, 1895), Vol.I, p.136; Mrs Gerald Porter, *Annals of a Publishing House: John Blackwood, Volume. III of William Blackwood and his Sons, Their Magazine and Friends* (Edinburgh and London: William Blackwood, 1898), p.268 has a slightly different version. Mrs Porter gives this letter a date of 12 December 1863, but though Shand does not give a date, its place in his narrative indicates December 1861, as do the extensive references to the *Trent* affair which are included in Mrs Porter's extract. Furthermore, Hamley had already written several articles on the war by December 1863.
12   Miller, 'Military Sketch', pp.245-46.

Chesney, lecturing at the same location a year later about the operations in Virginia, declared that it was 'simply impossible for anyone to study to advantage, any campaign of importance without taking into consideration what are generally called the general principles of war' and that 'these campaigns in America are no exception to the ordinary rules of warfare'.[13] These contemporary authors started the process of using the American war as a didactic example for their own theories. This tradition was later to be continued by men such as Henderson, Maurice, Liddell Hart, and Fuller.[14]

Miller wrote with a general expectation of a Northern victory, due to a simple calculation of the number of men that it could raise compared to the South and the lack of any compensating factors in fortifications, weapons, or mobility (Miller noted that the North had 100 miles of railroad for every 40 in the South). He believed that in April 1862 the war had reached a critical stage.

> The South must expect to see its trade ruined, its coasts invaded, its rivers made thoroughfares at the enemy's convenience, the divided states won by force, and then – then the resistance she might continue to offer must depend upon the unity of sentiment among all classes, and the degree of resolution which survived the trial.[15]

He predicted a contest full of bitterness and misery, where success for the South 'depends on moral qualities, of whose existence we cannot be sure until we have seen their effects'.[16]

Miller's analysis identified three critical factors in the progress of the war. The first was the initial lack of readiness for war and the 'unmilitary condition' of the armies formed by both sides. The second was the nature of the country and in particular the lack of roads that could enable an easy invasion of the South, and the resulting reliance on railways. The third was the nature of the conflict as a civil war. He concluded that the course of the war to date was entirely as expected for such a conflict. It had started with a fight for areas with disputed sympathy (West Virginia, Missouri, and Kentucky). This had been followed with a direct assault by the stronger side on the capital of the weaker, with diversions to draw the enemy's strength (Miller specifically identified the expeditions of Brigadier General Benjamin Butler at Hatteras Inlet, North Carolina, in August 1861; Brigadier General Thomas W. Sherman at Port Royal, South Carolina, in November 1861; and Brigadier General Ambrose Burnside at Roanoke, North Carolina, in February 1862). Only in the Northern invasion of

13   Chesney, 'The Recent Campaigns in Virginia and Maryland', *Journal of the Royal United Service Institution*, 7 (1864), pp.291-307 (p.291).
14   Reid, 'Military Intellectuals and the American Civil War', pp.133-49.
15   Miller, 'Military Sketch', pp.245-46.
16   Miller, 'Military Sketch', p.246.

Tennessee did he see a strategic operation 'more nearly allied to the art of war, but still to be traced by the sympathies of the inhabitants'.[17]

Hamley had by this time agreed to John Blackwood's request for an article for his magazine, which appeared in print the same month as Miller's lecture. Hamley also highlighted the Tennessee theatre as being of critical importance. This strategic significance sprang from the nature of the railroad network and the geographical impact of the Allegheny mountains. The railways that crossed the Alleghenies via the Potomac valley and to the north enabled the Union to readily transfer its forces. The Confederacy was only able to cross this mountain range in Georgia via Chattanooga, presenting the Union with the opportunity to assemble an overwhelming force along the Cumberland and Tennessee rivers and ultimately seize points along the Memphis railway, severing the Confederacy's artery to the Mississippi. Such an advance, Hamley observed, would be exceedingly strong strategically. 'Even if an army so advancing be attacked on its outward flank, and driven back upon the river, the heavy artillery of the flotilla would probably protect it from further disaster.' This is a broadly accurate summary of the events at Shiloh, fought on 6-7 April 1862. Hamley had written the article prior to the abandonment by the Confederates of Columbus, Kentucky, which had taken place on 2 March 1862, and so anticipated the nature of that critical battle.[18]

There was still comfort to be given however to *Blackwood's* pro-Southern readership. While the Mississippi plain lacked any strongly defensible positions, the opposite was true of the Allegheny passes. Here, Hamley wrote, the poor roads and the defensive advantages of mountain warfare would negate the North's numerical advantage and offer opportunities for guerrilla warfare. On these grounds he believed that the South could still resist – although he echoed Miller in observing that there was 'no sufficient proof that it will'.[19]

Hamley's belief that the West was the critical theatre was re-emphasised in December 1863, in an article that directly referenced his predictions 20 months earlier. In the East, he wrote, the Federal Army 'seeks only to push back the Southern frontier' whereas in the West it 'aims at the dissolution of the whole fabric of the South' through the lines of invasion via the Tennessee and Cumberland rivers that led 'straight to the heart of the Confederacy'. Drawing on the example of Sebastopol (where he had served during the Crimean War) he noted the difficulty of capturing an un-invested harbour such as Charleston; concluded that Richmond was safe until

17   Miller, 'Military Sketch', pp.260-62.
18   [Sir Edward Bruce Hamley], 'Spence's American Union', *Blackwood's Edinburgh Magazine*, 91 (1862), pp.514-36 (pp.530-31). Articles in *Blackwood's* were mostly published anonymously, and basing his information on Mrs Porter's biography of John Blackwood, Luvaas only identified one, 'Books on the American War' (December, 1863), as definitely written by Hamley. His biographer however noted that 'most of the articles on American affairs, whether political or military were written by him' (Shand, *Life of Hamley*, Vol.I, p.144), and I have gone with the attributions in the *Wellesley Index to Victorian Periodicals*.
19   Hamley, 'Spence's American Union', pp.532-34.

the Federals could repair their railroad communications; and expected Confederate success at Chattanooga where the Federals were reliant on a single line of communication (published in December 1863, the article had been written prior to Major General Grant's victory at Missionary Ridge on 25 November 1863 which drove the Confederate army away from the city). Most significantly however, in this article he urged his readers to understand the connection between the East and the West in order to understand the full meaning of the war.[20]

According to his biographer Hamley was a 'red-hot Southern sympathiser ... in cordial agreement with the line taken by the Magazine', and he often predicted the economic or military exhaustion of the North, although even John Blackwood suggested that his Southern sympathies had perhaps led him to underestimate the material advantage that the North had accumulated by this time.[21] He was not so politically biased however that he did not on occasion criticise the Southern generals. 'Little tactical talent was displayed on the side of the Confederates in the battles fought on the [Virginia] peninsular', he wrote, blaming them for relying upon frontal assaults and for not pressing home their hard fought victories.[22]

One of the publications that Hamley used as a source for his analysis was Chesney's *A Military View of Recent Campaigns in Virginia and Maryland* published in 1863. Like other contemporary European commentators, Chesney was disparaging of the quality of the American armies, particularly those of the North. The troops around Washington in March 1862 were described by him as 'not an army in the strict sense of the term, as we call an army, that is, composed of trained soldiers' and he had commented on how turning the flank of an American army (in this particular case the Confederate army at the battle of Fair Oaks in June 1862) 'seems to be disastrous [...] owing to their lack of discipline'.[23] Nevertheless, as a lecturer in military history, Chesney saw great value in studying the campaigns due to the numerous observers present from different nations and the different classes of opinion that this brought about. These enabled the war to be analysed 'in a way that no other such contest has been'.[24] Writing his study of the Eastern campaigns at a time when the Confederate cause was at its height, Chesney needed to explain the causes not of Southern defeat, but of Northern reverses. Part of this he put down to the superior quality of the Southern troops – 'an army entitled to the name, by the subordinate spirit, as well as the valour, of its soldiers'; part down to divided Northern command; but also due to

20   Hamley, 'Books on the American War', pp.768, 753. Blackwood sent the proof of 'Books on the American War' to Hamley on 16 November 1863, Mrs Porter, *Annals of a Publishing House*, p.269.
21   Shand, *Life of Hamley*, Vol.I, p.141; John Blackwood to Colonel E.B. Hamley, Edinburgh, 16 November 1863, in Mrs Porter, *Annals of a Publishing House*, p.268, also referenced in Luvaas, *Military Legacy*, p.102.
22   Hamley, 'Books on the American War', p.764.
23   Chesney, 'Campaigns in Virginia and Maryland', pp.295, 301.
24   Chesney, *Virginia and Maryland*, p.ix.

a disregard, and even contempt for, the principles of war by the Northern generals up to that time compared to an understanding and use of them by those of the South.[25]

Like Miller, Chesney first presented his analysis of the American campaigns at the Royal United Service Institution, in May 1863. His introduction to that lecture stated three 'general principles' to which he believed America presented no exception. The first was the importance to a modern army of a large volume of supplies, and the resulting need both to have a base and to maintain a line of communications with that base. The second was the capability of two or three small armies, faced by two or three larger armies, to combine and beat their larger opponents in succession. The third was the danger of a large army if divided of being attacked and defeated in detail.[26]

The Virginia theatre gave Chesney much material in support of his theories. Communications, in view of the poor condition of roads in the region, were dictated by the availability of railroads, although still 'very rough they are compared to our own'.[27] This explained Major General McClellan's campaign against Richmond via the Virginia Peninsula, since a single line railway was inadequate to maintain his army in a direct overland attack, McClellan's strategy enabled him to supply his army by sea. Also supporting Chesney's first principle was the influence of the Confederate ironclad CSS *Virginia* (referred to by British writers of the time by its former name, *Merrimac*) in disrupting the use of the more direct route via the James River, thereby limiting McClellan's supply line to the York River.[28] Chesney had no great regard for McClellan as a field commander, thinking him over-cautious, but did consider that he was an educated soldier 'well qualified to apply his theoretical knowledge in the practical school of a campaign'.[29] Chesney attributed McClellan's defeat to the Confederate leadership applying Chesney's second and third principles, drawing in their troops from North Carolina, the Shenandoah Valley, and Norfolk, Virginia, to mass their forces against McClellan and then defeat him in detail while his army was divided by the Chickahominy River.

The concentration of forces and the defeat of the enemy in detail were of course not novel doctrines. They were central to all contemporary teachings on the art of war, in particular the influential writings of Jomini, and essential to any discussion of the campaigns of the great commanders, especially Napoleon. But British authorities in the 1860s were quick to make use of examples from the American war as evidence of these supposedly immutable principles. In *Operations of War*, Hamley followed Chesney in using McClellan's defeat, and that of his successor Major General John Pope at Second Manassas in August 1862, to demonstrate the principle of interior lines, in preference to Napoleonic examples.[30] Sir Patrick MacDougall, another

---

25   Chesney, *Virginia and Maryland*, p.2.
26   Chesney, 'Campaigns in Virginia and Maryland', pp.291, 296.
27   Chesney, 'Campaigns in Virginia and Maryland', p.294
28   Chesney, 'Campaigns in Virginia and Maryland', pp.295-98.
29   Chesney, 'Campaigns in Virginia and Maryland', p.295.
30   Hamley, *Operations of War*, pp.169-78.

Commandant at the Staff College, used the example of the Federal's diversion of effort to North Carolina at the time of Fredericksburg, and also that of Lee's distribution of forces during the Gettysburg campaign of 1863, to demonstrate the fatal results of dispersion, the latter showing that it was not only Northern generals who avoided the basic principles of war at their peril.[31]

In 1865 Chesney turned his attention to the western theatre. Sherman's campaign against Atlanta was held up as a further example of the importance of communications in war, both threatening the enemy's and securing one's own. Yet it was still largely seen as conforming to the initial pattern of American strategic operations which had been observed by other early European commentators such as the Prince de Joinville, a French observer who had served on McClellan's staff in 1862, that they were tied to their lines of communications. William Tecumseh Sherman, however, was described by Chesney as a man 'of original genius; for he is the first person in this war who saw long ago that it was perfectly possible to conduct a campaign without keeping his army constantly within a day's march of a railroad, or a river covered with steamboats'. In Chesney's view here was something new to be learned from America, not mere butchery or indecisive skirmishes, but someone who was not only a master of the principles of war, but also a soldier of genius (Chesney uses the word on four occasions in his article), who knew when to lay aside the principles of war with impunity.[32]

Hamley at the time had a more reserved view of Sherman's success considering him 'never sufficiently tested'.[33] In the first edition of *Operations of War* he was dismissive of the March to the Sea as being unexceptional, comparing it to the *chevauchées* of the Hundred Years' War, and regarded it as having a very limited strategic objective. Although he used Sherman's Atlanta campaign as an example of how to turn an enemy's flank, he was nevertheless critical of Sherman's performance, writing that 'probably no commander ever obtained a reputation equal to Sherman's with so little fighting, and with such odds in his favour'.[34] Sherman himself, on reading the work, responded by sending Hamley a copy of his report of the campaign. A covering letter sent with the report included the following passage.

A good many of the English commentaries and criticisms err, because it is impossible for them to see why well-established principles of war had to be modified to suit the peculiar geography and forest nature of our country. Thus, I think,

31 Sir Patrick MacDougall, *Modern Warfare as Influenced by Modern Artillery* (London: John Murray, 1864), pp.139-40, 143-44.
32 Captain C.C. Chesney, 'Sherman's Campaign in Georgia', *Journal of the Royal United Service Institution*, 9 (1865), pp.204-20 (pp.205-06, 216, 219).
33 [Sir Edward Bruce Hamley], 'General McClellan', *Blackwood's Edinburgh Magazine*, 96 (1864), pp.619-44 (p.642).
34 Sir Edward Bruce Hamley, *The Operations of War Explained and Illustrated*, 1st edn (Edinburgh and London: W. Blackwood, 1866), pp.18-19, 198-99.

if Colonel Hamley were to visit the ground about Dalton and Resaca, he would modify his chapter treating of my dispositions there.[35]

Somewhat tongue in cheek perhaps, Sherman added that 'I like to see these criticisms, however, as they show that the rest of the world is interested in our youthful imitations of their grand games of war'.[36]

To Hamley's credit he did modify his judgement, declaring it 'unjust to Sherman's generalship' in subsequent editions, and in his correspondence with Sherman referring to him as a general 'who has commanded a great army with such brilliant results'.[37] Sherman's reply to Hamley is also of interest.

I don't think any of us claim to be great generals, in the strict sense of that term, or to have initiated anything new, but merely to have met an emergency forced on us, and to have ceased war the very moment it could be done. I beg you will consider me as one who fully accords to you the right to criticise strictly anything that will illustrate the principles of our art, which we, as military men, must claim to be based on principles as everlasting as Time [sic].[38]

This brief series of correspondence with Sherman, which Hamley's biographer saw as important enough to reproduce at length, demonstrates a number of points regarding the analysis of the war by British military academics such as Chesney and Hamley. Firstly, the limited sources that these early writers had to work from restricted their analysis – Hamley regretted the lack of a good map. Secondly, that the Americans themselves attributed much of the way that the campaigns were fought to the 'peculiar geography' of their country. Thirdly, that neither the British commentators nor the American participants believed at the time that the conflict had modified to any great extent the traditional principles of war.

Wolseley, writing several years later, re-iterated the importance of Sherman and the western theatre. In a series of articles written at the time of Sherman's death in 1891 he expressed the view that the Federal seizure of the Mississippi was the turning point of the war. 'The event has not, I think, been yet fully recognised at its full value by most American historians; General Sherman however, dwells forcibly upon the importance in his writings.'[39] Wolseley's articles in the *North American Review* also remarked upon the importance of water transport in the West and the great relevance

---

35   Sherman to B. Moran, 16 March 1867, quoted in Shand, *Life of Hamley*, Vol.I, pp.185-86; Hamley, *Operations of War*, 4th edn, p.200 (footnote).
36   Shand, *Life of Hamley*, Vol.I, p.186.
37   Hamley to Sherman, 12 April 1867, Shand, *Life of Hamley*, Vol.I, pp.187-88.
38   Sherman to Hamley, 10 May 1867, Shand, *Life of Hamley*, Vol.I, pp.188-89.
39   Wolseley, 'General Sherman', *United Service Magazine*, n.s., 3 (1891), pp.97-116, 193-216, 289-309 (p.204).

of this to British operations which often took place in 'wild and distant countries'.[40] Two of Wolseley's most famous campaigns, the Red River Expedition in Canada (1869) and the Gordon Relief Expedition in the Sudan (1884-85) had relied upon river transport in inhospitable terrain, and it is reasonable to assume that these heightened his awareness of this aspect of the Civil War.

Of all the campaigns in America, Wolseley believed that the most informative from a European point of view were those around the port of Charleston in South Carolina. This had drawn a lot of attention from British observers during the war and had particular relevance in a British context due to the nature of British power. Aside from the scenarios of an invasion of England and the defence of the land frontiers, any projection of British power would require transporting the army by sea, and against any major foe this would be likely to entail the capture of a harbour and the need for the reduction of an enemy fortress.[41] Wolseley had some experience of this from the Crimea and Egypt.

> This co-operating action, of the naval and military services, mutually supporting each other, and the fact that neither can be neglected without direct detriment to the other, seems to be among the most important lessons taught in the whole history of the American Civil War.[42]

It was a lesson that the British often failed to effectively apply. The Royal Navy's attack on the forts at Alexandria at the start of the Egyptian campaign in July 1882 took place independently of the arrival of the Army's expeditionary force a week later. Gunboats were used more successfully in support of riverine operations, the Nile campaign of 1898 and the Battle of Omdurman being reminiscent of the American operations in the West, where fire support had been an important element in the Battle of Shiloh for example.[43] The British congratulated themselves on their logistical organisation of the rapid despatch of troops by sea to South Africa in 1899-1902, but co-ordination between the Navy and Army failed again significantly during the First World War in the initial naval attack at Gallipoli in March 1915.[44]

Attempting to suppress fortifications through naval gunfire alone ignored the experience of similar attempts in America, from the initial failed naval attack on

---

40 Wolseley, 'An English View of the Civil War', pp.556-57.
41 Wolseley, 'An English View of the Civil War', pp.594-97, 556. The Gallwey mission as well Innes had visited Charleston, and the naval attack on Fort Sumter was closely analysed by Jervois.
42 Wolseley, 'An English View of the Civil War', p.597.
43 Barthorp, *War on the Nile*, pp.34-35, 152, 161; Philip Ziegler, *Omdurman* (New York: Dorset Press, 1987), pp.27-28, 92-93, 140. Henderson, 'Strategy and Its Teaching', p.761 quoted the example of Alexandria, and noted the failure of the Americans to learn the same lesson in the Philippines.
44 Henderson, 'The War in South Africa', pp.253-55.

Fort Donelson on the Cumberland River in Tennessee (February 1862), through the unsuccessful naval assault on Fort Sumter in Charleston Harbour (April 1863), up to the poorly conceived and executed first assault on Fort Fisher at the entrance to the Cape Fear river at Wilmington, North Carolina, in December 1864. The latter two examples were used by the prominent British naval theorist and historian Rear Admiral (later Vice Admiral) Philip Colomb in a lecture at Aldershot on combined operations in 1891. According to Colomb, the Federal capture of enemy ports during the Civil War was a new development in warfare, which had been made possible due to the steamship, and he agreed with Wolseley's view that combined attacks were required when seizing the approaches to ports, and that naval attacks alone were a waste.[45]

Wolseley drew further conclusions from the American war on the significance of a unified military command, and the need to keep political interference with that command to a minimum. His prime example of this was a comparison of the Union and Confederate command structures in Virginia in 1864. Grant, who President Lincoln had appointed to overall command all of the Union armies, was able to coordinate and control the operation of all his forces both north and south of Richmond, whereas Lee was only able to request assistance from General Beauregard, who initially commanded the Confederate troops south of Richmond at Petersburg, as a 'coequal ally'. Grant's authority was also compared favourably with the previous situation where Major General Henry Halleck, though nominally General in Chief, had held a position 'practically that of chief of staff to Mr Lincoln'. For Wolseley, the professional soldier, the Federal failures of 1862 orchestrated by Halleck were the result of political interference with the conduct of the war.[46] By 1889 when he wrote his analysis, these opinions were likely to have been influenced, and in his mind substantiated, by what he saw as the interference and vacillation of the British government on two occasions, the peace treaty with the Boers in 1881 and more significantly the delay in sending the Gordon Relief Expedition of 1884.[47]

One further contemporary observation on the strategy of the Civil War is worth noting, both because it demonstrates British awareness of the political aspects of strategy demonstrated through the war, and because it anticipates modern debate. Chesney questioned the wisdom of the Confederacy in attacking the North, as Lee did in his campaigns of Antietam and Gettysburg, suggesting that the South had

45   Rear Admiral P.H. Colomb, *Combined Military and Naval War Operations: With Some Remarks Upon the Embarkation and Disembarkation of Troops in the Presence of an Enemy*, *Lecture to Aldershot Military Society, Tuesday November 24 1891* (Aldershot: Gale and Polden, [1891]), pp.6, 20-21. Chesney also recognised the importance of fleets in augmenting the striking power of the army, Chesney, 'Recent Changes in the Art of War' in Chesney and Reeve, *Military Resources*, p.53.
46   Wolseley, 'An English View of the Civil War', pp.742-43, 23-24.
47   Kochanski, *Sir Garnet Wolseley: Victorian Hero*, pp.111, 156-58, 171, 174-76; Luvaas, *Military Legacy*, p.49.

thereby lost its moral advantage in exchange for dubious military gain. Chesney thought that this constituted 'throwing away a great political advantage to reduce a defensive struggle for rights to the mere level of a civil war for mastery'.[48] He advocated that a purely defensive strategy was the correct approach for the weaker side, and for the Confederacy had been the 'only safe one as regarded the ultimate issue, the assertion or surrender of independence'.[49]

* * *

From the very start of the American war, transportation was seen as a key factor in the conflict, and if this was not by water then it usually meant the railway. Miller noted that in America the railway often constituted the first form of communications in remote areas, while Chesney explained to his audience that in the New World railways had acquired a 'degree of usefulness and completeness, far out of proportion, to judge by European standards, to that of the ordinary roads'.[50] Another contemporary historian wrote that the American war was the first to provide extensive insight into how railways would come to affect both strategy and tactics. They provided the capacity to convey the greatly increased volumes of troops and supplies needed to conduct a modern war, but conversely were a point of weakness due to the need to protect that capacity from interruption.[51]

Hamley has been criticised for not appreciating the importance of railways until after the Civil War, since the first edition of *Operations of War* makes little mention of them. However, Hamley had clearly identified the strategic importance of railways in America in 1863, and in 1864 he noted how McClellan had viewed railways as a new element in war, particularly the seizure of railways in the rear of the enemy points of concentration. Such use of them he described as 'obvious', and thought that McClellan's explanation had only been necessary because he (McClellan) had been explaining strategy to an amateur (Lincoln). From the second edition onwards, *Operations of War* frequently made mention of railways, using examples from both America and the European wars of the mid-century, and prompting its readers to consider how railways would have altered historic campaigns, such as Waterloo.[52]

The American Civil War was not the first time that railways had been used in war, either at battlefield or strategic level. In the 1848 they had been used for strategic troop movements during the Austro-Sardinian War and the Hungarian and

48 Chesney, 'The Military Life of General Grant', p.243.
49 Chesney, 'The Military Life of General Grant', p.243.
50 Chesney, *Virginia and Maryland*, p.8; Miller, 'Military Sketch', p.261.
51 John Cannon, *History of Grant's Campaign for the Capture of Richmond, 1864–1865, with an outline of the previous course of the American Civil War* (London: Longmans & Co, 1869), p.68.
52 Luvaas, *Education of an Army*, p.145; Hamley, 'Books on the American War', p.753; Hamley, 'General McClellan', pp.620-21; Hamley, *Operations of War*, pp.48-49.

Saxon revolutions. In 1854 the British Army had laid a railway in the Crimea between Balaclava and Sebastopol. During the Franco-Austrian War of 1859 the French had poured troops into North Italy by means of the railway, while in the same war both the French, at Montebello (May 1859), and the Austrians, at Magenta (June 1859), were credited with bringing up reinforcements in battle two years before the similar event at First Bull Run. At Magenta, the Austrians had also taken tactical advantage of the railway's impact on the topography of the modern battlefield through the use of embankments and sleepers as protection from enemy fire, anticipating their later use in America at actions such as Second Bull Run.[53]

The country that is generally considered to have most been influenced by the use of railways in the Civil War was Prussia. The organisation of the Prussian General Staff in arranging the mobilisation of their armies via railways in 1866 and 1870 was a key part of their victories over Austria and France. British authors however had not been slow to recognise the importance of this new technology even before the war in America. Perhaps most notably, the Duke of Wellington had proposed the use of railways to provide a mobile force for the defence of the south coast of England as early as 1847.[54] Their potential usefulness in the colonies had also been recognised, the difficulties that had been experienced during the Indian Mutiny led one former officer in the Royal Engineers to write

> had the Home Government appreciated what was going on in India they would have understood, in 1830, that a railway, and not an old-fashioned carriage road, was the fitting requirement as a grand trunk communication between Calcutta and the north-west of India, and a railway in that direction would have been opened, which would have enabled the Government at once to crush any Sepoy mutiny, without exposing their Europeans to long and destructive summer marches.[55]

Railways were by the 1860s an important component of troop movements within Britain. When the Guards Brigade was deployed to Canada in December 1861 as a result of the *Trent* affair, it left London early in the morning, the first train carrying the troops arrived Southampton at half past ten, and by one o'clock in the afternoon

53   Captain H.W. Tyler, 'Railways Strategically Considered', *Journal of the Royal United Service Institution*, 8 (1864), pp.321-43 (pp.325-32); Captain C.E. Luard, 'Field Railways and their General Application in War', *Journal of the Royal United Service Institution*, 17 (1873), pp.693-724; Robert Self Henry, 'Civil War Railroads' *Civil War History*, 7 (1961), pp.229-30 (p.229); Armi E. Mruck, 'The Role of Railroads in the Atlanta Campaign', *Civil War History*, 7 (1961), pp.264-71 (p.264).
54   Strachan, *Wellington's Legacy*, p.201.
55   Lieutenant Colonel J.P. Kennedy, 'The Strategic And National Importance of Extending Railway Communications Throughout The British Colonies, More Especially Throughout India', *Journal of United Service Institution*, 2 (1858), pp.62-86 (p.85).

the two transports carrying the Brigade were steaming out of harbour. In another example, given in a lecture on the use of railways by Captain H.W. Tyler RE, the Railway Commissioner at the Board of Trade, some 15,000 men of the Volunteers travelled by rail from London to the south coast of England for their Brighton review in 1863 (among a total of 132,000 passengers carried for the day), with a journey time of two and a half hours.[56]

Britain had one of the densest railway networks in the world, and because it had a near-uniform gauge as standard throughout the country, the supply of rolling stock was almost unlimited for military purposes. In the event of invasion, Tyler identi-fied that towns containing important railway junctions would be critical strategic points. However, Tyler also noted that for moving troops laterally over short distances in defence of the coast, the strategic importance of railways in Britain was much more limited than in America because the time spent embarking, disembarking, and marching to the front outweighed the savings in travelling time. With the introduc-tion of railways to strategic operations hours, not miles, became the key to strategic calculation. Works such as Wolseley's *Soldier's Pocket Book* and Hamley's *Operations of War* duly provided detailed information to enable the calculation of the amount of rolling stock needed and the time required to despatch troops by rail, the former based upon American experience.[57]

In his lecture Tyler studied in some detail the influence of railways on the course of the American Civil War up to 1863. His view was that while railways were of impor-tance to the North, they were of even greater significance to the South. The North was mostly able to link their operations to the great rivers, especially in the West, whereas without the railroad Tyler believed that the South could not have carried out operations with the scale or the success that they achieved. They were the key to any inland operations, and his opinion was that it was the South's limited resources in rails and rolling stock, resulting in difficulties providing ammunition, that largely accounted for the failure of the Confederacy to follow up victories or sustain their armies in long battles. Writing in early 1864, Tyler concluded from the operations in America up to that time that the role of railways was more significant for the defen-sive, and that they were of more limited use by an aggressor (this was a view shared by Hamley).[58] He believed that they increased the advantage of an army operating on interior lines, and that 'the most instructive and interesting episode of the whole war' was Stonewall Jackson's combination of the use of railways and marching, adding

56 Anon, 'The Guards in Canada', *Journal of the Household Brigade for the year 1862* (London: W. Clowes and Sons, 1863), pp.153-55 (p.155); Tyler, 'Railways Strategically Considered', pp.324-25; also Captain Henry W. Tyler, 'The Volunteers and National Defence', *Quarterly Review*, 112 (1892), pp.110-45 (p.142). London to Brighton is about 50 miles, and the modern rail journey is timetabled to take slightly over an hour.
57 Hamley, *Operations of War*, pp.22-24; Wolseley, *Soldier's Pocket Book*, pp.307-09.
58 Tyler, 'Railways Strategically Considered', pp.333-40, 343; Hamley, *Operations of War*, pp.47-48.

that 'locomotives must not supersede legs'.[59] Tyler believed that a single line of track could be sufficient for the supply of an army in the field, but that it was dangerous to rely upon such a precarious lifeline in hostile country. For example, he thought the Richmond, Fredericksburg and Potomac Railroad in Virginia was too vulnerable to be relied upon for the continued supply of a large army, and like Chesney concluded that this explained McClellan's Peninsular Campaign.[60]

Tyler wrote before the Federal railway organisation reached the height of its powers in Georgia in 1864, when it defied his predictions by supplying an army of 100,000 men, over a supply line of 800 miles, and over a single track through hostile territory. British writers in the years immediately after the war consistently cited, as evidence of the United States' aptitude for war, the extraordinary engineering feats carried out by the Americans 'in a manner and with a rapidity which cast all engineering works executed in previous wars entirely into the shade'.[61] Tyler reported the repair by one Federal division of 1,200 feet of bridging in ten days, and even more remarkable feats were later remarked upon such as the repair of the Chattahoochie Bridge in Georgia, 740 feet long and 90 feet high, in just four and a half days.[62]

The British also recognised that this had only been achieved through the development of a highly sophisticated logistical and engineering organisation. Ten years after Tyler gave his lecture at the Royal United Service Institute, another officer in the Royal Engineers, Captain C.E. Luard, told his audience there that '[t]he fact should be understood that the management of railroads is just as much a distinct profession as is that of the art of war.'[63] Luard talked at some length about the importance of, and the management of, railways in the Civil War, and especially in Tennessee. Quoting a report by Major General Daniel McCullum, the Military Director and Superintendent of the Union railroads, he described the creation by the Federal authorities of the Construction Corps to organise skilled workers, and to supply them with material and equipment, as being of 'paramount importance', so much so that as an appendix to the lecture Luard included a complete breakdown of this organisation. Equally important, and quoted at length, were the orders to commanding officers to give the fullest support to railway officers and quartermasters to unload trains, and giving the Superintendent of the [Rail]Road full authority for all activities along the line of communications, with any interference or negligence in either respect being

59   Tyler, 'Railways Strategically Considered', p.336
60   Tyler, 'Railways Strategically Considered', p.335.
61   J.L.A. Simmons, *Defence of Canada Considered as an Imperial Question with Reference to a War with America* (London: Longman, Green, Longman, Roberts and Green, 1865), p.25.
62   Tyler, 'Railways Strategically Considered', p.341; Luard, 'Field Railways', p.695; Colonel Sir R.A. Shafto Adair, 'The Strategy Of Invasion, As Exemplified in the American and Austro-Prussian Wars, and in the War of Metz; with Remarks on Centres of Defence and the Training of National Forces', *Journal of the Royal United Service Institution*, 16 (1872), pp.153-67 (p.162).
63   Luard, 'Field Railways', pp.696.

Military railroad bridge over the Potomac Creek, 1864. 414 feet long, it was built in just forty hours. (Library of Congress)

a dismissible offence. Luard drew three conclusions from the American war; first the importance of such an organised and disciplined corps; second the rapidity with which the railways could be maintained once it was in place, and thirdly the large number of men that the Americans had found it necessary to employ.[64]

Luard was critical of the fact that Britain, unlike her continental rivals, had no recognised department for the military management of railways, and that most of the army was ignorant of railway management. Luard described the formation of units of dedicated railway engineers in the Russian and Italian armies, but how instruction in railway construction was very limited at the School of Military Engineering. Even by the start of the Boer War the British Army only had two troops of Royal Engineers specially trained for railway operations.[65]

This did not mean that there were no plans for the control of the British railways in time of war, but they were to remain primarily in civilian hands. In 1865 the Volunteer Engineer and Railway Transport Staff Corps had been formed, this comprised civilian railway staff including General Managers, eminent engineers, and railways contractors, to assist the military in planning the use of British railways and the modifications that would be needed in the event of a defensive war. The creation of this body therefore predates the Austro-Prussian (1866) and Franco-Prussian Wars (1870-71),which are supposed to have alerted the British military to the strategic value of

---

64   Luard, 'Field Railways', pp.695-696.
65   Luard, 'Field Railways', pp.704-07; Anon (ed.), *The Times History of the [Great] War*, 22 vols (London: The Times, 1914-21), Vol.VI (1915), p.162.

railways, and it would appear to have been primarily in response to observation of the Civil War (although the Prussian government had formed a Railway Section within their general staff in 1864, which had been employed in the war against Denmark that year). The setting up of the Corps applied the lesson learnt from America that railway logistics needed to be placed in the hands of a dedicated organisation.[66] The *Regulations for Organisation of the Line of Communications of an Army in the Field* (1878) stated that 'railways are of such paramount importance in war, and their proper use is so difficult and so liable to produce confusion, that full and complete instructions are requisite'.[67] Between 1865 and 1888 the Corps managed five formal exercises, gradually doubling the scale of rolling stock used. The annual Brighton review of Volunteers also continued to demonstrate the capability of the British railway system to move large numbers of men – 23,422 Volunteers in 1888, as well as 144,606 civilian passengers.[68]

In 1888 the Corps comprised 28 members, including Myles Fenton, General Manager of the South-Eastern Railway, who had the rank of Lieutenant Colonel in the Volunteers. Speaking at the Aldershot Military Society, Fenton compared the British system with that of Germany and France. In Britain the overall authority for the railways in time of war was a committee of railway inspectors at the Board of Trade. Each railway company would have a traffic manager receiving orders from the committee, and an army officer assigned to transmit those instructions to the troops. Civilian and military authorities at individual stations similarly received instructions from the civilian traffic managers. This fell well short of the absolute military control that had been so successful in America. Although the British system meant that those involved in directing the movements of troops were railway professionals, it also depended upon the co-operation of the military and civilian authorities, the relationship between which was neither clearly defined nor understood. In Germany the railways were owned by the state, and therefore effectively under military control, which would have been unacceptable in Britain. The French railways were private, but heavily state controlled, and from 1887 railway workers were organised so as to be part of the mobilisation process in the event of war. Britain's liberal democracy meant that railway workers had no such obligation, and very few were in the Volunteers. Fenton recommended a review of the regulations governing the control of the railways, and arrangements to organise railway workers in time of war along lines similar to the French.[69]

66   Colonel J.S. Rothwell RA, 'The Conveyance of Troops by Railway', *United Service Magazine*, n.s., 4 (1891-1892), pp.215-221, 310-320, (p.216); Lieutenant Colonel Myles Fenton, Engineer and Railway Volunteer Staff Corps, *British Railways and Their Capabilities for Home Defence, Lecture to Aldershot Military Society, Thursday December 6th 1888* (Aldershot: Gale and Polden, 1888), pp.3-4.
67   Fenton, *British Railways*, p.3. I have not been able to trace the original publication.
68   Fenton, *British Railways*, p.7.
69   Fenton, *British Railways*, pp.9-17. See also Major General T.B. Collinson, 'On the Present Facilities for the Invasion of England, and for The Defence Thereof', *Journal of the Royal*

Colonel J.S. Rothwell, the Professor of Military Administration at the Staff College, similarly took a critical view of the British arrangements for rail transport. Since it was impossible to know where operations overseas might take place, like Fenton he focussed on their use in home defence. He was sceptical of the value of the statistics from the Brighton review, since they did not involve the transport of artillery and horses, which was a much more complex logistical operation than moving quantities of men. He dismissed such a deployment as 'Brighton Volunteer field day without the spectators', and thought that if resorted to in the event of an invasion it would be effectively outnumbered and outclassed by any enemy force that was capable of making a landing.[70] His strategic solution was therefore to defend the line of march to London, massing the force to do so within three days of a landing. The organisation for this would fall under the Volunteer Engineer and Railway Transport Staff Corps. Although he doubted its capacity to do this, Rothwell agreed that civilian expertise was vital. The Regulation of the Forces Act of 1871 did allow for railways to be taken possession of in the event of war or threatened invasion, but Rothwell thought it madness for the military to take over completely, and that it should be left in the hands of the railway officials. He pointed to another piece of legislation, the National Defence Act of 1888, which allowed priority to be given to military traffic on the railways under certain circumstances. The problem remained that even while the military recognised the strategic importance of the railways and the probable need to use much of their capacity in the event of a major war, there was no clear mechanism for cooperation between civilian and military authorities, a disinclination to use the compulsory powers available, and limited opportunities to trial the process. The manoeuvres of August 1898 did incorporate the use of rail transport, but less than a single corps was moved by this method.[71]

At the operational or even tactical level, Tyler's ultimate conclusion about railroads had been that it was vitally important that 'every soldier should be trained to be more or less as an engineer', and he saw a positive step in this direction from the employment of soldiers on public works at Portland and Dover, which had been directed by the Commander in Chief. Specifically, he stated that every soldier should become proficient in destroying and repairing railroads.[72] Wolseley took up this idea in the *Soldier's Pocket Book*, stating that 'it is strongly recommended that all staff officers should carefully study the construction of railways as practised in America' and including a long section upon the destruction and reconstruction of railroads based upon his

---

United Service Institution, 21 (1877), pp1-91, (pp.70-71), who described the Railway Volunteer Staff Corps as having energy and zeal, but lacking links to the military, and not being 'strategically designed'; and Rothwell, 'The Conveyance of Troops by Railway', p.319, who doubted that it had the capacity to plan complex troop movements.

70   Rothwell, 'The Conveyance of Troops by Railway', pp.311, 319.
71   Rothwell, 'The Conveyance of Troops by Railway', particularly pp.217-19, 311-12, 318-20; 'Signalman', 'The Railways and the Manoeuvres', *United Service Magazine*, n.s., 18 (1898), pp.71-81 (pp.72-73).
72   Tyler, 'Railways Strategically Considered', p.342-43.

observations of the American Civil War.[73] Wolseley noted the lack of instruction on this in Britain, and from comments made at Fenton's lecture by Major General Philip Smith, who had also been in America during the Civil War, it was still lacking in 1888. It was American rather than European construction practice that was recommended by Wolseley, because the cheap construction methods used there were more practical to the temporary construction of railroads in remote areas.[74]

This reflected the fact that action in India or Africa, rather than in Europe, was the focus of British military operations at this time. A few years after the American war ended a British expedition constructed a temporary field railway, during the Abyssinian expedition of 1867-68. 'We were the first nation that demonstrated how feasible and useful it was to do so', wrote Wolseley.[75] By American standards the line, from the coast to the Suru Pass, was short (less than 12 miles) and the duration of construction long (four months), but the railway was constructed through a salt desert where wells had to be dug to obtain water, in intense heat, with very little skilled labour. Chinese labourers were brought in for the construction, the local population not being considered strong enough for the work. In the circumstances the creation of this railway represented a significant feat by the British.[76]

* * *

The real significance of the railway in war however was not just in engineering, logistics, and administration, it was far more fundamental than this. Wolseley believed that the impact of new weapons was 'trifling' compared to the railway and the telegraph. He gave the subject of railways much thought, and anticipated them altering the very nature of war. Writing in 1873 he considered that

> the great revolution in war that has lately taken place has been that instead of armies of comparatively limited numbers being used on both sides, whole nations now take the field as in the days of Attila or of Zenghis Khan; henceforth in estimating the number of soldiers possessed by any of the great military empires, one will have merely to ascertain from its census the number of men it possesses between the ages of 20 and 36. To collect, to move, and to supply with food and military stores the huge armies thus provided, is rendered possible only by means of railways.[77]

73   Wolseley, *Soldier's Pocket Book*, p.298.
74   Wolseley, *Soldier's Pocket Book*, p.298; Fenton, *British Railways*, p.17.
75   Wolseley, *Soldier's Pocket Book*, p.298.
76   Luard, 'Field Railways', pp.698-701; Frederick Myatt, *Marching to Magdala* (London: Leo Cooper, 1970), p.91; Darrell Bates, *The Abyssinian Difficulty* (Oxford: Oxford University Press, 1979), p.130.
77   Colonel Sir G.J. Wolseley, *The Use of Railways in War: A Lecture Delivered at Aldershot on the 29th January 1873* (London: [n.pub.], 1873), p.2 (HPL, Wolseley Archive, RLY 2/1).

British base at Zoola, Abyssinia, with field railway, 1868. (Anne S.K. Brown Military Collection)

The implication was that in the future sheer manpower would determine the strength of nations. Fourteen years later, Wolseley made a further prediction which demonstrated his ongoing interest in American affairs, and also logically follows from this idea. After stating that the American war 'must be regarded as a war fully equal in magnitude to the successful invasion of France by Germany in 1870', he went on to make a comment that, while rooted in the 19th Century, looks disturbingly prophetic from the perspective of the twenty-first.

> Think what a power the re-United [*sic*] States will be in another century! May it not be in the possible future that Armageddon, the final contest between heathendom and Christianity, may be fought out between China and North America?[78]

Chesney also saw in the outcome of the Civil War evidence of the way in which technology had transformed not tactics (a subject on which he remained highly conservative), but strategy overall, and the relative strength of nations.

---

78   General Viscount Wolseley, 'General Lee', *MacMillan's Magazine*, 55 (1887), pp.321-33 (p.325). Wolseley saw the rise of China primarily in military and territorial terms due to its population, see Colonel H. Elsdale, 'The Three Ruling Races of the Future', *United Service Magazine*, n.s., 4 (1892), pp.333-344; 385-94, 473-487 (pp.336-37).

What, in short, may be read in the history of the close of the American struggle – in the utter crushing of the splendid resistance offered by the South – more striking than the lesson that the advantage of superiority in population, in manufacturing power, and material wealth is increased beyond all former belief by the new resources of the railroad and the steam fleet.[79]

Just how these factors of technology and population would affect future warfare, though, was unclear at the time. The radical politician John Bright, speaking of the Franco-Austrian conflict in Italy, had believed that warfare was becoming 'a mere mechanical mode of slaughtering your fellow-men'. His fellow radical, Richard Cobden, observed 'something in the modern development of armaments which favours the defence over attack. This must tend to prolong the war, and make the issue dependent upon the comparative strength of the resources of the contending parties'.[80]

Chesney came to a different conclusion. He expected the growing industrialisation of war to increase the rapidity with which wars would be fought, and while recognising that the weapons of war had become more destructive, predicted that the over all suffering of war would be diminished by a restriction of the length of conflicts. Steam power, by land or sea, would allow the more rapid concentration of superior forces at the decisive strategic point. Furthermore, the more perfect the system of supply, the less likely inferior forces and governments were to be able to hold out. Chesney's main example was the swift defeat of the Danes in 1864, where the rapid Prussian deployment had forced the Danes into their entrenchments, creating a siege situation that could only be won by the better supplied and equipped Prussian forces. Counterfactually, Chesney argued that the American Civil War supported this view, on the basis that had the Federal government deployed overwhelming force at the start, the South would have capitulated sooner.[81]

One British observer of the time who thought that the war being fought in America gave a different prediction of the future of modern war was George Sala, a journalist with the *Daily Telegraph*. In early 1864, through his contacts with Northern contractors provisioning the army, Sala managed to find a way around the Federal government's restrictions on foreigners visiting the Army of the Potomac. Even before Grant's Overland Campaign in the late spring of that year, and before the adoption of trench warfare at Petersburg, he painted a picture of northern Virginia as a man-made desert, 'absolutely nothing but the abomination of desolation' where the countryside had been stripped bare by the opposing armies and the towns had become purely

---

79   Chesney, 'Recent Changes in the Art of War' in Chesney and Reeve, *Military Resources*, p.52.
80   Bright in *Hansard*, Vol. 155, p.199, and letter from Cobden to [George?] Scovell, both quoted in Cecil, 'The United States as an Example', p.275.
81   Chesney, 'Recent Changes in the Art of War', in Chesney and Reeve, *Military Resources*, p.18. Chesney's words support M. D Welch's hypothesis that the Victorians expected technology to 'perfect' warfare, Welch, *Science and the British Officer*, p.69.

military camps.[82] Sala observed the destructive power of modern weapons and wrote that in modern war 'more men can be killed than in the old time; but more men can be procured to be killed, and they can hold out much longer before they are killed'.[83] He even predicted poison gas, writing that in the future 'there may be perfected processes for destroying whole brigades by noxious gases, or razing fortresses by hydraulic pressure'.[84] Sala also put the reason for this stalemate down to the railroad.

> An average army in the last generation, which, fighting a hundred miles from its base, had lost ten thousand men, was virtually ruined; but now, within a dozen hours, a dozen railway trains can reinforce it to twice the amount of its casualties.[85]

Sala's images of northern Virginia in 1864 seem to anticipate those of northern France in 1914-18, and if the American Civil War is regarded as the prototype for the First World War it may appear that Chesney and the military establishment got it wrong, and that the politicians and journalists, such as Bright and Sala, got it right. However, taking a contemporary view, the question that British commentators were trying to answer is one that many historians have tried to resolve since: why did the North, with its overwhelming resources and technological superiority, take four years to suppress the Confederacy? Geography and the superior military abilities of the South were seen as two of the factors, but a third lay in the nature of the conflict itself. The contemporary, and relatively short, wars in Europe were linked to specific geo-political ends, and once those ends were achieved the wars could be concluded by diplomacy. The conflict in America was recognised by professional military men and 'amateurs' alike to be of a completely different kind, a war in which the deeply political nature of the conflict was always seen as being of enormous significance, and one that would shape the way in which it was fought. The objective of 'ordinary war' was to secure peace on favourable terms. But Hamley, trying to deduce the basis on which the war in America was being fought, drew upon a memo written in 1861 by McClellan which stated that in this instance it was 'necessary to crush a population sufficiently numerous, intelligent, and warlike, to constitute a nation'.[86] Hamley had previously concluded that '[t]he general design is not only vast but indefinite, being nothing less than the entire subjugation of the enormous territory of the Confederacy'.[87]

82   George Sala, *My Diary in America in the Midst of War*, 2 vols (London: Tinsley Brothers, 1865), Vol.I, pp.240, 266, 269-70.
83   Sala, *My Diary in America*, Vol.I, p.393.
84   Sala, *My Diary in America*, Vol.I, p.393.
85   Sala, *My Diary in America*, Vol.I, p.391.
86   Hamley, 'General McClellan', pp.619-44; Anon, 'Topography of the Seat of War in America and Present Position of the Belligerents', *United Service Magazine*, 436 (March 1865), pp.365-72 (p.368).
87   Hamley, 'Books on the American War', p.752.

Such a conflict would almost inevitably become one of attrition. Political commentators in Britain picked up on this aspect of the war almost from the start. In 1862, Robert Cecil MP (later to become Prime Minister as Lord Salisbury), commenting upon the war in the *Quarterly Review*, predicted a war of exhaustion, but one in which he thought that the South would end up independent. Searching for historical precedents, Cecil compared the war to the successful struggles for independence of Mexico, the United Provinces, and the United States itself.[88] It was not only the South whose existence was thought to be at stake in Britain. Republicans in the North were seen as being prepared to devastate the South rather than let the Union be dismembered, and it was suggested by another British commentator that failure could mean the possible break away of New York or the Western states. He regarded Lincoln's issuing of the Emancipation Proclamation in 1862 as a pivotal event in this analysis of the conflict, signifying just how far the North was prepared to go to preserve the Union itself. His article in *Blackwood's* declared that by evoking 'the unthinkable horrors of a servile war [...t]he die is cast. Henceforth it is a war of extermination.'[89]

By late 1864 Cecil had identified a Federal strategy of attrition to break down the military power of the South, 'if every two Federals can contrive to kill one Southerner, it is clear that the surviving Federals will find no difficulty in taking possession of the devastated Southern lands'.[90] He nevertheless believed that the South would fight on due to the implications of subjugation, and that success was still a matter of who would tire first.[91] Chesney also recognised that the focus of the Federal war effort was the suppression of the enemy's means to fight rather than traditional strategic objectives. In his biographical essay on Grant, published in 1874, he observed that, after Shiloh, Grant was convinced 'that the war would never end until the Southern armies were crushed and worn down, and that they, not forts or cities or territory, should be the chief objects of the strategy which controlled the greater resources of the North'.[92]

The nature of the conflict led to the growing escalation of violence until it reached a point where reconciliation became impossible. The *Edinburgh Review* in October 1862 referred to the increasing atrocities of the war, and Fletcher bore witness to Sherman's threat of reprisals against civilians in Memphis at the end of the same year.[93] The pro-Southern, or at least anti-democratic, bias of many of the writers and publications meant that it continued to be largely Federal actions that were publicised and

---

88   Robert Cecil, 'The Confederate Struggle and Recognition', *Quarterly Review*, 112 (July 1862), pp.535-70 (pp.563-64).
89   [R.H. Patterson], 'The Crisis of the American War', *Blackwood's Edinburgh Magazine*, 92 (1862), pp.636-46 (pp.641-42, 636).
90   Cecil, 'The United States as an Example', p.257.
91   Cecil, 'The United States as an Example', pp.258-59, 269.
92   Chesney, 'The Military Life of General Grant', in *Essays in Modern Military Biography*, p.242.
93   Head, 'The American Revolution', p.584; Fletcher, 'A Run Through the Southern States', p.496.

criticised. Cecil wrote that the brutality of the war reversed recent trends in Europe, which had limited war to the contending armies, and 'rolled back for two centuries the progress which civilisation has made in taming the savage passions of mankind'.[94] Actions such as those of Grant in Virginia, Gillmore's bombardment of Charleston, Sheridan's devastation of the Shenandoah Valley, and Sherman's campaign in Georgia, were likened to the 'ruthless devastation of barbaric hordes', and what had been the 'most peace-loving, of all nations, has suddenly become the most profuse and the most recklessly martial'.[95] Sala, writing from a Northern perspective, also commented on the escalation of the conflict.

> It is idle to talk about civilisation and humanity in the complexion this contest has come to. Those agreeable but impracticable figments have long been thrown overboard. "War to the bitter end" is the Federal mot d'ordre.[96]

British armies were not guiltless of excesses during the period, as the brutality with which the Indian Mutiny was suppressed demonstrates, but the rules of 'civilised' war were regarded somewhat differently. So Hamley favourably compared McClellan to Sherman because the former had waged war against armies and not civilians.[97] A similar comparison between the eastern and western theatres was also made by Chesney, for whom the operations in Virginia in 1862 presented

> a most favourable contrast to the excesses committed in Tennessee and Alabama during the same year, when every rule by which modern generals have softened the rigours of war has been thrown aside; when soldiers have been encouraged by their officers to plunder, excess, and cruelty; and the horrors of the Thirty Years' War have been revived, to the disgrace of the boasted civilisation of our age.[98]

A critic of *The Times'* coverage of the war wrote that '[i]n our ignorance of the cause of some great foreign disturbance, we judge of it partly by the way in which it affects our interests, and partly in accordance with certain traditional prejudices'.[99] British military writers certainly laboured under a level of ignorance of the situation in America, and equally certainly based their analysis upon traditional ideas of how war should be fought. Yet allowing for the difficulty of writing about a war in a country few of them had visited, their strategic analysis shows a great deal of understanding of the contemporary problems of transportation and logistics, the inter-relationship of the different

---

94   Cecil, 'The United States as an Example', pp.270-71.
95   Cecil, 'The United States as an Example', pp.273-75.
96   Sala, *My Diary in America*, Vol.I, p.261.
97   Hamley, 'General McClellan', p.642.
98   Chesney, *Virginia and Maryland*, p.36.
99   Sir Leslie Stephen ['L.S.'], *The Times on the American War* (London: William Ridgeway, 1865), p.6.

theatres of war, and the political nature of the war. In addition, they also commented upon the industrialisation of warfare, the mass mobilisation of the populations, the emergence of a strategy of attrition, and the conflict becoming a war of survival between competing cultures that therefore resulted in the extension of violence to the civilian population and widespread economic devastation. How though could these observations be applied to the British Army and its operations?

* * *

The role of the British Army in the late 19th Century was not codified in any formal sense until the Stanhope Memorandum of 1888. Issued by the Secretary of State for War, Edward Stanhope, this document gave as the Army's objectives the support of the civil powers within the United Kingdom; the provision of garrisons for India, and for fortresses and coaling stations at home and abroad; and the ability to mobilise three corps for home defence. Subject to these considerations a further aim was to be able to despatch abroad two army corps, but 'the probability of the employment of an army corps in the field of war in any European war is sufficiently improbable to make it the primary duty of the military authorities to organise efficiently for the defence of this country'.[100]

At first sight it could be thought that there was relatively little in the experience of the American Civil War at a strategic level that had any bearing on the defence of the United Kingdom, but some military writers did try to relate the American experience to the challenge of home defence. One of these was Sir Robert Alexander Shafto Adair, *aide-de-camp* to Queen Victoria, who as the commander of a militia artillery regiment was also prominent in military circles, and who would have been involved with the defence of south-east England in the event of invasion. He gave a number of lectures on this subject to the Royal United Service Institution, and that of 1873 is notable for his suggestion that a new form of war had emerged, which he dubbed the 'Strategy of Invasion'.

> Invasion means a war of a decisive and severe character. Invasion means a war not merely to occupy military posts, or islands, or to divert the course of commerce; but, as we have seen it exemplified in later years, it means that effort of armed force which shall substitute entirely one system of government and ideas for another; or, shall leave the vanquished party so helpless that for years to come it may probably be unable to emerge from the state of humiliation and defeat in which it has been left at the close of the contest.[101]

100 Spiers, *The Late Victorian Army*, p.209; Robertson, *From Private to Field Marshal*, p.92.
101 Adair, 'The Strategy of Invasion', p.154.

Adair thought that this new style of war was exemplified not only by the Prussian campaigns in Europe, but also by the American Civil War – 'a war of unanticipated duration, a war than the results of which, none have been more conclusive'.[102] Also symptomatic of the American implementation of this style of warfare was the tremendous flexibility of the logistical organisation and the mobilisation of the country's entire economic, technical and manpower resources. Adair attributed to America a 'stupendous aptitude for the struggles of war'. What was needed was for Britain to accept the need to be prepared for war, in which case she would be perfectly capable of achieving similar feats.[103]

Looking at how the defence of Britain would be carried out at a more practical level, Adair focussed upon the defence of London. His view was that the appropriate British strategy in the event of an invasion was a combination of static defence and mobile operations. The defences would be comprised of permanent fortifications – primarily earthworks; and temporary defences, in the form of infantry trenches. Adair believed that modern firearms and artillery now enabled the Militia and Volunteer forces to man these effectively. Britain's field forces would be limited, and his expectation was that these would operate on the more open terrain to the west of the city, this manoeuvring force presumably being made up of the more highly trained and mobile Regular Army. This is similar to some of the strategies adopted in American campaigns – the Seven Days or Second Bull Run for example – but without obvious strategic equivalents in the European wars of the time.[104]

More directly, G.F.R. Henderson also used his observations of the American war as the basis for instruction on the defence of southern England. His book *The Campaign of Fredericksburg* published in 1886, which first bought him to the attention of Wolseley, was primarily written as an instructive text for Volunteer officers. Henderson had been posted to Bermuda and then Halifax, Nova Scotia, in the early 1880s. The latter posting, echoing that of the wartime observers, had given him the opportunity to visit the battlefields of Virginia and Maryland. This familiarity with the battlefields of the eastern theatre in part explains the choice of subject for his book. Henderson later wrote similar instructional texts based upon his knowledge of French battlefields, and was an exponent of staff rides during his tenure at the Staff College.[105]

---

102 Adair, 'The Strategy of Invasion', p.159

103 Adair, 'The Strategy of Invasion', p.164.

104 Adair, 'The Strategy of Invasion', p.165. See also Colonel [Shafto] Adair, 'The Lines Of London: Defences by Works And Manoeuvre in the Field', *Journal of the Royal United Service Institution*, 6 (1862), pp.521-33 (especially p.530), and Colonel Shafto Adair, 'The Defence of London', *Journal of the Royal United Service Institution*, 4 (1860), pp.291-310 for his earlier ideas on the subject. Major H. Elsdale, 'The Defence of London and of England' written in 1886, also proposed that the multiplication of defensive power using artillery, machine guns and 'appliances' to counter enemy numbers, would free the best trained and most mobile battalions to conduct a vigorous counter-offensive.

105 Luvaas, introduction to *Soldier's View*, pp.2, 5-6.

The volunteer nature of the armies involved in America was explicitly cited as a reason for Henderson's selection of the Frederickburg campaign. However, there were also clear parallels to the possible strategic scenario that might be faced by volunteer officers in south-eastern England opposing an enemy advancing upon London, in that this was a defensive campaign shielding a capital city against an invading army. Although not stated explicitly by Henderson, it is possible that he regarded the similarity extended to the type of terrain that these officers might be expected to defend. While this may seem fanciful, Henderson himself compared the country in the Shenandoah Valley to that of England, while journalist Edward Dicey in 1862 had compared Georgetown, outside Washington DC, to a northern England manufacturing town, and the countryside of northern Virginia to that near the village of Albury in Surrey. Lee's defence of the Fredericksburg position was clearly being presented by Henderson as an indication of how the defence of south-east England might need to be conducted. This included recognition of the importance of taking a strategically defensive position fortified by fieldworks, which were particularly appropriate given the wooded nature of the country.[106]

Adair did not concern himself with the defence of Britain's Imperial possessions, except to note that he thought an invasion of Canada unlikely and that it was 'perfectly defensible as long as the people of Canada are determined in their own defence'.[107] Another writer however drew very different conclusions from the American Civil War and its implications for the Empire. John Lintorn Arabin Simmons, Colonel in the Royal Engineers, one time Major General in the Ottoman Army, and later a Field Marshal and Governor of the Royal Military Academy at Woolwich, wrote a pamphlet as the Civil War drew to a close which assessed the possible threat that the re-united United States would pose to Canada, and how it could be met.[108] Simmons considered that 50,000 Canadian militia would suffice to hold Montreal or Quebec against an army the size of Grant's at Richmond, which reflects the relative tactical advantages assumed for the defensive over the offensive, but given that only 30-40,000 men would be sent from Britain in the event of war Simmons concluded the population of Canada could not hope to hold out alone against a country the size of the United States. Standing on the strategic defensive therefore reduced the war to a Canadian problem, and invited defeat. One reason cited was the vulnerability of static defences to the type of flank attacks 'so eminently successful in Sherman's advance from Chattanooga to Atlanta [...] and now again in Grant's last successful attack of the lines in front of Richmond'.[109]

---

106 Henderson's preface to *The Campaign of Fredericksburg*, in Luvaas, *Soldier's View*, p.12; Lieutenant Colonel G.F.R. Henderson, *Stonewall Jackson and the American Civil War*, 2 vols (Secaucus NJ: Blue and Grey Press, [n.d.], originally published London: Longmans, 1900), Vol.I, p.237; Dicey, *Six Months in the Federal States*, Vol.II, pp.14, 16, 25.

107 Shafto Adair, 'The Strategy of Invasion', p.164.

108 Simmons, *Defence of Canada*, pp.257-59.

109 Simmons, *Defence of Canada*, p.23.

Simmons' answer was to adopt an offensive strategy on a global scale; for the Royal Navy to carry out a blockade and pin down large numbers of American troops in local defence; to utilise the resources of the whole empire – particularly India and Australia – in an attack on the West Coast; and to accept the possibility of a large war from the outset. He was highly critical of the limited commitment that had been made at the time of the *Trent* affair. Trying to limit the initial military commitment, as had been done in 1861, would only increase the enemy's confidence while lowering one's own, and ultimately would require the same force to be committed in order to achieve a successful conclusion.[110] This lesson from America would be one that British administrations would continue to have to re-learn.

Simmons wrote anticipating a conflict that never occurred and his pamphlet is now obscure, but he was not an insignificant figure in the British military establishment, and he had a high regard for the standard which the American army had reached, considering its generals 'adept at strategy and very skilful tacticians'.[111] Like Adair, he also considered the aptitude for war in the general population a key element of the American War, resulting in the rapid construction of ships, and an ability to pass natural obstacles 'in a manner and with a rapidity which cast all engineering works executed in previous wars entirely into the shade'.[112] The strategic importance of the railroads in North America was frequently mentioned, while also notable as lessons that appear to be drawn from the Civil War are his recognition of the power of the tactical defensive, while adopting a strategic offensive based upon maritime supremacy.[113]

The most interesting element of Simmons' pamphlet is his expectation of needing to mobilise, in the event of war with a major power, the military capabilities not only of Britain but also of the Empire. This is prophetic for the Boer War and subsequently the two World Wars of the next century. Simmons also did not consider the size of the armies raised by the United States particularly daunting, comparing them to 1813, when Britain had 853,000 men under arms in a population of eighteen million. Simmons anticipated that the British Army would have to expand in the event of a war with America, but not to unprecedented numbers.[114]

Simmons underestimated the American achievement in mobilising manpower for her armies. Of course the American Civil War was not the only war in this period which saw large armies put into the field. The Battle of Sadowa (Königgrätz), fought between Austria and Prussia in July 1866, was substantially larger than any in the American Civil War, and several battles in 1870 were of similar size to the largest

110 Simmons, *Defence of Canada*, pp.9, 18-19.
111 Simmons, *Defence of Canada*, p.24
112 Simmons, *Defence of Canada*, p.24
113 Simmons, *Defence of Canada*, pp.14,16-17, 21, 24-25.
114 Simmons, *Defence of Canada*, p.18. Simmons's numbers were based upon a speech by
        Lord Castlereagh in Parliament on 11 November 1813, and included the Army, Navy and
        Militia.

seen in 1861-65. American military writer Emory Upton observed that in 1870 when Prussia fought France she had put her army on a war footing in eight days, and in a further eight days had more than 400,000 men in France, whereas it had taken the United States from April 1861 until March 1862 to do the same, at a cost of 800 million dollars.[115] Nevertheless, the overall scale of the armies seen in America as a proportion of the population was of an order not seen before. After mobilisation, it was estimated by a British writer that the major European armies in the 1870s would have had around one in 30 of their men of military age under arms. In the Civil War, according to the same writer, over three and a half million men were recruited or drafted, or one in nine of the adult male population.[116]

In Britain there was no lack of recognition that as a result of conflicts on this scale war was no longer a matter of professional armies but a matter of armed populations. This was regarded as "'essentially retrograde" but retrograde or not this is the danger against which we need to provide.'[117] An official memorandum to the Secretary of State for War on the subject of reserve forces stated that

> War in the present day means a trial of national strength which cannot be tested by the contact of standing armies only, nor entered upon without the sanction of those who are actually to fight, embracing as it does the whole male population of the nation.[118]

The British Army of the day was substantially larger both in absolute numbers and in numbers per head of population than the US Army had been in 1861, but in comparison to its European rivals and in common with its American counterpart it had a similar problem: the lack of an immediate reserve that would be needed to enable it to match the numbers that could be mobilised by a continental army. Upton considered the non-expansive organisation of the British Army as a significant defect of the English system. With nearly half of the Regular army in India, only 100,000 regulars were left to defend England. Had one of the invasion scares of the period actually

115 Peter S. Michie, *Life and Letters of Emory Upton* (New York: Arno Press, 1979, originally published 1885), p.387.

116 Captain J.C. Ardagh, 'The Comparative Cost of the Armies of Different Nations and the Loss to Country by Conscription', *Journal of the Royal United Service Institution*, 20 (1876), pp.218-52 (pp.232-33). By 1914 both France and Germany were nearing the levels of mobilisation seen in the Civil War, with one in ten Frenchmen and one in thirteen Germans having some form of military training, M.A. Ramsay, *Command and Cohesion: The Citizen Soldier and Minor Tactics in the British Army, 1870-1918* (Westport CN: Prager, 2002), p.54

117 Henry William Lovett Hime, *Royal United Service Institution Prize Essay: Universal Conscription: The Only Answer to the Recruiting Question* (London: W. Mitchell, 1875), p.25, quoting Professor Cairnes' *Political Essays* (no further details).

118 TNA, WO 33/22/453, Lieutenant Colonel F. Robertson Aikman, untitled memorandum to Secretary of State for War, undated [c. November 1875], pp.4A-4B.

come about, unlikely though that may have been in view of the strength of the Royal Navy compared to its foreign rivals, the defence of the nation would have relied to a considerable extent on the part-time soldiery of the Militia and the Volunteers, and the performance in battle of newly formed and trained volunteer armies that had been seen in America was therefore of significant interest to the British.[119]

The Volunteer movement in Britain predated the American Civil War. It had emerged in response to the French invasion fears of 1858-59, which occurred when the army was still committed to the suppression of the Indian Mutiny, and also because the state of the Militia was judged to be poor. While the Militia were largely drawn from the agricultural labouring class in the counties, the ranks of the Volunteers, who provided their own arms, were filled by more prosperous individuals. By 1861 there were approximately 161,000 registered volunteers, although only half of these might be considered 'efficient' (an official term for Volunteers who had reached a certain level of proficiency, usually through attending a set number of drills). A little like the American state troops they fell under military command, through the Lords Lieutenants of each county, but remained independent of the regular army.[120] There was throughout the period some hostility in the British military press to the Volunteers, and doubts as to their usefulness. The evidence of the performance of volunteers of different nationalities in battle was regarded as mixed. They had been successful under Garibaldi in Italy in 1859, and in some colonial operations such as in New Zealand. However, Garibaldi's defeat by a Papal-French Army at Mentana in November 1867, and the later failure of the French *Garde Mobile* in the Franco-Prussian war, indicated that they could not stand up to regular forces. The rout of First Bull Run was seen as the likely fate of British volunteers facing battle for the first time.[121]

> Those among ourselves who know most of war are agreed that, however highly one may think of the spirit of the levies we call our Auxiliary forces, there is no ground whatever, beyond a vulgar national vanity, for the common belief that a mass of these, once beaten and panic stricken, would show conduct very different from that of McDowell's volunteers in 1861, or of the Mobiles of the Army of the Loire ten years later. 'Nations deceive themselves very much in this matter of their untrained troops'.[122]

119   Upton, *Armies*, p.268. Hime, *Universal Conscription*, p.23, states that of 194,227 men in the regular army in 1873, 62,844 were in India and 103,618 in Britain, of the latter only 62,334 were infantry. The lack of a reserve was not a new problem and earlier reforms had been attempted to solve it, see Strachan, *Wellington's Legacy*, pp.70-74, 204-11.

120   Tyler, 'The Volunteers and National Defence', pp.110-13; Colonel Willoughby Verney, *The Military Life of HRH George, Duke of Cambridge* (London: John Murray, 1905), pp.272-74; Fortescue, *History of the British Army*, Vol.XIII, pp.520-21.

121   Beckett, *The Amateur Military Tradition*, p.180; Beckett, *Riflemen Form*, pp.177-78.

122   Charles Cornwallis Chesney, 'A Memoir of General Lee' in *Essays in Modern Military Biography*, pp.357-414 (p.374-5) (a review of *Life of General Robert E Lee* by John Esten Cooke originally published in *Edinburgh Review*, 137 (April 1873) pp.363-398). The

A report in 1870 considered that although a million men had passed through their ranks, the majority of the Volunteers were still little better than raw recruits.

> Constituted as the force is, without the commonest principles of cohesion, or the establishment of a chain of responsibility and control from the higher to the lower grades, it would afford no substantial assistance to the Army in the presence of an enemy, but, on the contrary, might contribute to defeat and disaster.[123]

Another critic a few years later described the Volunteers in language usually attributed to European opinions of American Civil War armies, as 'a military mob', whose only reason for existence was 'the gratification of our national vanity', and predicted harmful effects from filling the country with 'mock colonels and majors who, if an invasion did take place, would cause incalculable harm by the tenacity with which they would cling to their relative rank'.[124] No reference was made to the Civil War here, but regular British officers clearly feared the influence of political and amateur officers such as had been seen in America. Lieutenant Colonel Henry Malet of the Grenadier Guards, who had visited the Northern army at Fredericksburg, had subsequently retired from his regiment in 1870 and joined a battalion of metropolitan Volunteers. He reported that on his arrival command had been an impossibility due to 'a system of committees', which appears to have been the British cultural equivalent of the American system of electing officers, and which Malet immediately suppressed even though it led to some resignations. The moral that Malet took from this tale echoes his observation from 1862 on the handling of volunteers, that they needed to be treated in the same way as regular troops, and that they should be commanded by regular officers.[125]

The wars in which Britain might be engaged differed from the context of an American War of Secession. In broad terms the British Army anticipated two types of war. The

---

final quotation, in Chesney's original text, was a remark by the commander of the Swiss Army. Ten years earlier, in *A Military View of Recent Campaigns in Virginia and Maryland* (footnote, p.13), Chesney had however rated the British volunteers as 'infinitely the superior' of American Militia, French National Guard or even Prussian reserves.

123 WO 33/22/453, Aikman memo, p.13; see also ibid, p.7.

124 Hime, *Universal Conscription*, p.24. The popular story that von Moltke described the American armies as 'armed mobs' is possibly apocryphal (see Dmitri Rotov, 'von Moltke's Armed Mobs', *Civil War Bookshelf* (11 March 2008),<http://cwbn.blogspot. co.uk/2008/11/richard-f.html> [accessed 16 August 2015], but British writers did use the term. For example Chesney, wrote of the Union Army in 1861 as being akin to 'an armed and dangerous mob', Chesney, *A Military View of Recent Campaigns in Virginia and Maryland*, p.14, quoted by Jay Luvaas, 'Through Foreign Eyes', p.139; also Lieutenant Colonel Henry Charles Fletcher, *Memorandum on the Militia System of Canada* (Ottawa: [n.pub.], 1873), p.7 'during the first campaign [in the Civil War] the troops were little better than armed mobs'.

125 George H. Hoste, 'The Further Development of the Volunteer Force', *Journal of the Royal United Service Institution*, 21 (1877), pp.799-820 (p.819).

first would take place abroad against an opponent from which there was little or no fear of invasion, and required a 'first reserve' of men who were obliged to serve abroad. The second involved a war against a power who might have the naval resources to temporarily gain possession of the English Channel and invade, this was the option in which the use of a 'second reserve' of militia and local troops was expected.[126] One difference in the latter scenario between volunteers in America and those in Britain was that whereas the American armies had been fighting similarly raised and equally inexperienced troops, it was expected that an invasion of Britain would be conducted by the elite of a professional European army, and that the British volunteer soldiers would not be trained well enough to resist. The strategy and tactics of the Civil War became reflected in British ideas about the use of volunteer troops under these conditions. The target for an invasion was expected to be the capital, just as it had been in Virginia. The forces available to defend London were reckoned to be around 50,000 regular troops, backed up by 50,000 Militia and 100,000 Volunteers. In the absence of expensive permanent works to defend London, it was envisaged that successive lines of concentric field entrenchments would be used to offset a lack of numbers and training. The railway network would, as in America, dictate the lines of attack and defence, and would be used to bring in reinforcements, move troops and create defensive lines based upon key communication hubs. Volunteers, field entrenchments, and railways were all seen as part of the overall strategic solution, and again the comparison to the campaigns in Virginia are striking.[127]

Colonel Henry Fletcher, an observer in 1862 and the author of the *History of the American War*, published in 1865-66, looked beyond the defence of England to how the British army could fight abroad, either in defence of her colonies or in the form of an expeditionary force. Fletcher recognised that a future European war would not be on a small scale. The armies engaged would be of vast size and approximate to militia rather than to the regular armies previously seen. If Britain fought a European war every able-bodied man in the opposing nations would need to be under arms, and it would be necessary for Britain to employ every resource. His solution to the problem, noting that historically powerful nations had recruited from all ranks of society, was to tap two hitherto unrealised national resources of manpower, the middle classes and the great colonies.[128]

With his experience in North America, Fletcher naturally used the Civil War as evidence for his arguments. He observed that an army formed from 'a class similar to

126   TNA, WO 33/17A/306, J. Peel, untitled memorandum on Army Reserves (December 1866).
127   Verney, *Military Life of HRH George, Duke of Cambridge*, p.275; Sir Francis Boyd Head, *The Royal Engineer* (London: John Murray, 1869), p.353; Tyler, 'The Volunteers and National Defence', p.143-45; Colonel [Sir R.A. Shafto] Adair, 'The Lines Of London: Defences by Works And Manoeuvre in the Field', *Journal of the Royal United Service Institution*, 6 (1862), pp.521-33 (p.530-31).
128   Fletcher, *Militia System of Canada*, pp.7-8; Colonel Henry Charles Fletcher, 'A Volunteer Force, British and Colonial in the Event of War', *Journal of the Royal United Service Institution*, 21 (1877), pp.631–58 (p.637, p.645). Hereafter Fletcher, 'Volunteer Force'.

that which forms our volunteers, may be found in the troops of the Southern States of America, that commenced the war with the victory of Bull Run'.[129] Companies that had been raised in the South included wealthy men who had taken service in the ranks. Once these men had been blooded in combat, they had recruited more troops and taken up appointments themselves as NCOs and officers. This reflected ideas that Fletcher had developed in Canada that the active and reserve Militias were the 'real army', while a professional cadre of officers should exist for training.[130] He did not only look to the South as his model. 'In a minor degree (as the war at its commence-ment was less national) the Northern States furnished regiments composed of men who could compare with those who fill the ranks of the best of our volunteer regi-ments', and he referred to having frequently seen a New York regiment composed of wealthy recruits undertaking siege work 'remarkably well'.[131]

While this clearly shows the social prejudices of the age, Fletcher was neverthe-less seeking to modernise the composition of the British Army. The purpose of his argument was to mobilise the 'middle strata of our society', who could be found in the ranks of the Volunteers but not in those of the regular army or the Militia, which were raised from the 'poorer classes' (or as another author less charitably put it, 'the dregs of the people').[132] Continental systems such as the Prussian achieved this through conscription, but Fletcher believed that 'the volunteer system and the responsibility thrown upon the officers and men for their efficiency appears to suit the English race'.[133]

Moreover, Fletcher did not anticipate a purely defensive war. Unlike Henry Tyler, for example, who saw the Volunteers as a home defence force, whose only contribu-tion to the projection of power was through bolstering public morale and freeing up regular troops to serve abroad, Fletcher proposed the integration of small numbers of Volunteer troops into an expeditionary force.[134] To do this he proposed a special roll of Volunteers prepared to serve overseas in the event of war. A mere two percent of the 165,000 men enrolled would give a brigade of 3,500, which Fletcher would have integrated into the regular expeditionary force. A defect of the American system, in Fletcher's view, had been that volunteers did not serve alongside regulars which would have improved their training and efficiency. He placed 'great stress on the necessity for this description of force being limited to a small proportion only of the army' since 'nothing can compensate for any want of the elements of stability, which disci-pline, training, and, I may add, professional instincts, can alone ensure'.[135] Reflecting

129 Fletcher, 'Volunteer Force', p.639.
130 Fletcher, 'Volunteer Force', p.639; Fletcher, *Militia System of Canada*, p.8.
131 Fletcher, in discussion on Hoste's lecture at the Royal United Service Institution, 13 April 1877, Hoste, 'The Further Development of the Volunteer Force', p.820.
132 Fletcher, 'Volunteer Force', p.634; Hime, *Universal Subscription*, p.17.
133 Fletcher, *Militia System of Canada*, p.15.
134 Tyler, 'The Volunteers and National Defence', p.123; Fletcher, 'Volunteer Force', pp.635-38.
135 Fletcher, 'Volunteer Force', p.639.

his friend Henry Malet's view of 1862, the Volunteers would be subject to the same military discipline as the regulars, subject to the Mutiny Act, and with the same regulated pay and allowances.[136]

In 1872 Fletcher had taken the position as private secretary to Lord Dufferin, who had been appointed Governor General of Canada. One of his tasks had been to develop the Canadian military in order that Canada could contribute more to her own defence.[137] In doing so Fletcher had looked to the American model of a small regular force to provide officers supplemented by the militia, believing that this was the correct application of the European principles of large armies within the social structure in North America. The Canadian Militia had similarities with both the Militia and the Volunteers back in Britain. Canadians were believed, due to their occupations and way of life, to have the qualities to make good soldiers, and Fletcher pointed to Wolseley's Red River campaign of 1869 and to Denison's activities against the Fenians in 1866 as evidence of this. He had lectured in Ottawa in 1873 on how the Canadian militia should be organised for local defence, and in 1877 he anticipated the events of 1914 by proposing that Canada, though not Australia which he thought too remote, should provide manpower to Britain in the event of a European war.[138]

Perhaps influenced by his observations in America and the problems of political officers, Fletcher also warned against 'ambitious men raising companies and regiments in order to obtain commissions' and would have forbidden any but efficient Volunteers to enrol in his expeditionary brigade.[139] He had observed in Canada that short service recruits need highly educated officers and trained NCOs, and he proposed mainly ex-officers to lead the Volunteers, likening them to the men who had formed and led Indian irregulars.[140]

In 1879, two years after Fletcher's proposal for Canadian troops to be used in Europe, Sir Patrick MacDougall became Commander of British troops in Canada. In response to concerns over the threat of war with Russia, MacDougall and the Canadian government did indeed offer to furnish a Canadian contingent.[141] MacDougall's recommendation was for a Military Reserve of 10,000 men, separate from the militia and volunteers, who would not only be liable for colonial service but would serve anywhere in the world. The offer was repeated again the following year by the Canadian Prime Minister Sir John A. MacDonald, in giving evidence to the

136 Fletcher, 'Volunteer Force', pp.641.
137 Richard A. Preston, entry for Henry Charles Fletcher in *Dictionary of Canadian Biography Online:* <http://www.biographi.ca/en/bio/fletcher_henry_charles_10F.html> [accessed 5 April 2015].
138 Fletcher, *Militia System of Canada*, p.7; Fletcher, 'Volunteer Force', p.644.
139 Fletcher, 'Volunteer Force', pp.638-639.
140 Fletcher, *Militia System of Canada*, pp.7-8; Fletcher, 'Volunteer Force', p.640.
141 Jay Luvaas, 'General Sir Patrick MacDougall, The American Civil War and the Defence of Canada', *The Canadian Historical Association*, (June 1962), pp.45-54 (pp.53-54) (reprint held in Kings College London, Liddell Hart Archive, 15/1/39).

Royal Commission on the Defence of British Possessions and Commerce Abroad, considered to be the first scheme for systematic Imperial Defence.[142] There does not appear to be direct evidence that Fletcher's ideas influenced MacDougall's offer, but the timing is suggestive. A further connection to the Civil War was the presence on the Commission of Sir Lintorn Simmons, who had written the pamphlet proposing an Imperial solution to the problem of defending Canada. Simmons, like Fletcher, was in favour of trained officers to lead MacDougall's reserve, commenting that in the Civil War the best officers had been those with a West Point education.[143]

Wolseley also looked to America for indications of how volunteers would perform in war. In some of his writings he appeared to share the professional soldier's prejudices against the amateur volunteers. From the failings of the US military early in the war, he concluded that an improvised civilian army could not achieve great military success quickly. He was critical of the impatience of the American politicians, which drove weak generals into premature action, and believed that regular troops backed by a good staff would have exploited victory better, resulting in fewer indecisive actions, and would not have been surprised as Grant and Sherman had been at Shiloh.[144]

Wolseley nevertheless saw that Britain would need to create a large army in the event of a war against some of its potential opponents, and also turned his attention to this in 1878 when war with Russia seemed possible. In a paper on the subject he referred to the United States raising large numbers of militia and volunteers during the Civil War as evidence that Britain could do so as well. He based this view upon the volunteer system and the natural 'martial spirit' of the English, something 'that did not exist in the Northern States of America in 1862'.[145] He proposed that the rank and file should enlist for 12 years but only be with the colours for three years or the duration of the war, avoiding the problems America had experienced with men's terms of enlistment expiring while on campaign. He also proposed that the additional troops raised would be added to existing regiments, retaining the *esprit de corps*, rather than creating new formations.[146] This principle had been recommended by Sherman as a result of the Civil War, and would be used in the British Army in the First World War, through the process of adding new battalions to the Regular and Territorial battalions that already existed within the regiments.[147] In order to find officers with military experience to direct the greatly increased army Wolseley suggested that those who had retired following the

---

142 Alice R. Stewart, 'Sir John A. Macdonald and the Imperial Defence Commission of 1879', *Canadian Historical Review*, 35-2 (June 1954), pp.119-139 (pp.119, 130, 133-34).

143 Stewart, 'Sir John A. Macdonald and the Imperial Defence Commission of 1879', p.138.

144 Wolseley, 'General Sherman', p.199; Wolseley, 'General Lee', p.327.

145 TNA, WO 147/49, Major General G.J. Wolseley, untitled confidential memo on war between Britain and Russia, 30 March 1878, p.2

146 TNA, WO 147/49, Wolseley Memo, p.5.

147 General William Tecumseh Sherman (USA), *Memoirs*, 2 vols (New York: Appleton, 1875), Vol.II, p.387-88; Fortescue, *History of the British Army*, Vol.XIII, p.572.

abolition of the purchase system in 1871 under the Cardwell reforms could resume their commissions.[148]

Not everyone who had observed the American armies in action concluded that the volunteer system was the best solution for establishing a reserve for the British Army. Henry Malet considered that without conscription Britain could never have an effective reserve. His reasons reflect the observations he made during the war on the limitations of volunteers regarding discipline.

> All men of the military age are morally as much bound to serve the State in war, as to obey its laws but to serve it efficiently they must have learnt discipline and the use of arms, not as Volunteers only, but, as on the Continent, in the ranks.[149]

Recognising the numbers of militia and volunteers that could be put in the field by Britain, Malet questioned how this force would be armed, supplied, organised, administered, and, perhaps most significantly, officered. While suggesting that sooner or later conscription would need to be adopted, he went on to propose how the existing Volunteer organisation could be organised on regional grounds. Like other writers recommending ways of defending Britain, Malet saw the railway network as essential to the concentration of the volunteer forces and the distribution of supplies.[150]

Even though both North and South had finally resorted to some form of conscription, the example of America could still be used by its opponents. One such author denied the need for the draft in favour of the volunteer principle.

> [D]uring the struggle for existence in America during which 3,700,000 men were under arms on both sides, (about one ninth of the entire population), there was *no* time that a substitute could not be procured, although the price sometimes ran very high. It was enthusiasm and patriotism which bought the best men in America into the army, and not the complication of the draft.[151]

The conclusion of this author was that small cadres of regulars and large volunteer reserves might render a resort to conscription unnecessary. An earlier official memorandum had also suggested that a cadre system would be better than a large number of

---

148 WO 147/49, p.2.
149 Lieutenant Colonel Henry Malet, 'Our Reserve Forces', *Journal of the Royal United Service Institution*, 20 (1869), pp.160-80 (pp.162-63).
150 Malet, 'Our Reserve Forces', pp.168, 177; Major Arthur Leahy, 'Army Organisation, our Infantry Forces and Infantry Reserves', *Journal of the Royal United Service Institution*, 12 (1868), pp.310-58 (pp.335-36); Rothwell, 'The Conveyance of Troops by Railway', pp.310-17.
151 Ardagh, 'The Comparative Cost of the Armies of Different Nations', pp.233-34. Original italics.

poorly drilled men.[152] These views are interesting to compare again to those of Emory Upton. He also regarded regular troops as superior to both militia and volunteers, and supported both a cadre system and a regional system of territorial districts, ideas which can be seen in contemporary British thought. Upton however thought conscription the best means of providing the reserve that supported the regular cadres, along the German practice, while also recognising that it was unacceptable to American society.[153]

One supporter of the volunteer principle had actual experience of fighting in the Civil War. William Watson was a Scottish businessman in Baton Rouge at the start of the war who had enlisted in the Confederate service and served in the 3rd Louisiana Regiment. In 1887 he published his memoirs of his experiences, in part because he thought that they

> may be of interest in showing something of the utility of the Volunteer system, and how a nation may be strengthened in time of necessity and large and effective armies raised upon that system, and also in relating a test of the experience of citizen soldiers and their capabilities in actual warfare.[154]

Watson dedicated his work to Colonel John Scott, commander of the local volunteer artillery battery, who he thought typified the involvement of the British industrial and commercial classes, and their commitment to the military defence of the country.[155]

Watson suggested that the European systems of conscription would become unsustainable as popular government extended throughout the continental powers, and that the British and American system of volunteers would become 'the strong arm of all civilised nations'.[156] He was referring here not to the enlistment system of the regular service but to an army 'composed not of the residuum of society but rather of the elite', the middle classes who were patriotic and diligent enough to undergo military training but not prepared to abandon other pursuits or personal freedoms in time of peace.[157] Such an army, well drilled and skilled in arms, would display pride in their corps and country and not abandon the field in panic when defeated. Compulsory service, in Wilson's view, could not produce the same level of *morale* as that generated by a volunteer system, writing that his regiment had retained their volunteer status in 1862 rather than accepting conscription since 'as conscripts they would be serfs'.[158]

152 Ardagh, 'The Comparative Cost of the Armies of Different Nations', p.234; WO 33/22/453, Aikman memo, pp.7-8.

153 Russell F. Weigley, *Towards an American Army* (New York, London: Columbia University Press, 1962), pp.101, 105, 118, 123-24.

154 William Watson, *Life in the Confederate Army: Being the Observations and Experiences of an Alien in the South during the American Civil War*, ed. by Thomas W. Cutrer (Baton Rouge and London: Louisiana State University Press, 1995), p.viii.

155 Watson, *Life in the Confederate Army*, p.iii.

156 Watson, *Life in the Confederate Army*, p.135.

157 Watson, *Life in the Confederate Army*, p.135.

158 Watson, *Life in the Confederate Army*, p.358.

To those critics of the Volunteers who could only see merit in parade ground drill, he described the success of his own regiment in overcoming a battalion of US regulars at the Battle of Oakhill (Wilson's Creek, Missouri) in August 1861, which he ascribed to superior marksmanship and to the regulars using rigid close order formations. Watson concluded his work by saying that volunteers were more resilient in defeat than regulars, and that the most striking feature of the Civil War was the success of the volunteer system in raising a large and effective army in such a short space of time.[159]

F.N. Maude characteristically drew upon both Germany and America as models for his opinions in the debate between voluntary and compulsory service. Describing the Volunteers as the 'military school of the nation' he was critical of a specialist professional army and long service in time of peace.[160] This ran counter to the prevailing thought in the War Office, which did not like three-year enlistments because they were not efficient to train troops for use in small wars.[161] Maude was more interested in countering the threat of invasion, which he thought remote but not impossible. He saw the wars of Prussia in 1866 and 1870 as vindication of the short-term principle and universal service, which led to a higher level of intelligence in the Prussian ranks, and higher standards amongst the officers who had to train them. In comparison with European armies Maude also thought that Britain was closer to the German model, with its aristocratic elite, than to France's more professional officer corps.[162]

From this it might be expected that Maude would support conscription, but he then drew on American experience to support voluntary service and argue against a conscript army. The Civil War provided Maude with evidence that volunteer armies could fight with high levels of efficiency even when raised 'under every conceivable disadvantage of time and circumstance'.[163] Maude was particularly concerned with the ability of troops to sustain casualties, which he saw as key to battlefield success under modern conditions, and he used the Irish Brigade at Fredericksburg, Pickett's Division at Gettysburg, and the 1st Maine Heavy Artillery at Spotsylvania as examples of the resilience of relatively raw volunteers and their capacity to undergo punishment. In comparison, when the ballot was introduced, Maude wrote, the fighting value of the armies fell away. There was a 'closer resemblance that exists between our own race and our cousins across the Atlantic than between ourselves and any other nation on the continent' and Maude concluded that the military evidence was against compulsion.[164]

159 Watson, *Life in the Confederate Army*, pp.215-17, 453.
160 Captain F.N. Maude, *Voluntary Versus Compulsory Service: An Essay* (London: Edward Stanford, 1897), p.xi.
161 Halik Kochanski, 'Field Marshal Viscount Wolseley as Commander in Chief, 1895–1900: A Reassessment', *Journal of Strategic Studies*, 20 (1997), pp.119–39 (p.127).
162 Maude, *Voluntary Versus Compulsory Service*, pp.63, 76, 116.
163 Maude, *Voluntary Versus Compulsory Service*, p.77.
164 Maude, *Voluntary Versus Compulsory Service*, pp.77-78.

G.F.R. Henderson was critical of the value of the British non-regular forces by 1899, pointing to the poor showing of militia units in South Africa and their lack of training in skirmishing, outpost work, and scouting. The value of volunteers he also thought low due to their limited training, though this was offset by their higher intelligence.[165] Yet he too was not in favour of conscription, citing the South African War, as well as the Peninsular War and the American Civil War, as evidence of 'the triumph for the principle of voluntary service', and the superior moral of volunteers to conscripts.[166] He later wrote that 'the War of Secession affords the most ample evidence of the truth of the old proverb that one volunteer is worth three pressed men'.[167] Henderson criticised conscripts as more prone to panic, less forward in attack, less stubborn in defence, and more prone to insubordination, and singled out a Confederate regiment that had broken at Fredericksburg by identifying them as conscripts.[168]

The relevance of American experience to discussion on the effectiveness of volunteers has the same characteristics as other issues where the Civil War was used by British writers to support their own views. There were certain clear parallels with British problems which led to common solutions, such as the use of field entrenchments and railways, which did take account of American lessons even where not explicitly acknowledged as doing so. There were also differences in the strategic situation – principally the need to either send the expanded army abroad or to plan against invasion by a continental standing army and its system of conscripted reserves – that meant American practices were seen as less relevant, particularly after 1870. Those with experience of or an ongoing interest in America, such as Fletcher, Wolseley, Maude, and Henderson, still saw the racial and cultural ties between the two nations as significant and therefore of relevance to the British situation. Britain held faith in the volunteer system in contrast to European practice, and over 230,000 volunteers served in the Boer War, well in excess of the small number envisaged by Fletcher as supporting the regulars in an overseas war.[169] Only the enormous demands on manpower in the First World War finally forced the adoption of conscription.

*   *   *

The extreme nature of the American war was also seen to be of relevance as a parallel with colonial wars. At the end of the century Spenser Wilkinson, the influential

---

165 Henderson, 'The British Army', in *Science of War*, pp.422-24.
166 Henderson, 'Foreign Criticism', in *Science of War*, p.379.
167 Henderson, 'The British Army', in *Science of War*, p.385.
168 Henderson, 'The British Army', in *Science of War*, pp.422-24; Henderson, 'Campaign of Fredericksburg', in Luvaas, *Soldier's View*, p.79. A detailed footnote by Luvaas challenges Henderson's view of the unit in question, Orr's Regiment of Rifles.
169 Stephen M. Miller, *Volunteers on the Veldt* (Norman: University of Oklahoma Press, 2007), p.48, gives 230,785. Thomas W. Cutrer, in his introduction to Watson, *Life in the Confederate Army*, pp.1-16 (p.16) gives a much higher number of 288,470.

military correspondent for the London *Morning Post*, compared the Federal war aims directly with those of the British in South Africa. The Boers' struggle was portrayed by Wilkinson as a mirror to that of the South. Underpinned by the suppression of the black population, which echoed slavery, the Boers were similarly fighting for their independence, and had the same advantage of defending their own soil. In Wilkinson's analysis, the British were the party fighting for personal freedom, just as the North had been the true champions of freedom in the American War, and the Boers had underestimated the British determination in this fight just as the South had unsuccessfully relied upon Northern exhaustion to obtain victory. Since the American struggle was 'one of those which could only be terminated by the military annihilation of the adversary', Wilkinson correctly predicted in June 1900 that the South African war would also become one of extreme measures, and that the Boers would resort to guerrilla warfare.[170]

Another writer on South Africa turned again to McClellan's memo of 1861 to demonstrate the parallels between the American Civil War and the British position in South Africa in 1900.

> The object of the present war differs from those in which nations are usually engaged, mainly in this: that the purpose of ordinary war is to conquer a peace and make a treaty on advantageous terms. In this contest it has become necessary to crush a population sufficiently numerous, intelligent and warlike, to constitute a nation. We have not only to defeat their armed and organised forces in the field, but to display such an overwhelming strength as will convince all our antagonists of the utter impossibility of resistance. Our late reverses make this course imperative, had we been successful in the recent battles it is possible that we might have been spared the labour and expense of a great effort.[171]

These words of McClellan's in 1861 provided an accurate description of the situation that the British found themselves in at the end of 'Black Week' in December 1899. The writer, Major E.S. Valentine, elaborated on this with a list of the similarities between Britain and the North at the start of the respective conflicts, high among them being: overconfidence; the fault of underestimating the enemy but at the same time over-estimating enemy numbers; the natural military capabilities of their opponents at an individual level; a lack of scouting and adequate maps; and the lack of mobility due to inferior numbers of cavalry.[172]

---

170 Spenser Wilkinson, 'The American Civil War and the South African Affair', in *War and Policy: Essays* (Westminster, UK: Constable, 1900), pp.422-39 (p.429), originally printed in the *Contemporary Review*, June 1900.

171 E.S. Valentine, 'An American Parallel to the Present Campaign', *Fortnightly Review*, n.s., 17 (1900), pp.660-67 (p.660). The quote is from McClellan on 4 August 1861; Valentine cites that it is taken from *Records of the Rebellion*, Vol.II. The modern reference is OR Series 1, Vol.5, p.6.

172 Valentine, 'An American Parallel to the Present Campaign', pp.662-66.

We believe that a greater interest may pertain not only to the exhibition of parallels between tactical and strategic details, but to the extraordinary similitude
of the one general situation to the other in the opening months of the war.
Seemingly, the lesson of the earlier strife has failed to teach the great British
nation many things it might have learnt.[173]

While Valentine was perhaps the first commentator to directly state that the British
had failed to learn from the American war, he was rather too keen to find parallels
between the two conflicts, and to find similarities between the Boers and the South.
For example he made the rather dubious assertion that the Confederate generals
adopted defensive tactics based upon the prowess of the individual soldier – 'tactics
the Union commanders had yet to learn' and therefore by inference tactics the British
also needed to learn from the Boers.[174] Both Victorian and modern authorities have
identified the Confederate generals as being equally if not more likely to adopt offensive tactics as their Federal counterparts.[175]

In fact G.F.R. Henderson, the most eminent student of the American Civil War
at the time, had noted immediately prior to the Boer War that 'it is difficult to
bring strategy into play against enemies who have no vulnerable or vital points, no
lines of communication, no capitals, no fortresses, and no bases of operations, and
who move with the rapidity of cavalry'.[176] At the same time he had urged that the
study of strategy, and in particular the strategy of the Civil War, was of relevance
to the British officer. In 1898 Henderson completed his major work, *Stonewall
Jackson and the American Civil War*: just as *The Campaign of Fredericksburg* had been
written as an instructional text for volunteer officers, so *Stonewall Jackson* was in
part a treatise on Henderson's theories of war.[177] Henderson's supposed weakness
was his concentration on the campaigns in the East. However, if his writings are
considered as educational works for the British officer, there is logic behind his
choice of subject. One of Britain's main strategic constraints was the numerical
weakness of the British Army compared to its potential opponents, and a key strategic challenge was how it could defeat a superior enemy. The operations of Lee and
Jackson in Virginia were used as an example of how the concentration of numbers
on the battlefield, the selection of strong positions and entrenchment, the use of
surprise, and the effect of *morale* could offset superior numbers. While Henderson
was therefore appreciative of the talents of the Northern generals, for him the

173 Valentine, 'An American Parallel to the Present Campaign', p.667.
174 Valentine, 'An American Parallel to the Present Campaign', pp.663-64.
175 Hamley, 'Books on the American War', p.764; for a modern view see Grady McWhiney
     and Perry D. Jamieson, *Attack and Die: Civil War Military Tactics and the Southern Heritage*
     (Tuscaloosa: University of Alabama Press, 1990, originally published 1982).
176 Henderson, 'Strategy and its Teaching', in *Science of War*, p.767-71.
177 Henry Brackenbury, 'Stonewall Jackson', *Blackwood's Edinburgh Magazine*, 164 (1898),
     pp.721-38 (p.721).

experiences of the Confederacy, being the weaker side, were more relevant for the British Army at the end of the 19th Century, and this drove his choice of subject.[178] The relevance of manoeuvre and counter-attack for the smaller army was explicitly stated in a passage that has distinct parallels to the situation facing the British Expeditionary Force in 1914.

> The enemy is permitted to advance and pushes forward in the hope of winning a decisive victory; but before he can achieve his end he finds his march embarrassed by topographical obstacles, and he is met when he least expects it by a vigorous counter-stoke. It is the waiting game – the strategy which paves the way for counter-stroke, and counter-stroke in superior force – which enables small armies to conquer great; and the study of this game may be especially recommended to English soldiers. It is often argued that if our two army corps were to take part in a European war that they must always expect to be met by superior numbers. This, however, is as much to say that the strategy which would direct our two army corps would be indifferent, for it is only the unskilful leader who commits his troops to battle with the odds against him.[179]

Henderson recognised the advantages of the tactical defensive, but believed that *only* acting on the defensive was a fatal strategy for the smaller army. Only by outmanoeuvring the enemy to bring superior numbers to bear could physical and moral supremacy be obtained and victory achieved.

Also, Henderson noted, the strategic problems of the British Army were unlike those of its European peers. While they fought a small number of great wars often decades apart, Britain fought numerous small campaigns every year. Aside from the defence of the United Kingdom and India, it was impossible to predict under what circumstances Britain might be called upon to fight – 'it is as useless to anticipate in what quarter of the globe our troops may have to be next employed as to guess at the tactics, the armament, and even the colour [...] of our next enemy'.[180] Other European powers had much simpler strategic situations, with obvious enemies and clearly defined frontiers to protect. British officers joining a major expedition could also be expected to suffer from the same difficulties that American officers had faced in 1861: scattered around the world they lacked experience of directing large bodies of troops or time to study the higher branches of their profession.[181] Jackson, with his career spanning the peacetime US Army, the colonial style campaign in Mexico, independent command in the Valley, and corps command under Lee, and consistently

---

178 Luvaas, *Military Legacy*, pp.180-81; Henderson 'Strategy and its Teaching', p.767.
179 Henderson, 'Strategy and its Teaching', p.767.
180 Henderson, 'Strategy and its Teaching', p.774; Henderson, 'The War in South Africa', p.251.
181 Brigadier General Gobbet, discussion on G.F.R. Henderson's lecture 'Lessons from the Past for the Future', p.1200.

fighting and defeating larger opponents, was a logical choice for Henderson to choose as the role model for English officers wishing to learn their profession.

The initial observations on the strategy of the Civil War were clearly rooted in the consensus of military thought generated by European military writers of the first half of the 19th Century and primarily based upon the operations of the great European commanders, particularly Frederick the Great and Napoleon. If American examples are relatively lacking in Hamley, examples of the art of war as practised by English generals are also rare. However, this predominance of European thinking was also prevalent in American thought of the time, with the theories expounded by authorities such as Jomini forming the basis for military education and practice in the Civil War.[182] British writers looked to find confirmation of basic principles of war in the American conflict, but they were also perceptive in identifying critical geographic and political elements of strategy. In particular the importance of the western theatre and the pivotal significance of the river systems of central Tennessee and the Mississippi were recognised early in the war. Another significant observation was the way in which railways had altered the nature of military logistics and the ability to sustain large armies in the field. The lessons derived by the British in utilising railways to support logistics were applied to their colonial expeditions, such as Abyssinia and the Sudan, where other forms of transport were limited. These were more closely aligned to the American experience of using railways to transport troops and war material over large expanses of wilderness than the Prussian use of railways to achieve strategic concentration of forces in the much more extensive rail networks of Europe.

The Civil War also stimulated some new developments in British strategic thinking. For the first time in the century a significant potential enemy with substantial armed forces, organised and equipped upon European lines, had a direct land border with a British overseas territory. This meant that the British had to consider the means of defending this border. At what would now be considered the operational level of warfare, the problem had been addressed through the Commissions sent to review the defences of Canada, and in particular Jervois' plans for how a campaign against the United States would be fought. Simmons' view of the problem rose above the operational and considered how the full resources of the British Empire could be brought to bear against such an enemy. Some of Simmons' ideas, including the mobilisation of Dominion forces in support of other threatened areas of the Empire and the use of naval supremacy to move troops, were to come to pass in the response to the Boer War with the deployment of Canadian and Australian (though not, in this case, Indian) contingents, and subsequently the similar mobilisation of Imperial resources in the

---

182 Strachan, *European Armies and the Conduct of War*, p.73; W.J. Wood, *Civil War Generalship* (New York: Da Capo Press, 2000), pp.12, 15-19; Nosworthy, *The Bloody Crucible of Courage*, pp.394-98. The influence of Jomini on Civil War generals is much debated, but there was certainly no equivalent American theoretical school of military thought.

Great War. Simmons' strategy of using naval supremacy to blockade the Empires' enemies was also adopted, and while neither the Boers nor Germany had strategically vital points vulnerable to naval attack to distract and diffuse the enemy's efforts, there is some similarity between these proposals of Simmons and the peripheral attacks carried out against Germany's allies. While there is no direct link between Simmons and the strategic decisions of 1899-1902 and 1914-18, his observations resulting from the American Civil War were perhaps the first occasion that an Imperial solution to a British strategic problem had been proposed.

Another new theme in writings on the Civil War was the recognition of the potential for future wars not to be short affairs fought over limited political ends, but to become conflicts in which the whole of a nation's resources would need to be committed in order to overcome the enemy's will to fight and bring about fundamental change in the enemy's political system. This did not arise solely out of the Civil War, Adair for example recognised a commonality with the mass mobilisations of the Franco-Prussian conflict. There are also indications here of trends in contemporary European military theory merging with the actual observation of conflict in America. The escalation of the intensity of the conflict in the American Civil War, from an initial short-term mobilisation of volunteers to suppress what was perceived as a limited rebellion, to the mobilisation of the entire resources of the nation to totally suppress an external political entity through the subjugation of the enemy's will to fight, is much as described in the writings of Clausewitz. Adair does not explicitly reference Clausewitz, and the timing of his lecture slightly predates the first English translation of *On War*, but it is possible that he was familiar with European publications of the text and it is tempting to see here a fusion of European theory with British observation.[183] In 1899, faced with an enemy of European extraction but with significantly different political, social and economic traditions, the British were forced both to mobilise extensive resources and to adopt more extreme forms of war such as concentration camps, and the similarities with the political context of the American Civil War were noted by contemporaries.

* * *

Other writers have concluded that the British military establishment rejected the evidence of the Civil War that future wars would be lengthy, and characterised by extreme violence, either through a deliberate rejection of the mass mobilisation of

---

183 Clausewitz, *On War*, pp.104-05. The first English translation of *On War*, by Colonel J.J. Graham, was published in 1873. In his *Precis of Modern Tactics* published the same year, Major Robert Home referenced the 1849 French edition of Clausewitz' as being a valuable work and noted the publication of Graham's translation. Adair's lecture was in March 1872. Henderson's references to the moral effects at a strategic (rather than tactical) level also seem to reflect Clausewitz' theories without explicitly referencing his work, see Henderson 'Strategy and its Teaching' pp.765-69; Clausewitz, *On War*, pp.251-52.

the economy practised by the North in favour of a more traditional form of warfare, or through a lack of an intellectual foundation for war on such a scale.[184] Neither of these conclusions seems to be justified. People like Chesney, Simmons and Adair were not blind to the nature of the war in America, and the Napoleonic Wars were a precedent for a war engaged by the whole economic and military resources of the nation. Yet in comparison with continental armies, with their limited set of external threats to consider, the British army lacked a clear strategic paradigm to work within. The invasion scares of the middle of the century and the subsequent attempts to identify a means of defending Britain, or Canada, against an enemy bringing large forces to bear show that this did for a short period get the attention of British strategists. However, this period of anxiety was short lived, and the nature of the warfare that was practised by the British Army during the remainder of the century did not require it to create plans for a war on a continental scale. The average operation carried out was of limited extent, for limited political objectives, and, as Henderson observed, against enemies where little strategic thought was required. The basic 'strategy' of Britain's colonial campaigns was to advance directly on the enemy by the most easily supplied route, and to rely on superior technology and hard fighting to do the rest – an operational approach, and one which served the British remarkably well in most cases.[185]

Only when faced by the Boers – an army equally well armed, capable of a defensive strategy of exhaustion able to wear down the British advantage of numbers, and not prepared to surrender even when beaten in traditional battle – was a more radical strategy needed. With regards to European wars, Britain's policy up to the end of the century remained one of intervention with an expeditionary force of limited size, and it was not unreasonable for men like Henderson to put their intellects to considering what strategy an inferior force should adopt in such a scenario. The numerically inferior Confederacy seemed to offer a model for this; though given the emphasis placed upon the Royal Navy in political strategy more attention should probably have been paid to Wolseley's observations that amphibious operations were the most important lessons to be drawn from the Civil War.

British writers in the 19th Century were not blind to the operational and strategic significance of the American Civil War, either in its detail or in its overall context. Colonial by the nature of its terrain, Napoleonic in scale and political significance, and fought by English-speaking armies, its execution was of particular interest to the British. The writers who studied the war did so specifically with the object of identifying lessons of relevance. The clearest parallel to the American experience would have been the defence of south-east England against a continental opponent, but this

---

184 Dubrulle, 'A Military Legacy of the Civil War: the British Inheritance', pp.153-80 particularly pp.179-80; David Gates, *Warfare in the 19th Century* (Basingstoke: Palgrave, 2001), p.180.
185 Henderson, 'Strategy and its Teaching', pp.765-66.

was a military problem which never had to be faced in reality. Overall, the British Army lacked both a defined strategic agenda against which to apply their observations, and a body such as the German General Staff with which to do so. As a result, the learning process was individual rather than institutional, and its influence on the actual conduct of campaigns was limited.

Conclusions

The starting point for this book was that the traditional view presented in most military histories is that the British Army generally failed to learn from the American Civil War, and that this view is flawed due to a tendency to judge the process from a 20th Century viewpoint. Through examination of a wide range of sources it has identified that the war featured more widely in Victorian military thought than has been previously shown; has argued that both the British observers of the American Civil War and those writers who subsequently used the evidence of the conflict were more perceptive of its significance than has previously been acknowledged; and as a result has put forward a more positive view of the British Army's acceptance of the need for change in the light of the American experience than has previously been suggested.

In making the final assessment of whether the British Army's evaluation of the lessons of the Civil War was successful or not, three approaches will be used. The first reconsiders the existing historiography in the light of the new evidence and assesses which if any of the views of previous authorities still hold. The second looks at how different elements of the Victorian Army evaluated lessons from the war, and how it was interpreted and used by the organisation. The final approach looks at the main developments and lessons which modern historical and military opinion attribute to the American Civil War, and asks whether these were reflected in the Army's doctrines and actions.

J.F.C. Fuller's identification of the similarities between the conduct of the Civil War and that of the First World War has influenced all subsequent historiography. The parallels as presented by Fuller are certainly striking, but he was not the first to depict the war as a source of lessons missed by the British. In 1900, E.S. Valentine had drawn parallels between the Civil War and the Boer War with much the same object as Fuller, to demonstrate how unprepared the peacetime army had been for a substantial conflict against an implacable foe. Several of Fuller's criticisms were overstated. For example, he suggested that 'scientific' analysis of modern weaponry would have been able to predict the nature of the Civil War before it was fought.[1] Such analysis was the basis of Sir Henry Whatley Tyler's lectures to the Royal United

---

1   Major General J.F.C. Fuller, 'The Place of the American Civil War in the Evolution of War', *Army Quarterly*, 26 (1933), pp.316-325 (p.318).

Service Institution in the 1850s, and several of Tyler's predictions were seen in the American war. Fuller was also scathing of tactical theories that placed the bayonet as the arbiter of battle, which he claimed were dominant in 1861 and 1914.[2] However, the writings of the late Victorian period clearly identify firepower as the decisive factor in battle, with the bayonet charge becoming viable only through the moral ascendency gained from the effects of fire.

Fuller's suggestion that studying the Civil War would have prevented the mistakes of the First World War seemingly contradicts his own dictum that the lessons of earlier wars cannot be the foundation of new tactics unless weaponry does not change. Fuller wrote this to support his view that the tactics of the Great War needed to be modified in the 1930s to meet the new technologies of the tank, aeroplane, and submarine.[3] In the same way, British authorities after 1870 favoured European tactical models over American precisely because the rifled musket that formed the principal infantry weapon of the Civil War was obsolete and new tactics had to be introduced as a result of breech-loading rifles. By the end of the century the magazine rifle and quick-firing artillery had further changed the expectations of how modern wars would be fought and made the tactics of Gettysburg as obsolete as those of Waterloo. The ideas that the British expected the next European war to be a repeat of the last is not true: they expected future wars to be conflicts of massed armies in which army corps would be mere units, as shown by the following passage which anticipates several features of the First World War.

> The fact that decisive battles in the next great Continental war will probably last more than one day, that positions of great strength will have to be frontally attacked, that attacks will be slow in progress and last many hours, that ground once gained must be retained at all cost as in a siege, that attempts will be made to secure vantage ground under cover of darkness – all point to the conclusion that a judicious use of the spade will be one of the features of future warfare.[4]

The work quoted from is the second edition (1896) of Home's *Precis of Modern Tactics*, a popular treatise. The author did not directly reference the American Civil War, but nor was his prediction contrary to aspects of the later stages of that conflict which are seen as portents of the First World War, such as the prolonged nature of battles, their resemblance to sieges, and the importance of entrenchment.

Liddell Hart was equally critical of the British military establishment as a result of the First World War. His contention was that it failed to draw appropriate lessons from the Civil War largely because British writers had focussed upon the eastern

2 Fuller, 'The Place of the American Civil War', p.325.
3 Fuller, 'The Place of the American Civil War', p.317.
4 Lieutenant Colonel Sisson C. Pratt, *[Home's] Precis of Tactics*, 2nd edn revised and rewritten (London: HMSO, 1896), p.53.

campaigns, and that this not only anticipated but actually produced the staleness of thought that led to the frontal attacks of the Western Front.[5] This view cannot be justified from the evidence. During the Civil War itself it is true that the majority of observers made their way to Virginia and the north-eastern states, but this was largely due to practical constraints. Several did manage to travel to a much wider range of locations and to report on what they found there. Contemporary journals such as the *Army and Navy Gazette* covered the eastern theatre extensively, but this was not to the exclusion of major events in the West, and was mostly driven by the availability of reports received from the American press. With the two capitals of Richmond and Washington so close to each other, and with the largest and most well-equipped armies of the war campaigning between the two cities for four years, the newspapers understandably focussed on the events in Virginia. Contemporaries analysing the war such as Chesney and Hamley were acutely aware of the importance of the western theatre in their writings. The maligned Hamley, while not considering that there was much of military significance in Sherman's Georgia campaign, nevertheless used it as an example of how to threaten multiple objectives and therefore deceive the enemy as to one's intentions. This anticipated some aspects of Liddell Hart's use of Sherman's advance to illustrate the 'indirect approach' by over fifty years.

Even if it is accepted that by the turn of the century Henderson's work on Stonewall Jackson had led to an undue focus in Britain on the campaigns in Virginia, and the Shenandoah Valley in particular, this cannot be construed as a blind intent to adopt a 'direct approach' of frontal assaults against the enemy's main strength.[6] Such a view is the very antithesis of what Henderson aimed to teach, and static trench warfare to Henderson's eyes would have been a failure of strategy. Henderson selected his subjects, whether from the Franco-Prussian War or from the American Civil War, because he believed that they had specific relevance to preparing his chosen audience, which ranged from volunteer officers to Staff College students, for the problems that they would face in wartime. The battlefields of Virginia were chosen specifically because they had parallels to the defence of south-east England. Jackson's campaign in the Valley reflected the likely scale of operations in which it was anticipated most British officers would be engaged.

Henderson did on occasion seem to emphasise Jackson's support for aggressive tactics and the bayonet, but *Stonewall Jackson* is as much a vehicle for Henderson's views on strategy as his views on tactics. These stressed two aspects, firstly the use of superior manoeuvring and generalship to bring about tactical superiority on the battlefield, either in terms of numbers or position, and secondly the importance of the moral element in warfare. The latter can be misrepresented as suggesting that superior *morale* on the part of attacking troops would enable even frontal assaults against modern weaponry to succeed, but this was clearly not Henderson's intent, as his earlier

5   Liddell Hart, *The British Way in Warfare*, pp.74-76.
6   Luvaas, *Military Legacy*, pp.187-89.

repetition of MacDougall's view on the invincibility of well dug in infantry demonstrates. The 'moral factor' in Henderson's eyes was a strategic as well as a tactical concept, and as much about the personal *morale* of the general as that of his troops. According to Henderson, Jackson's victories were the result of his reading of his opponent's intent, his outmanoeuvring of the enemy to put him at a moral disadvantage, and the use of superior mobility to bring about tactical superiority when battle was joined. Anticipating a war where the enemy's superior numbers would need to be met by superior skill, training and morale, Jackson was a logical role model. This is not much different from Liddell Hart's view that the British way of warfare was to avoid a direct assault on the enemy's main force, and to defeat him indirectly through mobility and generalship. Liddell Hart stressed the economic aspects of Sherman's later operations, whereas Jackson's campaigns were founded upon the political objectives associated with the threats to the two capitals, and Washington DC was a moral objective, just as described by Liddell Hart in his theories in the 1920s.[7]

While Liddell Hart's own thinking on the Civil War has been criticised by modern revisionists, his indirect influence through his disciple Jay Luvaas has persisted. Luvaas' findings have not been seriously challenged, and to this day remain the basis for the popular idea that the European military establishment ignored the Civil War.[8] On re-examination both his chronological narrative and his conclusion on how the war was interpreted need to be reviewed. Luvaas described British historical interest in the Civil War as falling into a series of phases. The first was the initial period of intense interest while the war was fought; the second a period of indifference due to a focus on European conflicts. There was then a revival of interest under Henderson, that according to Luvaas was distorted by the conservative military system, and finally a re-appraisal after the First World War by writers such as Fuller and Liddell Hart.[9] This breakdown still has some value as a narrative framework. However, Luvaas' focussed his research on published writings that directly addressed the subject of the Civil War, rather than looking at where its influences might be seen in the wider military literature and doctrines of the time. This has understated the level to which the British were influenced by the American experience throughout the late Victorian period, and overstated the extent to which some of those who did comment on the war conflicted with mainstream thought.

---

7   Sir Basil Liddell Hart, *Paris, or The Future of War* (London: Kegan Paul, Trench, Trubner & Co., 1925), pp.30-31, described Paris as a morale objective; but seems to have failed to see that Washington and Richmond had the same significance in the Civil War.

8   An example is Kevin M. Levin, 'Did the Civil War Affect European Military Culture', *Civil War Memory* (10 March 2010) <http://cwmemory.com/2010/03/31/did-the-civil-war-affect-european-military-culture> [accessed 10 December 2012], with a discussion based upon Luvaas' book.

9   Luvaas, *Military Legacy*, pp.14-51, 100-18, 170-202, 203-25. In particular pp.202-204 for the comparison between the 'Henderson Legacy' and post-1918 writers.

Up until 1870 the American Civil War was the largest and most significant war since Napoleon. As well as being the most recent proving ground of many modern weapons, it had particular relevance to the British because of cultural ties, and because of the strategic threat posed by the expanded American military to the British possessions in Canada. This pre-eminent position of the war in British military writing inevitably declined as technology advanced and made the tactics of the war appear less relevant, and as the threat to British interests from the United States lessened. The Franco-Prussian War accelerated this decline in interest due to the magnitude of the change in the European balance of power, and also because of the mass of continental writings about that war and the wealth of new evidence it provided about the impact of new technology on tactics and strategy in a European context. In comparison, no new information was coming to light regarding the American Civil War. Yet there was not, as Luvaas suggested, a total rejection in this second period of American lessons in favour of all things German, and the period from the Franco-Prussian War in 1870 to the publication of Henderson's *Campaign of Fredericksburg* in 1884 was not quite the wasteland of observation on the American war as it is portrayed. British authors addressing the issues of the 1870s did find occasion to look back to the Civil War for examples and lessons. This happened in the case of field entrenchments in the wake of the Russo-Turkish War of 1877-78, and during debates about the future of cavalry and mounted infantry in modern warfare. The ability of the United States to mobilise the full resources of the country for war, and to raise large volunteer armies rapidly, was not lost at the time on those concerned about Britain's ability to defend itself against the much larger armies of its potential continental foes. These writers were looking at a range of recent historical lessons to answer the important military questions of the day as they saw them, and while more recent events were not unreasonably given more attention, the American experiences were not ignored.

The emergence in the 1880s of new information about the American war in the form of memoirs and official records gave an impulse to historical writings on the war that was just as significant as the supposed backlash against German military thought in influencing Henderson and others. Henderson was a student of both European and American wars, and drew conclusions and comparisons from both, sometimes regarding German examples as more relevant, and at other times considering American methods, particularly those of the cavalry, as superior.[10] Maude too drew from a wide range of sources both European and American, contemporary and historical, to support his theories. The use by Maude of examples from America to support his aggressive tactical theories at first seems to support Luvaas' final conclusion, which was that the observers and commentators took what they wanted from the Civil War to reinforce their existing opinions.[11] While there is truth in this, it reflects the way in which military works were written at the time, and should not be interpreted as meaning that there was uniform rejection of the 'modern' aspects of the

10   Luvaas, *The Education of an Army*, pp.221-23, 225-27.
11   Luvaas, *Military Legacy*, p.233.

war due to an innate conservatism. There were aspects of the Civil War that could, if necessary, provide evidence in support of traditional practices, from the views of Lee and Seymour on the usefulness of muzzle loaders, to the deep columns of attack used by Upton at Spotsylvania. Nevertheless, the reaction of conservatives to the war was more likely to be a statement of its irrelevance due to its peculiar circumstances, as in the case of the limited opportunities for traditional cavalry action, rather than citing evidence from it in support of their own views. Turning Luvaas' conclusion around, rather than reinforcing conservative opinions, evidence from the Civil War was more often used by reformers to support their views that modern warfare, whether at a tactical, operational or strategic level, did in fact require the British Army to change.

* * *

Those views covered a wide range of opinion and do not fall easily into previous classifications of schools of thought within the British Army. There existed a small group of people, notably Wolseley, Fletcher, and Hewett, whose first-hand experience of America seems to have directly influenced their careers and views, and others who made or enhanced their scholarly reputations through studying the Civil War such as Chesney and Henderson. These did not constitute a separate 'American school', but nevertheless the war had a significant influence on their military thought. The way in which the American Civil War was studied and used to support opinions by other authors who had less immediate experience of America throughout the period indicates the existence of a number of interest groups within the Army, each of which used the lessons of the Civil War in different ways.

The first such group was the engineers. The professional branches of the service were becoming more significant in the Army, and by their nature engineers were inclined to stress the growing importance of technology in warfare. They were also likely to take a forward-looking view of how technology might be refined and developed in the future, and to extrapolate the nature of future war from current trends. This was the type of thinking that had informed Tyler's lectures in the 1850s. For this group, the widespread use of field fortifications and the importance of siege-like tactics in the later stages of the Civil War were vindication of their predictions. Post-war, lecturers like Schaw continued to use American examples where relevant to prove points, and younger engineer officers like Clayton and Fraser continued to demonstrate knowledge of the Civil War in their discussion of field fortifications. Engineers were naturally inclined to see technology as the basis for military developments. Sir Francis Head for example, in 1869, attributed the widespread use of field fortifications during the war to the power of the rifle. He also promoted his profession within the Army by suggesting that the nature of modern warfare meant that in future it would be appropriate for armies to be led by engineer generals.[12]

12 Sir Francis Boyd Head, *The Royal Engineer* (London: John Murray, 1869), pp.330, 353.

The second group, and one given prominence by Luvaas, were the supporters of mounted infantry. The motives of this group varied – Havelock was primarily interested in how to defend India, Denison and Chevenix Trench in the most effective way to train and equip light cavalry, and Hutton, at least in part, in how to equip auxiliary and colonial forces. Their great conclusion from the Civil War was an alternative response to that of the engineers. Rather than accepting that future warfare would be one of entrenchments, sieges and engineering works, they sought a means to provide tactical mobility on the battlefield through the only means possible at the time, the horse. They saw this opportunity not in the form of mounted tactics, but through using the horse as a means of conveyance, allowing the infantry to seize vital positions for defence or to manoeuvre into a position to make traditional infantry attacks on the flanks or rear of the enemy. Such tactics had historical forebears in Europe in the form of the traditional dragoon, and in the colonies in the raising of auxiliary or temporary mounted formations during campaigns, but the main model for their ideas was the employment of mounted troops in a dismounted role by American commanders such as Forrest and Sheridan. The development and use of mounted infantry in the period indicates a willingness within the British Army to adopt and adapt new methods of operation. However, caught up in the rivalry between the infantry and cavalry, mounted infantry never became an entirely separate combat arm fulfilling modern definitions of military innovation.[13]

The regular British cavalryman has been portrayed by Luvaas and others as a conservative figure, ignoring the evidence of the Civil War on the importance of dismounted action and clinging to outmoded ideas of the grand cavalry charge with sabre or lance.[14] Re-examination of the material written in the period indicates that the lessons drawn by cavalrymen were more complex than this, and that cavalry reformers such as Denison and Trench were more aligned to mainstream thinking than Luvaas depicted. On the one hand the British cavalry officer regarded the American horseman as a poor exponent of the cavalry art compared to his European contemporary, incapable of effective shock action or vigorous pursuit, and saw little to learn from them tactically in this respect. On the other, confronted by the evidence that the battlefield role of cavalry had been permanently diminished by the new arms of precision, and fearing conversion to mounted infantry or even abolition, cavalrymen promoted a new vision of their role as a strategic arm acting independently of the army to conduct reconnaissance in strength and raids upon the enemy lines of communication.

13   A similar observation that internal rivalries have constrained innovation has been made of modern mechanised infantry in the US Army, Major Ros A. Coffey (USA), 'Doctrinal Orphan or Active Partner? A History of U.S. Army Mechanised Infantry Doctrine' (Thesis for the Degree of Master of Military Art and Science, U.S. Army Command and General Staff College, Fort Leavenworth Kansas, 2000), cited in Grissom, p.916.
14   Luvaas, *Military Legacy*, pp.193-98; Preston, 'Military Lessons of the American Civil War', p.235; Craddock, 'The American Civil War and its Influence on the British Army', pp.44, 105-06, 179.

The British cavalry's response to the lessons of the Civil War supports some modern theories about military change. The cavalry saw itself competing for scarce resources, and in particularly with the new mounted infantry school, in what would now be termed 'contested mission areas'. At the same time some cavalrymen put forward new 'theories of victory' based upon mobility and operations against the enemy rear. The focus by historians on the retention of the doctrine of mounted action has understated the cavalry's capability for self-examination and its willingness to adopt other change in this period. While the individual American trooper was often dismissed as a mere mounted infantryman, the exploits of the American cavalry as a whole were held up as exemplars of this new form of cavalry warfare that would justify their continued existence.

No such existential threat from modern weapons applied to the artillery. Throughout the late Victorian period the capability of this arm increased both in range and in destructive firepower. During the Civil War itself the Royal Artillery showed great interest in the technical developments of the period. It was represented in both of the formal missions, and American ordnance was obtained for experimental purposes. In the longer term however nothing of great note was taken from the Americans. With one or two exceptions the American topography did not lend itself to mass artillery bombardments, and the European experiences of Sadowa and Sedan were seen as more indicative of the future capability of artillery than Malvern Hill or Gettysburg.[15] The artillery arm retained ownership of the machine gun for most of the period, a relationship entirely consistent with, though not directly justified by, the tactical use of multiple-barrelled rifle-bore weapons in the Civil War.

Those interested in infantry tactics also rarely referenced the Civil War directly in their writings. There was some early support for American ideas such as the more widespread use of 'fours' in the years immediately following the war, but the 1867 drill manual showed no acknowledgement of any tactical revolution in the American war. By comparison the success of the Prussian infantry in 1866 and 1870 transformed the drill manuals for the infantry attack beyond recognition. When the reaction against the Prussian 'skirmisher swarm' set in, however, it was mostly justified by a return to traditional British methods and tactics rather than attributing any superiority to Civil War formations, which were largely seen as derivative of European practice. The main conclusion drawn specifically from the war was the ability of volunteer infantry to take substantial losses in the assault, arguably a negative lesson given later developments. However, although the conclusion must be that the Civil War had limited

---

15 Wagner, *The Campaign of Königgrätz*, pp.95-97, accepted that artillery tactics up to 1866 including the Civil War had not changed much since Wagram. Major E.S. May, *Achievements of Field Artillery* (London: Royal Artillery Institution, 1893), pp.64-75 considered Malvern Hill, Second Manassas, and Gettysburg significant artillery engagements, but the 1877 work by Captain Henry Knollys used no Civil War examples even though Knollys had visited the United States during the war (Knollys, *The Elements of Field Artillery*, pp.141-63 covers the relevant period).

direct impact on British infantry tactics, it should not be inferred that these were static during the period. Based upon the evidence of the drill manuals, the recommended tactics for use against a European enemy underwent substantial change as a result of theoretical ideas about the future nature of battle, some of which drew on observation from the Civil War. Their use in action was constrained by the actual tactical situations encountered by the British in the field.[16]

Beyond the tactical considerations of different branches of Army, a more limited group of writers was looking at wider issues of how to project and protect British power. Those who took an imperial view of British defence were most likely to turn to the American experience as a source of ideas, as the great distances and limited communications in much of the British Empire had parallels to the problems facing American generals. Fletcher and Hutton, in their development of the Canadian and Australian military respectively, looked in some degree to American models for inspiration, and in particular saw relevance in the use of irregular cavalry or mounted infantry in the colonies. Simmons looked at the problem of defending Canada against the United States, and anticipated the application and concentration of global military resources in the event of a war. Wolseley noted the importance of combined operations, and looked to the Civil War for lessons in how to apply technology such as the railway and telegraph to future campaigns.

Those whose main concern was how Britain would fight a European war were less inclined to look to the Civil War for lessons. The marked differences between Europe and America particularly in terms of geography and infrastructure, as well as the different nature of European and American armies, were seen by 'continentalists' as factors that limited the relevance of American methods and tactics, particularly in relation to the cavalry. Nevertheless, it was still occasionally cited in the context of national defence, particularly regarding how to augment the relatively small regular forces based in Britain with the volunteer and militia corps in the event of invasion. The example of the American volunteer was used to support the principle of voluntary over compulsory service in raising a mass army, and Adair and Henderson both looked to the Civil War as a model for the defence of London and the south-east.

Since the evidence points to there being a widespread awareness in the British military of the American Civil War, this begs the question: why was the Army unprepared for the Boer War in 1899, and criticised for not having learnt from America and from the unprepared state of the United States Army in 1861? It cannot simplistically be ascribed to ignoring the lessons of the American Civil War, or any other conflict that took place in the period. Many officers fully recognised the many changes that had taken place in the art of war since 1861, and in a few individuals, some of whom

---

16   Stephen Rosen suggests peacetime innovation is the result of military communities evaluating the future character of war, the generation of future theories of victory and consequent changes in the officer corps, Rosen *Winning the Next War*, pp.19-21, 52. The British invested considerable thought into the nature of future war regarding the infantry, but this did not lead to any organisational changes in the period.

were in positions of influence, the level of interest in and recognition of the lessons of the Civil War was quite substantial. One factor limiting their impact was the lack of formal institutions within the army to properly evaluate the results of previous conflicts. Modern theory views learning as a three-stage knowledge management process of acquisition, analysis, and dissemination. Modern armies have a substantial intellectual infrastructure to support this type of process which the Victorian British Army lacked. The application of the lessons of the Civil War therefore depended upon the individual rather than being promulgated as doctrine.[17]

An exception that proves the rule is the sphere of technology. At a technical level the British appear to have absorbed the material gleaned from the war quite effectively. The reasons for this success can be attributed to the fact that technical questions allowed the application of scientific method to their answer, and to the existence of institutions within the Army that could apply these methods. Gallwey, the head of the 1864 mission, was a member of the Ordnance Select Committee, and this group processed the reports from the missions sent to the United States, and from some of the individual engineering and artillery officers who took the opportunity to visit the war. American intelligence and practices informed a number of other committees and reports on subjects such as breech-loading rifles, signals, and torpedoes (mines), as well as experiments or trials with balloons and primitive machine guns. The British procured several American weapons for formal trials, those of large cast iron guns continuing for some years after the conclusion of the Civil War. It is true that certain conservative technical biases delayed the take-up of some advances in weaponry, such as the resistance to introducing capped cartridges containing the means of ignition, but even in this case once experimentation took place the argument was settled in favour of the new technology.

Although writers from Fuller onwards have claimed technical innovation as a feature of the war, American progress in weapons during this period was not substantially in advance of other military powers, and in many aspects American practices were technically conservative. Machine guns, balloons, and torpedoes all had precedents in European warfare, and were progressed by the British Army with due recognition of both their utility and their limitations as evidenced in the Civil War. The adoption of the breech-loading rifle in the British service was in advance of that in the Unites States Army. Smoothbores remained a weapon of choice for many American artillerymen even when they were deemed obsolete in Britain and Europe. Given the speed of technological change during the period, the significance of the British interest in American technology is not so much whether it was adopted or not, for example the cast iron ordnance used in the war was obsolete a decade later, but in the

17   Catignani, 'Coping with Knowledge', pp.36-37. Nagl, *Learning to Eat Soup with a Knife*, p.10, has a similar model, Nagl adds three additional phases; the initial targeting of a learning opportunity, and its short and long term application in the field. In the Victorian era individual writers could only go so far in acquiring and analysing lessons from the Civil War in the absence of institutions to build consensus and disseminate these lessons.

readiness of the British establishment to look at American technology and to evaluate it on its merits.[18]

Luvaas was critical of the lack of attention paid to the Civil War by the Army's educational institutions.[19] The military colleges which existed in this period were focused on the training of officers in the practical skills required to perform their duties in their regiments or in the field. The Professors at the Staff College were primarily lecturers and tutors, not academic historians as we would recognise them today, and the study of military history was in its infancy. There was no systemic process of analysis of the lessons of Civil War, or indeed any other contemporary conflict.[20] This did not mean that the British did not recognise the need for change, but the result was a plethora of views that drew their evidence from a range of sources, which sometimes included the Civil War in their examples, but which rarely achieved universal acceptance. The lack of any extensive practical experience of actions against a well-armed, well trained enemy in this period contributed to this, as in the context of European conflict these views were largely drawn from second-hand writings and observation.

Furthermore, and partly as a result of observation of the Civil War, there was a recognition that the extended modern battlefield meant a need to devolve responsibility to the officer on the spot. This meant that the adoption of a particular tactical approach largely came down to the field experience and capabilities of individual officers. The global stretch of the Army meant that not only were the British obliged to retain tactics at odds with those required in modern war, but that the experiences and training of officers and men were varied and inconsistent. It supported a culture of independence and initiative that should have suited the new battlefield conditions, but individuals were found lacking in war against a well-equipped foe when they did not have personal experience of fighting against modern weapons.

The absence of an institutional basis for deriving lessons was an even greater limitation on operational and strategic thinking. Once again this became a matter of prominent individuals studying the war and drawing their own conclusions. Hamley was a more astute observer of the war than is sometimes credited. His writings during the conflict show an awareness of the importance of geographical and economic factors, though like most contemporaries he overestimated the capability of the South to resist

18   The British approach supports Stephen Rosen's characterisation of technological change as being driven by the need to develop strategies for managing uncertainty. Rosen, *Winning the Next War*, p.53.
19   Luvaas, *Military Legacy*, pp.115-16.
20   Captain Charles E. Callwell, 'Lessons to be Learnt From the Campaigns in Which British Forces Have Been Employed Since the Year 1865', *Journal of the Royal United Service Institution*, 31 (1887), pp.357-412, is a partial exception, but this appears to be a privately produced paper not officially commissioned. Callwell later expanded his essay into his book *Small Wars: Their Principles and Practice* (1896), and would rise to the rank of major general.

and underestimated the determination of the North to prevail. However, although prepared to revise his observations to an extent when presented with new evidence, as revealed by his correspondence with Sherman, he did persist in using the war to demonstrate pre-existing and constant principles, and the adoption of his work as the standard text on strategy by the Army perpetuated this approach. Proving general principles was also Chesney's initial intent from studying the war, but unlike Hamley he saw in it evidence that substantial change would come about in European conflicts, not so much from tactical developments, but from the way in which the railway, telegraph, and steamship enabled the larger power to bring overwhelming superiority to bear against the weaker at an operational and strategic level.

Henderson's objective was the training of both regular and volunteer officers to meet practical problems that they would face in the field, and he took specific examples from the Civil War to teach what he saw as important tactical or operational principles. Although Brackenbury described his biography of Jackson as part thesis on the art of war, Henderson never published an overall theory of war based upon objective analytical review of the Civil War as a whole, nor do his writings contain any definitive predictions for the future based upon his studies of the past. Henderson himself identified that the lack of institutions whose objective was to carry out such studies limited the operational readiness of the army, writing that 'a body of staff officers devoted to the study of war would have paid special attention to the campaigns of the United States' and attributing the organisational failures of 1899 to a similar lack of responsibility for any organisation or individual within the army 'to note, to analyse, and to apply the teachings derived from the operations and the constitution of foreign armies'.[21]

* * *

Clearly the Victorian Army was not without contemporary, as well as more modern, critics of its ability to learn from historic conflicts. Equally, there were individuals at the time who did see that aspects of the American Civil War would anticipate future developments in the art of war throughout the Victorian period and into the next century. The final stage of assessing how well the British learnt from the Civil War is to review it against what are now perceived of as the lessons of the war at tactical, operational, and strategic levels, and their application at the time, in order to arrive at an objective view of what the British did or did not derive from American experiences.[22]

Perhaps the most popular misconception regarding the British Army's failure to adopt modern tactics as it entered the Boer War, and indeed the First World War

21   Henderson, 'The British Army' in *The Science of War*, pp.419, 433.
22   The list of key lessons from a modern perspective is based partly but not exclusively upon those in Brinkmann, 'German Observations and Evaluations of the U.S. Civil War'.

15 years later, is the supposed lack of attention given to field fortification. Surely the evidence of the Wilderness, Atlanta, and Petersburg, to name only the most prominent campaigns, should have forewarned the British of the emergence of trench warfare? The fact is that that the British Army was fully aware of the need to protect its troops against unnecessary loss, and the use of shelter trenches and earthworks to do so. While it is possible to identify occasions such as Isandlwana or Majuba where the lack of prepared defences may have contributed to British defeat, these must be attributed to mistakes by the local commanders and not down to doctrine. The importance of shelter trenches, not only in defence but also where necessary in attack, was part of the British drill book as early as 1870. It is true that senior officers worried, as did commanders in the Civil War, about the potential loss of offensive spirit that would result from prolonged periods in static positions. At the same time, however, it was considered that entrenchment was a means of bolstering the morale of inexperienced troops as well offsetting numerical superiority. This was an essential component of plans to defend Canada against the United States in the 1860s and of those to defend south-east England against continental invasion. Where the British Army can be criticised is in its practical arrangements for constructing entrenchments, as throughout the period the tools required for entrenchment were managed at battalion level rather than being part of the individual soldier's equipment.

The field manual clearly stated that the purpose of entrenchment was to provide shelter for the troops, whether in attack or defence, from the enhanced firepower of modern weapons. In this respect the Victorian military endorsed the mainstream view of modern historiography that it was the lethality of modern small arms that resulted in the widespread adoption of entrenchments in the Civil War. However, Chesney had drawn a different conclusion as to why the practice of field entrenching was so widespread, stating that it was due to the need for security when two armies were close by and to prevent surprise attacks. This was the context for British entrenchments in Zululand in 1879, when the enemy had few modern weapons. The truth would appear to be that both protection from firepower and the traditional raising of fortification to defend against surprise attack were contributing factors to both Civil War and to British practice, but that the specific inclusion of shelter trench drill in the 1870 manual must be ascribed to the perceived capability of the new rifle rather than tactical considerations of security.

The second response to the new firepower ascribed to the Civil War was the adoption of looser formations. The popular image of late Victorian infantry is of the British redcoat firing volleys in close order lines or squares to breakup attacks by fanatic but poorly armed tribesman, or being shot down by Boer marksmen through adoption of similar outmoded formations. This image fails to recognise the substantial changes that took place in tactical infantry formations throughout the period, and the considerable variety of formations and tactics that were considered and employed throughout the period. Although the 1867 drill manual for the infantry did not modify the official tactics in any way as a result of either the Civil War or contemporary European conflicts, British writers had by this time already recognised the limitations of the traditional linear formations under the new conditions of war. Wolseley, Maurice, and Clery were among those emphasising the need to adopt looser formations. However, new formations were not initially modelled on the Civil War, where extended skirmish lines were seen as ineffective, and as one of the reasons for the indecisive nature of many battles, but on the way in which the Prussians had been observed to operate in 1870.[23]

The search for an infantry formation that both limited casualties and allowed offensive action was the fundamental dilemma of infantry tactics in the period. If any form of offensive action was to be successful then superior firepower had to be concentrated at the point of attack, but skirmish lines meant both a dispersal of fire, and a loss of the command and control that made concentration possible. The rejection of the Prussian 'skirmisher swarm' in the 1880s came about due to the undesirability of the intermingling of formations and resulting loss of control. This was also a concern of officers with experience in the Civil War, as demonstrated in Upton's manual of 1867. The reversion to a more traditional formation of skirmish screen, main body and support, operating in extended formation when under fire, and with limited frontages for individual battalions, all resulted from the desire to retain control. It was not directly derived from, but it did have similarities to, the formations used in the Civil War. By the last decade of the century the attack in extended order, with the successive re-enforcement of the firing line to achieve fire supremacy prior to the actual assault, was the official British practice for an assault on a European or 'civilised' enemy armed with modern weapons.

Close order tactics remained the standard in so-called 'savage wars' because the threat from the enemy's firepower was lower and the retention of unit cohesion was seen as more important in hostile territory where the threat of sudden attack from any direction was constant. It was this threat that led to the retention of the square in colonial tactics long after it was recognised as obsolete and vulnerable against modern firearms and artillery. The square itself was regarded as a means of bringing concentrated firepower to bear while retaining security. In effect it was a mobile equivalent of the American use of regular and frequent entrenchment to provide defence against surprise attack. Even in savage wars the importance of firepower was seen as paramount, although the bayonet remained an important auxiliary weapon.

Field entrenchment and the adoption of looser formations in the face of modern firearms were just two aspects of a more general tactical lesson that is attributed to the Civil War: that the defensive had become the stronger form of war. The retention of drills for frontal attack and in particular the role of the bayonet, believed and portrayed by some 19th Century writers to be an essentially British weapon, have fuelled criticism of the British Army as an essentially conservative institution.[24]

---

23   Nosworthy, *The Bloody Crucible of Courage*, pp.633-40, argues that the Prussian tactics were more revolutionary than those in America and that their prominence in European thought was therefore justified.

24   Craddock, 'The American Civil War and its Influence on the British Army', pp.212, 91-93, 303.

This once again simplifies a complex debate. Throughout the 1850s some British authorities had looked at the increasing precision and penetrative power of the new weapons and recognised that they changed the relative capabilities of different arms and would require new tactics. For example, the works of Tyler, MacDougall, Nolan, and Wolford, all considered the effect of improved firepower to some extent. It also needs to be recognised that neither the technology not the tactical thinking of the day was static, and that contrary to Fuller's proposition, war is not a simple matter of scientific calculations. At the time of the Civil War the predominant infantry weapon, the muzzle-loading musket certainly gave a great advantage to troops taking the defensive. The terrain in America also limited possible advantages to the offensive because it nullified the long-range firepower of rifled artillery. European wars with different terrain and different combinations of weaponry provided different lessons that seemed to indicate that the offensive could still be successful when undertaken by a skilful general and highly trained troops. Direct frontal assaults on strongly held defensive positions were recognised as suicidal, whether executed by Virginian volunteers at Gettysburg or by Prussian guardsmen at St Privat, but the argument was that the breech-loading rifle and long range rifled artillery could provide the attacker, given a suitable numerical advantage, with the means to prevail through superior firepower and enfilade fire. The bayonet was not portrayed as a superior weapon to the rifle, it was the physical symbol of the moral ascendency achieved in the firefight.

If the relative decline in the significance of the *arme blanche* compared to the impact of the vastly enhanced firepower of modern weapons was important to the infantry, in the cavalry it became a matter that seemed to threaten their very existence as a distinctive arm. This fuelled the heated debate around the role of cavalry on the modern battlefield. In hindsight, the extensive use of dismounted firepower-based cavalry tactics observed in America can be seen to be more indicative of the future than the European emphasis on the continued importance of mounted action, and the retention of the sabre and lance as the primary cavalry weapons. However, the issues were not so obvious from the viewpoint of the 19th Century. The retention of the *arme blanche* was partly due to the ongoing belief in the psychological impact of the cavalry charge in battle, partly a response to its retention by possible European opponents, and partly a political defence against the fear that cavalry and yeomanry regiments would be converted into mounted infantry and lose their *esprit de corps*. However, the cost of retaining specialist heavy cavalry, the limited number of regular cavalry regiments, and the wide range of tactical environments in which British cavalry needed to operate, meant that it was necessary for them to adopt dismounted tactics increasingly over the period. By the end of the century British cavalry doctrine had accepted that firepower, including the support of machine guns, was an essential part of cavalry operations.

It has been suggested that massed artillery fire was a tactical lesson from the American Civil War.[25] At the start of the Civil War batteries were arranged upon

25   Brinkmann, 'German Observations and Evaluations of the U.S. Civil War', pp.116-18.

British lines, attached to and subordinated to the infantry. Later organisations, initially in the Confederate service, created artillery battalions independent of the infantry command structure. There were occasions when artillery firepower was concentrated, but there were Napoleonic precedents for massed batteries and the Prussian use of concentrated long-range artillery fire in 1870 was a more significant development than anything seen in the Civil War. In recognition of its greater range and effectiveness, and the need for specialist direction of the artillery in battle, British regulations did relax the requirement for the artillery to conform tactically to infantry movements in 1874, and also emphasised the importance of concentrated artillery fire in the support of attacks on prepared positions. Artillery was also intended to be operated outside of the effective range of infantry firepower;[26] the fact that this was ignored by some aggressive artillery commanders such as Colonel Long at the Battle of Colenso was not due to an ignorance of the Civil War, but instead suggests a throwback to the close combat tactics practised by American artillerists. Nevertheless, since in the British Army organisations above the battery were rarely used in the field due to the small scale of troop deployments during the period, the impact of the Civil War on the artillery arm was limited.

By the end of the 19th Century the essence of British tactical doctrine was that firepower decided the battle, whether this was provided by infantry, artillery or cavalry. The objective of gaining the firepower superiority was to break the enemy *morale* which would then enable a final assault. Without the assault, defended positions could not be taken unless the enemy had been annihilated by firepower. A defensive posture was recognised as having substantial tactical advantage over the offensive, but was not seen as being always possible, and offensive action might well be required in order to gain the necessary defensible positions. Particularly in the context of colonial warfare a focus on offensive action was not irrational. Even against a European style enemy a purely defensive posture against an opponent in superior numbers with a freedom to manoeuvre had been demonstrated to lead to defeat, as evidenced by the campaign before Atlanta between Sherman and Johnson. Frontal offensives against a prepared enemy were recognised as sometimes necessary, but also to be the most difficult tactical operation of war, and they were generally to be avoided. Open and extended order were the regulation attack formations against an enemy in position, and flank attacks were the preferred approach, using mobile forces such as cavalry and mounted infantry where appropriate. At a tactical level therefore, with possible reservations over the retention of a battlefield role for the mounted cavalry charge, it is difficult to see where the British Army's practices were incompatible with the lessons of the Civil War.

26   Anon, *Field Exercises and Evolutions of the Infantry, 1874*, Pocket edn (London: HMSO, 1874), pp.280-84; Anon, *Infantry Drill* (1889), p.208.

According to Luvaas most Europeans writing about the Civil War up to 1914 focused on the tactics of the war not the strategy.[27] This introduced Luvaas' final chapters on the theories of Fuller and Liddell Hart, with their more strategic views on the war's importance, but it is not born out by the opinions being expressed by British authors. By the end of the 19th Century the Civil War was being held up as a source of strategic lessons, but of relatively little use for detailed tactical lessons. This was in part due to the changed nature of modern weapons, and also due to a perception that Civil War tactics had been indecisive and failed to achieve what the strategy had aimed at. While the tactics of 1870 were considered superior to those of 1865, the strategies of the American generals were still seen as relevant.[28]

'Strategy' in this period referred primarily to what would normally now be termed 'Operations', and focussed on the bringing to bear of superior forces on the battlefield. British writers up to and including Henderson mostly looked upon strategy in terms of manoeuvring so as to bring about decisive battle, a pattern of military thought in line with both Jomini and Clausewitz. Modern operational theory considers that the decisive battle is only one aspect of operations, and the origins of this can be assigned to the later campaigns of the Civil War. Grant's Overland Campaign replaced the traditional decisive battle with a deliberate policy of wearing down the enemy's army, while Sherman's campaign in Georgia applied military force against the enemy's economy and the civilian population's will to fight.[29] It is in comparison to these new ways of waging warfare that Hamley's *Operations of War* can be criticised as conservative and unoriginal.[30] British generals did remain fixated on decisive battle, but this was largely because in colonial campaigns, where British armies were outnumbered, operating in both geographically and politically hostile territory, and where public opinion back home would not accept heavy casualties, they needed quick victories and could not afford long drawn out campaigns. The Boer War demonstrated what happened if no quick decisive battle took place. Operations became extended, sieges occurred, and the war became one of attrition that was also directed upon the civil population. Even though very different tactically, the operational objectives of the late stages of the Boer War, the reduction of the enemy's will and capability to continue the fight, were those of Sherman and Grant.

27   Luvaas, *Military Legacy*, p.230.
28   Major E.S. May, 'History of the Civil War in America' [A review of John Codman Ropes' *The Story of the Civil War Vol. 1*], *Minutes of the Proceedings of the Royal Artillery Institution*, 22 (1895), pp.109-12 (pp.109-10).
29   Brinkmann, 'German Observations and Evaluations of the U.S. Civil War', p.95. Weigley, *A Great Civil War*, pp.328-29, sees the Civil War as the start of the concept of the operational art of war; and in *Towards an American Army*, pp.81-82, compares the Clausewitzian objective of destroying the enemy's army with Grant and Sherman's conduct of war against the enemy's society and economy.
30   Luvaas, *Education of an Army*, p.165.

Prolonged campaigns required a greater emphasis on logistics and critical to the maintenance of modern armies was the railway. The significance of railways in the Civil War did not come as a surprise to the British, but it was seen largely as a consequence of the relatively undeveloped infrastructure in America. Particularly in the West, the only means by which armies of the scale raised during the war could be maintained in the field were by water or by the railway. The British subsequently used railways themselves in colonial wars to supply their armies in hostile terrain, in Abyssinia and in the Sudan, and Wolseley recommended the adoption of American rather than European practice in the construction of such railways. In European warfare the much denser railway networks presented a different set of operational circumstances. The events of the Austro-Prussian and Franco-Prussian Wars focussed attention on the way in which railways could be used for rapid mobilisation in a European context, rather than the use of railways to support troops in remote locations. Both these aspects of the use of railways did feature in British thought, but what did not happen was the establishment of a military organisation to manage the railways in time of war equivalent to those of the European powers.

What was not fully anticipated was the contribution of the railway to the prolonging of campaigns and to the indecisiveness of battle in a major war. By allowing the concentration of larger armies and their supply and reinforcement in position on an unprecedented scale, the tactical defeat of an army was less likely to result in strategic withdrawal. Increased dependency on railways had another major operational impact, it resulted in an increased vulnerability of the lines of communications. In America this had led to the development of the concept of what are now called 'deep operations' through the cavalry raid, used both offensively, mostly by Union generals, and on the strategic defensive, by Confederate raiders such as Forrest and Morgan. British military thought did not ignore this development, but its application during British campaigns was rare, mostly due to the limited numbers of cavalry that were available to be deployed. However, the actions of Drury-Lowe's Cavalry Division after Tel-el-Kebir shows that the bold use of cavalry at an operational level was not the sole preserve of American generals. The successes of Russian cavalry both in manoeuvres and in the Russo-Turkish war were recognised as a development of American practice, but in the context of the defence of Britain or a campaign in western Europe, where the communications infrastructure was more sophisticated and the capacity to guard it much greater, the ability to conduct American style raids was expected to be constrained. The Boer War raised the profile of mounted troops and deep operations, drawing parallels with the Civil War again, but the opportunities for these types of attacks on the railway and logistical infrastructure rested mainly with the Boers, not with the British.

Steam power had also revolutionised the capability of naval power to project armies against vulnerable points on the enemy coast or inland waterways, attacks which could be either military or economic in their objective. This was a feature of the Civil War that should have resonated very strongly with the British, and indeed Wolseley regarded it as highly significant, citing the siege of Charleston as the most important source of lessons for Britain. Yet in spite of Wolseley's interest, the actual development of a theory of combined operations was minimal. Actions such as Charleston and Fort Fisher should have clearly demonstrated the importance of collaboration between the Navy and the Army, and on some occasions such as at Omdurman this did occur, but on a limited scale. The attack on Alexandria in 1882 revealed a poor level of collaboration between the two services, and lessons had still not been learnt by the Dardanelles campaign in 1915.

A final point to note is the awareness of the British to the changes in command, control, and communications, or 'C3' in modern parlance, which were observed in the Civil War. At an operational level this was most marked in the recognition of the importance of the telegraph. Already identified in the British Army as a significant new technology, its use in America was particularly publicised by Wolseley who thought it even more important than the railway in changing the future of warfare. By enabling near instant communication between widely separated forces, the new telegraphy and signalling technologies offered the opportunity to co-ordinate their movements. This was expected to allow greater opportunities at a tactical level for outflanking movements. It also facilitated the deployment of larger forces and the extension of the operational theatre, even to the grand strategic level. The advances made in this respect in the American War were further developed by the actions of the Prussians in 1866 and 1870.[31]

Overall the assimilation of operational lessons from the Civil War by the British has to be judged as incomplete. All of the more significant developments in the Civil War were recognised by British writers, but by the end of the century relatively little had been done at an official level to respond. The desire to bring about a decisive battle may be excused given the geographic circumstances, and usually limited political objectives, of British campaigns in the period. However, there was little consideration of how cavalry should be equipped to carry out deep operations; how joint command structures should be set up to conduct combined operations; or how to establish organisations for the effective management of railways for military purposes, either at home or more importantly overseas. The lack of effective institutions responsible for considering such matters meant that awareness and debate were not translated into practical actions.

Strategy, in its modern context of employing all aspects of national power to achieve a political objective, was an almost unknown concept at the time of the Civil War. Historians have seen in the war the origins of a number of features which in combination make up the model of modern 'total war' as seen in the 20th Century. These include the application of the entire resources of the nation to the war; the corresponding attack on the enemy's economic production; the mass enlistment of the

31   Charles Cornwallis Chesney, 'The Military Growth of Prussia' in Chesney Reeve *Military Resources*, pp.58-125 (p.112); Maurice, 'How Far the Lessons of the Franco–German War are out of Date', pp.560-61, 575.

population into the army; and the interdependence and cooperation of the political and military establishments.[32]

To some extent all of these features were identified by different British commentators and analysts of the Civil War. While in the early stages of the war the Americans were mocked for their amateurism, and continued to be criticised for the enormous cost of the war in material and lives, the effort that the nation had put into the conflict was recognised, and held up after the war as a model for how Britain might need to mobilise her resources in the future. Chesney recognised that 'the advantage of superiority in population, in manufacturing power, and material wealth is increased beyond all former belief by the new resources of the railroad and the steam fleet' and Adair that 'the indomitable spirit and inexhaustible resources' of the United States had led to the total defeat of the Confederacy.[33] There were also similarities between the Boer War and the Civil War in respect of targeting civilian support for the enemy war effort.

Strategically the Boer War also saw the first substantial mobilisation of imperial forces from Australia and Canada and the raising of large numbers of volunteer units from Britain for foreign service. The creation of mass volunteer armies had been one of the most outstanding features of the Civil War. Britain had a small peacetime regular army and a very limited regular reserve compared to her potential continental foes, and since conscription was rejected as politically unacceptable the British were dependent upon part-time and part-trained volunteers to provide numbers of troops to defend against invasion. The American experience should have been particularly relevant therefore, but while recognising the achievement of both sides in the war of raising such large numbers of troops, the British response to it was once again limited, and did not contribute in any substantial way to the recruiting or training of British volunteers. Certain authors drew comparisons from the American war to promote the volunteer movement or in Henderson's case to educate them, but there was no systematic learning from the Civil War of the nature of the volunteer armies, how they should be trained or used, and most significantly how they could be officered. The British stuck to the notion that only regular trained officers were appropriate to lead substantial formations of troops.

The emergence of 'total war' closely linked to political objectives, and its role in enabling the North to defeat the South, was seen by the British, but it was not adopted by them. In part this was due to an aversion to the brutality of some of the methods, which were not viewed as in accord with contemporary civilised values. There was also no occasion during the period in which Britain needed to fight a war where national survival was at stake, and which therefore could have led to the introduction of measures such as conscription. A third reason was the fact that the Army was never called

---

32   Brinkmann, 'German Observations and Evaluations of the U.S. Civil War', p.87.
33   Chesney, 'Recent Changes in the Art of War', in Chesney and Reeve, *Military Resources*, p.52; Adair, 'Strategy Of Invasion', p.161.

upon politically to carry out a thorough review its role in national or imperial policy. The nearest Victorian equivalent to a modern 'Strategic Defence Initiative' was the Stanhope Memorandum of 1888, which assigned the Army relatively limited and primarily defensive goals. A few individuals like Fletcher and Simmons considered issues of imperial defence, but while imperial troops were used in colonial actions there was again no organisation that was tasked with producing a strategic plan to bring the full resources of the Empire to bear in a war against a major power.[34] The most the Memorandum considered was an expeditionary force provided that the home country and India were secure from invasion. The campaigns on which the army embarked during the period were limited in scope and political objectives, and largely reactive to events. In these circumstances the 'total war' fought in the later stages of the American conflict seemed irrelevant to British strategic requirements both politically and militarily.[35]

*   *   *

Luvaas, influenced by 20th Century criticism of the Victorian and Edwardian army, argued that the tactical lessons of the war had been largely ignored whereas the changes in strategy had been acknowledged. The conclusion from this analysis is that the reverse is true. The operational impact of steamships, railways, and the telegraph upon warfare, and the growing importance of logistics, were all recognised and their use was vital in some campaigns, but the operational art of war nevertheless lagged behind that seen in the Civil War. At the strategic level the appearance during the Civil War of something approaching the 20th Century concept of total war had also been noted. However, 20th Century concepts of strategy were not something which the British needed to apply during the 19th Century, although the latter stages of the Boer War did begin to take on some of the features of 20th Century wars, such as the targeting of civilians to undermine support for the enemy's combat troops, and the mobilisation of the resources of the Empire in support of its political objectives.

In contrast, by the end of the 19th Century the Army's tactical instructions for fighting a European enemy armed with modern weapons were significantly more advanced than usually credited. The strength of the tactical defensive and the fact

34   Indian and Australian troops were used in the Sudan and Australians and Canadians in South Africa. West Indian troops were used in West Africa. Henry Charles Fletcher suggested the use of Indian troops in the event of war against Russia in 1878, Colonel Henry Charles Fletcher, 'On the Employment of the Reserve Forces in Case of an Expeditionary Force Being Sent Abroad', *Journal of the Royal United Service Institution*, 22 (1878), pp.350-68 (p.351).

35   Deborah Avant, *Political Institutions and Military Change: Lessons from Peripheral Wars* (Ithaca, Cornell University Press, 1994), pp.102-14, argues that the Army's doctrine and strategic objectives were well aligned to those of Britain's political establishment, which minimised conflict between the two and enhanced the Army's ability to adapt during the Boer War, but also led to short-termism.

that firepower had become more destructive and had transformed the battlefield was clearly recognised. Lessons attributed to the Civil War such as the use of field fortifications, the need for more open formations, the importance of artillery in attacking strongly held positions, and the use of mobile firepower to attack the enemy flanks and rear were all included in contemporary manuals, and there was an expectation that modern European warfare would result in long drawn out battles resembling sieges that were typical of the American campaigns of 1864-65.

This book has aimed to judge the British Army by how well it used its knowledge of the Civil War to solve the problems that it faced in the 19th Century. Its deficiencies were due to the immaturity of its institutions; to the type of campaigns on which it embarked; and to the varied nature of its military problems and the resultant wide range of experience and competence shown by individuals, rather than to any fundamental resistance to the learning process or failure to observe changes in warfare. When judged by contemporary standards, the evidence is that between 1861 and 1899 it had learned a great deal more than previously recognised. Britain's particular affinity with America and the resulting study of the Civil War contributed to this to a significant extent. While the study of the war was not the only reason for change or the only source of lessons, it had nevertheless played an important role in preparing the Army for the next century.

Sources and Bibliography

Primary Unpublished Sources

Private Papers
Bentley Papers, British Library, Additional Manuscripts
Dearborn Collection, Houghton Library, Harvard University
Doyle, General Sir Hastings, Letters to Sir William Fenwick Williams, Museum of New Brunswick, St John
Evans, Henry, Diary Transcript, University of Wales, Bangor
Layard, Sir Austen Henry, Papers, British Library, Additional Manuscripts
Liddell Hart Papers, Liddell Hart Archive, Kings College London
Malet Family Papers, British Library, Western Manuscripts Microfilm RP.886; originals in Duke University, Durham, NC
Wolseley, Field Marshal Viscount Garnet Joseph, Papers, Hove Public Library, Sussex

War Office Papers
WO 17 Office of the Commander in Chief: Monthly Returns to the Adjutant General
    WO 17/1565 through 1569 Monthly Returns to the Adjutant General, Canada, 1861-1865
    WO 17/2409 through 2412 Monthly Returns to the Adjutant General, Nova Scotia, 1862-1865
WO 25 Secretary-at-War, Secretary of State for War, and Related Bodies, Registers
    WO 25/1191 through 1192 Disembarkation returns, 1861-3
    WO 25/3913 Records of Service – Officers – Royal Engineers
WO 32 Registered Files (General Series). This series comprises registered files of the War Office dealing with all aspects of the administration of the departments and the armed forces.
    WO 32/6062 Lecture given in Paris by Col. A. Lynch MP on the role of English Military Balloons in the South African War
    WO 32/6067 Report by Major H. Elsdale, Royal Engineers, on the comparable position of British and Foreign Ballooning. Question of expenditure to maintain and train British Balloon Detachment [1885-1886]

WO 32/6068 Proposed Balloon Depot and Training Establishment at Chatham. Requirements and estimates and memorandum on Balloon Photography by Major El[m]sdale [1886-1887]

WO 32/6930 *Final Report of Committee on Ballooning* (1904)

WO 33 Reports, Memoranda and Papers. This series contains confidential printed reports, memoranda etc. which were specially printed and given a limited circulation.

a) Minutes of the Ordnance Select Committee and its Successors

WO 33/10/0140 *Abstract of Proceedings of the Ordnance Select Committee From 1st January to 31st March 1861*

WO 33/10/0146 *Abstract of Proceedings of the Ordnance Select Committee from 1st April to 30th June 1861*

WO 33/10/051 *Abstract of Proceedings of the Ordnance Select Committee from 1st July to 30th September 1861*

WO 33/11/0159 *Abstract of Proceedings of the Ordnance Select Committee from 1st October to 31st December 1861*

WO 33/11/0164 *General Index to the Abstracts of Proceedings and Reports of the Ordnance Select Committee for the Year 1861*

WO 33/11/0169 *Abstract of Proceedings of the Ordnance Select Committee From 1st January to 31st March 1862*

WO 33/11/0173 *Abstract of Proceedings of the Ordnance Select Committee from 1st March to 30th June 1862*

WO 33/11/0178 *Abstract of Proceedings of the Ordnance Select Committee from 1st July to 30th September 1862*

WO 33/12/0186 *Abstract of Proceedings of the Ordnance Select Committee from 1st October to 31st December 1862*

WO 33/12/0189 *General Index to the Abstracts of Proceedings and Reports of the Ordnance Select Committee for the Year 1862*

WO 33/12/0192 *Abstract of Proceedings of the Ordnance Select Committee From 1st January to 31st March 1863*

WO 33/12/0199 *Abstract of Proceedings of the Ordnance Select Committee from 1st March to 30th June 1863*

WO 33/12/0203 *Abstract of Proceedings of the Ordnance Select Committee from 1st July to 30th September 1863*

WO 33/13/0214 *Abstract of Proceedings of the Ordnance Select Committee from 1st October to 31st December 1863*

WO 33/13/0220 *General Index to the Abstracts of Proceedings and Reports of the Ordnance Select Committee for the Year 1863*

WO 33/13/0226 *Abstract of Proceedings of the Ordnance Select Committee for the Quarter Ending 31st March 1864*

WO 33/14/0230 *Abstract of Proceedings of the Ordnance Select Committee for the Quarter Ending 30th June 1864*

WO 33/14/0234 *Abstract of Proceedings of the Ordnance Select Committee for the Quarter Ending 30th September 1864*

WO 33/14/0249 *Abstract of Proceedings of the Ordnance Select Committee for the Quarter Ending 31st December 1864*

WO 33/15/0254 *General Index to the Abstracts of Proceedings and Reports of the Ordnance Select Committee for the Year 1864*

WO 33/15/0255 *Abstract of Proceedings of the Ordnance Select Committee From 1st January to 31st March 1865*

WO 33/15/0259 *Abstract of Proceedings of the Ordnance Select Committee from 1st March to 30th June 1865*

WO 33/15/0266 *Abstract of Proceedings of the Ordnance Select Committee from 1st July to 30th September 1865*

WO 33/16/0270 *Abstract of Proceedings of the Ordnance Select Committee from 1st October to 31st December 1865*

WO 33/17A/0276 *General Index to the Abstracts of Proceedings and Reports of the Ordnance Select Committee for the Year 1865*

WO 33/17A/0285 *Abstract of Proceedings of the Ordnance Select Committee for Quarter Ending 31st March 1866*

WO 33/17A/0294 *Abstract of Proceedings of the Ordnance Select Committee for the Quarter ending 30th June 1866*

WO 33/17A/302 *Abstract of Proceedings of the Ordnance Select Committee for the Quarter ending 30th September 1866*

WO 33/18/0309 *Abstract of Proceedings of the Ordnance Select Committee for the Quarter ending 31st December1866*

WO 33/18/0310 *General Index to the Abstracts of Proceedings and Reports of the Ordnance Select Committee for the Year 1866*

WO 33/18/0320 *Abstract of Proceedings of the Ordnance Select Committee for Quarter Ending 31st March 1867*

WO 33/18/0324 *Abstract of Proceedings of the Ordnance Select Committee for Quarter Ending 30th June 1867*

WO 33/18/0332 *Abstract of Proceedings of the Ordnance Select Committee for Quarter Ending 30th September 1867*

WO 33/18/0337 *Abstract of Proceedings of the Ordnance Select Committee for Quarter Ending 31st December 1867*

WO 33/19/0347 *General Index to Abstracts of Proceedings for Ordnance Select Committee, 1867*

WO 33/19/0353 *Abstract of Proceedings of the Ordnance Select Committee for Quarter ending 31st March 1868*

WO 33/19/0354 *Abstract of Proceedings of the Ordnance Select Committee for Quarter ending 30th June 1868*

WO 33/19/0356 *Abstract of Proceedings of the Ordnance Select Committee for Quarter ending 30th September 1868*

WO 33/20/0364, *Abstract of Proceedings of the Ordnance Select Committee from 1st October to 7th December 1868 and of the Department of the Director General of Ordnance from 8th December to 31st December 1868*

WO 33/20/0374 *General Index to Abstracts of Proceedings for Ordnance Select Committee, 1868*

WO 33/20/0378 *Abstract of Proceedings of Department of the Director General of Ordnance for Quarter Ending 31st March 1869*

WO 33/20/0392 *Abstract of Proceedings of Department of the Director General of Ordnance for Quarter Ending 30th June 1869*

WO 33/21A/0428 *Abstract of Proceedings of the Department of the Director of Artillery for the Quarter Ending 30th September 1870*

WO 33/22/0411 *General Index to Abstracts of Proceedings of Department of the Director General of Ordnance 1869*

WO 33/22/0469 *General Index to abstracts of Proceedings of Department of the Director General of Artillery 1870*

WO 33/23/0492 *Abstract of Proceedings of the Department of the Director of Artillery for the Quarter Ending 30th September 1871*

WO 33/24/0514 *General Index to Abstracts of Proceedings of Department of the Director Of Artillery 1871*

WO 33/25/0543a *Abstract of Proceedings of the Department of the Director of Artillery for the Quarter Ending 30th September 1872*

WO 33/25/0546 *General Index to Abstracts of Proceedings of Department of the Director of Artillery 1872*

WO 33/29/0630 *Abstract of Proceedings of Department of Director of Artillery for Quarter Ending 30th June 1876*

b) Other Reports and Memoranda

WO 33/11/0155 *List of Troops and Stores Embarked for British North America* (1861)

WO 33/11/0163 *Reports and Papers on Foreign Artillery* (1861)

WO 33/11/0165 Burgoyne, Field Marshal Sir John, *Memorandum by Sir J.F. Burgoyne, on the Defence of Canada – February 1862* (1862)

WO 33/11/0174 *Report of Officers of the British Army on American Arms* (1862)

WO 33/11/0185 *Report of the Commissioners Appointed to Consider the Defences of Canada* (1862)

WO 33/12/0204 *Report of Ordnance Select Committee No. 3065 6th November 1863: The Relative Penetration into Earth of Projectiles From Rifled and Smooth Bore Guns, and on Several Varieties of Percussion Fuze* (1863)

WO 33/14/0229 Gallwey, Lieutenant Colonel, and Alderson, Captain, *Report upon the Military Affairs of the United States of America* (1864)

WO 33/14/0241 *Report of the Committee on Small Arms* (1864)

WO 33/15/0242 *Report of Ordnance Select Committee on various plans of Breech-Loading Small Arms Submitted between 1859 and 1864* (1864)

WO 33/15/0256 *Report of Ordnance* (1864)

WO 33/15/0257 *Memorandum by the Defence Committee on the Report by Lieutenant Colonel Jervois on the Defence of Canada* (1865)

WO 33/15/0265 Jervois, Lieutenant Colonel William F. Drummond, *Report on the Defence of Canada, Made to the provincial government on the 10th November 1864, and of the British Naval Stations in the North Atlantic: Together with Observations on the Defence of New Brunswick, etc.* (1865)

WO 33/17A/0288 *Memoranda Relative to Transport for an Army in the Field* (1866)

WO 33/17A/0297 Jervois, Lieutenant Colonel William F. Drummond, *Report with Reference to the Progress Made in the Construction of the Fortification for the Defence of the Dockyards and Naval Arsenals of the United Kingdom* (London: HMSO, 1867)

WO 33/17A/0298 *Papers relating to the Question of Arming the Infantry with Breechloaders*

WO 33/17A/0299 W.D.F. J[ervois], *Experiments upon a Casemated Structure for Granite, with Iron Shields at the Embrasures, carried on at Shoeburyness in May and November 1865* (1866)

WO 33/17A/0300 *Memorandum by Floating Obstructions Committee on Extemporizing Torpedoes* (1865)

WO 33/17A/0305 *Report on Passive Obstructions For The Defence Of Harbours And Channels, by the Committee on Floating Obstructions and Submarine Explosive Machines* (1866)

WO 33/17A/0306 Peel, J., *Untitled Memorandum on Army Reserves* (1866)

WO 33/17B *Report on Arming of Infantry with Breach Loading Rifles* (1864)

WO 33/19/0357 *Report on Active Obstructions For The Defence Of Harbours And Channels, etc., and on the Employment Of Torpedoes For Purposes Of Attack, by the Committee on Floating Obstructions and Submarine Explosive Machines* (1868)

WO 33/19/0358 *Confidential report on Reserve forces 1868-9* (1869)

WO 33/20/0382 *Report of a Special Committee on Breech-loading Rifles* (1868)

WO 33/20/0384 *Considerations on the Military Position of Great Britain with respect to the United States* (1868)

WO 33/21A/0402 Fosberry, Major George V., *Report on the Construction of the Mitrailleur Christophe-Montigny; its Rifling, Cartridges, and Projectiles* (1870)

WO 33/21A/0424 *Departmental Papers Relating to Muzzle Loading versus Breech Loading Rifled Field Guns* (1870)

WO 33/21A/0425 Morshead, O.H., *Memorandum on Militia Recruiting* (1870)

WO 33/21B/0426 *Report of the Committee appointed to inquire into the Financial State and Internal Organization of the Volunteer Force in Great Britain* (1870)

WO 33/22/0445 *Minute by the Director of Artillery, upon the Report of the Special Committee on Mitrailleurs* (1870)

WO 33/22/0450 *Martini Henry Rifles* (1871)

WO 33/22/0453 Balfour, Major General Sir George, *Militia and Volunteers Training of Population by Voluntary Attendance at Drill* (1870)

WO 33/22/0453 Robertson-Aikman, Lieutenant Colonel F., untitled Memo, [1870]

WO 33/22/0454 Hamley, Colonel E.B., *Mitrailleuses* (1871)

WO 33/22/0465 Mansfield, Lieutenant General W.R., *The Future Recruitment of the Army* (1871)

WO 33/22/0519 *Report of the Special Committee on Mitrailleurs* (1870)

WO 33/24/0539 *Second Report of the Special Committee on Mitrailleurs* (1871)

WO 33/30/0648 *Second Report of the Special Committee on Siege Batteries* (1877)

WO 33/30/0649 *Proceedings of a Committee to consider the Medical Arrangements for an Army in the Field* (1877)

WO 45 Ordnance Office and Office of the Commander in Chief: Reference Books to Correspondence. Registers of the in-letters of the Board of Ordnance.

WO 45/289 through 293 covers the period 1861-1865

WO 147 Field Marshal Viscount Garnet Joseph Wolseley, Adjutant General of Army: Papers. An accumulation of some of the private papers of Field Marshal Viscount Wolseley

WO 147/49 Wolseley, Field Marshal Viscount Garnet Joseph, 'War Between England and Russia', untitled confidential memorandum (1878)

WO 147/49 Wilde, Brigadier General A., 'Report on equipment of the Hazarrah Field Force' (1868)

Miscellaneous War Office Records

DEFE 1900 Thomas, Major General V.D., *A Short Review of the History and Development of British Amphibious Warfare* (1954)

SUPP 5/908 *Trials of Magazine Rifles in England from 1879, a Memorandum by Colonel C.G. Slade* (1887)

SUPP 6/12 *Extracts from the Reports and Proceedings of the Ordnance Select Committee, Vol. 2. January–December 1864* (London: HMSO, 1865)

WO 279/860, *Report of the Torpedo Committee appointed 29 July 1870 by HRH the Field Marshal Commanding in Chief for the Purpose of Deciding on the Form, Composition and Machinery of Torpedoes* (1876)

WO 1/1138 *Commander in Chief Loose Letters* (1845-1868)

Air Ministry Papers

AIR 1/2404/303 War Office Ordnance Select Committee: Employment of Balloons in Warfare, (1862-1885).

Colonial Office Papers

CO 880/6/1, *Canada: Defences of Canada* (1864)

Foreign Office Papers

FO 5 Foreign Office: Political and Other Departments: General Correspondence before 1906, United States of America, Series 2

FO 5/829 through 831, Lord Lyons and Mr Stuart; Correspondence, 1862

FO 5/896 through 898, Lord Lyons; Correspondence, 1863
FO 5/904, Consular Correspondence, 1863
FO 5/915, Consular Correspondence, 1863
FO 5/938 through 950, Lord Lyons; Correspondence, 1864
FO 5/966, Consular Correspondence, 1864
FO 5/1149 through 1153, Blockade runners, imprisonment of British Subjects,
vols 1-5 (1863-1864)
FO 115 Foreign Office: Embassy and Consulates, United States of America: General
Correspondence
FO 115/359 through 367 Correspondence from United States Government, 1863
FO 115/402 Correspondence from Foreign Office, 1864
FO 881 Foreign Office: Confidential Print
FO 881/1254 *Confidential Report by Captain Goodenough, R.N. On the Naval
Resources of the United States* (1864)

Parliamentary Papers
Army Medical Department, *Statistical Sanitary and Medical Reports, Vol. VI for the
Year 1864* (1866)
British Parliamentary Papers, 1864, 62 (cmd 299)
House of Commons, *First Report of the Royal Commission Appointed to Inquire into
the Present State of Military Education and into the Training of Candidates for
Commissions in the Army,* 1868-69 *(*cmd 4221)
House of Commons, *Report from the Select Committee on Ordnance; together with the
Proceedings of the Committee, Minutes of Evidence, Appendix, and Index* (1862)
House of Commons, *Report from the Select Committee on Ordnance; together with the
Proceedings of the Committee, Minutes of Evidence, Appendix, and Index* (1863)
Parliamentary Debates, 3rd Series, vols 167-175 (1862-1864)

Primary Published Sources

Bibliographic Notes
Several authors published both under their own names and also anonymously or
under pseudonyms; and their formal titles and ranks changed during the period being
researched. In order to clearly group works of common authorship, I have taken the
approach of using the most complete name and the highest known rank or title from
any of the publications used, while noting pseudonyms used in the original publication where appropriate to clearly identify the source.

Modern reprints and collections of original works are included here under their original authors with their editors and translators indicated.

Books and Pamphlets

Acton, John Emerich Edward Dalberg, *Essays in Religion, Politics, and Morality*, edited by J. Ruffin Fears (Indianapolis: Indianapolis: Liberty Classics, 1988)

Anderson, Colonel R.P., *Victories and Defeats: An Attempt to Explain the Causes Which Have Led to Them* (London: Henry S. King, 1873)

Anon, *American War: the Mode in Which it is Waged by the Federals, as Recorded by Both Parties* (London: Society for Promoting the Cessation of Hostilities in America, [1864])

Anon ['An Adjutant'], *An Essay on Tactics (Wellington Essay Prize)* (London: W. Mitchell, 1872)

Anon ['An Adjutant of Militia'], *British Infantry Tactics, or the Attack Formation Explained with Some Introductory Remarks on Infantry Tactics in General* (London: Mitchell & Co, [1877])

Anon ['R.R.'], *British Infantry Drill as it Might Be* (London: Simpkin Marshall and Co, 1868)

Anon, *Catalogue of the War Office Library Volume 1.2* (London: Unknown Publisher, 1906)

Anon, *Hart's Army List No. 87, July 1860* (London: John Murray, 1860)

Becke, Captain A.F., *Introduction to the History of Tactics 1740-1905* (London: Hugh Rees,1909)

Bell, Sir George, *Soldier's Glory: Being Rough Notes of an Old Soldier*, edited by Brian Stuart (London: Spellmount, 1991, originally published London: Day, 1867)

Blackford, Lieutenant Colonel William Willis, (CSA), *War years with Jeb Stuart* (New York: Charles Scribner, 1946)

Bowdler-Bell, Captain C., *Catechism of Reconnaissance, Marches and Outposts. Founded on the Authorised Instructions for the Regular and Auxiliary Cavalry* (London: W. Mitchell, [1877])

Brialmont, Colonel Alexis Henri, *La Fortification Improvisée* (Brussels: C Muquardt, 1870)

Britten, Bashley, *Rifled Cast-Iron Ordnance. The Power and Endurance of the Smooth Bore and Rifled Cast-iron Ordnance of the United States, Employed in the Late American War* (London: W. Mitchell, [1872])

Butler, Colonel Sir W.F., *The Campaign of the Cataracts* (London: Sampson Low, Marston, Searle and Rivington, 1887)

Caffey, Thomas ['T.E.C.'], *Battle-fields of the South, from Bull Run to Fredericksburg; With Sketches of Confederate Commanders, and Gossip of the Camps*, 2 vols (London: Smith, Elder, and Co., 1863)

Cairnes, W.E. ['A Staff Officer'], *An Absentminded War* (London: John Milne, 1900)

Cairnes, W.E. ['Author of *An Absentminded War*'], *A Commonsense Army* (London: John Milne, [1901])

Cannon, John, *History of Grant's Campaign for the Capture of Richmond, 1864-1865, with an Outline of the Previous Course of the American Civil War* (London: Longmans & Co., 1869)

Chesney, Lieutenant Colonel Charles Cornwallis, *A Military View of Recent Campaigns in Virginia and Maryland* (London: Smith, Elder, and Co., 1863)

Chesney, Lieutenant Colonel Charles Cornwallis, and Henry Reeve, *The Military Resources of Prussia and France and Recent Changes in the Art of War* (London: Longmans Green and Co. 1870)

Chesney, Lieutenant Colonel Charles Cornwallis, *Essays in Modern Military Biography* (London: Longman, Green & Co, 1874)

Chesney, Lieutenant Colonel Charles Cornwallis, *On The Value of Fortresses and Fortified Positions on Defensive Operations: An Essay written on a vacation tour in 1864 to accompany an application for the professorship of Military History at the Staff College*, 2nd edn Revised (London: Byfield, Stanford and Co, 1868)

Chesney, Lieutenant Colonel Charles Cornwallis, *The Study of Military Science in Time of Peace* (London: Harrison and Sons, [c.1871]

Chesney, Lieutenant Colonel Charles Cornwallis, *The Tactical Use of Fortresses: A farewell lecture concluding a course of military history for military engineers* (London: Byfield, Stanford and Co, 1868)

Chevenix Trench, Colonel F., *Cavalry in Modern War* (London: Kegan Paul, 1884)

Clausewitz, Carl von, *On War*, trans. by Colonel J.J. Graham (London: N. Trübner & Co., 1873)

Clausewitz, Carl von, *On War*, trans. by F.N. Maude, ed. by Anatol Rapoport (London: Pelican, 1968, originally published 1832, translated 1908)

Clery, Lieutenant Colonel C.F., *Minor Tactics* (London: Henry S. King, 1875)

Clarke, Major Sir George Sydenham, *Fortification: its past achievements, recent development, and future progress* (London: John Murray, 1890)

Clifford, Lieutenant W.R., *A Resume of the Tactical Portions Contained in parts VI, VII, VIII and IX of the 'Infantry Drill, 1889'* (London: William Clowes, 1890)

Collen, Lieutenant E.H.H., *The Battle of Worth. Staff College Essay Prize, 1872* (London, W Mitchell, 1872)

Colomb, Rear Admiral P.H., *Combined Military and Naval War Operations: With Some Remarks Upon the Embarkation and Disembarkation of Troops in the Presence of an Enemy, Lecture to Aldershot Military Society, Tuesday November 24th 1891* (Aldershot: Gale and Polden, [1891])

Colomb, Rear Admiral P.H., *Co-operation between the Army and Navy, Lecture to Aldershot Military Society, Wednesday January 19th 1891* (London: Edward Stanford, 1898)

Creswicke, Louis, *South Africa and the Transvaal War* (Edinburgh: T.C. and E.C. Jack, 1900)

Cunningham-Robertson, Major General, *Field Intrenching* (Edinburgh: Thomas and Archibald Constable, 1878)

Davitt, Michael, *The Boer Fight for Freedom* (New York and London: Funk and Wagnalls, 1902)

Dawson, Captain Francis W., (CSA), *Reminiscences of Confederate Service 1861-65* (Charleston: The News and Courier Book Presses, 1882)

Day, Samuel Philips, *Down South: or, An Englishman's Experience at the Seat of the American War* (London: Hurst and Blackett, 1862)

De Cosson, Major E.A., *Fighting the Fuzzy-Wuzzy: Days and Nights of Service with Sir Gerald Graham's Field Force in Suakin* (London: Greenhill Books, 1990, originally published London: John Murray, 1886)

Denison, Lieutenant Colonel George Taylor, *A History of Cavalry: From the Earliest Times, With Lessons for the Future* (London: MacMillan, 1877)

Denison, Lieutenant Colonel George Taylor, *Modern Cavalry* (London: T. Bosworth, 1868)

Denison, Lieutenant Colonel George Taylor, *Soldiering in Canada: Recollections and Experiences*, 2nd Edn (Toronto: George N. Morang, 1901)

Denison, Lieutenant Colonel George Taylor, *The National Defences: or, Observations on the Best Defensive Force for Canada* (Toronto: Unknown Publisher, 1861)

Dicey, Edward, *Six Months in the Federal States* (London and Cambridge: Macmillan, 1863)

Douglas, Henry Kyd, *I Rode with Stonewall* (London: Putnam, 1940, originally written 1899)

Dundonald, Lieutenant General the Earl of, *My Army Life*, New edn (London: Edward Arnold, 1934)

Engels, Friedrich, *Engels as Military Critic*, edited by W.O. Henderson and W.H. Chaloner (Manchester: Manchester University Press, 1959; articles originally published 1860-66)

Engels, Friedrich, *Engels: Selected Writings*, edited by W.O. Henderson (London: Pelican Books, 1967, original material from 1852-66)

Essays Written for the Wellington Prize (Edinburgh: Wm. Blackwood & Sons, 1872)

Fenton, Lieutenant Colonel Myles, *British Railways and Their Capabilities for Home Defence, Lecture to Aldershot Military Society, Thursday December 6th 1888* (Aldershot: Gale and Polden, 1888)

Fletcher, Colonel Henry Charles, *A Lecture Delivered at the Literary and Scientific Institute Ottawa* (Ottawa: Unknown Publisher, 1875; Microfiched by Canadian Institute for Historical Microproductions, 1981)

Fletcher, Colonel Henry Charles, *A Volunteer Force, British and Colonial, in the Event of War* (London: Harrison, [c.1877])

Fletcher, Colonel Henry Charles, *History of the American War*, 3 vols (London: R. Bentley, 1865–66)

Fletcher, Colonel Henry Charles, *Memorandum on the Militia System of Canada* (Ottawa: Unknown Publisher, 1873)

Fletcher, Colonel Henry Charles, *Report on the Military Academy of West Point U.S.* (Unknown Publisher, c.1874)

Fraser, Brevet Major [Captain] T., RE, *The Defence of a Position Selected as a Field of Battle: Royal Engineer Prize Essay for 1875* (Woolwich: Unknown Publisher, 1875)

Fremantle, Lieutenant Colonel Arthur James Lyon, *Three Months in the Southern States, April-June 1863* (Electronic edn) (Chapel Hill: University of North Carolina 2000, originally published Mobile, S.H. Goetzel, 1864)

Fremantle, Lieutenant Colonel Arthur James Lyon, *Three Months in the Southern States, April-June 1863*, ed. by Gary Gallagher (Lincoln: University of Nebraska Press, 1991, originally published New York, J. Bradburn, 1864)

Gall, Captain H.R., *Tactical Questions and Answers on the Infantry and Artillery Drill Books, 1889* (London: W.H. Allen, 1890)

Gillmore, Major General Q.A., (USA), *Engineer and Artillery Operations during the Defences of Charleston Harbour in 1863* (New York: Van Nostrand, 1865)

Gillmore, Major General Q.A., (USA), *Official Report of the United States Engineer Department of the Siege and Reduction of Fort Pulaski, Georgia* (New York: Van Nostrand, 1862)

Glenn, William Wilton, *Between North and South* ed. by Bayly Ellen Marks and Mark Norton Schaz, (London: Associated University Press, 1976)

Goldie, Lieutenant Colonel M.H.G. *Tactical Application of Field Defences in Battles of Recent Campaigns, Lecture to Aldershot Military Society, Tuesday March 2 1897* (London: Edward Stanton, 1897)

Gurowski, Adam von, *Diary [kept during the civil war in the United States of America] from 1861 [-65]* (Electronic edn, originally published Washington, DC: Unknown Publisher, 1862-66)

Hale, Colonel Lonsdale, *The Spirit of Tactical Operations of To-day, Lecture to Aldershot Military Society, Wednesday 11 April 1888* (Aldershot: Aldershot Military Society, 1888)

Halford, Colonel Sir Henry St John, *New Service Magazine Rifle, Lecture to Aldershot Military Society, Thursday 2 Feb 1888* (Aldershot: Aldershot Military Society, 1888)

Hamley, Lieutenant Colonel Edward Bruce, *The Operations of War Explained and Illustrated*, 1st edn (Edinburgh and London: W. Blackwood, 1866)

Hamley, Lieutenant Colonel Edward Bruce, *The Operations of War Explained and Illustrated*, 4th edn (Edinburgh and London: W. Blackwood, 1878)

Harrison, General Richard, *Recollections of the life in the British Army during the Latter Half of the 19th Century* (London: Smith, Elder & Co, 1908)

Harrison, General Richard, *The Organization of an Army for War, Lecture to Aldershot Military Society, Thursday January 3 1889* (Aldershot: Gale and Polden, 1889)

Hatfield, Major Samuel P., (USA), *History of the First Connecticut Artillery and of the Siege trains of the Armies Operating against Richmond, 1862-65* (Hartford, CN: Case, Lockwood and Brainard, 1893)

Havelock-Allen, Major Henry, *Three Main Military Questions of the Day* (London: Spottiswoode, 1867)

Head, General Sir Francis Boyd, *The Royal Engineer* (London: John Murray, 1869)

Henderson, Lieutenant Colonel George Francis Robert, *First lecture on 'The American Civil War, 1861-65 – the Composition, Organization, System, and Tactics of the Federal and Confederate Armies'* (Aldershot: Gale & Polden, 1892)

Henderson, Lieutenant Colonel George Francis Robert, *Second lecture on 'The American Civil War, 1861-65 – a Resume of some of the Principal Events of the War, Illustrative of the Strategy and Tactics of the Belligerents'* (Aldershot: Gale & Polden, 1892)

Henderson, Lieutenant Colonel George Francis Robert, *Stonewall Jackson and the American Civil War*, 2 vols (Secaucus NJ: Blue and Grey Press, [n.d.], originally published London: Longmans, 1900)

Henderson, Lieutenant Colonel George Francis Robert, *The Battle of Gettysburg, July 1st, 2nd, and 3rd, 1863* (Aldershot: Gale & Polden, [1893])

Henderson, Lieutenant Colonel George Francis Robert, *The Battle of Spicheren August 6 1870 and the Events that Preceded it: a Study in Practical Tactics and War Training* (London: Gale and Polden, [n.d.])

Henderson, Lieutenant Colonel George Francis Robert, *The Campaign of Fredericksburg, Nov-Dec 1862: a Tactical Study for Officers* (London: Gale and Polden, 1886)

Henderson, Lieutenant Colonel George Francis Robert, *The Civil War: A Soldier's View. A Collection of Civil War Writings by Col. G.F.R. Henderson*, ed. by Jay Luvaas (Chicago: University of Chicago Press, 1958, original material from 1886-95)

Henderson, Lieutenant Colonel George Francis Robert, *The Science of War: A Collection of Essays and Lectures, 1892–1903* (New York: Longmans, Green, and Co., 1905)

Henty, G.A., *With Lee in Virginia: a Story of the American Civil War* (London: Blackie & Son, 1890)

Hime, Lieutenant Colonel Henry William Lovett, *Royal United Service Institution. Prize Essay: Universal conscription: the only answer to the recruiting question* (London: W. Mitchell, 1875)

Hime, Lieutenant Colonel Henry William Lovett, *Stray Military Papers* (London, New York and Bombay: Longmans, Green, and Co, 1897)

Hime, Lieutenant Colonel Henry William Lovett, *The Minor Tactics of Field Artillery* (London and Woolwich: Unknown Publisher, 1872), reprinted from *Proceedings of the Royal Artillery Institution* 7 (1872)

Home, Major Robert, *A Precis of Modern Tactics: Compiled from the Works of Recent Continental Writers at the Topographical and Statistical Department of the War Office* (London: HMSO, 1873)

Home, Major Robert, *A Precis of Modern Tactics*, 2nd edn revised and rewritten by Lieutenant Colonel Sisson C. Pratt, (London: HMSO, 1896)

Hood, General John Bell, (CSA), *Advance and Retreat* (Edison NJ: Blue and Grey Press, 1985 originally published 1880)

Humel, Captain H.W., *The discipline of the Volunteer Force: A lecture delivered at the Royal United Service Institution, 9th July 1877* (London: W. Mitchell, [1877])

Hutton, Lieutenant General Edward Thomas Henry, *Mounted Infantry its Present and Future, Lecture to Aldershot Military Society, Thursday March 21 1889* (Aldershot: Gale and Polden, 1889)

James, Captain W.H., *The Role of Cavalry as Affected by Modern Arms of Precision* (Aldershot: Gale and Polden, 1894)

James, Major W.C., *The Development of Modern Cavalry Action in the Field* (Aldershot: Gale and Polden, [1881])

Johnson, Robert Underwood, and Clarence Clough Buel (eds), *Battles and Leaders of the Civil War*, 4 vols (Secaucus NJ: Castle 1983, originally published 1887)

Kenneway, John H., *On Sherman's Track: or, The South after the War* (London: Seeley, Jackson, and Halliday, 1867)

Knollys, Captain Henry, RA, *The Elements of Field Artillery* (Edinburgh and London: William Blackwood and Sons, 1877)

Lawrence, George Alfred, *Border and Bastille* (New York: W.I. Pooley, 1863),

Liddell, Colonel R.S., *Modern Cavalry on the Field of Battle, Lecture to Aldershot Military Society, Monday August 6 1888* (Aldershot: Gale and Polden 1888)

Lippitt, Francis J., *Reminiscences of Francis J. Lippitt, written for his family, his near relatives and intimate friends* (Providence RI: Preston & Rounds Co, 1902)

Lippitt, Francis J., *A Treatise on the Tactical Use of the Three Arms, Infantry, Artillery, and Cavalry* (New York: Van Nostrand, 1865)

Longstreet, Lieutenant General James, (CSA), *From Manassas to Appomattox: Memoirs of the Civil War in America* (New York: Da Capo Press, 1992, originally published Philadelphia: J.B. Lippincott and Co, 1896)

Lothian, Marquess of, *The Confederate Secession* (Edinburgh: W. Blackwood & Sons, 1864)

Lyman, Theodore, *Meade's Army: The Private Notebooks of Lieutenant Colonel Theodore Lyman*, ed. by David W. Lowe (Kent: Kent State University Press, 2007)

Lyman, Theodore, *Meade's Headquarters 1863-1865. Letters of Theodore Lyman From The Wilderness to Appomattox*, selected and edited by George R. Agassiz (Freeport NY: Books for Libraries Press, 1970)

Macdonald, Lieutenant Colonel J.H.A., *Memorandum of Instructions for a New System of Infantry Attack* (Edinburgh: Wm. Blackwood & Son, [1884])

MacDougall, General Sir Patrick L. ['An Officer'], *Forts Vs Ships: Also Defence of the Canadian Lakes and its Influence on the General Defence of Canada* (London: James Ridgway, 1862)

MacDougall, General Sir Patrick L., *Modern Warfare as Influenced by Modern Artillery* (London: John Murray, 1864)

MacDougall, General Sir Patrick L., *The Theory of War Illustrated by Numerous Examples from Military History* (London: Longman, Brown, Green, Longmans & Roberts, 1856)

MacPherson, James F. ['An Adjutant'], *An Essay in Tactics* (London: W. Mitchell, 1872),

Maguire, T. Miller, *Importance of the American War 1861-5 as a Strategic Study, Lecture to Aldershot Military Society, Tuesday November 1 1892* (Aldershot: Gale and Polden, 1893)

Mahan, Asa, *A Critical History of the Late American War. With an Introductory Letter by Lieutenant General M.W. Smith* (London: Hodder and Stoughton, 1877)

Majendie, Captain V.D. and Captain C.O. Browne, *Military Breech-Loading Rifles* (London: Royal Artillery Institution, 1869)

Malet, Captain J.W., *Handbook to Field Training in the Infantry* (Chatham: Gale & Polden, 1891)

Maude, Lieutenant Colonel Frederic Natusch, *Attack or Defence: Seven Military Essays* (London: J.J. Keliher, 1896)

Maude, Lieutenant Colonel Frederic Natusch, *Cavalry versus Infantry and Other Essays* (Kansas City: Henderson-Kimberley, 1896)

Maude, Lieutenant Colonel Frederic Natusch, *Cavalry: Its Past and Future* (London: William Clowes, 1903)

Maude, Lieutenant Colonel Frederic Natusch, *Letters on Tactics and Organisation or, English Military Institutions and the Continental Systems* (Leavenworth: G.A. Spooner, 1891)

Maude, Lieutenant Colonel Frederic Natusch, *Voluntary Versus Compulsory Service* (London: Stanford, 1897)

Maurice, Major General Sir John Frederick, *Wellington Prize Essay on The System of Field Manoeuvres Best Adapted for Enabling our Troops to meet a Continental Army* (London: William Blackwood and Sons,1872)

Maurice, Major General Sir John Frederick, *War* (London: Macmillan & Co., 1891)

May, Major E.S., *Achievement of Field Artillery* (London: Royal Artillery Institution, 1893)

May, Major E.S., *The Problem of the Attack, Lecture to Aldershot Military Society, Tuesday April 5 1898* (London: Edward Stanford, 1898)

Mayer, Captain Edgar J., *The Attack Formation by Sections. As it can be Carried out in Accordance with 'Field Exercises, 1884' Without Mixing Companies* (London: T.G. Johnson, 1885)

Michie, Peter S., *Life and Letters of Emory Upton* (New York: Arno Press, 1979, originally published 1885)

Nevill, Captain H.L., *North-West Frontier: British Army Campaigns on the North-West Frontier of India 1849-1908* (London: Tom Donovan, 1992, originally published 1912),

Newdigate, Sir Edward, *Experimental Tactics of Infantry in the Year 1872: Extracts From 'Militair Wochenblatt'* (London: Unknown Publisher, 1873)

Nolan, Captain L.E., *Cavalry: Its History and Tactics*, 3rd edn (London: Bosworth & Harrison, 1860, originally published 1853)

Nolan, Captain L.E., *Cavalry: Its History and Tactics*, with an introduction by Jon Coulston (Yardley PA: Westholme, 2007, originally published 1853)

Patton, Colonel Bethune, *Attack Formations* (London: Wm. Clowes, 1885)

Ropes, John Codman, *The Story of the Civil War* (London, New York: GP Putnam, 1894-98)

Ross, Fitzgerald, *A Visit to the Cities and Camps of the confederate States* (Edinburgh and London: W. Blackwood 1865)

Rothwell, Captain J.S., *Narrative of the Field Operations connected with the Zulu War of 1879* (London: Greenhill Books, 1989, originally published 1881)

Russell, William Howard, *My Diary North and South* (Boston: T.O.H.P. Burnham, 1863)

Saint Maur, Lord Edward Adolphus Ferdinand, and Lord Edward St Maur, ed. by Guendolen Ramsden, *Letters of Lord St. Maur and Lord Edward St. Maur, 1846 to 1869* (London: n. pub., 1888)

Sala, George, *My Diary in America in the Midst of War*, 2 vols (London: Tinsley Brothers, 1865)

Savage, Major J.W., *The Application of Fortification to the Requirements of the Battlefield, Lecture to Aldershot Military Society, Thursday, February 21 1889* (Aldershot: Gale and Polden, 1889)

Schaw, Colonel Henry, *Defence and Attack of Positions and Localities*, 5th edn (London: Kegan Paul, Trench, Trübner, 1893, originally published 1875)

Scheibert, Captain Justus, *Seven Months in the Rebel States During the North American War*, translated from the German by Joseph C Hayes (Tuscaloosa: Confederate Publishing Company, 1958)

Scheliha, Karl Rudolph, *A Treatise on Coast-defence Based on the Experience Gained by Officers of the Corps of Engineers of the Army of the Confederate States, and Compiled from Official Reports of Officers of the Navy of the United States* (London: E. & F.N. Spon, 1868)

Scherff, Wilhelm Carl Friedrich Gustav Johann von, *The New Tactics of Infantry*, translated by Colonel Lumley Graham (London: Henry S. King & Co., 1873)

Sherman, General William Tecumseh, (USA), *Memoirs*, 2 vols (New York: Appleton, 1875)

Simmons, General John Lintorn Arabin, *Defence of Canada considered as an imperial question with reference to a war with America* (London: Longman, Green, Longman, Roberts, & Green, 1865)

Smith, General M.W., *Modern Tactics of the Three Arms* (London: W. Mitchell, 1869)

St Alcock, Colonel Thomas, *The Relative Power of Nations* (London and Edinburgh: Williams & Norgate, 1872)

Stephen, Sir Leslie ['L.S.'], *The 'Times' on the American War: an Historical Study* (London: William Ridgeway, 1865)

Stone, Captain F.G., *The Maxim Machine Gun, Friday July 6 1888*. (Aldershot: Gale and Polden, 1888)

Upton, Brevet Major General Emory, (USA), *The Armies of Asia and Europe. Embracing Official Reports On the Armies of Japan, China, India, Persia, Italy, Russia, Austria, Germany, France, and England. Accompanied by Letters Descriptive of A Journey from Japan to the Caucasus* (New York: Appleton, 1878)

Verdy Du Vernois, Julius Adrian Friedrich Wilhelm von, *A Tactical Study, Based on the Battle of Custozza*, trans. by Major G.F.R. Henderson (London: George Allen, 1894)

Von Borcke, Heros and Justus Scheibert, *Die Grosse Reitershlacht bei Brandy Station*, translated by Stuart T. Wright and F.D Bridgewater (Winston-Salem: Palaemon, 1976, originally published Berlin, 1893)

Von Borcke, Heros, *Memoirs of the Confederate War of Independence*, 2 vols (London: William Blackwood and Sons, 1866)

Wagner, Arthur Lockwood, *The Campaign of Königgratz: A study of the Austro-Prussian Conflict in the Light of the American Civil War* (Fort Leavenworth: Unknown Publisher, 1889)

Watson, William, *Life in the Confederate Army: Being the Observations and Experiences of an Alien in the South during the American Civil War* (London: Chapman & Hall, 1887)

Watson, William, *Life in the Confederate Army: Being the Observations and Experiences of an Alien in the South during the American Civil War*, ed. by Thomas W. Cutrer (Baton Rouge and London: Louisiana State University Press, 1995)

Wilkinson, Spenser, *War and Policy: Essays* (Westminster UK: Constable,1900)

Wilson, Sir Charles, *From Kurti to Khartoum*, 4th edn (London: Blackwood, 1886)

Wolseley, Field Marshal Viscount Garnet Joseph, *Story of a Soldiers Life* (Westminster: Archibald Constable, 1903)

Wolseley, Field Marshal Viscount Garnet Joseph, *Soldier's Pocket Book*, 2nd edn (London and New York: MacMillan, 1871)

Wolseley, Field Marshal Viscount Garnet Joseph, *The American Civil War: An English View*, ed by James A. Rawley (Charlottesville: University Press of Virginia, 1964)

Wolseley, Field Marshal Viscount Garnet Joseph, *The Use of Railways in War: A Lecture Delivered at Aldershot on the 29th January 1873* (London: Unknown Publisher, 1873)

Wood, General Sir Evelyn, *Achievements of Cavalry, with a chapter on Mounted Infantry* (London: George Bell and Sons, 1897)

Wood, General Sir Evelyn, *Mounted Riflemen – A lecture delivered at the Royal United Service Institution, March 4 1873* (London: W. Mitchell & Co, 1873)

Drill Manuals

Anon, *Cavalry Drill* (London: HMSO, 1891)

Anon, *Cavalry Drill* (London: HMSO, 1896)

Anon, *Combined Training* (London: HMSO, 1902)

Anon, *Field Exercises and Evolutions of Infantry* (London: HMSO, 1861)

Anon, *Field Exercises and Evolutions of Infantry* (London: HMSO, 1867)

Anon, *Field Exercises and Evolutions of Infantry* (London: HMSO, 1870)

Anon, *Field Exercises and Evolutions of Infantry*, Pocket Edition (London: HMSO, 1874)

Anon, *Field Exercises and Evolutions of Infantry* (London: HMSO, 1877)

Anon, *Infantry Drill* (London: HMSO, 1889)

Anon, *Infantry Drill (Provisional)* (London: HMSO, 1892)

Anon, *Instructions for the Sword, Carbine, Pistol, and Lance Exercise; together with Field Gun Drill* (London: HMSO, 1871)

Anon, *Manual of Field Artillery Exercise* (London: HMSO, 1875)

Anon, *Regulations and Field Service Manual for Mounted Infantry* (London: HMSO, 1889)

Anon, *Regulations for Mounted Infantry* (London: HMSO, 1884)

Anon, *Regulations and Instructions. Mounted Infantry* (London: HMSO, 1895)

Anon, *Regulations for the Instructions and Movements of Cavalry* (London: HMSO, 1865)

Anon, *Regulations for the Instructions and Movements of Cavalry* (London: HMSO, 1876)

Anon, *Regulations for the Instructions and Movements of Cavalry, 1887 Alterations and additions* (London: HMSO, 1887)

Anon, *Rifle Exercises and Musketry Instruction. Appendix to the Field Exercise 1874; revised 1877* (London: HMSO, 1877)

Anon, *Yeomanry Regulations 1853* (London: HMSO, 1853)

Bower, Lieutenant Colonel J., *Manual of Drill for Mounted Rifle Volunteers, or Volunteer Irregular Cavalry* (London: Unknown Publisher, 1863)

Hardee, William J., *Rifle and Light Infantry Tactics* (New York: J.O. Kane, 1862)

Hardee, William J., *The Rifle and Light Infantry Tactics: For the Exercise and Manoeuvres of Troops*, 2 Volumes (Philadelphia: Lippincott, Grambio & Co., 1855)

Upton, Brevet Major General Emory, (USA), *A New System of Infantry Tactics Double and Single Rank, Adapted to American Topography and Improved Fire Arms* (New York: D. Appleton, 1868)

Chapters

Roberts, Field-Marshal Lord, 'Memoir' in G.F.R. Henderson, *The Science of War* (New York: Longmans, Green, and Co., 1905), pp.xiii-xxxviii

Wagner, Arthur Lockwood, 'The Army' in *The United States Army and Navy* (New York: Werner, 1899), pp.5-103

Wolseley, Field Marshal Viscount Garnet Joseph, 'The Standing Army of Great Britain' in *The Armies of Today: A Description of the Armies of Leading Nations at the Present Time* (London: Osgood, 1893), pp.59-96

Journals and Newspapers

Army and Navy Gazette

Army and Navy Journal

Blackwood's Edinburgh Magazine

Cornhill Magazine

Evening Star

Fortnightly Review

Fraser's Magazine
Illustrated Naval and Military Magazine
Journal of the Household Brigade
Journal of the Royal United Service Institution
Minutes of the Proceedings of the Royal Artillery Institution
19th Century
North American Review
Quarterly Review
*Royal Engineers' Professional Papers (*formerly *Papers on Subjects Connected with the
    Duties of the Corps of Royal Engineers)*
The Times
United Service Magazine (formerly *Colbourn's United Service Magazine)*

Articles
Adair, Colonel Sir R.A. Shafto, 'The Defence of London ', *Journal of the Royal United
    Service Institution*, 4 (1860), pp.291-310
Adair, Colonel Sir R.A. Shafto, 'The Lines of London: Defences by Works And
    Manoeuvre In The Field', *Journal of the United Service Institution*, 6 (1862),
    pp.521-33
Adair, Colonel Sir R.A. Shafto, 'The Militia, and its Defensive Uses in the Event Of
    Invasion', *Journal of the United Service Institution*, 2 (1858), pp.379-405
Adair, Colonel Sir R.A. Shafto, 'The Strategy of Invasion, as Exemplified in the
    American and Austro-Prussian Wars, and in the War of Metz; with Remarks
    on Centres of Defence and the Training of National Forces', *Journal of the Royal
    United Service Institution*, 16 (1872), pp.153-67
Alexander, Sir J.E., 'United States Military Academy, West Point', *United Service
    Magazine*, 310 (September 1854), pp.7-23
Altham, Captain E.S., 'The Cavalry Revival – A Plea for Infantry', *United Service
    Magazine*, n.s., 2 (1890), pp.17-33
Anon, '[Review of Denison's] A History of Cavalry', *United Service Magazine*, 586
    (1877), pp.15-22
Anon, '[Review of Emory Upton's] Armies of Asia', *United Service Magazine*, 598
    (September 1878), pp.87-95
Anon ['R.D.'], 'Boston, New York and Washington', *Journal of the Household Brigade
    for the year 1862*, (London: W. Clowes and Sons, 1863), pp.192-96
Anon, 'Canada – Its Several Invasions', *Journal of the Household Brigade for the year
    1862* (London: W. Clowes and Sons, 1863), pp.150-51
Anon, 'Coast Defence', *United Service Magazine*, 475 (June 1868), pp.241-47 and 477
    (August 1868), 493-99
Anon, 'Democracy on its Trial', *Quarterly Review*, 110 (July 1861), pp.247-88
Anon, 'Ironclad Ships of War and our Defences', *Blackwood's Edinburgh Magazine*, 89
    (1861), pp.304-17
Anon, 'Military Mines', *United Service Magazine*, 480 (November 1868), pp.440-45

Anon, 'Notes on Hasty Entrenchments', *United Service Magazine*, 598 (September 1878), pp.95-101

Anon ['W.C.'], 'On the Defence of our Dockyards against Iron-Plated Vessels, *United Service Magazine*, 428 (July 1864), pp.339-44

Anon, 'Our Critics in Germany', *Illustrated Navy and Military Magazine* 6 (1890), pp.69-77

Anon [Sir Bruce Hamley?], 'Our Rancorous Cousins', *Blackwood's Edinburgh Magazine*, 94 (November 1863), pp.636-52

Anon, 'Siege of Charleston', *United Service Magazine*, 439 (June 1865), pp.170-83

Anon [Sir Francis Ottiwell Adams?], 'The American War: Fort Sumter to Fredericksburg', *Quarterly Review*, 113 (April 1863), pp.322-53

Anon ['Cold Steel'], 'The Bayonet as a Weapon', *United Service Magazine*, n.s., 18 (1898), pp.82-85

Anon, 'The Big Guns of all Nations', *United Service Magazine*, 478 (September 1868), pp.83-93

Anon, 'The Efficiency of British Cavalry', *United Service Magazine*, 478 (September 1868), pp.94-100

Anon, 'The Guards in Canada', *Journal of the Household Brigade for the year 1862* (London: W. Clowes and Sons, 1863), pp.153-55

Anon, 'The Last Campaign in America', *United Service Magazine*, 444 (November 1865), pp.369-81

Anon, 'The Spade in a Campaign', *United Service Magazine*, 440 (July 1865), pp.364-76

Anon ['Signalman'], 'The Railways and the Manoeuvres', *United Service Magazine*, n.s., 18 (1898), pp.71-81

Anon, 'The War in South Africa', *Edinburgh Review*, 192 (1900), pp.271-306

Anon, 'Topography of the Seat of War in America and Present Position of the Belligerents', *United Service Magazine*, 436 (March 1865), pp.365-72

Ardagh, Captain J.C., 'The Comparative Cost of The Armies of Different Nations and the Loss to Country by Conscription', *Journal of the Royal United Service Institution*, 20 (1876), pp.218-52

Armit, Captain R.H., 'Machine-Guns, Their Use and Abuse', *Journal of the Royal United Service Institution*, 30 (1886), pp.37-68

Baden-Powell, Lieutenant B[aden], 'Military Ballooning', *Journal of the Royal United Service Institution*, 12 (1868), pp.735-57

Baillie Hamilton, Major W.A., 'The Truth about the Yeomanry Cavalry', *United Service Magazine*, n.s., 3 (1891), pp.433-40

Bainbridge, Major General, 'Notes on the Changes in Field Operations Likely to be Caused by the Adoption of Rifled Arms, and their Effect on the Engineer Equipment', *R.E. Professional Papers*, 11 (1862), pp.240-42

Bainbridge, Major General, 'Notes on the Changes in The Construction of Fortifications Which Appear Likely to be Required in Consequence of the General Adoption of Rifled Guns', *R.E. Professional Papers*, 13 (1864), pp.121-26

Baker, Colonel Valentine, 'Organisation and Employment of Cavalry', *Journal of the Royal United Service Institution*, 17 (1873), pp.375-410

Beaumont, Captain Frederick F. E, 'On Balloon Reconnaissance as Practised by the American Army', *R.E. Professional Papers*, 12 (1863), pp.94-103

Beaumont, Captain Frederick F.E., 'Balloon Reconnaissance', *Journal of the Royal United Service Institution*, 8 (1864), pp.52-66

Benson, Lieutenant G.E., 'A Machine-Gun Battery and its Equipment', *Journal of the Royal United Service Institution*, 30 (1886), pp.69-76

Bigge, Major T.S., 'Proposed Formation of a Battalion for the Attack', *Journal of the Royal United Service Institution*, 18 (1874), pp.152-56

Boulderson, Major S., 'The Armament and Organisation of Cavalry and Their Influence on its Tactics', *Journal of the Royal United Service Institution*, 22 (1878), 3 pp.78-96

Bourke, Robert [Anon], 'A Month with the Rebels', *Blackwood's Edinburgh Magazine*, 90 (1861), pp.755-67

Bourke, Robert [Anon], 'Canada – Our Frozen Frontier', *Blackwood's Edinburgh Magazine*, 91 (1862), pp.102-17

Brackenbury, General Henry, 'Stonewall Jackson', *Blackwood's Edinburgh Magazine*, 164 (1898), pp.721-38

Brackenbury, General Henry, 'The Tactics of the Three Arms as Modified to Meet the Requirements of the Present Day', *Journal of the Royal United Service Institution*, 17 (1873), pp.617-47

Burgoyne, Field Marshal Sir John, 'On Hasty Entrenchments in the Field', *R.E. Professional Papers*, 18 (1870), pp.93-96

Burrell, G.R., 'On the Progress of the Military Sciences', *Journal of the Royal United Service Institution*, 7 (1863), pp.395-425

Butler, General Benjamin F., (USA), 'Defenseless Canada', *North American Review*, 147 (1888), pp.441-52

Cairnes, W.E. ['Author of *An Absent Minded War*'], 'The Empire and the Army', *Fortnightly Review*, n.s., 70 (1901), pp.13-25

Callwell, Major General Sir Charles E., 'Lessons to be Learnt From the Campaigns in Which British Forces Have Been Employed Since the Year 1865', *Journal of the Royal United Service Institution*, 31 (1887), pp.357-412

Cecil, Robert, 'The Confederate Struggle and Recognition', *Quarterly Review*, 112 (July 1862), pp.535-70

Cecil, Robert, 'The United States as an Example', *Quarterly Review*, 117 (January 1865), pp.249-86

Chesney, Lieutenant Colonel Charles Cornwallis, 'Sherman and Johnston in the Atlanta Campaign', *Fortnightly Review*, 18 (December 1875), pp.611-24

Chesney, Lieutenant Colonel Charles Cornwallis, 'Sherman's Campaign in Georgia', *Journal of the Royal United Service Institution*, 9 (1865), pp.204-20

Chesney, Lieutenant Colonel Charles Cornwallis, 'The Compte de Paris' Campaigns on the Potomac', *Edinburgh Review* 164 (1876), pp.79-103

Chesney, Lieutenant Colonel Charles Cornwallis, 'The Recent Campaigns in Virginia and Maryland', *Journal of the Royal United Service Institution*, 7 (1864), pp.291-307

Chesney, Sir George T. [Anon], 'A True Reformer' (Part XIV), *Blackwood's Edinburgh Magazine*, 113 (April 1873), pp.446-75

Chevenix Trench, Colonel F., 'On the Progress That Has Been Made During Recent Years In Developing The Capabilities of Cavalry', *Journal of the Royal United Service Institution*, 21 (1877), pp.990-1011

Clarke, Charles Sidney, 'The Volunteer in War', *United Service Magazine*, n.s., 18 (1898), pp.301-08

Clayton, Captain Emilius, 'Field Intrenching: Its Application on the Battlefield and its Bearing on Tactics', *Journal of the Royal United Service Institution*, 23 (1879), pp.281-338

Clive, Colonel Edward, 'On the Influence of Breechloading Arms on Tactics, and on the Supply of Ammunition in the Field', *Journal of the Royal United Service Institution*, 22 (1878), pp.814-63.

Collinson, Major General T.B., 'On the Present Facilities for the Invasion of England, and for the Defence Thereof', *Journal of the Royal United Service Institution*, 21 (1877), pp.1-91

Copper, Colonel, Captains Thynne and Cooper, and Lord Dunmore, 'Hunting Tour in the Western Prairies', *Journal of the Household Brigade for the year 1862* (London: W. Clowes and Sons, 1863), pp.200-203

Cox, Captain J.C., 'Proposal for the Formation of a Corps of Riflemen for Immediate Service on the Frontier (India)', *Journal of the Royal United Service Institution*, 8 (1864), pp.437-42

Davis, Jefferson, 'Lord Wolseley's Mistakes', *North American Review*, 149 (1889), pp.472-82

De La Bere, Captain, 'The Musketry Training of Infantry Volunteers', *United Service Magazine*, n.s., 19 (1899), pp.58-63

Dilke, Charles W., 'Guerrilla and Counter-Guerrilla', *Fortnightly Review*, n.s., 70 (1901), pp.927-33

Dixon, R.A., 'The Rifle–Its Probable Influence on Modern Warfare', *Journal of the United Service Institution*, 1 (1858), pp.95-120

Edwards, Major C.J., 'The Yeomanry Cavalry as an Auxiliary and Reserve Force', *Journal of the Royal United Service Institution*, 27 (1883), pp.329-356

Elias, Lieutenant Colonel R., 'The Land Forces of Australia', *Journal of the Royal United Service Institution*, 34 (1890), pp.205-28

Elsdale, Colonel H., 'The Defence of London and of England', *Journal of the Royal United Service Institution*, 30 (1886), pp.601-670

Elsdale, Colonel H., 'The Three Ruling Races of the Future', *United Service Magazine*, n.s., 4 (1892), pp.333-344; 385-94, 473-487

Farquharson, Lieutenant Colonel J.F., 'The Military Organisation Best Adapted for Imperial Needs', *Journal of the Royal United Service Institution*, 34 (1893), pp.329-60

Featherstonhaugh, Captain Albany, 'Narrative of the Operations of the British North American Boundary Commission, 1872–76', *R.E. Professional Papers,* 23 (1876), pp.24–69

Featherstonhaugh, Captain Albany, 'Notes on the Defence of Petersburg', *R.E. Professional Papers,* 14 (1865), pp.190-94

Fergusson, James, 'On a Proposed New System of Fortification', *Journal of the Royal United Service Institution,* 4 (1861), pp.178-96

Fergusson, James [Anon], 'Some Account of Both Sides of the American War', *Blackwood's Edinburgh Magazine,* 90 (1861), pp.768-79

Firth, J.B., 'The Guerrilla in History', *Fortnightly Review,* n.s., 70 (1901), pp.803-11

Fletcher, Colonel Henry Charles, 'On the Employment of the Reserve Forces in Case of an Expeditionary Force Being Sent Abroad', *Journal of the Royal United Service Institution,* 22 (1877), pp.350-68

Fletcher, Colonel Henry Charles [Anon], 'A Run Through the Southern States', *Cornhill Magazine,* 7 (1863), pp.495–515

Fletcher, Colonel Henry Charles, 'A Volunteer Force, British and Colonial in the Event of War', *Journal of the Royal United Service Institution* 21 (1877), pp.631–58

Fletcher, Colonel Henry Charles, 'On the Causes that lead to Pre-eminence in War', *Journal of the Royal United Service Institution,* 21 (1877), pp.423-54

Fletcher, Colonel Henry Charles, 'The Employment of Mitrailleurs During the Recent War and their Use in Future Wars', *Journal of the Royal United Service Institution,* 16 (1872), pp.28-52

Fletcher, Lieutenant Colonel Henry Charles and Lieutenant Colonel Edward Neville, 'Visit to the Army of the Potomac', *Journal of the Household Brigade for the year 1862* (London: W. Clowes and Sons, 1863), pp.197-99

Forsyth, William [Anon], 'The American Crisis', *Quarterly Review,* 111 (January 1862), pp.239-80

Fosbery, Captain D.C., 'The Umbeyla Campaign', *Journal of the Royal United Service Institution,* 11 (1868), pp.548-68

Fraser, Brevet Major T., 'Field Intrenching: its Application on the Battlefield and its Bearing on Tactics', *Journal of the Royal United Service Institution,* 23 (1880), pp.339-401

Fraser, Brevet Major T., 'Notes on the Battlefield and its Bearing on Tactics', *Journal of the Royal United Service Institution,* 23 (1880), pp.339-401

Fremantle, Lieutenant Colonel Arthur James Lyon ['An English Officer'], 'The Battle of Gettysburg and the Campaign in Pennsylvania: Extract from the Diary of an English Officer Present with the Confederate Army', *Blackwood's Edinburgh Magazine,* 94 (1863), pp.365-94

Fry, James B., 'Lord Wolseley Answered', *North American Review,* 149 (1889), pp.728-40

Gall, Captain H.R., 'Infantry', *Illustrated Naval and Military Magazine,* 2 (1889) pp.1223-26

Gall, Captain H.R., 'Tactical Use of Mounted Infantry', *Illustrated Naval and Military Magazine*, 4 (1889) pp.453-56,

Gallwey, Lieutenant Colonel T.L., 'The Influence of Rifled Guns on the Attack and Defence of Fortresses', *R.E. Professional Papers*. 14 (1865), pp.25-55

Gillmore, Major General Q.A. (USA), 'Extracts from the Report of the Siege of Fort Pulaski, Georgia', *R.E. Professional Papers*, 13 (1864), pp.147-52

Gleig, George Robert [Anon], 'Defence of Canada', *Blackwood's Edinburgh Magazine*, 91 (1862), pp.228-58

Graham, Lieutenant General Sir Gerald, 'Shelter Trenches or Temporary Cover for Troops in Position', *Journal of the Royal United Service Institution*, 14 (1871), pp.448-78

Graham, Colonel Lumley, 'The Company As a Military Body. – Its Establishment. – The Best Number of Companies in the Battalion', *Journal of the Royal United Service Institution*, 19 (1875), pp.567-87

Graham, Colonel Lumley, '[Review of] A New System of Infantry Tactics', *United Service Magazine*, 470 (January 1868), pp.129-30

Graham, Lieutenant General Sir Gerald, 'Infantry Fire Tactics: Attack Formations and Squares', *Journal of the Royal United Service Institution*, 30 (1886), pp.233-274

Graham, Lieutenant General Sir Gerald, 'Suggestions for Adapting Fortifications to the Present Means of Attack', *R.E. Professional Papers*, 11 (1862), pp.156-68

Graves, Colonel F.J. [Colonel F.T. Graves], 'Cavalry Equipment, Organisation and Distribution', *Journal of the Royal United Service Institution*, 34 (1891), pp.695-712

Grover, Lieutenant [George Edward], 'On Reconnoitring Balloons', *R.E. Professional Papers*, 12 (1863), pp.87-93

Grover, Lieutenant [George Edward], 'On the Use of Balloons in Military Operations', *R.E. Professional Papers*, 12 (1863), pp.71-86

Hamilton, Mark, 'The Smoke Attack: As Shown to the German Emperor by Colonel Crease on the 7th August', *United Service Magazine*, n.s., 1 (1890), 5 pp.51-55

Hamley, Lieutenant Colonel Edward Bruce [Anon], 'Books on the American War', *Blackwood's Edinburgh Magazine*, 94 (1863), pp.750-68

Hamley, Lieutenant Colonel Edward Bruce [Anon], 'Democracy Teaching By Example', *Blackwood's Edinburgh Magazine*, 90 (1861), pp.395-405

Hamley, Lieutenant Colonel Edward Bruce [Anon], 'The Convulsions of America', *Blackwood's Edinburgh Magazine*, 91 (1862), pp.118-30

Hamley, Lieutenant Colonel Edward Bruce [Anon], 'Disruption of the Union', *Blackwood's Edinburgh Magazine*, 90 (1861), pp.125-34

Hamley, Lieutenant Colonel Edward Bruce [Anon], 'General McClellan', *Blackwood's Edinburgh Magazine*, 96 (1864), pp.619-44

Hamley, Lieutenant Colonel Edward Bruce [Anon], 'Our Neutrality', *Blackwood's Edinburgh Magazine*, 95 (1864), pp.447-61

Hamley, Lieutenant Colonel Edward Bruce [Anon], 'Spence's American Union', *Blackwood's Edinburgh Magazine*, 91 (1862), pp.514-36

Harrison, General Richard ['An Officer of the Royal Engineers'], 'A Trip to Meade's Army on the Rappahannock', *United Service Magazine*, 428 (July 1864), pp.329-39

Harrison, General Richard, 'The Use of Field Works in War', *United Service Magazine*, n.s., 9 (1894), pp.111-27

Harvey, Major Talbot, 'The Progressive and Possible Development of Infantry Drill and Manoeuvres', *Journal of the Royal United Service Institution*, 8 (1865), pp.294-95

'HCW', 'Future Infantry Tactics', *Illustrated Naval and Military Magazine* 4 (1889), pp.418-24

Head, E.W. [Anon], 'The American Revolution', *Edinburgh Review of Books*, 116 (1862), pp.549-94

Henderson, Lieutenant Colonel George Francis Robert, 'Lessons from the Past for the Future', *Journal of the Royal United Service Institution*, 38 (1894), pp.1183-1206

Henderson, Lieutenant Colonel George Francis Robert [Anon], 'The War in South Africa', *Edinburgh Review*, 191 (January 1900), pp.247-78

Henderson, Lieutenant Colonel George Francis Robert ['The Author of *The Campaign of Fredericksburg*'], 'Military Criticism and Modern Tactics', *United Service Magazine*, n.s., 3 (1891), pp.396-415, 553-67; 4 (1891), pp.51-65

Henderson, Lieutenant Colonel George Francis Robert, 'Strategy and Its Teaching', *Journal of the Royal United Service Institution*, 42 (July 1898), pp.761-86

Hime, Lieutenant Colonel Henry William Lovett, 'On the Development of Infantry Formations, With Special Reference to the Present Prussian Company', *United Service Magazine*, 597 (August 1878), pp.405-15

Hime, Lieutenant Colonel Henry William Lovett, 'Duties of Partisan Cavalry', *United Service Magazine*, 578 (1877), pp.1-12

Hoste, George H., 'The Further Development of the Volunteer Force', *Journal of the Royal United Service Institution* 21 (1877), pp.799-820

Hozier, Major John Wallace ['JWH'], '[Review of Denison's] History of Cavalry', *Journal of the Royal United Service Institution*, 22 (1878), pp.1225-32

Hutton, Lieutenant General Edward Thomas Henry, 'The Tactical and Strategic Power of Mounted Troops in War', *United Service Magazine*, n.s., 10 (1895), pp.431-49

Hutton, Lieutenant General Edward Thomas Henry, 'Mounted Infantry', *Journal of the Royal United Service Institution*, 30 (1886), pp.695-738

Hutton, Lieutenant General Edward Thomas Henry, 'The Mounted Infantry Question in its Relation to the Volunteer Force of Great Britain', *Journal of the Royal United Service Institution*, 35 (1891), pp.785-814

Inglis, Lieutenant Colonel, 'Experiments on Iron Armour', *R.E. Professional Papers*, 16 (1868), pp.125-144

Innes, Lieutenant, 'Notes on the Defences of Charleston, South Carolina', *R.E. Professional Papers*, 13 (1864), pp.16-23

James, Captain Walter H., 'Modern Fire: Its influence on Armament, Training and Tactics', *Journal of the Royal United Service Institution*, 17 (1873), pp.378-403

Jervois, Colonel William F. Drummond, 'Coast Defences, and the Application of Iron to Fortification', *Journal of the Royal United Service Institution*, 12 (1868), pp.549-69

Kennedy, Lieutenant Colonel J.P., 'The Strategic and National Importance of Extending Railway Communications Throughout the British Colonies, More Especially Throughout India', *Journal of United Service Institution*, 2 (1858), pp.62-86

Ker Fox, Major J.C., 'The Training of the German Cavalry as Compared with that of the English', *Journal of the Royal United Service Institution*, 34 (1890), pp.805-28

Knollys, Colonel W.W., 'The Effect of Smokeless Powder on the Wars of the Future', *United Service Magazine*, n.s., 4 (1891), pp.66-74

Knollys, Colonel W.W., 'The Fighting of Cavalry on Foot', *United Service Magazine*, 589 (1877), pp.403-10

Knollys, Colonel W.W., 'Lessons Taught by the Franco-German War', *United Service Magazine*, 705 (August 1887), pp.93-119

Knollys, Colonel W.W., 'The New System of Tactics', *United Service Magazine*, 584 (July 1877), pp.271-79

Knollys, Colonel W.W., 'What we Have Learnt from the War', *United Service Magazine*, 591 (February 1878), pp.135-43

Lane Fox, Lieutenant Colonel, 'On the Improvement of the Rifle as a Weapon for General Use', *Journal of the United Service Institution*, 2 (1859), pp.453-493

Lawley, Francis Charles, 'General Lee', *Blackwood's Edinburgh Magazine*, 111 (March 1872), pp.348-63

Lawley, Robert Neville, 'The Prospects of the Confederates', *Quarterly Review*, 115 (April 1864), pp.289-311

Lawrence, James, 'The Principles of Rifled Cannon and Projectiles', *Journal of the Royal United Service Institution*, 6 (1862), pp.116-27

Leahy, Lieutenant Colonel Arthur, 'Army Organisation, our Infantry Forces and Infantry Reserves', *Journal of the Royal United Service Institution*, 12 (1868), pp.310-58

Leahy, Lieutenant Colonel Arthur, 'Military Bridge Construction', *Journal of the Royal United Service Institution*, 19 (1876), pp.689-722

Leverson, Captain G.F., 'Tactical Guides for the Cavalry Division – translated from the German', *United Service Magazine*, n.s., 2 (1890), pp.138-52, 222-41, 340-56, 440-63, 553-63; 3 (1891), pp.33-41, 165-69, 240-54

Leverson, Captain G.F., 'The Cavalry Division as a Body in the Fight – translated from the German', *Journal of the Royal United Service Institution* 34 (1890), pp.46-100

Luard, Captain C.E., 'Field Railways and their General Application in War', *Journal of the Royal United Service Institution*, 17 (1873), pp.693-724

Macdonald, Lieutenant Colonel J.H.A., 'On the Best Detail Formation for Infantry in Line', *Journal of the Royal United Service Institution*, 22 (1878), pp.556-82

Mackinson, Colonel W., 'Bisley and the National Rifle Association', *United Service Magazine*, n.s., 4 (1892), pp.497-505

Maguire, T. Miller, 'The American War', *The Illustrated Naval and Military Magazine* 4 (1890), pp.259-76, 565-86; 5 (1890), pp.576-96; 6 (1890), pp.481-502

Maguire, T. Miller, 'Guerrilla or Partisan Warfare', *United Service Magazine*, n.s., 23 (1901), pp.127-34, 264-71, 353-64, 473-85, 583-92

Majendie, Captain V.D., 'Military Breech-Loading Small Arms', *Journal of the Royal United Service Institution* 11 (1867), pp.190-217

Malet, Lieutenant Colonel Henry, 'Our Reserve Forces', *Journal of the Royal United Service Institution*, 13 (1869), pp.160-80

Maude, Lieutenant Colonel Frederic Natusch, 'Cavalry on the Battlefield, *United Service Magazine*, n.s., 3 (1891), pp.310-23

Maurice, Major General Sir John Frederick, 'How Far the Lessons of the Franco-German War are out of Date', *United Service Magazine*, n.s., 10 (1895), pp.555-77

May, Major E.S., 'The Handling of Masses of Artillery, With Special Reference to the Preparation for the Infantry Attack, as Illustrated by the French Experience at the Camp of Chalons in 1892', *Journal of the Royal United Service Institution*, 37 (1893), pp.837-966

May, Major E.S., 'History of the Civil War in America' [A review of John Codman Ropes' *The Story of the Civil War Vol.1*], *Minutes of the Proceedings of the Royal Artillery Institution*, 22 (1895), pp.109-12

McCartney, Major, 'Modern Rifle Fire', *United Service Magazine*, n.s., 10 (1894), pp.31-41

Middleton, Lieutenant General Sir Frederick, 'Mounted Infantry', *United Service Magazine*, n.s., 5 (1892), pp.178-84

Miller, Major F., 'Military Sketch of the Present War in America', *Journal of the Royal United Service Institution*, 6 (1863), pp.241-62

Molyneux, Major W.C.F., 'Notes on Hasty Defences as Practised in South Africa', *Journal of the Royal United Service Institution*, 24 (1881), pp.806-14

Morris, General William H. (USA), 'On The Best Method Of Arming, Equipping, and Manoeuvring Infantry', *Journal of the Royal United Service Institution*, 10 (1866), pp.209-24

Morris, William O'Connor, 'General Sheridan', *Illustrated Naval and Military Magazine*, 2 (1889) pp.483-95

O'Hea, Captain J., 'Cartridges for Breech-Loading Small Arms, and the Best Form of Projectile', *Journal of the Royal United Service Institution*, 12 (1868), pp.105-26

O'Shea, John Augustus, 'Lessons of the American War', *United Service Magazine*, 704 (July 1887), pp.45-54

Otey, William Newton Mercer, 'Operations of the Signal Corps', *Confederate Veteran*, 8 (March 1900), pp.120-30

Owen, Major C.H., RA, 'The Present State of the Artillery Question', *Minutes of Proceedings of the Royal Artillery Institution*, 5 (1867), pp.212-249 (reprinted from *Journal of the Royal United Service Institution* 9 (1865), pp.342-370)

Patterson R.H. [Anon], 'The Crisis of the American War', *Blackwood's Edinburgh Magazine*, 92 (1862), pp.636-46

Peel, Captain Cecil Lennox ['CLP'], 'A Short Campaign With the Federal Army of the Potomac', *Journal of the Household Brigade for the year 1863* (London: W. Clowes and Sons, 1864), pp.190-99

Pritchard, H. Baden, 'The Application of Photography to Military Purposes', *Journal of the Royal United Service Institution*, 13 (1869), pp.419-34

'Q', a Company Officer, 'The Critics and the Infantry Attack' *United Service Magazine*, n.s., 13 (1896) pp.238-253

Raper, Colonel A.J., 'Notes on Organisation and Training, by a Regimental Officer', *Journal of the Royal United Service Institution*, 36 (1892), pp.1-15

Ross, Fitzgerald ['A Cavalry Officer'], 'A Visit to the Cities and Camps of the Confederate States', *Blackwood's Edinburgh Magazine*, 96 (1864), pp.645-70; and 97 (1865), pp.26-48, 151-76

Rothwell, Colonel J.S., 'The Conveyance of Troops by Railway', *United Service Magazine*, n.s., 3 (1891-92), pp.215-21, 310-20

Russell, Major Frank S., 'Cavalry', *Journal of the Royal United Service Institution*, 20 (1876), pp.179-95

Russell, William Howard, 'Recollections of the Civil War', *North American Review*, 166 (1898), pp.234-49, 362-73, 491-502, 618-30, 740-50

Schaw, Captain Henry, 'The Amount of Advantage which the New Arms of Precision give to the Defence over the Attack', *Journal of the Royal United Service Institution*, 14 (1870), pp.377-94

Schaw, Captain Henry, 'The Present State of the Question of Fortification', *Journal of the Royal United Service Institution*, 10 (1866), pp.442-62

Schaw, Captain, Henry, 'Military Telegraphs', *R.E. Professional Papers* 11 (1862), pp.111-24

Scheibert, Major J., 'Letter from Major Scheibert of the Prussian Royal Engineers', *Southern Historical Society Papers*, 5 (Jan-June 1878), pp.90-93

Scott, Commander R.A. (RN), 'Progress of Artillery Abroad Compared With That at Home', *Journal of the Royal United Service Institution*, 8 (1864), pp.443-66

Scott, Captain Sir Sibbald David, 'On the History of the Bayonet', *Journal of the Royal United Service Institution*, 7 (1863), pp.333-48

Selwyn, Captain J.H. (RN), 'Breech-Loaders, with Reference to Calibre, Supply and Cost of Ammunition', *Journal of the Royal United Service Institution*, 11 (1867), pp.16-26

Sherman, General W.T., (USA), 'Grant, Thomas, Lee', *North American Review*, 144 (1887), pp.437-50

Smith, General M.W., 'Cavalry: How Far its Employment is Affected by Recent Improvements in Arms of Precision', *Journal of the Royal United Service Institution*, 12 (1868), pp.147-68

Smyth, Major H.A., 'Account of the Final Attack and Capture of Richmond, by the Federal Army, Commanded by General Grant', *Minutes of the Proceedings of the Royal Artillery Institution*, 4 (1865), pp.363-70

Smyth, Major H.A., 'Some Observations Amongst German Armies During 1870', *Minutes of the Proceedings of the Royal Artillery Institution*, 7 (1870), pp.184-202

Spence, James, 'The Close of the American War', *Quarterly Review*, 118 (July 1865), pp.106-36

St Maur, Lord Edward [Anon], 'Ten Days in Richmond', *Blackwood's Edinburgh Magazine*, 92 (1862), pp.391-402

Steinmetz, Lieutenant A., 'Musketry Instruction For The Cavalry Carbine And Pistol, Recently Issued To The French Cavalry With Suggestions For The Training Of Cavalry, And Its Important Functions In Future Battles', *Journal of the Royal United Service Institution*, 5 (1861), pp.454-96

Steinmetz, Lieutenant A., 'On the Formation of Troops for Battle with Reference to the Modern Improvement in Firearms', *United Service Magazine*, 429 (September 1864), pp.11-21

Steinmetz, Lieutenant A., 'Past and Future of Cavalry', *United Service Magazine*, 439 (June 1865), pp.159-79

Steinmetz, Lieutenant A., 'The Soldier's Why and Because: or the Theoretical Principles of Drill; and the Chief Battalion Movements Exemplified in Battle', *United Service Magazine*, 428 (July 1864), pp.339-44

Stephen, Sir James Fitzjames, 'England and America', *Fraser's Magazine*, 68 (October 1863), pp.419-37

Steward, Captain E. Harding, 'Notes on the Employment of Submarine Mines in America During the Late Civil War', *R.E. Professional Papers*, 15 (1866), pp.1-28

Stothard, Captain R.H., 'The Electric Telegraph and Visual Signalling in Connection with Future Military Operations', *R.E. Professional Papers*, 18 (1870), pp.100-106

Stowell Jones, Major Alfred, 'Present Condition of Our Cavalry', *Journal of the Royal United Service Institution*, 6 (1863), pp.423–35

Thesiger, Frederick, Lieutenant Colonel [Lord Chelmsford],'Is a Radical Change in the Tactical Formation of our Infantry Really Necessary', *Journal of the Royal United Service Institution*, 17 (1873), pp.411-23

'Three Field Officers', 'The Critics and the Infantry Attack' *United Service Magazine*, n.s., 13 (1896) pp.368-374

Townsend, George Alfred [Anon], 'Richmond and Washington during the War', *Cornhill Magazine*, 7 (1863), pp.93-102

Turner, Colonel Alfred E. (et al.), 'The Battle of Vionville: a discussion', *United Service Magazine*, n.s., 10 (1894), pp.42-55

Tyler, Captain Henry W., 'Railways Strategically Considered', *Journal of the Royal United Service Institution*, 8 (1864), pp.321-43

Tyler, Captain Henry W., 'Spithead and Harbour Defence', *Journal of the Royal United Service Institution*, 8 (1864), pp.139-57

Tyler, Captain Henry W., 'The Effect of the Modern Rifle upon Siege Operations, and the Means Required for Counteracting it', *Journal of the United Service Institution*, 2 (1858), pp.225-53

Tyler, Captain Henry W., 'The Rifle and the Rampart; or, the Future of Defence', *Journal of the Royal United Service Institution*, 4 (1861), pp.331-63

Tyler, Captain Henry W., 'The Rifle and the Spade, or the Future of Field Operations', *Journal of the Royal United Service Institution*, 3 (1859), pp.170-94

Tyler, Captain Henry W., 'The Volunteers and National Defence', *Quarterly Review*, 112 (July 1862), pp.110-45

Vandenburgh, General O. (NYSM), 'A New System of Artillery for Projecting a Group or Cluster of Shot', *Journal of the Royal United Service Institution*, 6 (1862), pp.378-90

Valentine, E.S., 'An American Parallel to the Present Campaign', *Fortnightly Review*, n.s., 67 (1900), pp.660-67

Vincent, Colonel Sir Howard, 'Lessons Of The War: Personal Observations And Impressions Of The Forces And Military Establishments Now In South Africa', *Journal of the Royal United Service Institution*, 44 (1900), pp.606-62

Vizetelly, Frank, 'Charleston Under Fire', *Cornhill Magazine*, 10 (1864), pp.99-110

Walker, Lieutenant Arthur, 'Breechloaders for the Army, and Gun Cotton as an Explosive Agent in Modern Warfare', *Journal of the Royal United Service Institution*, 8 (1863), pp.396-426

Watson, Colonel C.M., 'Military Ballooning in the British Army', *R.E. Professional Papers*, 28, (1902), pp.39-59

Welch, Lieutenant Francis, 'Military Notes around Plevna and on the Danube, during December 1877 and January 1878', *Journal of the Royal United Service Institution*, 22 (1878), pp.328-49

Wilford, Lieutenant Colonel, 'On The Rifle; Showing the Necessity for its Introduction as a Universal Infantry Weapon', *Journal of the United Service Institution*, 1 (1858), pp.238-53

Williams, Lieutenant Colonel W.J., 'On Infantry Tactics', *Journal of the Royal United Service Institution*, 16 (1872), pp.768-73

Wolseley, Field Marshal Viscount Garnet Joseph ['An English Officer'], 'A Month's Visit to the Confederate Headquarters', *Blackwood's Edinburgh Magazine*, 93 (1863), pp.1-29

Wolseley, Field Marshal Viscount Garnet Joseph, 'An English View of the Civil War', *North American Review*, 148 (1889), pp.538-63; and 149 (1989), pp.30-43, 164-81, 278-92, 446-59, 594-606, 713-27

Wolseley, Field Marshal Viscount Garnet Joseph, 'Field-Marshal Von Moltke', *United Service Magazine*, n.s., 3 (1891-92), pp.1-22, 481-97

Wolseley, Field Marshal Viscount Garnet Joseph, 'General Forrest', *United Service Magazine*, n.s., 5 (1892), pp.1-14, 113-24

Wolseley, Field Marshal Viscount Garnet Joseph, 'General Lee', *MacMillan's Magazine*, 55 (1887), pp.321-31

Wolseley, Field Marshal Viscount Garnet Joseph, 'General Sherman', *United Service Magazine*, n.s., 3 (1891), pp.97-116, 193-216, 289-309

Secondary Unpublished Sources

Unpublished Theses

Badsey, Stephen 'Fire and the Sword: the British Army and The Arme Blanche controversy 1871-1921' (PhD Thesis, University of Cambridge, 1981)

Bou, Jean, 'The Evolution and Development of the Australian Light Horse, 1860-1945' (Thesis submitted for the degree of Doctor of Philosophy in the School of Humanities and Social Sciences, University of New South Wales, 2005)

Brinkmann, Lieutenant Colonel Kay, (German Army) 'German Observations and Evaluations of the U.S. Civil War: A Study in Lessons Not Learned' (Thesis for the Degree of Master of Military Art and Science, U.S. Army Command and General Staff College, Fort Leavenworth Kansas, 2000)

Coffey, Rod A., Major, (USA), 'Doctrinal Orphan or Active Partner? A History Of U.S. Army Mechanised Infantry Doctrine' (Thesis for the Degree of Master of Military Art and Science, U.S. Army Command and General Staff College, Fort Leavenworth Kansas, 2000)

Craddock, Patrick C., 'The American Civil War and its influence on the British Army 1865-1902' (PhD Thesis, University of Aberystwyth, 2001)

Grimes, Scott Thomas, 'Lord Lyons and Anglo-American Diplomacy during the Civil War' (PhD Thesis, London School of Economics, July 2004)

Jones, Spencer, 'The Influence Of The Boer War (1899 – 1902) On The Tactical Development Of The Regular British Army 1902 – 1914' (PhD Thesis, University of Wolverhampton, 2009)

Kerr, Richard E., Jr, Major, (USA), 'Wall Of Fire – The Rifle And Civil War Infantry Tactics' (Thesis for the degree of Master Of Military Art And Science, U.S. Army Command and General Staff College, Fort Leavenworth, Kansas, 1990)

Luvaas, Morten Jay, 'Through English Eyes: The Impact of the American Civil War on British Military Thought' (Thesis for the degree of Master of Arts, Duke University, 1951)

Luvaas, Morten Jay, 'Through Foreign Eyes: The American Civil War in European Military Thought' (Thesis for the degree of Doctor of Philosophy, Duke University, 1956)

Mitchell, Stuart Bruce Tylor, 'An Inter-disciplinary Study of Learning in the 32nd Division on the Western Front, 1916-1918' (PhD Thesis, University of Birmingham, 2015)

Winrow, Andrew Philip, 'The British Regular Mounted Infantry 1880 – 1913: Cavalry of Poverty or Victorian Paradigm?' (DPhil Thesis, University of Buckingham, 2014)

Secondary Published Sources

Books

Adams, Ephraim Douglass, *Great Britain and the American Civil War* (Electronic edn) (New York: Diversion Books, 2008, first published 1924)

Addington, Larry H., *The Patterns of War since the Eighteenth Century*, 2nd edn (Bloomington and Indianapolis: Indiana University Press, 1994)

Alexander, Bevan, *Robert E. Lee's Civil War* (Holbrook, MA: Adams Media, 1998)

Anglesey, Marquess of, *A History of the British Cavalry: 1816-1919* (London: Leo Cooper, 1973-1997)

Anon, (ed.), *The Times History of the [Great] War*, 22 vols (London: The Times, 1914-21)

Argyris, Chris, *On Organizational Learning* (Oxford: Blackwell, 1992)

Argyris, Chris and Donald A. Schön, *Organizational Learning: A Theory of Action Perspective* (Reading MA: Addison-Wesley, 1978)

Arnold, James R., *The Armies of U.S. Grant* (London: Arms and Armour Press, 1995)

Avant, Deborah, *Political Institutions and Military Change: Lessons from Peripheral Wars* (Ithaca: Cornell University Press, 1994)

Badsey, Stephen, *Doctrine and Reform in the British Cavalry 1880-1918* (Aldershot: Ashgate, 2008)

Bailey, D.W., *British Military Longarms 1715-1865* (New York, London, Sydney: Arms and Armour Press, 1986)

Barthorp, Michael, *The Anglo-Boer Wars: The British and the Afrikaners, 1815-1902* (London: Blandford, 1987)

Barthorp, Michael, *The Armies of Britain 1485-1980* (London: National Army Museum, 1980)

Barthorp, Michael, *War on the Nile* (Poole: Blandford, 1984)

Bates, Darrell, *The Abyssinian Difficulty* (Oxford: Oxford University Press, 1979)

Becke, Captain A.F., *An Introduction to the History of Tactics 1740-1905* (London: Hugh Rees, 1909)

Beckett, Ian F.W., *Riflemen Form* (Barnsley: Pen and Sword, 2007, originally published Aldershot, Ogilvy Trust 1982)

Beckett, Ian F.W., *The Amateur Military Tradition 1558-1945* (Manchester: Manchester University Press, 1991)

Berkeley, Edmund and Dorothy Smith Berkeley, *George William Featherstonhaugh: The First US Government Geologist* (Tuscaloosa and London: University of Alabama Press, 1988)

Bidwell, Shelford and Dominick Graham, *Fire-Power: The British Army Weapons and Theories of War 1904-1945* (Barnsley: Pen and Sword, 2004, first published London: Allen & Unwin, 1982)

Black, Jeremy, *The Age of Total War* (Westport and London: Praeger Security International, 2006)

Blackett, R.J.M., *Divided Hearts: Britain and the American Civil War* (Baton Rouge: Louisiana State University Press, 2001)

Bond, Brian, *The Victorian Army and the Staff College, 1854–1914* (London: Eyre Methuen, 1972)

Bou, Jean, *Light Horse: A History of Australia's Mounted Arm* (Cambridge: Cambridge University Press, 2010)

Brighton, Terry, *The Last Charge: The 21st Lancers and the Battle of Omdurman* (Ramsbury: Crowood Press, 1998),

Broadwater, Robert P., *Civil War Special Forces: The Elite and Distinct Fighting Units of the Union and Confederate Armies* (Santa Barbara: Praeger, 2014)

Brogan, Hugh, (ed.), *The American Civil War: Extracts from the Times 1860-1865* (London: Times Books, 1975)

Callwell, Major General Sir Charles E. and Major General Sir John Headlam, *History of the Royal Artillery*, 3 vols (London: Royal Artillery Institution, 1931-40)

Catton, Bruce, *Grant and the American Military Tradition* (Boston: Little Brown, 1954)

Clark, Christopher, *The Sleepwalkers: How Europe Went to War in 1914* (London: Allen Lane, 2012)

Conyer, A.L., *The Rise of U.S. Grant* (New York: Century, 1931)

Coppée, Henry, *Grant and his Campaigns: A Military Biography* (New York: Charles B. Richardson 1866)

De Groot, Gerard J., *Douglas Haig 1861-1928* (London: Unwin Hyman, 1988)

Donald, David, (ed.), *Why the North Won the Civil War* (London & New York: Collier Macmillan, 1962)

Downie, Richard D., *Learning from Conflict: The US Military in Vietnam, El Salvador and the Drug War* (Westport: Praeger, 1998)

Driver, Hugh, *The Birth of Military Aviation: Britain, 1903-1914* (Woodbridge (Suffolk) and Rochester NY: Royal Historical Society (Boydell Press), 1997)

Drury, Ian and Tony Gibbons, *The US Civil War Military Machine* (Limpsfield: Dragon's World, 1993)

Dupuy, Colonel Trevor N., *Understanding War* (New York: Paragon, 1987)

Dutton, Roy, *Forgotten Heroes: The Charge of the 21st Lancers at Omdurman* (Prenton: InfoDial, 2012)

Evans, Charles M., *The War of the Aeronauts: A History of Ballooning during the Civil War* (Mechanicsburg PA: Stackpole Books, 2002)

Farwell, Byron, *Queen Victoria's Little Wars* (Ware: Wordsworth, 1999, originally published 1973)

Forbes, Arthur, *History of the Army Ordnance Services*, 3 vols (London: Medici Society 1929)

Foreman, Amanda, *World on Fire* (London: Allen Lane, 2010)

Fortescue, Sir John William, *A History of the British Army*, 13 vols (London: Macmillan, 1899-1930)

Fryer, Mary Beacock, *Battlefields of Canada* (Toronto and Reading: Dundurn Press, 1986)

Fuller, Major General J.F.C, *The Conduct of War, 1789–1961* (London: Eyre and Spottiswoode, 1961)

Fuller, Major General J.F.C, *War and Western Civilization, 1832–1932: A Study of War as a Political Instrument and the Expression of Mass Democracy* (London: Duckworth, 1932)

Fuller, Major General J.F.C., *The Generalship of Ulysses S. Grant* (London: John Murray, 1929)

Gat, Azar, *A History of Military Thought: From the Enlightenment to the Cold War* (Clarendon: Oxford University Press, 2001)

Gates, David, *Warfare in the 19th Century* (Basingstoke: Palgrave, 2001)

Glover, Michael, *Warfare from Waterloo to Mons* (London: Cassell, 1980)

Gooch, John, *Armies in Europe* (London: Routledge and Kegan Paul, 1980)

Graves, Charles L., *Life and Letters of Alexander MacMillan* (London: MacMillan, 1910)

Griffith, Paddy, *Battle in the Civil War* (Camberley: Field Books, 1986)

Griffith, Paddy, *Rally Once Again: Battle Tactics of the American Civil War* (Ramsbury: Crowood Press, 1987)

Hagerman, Edward, *The American Civil War and the Origins of Modern Warfare: Ideas, Organization, and Field Command* (Bloomington: Indiana University Press, 1992)

Harwell, Richard B., *The Civil War Reader: The Confederate Reader* (New York: Konecky and Konecky, [n.d.], originally published 1957)

Hassler, William Wood, *Colonel John Pelham* (Chapel Hill: University North Carolina, 1960)

Haythornewaite, Philip, *The Colonial Wars Source Book* (London: Caxton, 2000)

Heathcote, Tony, *The British Field Marshals 1736–1997* (London: Leo Cooper, 1999)

Hess, Earl J., *Field Armies and Fortifications in the Civil War: The Eastern Campaigns 1861-64* (Chapel Hill: University of North Carolina Press, 2005)

Hess, Earl J., *The Rifle Musket in Civil War Combat Reality and Myth* (Lawrence: University of Kansas, 2008)

Hess, Earl J., *Trench Warfare Under Grant and Lee* (Chapel Hill: University of North Carolina Press, 2007)

Hogg, Ian V., *Weapons of the Civil War* (New York: Military Press, 1986)

Hogg, Ian V., *Machine Guns: A Detailed History of the Rapid-Fire Gun 14th Century to Present* (Iola WI: Krause, c. 2002),

Holden-Reid, Brian, *Studies in British Military Thought: Debates with Fuller and Liddell Hart* (Lincoln: University of Nebraska Press, 1998)

Holden-Reid, Brian, *The American Civil War and the Wars of the Industrial Revolution* (London: Cassell, 1999)

Hoole, William Stanley, *Lawley Covers the Confederacy (Confederate Centennial Studies Number 26)* (Tuscaloosa: Confederate Publishing Company, 1964)

Hoole, William Stanley, *Vizetelly Covers the Confederacy (Confederate Centennial Studies Number 4)* (Tuscaloosa: Confederate Publishing Company, 1957)

Horn, Stanley, *The Robert E. Lee Reader* (New York: Smithmark, 1995, originally published 1949)

Houghton, Walter E., Josef L. Altholz [et al.], ed,*Wellesley Index to Victorian periodicals, 1824-1900*, (Toronto: University of Toronto Press; London: Routledge, 1966-89)

Howard, Michael, *The Franco-Prussian War* (London: Methuen, 1981)

Howard, Michael, *War in European History* (Oxford: OPUS, 1976)

Hutchison, Lieutenant Colonel G.S., *Machine Guns: Their History and Tactical Employment* (London: MacMillan, 1938)

Jaeger, Michael and Carol Lauritzen, (ed.), *Memoirs of Thaddeus S.C. Lowe, Chief of the Aeronautic Corps of the Army of the United States during the Civil War: My Balloons in Peace and War* (Lewiston NY; Lampeter: Edwin Mellen Press, c. 2004)

Jamieson, Perry D., *Crossing the Deadly Ground: United States Army Tactics 1865–1899* (Tuscaloosa: University of Alabama Press, 1994)

Jones, Spencer, *From Boer War to World War: Tactical Reform of the British Army 1902 – 1914* (Norman: University of Oklahoma Press, 2012)

Katcher, Philip, *The Army of Robert E. Lee* (London: Arms and Armour Press, 1994)

Keegan, John, *The Mask of Command* (London: Penguin, 1987)

Keir, Elizabeth, *Imagining War: French and British Military Doctrine Between the Wars* (Princeton: Princeton University Press, 1997)

Knight, Ian, *Brave Men's Blood* (London: Guild, 1990)

Knotel, Richard, Herbert Knotel and Herbert Sieg, *Uniforms of the World* (New York: Charles Scribner and Sons, 1980)

Koch, H. W, *Modern Warfare* (London: Bison, 1983)

Kochanski, Halik, *Sir Garnet Wolseley: Victorian Hero* (London: Hambledon Press, 1999)

Kruger, Rayne, *Good-bye Dolly Gray: The Story of the Boer War* (London: Pan, 1974)

Lehmann, Joseph, *The First Boer War* (London: Military Book Society, 1972)

Lehmann, Joseph, *All Sir Garnet: A Life of Field Marshal Lord Wolseley* (London: Jonathan Cape, 1964)

Lewis, Lloyd, *Sherman, Fighting Prophet* (New York: Smithmark, 1994, originally published 1932)

Liddell Hart, B.H., *The British Way in Warfare* (London: Faber and Faber, 1932)

Liddell Hart, B.H., *Paris, or The Future of War* (London: Kegan, Paul, Trench, Trubner & Co., 1925)

Liddell Hart, B.H., *Sherman* (New York: Da Capo Press, 1993, originally published 1929)

Liddell Hart, B.H., *Strategy* (New York: Praeger, 1961)

Liddell Hart, B.H., *Thoughts on War* (London: Faber and Faber, 1944)

Lonn, Ella, *Foreigners in the Confederacy* (Chapel Hill: University of North Carolina Press, 2002, originally published 1940)

Lonn, Ella, *Foreigners in the Union Army and Navy* (Baton Rouge: Louisiana State University Press, 1951)

Low, Charles Rathbone, *General Lord Wolseley of Cairo: A Memoir*, 2nd edn (London: Richard Bentley, 1883)

Luvaas, Jay, *The Education of an Army: British Military Thought, 1815–1940* (Chicago: University of Chicago Press, 1964)

Luvaas, Jay, *The Military Legacy of the Civil War: The European Inheritance* (Chicago: University of Chicago Press, 1959)

Luvaas, Jay, *The Military Legacy of the Civil War: The European Inheritance*, 2nd edn (Lawrence: University of Kansas Press, 1988)

Marshall-Cornwall, James, *Grant as Military Commander* (London: Batsford, 1970)

Maurice, Major General Sir Frederick, and Captain Maurice Harold Grant, *History of the War in South Africa*, 4 vols (London, Hurst and Blackett, 1906-10),

Maxwell, Leigh, *My God – Maiwand!* (London: Leo Cooper, 1979)

McEllwee, William, *The Art of War Waterloo to Mons* (London: Weidenfeld and Nicolson, 1974)

McWhiney, Grady and Perry D. Jamieson, *Attack and Die: Civil War Military Tactics and the Southern Heritage* (Tuscaloosa: University of Alabama Press, 1990, originally published 1982)

Miller, Stephen M., *Lord Methuen and the British Army: Failure and Redemption in South Africa* (London: Frank Cass, 1999)

Miller, Stephen M., *Volunteers on the Veldt* (Norman: University of Oklahoma Press, 2007)

Mollo, Boris, *The Indian Army* (Poole: New Orchard, 1986, originally published 1981)

Montgomery of Alamein, Viscount, *History of Warfare* (London: Collins, 1968)

Myatt, Frederick, *Marching to Magdala* (London: Leo Cooper, 1970)

Nagl, J.A., *Learning to Eat Soup with a Knife: Counter-insurgency Lessons From Malaya and Vietnam* (Chicago: University of Chicago Press, 2005)

Newell, Clayton R. and Charles R. Schrader, *Of Duty Well and Faithfully Done: A History of the Regular Army in the Civil War* (Lincoln: University of Nebraska, 2011)

Nosworthy, Brent, *The Bloody Crucible of Courage* (New York: Carroll and Graf, 2003)

Pakenham, Thomas, *The Boer War* (London: Weidenfeld and Nicholson, 1979)

Palazzo, Albert, *Seeking Victory on the Western Front* (Lincoln and London: University of Nebraska Press 2000)

Pemberton, W. Baring, *Battles of the Boer War* (London: Batsford, 1964)

Porter, Mrs. Gerald [Mary], *Annals of a Publishing House: John Blackwood, Volume. Ill of William Blackwood and his Sons, Their Magazine and Friends* (Edinburgh and London: William Blackwood, 1898)

Porter, Major General Whitworth, C.M. Watson, and others, *History of the Corps of Royal Engineers*, 3 vols (London: Longmans & Co, 1889-1915)

Posen, Barry R., *The Sources of Military Doctrine: France Britain and Germany Between the World Wars* (Ithaca: Cornell University Press, 1984)

Powell, Geoffrey, *Buller: A Scapegoat?* (London: Leo-Cooper, 1994)

Ramsay, M.A., *Command and Cohesion: The Citizen Soldier and Minor Tactics in the British Army, 1870-1918* (Westport CN: Prager, 2002)

Randall, J.G., *Lincoln the President: Midstream* (New York: Dodd, Mead & Co., 1952)

Ransford, Oliver, *The Battle of Majuba Hill* (London: John Murray, 1967)

Roads, Christopher H., *The British Soldier's Firearm 1850-1864* (London: Herbert Jenkins, 1964)

Roads, Christopher H., *The Gun* (London: BBC, 1978)

Robertson, Field Marshal Sir William, *From Private to Field Marshal* (London: Constable and Company, 1921)

Rogers, Colonel H.C.B., *A History of Artillery* (Secaucus NJ: Citadel Press, 1975)

Ropp, Theodore, *War in the Modern World* (Durham NC: Duke University Press: 1959)

Rosen, Stephen Peter, *Winning the Next War: Innovation and the Modern Military* (Ithaca: Cornell University Press, 1991)

Rowland, Thomas J., *George B McClellan and Civil War History* (Kent: Kent University Press, 1998)

Royster, Charles, *The Destructive War: William Tecumseh Sherman, Stonewall Jackson, and the Americans* (New York: Random House, 1991)

Senge, Peter, *The Fifth Discipline: The Art and Practice of the Learning Organization* (New York: Doubleday, 1990)

Shand, Alexander Innes, *The Life of General Sir Edward Bruce Hamley* (Edinburgh and London: William Blackwood and Sons, 1895)

Sheffield, Gary and Dan Todman, (ed.), *Command and Control on the Western Front: The British Army's Experience* (Staplehurst: Spellmount, 2004)

Spiers, Edward M., *The Army and Society* (London and New York: Longman, 1980)

Spiers, Edward M., *The Late Victorian Army 1868–1902* (Manchester: Manchester University Press, 1999)

Starr, Stephen Z., *The Union Cavalry in The Civil War* (Baton Rouge: Louisiana University Press, 1979-85)

Strachan, Hew, *European Armies and the Conduct of War* (London: Allen & Unwin, 1983)

Strachan, Hew, *From Waterloo to Balaclava: Tactics, Technology and the British Army 1830-54* (Cambridge: Cambridge University Press, 1985)

Strachan, Hew, *Wellington's Legacy: The Reform of the British Army 1830-54* (Manchester: Manchester University Press, 1984)

Terraine, John, *The Smoke and the Fire: Myths and Anti-Myths of War 1861–1945* (London: Sidgwick and Jackson, 1980)

Trask, David F., *The War With Spain* (New York: Bison Books, 1996, originally published Simon and Schuster, 1981)

US Army, *Field Manual FM 3–0: Operations* (Washington: Department of the Army, 2008)

Urwin, Gregory J.W., *The United States Cavalry: an Illustrated History* (Poole: Blandford, 1983)

Urwin, Gregory J.W., *The United States Infantry: an Illustrated History* (London: Blandford, 1988)

Verney, Colonel Willoughby, *The Military Life of HRH George, Duke of Cambridge* (London: John Murray, 1905)

Waller, John H., *Gordon of Khartoum: The Saga of a Victorian Hero* (New York: Atheneum, 1988)

Ware, Jean and Hugh Hunt, *The Several Lives of a Victorian Vet* (London: Bachman & Turner, 1979)

Weigley, Russell F., *History of the United States Army* (London: Batsford, 1968)

Weigley, Russell F., *A Great Civil War* (Bloomington: Indiana University Press, 2000)

Weigley, Russell F., *The American Way of War, a History of United States Military Strategy and Policy* (New York and London: Macmillan, 1973)

Weigley, Russell F., *Towards an American Army* (New York, London: Columbia University Press, 1962)

Weinart, Richard P., *The Confederate Regular Army* (Shippensburg: White Mane, 1991)

Welch, M.D., *Science and the British Officer: The Early Days of the Royal United Service Institute for Defence Studies* (London: Royal United Institution for Defence Studies, 1998)

Wheeler, Richard, *Witness to Gettysburg* (New York: Harper and Row, 1987)

Williams, T. Harry, *Lincoln and his Generals* (London: Hamish Hamilton, 1952)

Williams, T. Harry, *McClellan, Sherman and Grant* (New Brunswick NJ: Rutgers University, 1962)

Wyeth, John Allan, *Life of Bedford Forrest* (Edison NJ: Blue and Grey Press, 1996, originally published 1918)

Ziegler, Philip, *Omdurman* (New York: Dorset Press, 1987)

Zulfo, Ismat Sultan, *Karari: The Sudanese Account of the Battle of Omdurman*, translated by Peter Clark (London: Frederick Warne, 1980)

Chapters

Bailes, Howard, 'Technology and Tactics in the British Army 1866-1900' in *Men Machines and War* ed. by Ronald Hapcock and Keith Nielson, (Kingston: Wilfred Laurier University Press, 1984), pp.21-47

Bond, Brian, 'Doctrine and Training in the British Cavalry, 1870–1914' in *The Theory and Practice of War: Essays Presented to Captain B H Liddell Hart*, ed. by Michael Howard (London: Cassell, 1965), pp.97-125

Degler, Carl N., 'The American Civil War and the German Wars of Unification: the Problem of Comparison' in *On the Road to Total War: The American Civil War and the German Wars of Unification*, ed. by Stig Förster and Jörg Nagler (Cambridge: Cambridge University Press, 1997), pp.53-71

Farrell, Theo, and Terry Terriff, 'The Sources of Military Change' in Theo Farrell and Terry Terriff (Eds.), The Sources of Military Change: Culture, Politics, Technology (Boulder: Lynne Riener, 2002), pp.3-17

Reid, Brian Holden, 'Military Intellectuals and the American Civil War: Maurice, Fuller and Liddell Hart' in *Studies in British Military Thought: Debates with Fuller and Liddell Hart* (Lincoln: University of Nebraska Press, 1998), pp.133-49

Katzenbach, Edward L., Jr, 'The Horse Cavalry in the 20th Century: A Study in Policy Response' in *American Defense Policy*, 4th Edn ed by John E. Endicott and Roy W. Stafford Jr (Baltimore and London: John Hopkins University Press, 1977), pp.360-73. Originally published in *Public Policy*, 7 (1958)

Murray, Williamson, 'Innovation Past and Future' in *Military Innovation in the Interwar Period*, ed. by Williamson Murray and Allan R. Millett (Cambridge: Cambridge University Press, 1998, originally published 1996), pp.300-328

Van der Ven, Hans, 'A Hinge in Time: The Wars of the Mid-19th Century' in *Cambridge History of War Volume 4: War in the Modern World* (Cambridge: Cambridge University Press, 2012), pp.16-44

Wawro, Geoffrey 'War, Technology and Industrial Change' in *Cambridge History of War Volume 4: War in the Modern World* (Cambridge: Cambridge University Press, 2012), pp.45-68

Journal Articles

Atkins, John, 'Early History of the Army School of Musketry in Hythe, Kent', *Black Powder* (Winter 2007), pp.35-37

Badsey, Stephen, 'The Boer War (1899-1902) and British Cavalry Doctrine', *Journal of Military History*, 71 (2007), pp.75-98

Badsey, Stephen, 'Forum II: Confederate Military Strategy in the U.S. Civil War Revisited', *Journal of Military History*, 73 (2009), pp.1273-1278

Badsey, Stephen, 'Mounted Combat in the Second Boer War, *Sandhurst Journal of Military Studies*, 2 (1991), pp.11-28

Bailes, Howard, 'Patterns of thought in the late Victorian Army', *Journal of Strategic Studies*, 4 (1981), pp.29-45

Beckett, Ian F.W., 'The Pen and the Sword: Reflections on Military Thought in the British Army 1854-1914', *Soldiers of the Queen*, 68 (March 1992), pp.3-7

Bou, Jean, 'Cavalry, Firepower, and Swords: The Australian Light Horse and the Tactical Lessons of Cavalry Operations in Palestine, 1916-1918', *Journal of Military History*, 71 (2007), pp.99-125

Broke-Smith, Brigadier P.W.L., 'Aeronautics, the History of Early British Military Aeronautics', *Royal Engineers Journal*, 66 (1952), pp.1-20, 105-21, 208-226

Carroll, Francis M., 'The American Civil War and British Intervention: The Threat of Anglo-American Conflict', *Canadian Journal of History*, 47 (2012), pp.87-115

Castel, Albert, 'Liddell Hart's Sherman: Propaganda as History', *Journal of Military History*, 67 (April 2003), pp.405-26

Catignani, Sergio, 'Coping with Knowledge: Organizational Learning in the British Army?', *The Journal of Strategic Studies*, 37 (2014), pp.30-64

Cunliffe, Marcus, 'Recent Writing on the American Civil War', *History*, 50 (1965), pp.26-35

DiBella, Anthony J., Can the Army Become a Learning Organization? A Question Reexamined', *Joint Force Quarterly* 56 (2010), pp.117-22

Dubrulle, Hugh, ' "We are Threatened with Anarchy ...and Ruin": Fear of Americanization and the Emergence of an Anglo-Saxon Confederacy in England during the American Civil War', *Albion*, 33.4 (Winter 2001), pp.583–613

Dubrulle, Hugh, 'A Military Legacy of the Civil War: The British Inheritance', *Civil War History*, 49 (2003), pp.153-80

Farrell, Theo, 'Improving in War: Military Adaptation and the British in Helmand Province, Afghanistan, 2006-2009, *Journal of Strategic Studies*, 33 (2010), pp.567-94

Foley, Robert T., 'Dumb donkeys or cunning foxes? Learning in the British and German armies during the Great War', *International Affairs* 90 (2014), pp.279–98

Foley, Robert T., Stuart Griffin and Helen McCartney, '"Transformation in Contact": Learning the Lessons of Modern War', *International Affairs*, 87 (2011), pp.253-70

Fuller, J F.C., 'The Place of the American Civil War in the Evolution of War', *Army Quarterly*, 26 (July 1933), pp.316–25

Grissom, Adam, 'The Future of Military Innovation Studies', *The Journal of Strategic Studies*, 29 (2006), pp.905-34

Harvey, A.D., 'Was the American Civil War the First Modern War?', *History*, 97 (2012), pp.272-80

Henderson, W.O., 'The Cotton Famine in Lancashire', *Transactions Of The Historic Society Of Lancashire And Cheshire*, 84 (1932), pp.37-62

Henry, Robert Self, 'Civil War Railroads', *Civil War History*, 7 (1961), pp.229-30

Hernon, Joseph, 'British Sympathies in the American Civil War: A Reconsideration', *The Journal of Southern History*, 33 (1967), pp.357-67

Kirkpatrick, David, 'A Tale of Three Forts', *RUSI Journal*, 152 (2007), pp.68-73

Kochanski, Halik, 'Field Marshal Viscount Wolseley as Commander in Chief, 1895–1900: A Reassessment', *Journal of Strategic Studies*, 20 (1997), pp.119-39

Luvaas, Jay, 'General Sir Patrick Macdougall, The American Civil War and the Defence of Canada', *The Canadian Historical Association* (1962), pp.45-54

Luvaas, Jay, 'G.F.R. Henderson and the American Civil War', *Military Affairs*, 20 (1956), pp.139-53

Margrave, Tony, '"brits in blue or gray": Thomas Morley, 12th Pennsylvania Cavalry' *Crossfire*, 96 (August 2011), pp.6-12

Margrave, Tony, 'British Officers Observe the Civil War in America', *Crossfire*, Part 1 No 104 (Spring 2014), pp.13-20; Part 2 No.105 (Summer 2014), pp.13-15; Part 3 No 106 (Winter 2014), pp.12-16; Part 4 No 107 (Spring 2015), pp.17-21

Mruck, Armi E., 'The Role of Railroads in the Atlanta Campaign', *Civil War History*, 7 (1961), pp.264-71

Negus, Samuel, '"A notorious nest of offence": Neutrals, Belligerents and Union Jails in the Civil War Blockade-running Trade', *Civil War History*, 56 (2010), pp.350-85

Phillips, Gervase, 'Scapegoat Arm: 20th Century Cavalry in Anglophone Historiography', *Journal of Military History*, 71 (2007), pp.37-74

Preston, Adrian, 'British Military Thought 1856-1890', *Army Quarterly*, 88 (1964), pp.57-74

Preston, R.A., 'A Letter from a British Military Observer of the American Civil War', *Military Affairs*, 16 (1952), pp.49-60

Preston, R.A., 'Military Lessons of the American Civil War', *Army Quarterly*, 65 (1953), pp.229-37

Reid, Brian Holden, '"A Signpost That Was Missed"? Reconsidering British Lessons from the American Civil War', *The Journal of Military History*, 70 (2006), pp.385–414

Rosen, Stephen Peter, 'New Ways of War: Understanding Military Innovation', *International Security*, 13/1 (1988), pp.134-68

Rowland, Kate Mason, 'English Friends of the Confederacy', *Confederate Veteran*, 25 (June 1917), pp.198-202

Somerville, Michael, 'Aerial Observers: The British Legacy from the United States Balloon Corps', *Crossfire*, 118 (Winter 2018), pp.25-32

Somerville, Michael, '"English Enterprise": The Earl of Dunmore and the Confederacy', *Crossfire*, 117 (Summer 2018), pp.16-21

Somerville, Michael, 'The Siege of Petersburg: The British View', *Crossfire*, 104 (Spring 2014), pp.21-25

Stewart, Alice R, 'Sir John A MacDonald and the Imperial Defence Commission of 1879', *Canadian Historical Review*, 35-2 (June 1954), pp.119-139

Sullivan, A.E., 'The 1860s and the 1960s: a Parallel', *Army Quarterly*, 88 (1964), pp.188-94

Travers, Tim, 'The Offensive and the problem of Innovation in British Military Thought, 1870-1915', *Journal of Contemporary History*, 13 (1978), pp.531-53

Vallely, Tom, 'Why Liverpool and Manchester supported different sides in the American Civil War', *Crossfire*, 118 (Winter 2018) pp.20-24

Wheatley, Margaret J., 'Can the U.S. Army Become a Learning Organization?' *The Journal of Quality and Participation*, 17 (1994), pp.50-56

Online Resources

Ancestry.com genealogical website: <http://home.ancestry.co.uk>

Andrews, Evan, '8 Unusual Civil War Weapons', (9 April 2013) <http://www.history.com/news/history-lists/8-unusual-civil-war-weapons>

Anon, 'Confederate Link with Mayfair', *American Civil War Round Table UK* ([n.d.]) <http://www.acwrt.org.uk/uk-heritage_Confederate-Link-with-Mayfair.asp>

Anon, 'Stephen Winthrop – Rebel Without a Cause', *American Civil War Round Table UK* (2001, originally published 1993) < http://www.acwrt.org.uk/uk-heritage_Stephen-Winthrop---Rebel-Without-A-Cause.asp>

Anon, 'Obituary of Sir George Edward Grover (1840-1893), Institution of Civil Engineers', on *Grace's Guide to British Industrial History*, <https://www.graces-guide.co.uk/George_Edward_Grover#cite_note-1> [accessed 02/10/2017].

Bank of England Historic Currency Converter <http://www.bankofengland.co.uk/education/Pages/resources/inflationtools/calculator/index1.aspx>

Cowan's Auctions: Brady Album Gallery Card of British Observers at Falmouth, Va <http://www.cowanauctions.com/auctions/item.aspx?ItemId=15800>

Dictionary of Canadian Biography Online: <http://www.biographi.ca>

Dubrulle, Hugh, <http://www.anselm.edu/academic/history/hdubrulle/professor/text/research%202.htm>

Hamill, John, 'Civil War Tactics in Perspective' (2008-2015) <http://johnsmilitary-history.com/cwarmy.html>

Hutchison, Will, Official website <http://willhutchison.com/british-military-observers-in-the-american-civil-war/>

Irish Emigration Database <http://www.dippam.ac.uk/ied>

Levin, Kevin M., 'Did the Civil War Affect European Military Culture', *Civil War Memory* (10 March 2010) <http://cwmemory.com/2010/03/31/did-the-civil-war-affect-european-military-culture>

Masterton, Heather, 'Who was Colonel Hamby? British Observer with W.T. Sherman, c. 1864', *Civil War Talk* (February 2011) <http://civilwartalk.com/threads/who-was-colonel-hamby-british-observer-with-wt-sherman-c-1864.22091/>

Muzzle Loaders Association of Great Britain, <http://www.mlagb.com/black-powder/200704_hythe.pdf>

Rotov, Dmitri, 'von Moltke's Armed Mobs', *Civil War Bookshelf* (11 March 2008) <http://cwbn.blogspot.co.uk/2008/11/richard-f.html>

Royal United Service Institution <https://www.rusi.org>

San Juan Island National Historical Park, 'The Pig War', <http://www.nps.gov/sajh/historyculture/the-pig-war.htm>

Shotgun's Home of the American Civil War, 'Civil War Firsts' (15 Feb 2002) <http://www.civilwarhome.com/civilwarfirsts.htm>

The Peerage genealogical website: <http://www.thepeerage.com/p4805.htmi48050>

The War of the Rebellion: a Compilation of the Official Records of the Union and Confederate Armies, electronic edn, Cornell University (2015), <http://ebooks.library.cornell.edu/m/moawar/waro.html>

Unit History: Cape Mounted Rifles, *Forces War Records,* <http://www.forces-war-records.co.uk/units/5147/cape-mounted-rifles>

Vetch, R.H. and Lunt, Rev. James, 'Smyth, Sir Henry Augustus (1825–1906)', *Oxford Dictionary of National Biography,* online edn (January 2008), <http://www.oxforddnb.com/view/article/36174>

Virginia Foundation for the Humanities, *Encyclopedia Virginia,* <http://www.encyclopediavirginia.org/Davis_Burke_1913-2006>

Index

People

Places

Formations & Units

General

Wolverhampton Military Studies

www.helion.co.uk/wolverhamptonmilitarystudies

Submissions

The publishers would be pleased to receive submissions for this series. Please contact us via email (info@helion.co.uk), or in writing to Helion & Company Limited, 26 Willow Road, Solihull, West Midlands, B91 1UE.

Titles